THE
COMPLETE
FISHERMAN'S
CATALOG

Also by Harmon Henkin:

The Environment, the Establishment and the Law
Fly Tackle: A Guide to the Tools of the Trade
Crisscross, *a novel*

THE COMPLETE FISHERMAN'S CATALOG

HARMON HENKIN

J. B. LIPPINCOTT COMPANY
PHILADELPHIA · NEW YORK

U.S. Library of Congress Cataloging in Publication Data

Henkin, Harmon.
  The complete fisherman's catalog.

  Includes index.
  1. Fishing tackle. I. Title.
SH447.H45   688.7'9   76-56200
ISBN-0-397-01186-5
ISBN-0-397-01205-5 (pbk.)

To Ada, what's left of Montana and, of course, Bill.

Staff

Written and compiled by Harmon Henkin
Edited by William T. Vaughn

Design	*William T. Vaughn*
Research Director	*Jennifer O'Loughlin*
Editorial Staff	*Laurel Desnick*
	Donna Mellin
	Billie Miller
	Marianne Painter
	Eric Seymour
	John Waite
Production Staff	*Glenn Law*
	John K. Maillet

"Modern fishing is as complicated as flying a B-53 to Tacoma. Several years of preliminary library and desk work are essential just to be able to buy equipment without humiliation."

Russell Baker, "Observer" column, *New York Times*, July, 1964.

CONTENTS

CONTENTS

INTRODUCTION

What sums up the *Complete Fisherman's Catalog*? The unusual and the offbeat. The best buys and most practical gear. The ultimate commodities whether in equipment or writers. In essence, it's just like the sport itself — a composite of viewpoints, preferences and idiosyncrasies.

For most anglers, knowledge about their sport is incredibly diffuse. It's found in innumerable catalogs, thousands of books and pamphlets spanning five centuries and in casual conversations in tackle shops around the country. These are the sources we tapped in a year of scouring the literature of fishing.

And it was a helluva job! Every manufacturer claims it makes only the best possible equipment, and every expert in a sport with nothing but experts says he knows the way to catch the big ones. This is what we had to wade through, separating fact from fiction.

But there is a method to our tackle madness. Though we certainly don't have every bit of quality equipment listed in the thousand or so commodities in the book, every one we list should be of real value to the angler. The same is true of the original contributions by some of the better-known angling writers in the country and the compilation of excerpts from the rich literary heritage of fishing.

They aren't the last words on the subject but good first ones at least. They, like the equipment listings, are a starting point for the angler trying to make sense of the myriad of sources available.

The book also has another important function to fulfill. There are few sources that compare gear with other similar products. We don't have anything to sell in the *Catalog*. Like other anglers we are consumers of tackle and want the most for our money. Whether you are after high-quality dry flies or a medium-range close-faced spinning reel, this book can help you wend through the maze of those offerings and make some sense of them.

Likewise with excerpts. They are a starting point for anglers trying to figure out which books, current and past, should be added to their library, which writers address the problems they are interested in solving and the chronology of theoretical developments.

Undoubtedly we are guilty of sins of omission. There was just too much to cover in a limited space, even one as large as this one.

But we did our best and hope that anglers will enjoy our offering. For most of all, this book should be fun. Not as much fun as fishing itself — that would be impossible. But, nonetheless, fun.

Harmon Henkin
Missoula, Montana

DEAR GENTLE READER:

The Best & The Most Expensive Are Usually The Same

Let's face it. All anglers may be created equal, but they aren't treated equally in the manufacture and merchandising of fishing tackle.

It's usually not discussed but the average national income of fly anglers ranks higher than the average incomes of other anglers such as spincasters, baitcasters and trollers. Now this is, again, the average income and there are undoubtedly millionaire spincasters and dirt-poor fly casters. But we are not talking about the exceptions.

What this means practically is simple: The higher the social and economic scale of a group, the better the variety and quality of the equipment offered to that group. Taste, quality and economics are intertwined.

Almost all anglers, whether as kids or adults, begin with the basic sort of equipment — most often a spincasting rig but sometimes with a fundamental fly or open-faced spinning rig. At this point things are more or less equal because you have to have more money than sense to splurge on top-quality equipment for your first outing.

But then the differences begin. For instance, though there are good-quality spin-casting reels available, there is a remarkable sameness among them. The metals used in their construction, their design and their capabilities don't vary enough, except in extreme cases, to matter much to the practical angler. Examination and equipment tests brought this fact home to us persistently.

In the case of cheaper spinning and spincasting rods this was particularly true. There aren't many companies producing glass rod blanks, and many of the rods marketed by different companies come from just a few factories.

In choosing products to list we faced the problem of real vs. illusory ad-agency differences in products and tried to make the best of it. Mass-produced products are just that and will never approach the quality and design differences of individually-crafted equipment. That's a simple fact.

If this book seems weighed in favor of the more expensive equipment, it was unavoidable. The top-of-the-line equipment and the most expensive equipment are usually the best — with some exceptions, such as Japanese open-faced reels which seem to be as good as anything available. The smaller operations which turn out the higher-priced stuff seem most capable of producing the most interesting and capable gear.

Fly fishing is the last angling repository of true quality, and in the handcrafted bamboo rods costing hundreds of dollars there are the kinds of differences that provide real options. No mass-produced items receive the tender loving care that fine tackle does. That's a simple fact.

We have tried to make the best of this situation by listing what real differences and strengths the tackle has. But the only way that all tackle will have top quality is if its users demand it. That's the way it goes.

—Harmon Henkin

A Disclaiming Word

Before embarking on the journey through this big book, please understand its limitations. This is a guide to the wonders of fishing tackle, not an encyclopedia of ordering instructions. It was compiled during a period of extensive model changes and price fluctuations in the fishing tackle industry. And it is very possible that by now certain products may be no longer available.

What this means to you is simple. Before sending off your money, check the most recent catalogs of the manufacturers and mail order houses listed with the commodities in this book.

We may be clever, but we ain't foolproof.

—Harmon Henkin

How To Use This Book

This is a simple book to use.

In each equipment category we list the top-of-the-line equipment. By this we mean the items have been judged to be the leading equipment of their kind, the cream of the crop, as it were. They may not be the only cream but they are definitely part of it.

The category "Ultimate Commodity" means the one product that we judged to be the best in its particular field. All judgments in matters of tackle are ultimately subjective or personal. We're just giving our opinions.

Other than that, the book explains itself and, we hope, in an enjoyable way.

— W. T. Vaughn

Our Experts

We asked 100 angling experts their favorite brands in several categories of fishing tackle. Included on our panel were well-known angling writers and regional authorities. We are grateful for their help and would like to thank them here for faithfully completing and returning our questionnaires.

FLY FISHING TACKLE

 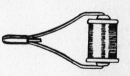

AN OBJECT OF WORSHIP:
The split cane rod is one of the finer things in life

By Harmon Henkin

There is little doubt that the split bamboo fly rod represents the pinnacle of sporting equipment. With a simple elegance and strict organic functionalism, its handcrafted lines surpass all but a few of the most pedigreed shotguns, leaving far behind in the tacky jungle of discount houses such gaming appliances as tennis rackets, golf clubs, football tables and rifles with plastic stocks.

The cane rod has been babied and adored since its birth in America during the mid-19th Century but in the last decade — fly fishing's most spectacular renaissance — it has become an object of worship. The crafting of bamboo rods and fly fishing itself have emerged from the eclipse of the 1950s, when U.S. Cold War policy forbidding trade with China stopped the flow of superior Tonkin cane, when our perpetual infatuation with gadgetry led to a tawdry affair with the spinning outfit and when economic attrition made the long apprenticeship in rod building less attractive than peddling insurance.

Though specialized, nylon-coated fly lines had made fly casting much easier by the 1960s, the rod craft industry had degenerated except for a few stars like Orvis and Leonard.

Hapless refugees from spincasting would read the classics of angling with their lyrical descriptions of treasured Paynes and Thomases but were usually forced to choose between this or that gold-wrapped, tinsel-coated, three-guided beast that would be enough to chase away Ernie Schwiebert from the sport. The output of the bamboo companies was never large. During this nadir it was minuscule. Cheap, ill-conceived production glass rods pretty well defined the market.

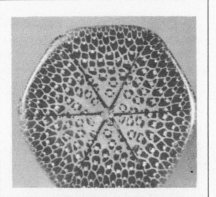

A cross-section of a glued, impregnated bamboo rod, showing the dense, unidirectional power fibers. *(Courtesy of the Orvis Company, Inc.)*

But though the process is sometimes very perverse, demand will often force some reply. Manufacturers began to notice the burgeoning fly fishing market. Even so, many of the bamboo rods initially built during the revival were just awful. Without a tradition to guide them newcomers to the sport were often shunted down dead-end streets. There was many a 1-ounce, 6-foot rod taking No. 8 line sold as an "ultra-light" outfit. Opposite such rug beaters were 7- and 8-footers so soft they were suffering from angling impotence.

But everyone knows what they say about fooling all of the people all of the time. By 1975 there was some discretion involved in the bamboo rod picture. Anglers were demanding that a rod that carried a midge be a really light rod that carried a light line as well. Experts like Leonard Wright, arguing against the tiny rod fetishism of people like Arnold Gingrich, stood up for the marked advantages of the long rod. As spokesmen

for various types of rods emerged the neophyte began getting a wide variety of meaningful choices in his tackle.

New brands of bamboo such as Thomas & Thomas appeared with dozens of options in taper, weight and appearance. Craftsmen resuscitated the patterns of master builders like Jim Payne and Ev Garrison and soon the buyer had an overwhelming number of choices before him. From one extreme to another.

The only limitation in fulfilling your heart's desire today is the steep prices being asked not only for the top-quality crafted rods but also for second-hand bamboo. A little homework is a good idea. Talk around trout shops these days often includes such arcane topics as ferrule construction, node staggering, casting arcs and the like. It is only the angler with much more money than sense who buys a $200-$300 rod merely because he likes the way it looks or because it can cast 75 feet.

Though the classic bamboo trout rod can be one of the most pleasurable things to own, it certainly isn't for everyone. It's not for the beginner with undefined tastes, someone who has a sado-masochistic relationship with equipment, or the dilettante who heard that everyone who's anyone owns a bamboo rod. It is for the angler who has refined his sensibilities to the point where the appreciation of a traditional rod designed for a particular task is natural.

The choice of a cane rod is ultimately a matter between the angler and his conscience. But the more you know before you buy the more you're going to be rewarded. And be sure to check for open seams!!

FLY RODS: THINK ABOUT THEIR ACTIONS

By Harmon Henkin

It takes time before an angler develops enough savvy to begin thinking about fly rods in terms of their actions. In the same way that wine is more than something that merely accompanies a meal, a fly rod is more than something that merely casts out the line.

Fly rods are available today with a larger variety of actions than ever before. In the earlier days of the sport, when bamboo was a new development, rods were long and usually willowy, which was fine for the wet flies that were fashionable.

But with the emergence of the dry fly, discriminating anglers wanted tackle that could handle the new style. Shortly after the turn of the century the dry-fly action rod emerged. Exactly who developed it is unknown, though Edward Payne is credited in some places. The tippy, fast dry-fly action cane rod worked well. The casts it made were usually short; when the fly was whipped back and forth it would dry quickly. It was especially good for what is called pocket fishing — where the angler blipped the fly into little pockets of still water, often near rocks. The unencumbered drift was usually very short before the line would be picked up and flipped to another pocket.

In the 1930s under the aegis of Frenchman Charles Ritz, the parabolic rod, still favored by many experienced anglers, was developed. This action, perfected by Paul Young, was slow and deep though it really had little or nothing to do with the concept in physics of the parabola. It has come to mean a rod whose action moves through its length rather than centering in the tip like dry-

(continued on page 10)

THE LAST HATCH
A FISHING MYSTERY
HARMON HENKIN

FREDERICK HALFORD ROUNDED Johnson Spring Creek's last curve and drifted placidly on his stomach with the slow current in the pool at the mouth. A fancy Abercrombie & Fitch gaff, the $39.95, mahogany-handled, stainless steel model, trailed from an ugly hole below the famous novelist's left ear.

Several things happened.

A pair of 18-inch brown trout that had been feeding politely in the pool on tiny cianis nymphs bolted back into their den in the undercut below the bank Paul Skues had spent 15 patient minutes on his hands and knees trying to approach. A little group of brookies scattered. Paul screeched with anger and dropped his Winston fly rod.

Then for the first time he saw the author of *My Stream Never Sleeps*, as Halford slipped into the turbulent Bitterroot River. Like a well-trained Labrador, Paul leaped into the frigid water after him.

A few minutes later he dragged the soggy mortal remains ashore to a soft sandbar. Halford's eyes were still open. Dead. No question about it. There would never be a sequel to *Loudly Flows the Madison*.

Paul stood up and gazed downstream in the late afternoon glare to a point where the choppy river seemed to disappear into the Bitterroot Mountains. He checked his emotions — shock, of course. And an exhilarating sense of pure joy. This had been the best July of his life, he decided, and broke into a loud, terrible chorus of "This Land Is My Land." Back on the bank he picked up his fly rod, dusted it off and started briskly up the game trail that led through the cottonwood grove by the river.

Two-hundred yards later he crawled between the bottom strands of a five-foot barbed wire fence with the expertise that comes from growing up in modern Montana, where they believe in fencing you in as well as out. On the other side, hand-lettered in red, a sign proclaimed,

NO TRESPASSING. SURVIVORS WILL BE PROSECUTED.
F. W. HALFORD, ESQ.

Tacked on a scrawny lodgepole pine a few yards away from that was a professional-looking announcement that said,

FUTURE HOME OF TROUTFISH ACRES, LEISURE LIVING FOR LEISURELY AMERICANS

A local phone number and address were listed below as if poachers like

(continued on page 20)

top of the line

ANGLERS' WORLD. Have to have the most expensive bamboo fly rod around? Try one of these Anglers' World models. Available in trout sizes at 6½, 7 and 8 feet, these two-piece, impregnated cane rods sell in the neighborhood of $550. They have nickel-silver ferrules, high-class reel seats and the other goodies that make up a deluxe wooden rod. Are they worth it? That's something for you and your banker to decide. Also available in salmon sizes at even more staggering prices.

DENNIS BAILEY. Dennis Bailey is one of the few remaining top-quality English rod makers who puts intermediate windings up the cane. His products are fine-looking pieces of equipment fitted in mahogany cases, no less. Bailey wants American customers for his handmade rods and will deal directly. Worth dropping a line for detailed information.

HARDY. This is one of the great traditional names in angling that has been undergoing great changes recently. From once offering perhaps the largest line of cane fly rods in the world, the venerable English firm, whose importer in this country is Harrington & Richardson, now offers just a few rods in the Palakona series.

Though still put up in a very elegant style, at times the Hardys seem to have lost the spirit for bamboo as the empire has set. But in the medium ranges around 8 feet they are still capable of turning out a very acceptable cane rod especially for those who prefer the crispy action that characterizes them.

LEONARD. *The* name in American bamboo rods has also been undergoing all sorts of changes since a fire in 1964 destroyed all of

WHAT WE LOOKED FOR IN QUALITY

The angler looking for a bamboo rod should be looking for a specialized product. Just about any bamboo produced today is well-made — for the kind of money being asked that's the least you can expect. We considered how refined the action was compared to the rod's intended use. Of course, there was lots of misty-eyed sentiment that clouded our judgement. We couldn't help it but that's what bamboo fly rods are all about these days.

DENNIS BAILEY

HARDY

"I have laid aside business, and gone a-fishing."
IZAAK WALTON, *The Compleat Angler*

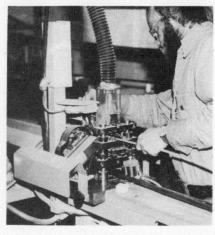

Building the split cane rod

(upper left) Selecting care for straightness, hardness, wall thickness, color and proper node placement. **(above)** Leonard claims its beveler can cut taper designs to tolerances of 1/10,000 of an inch. Each strip of bamboo is hand-fed and six strips will be matched to make a "joint" or rod selection. **(lower left)** After heat treating, each joint is individually glued and wrapped under pressure. **(below)** Filing 1/1000 to 2/1000 of an inch of the surface bark from a bamboo "joint." Care must be taken to avoid shearing the dense power fibers that give bamboo rods their strength. **(more photos on next page)**

H. L. Leonard Rod Co. photos

top of the line

Leonard's facilities, culminating in its sale to a publishing company in 1973. It has recently been putting out a very glossy catalog which de-emphasizes the bamboo rods that gave the company its superb reputation.

Hiram Leonard, who opened his Bangor, Maine, plant in the 1870s and built the first commercial 6-strip cane rod, was the first full-time bamboo producer in the country. All other builders are derived from this tradition.

The finish on the Leonard rods has always been one of their strong points. Throughout the last century many of the rods have been as fine as those made by anyone, anywhere. The most popular Leonard in recent times has been the 38H, 7-foot, basically dry fly rod built for a No. 4 line. But now it is difficult to forecast what models and what changes will occur in the line.

Along with the light trout rods, Leonard's other specialty was the salmon dry fly rod. These long, three-piece rods, usually running around nine feet, were often masterpieces.

Among the other delights of Leonard is the delicate 36L, a one-ounce 6-footer that balances with a No. 2 line. It is the only rod produced in the world specifically for No. 28 flies fished on 8x tippets. The whole Letort Series rods are for the experienced angler only.

Some of the "H" models in the Ausable Series are objected to as being a touch clubby while others claim the "L" models are too soft. But there are many experienced anglers who claim these unique tapers are unsurpassed.

ORVIS. Though the company made its appearance a century ago with the first perforated fly reel — which was patented by Charles F. Orvis — it has been among the leaders in bamboo production only since it

top of the line

began marketing impregnated rods after WWII.

The impregnation process, which has been adopted by other makers as well, consists of baking epoxide glues into the cane. This gives the rod more strength and durability than those put together with animal or other natural glues but can also make the rod seem a bit "woody," something most objected to by sticklers who like their tackle *au naturel*.

Orvis, under the spell of pioneering ultra-lighter Lee Wulff, once produced a complete line of rods under 7 feet that took a No. 6 or heavier line. In recent years the company has gotten away, at least somewhat, from the production of these shorties.

Despite being very innovative in rod design, Orvis is very traditional in building rods sticking to a wooden reel seat for most of the larger models, and all-cork seats for smaller ones, wrapped in a pleasing dark brown.

The top of the Orvis line is the Wes Jordon, a very elegant rod named after the Orvis ex-master builder. The 7½- and 8-footers are very good basic trout rods.

Orvis also produces a complete line of Battenkill Rods, the company's mainstay, and a less expensive 1-tip Madison plus specialized rods for everything from midge fishing to a gargantuan SSS for battling tarpon and other large finny beasts.

PEZON ET MICHEL. These rods have been on the scene in varying quantities for a few decades. Designed basically by master angler Charles Ritz, these French-made products are now being imported by Stoeger. What sets them apart from most other rods is their action. Some of the models are full parabolic, not the semi-parabolics made by the Paul Young people. They're beautifully

Building the split cane rod

(upper left) Making nickel-silver ferrules. **(upper right)** Turning down a handle to be mounted onto a rod. **(lower right)** Hand varnishing a rod. Leonard claims its drying room is maintained at a constant 90° to ensure proper drying conditions. **(more photos on preceding page)**

H. L. Leonard Rod Co. photos

top of the line

done and very powerful once you get the feel.

In England, where these rods are very popular, the 7-foot, 7-inch Colorado is most favored. Very well put up, though a bit heavy, the Pezons are available in various models from 6 feet, 10 inches to a two-handed salmon monster at 14 feet. May have a big future in this country if distribution is perfected.

WALTON POWELL. The son of the famed West Coast rod maker E. C. Powell, Walt continues in his father's tradition, building a variety of custom bamboos starting at about $250. He makes some rods that are quite peculiar in taper and design but others that are in the West Coast traditions.

THOMAS & THOMAS. What is old and very traditional is what's usually revered in cane rods. But in a relatively short time Thomas & Thomas has become one of the major exceptions to that rule.

Since it was founded in the 1960s, T&T, started by a couple of University of Maryland teaching types, has grown by leaps and bounds. Its biggest single leap was the acquisition of Sewell Dunton Rod Company in Massachusetts and the ensuing move to larger facilities in New England.

In an era when many cane companies were cutting back on their model numbers, T & T began offering a surprisingly large selection of possibilities. Their catalog boasts that you can order any of their rods from the tiniest to the mightiest in your choice of impregnated or regular glue construction. This is something that no other company offers. They'll also give you options of reel seat, handle shape, winding color or what-

THOMAS & THOMAS

LEONARD FERRULE PLUGS

In the olden days many fine rods came with plugs to prevent damage to hand-wrought ferrules. They kept dirt and dust from sneaking in and were an elegant addition to fancy rods. Leonard is now selling them in silver or black in ferrule sizes 6/64 through 18/64 inch. Tell them what model rod you have when ordering.

An old name is back.

PAYNE. The long-awaited revival of the Payne Rod has arrived. But the $575-$675- and $650-price tag will scare away all but the most devout. Leo Decker and Walt Carpenter are handling the operation for Gladding, which owns the Payne name. Jim Payne was considered probably the best rod maker of them all and these new Paynes are the same models that Jim constructed. They come in standard sizes in two or three pieces plus salmon dry fly rods, two models of Parabolic and some custom models, including a bass bugger and streamer rod. Only the best of modern materials and techniques are used for these traditional rods, according to their makers, but only time will tell if they catch on.

"Memory is especially merciful to fishermen."
LEONARD WRIGHT

THE CLASSIC BAMBOO ROD 7

top of the line

ever. If that weren't enough they'll make you any sort of rod your little heart desires.

They seem to have overcome their predilection for the shorter-length, heavyish line rods popularized basically by Lee Wulff and Orvis and have gotten more and more into the longer, lighter rods now so popular among practical anglers. They also offer excellent rods for salmon fishers, including some extraordinary 1-piecers and some semi-parabolic types outstanding for western nymph fishing.

One of their most interesting types of rods is the brush or pond rod that takes a No. 2 or No. 3 line. They really work, unlike most other tiny tackle.

All in all, T&T makes lots of rods worth serious consideration.

USLAN. Uslan 5-strip cane rods were once heavily touted by no less a rod authority than Al McClane. Then cane went sorta out of fashion and Nate Uslan retired to Florida where he made an occasional glass rod for the saltwater crowd. Well, now bamboo is definitely back in favor with lots of fly fishers and the 5-siders with their distinct and usually powerful actions are back on the market. Available in a standard range of sizes and priced below most other comparable cane, these come as close to a bargain as there is in a good bamboo rod.

WEIR AND SONS. Weir and Sons of Los Gatos, California, is one of those relatively small makers of cane rods that offers some nice choices as well as a complete repair service for all rods. They boast a wide range of models and actions at reasonable prices.

LEONARD

PEZON & MICHEL

ORVIS

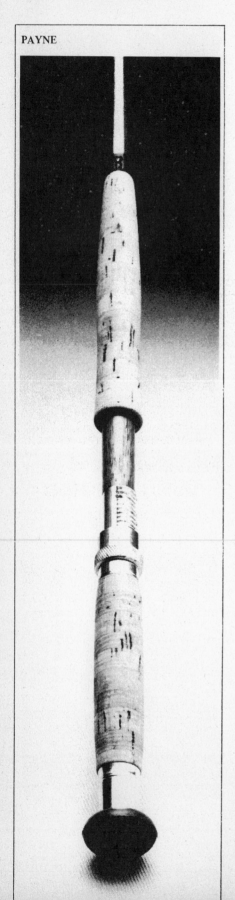

PAYNE

top of the line

WINSTON. These light-colored bamboo rods have been treasured by West Coast anglers ever since Lew Stoner and Ted Johnson started the San Francisco firm in the 1930s.

Their popularity was ensured by anglers who felt that the effete eastern rods made by Leonard and others just couldn't do the job in the bigger western waters. One of the early favored Winstons was an 8½-foot dry fly rod perfect for reaching out with Wulff and other attractor patterns.

Winston, under the aegis of Doug Merrick, began producing fine light- and ultra-light rods in the early 1960s and also offered a custom-building service to meet any specialized needs.

The company was taken over by Montanan Tom Morgan in 1972 and continues to produce fine rods.

PAUL YOUNG. The rods made by this original designer are certainly not the best-looking sticks around but many enthusiasts, including Ernie Schwiebert and Arnold Gingrich, claim they are among the best-casting.

Today these rods are being produced by son Jack Young and Bob Summers, who are continuing the founder's work. The rods most desired are the 6¼-foot Midge and the 7½-foot Perfectionist, which takes a No. 4 line as well as any rod around, the 7½-foot Martha Marie and the 8-foot Para 15 for No. 5 lines. Young rods are characterized by a semi-parabolic action that makes for long casting — especially for nymphs — and a deep, dark, very distinctive bamboo.

Young also makes a number of very powerful longer rods which have the tendency to be heavier than most

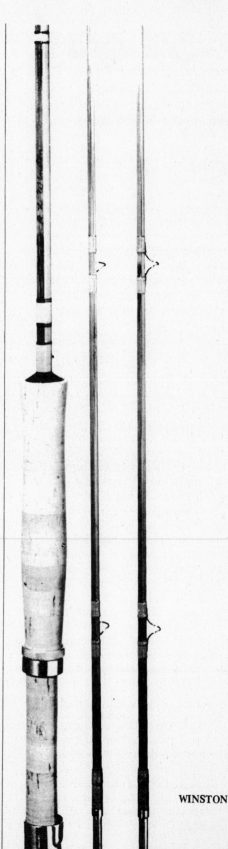

WINSTON

ORVIS

modern anglers weaned on glass and graphite care for.

These rods have been eulogized as strongly as any, including the famed Paynes and Garrisons, especially in Michigan, where generations of anglers have grown up passing around Youngs since the 1930s.

Characteristics of these rods, aside from bamboo color, are very simple sliding bands or screw-lock reel seats. Production is very limited and a two-year wait is common.

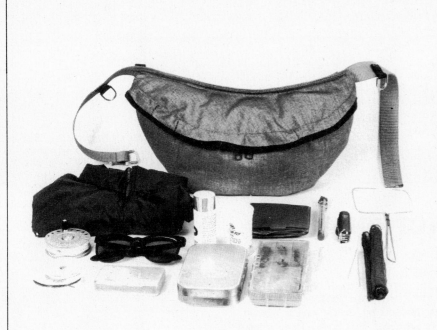

HIPPAK

Hippak was designed as a warm-weather alternative to the fishing vest. It will hold just about everything a fly fisherman needs, in a well-organized arrangement, and is a pleasure to wear. All of the contents are quickly accessible and yet secure. Each of the seven inside pockets has an elastic collar. A double slide zipper provides access to any one, leaving the others protected. The eighth center compartment is large enough to carry a good-size fish. Hippak can be worn in different ways to suit your mood or type of fishing. Wear it on your hip, behind your back. When wading deep, sling the strap over a shoulder and across your chest and it tucks under your arm.

The shell is tan waterproofed Cordura nylon, and the pocket material is waterproof. It is sewn with nylon thread, rivetted at points of stress, and D-rings are rivetted to the heavy nylon web belt. All hardware is non-reflective. The optional, adjustable bandolier has additional hangers which can be positioned to suit your needs. You may never wear a vest again.

Leonard Presentation Rods

Leave it to the Leonard Rod Company to outsnazz everyone else. The century-old company is producing 25 presentation rods a year for the dazzling price of $1400 each. Hold it! Read on. These rods, in either 2 or 3 pieces, come in lengths from 7 to 8 feet, are custom-fitted for the buyer through the use of tri-rods like the tri-guns fancy shotgun makers use. The action is fitted to the buyer's exact casting standard. They come in either a walnut or leather case. The sterling silver fittings are engraved and the rod has intermediate windings. Along with all those goodies you get a Bogdan trout reel, undoubtedly the most elegant reel around. Each rod is serial-numbered. It's available only through the Central Valley Store. Write before you send off your money.

"Let the blessings of St. Peter's Master be ... upon all that are lovers of virtue, and dare trust in his providence, and be quiet and go a-angling." **IZAAK WALTON,** *The Compleat Angler*

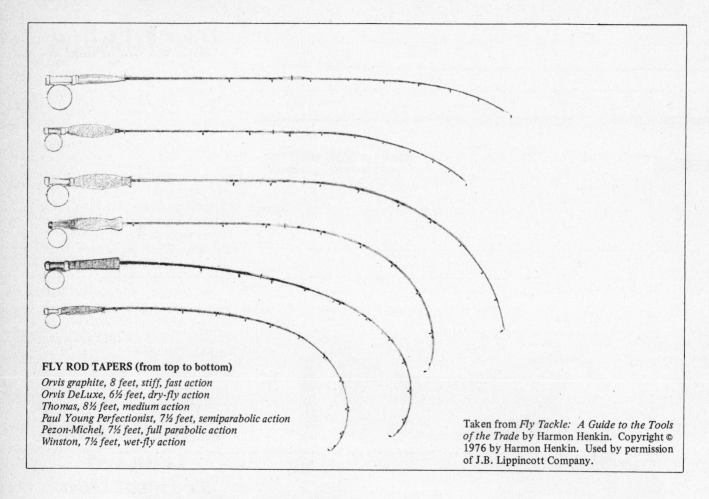

FLY ROD TAPERS (from top to bottom)

Orvis graphite, 8 feet, stiff, fast action
Orvis DeLuxe, 6½ feet, dry-fly action
Thomas, 8½ feet, medium action
Paul Young Perfectionist, 7½ feet, semiparabolic action
Pezon-Michel, 7½ feet, full parabolic action
Winston, 7½ feet, wet-fly action

Taken from *Fly Tackle: A Guide to the Tools of the Trade* by Harmon Henkin. Copyright © 1976 by Harmon Henkin. Used by permission of J.B. Lippincott Company.

FLY ROD ACTIONS

(continued from page 2)

fly action rods. The advantage of parabolics or semi-parabolics, according to their devotees, is that a slow, powerful rod gives more control than those with quicker actions.

Other rod tapers that are currently marketed include the so-called progressive action, which theoretically incorporates more and more of the rod as longer and longer lengths are cast. Often, however, these rods do not function well on long casts when lots of line has to be held up.

Slow-action rods, which have been favored by such noted anglers as Joe Brooks, are generally similar to the parabolics but their power arc is not as severe. Orvis continues to market slow action bamboo rods which are especially good in handling big flies and streamers.

The best of the long, light-line rods now favored by caddis and midge anglers are those that have a little spunk. Without backbone, these rods are merely regressions back to the Old English wet-fly sticks.

There still is a market for the stubby, six-footers that take No. 6 or even heavier lines. These rods, dubbed rug-beaters, have a place for the angler who wants to play around with small, light rods. But they are usually so powerful that delicate presentation is a problem.

Unless you're looking for a specific function, rods that have their action distributed at least fairly well along their lengths usually work out best. Avoid the ultra-tippy or ultra-deep rods. They are often difficult to master and are less forgiving than the standard actions.

By Leonard Wright

Fly rods come in all lengths from batons of 4 or 5 feet to wagon tongues of 18 or 20, if you count European salmon rods. Your final selection is a highly personal affair, but longer-than-average rods do offer the angler certain provable advantages — especially for fishing running water — if they don't overpunish his arm.

First, and most important, long rods let you keep more line off the water surface for a given presentation distance than short ones do. The less line and leader on the water when dry-fly fishing on streams, the less chance there is that your fly will be dragged unnaturally over the fish's lie by some intervening tongue of current.

A longer rod is more efficient for nymph, wet fly and streamer fishing, for much the same reason. You can control the direction and speed of travel of a sunken fly far more effectively if your rod-tip reaches out farther over the flowing water.

There's been a trend towards shorter fly rods over the past few decades due to a belief that shorter rods are lighter and therefore magnify the fight of the fish. Actually, this is pure myth. A fishing rod is basically a lever, the fulcrum of which is either your hand or your elbow, depending on how you hold it, and the tip of a longer rod is farther from the fulcrum than the tip of a shorter rod. Thus, the mechanical advantage in using a long rod is against the angler and in favor of the fish.

Take, for example, two trout rods designed for 5-weight lines — one of 6 feet and the other of 9. Both rods should bend equally in response to the same pull of a fish, for both are built to bend and cast best with 120 grams of line activating the rod. But the 9-footer is 50 per cent longer than the 6-footer, thereby giving the struggling fish half-again as much leverage *against* the angler's hand. Anyone with a smattering of physics can tell you that the 9-footer will make playing even a small fish into more of a struggle than the shorter rod will.

If, then, longer rods are more efficient fish-catchers and more pleasurable fish-players, why doesn't everyone use rods 12 to 18 feet long as they did a couple of hundred years ago? The light-rod fallacy mentioned earlier is part, but only part, of the reason. Long rods with their mechanical advantage against the angler work against him when casting, too. An aching arm, shoulder, or back can take the joy out of fishing — no matter how many you catch.

It's probably best to strike a compromise between the ultimate in fish-taking and the utterly fatigue-free. The length of rod this turns out to be in your case depends on many factors. Only you can make a final judgment. You will probably feel most comfortable with a rod of 9 feet or less if you fish the dry fly steadily for long hours in fast water or have a less-than-average physique. On the other hand, if you fish slow-moving waters or a lot of sunken flies where the place of casting is more relaxed, or if you have the arm of a blacksmith, you may well feel quite comfortable with a rod of 10 feet or perhaps slightly more if it's made of one of the light new synthetic fibers.

In any event, try out some of the new longer, lighter fly rods that are being produced today. They'll definitely help you catch more fish on running waters. Even on still waters, where their other advantages are negligible, they'll make playing a fish a bigger event. And that's what you really go fly fishing for, isn't it?

The advantages of the long rod

NEW TECHNIQUES & MATERIALS HAVE MADE THE FEATHERWEIGHT FLY ROD EASIER TO USE

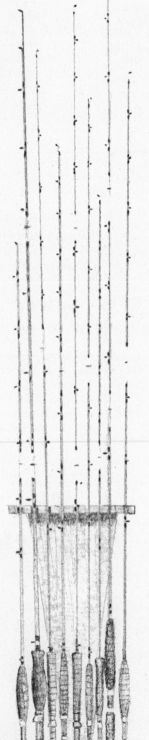

Fly fishermen have long believed that very light rods are not only hard to handle but won't make long casts. That used to be true, but modern techniques have made the featherweight fly rod much easier to use and have increased its range greatly. Important in these techniques is full use of the arm in casting.

Some years ago, in writing my *Handbook of Freshwater Fishing*, I described fly casting much as everyone else did, emphasizing movement of the wrist rather than of the arm, and warning against bringing the rod back much past the vertical on the back cast. At that time I had only limited experience with featherweight fly rods of 2 to 2½ ounces (scale weight of the complete rod). But since then, consistent, season-long fishing with such rods has convinced me that light rods are not only practical but that best results will be obtained with them when full use is made of the casting arm. Limiting the rod to the vertical point on the back cast, I've found, hinders rather than helps the cast.

In the traditional method, length and stiffness of the rod provide the casting power. And since the combined weight of the longer rod and the line-filled reel is great enough to make full-arm movement fatiguing, casting is achieved by wrist motion. (Almost every fly fisherman has been told that the perfect caster can hold a book against his body with the elbow of his casting arm while he's in action.) But with short rods the limited power of the wrist simply isn't enough to throw a light line.

A second factor favoring the use of lighter gear is the improvement of rod materials in the past quarter-century. The impregnation of bamboo with Bakelite, and the development of fine rods of glass fiber have given us lightness *and* durability. Glass fiber has the greatest strength for its weight, but there is a certain delicacy that's combined with power in split bamboo. Glass rods are more uniform, more durable.

In light rods it is the continuous casting, rather than the playing of fish, that causes deterioration and breakage. I enjoy casting and always work my rods relatively hard. And I cast them to the limit of my strength whenever there's a particularly distant spot I want to reach. In the past I could count on only about one month of life for a very light rod. Now they stand up, season after season, with practically no breakage.

A third factor lengthening the casts of short fly rods is the forward-taper fly line. Its advantage over the old double-taper comes only when the line really begins to stretch out and thirty-five feet or more are off the reel. Then the lighter line gets extra distance with the same amount of effort. Extra distance over a normal cast isn't so important with the usual 8½- or 9-foot rod, but the long "shoot" permitted by the forward-taper line makes it possible to reach out to all normal fishing distances with a rod of seven feet or less.

Obviously, the casting power of any fly rod is mainly limited by the weight of line it will handle in the air. And weight for weight, you get more line out with the featherweight outfit. However, there is a weight limit for any outfit. But supposing it's reached at fifty-five feet, say, you can still add length to the casts, and yet not overstrain the rod by using a long leader and learning how to snap it out.

From *Fishing with Lee Wulff* by Lee Wulff. (C) 1972 by Lee Wulff. Used by permission of Alfred A. Knopf.

"For you catch your next fish with a piece of the last."
O. W. HOLMES, *Verses for After Dinner*

THE CLASSIC BAMBOO ROD 13

HOW I FINALLY FISHED ROCK CREEK

By Harmon Henkin

"Rock Creek?" Why it's just up that dirt road. Can't miss it." I quickly thanked the woman behind the counter of the cafe, rushed back to my car and headed up the dusty road.

This was it. For five years I had planned to move out West and fish the fantastic trout waters I had drooled over in the outdoor magazines. Now here I was on my first day out — which also happened to be the last day of the season.

I had begun the morning dutifully unpacking my household belongings. But the warm October afternoon sun disarmed me and I threw responsibility to the wind and went fishing. I decided that my first outing would be on famous Rock Creek, that wild, wonderful stream 20 miles east of my new home in Missoula.

The road curved for a few miles and then a small creek came into sight. I slowed down and peered.

"That's the famous Rock Creek?" It was about six feet wide, shallow, slow and had almost cover. Maybe it was a spring creek? Well, this is where she told me it was. I got out and looked some more. I couldn't see any fish but maybe it was like those little eastern streams where you had to sneak up on the lunkers.

But deep inside I felt like a kid who had just had his first intimation that there wasn't any Santa Claus. I wasn't giving up though. I put on a 10-foot leader, and after debating for a couple of minutes, tied on a Royal Wulff. That was a good western-sounding fly.

I crept up to the bank and made the most graceful cast of my life. The fly drifted aimlessly back to me. Well, that was just the first cast.

Two hours, two hundred casts and some few hundred yards later I was still on my knees and the sun was heading home. I hadn't seen a trout or even a place where any self-respecting trout would hang its hat.

Then I got the strange feeling that someone was watching. I looked back and saw a rancher in an old pickup truck giving me a strange look. I stood up and looked back.

"Son, what you doing fishing that irrigation ditch?"

Irrigation ditch? Is that what they've done to my Rock Creek? Turned it into an irrigation ditch. I charged over to the truck.

"You'd be a lot smarter driving up the road a half mile and fishing Rock Creek. I lived here 60 years and never seen a fish in that little ditch. We just use a little of the creek water for our vegetable garden."

If I could have disappeared into my waders I would have. The rancher shook his head slowly like he had discovered another variety of nut and drove off.

A half mile up the road was the most beautiful mountain stream imaginable, with big boulders and white water, looking all the world like a housing development for trout.

But it was cold and almost dark and my first day of fishing in the glorious West came to an end.

This article appeared originally in *Montana Outdoors,* July/August 1974.

GAMEFISH: SPANISH MACKEREL

NAMES
Sierra mackerel, cero, spotted mackerel. *(Scomberomorus maculatus)*

DISTRIBUTION
The Spanish mackerel is a fish of the Atlantic, ranging from Cape Cod to Brazil. They are most abundant around the Carolinas and the coast of Mexico.

DESCRIPTION
The Spanish mackerel is a slender fish of beautiful green or blue coloring on the back with iridescent silver sides. The sides are marked with large orange or bronze spots. The dorsal fin is divided into two sections.

SIZE
The average Spanish mackerel is between 2 and 4 pounds. Larger catches have ranged as high as 20 pounds.

HABITAT
Although the Spanish mackerel prefers the open waters, they are often found in bays and inlets in search of food. They are a school fish and can be seen cruising on the surface.

FEEDING HABITS
The Spanish mackerel feeds on baitfish and small crustaceans. Among their favorite foods are glass minnows. Spring and summer are the best times to go after these fish.

TACKLE
This game fighter and great dinner falls victim most often to light- to medium-equipped trollers with large hooks and stripped baits.

specifications

BRAND-MODEL	LENGTH	WEIGHT (OZ.)	LINE SIZE	PIECES
HARDY				
	.6'	.2 1/2	.5	.2
	.6'8"	.3	.5	.2
	.7'2"	.3 1/4	.5	.2
	.7'6"	.3 1/2	.6	.2
	.8'	.4 1/2	.6	.2
	.8'6"	.5 1/4	.6	.2
	.8'9"	.5 1/2	.7	.2
Wye Salmon Fly Rod				
	.12'6"	.18	.9	.3
HUNTER'S WORLD: ANGLER'S WORLD				
Model Deluxe Rods				
A-1202	.6'6"	.2 1/8	.DT4	.2
A-1205	.7'	.2 1/2	.5	.2
A-1208	.8'	.4	.6	.2
Salmo Salar				
A-1210 (two-handed)	.12'	.15	.DT9, 10	.3
A-1212 (single handed)	.9'	.6 1/4	.DT9, WF9	.3
Impercane Salmon, Steelhead, Saltwater Rods				
A-1418 (two handed)	.12'6"	.16	.9	.3
A-1420 (single handed)	.9'	.6 3/4	.7, 8	.2
Impercane Offset Ferrule Rods				
A-1404	.8'3"	.4 1/2	.5, 6	.2
A-1406	.8'5"	.4 1/4	.5, 6	.2
A-1408	.8'8"	.5	.5, 6	.2
Impercane Superlight Series				
A-1410	.7'	.3 1/4	.5	.2
A-1412	.7'6"	.4	.5	.2
A-1414	.5'10"	.1 5/8	.6	.1
A-1416	.6'	.1 7/8	.6	.2
LEONARD				
Yellowstone Series				
37H 1850	.6'6"	.2 7/8	.DT4F	.2
38H 1854	.7'	.3 1/4	.DT5F	.2
39H 1858	.7'6"	.3 3/4	.6	.2
40H 1862	.8'	.4 1/2	.7	.2
41H 1866	.8'6"	.5 1/4	.8	.2
50H 1870	.8'	.4 5/8	.7	.2
51H 1872	.8'6"	.5 1/4	.8	.2
Ausable Series				
38 1852	.7'	.3 1/8	.DT4F	.2
39 1856	.7'6"	.3 5/8	.DT5F	.2
40 1860	.8'	.4 1/8	.6	.2
41 1864	.8'6"	.4 7/8	.7	.2
50 1868	.8'	.4 1/4	.6	.2
Letort Series				
38L 1874	.7'	.2 1/8	.DT3F	.2
39L 1876	.7'6"	.2 3/8	.DT4F	.2
40L 1878	.8'	.3 1/4	.DT5F	.2
41L 1809	.8'6"	.3 5/8	.6	.2

BRAND-MODEL	LENGTH	WEIGHT (OZ.)	LINE SIZE	PIECES
Miramichi Series (fresh, salt)				
60 1880	.8'	.5 1/8	.7	.2
61 1882	.8'6"	.5 1/2	.8	.2
62 1801	.9'	.5 7/8	.9	.2
70 1803	.8'	.5 1/2	.7	.2
71 1884	.8'6"	.5 3/4	.8	.2
72 1805	.9'	.6 1/8	.9	.2
73 1807	.9'6"	.6 3/4	.10	.2
Duracane Series (2-tips)				
654 1811	.6'6"	.2 5/8	.4	.2
704 1813	.7'	.2 5/8	.4	.2
705 1815	.7'	.2 7/8	.5	.2
754 1817	.7'6"	.3 1/4	.4	.2
755 1819	.7'6"	.3 1/2	.5	.2
756 1821	.7'6"	.3 5/8	.6	.2
805 1823	.8'	.3 3/4	.5	.2
806 1825	.8'	.4 3/8	.6	.2
807 1827	.8'	.4 1/2	.7	.2
856 1829	.8'6"	.4 3/4	.6	.2
857 1831	.8'6"	.4 3/4	.7	.2
806-3 1833	.8'	.4 7/8	.6	.3
857-3 1835	.8'6"	.5 1/8	.7	.3
807-SDF 1837	.8'	.4 3/8	.7	.2
858-SDF 1839	.8'6"	.5 1/4	.8	.2
909-SDF 1841	.9'	.5 5/8	.9	.2
858-3-SDF 1843	.8'6"	.5 3/8	.8	.3
909-3-SDF 1845	.9'	.5 3/4	.9	.3
ORVIS				
Battenkill				
M9650-2	.6'6"	.2 7/8	.6	.2
M9701-2	.7'	.3 3/8	.6	.2
M9751-2	.7'6"	.3 7/8	.6	.2
M9707-2 (with 2 interchangeable tips)	.7'/7'3"		.6	.2
M9809-2	.8'	.4 1/8	.6	.2
M9801-2	.8'	.4 3/8	.8	.2
M9855-2	.8'6"	.4 3/4	.8	.2
M9764-2 (with extra tip)	.7'6"	.3 5/8	.5	.3
M9808-2 (with extra tip)	.8'	.4 1/2	.7	.3
M9859-2 (with extra tip)	.8'6"	.4 5/8	.7	.3
M9650-1	.6'6"	.2 7/8	.6	.2
M9701-1	.7'	.3 3/8	.6	.2
M9751-1	.7'6"	.3 7/8	.6	.2
M9809-1	.8'	.4 1/8	.6	.2
M9801-1	.8'	.4 3/8	.8	.2
M9855-1	.8'6"	.4 3/4	.8	.2
Madison				
M9656-11	.6'6"	.2 3/8	.4	.2
M9702-11	.7'	.2 3/4	.3	.2
M9758-11	.7'6"	.3 1/4	.5	.2
M9652-1	.6'6"	.2 7/8	.6	.2
M9703-1	.7'	.3 3/8	.6	.2
M9753-1	.7'6"	.3 7/8	.6	.2
M9810-1	.8'	.4 1/8	.6	.2
M9813-1	.8'6"	.4 1/2	.6	.2

"You must lose a fly to catch a trout."
GEORGE HERBERT, *Jacula Prudentum*

THE CLASSIC BAMBOO ROD 15

specifications

BRAND-MODEL	LENGTH	WEIGHT (OZ.)	LINE SIZE	PIECES
M9803-1	8'	.4 3/8	.8	2
M9857-1	8'6"	.4 3/4	.8	2
M9820-1	8'9"	.5 7/8	.10	2

Wes Jordan

BRAND-MODEL	LENGTH	WEIGHT (OZ.)	LINE SIZE	PIECES
M9750-2 (with extra tip and leather case)	7'6"	.3 7/8	.6	2
M9800-2 (with extra tip and leather case)	8'	.4 3/8	.8	2

Limestone Special

BRAND-MODEL	LENGTH	WEIGHT (OZ.)	LINE SIZE	PIECES
M9812-2 (with extra tip)	8'6"	.4 1/2	.6	2

S-S-S Rod

BRAND-MODEL	LENGTH	WEIGHT (OZ.)	LINE SIZE	PIECES
M9815-2 (with two tips)	7'6"/7'9"		.5	2

Special Function Rods

BRAND-MODEL	LENGTH	WEIGHT (OZ.)	LINE SIZE	PIECES
M9759-1 (midge with single tip)	7'6"	.3 5/8	.5	2
M9759-2 (midge with extra tip)	7'6"	.3 5/8	.5	2
M9765-2 (midge/nymph with extra tip)	7'6"/7'9"		.5	2
M9505-1	5'9"	.1 7/8	.4	2
M9657-1	6'6"	.2	.4	2
M9657-2 (with extra tip)	6'6"	.2	.4	2

Orvis 7/3

BRAND-MODEL	LENGTH	WEIGHT (OZ.)	LINE SIZE	PIECES
M9353-2 (with extra tip)	7'	.2 3/8	.3	2

Orvis 7/4

BRAND-MODEL	LENGTH	WEIGHT (OZ.)	LINE SIZE	PIECES
M9705-2 (with extra tip)	7'	.2 3/4	.4	3

Rocky Mountain Travel Rods

BRAND-MODEL	LENGTH	WEIGHT (OZ.)	LINE SIZE	PIECES
M9659-2 (with extra tip)	6'6"	.3 1/4	.6	3
M9660-2 (fly and spin with extra tip)	6'6"	.3 1/8	.6	3

Rocky Mountain Presentation Set

M9663 (fly/spin) . . . . . 6'6" . . . . . With CFO III Fly Reel, WF6F Orvis line, 50 yards backing, Orvis leader selection, 2 Wheatley Fly Boxes stocked with dry and wet flies, Orvis Angler's Clip, Orvis Fly Threader and Orvis 50A Spin Reel (51A for left hand) loaded with 4 lb. test line, extra 50A spool with 2 lb. test line, 6-lure mini-lure selection in 1/8 oz. class, Fearsome Foursome Lure Selection in 1/4 oz. class, suede reel case for spin or fly reel.

Fly and Spin Pak Rod

BRAND-MODEL	LENGTH	WEIGHT (OZ.)	LINE SIZE	PIECES
M9352-2 (with extra tip)	7'	.3 1/2		4

E. F. PAYNE

3-Piece Rods

BRAND-MODEL	LENGTH	WEIGHT (OZ.)	LINE SIZE	PIECES
197	7'6"	.3 1/2-3 5/8	.5	3
198	7'6"	.3 3/4-3 7/8	.6	3
200	8'	.3 5/8-3 3/4	.4	3
201	8'	.3 7/8-4	.5	3
202	8'	.4 1/8-4 1/4	.6	3
204	8'6"	.4 1/8-4 1/4	.5	3
205	8'3"	.4 1/2-4 5/8	.6	3
206	8'6"	.5-5 1/4	.7	3
207	9'	.4 3/4-4 7/8	.7	3
208	9'	.4 3/4-5	.7	3
209	9'	.5 1/4-5 3/4	.8	3
210	9'	.5 1/2	.9	3
212	9'6"	.5 5/8-5 3/4	.8	3
214	9'6"	.6-6 1/8	.9	3

Payne 2-Piece Rods

BRAND-MODEL	LENGTH	WEIGHT (OZ.)	LINE SIZE	PIECES
95	6'	.1 5/8	.3, 4	2
96	6'6"	.2 1/4-2 3/8	.4	2
97	7'	.5/8-2 3/4		2
98	7'	.2 7/8-3	.5	2
100	7'6"	.3 1/4-3 3/8	.4	2
101	7'6"	.3 1/2-3 3/4	.5	2
102	8'	.3 5/8-3 7/8	.5	2
103	8'	.4-4 1/8	.6	2
104	8'6"	.4 1/8-4 3/8	.6	2
105	8'6"	.4 5/8-4 3/4	.7	2
106	8'6"	.4 5/8-4 3/4	.7	2
107	8'10"	.4 5/8-5 1/8	.8	2
108	9'	.5-5 1/4	.8	2
110	9'	.5 3/8-5 1/2	.9	2

Dry Fly Salmon Rods

BRAND-MODEL	LENGTH	WEIGHT (OZ.)	LINE SIZE	PIECES
400	9'	.6 5/8-6 3/4		3
405	9'3"	.7-7 1/8		3
410	9'6"	.7 1/8-7 3/8		3
430	9'	.6-6 1/4		2
435	9'6"	.7-7 1/8		2

Parabolic Rods

BRAND-MODEL	LENGTH	WEIGHT (OZ.)	LINE SIZE	PIECES
	7'1"	.2 7/8	.3, 4	2
(regular)	7'9"	.3 3/4	.4, 5	2
(heavier)	7'9"		.6, 7	2

Special Rods

BRAND-MODEL	LENGTH	WEIGHT (OZ.)	LINE SIZE	PIECES
Bass Bug	9'	.6 1/2-6 5/8		
Streamer	8'3"	.5 5/8-5 3/4		
Streamer	9'	.6-6 1/4		
Trout	8'	.3 5/8-4 1/8		

PEZON ET MICHEL

Parabolic PPP

BRAND-MODEL	LENGTH	WEIGHT (OZ.)	LINE SIZE	PIECES
CS262S	7'2"	.3 15/16	.5	2
CS279S	7'5"	.4 3/4	.5	2
CS263S	7'7"	.3 7/8	.5	2

specifications

BRAND-MODEL	LENGTH	WEIGHT (OZ.)	LINE SIZE	PIECES
CS276S	8'1"	5 1/16	4, 5	2
CS264S	8'3"	5 1/4	5, 6	2
CS270S	8'3"	5 3/8	6, 7	2
CS266S	8'5"	5 5/16	6	2
CS274S	8'7"	6 1/4	6, 7	2

Parabolic Royale (weight differs with type of reel seat)

	LENGTH	WEIGHT (OZ.)	LINE SIZE	PIECES
	6'10"	3-3 7/8	5	2
	7'4"	3 1/4-4 3/16	5	2
	7'9"	3 1/2-4 3/8	5	2
	8'3"	4 3/8-5 1/4	5	2
	8'8"	5 3/4	7	2
	9'3"	6 7/16	9	2

Parabolic Extra Series

BRAND-MODEL	LENGTH	WEIGHT (OZ.)	LINE SIZE	PIECES
CS242	8'2"	5 7/8	5, 6	2
CS244	8'2"	5 3/4	5	2
CS229	8'5"	4 7/8	5, 6	2
CS243	8'10"	5 3/8	6	2
CS241	9'6"	6 3/16	5, 6	2

Parabolic Prima

	LENGTH	WEIGHT (OZ.)	LINE SIZE	PIECES
	8'	5 3/16	4, 5	2
	8'6"	4 7/8	5, 6	2
	9'	5 1/2	6, 7	2

Parabolic Salmon

BRAND-MODEL	LENGTH	WEIGHT (OZ.)	LINE SIZE	PIECES
CS310	10'6"	10 3/4	7	2
CS312	12'	13 5/16	10	3
CS312	14'	20 5/16	11, 12	3

THOMAS & THOMAS

Individualist Rods (standard or custom-made with grip and reel seat options)

Montana (2- or 3-piece)

	LENGTH	WEIGHT (OZ.)	LINE SIZE
	6'6"	2 1/8	4
	7'	2 3/8	4
	7'	2 1/2	5
	7'6"	3 1/4	5
	7'6"	3 3/4	6
	8'	4	6
	8'	4 1/8	7
	8'6"	4 3/4	8

Hendrikson (2- or 3-piece)

	LENGTH	WEIGHT (OZ.)	LINE SIZE
	6'	1 3/4	4
	6'6"	2 1/8	4
	7'	2 1/4	3
	7'	2 3/8	4
	7'	2 1/2	5
	7'6"	3 1/4	5
	7'6"	3 3/4	6
	8'	3 3/4	5
	8'	4	6
	8'6"	4	5

Midge (2- or 3-piece)

	LENGTH	WEIGHT (OZ.)	LINE SIZE
	6'6"	2 1/8	4
	7'	2 3/8	4
	7'6"	3	4
	7'6"	3 1/4	5
	8'	3 1/2	4

BRAND-MODEL	LENGTH	WEIGHT (OZ.)	LINE SIZE	PIECES
	8'6"	3 7/8	4	3
	9'	4 1/4	4	3

Sans Pareil Custom Rods (contact Thomas & Thomas)

	LENGTH
	6'
	6'6"
	7'
	7'6"
	8'
	8'6"
	9'
	9'6"
	10'

Salmon XL Rods

	LENGTH	LINE SIZE	PIECES
	8'	6	2
	8'	7	2
	8'6"	8	2
	8'6"	8	3
	9'	8	3
	9'6"	9	3

Salmon SL Rods

	LENGTH	LINE SIZE	PIECES
	8'6"	8	3
	9'	8	3
	9'6"	8	3
	9'6"	8	3
	10'	8	3
	10'	9	3

Double-Handed Rods

	LENGTH	LINE SIZE	PIECES
	10'6"	9	3
	12'	8	3
	12'	10	3
	14'	10	4

Classic Rods

	LENGTH	WEIGHT (OZ.)	LINE SIZE	PIECES
	6'6"	2 1/8	4	2
	7'	2 1/4	3	2
	7'	2 3/8	4	2
	7'	2 1/2	5	2
	7'6"	3 1/4	5	2
	7'6"	3 3/4	6	2
	8'	3 3/4	5	2
	8'	4	6	2

USLAN

BRAND-MODEL	LENGTH	WEIGHT (OZ.)
7011	7'	2 1/4
7012	7'	3
7513	7'6"	4
8014	8'	4 1/4
8515	8'6"	4 3/4
9016	9'	5 3/4

3-piece Salmon Rod

WEIR & SONS

Lightweight Rods

BRAND-MODEL	LENGTH	WEIGHT (OZ.)	LINE SIZE
LW/M601	6'	1 1/4	2L.
D601	6'	1 5/8	DT3, WF4

specifications

BRAND-MODEL	LENGTH	WEIGHT (OZ.)	LINE SIZE	PIECES
LW/M763	7'6".	2 1/2	DT3, WF4	
LW/M803	8'	3 3/4	DT4, WF5	
Medium-Action Rods				
M761	7'6".	3 3/4	DT5, WF6	
M762	7'6".	3 3/4	DT5, WF6	
M763	7'6".	3 3/4	DT5, WF6	
M801	8'	4	DT6, WF7	
M802	8'	4	DT6, WF7	
M803	8'	4	DT6, WF7	
Dry Fly Rods				
D701	7'	2 1/2	DT3, WF4	
D702	7'	2 1/2	DT3, WF4	
D703	7'	2 1/2	DT3, WF4	
D761	7'6".	3 7/8	DT5, WF6	
D762	7'6".	3 7/8	DT5, WF6	
D763	7'6".	3 7/8	DT5, WF6	
D801	8'	4 1/8	DT6, WF7	
D802	8'	4 1/8	DT6, WF7	
D803	8'	4 1/8	DT6, WF7	
D861	8'6".	4 1/2	DT7, WF8	
D862	8'6".	4 1/2	DT7, WF8	
D863	8'6".	4 1/2	DT7, WF8	

Contact Weir and Sons for information on available options for custom bamboo rods.

R. L. WINSTON

Leetle Feller

	LENGTH	WEIGHT (OZ.)	LINE SIZE	PIECES
	5'6".	1 3/4	DT3	2
	6'	2	DT3	2
	6'6".	2 1/8	DT3	2
	7'	2 1/2	DT3	2

BRAND-MODEL	LENGTH	WEIGHT (OZ.)	LINE SIZE	PIECES
	7'6".	2 3/4	DT3	2
	7'	2 5/8	DT4	2
	7'6".	2 7/8	DT4	2
Light Trout Rods				
	5'6".	2	DT4	2
	6'	2 1/4	DT4	2
	6'	2 1/2	DT5	2
	6'6".	2 1/2	DT4	2
	6'6".	2 3/4	DT5	2
	7'	2 7/8	DT5	2
	7'6".	3	DT5	2
	7'6".	3 1/4	DT6	2
Trout Rods				
	8'	3 5/8	DT4	2
	8'	3 3/4	DT5	2
	8'	4	DT6	2
	8'6".	4	DT4	2
	8'6".	4 1/8	DT5	2
	8'6".	4 1/4	DT6	2
	8'6".	4 1/2	DT7	2
	8'6".	4 3/4	DT7, WF8	2
	8'9".	4 5/8	DT6, WF7	2
	8'9".	4 3/4	DT7, WF8	2
	9'	4 7/8	DT6, WF7	2
Steelhead and Salmon Rods				
	8'9".	5	WF8, ST9	2
	9'	5	WF7, ST8	2
	9'	5 1/4	WF9, ST9	2
	9'	5 1/2	WF9, ST10	2
	9'3".	5 1/2	WF9, ST10	2
	9'3".	5 3/4	WF10, ST11	2
	9'6".	6	WF10, ST11	2

WALTON POWELL

For custom bamboo rods, contact Walton Powell, 1148 West 8th Avenue, Chico, California 95926.

DENNIS BAILEY

For custom bamboo rods, contact Dennis Bailey, Principal, Coventry & Birmingham School of Casting, 288 Allesley Old Road, Coventry CV5 8GH, England.

GLASS AND GRAPHITE RODS ARE GETTING BETTER AND BETTER

By Harmon Henkin

Except for the perfectionist, traditionalist and social climber most anglers are using fly rods that come from the new inorganic technologies that sprang up after World War II.

Glass rods have gained enormously in finesse over the last 30 years and graphite rods have been slowly but steadily improving since Fenwick introduced them five years ago. The devotees of artificials have come to completely dominate the rod market except for the vociferous minority who still pledge allegiance to its bamboo.

But unless you're an angler who has a very compelling reason to use a bamboo rod go with glass or graphite, especially if you're just getting started. Good cane rods start out at $250 and the better ones are designed for very specific duties. The cream of today's cane rods are designed for light lines and small flies and don't you believe anything else. Since most glass and graphite is mass-produced there is a great deal more variety in taper design available.

None of this means much to the angler who just wants a fly rod. It's when you want a fly rod to cast a No. 3 line with No. 24 caenis imitations that you should start browsing through cane.

On bigger rods, say those that carry a No. 7 line or heavier, glass and graphite have a far superior weight-to-power ratio. A 9-foot, 4½-ounce glass rod or a 3-ounce graphite which carries a No. 9 line will cast that big steelhead fly much more efficiently over the course of a hard day's angling than the 6-or so-ounce cane rod that Joe Brooks used to favor. There's some who prefer the long, powerful wood rods but usually for reasons of tradition, as in Atlantic Salmon fishing, or just as a rationale because they own a big club.

If you avoid the assembly-line glass rods and get one that has been crafted by someone like Russ Peak or Vince Cummins there are nuances available to satisfy everyone but the bamboo fanatic. Peak will make you anything from a small, heavy-line rod that used to be in vogue a few years back to the long, willowy sticks for ultra-light lines that are now so chic.

Even in the mass-produced rods there ar[e] lots of different actions that can be bough[t] in the under-$100 category. The Winsto[n] Company among others offers a complet[e] variety of glass rods nicely put-up and Scien[tific] Angler System rods remain the stapl[e] they've been since late casting champion Jo[n] Tarantino designed them.

When glass rods were first marketed 2[0] years ago they were, for the most part, jus[t] awful. They were sold before much thinkin[g] had gone into their design and were eithe[r] board-stiff or noodle-soft. It was anothe[r] case where theory outdistanced practice an[d] marketing forgot the consumer. But as th[e] taste of anglers became more refined in th[e] 1960s with the development of highly spe[cialized] synthetic fly lines, producers re[sponded] with tubular glass rods that re[spected] this new sophistication. No longe[r] was every rod peddled as an all-around stic[k] and no longer were 8-foot rods for No. [] lines sold as dry fly specials. It became po[ssible] to find a glass rod for a No. 4 line, on[e] that worked well with nymphs or could cas[t] a dry fly with ample discretion.

Graphite rods on the other hand still hav[e] a ways to go. Admittedly, they can heave [a] line out great distances with incredible eas[e] but that doesn't really make a fly rod. Ex[cept] for certain specialized kinds of fishin[g] such as steelheading and lake fishing, it take[s]

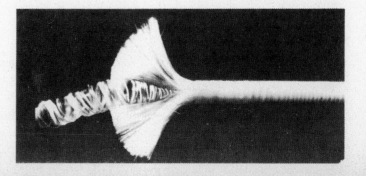

Shakespeare's Howald process for the construction of glass rods encases a continuous fiber spiral from butt to tip with continuous individual fibers running parallel to the full length of the blank.

ore than mere casting to make a decent fly
d. Graphites haven't as yet developed the
ndling ease that characterizes the best
ass or bamboo. The lightness and strength
graphite, originally developed in England
a space technology by-product, makes for
rod that generates incredible line speed, a
ght loop and all the rest of modern cast-
g's catechism. But even the best of the
aphites seem to lack the ability to really
ndle a 7X tippet and a No. 22 fly well.

Like glass in its time, graphite seems to
ve been marketed too soon. Now the
anufacturers are playing catch-up with
eir slogans, claiming that each year's offer-
g is vastly improved over the last. But with
ices usually starting at more than $100
ere are still lots of ifs and whens in the
aphite field.

Another problem is that no one yet has
fined what a "graphite rod" really is,
ough manufacturers are trying to set some
ndards. Is a rod that's 5 per cent graphite
apped with 95 per cent fiberglass a
raphite rod"? Good question. No answer
t. Graphite rods have varied from being
-graphite, and therefore rather brittle, to
cks that only have a small percentage of
phite fibers and therefore lack the weight-
-power ratio of full graphite.

But all this negativism is not to say that
phite isn't without its place. If you can

afford it, graphite rods, with their acceler-
ated line speed, are wondrous for the beginner who usually suffers from third-degree
line sag. Delicacy isn't a major consideration
and a graphite rod is easier to handle all day
without fatigue. Also, there's nothing like a
graphite rod for getting the line out. Undoubtedly, before too long the industry will
be producing graphites that can genuinely
take advantage of the subtleties of rod taper
developed over the past decade.

The standards for picking a decent piece
of glass or graphite should concentrate on
the desired action, the ferrules, the guides
and the way it's put up. The action is the
one constant — it can't be changed. The rod
can be rewrapped, the handle modified or
the ferrules repaired but you're stuck with
the action.

A few years ago there was a real danger in
buying cheaper rods since many of them
were equipped with half the number of requisite guides, tinny ferrules and reel seats
that froze at the slightest pressure. Today,
however, reputable manufacturers, even of
less expensive rods, have gotten their act together. Most fly rods will be at least close to
the one-guide-per-foot rule of thumb and
will carry a reel seat that will open and shut
easily.

For both kinds of rods under $100 look

for glass or built-up graphite ferrules. With a
few exceptions such as Vince Cummins, who
goes with nickel-silver ferrules on both his
graphite and glass, most makers today have
gone over to built-up ferrules. How
Cummins manages to produce the quality
ferrule he does in an $85 rod remains a mys-
tery. Metal ferrules on rods at the low end of
the line are very cheesy — so go with glass
unless you know better.

A reel seat should be in balance with the
rest of the rod in weight and size. And, yes,
it should hold your reel. You'd be surprised
how many anglers have bought rods which
they discover upon taking home don't hold
their favorite Pflueger or Hardy. The seat
should also be put on firmly but not in such
a way that it can't be replaced.

The guides should be wrapped on and
then lacquered rather than taped and glued
with weird compounds, as is sometimes the
case with discount-house rods. The guides
themselves should have no abrasive edges to
rub the fly line and they should be perfectly
even.

And lastly, the rod itself should look
decent. You have to spend lots of time holding your fly rod and you should be able to
look it in the guides without blanching. The
sleazy finish of some of the lesser rods is
usually an attempt to cover up a multitude
of sins.

Shakespeare began experimenting
with graphite in the early 1960s.
The company's graphite blanks
are built with the Howald process
described at left.

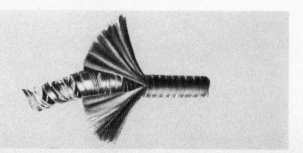

"The fish, once wounded by the treacherous hook, Fancies the barb concealed in every food."
Epistulae ex Ponto

A note on casting with graphite

There's a reel difference between a casting rod and a fishing rod — buyers of graphite should be aware of this difference.

Things are getting better a few years after the introduction of graphite fly rods but they still aren't great. Most of the early models made from this space-technology material were casting machines — but you couldn't fish with them. Despite all the touting of them by outdoor writers and manufacturers, they were not really fit for the delicate presentation required by fly fishing. They could get your fly out but the process was like a banzai pilot on his last mission.

In buying a rod, casting performance is only half the picture. Delicacy and accuracy, especially with light tippets, are the other half. Lots of affluent beginners who forked over $150 for an early graphite learned to put out 60 feet of tight-looped line with remarkable speed but they still had to learn how to put a fly in front of a fish.

Graphite rods, because of their relative stiffness, develop incredible line speeds even in the hands of a novice. But for most anglers this velocity can be overwhelming. Control is difficult. The slower that your line travels, within limits, the more forgiving of errors it is and the more time you have for judging fly approach.

Fine graphites on the market today include Winston and Leonard eight footers or longer that take a No. 4 line. They're wondrous things for getting out either a long or short light line with enough length to control and mend your line. This is where graphite seems to excel. Bamboo and even glass rods of this length never seem to behave well at extremes. They tend to get floppy at reaches of more than 40 feet.

But remember: actual fishing conditions are never anything like casting a rod in front of a fly shop. Practice in the field. Like any other fishing rod, graphites are only as good as their angling capability.
— H.H.

THE LAST HATCH
A FISHING MYSTERY
HARMON HENKIN

(continued from page 2)

Paul were considered likely customers for an overpriced quarter-acre mobile home tract on the floodplain.

Paul shook his head slowly and surveyed the Halford place, crouched on a gentle rise in the near distance. The sprawling main house, an over-sized two-story affair made of white pine logs, had been built by an atoning mining executive in the 1920s as a hide-out far from the scene of his company's environmental crimes. Halford had bought the place ten years before and immediately celebrated it in his epic work, *The Woodpecker Knocks Loudly*, which more than paid for it. With the excess he had built a tennis court, a four-car garage, a sauna and a stable.

As Paul approached the clearing he glanced at the stable. A man in the door was peering at him through a pair of Leitz Trinovids. Paul kept walking. The man lowered the binoculars, yelled something menacing and disappeared inside. A minute later he popped back out with a double-barreled Churchill shotgun aimed at Paul.

"Hey, you. This is private property. Get off or I'll pepper your hide."

Paul ignored him and elbowed the barrel away as he strode past on his way to the main house.

"Don't be rude. Put that away."

The man's tweed jacket seemed to rumple at Paul's impertinence. The shotgun stirred a little. The man was obviously very nervous and getting more so every second. But they both knew the bluff had been called. He was obviously used to taking orders from those in authority and passing them down to the serfs. A young, scruffy man in faded Levis, dirty sneakers, badly managed hair and a ragged fishing vest didn't figure into his understanding of the pecking order. Changing times and all. His face sagged, and the deep lines around his eyes made him suddenly look more worn than his 40 years. He lowered the barrel.

"What do you want here, anyway?" he called after Paul.

"Telephone."

"It's not public."

Paul stopped and turned around slowly in the middle of the patio, filled with strategically placed wicker furniture.

"Look, Wyatt Earp, I —"

"It's Andrew Dun. Mr. Halford's confidential secretary."

"Dun, I've just had a day's fishing ruined because of your boss.

(continued on page 45)

"No human being, however great, or powerful, was ever so free as a fish."
JOHN RUSKIN, *The Two Paths*

THE NEW TECHNOLOGY 21

GRAPHITE IS HERE TO STAY

Although there's no such thing as the perfect fly rod, graphite rods are the best casting tools ever made

By Russell Chatham

"What are you working on?" my lady friend asked, curious to know what kind of phone call could compete successfully with her invitation to go discotheque dancing.

"An article about a new kind of fishing rod," I answered sniffishly, covering the receiver with one hand.

"Oh, those pencil things you're always talking about," she came back impatiently.

Graphite does mean pencil lead. It's also a black powder you put on squeaky door hinges and a substance found in many paints. But that's natural graphite, a mineral.

Today's graphite composites are very different, man-made by a process which rearranges carbon atoms into graphite molecules to produce a new structural material which can be as much as nine times stronger than steel and 75 per cent as light.

One morning I met Steve Rajeff at the pools of the Golden Gate Angling and Casting Club in San Francisco to try out his set of graphite fly rods. Young Rajeff, considered one of the finest casters in the world, had recently broken the late Jon Tarantino's one-handed trout fly distance record of 201 feet with a long cast of 208, capturing what is perhaps the most difficult and coveted record in tournament fly casting.

Rajeff holds other records as well — accuracy and distance — and all have been set with graphite rods. An enthusiastic angler, he now uses them exclusively not only for tournament casting but for all his fishing.

"These rods won't make you a better caster," he told me, "but if you're already good they'll make the whole thing easier."

Rajeff began false casting an extremely light, slender Fenwick FF 908 with a No. 8 forward line,

a conventional cork bass bug tied to the leader. This was purely a fishing outfit, one that he was going to use later that day for black bass.

In response to precise timing, the line slid out in perfect narrow loops, the ungainly bass bug behaving as if it weren't there at all.

"A hundred and five feet," Rajeff said softly. "Not bad. I've gotten a hundred ten a couple of times though. Here, try it."

Bracing for possible embarrassment, I tentatively worked some line out. Then a bit more until the overhang was pushing the edge of reasonable limits. When I cast, the bug turned over cleanly at a measured 100 feet. The whole line was out.

Seeing that I might know a ferrule from a reel seat and that I had managed to keep from turning his fly line into macramé, Rajeff warmed to the project.

He offered me another stick. "Here's a glass rod with the same kind of line and bug on it. I think you'll find you can cast just as far. But compare the two."

He was right, I could cast as far — but with twice the effort. And there were other differences: the graphite rod required a shorter power stroke, it weighed noticeably less, and its excellent damping characteristics helped keep the normally awkward bass bug from bouncing.

Damping has to do with how a material returns to its original position after being flexed. It's a matter of speed but more importantly, vibration. Graphite recovers rapidly with almost no residual vibrations.

The new graphite tennis rackets, for example, stop vibrating immediately after the ball is struck. Vibrations are not transmitted up through the handle of the racket and the instances of tennis elbow are reduced.

In fly casting, line speed is distance. To obtain

> These rods won't make you a better caster, but if you're already good they'll make the whole thing easier.

(continued on page 28)

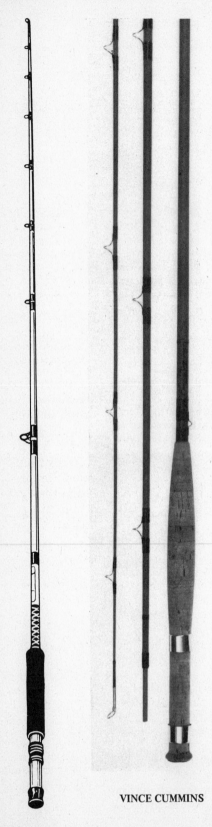

VINCE CUMMINS

DAIWA VIP

top of the line

Glass

F. M. CLAUDIO. F. M. Claudio makes a very pretty glass rod of special interest to the long-casting West Coast steelheader. With extension butts and other attractions for the heavy liner, Claudio lists some of his rods not in the standard line weights, but in grams, which are of concern to the shooting header. Standard rods are also available for the trout angler but the saltwater fanatic or big river fan should pay special attention to this San Francisco-based outfit.

VINCE CUMMINS. This New York state builder puts together some of the best light, medium-priced rods available. His Super-Lite models, which take lines as light as No. 3 and No. 4, are excellent casters. They don't have the mechanical feeling some other production glass rods seem to need to get a small line out. Among the best rods Vince makes is his 3-piece, 7-footer for a No. 3 or No. 4 that weighs in at under 2 ounces. This rod can take one of those lines out 50 feet with ease and is a great pack rod for those going back into small streams or lakes. It also fits into a suitcase for someone flying to a trouty spot. Vince also makes a lower priced River-Rat line and standard models as well. But look his lightweights over carefully if you want a good one for under $100.

DAIWA VP. For those who like a touch of the modern in their tackle. Marketed in 7½-, 8- and 8½-foot models for No. 6, No. 7 and No. 8 lines, these rods have translucent glass blanks, dark Dura-cork handles, royal purple diamond wrappings, stainless-steel rings on the guides and glass-to-glass ferrules. Very durable products especially good around corrosive salt water.

WHAT WE LOOKED FOR IN QUALITY

These days you can expect to get a lot for your money in glass fly rods. Besides such considerations as an adequate number of guides, a reel seat that clasped tightly, and overall good construction we wanted a well-designed action. There is no longer any reason to accept a clubby rod that merely heaves out line. This is why many of our Top of the Line rods were medium-priced models intelligently conceived. We looked for rods that allowed the control and delicacy modern, specialized fly fishing requires. This is why we emphasized the blank itself as the heart of the rod.

top of the line

TIM DURKOS ULTRA-LIGHT PREMIUM. Shades of the ultra-ultra-short and light craze of the early 1960s is Tim Durkos' custom glass in the West Fork Series. There is a 4-foot, 1-ouncer, a 5-foot, 1.2-ouncer, both taking No. 3 lines, and a 5-foot, 1.3 ouncer for a No. 4 line. All have medium actions. They sure aren't right for everyone but they're pretty little rods for tiny, brushy streams, farm ponds and the like. Takes a while to get one but worth it for that special need.

FENWICK. Though this is about Fenwick fly rods, ditto their spinning rods. When this company started putting out their mass-produced glass rods way back in the 1960s, they were the classiest in their league. Almost all the other companies were putting out either buggy whips or telephone poles with guides and ferrules. Their glass-ferruled, sufficiently guided rods in a variety of lengths were considered the best this side of custom rods. Today, that seems like another world: everyone and their sister can find a decent enough rod in their neighborhood discount shop. The FF855 and FF856, at 8½ feet for No. 5 and No. 6 line respectively, are still nice-actioned items that are hard to beat for the money. They've always made a variety of special purpose rods, as well, ranging from a tiny 5 foot 3 inch, 1¾ ouncer, for a No. 5, to a king-sized 9 footer that at 6¾ ounces takes a clothesline No. 12. A good line of decently put-up rods.

HARDY. Hardy glass fly rods aren't the easiest thing to find in America, but this traditional maker of high grade tackle puts out some very nice ones. The 6-foot, 3-inch Fibalite, which takes a No. 3½ line (available in some U.S. specialty tackle shops) is a delightful little rod both in appearance and casting per-

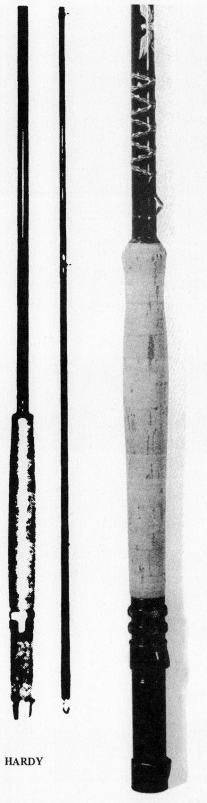

HARDY

FENWICK

A description of the Nineteenth-Century joys of salmon fishing

Days and nights of salmon fishing

Out came my trusty rod from a case of "filthy dowlass." Top varnished it was, and the work of the famous Higginbotham: not he the hero of an hundred engines, "who was *afeard* of nothing, and whose fireman's soul was all on fire;" but Higginbotham of the Strand, who was such an artist in the rod line as never appeared before, or has ever been since. "he never joyed since the price of hiccory wood rose," and was soon after gathered to the tomb of his fathers. I look upon him, and old Kirby the quondam maker of hooks, to be two of the greatest men the world ever saw; not even excepting Eustace Ude, or Michael Angelo Buonarotti.

But to business. The rod was hastily put together; a beautiful new azure line passed through the rings; a casting line, made like the waist of prior's Emma, appended, with two trout flies attached to it of the manufacture even of me, Harry Otter. An eager throw to begin with: round came the flies intact. Three, four, five, six throws – a dozen: no better result. The fish were stern and contemptuous. At length some favourable change took place in the clouds, or atmosphere, and I caught sundry small trout; and finally, in the cheek of a boiler, I fairly hauled out a two-pouner. A jewel of a fish he was – quite a treasure all over. After I had performed the satisfactory office of bagging him, I came to a part of the river which, being contracted, rushed forward in a heap, rolling with great impetuosity. Here, after a little flogging, I hooked a lusty fellow, strong as an elephant, and swift as a thunderbolt. How I was agitated say ye who best can tell, ye fellow tyros! Every moment did I expect my trout tackle, for such it was, to part company. At length, after various runs of dubious result, the caitiff began to yield; and at the expiration of about half an hour, I wooed him to the shore. What a sight

(continued on page 26)

top of the line

formance. Besides the standard sizes for regular intermediate line weights, Hardy also makes some oversized rods for salmon and steelhead fishing as long as 14 feet — far bigger than most other competitors. All in all Hardy glass rods are worth looking at . . . and fishing.

ORVIS. The famed maker of impregnated cane rods also produces some excellent glass rods. Best designed are the Golden Eagle rods, which are put up almost as beautifully as the bamboo rods. They also carry those very nice wooden reel seats. Orvis' Fullflex glass rods, while not as good as the Golden Eagles, are also very suitable for the intermediate angler. Orvis has had lots of experience designing good casting equipment — it shows in their glass rods.

WALTON POWELL. Walton Powell glass rods, made by the son of the famous cane builder E. C. Powell, have made a splash recently. Available through the standard size spectrum, Walton's rods usually have a nice feel, though there have been some complaints about the weighty metal reel seat he seems to favor. Like all rod makers of note, Walton is very opinionated about what makes a good rod; but his ideas translate into good-looking and very serviceable pieces of equipment. Definitely worth a look.

WINSTON. Under the tutelage of Tom Morgan the recently revitalized Winston Rod Company makes the best production glass rods in the country with only a few challengers. Winston glass is available in all imaginable sizes including some willow wands for No. 2 lines and a fine practical caster at 8½ feet for a No. 4. They also come in a handsome dark finish in favorite old sizes such as 7½ feet for a No. 5 and 8 feet for a No.

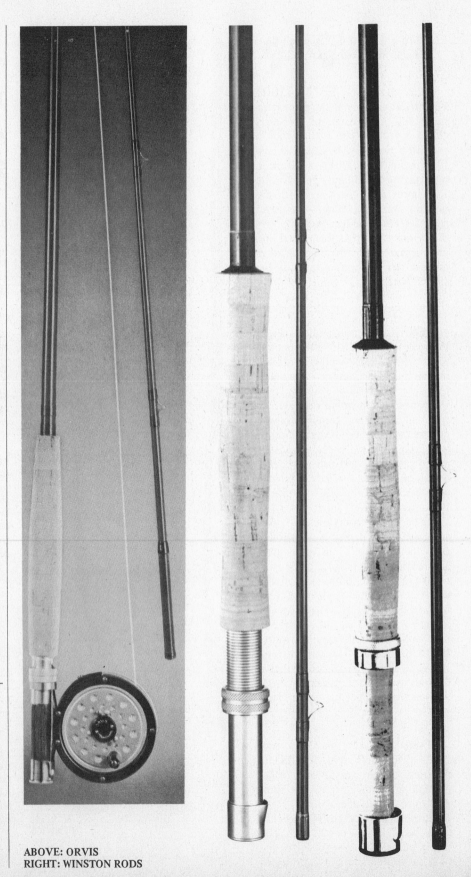

ABOVE: ORVIS
RIGHT: WINSTON RODS

"You will find angling to be like the virtue of humility, which has a calmness of spirit and a world of other blessings attending upon it."
IZAAK WALTON, *The Compleat Angler*

THE NEW TECHNOLOGY 25

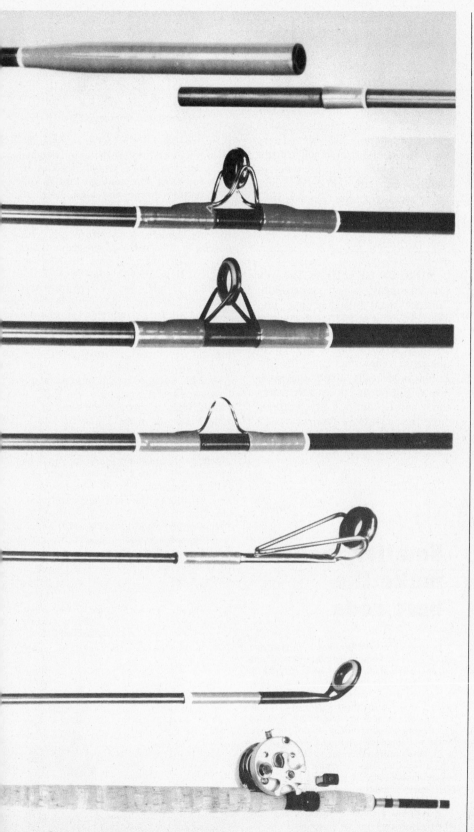

LAMIGLASS

top of the line

6. Winston has just about any rod you could want and on special order will make it in more than two pieces — practical for a longer rod that you'll haul about. Since they're glass-to-glass ferruled, three or four pieces doesn't present a problem. Winston glass looks much better with an all-cork reel seat but they make a metal seat for bigger models. Excellent equipment.

Graphite

LAMIGLASS. Lamiglass has grabbed a sizable chunk of the market. They'll either sell you a completed rod from their assortment of 20 models or the blank for any one of them. They even make a 7-foot rod for a No. 2 or No. 3 line and a 10½-footer for No. 8 or No. 9. They have all the features and versatility that have made graphite the coming material. Priced within reason and something for everyone.

LEONARD. The 8½-footer, which takes a No. 4 line, is one of the most delightful as well as practical graphite fly rods. Leonard makes lots of other good graphites but this one is very close to an all-around dry-fly rod since the stiffness of graphite allows for smooth casting even in relatively windy conditions. This rod will easily take flies as large as No. 10 or as small as No. 20. Its long length allows for good line control. Lots of fun playing fish and great for Len Wright's "sudden inch" method of using caddis flies.

SHAKESPEARE GRAFLITE. Until the invasion of the second generation of graphite rods the Shakespeare eight-foot Graflite fly rod was certainly the most sensitive one around. Now it has a lot more competition. But this under-two-ounce rod is a good bet for the graphite freak who wants something that does

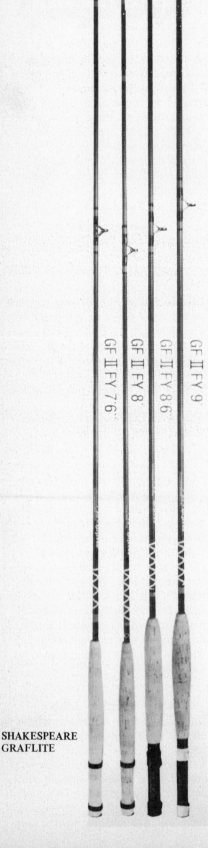

GF II FY 7'6"
GF II FY 8'
GF II FY 8'6"
GF II FY 9'

SHAKESPEARE
GRAFLITE

top of the line

more than merely cast a line. Taking a No. 6 line, it is as close to an all-around rod as one can get. It is sensibly put up with traditional snake guides, an all-cork reel seat and very little of the stylistic embellishments that mar some of the newcomers. Shakespeare also produces three other sized graphites ranging from 7½ to 9 feet, but the cream of the crop is definitely the eight-footer.

WINSTON GRAPHITE. The Winston Company, which started with bamboo then branched out into glass, came out in 1976 with graphite rods that are among the best around, the most sensitive rod of any type in this range. They are among the first graphites to really reflect the issues involved in putting down a fly with a rod; that is, the rod is something more than a stick used to heave out a line. Don't buy a graphite until you have at least checked out Winston.

Smaller makers make the best rods

In looking over this chapter on glass and graphite it will be apparent that most of the rods listed are made by smaller outfits. There is a definite reason for this.

As we delved into the tackle we discovered that for the most part rods made by the specialized and smaller makers give the angler more for the money than those made by the big companies. Within a margin of $20 or so, much more value can be had by getting a Winston, Cummins or similar rod than by buying mass-produced products. This, however, doesn't hold true for other types of rods.

Exceptions include Fenwick, a company that really knows how to design glass rods for the advanced angler.

That's just our opinion, of course.

Days and nights

(continued from page 23)

then struck my optics! a fair five-pounder at the least; not fisherman's weight, mark me, but such as would pass muster with the most conscientious lord mayor of London during the high price of bread. Long did I gaze on him, not without self-applause. All too large he was for my basket; I therefore laid the darling at full length on the ground, under a birch tree, and covered over the precious deposit with some wet bracken, that it might not suffer from the sunbeam.

I had not long completed this immortal achievement ere I saw a native approaching, armed with a prodigious fishing rod of simple construction guiltless of colour or varnish. He had a belt round his waist, to which was fastened a large wooden reel or pirn, and the line passed from it through the rings of his rod: a sort of Wat Tinlinn he was to look at. The whole affair seemed so primitive; there was such an absolute indigence of ornament, and poverty of conception, that I felt somewhat fastidious about it. I could not, however, let a brother of the craft pass unnoticed, albeit somewhat rude in his attire; so, "What sport," said I, "my good friend?"

"I canna say that I hae had muckle deversion; for she is quite fallen in, and there wull be no good fishing till there comes a spate."

Days and Nights of Salmon Fishing in the Tweed (1843).
By William Scrope.

RUSS PEAK GLASS RODS

It's a simple fact of fly-fishing life that Russ Peak of Pasadena, California, makes the best glass fly rods that money can buy.

They're best for a number of reasons.

In the first place Russ makes his own blanks. Now lots of outfits claim to use custom blanks and they do. But they custom-order them from one of the large blank makers. Only a few outfits make blanks. Lots make rods but only a few control things from the bottom. Because of Russ's longtime experience as a glass-maker he has a special arrangement with the well-known Conolon rod company to use on weekends their multi-million-dollar facilities, where he can fashion blanks to his own ultra-exacting specifications.

Russ markets a number of standard models (starting with the Zenith and ranging into the better-finished Golden Zenith) and has recently started making some interesting graphite rods. But the rod designed for the advanced angler who knows what he wants is what Russ is best at. He'll make any type of rod you can imagine and translate your rough ideas into a practical, beautiful piece of casting equipment.

Save your pennies, wait the year or so necessary and get ye a Peak.

Laura Berg gets a casting lesson from master rod designer Russ Peak (right) while Harmon Henkin (left) looks on.

(continued from page 21)

GRAPHITE IS STRONG AND LIGHT, BUT IT DOESN'T BEND OR STRETCH

this speed the loops of the false cast should flow as nearly parallel to the ground as possible. The loops must also be narrow or "tight." And above all, they must be smooth.

Because of graphite's excellent damping characteristics, there is no wobble at the end of the power stroke, hence, no undesirable waves in the fly line. The energy ceases when you want it to cease and conversely, power is transmitted instantaneously.

Obviously, not all kinds of fly fishing demand distance from the caster. In fact, most do not. Precision more than distance is the essence of trout fishing as it is in sight fishing tarpon on the flats. Here is where graphite's lightness delivers.

Fly fishermen have been perennially concerned with reducing the overall weight of the fly rod itself. I once heard a man who hunted upland game a great deal denounce this concern by saying he carried a 7-pound shotgun all day and that didn't bother him and he thought these fly fishermen were being awfully effete worrying about an ounce this way or that. Ted Trueblood was there to remind him that he didn't carry his shotgun all day by one end.

Rajeff uses a graphite rod in the trout fly accuracy games, as he does in trout fishing — not because it is intrinsically more accurate than glass or bamboo, but because it's so much lighter than either. Being less tired means accuracy over a longer period of time; in short, greater accuracy.

He who hesitates is not lost

The early graphite rods were exceedingly stiff and revealed no clue about how they would behave under line stress. This is because they were made of high modulus fibers with little epoxy or fiberglass added to soften or otherwise control the action.

"Very poor for living room shaking," as one friend of mine put it.

They also broke in half the minute you tried to pull in a fish, hardly a desirable quality in a fishing rod.

To help diffuse some of the graphite rod mystique, you can start by substituting the word stiffness for the term modulus. Graphite fibers can be given a higher modulus by subjecting the original material to more intense heat. This stiffness is a reflection of an increase in tensile strength.

On the other hand, as the tensile strength is raised, the compressive strength, or the material's ability to flex without breaking, is lowered. Making fly rods out of high modulus graphite is, in one important sense, doing something antipathetic to the nature of the material. Graphite is strong and light, but it doesn't bend or stretch.

This problem is resolved by adding another material — fiberglass. To begin with, graphite fibers are imbedded in a sheet of epoxy plastic, forming what's called a tape. To make a fly rod this tape is wrapped around a mandrel.

To increase the compressive strength of a graphite rod blank, a scrim in the form of a separate fiberglass tape is included. Here, it is a question of degree — too much glass increases the rod weight and begins to dilute the qualities of graphite. Too little and you're back to a rod that breaks.

Another way of altering rod action and compressive strength is to use lower modulus graphite fibers. Fiberglass must still be added but now there are two important variables to juxtapose: a range of stiffness in the graphite itself, and the quantity of fiberglass.

Critics of this process claim there is no standard of how much graphite must be present before the product can be labeled and sold as a graphite rod.

To be sure, some discount models will appear, bound to contain precious little of the expensive graphite. However, the addition of glass has brought the graphite fishing rod into focus as a practical marketable tool.

Graphite is here to stay. Some tackle manufacturers, noticeably the 3M Company, which owns Phillipson and Scientific Anglers and the small independent makers such as R. L. Winston and Russ Peak, held off production because of the limited market, high costs, and what they felt to be insufficient technical data. But the rods they have begun producing are excellent, refuting the notion that he who hesitates is lost.

Conolon, Shakespeare, Cortland, Fenwick, Orvis and Leonard are all offering versions of the graphite fly rod. Angler opinion is varied, though most negative appraisals seem to stem from experiences with the early prototype rods.

The early graphite rods broke in half the minute you tried to pull in a fish.

(continued on next page)

Graphite has a brilliant future

(continued from preceding page)

Some rods get more abuse than use. Fiberglass has provided an inexpensive, extremely tough, resilient material which fills the need. Of course, not all glass rods are made for knocking about. Russ Peak makes some which are works of art in their own right.

Bamboo is another matter entirely, remarkable for its natural properties. Each rod made from it is a unique product of the craftsman's hand. The most highly prized fly rods in the world are made of split Tonkin cane.

Graphite, while still in its infancy, looks forward to a brilliant future. The material is controllable, completely unaffected by moisture, heat or cold, and literally cannot be fatigued by flexing. Its outstanding qualities are its light weight, sensitivity and excellent damping chracteristics.

Aside from lessened casting fatigue, the lightness of the material means that rods can be made longer without making them heavier. If you had a seven foot bamboo rod which took a No. 6 line and a graphite rod eight feet long which also took a No. 6 line, the graphite would probably weigh even less than the bamboo while at the same time doing a much easier job of casting.

Steelhead fishermen will appreciate this fact when they try the 10½ foot graphite rod which casts a No. 10 line. Imagine wading chest deep into a river and having an extra 18 inches of loft in a rod lighter than the 9 footer you'd been used using. Not only lighter and longer, but faster, so you cast with less effort.

Some trout fishermen have complained that the stiffness of graphite in the lighter models too easily broke light leaders. True perhaps, with the earlier models, but the newer rods are softer. Also, there is little reaction to the action of setting the hook because of the damping quality. And the lightness helps prevent unwanted follow-through.

It's been said that every poet finds his place in the company of poets and there is no necessity for killing one poet to make room for another. Graphite fly rods are not going to replace hand-made split bamboo, or even glass for that matter.

Cecil Jacobs, a technician with 3M, explains it like this: "When deciding what kind of fishing rod you want, first determine what kind of fishing you are going to do. Then pick a rod to suit it."

In other words don't let the tail wag the dog. Graphite is not the solution to the problem of finding the perfect fishing rod. There is no such thing. The matter is far more subjective than that. Does a golfer use his driver to putt simply because it has a graphite shaft?

The breakage problem has been largely overcome through fiberglass reinforcement. Ferrule design, extremely critical in a graphite blank, has been improved, again with fiberglass. And while I would no more try to winch up a sounding amberjack with a graphite fly rod than I would with a cane Leonard, the rods currently available are clearly the best casting tools ever made.

Match your rod to the kind of fishing you'll be doing.

GAMEFISH: BLACK DRUM

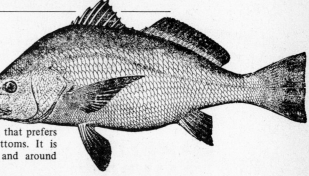

NAMES
Sea drum, grey drum, striped drum, drum.
(Pogonias cromis)

DISTRIBUTION
The black drum is a fish of the Gulf and Atlantic. It is plentiful from New York to Texas.

DESCRIPTION
The black drum is a short fish of over-all grey color. At times, the sides may take on a coppery cast. The back is somewhat humped and there are chin barbels.

SIZE
Although the black drum reaches a maximum of 150 pounds, the average fish weighs between 3 and 8 pounds.

HABITAT
The black drum is a school fish that prefers shallow waters with shady bottoms. It is found in inlets, bays, lagoons and around wharves and pilings.

FEEDING HABITS
A bottom feeder, the black drum feeds on mollusks, crustaceans and small fish.

TACKLE
The black drum is a fun stillfishing saltwater beast that requires simple pieces of crab or squid and tackle just heavy enough to get down to where the fish are feeding.

"That fish will soon be caught that nibbles at every bait."
THOMAS FULLER, *Gnomologia*

CHOOSING A ROD FOR ATLANTIC SALMON

By Leonard Wright

The first decision you must make in choosing a rod for Atlantic salmon fishing is whether you expect to own only one rod, two or even more. There are, after all, many different types of salmon water and at least two distinct styles of fishing to consider.

If you are to have one rod only, it should probably be a compromise between the optimum for wet-fly fishing and the most convenient size for the dry fly. Much longer rods can be used with advantage and with ease when fishing the conventional wet fly. Extra length of rod, here, helps control the speed of your fly (perhaps the single most important factor in this type of fishing) and makes mending your line to thwart irksome currents far easier. A rod of 9½, 10, even 10½ feet in this type of fishing can be, not only helpful, but also comfortable, since you'll be working at the leisurely pace of about two casts per minute.

Though more than 95 per cent of all Atlantic salmon are taken on the classic wet fly there are times when the dry fly is critical to success. A perfect wet-fly rod can turn into an arm-buster when the staccato and false casting of dry-fly fishing becomes necessary. If the water is slow, low, warm or all three, the dry fly may be your only chance. A rod of 8½ or 9 feet can spare you agony under these conditions.

The best compromise rod I've found is one of 9½ feet that takes a No. 7 line. I have one of 8 feet, 9 inches handling a No. 7 line that's even more comfortable for extended dry-fly casting. I also have one of 10½ feet taking a No. 9 line that gives wonderful command when presenting the wet fly, but neither one is a good all-purpose rod.

If you feel the need for a third rod, the only important addition (beyond the joy of variety, collecting and possession) would be a European-style, two-handed rod of 12 to 14 feet. This you might not use often. But it could be invaluable during high water or on very deep pools on the largest rivers when huge flies from size No. 1 to No. 5/0 or even bigger are needed. Casting these monsters with conventional fly tackle can become an abomination.

Admittedly, salmon can be hooked and played on conventional trout tackle, but you'll hook even more with scaled-up equipment and you'll have more fun playing your fish, too. Only a heftier rod will let you exert more pressure on the fish and thus enjoy their greater strength.

So my advice boils down to this. One rod: a 9 to 9½ footer taking a No. 7 or No. 8 line. Two rods: an 8½ to 9 foot rod for a No. 7 line and a 10 to 10½ footer for No. 8 to No. 10 line. A third rod? A 13-footer taking a No. 9 or No. 10. In all lengths, bamboo is beautiful and vintage, but the new graphites are arm-savers. Humor yourself on actions and fittings. If you decide to own four or more, well, happy collecting. I'll have to admit I'm guilty of this and it's one of the few luxuries that seem worth the extra money.

GAMEFISH: RAINBOW TROUT

NAMES

Steelhead, redsides, Kamloops trout. *(Salmo gairdneri)*

DISTRIBUTION

The rainbow trout was originally found in a range from Mexico to Canada and Alaska. Due to extensive stocking, it is now found throughout the United States, Canada and South America.

DESCRIPTION

The three forms of the rainbow trout are the rainbow, which lives its entire life in fresh water to spawn, and the Kamloops, which is mainly found in British Columbia. All of these fish are similar in appearance, basically colored olive or light green on the back and silver on the sides. The upper body is sprinkled with small black spots and a wide stripe of red or magenta runs laterally from the head to the tail.

SIZE

The size of a rainbow trout varies greatly depending on its form and location. The Kamloops and the steelhead are the largest of the rainbows, reaching weights of up to 25 pounds. The inland rainbow is usually smaller. Its average length is about 6 to 18 inches.

HABITAT

The rainbow prefers clear, cold waters although it is an extremely versatile fish. It is found in both large and small streams and lakes from the north and into the southern climates.

FEEDING HABITS

The rainbow trout feeds primarily on insect life taken both from the surface and the bottom. It also feeds on small crustaceans and bait fish. The Kamloops favors a diet of Kokanee salmon.

BEST FEEDING TEMPERATURE

Between 50° and 68°.

TACKLE

When it's a steelhead charging up a stream to spawn, these tacklebusters might require a long spinning or baitcasting rig, especially in winter when bait is sometimes necessary. When it's just a high jumping rainbow in a lake or stream a fly rod suited for the size of the water or a light spinning outfit will be fine. When deep, a medium trolling outfit plumbs the lakes for this fine fish.

"The man that weds fro greedy wealth,
He goes a fishing fair,
But often times he gets a frog,
Or very little share."   UNKNOWN, *Pepysian*

Brand-Model	Length	Weight (Oz.)	Line Size	No. Pieces	No. Guides	Material
DAIWA						
Alpine Pack Rods (spin, baitcast, fly)						
3053	6'6"				5	glass
VIP Series (fresh water)						
43	7'		5-6	2	7	glass
44	7'6"		6-7	2	8	glass
45	8'		7-8	2	8	glass
46	8'6"		8-9	2	8	glass
VIP Series (saltwater)						
47	9'		11-12	2	9	glass
Regal Series (fresh water)						
5344	7'6"		6	2	7	glass
5345	8'		7	2	7	glass
5346	8'6"		8	2	7	glass
5347	9'		8	2	7	glass
1300 Series						
1345	8'		7-8	2	8	glass
TIM DURKOS						
West Fork Series						
WF4013	4'	1	3			glass
WF5013	5'	1.2	3			glass
WF5014	5'	1.3	4			glass
Spring Creek Series						
SC	6'	1.4	3			glass
SC604	6'	1.6	4			glass
SST Rod (salmon, steelhead, trout)						
			6-7	1		glass

(Other sizes and models available to your specifications.)

Brand-Model	Length	Weight (Oz.)	Line Size	No. Pieces	No. Guides	Material
FENWICK						
HMG Graphite Rods						
GFF-634	6'3"	1 7/8	4			graphite
GFF-704	7'	2 1/4	4			graphite
GFF-755	7'6"	2 5/8	5			graphite
GFF-805	8'	2 3/4	5			graphite
GFF-905	9'	3 1/8	5			graphite
GFF-806	8'	2 3/4	6			graphite
GFF-856	8'6"	3 1/8	6			graphite
GFF-857	8'6"	3 1/4	7			graphite
GFF-858	8'6"	3 1/2	8			graphite
GFF-908	9'	3 3/4	8			graphite
GFF-1059	10'6"	4 5/8	9			graphite
GFF-9010	9'	4	10			graphite
GFF-9012	9'	5 1/4	12			graphite
Fiberglass Rods						
FF535	5'3"	1 3/4	5			glass
FF605	6'	2 1/8	5			glass
FF705	7'	2 5/8	5			glass
FF755	7'6"	3	5			glass
FF805	8'	3	5			glass
FF855	8'6"	3 1/4	5			glass
FF706	7'	2 7/8	6			glass
FF756	7'6"	3	6			glass
FF806	8'	3 1/8	6			glass

Brand-Model	Length	Weight (Oz.)	Line Size	No. Pieces	No. Guides	Material
FF856	8'6"	3 3/8	6			glass
FF807	8'	3 3/8	7			glass
FF857	8'6"	3 5/8	7			glass
FF858	8'6"	3 7/8	8			glass
FF908	9'	4 3/4	8			glass
FF909	9'	4 7/8	9			glass
FF9010	9'	5	10			glass
FF9310	9'3"	5 1/8	10			glass
FF9012	9'	6 3/4	12			glass
Voyageur Rods						
FF756-4	7'6"	3	6	4		glass
FF806-4	8'	3 3/8	6	4		glass
FF856-5	8'6"	3 1/2	6	5		glass
FF858-5	8'6"	3 3/4	8	5		glass
SF74-4	7'	4 3/4	6	4		glass
SF75-5	7'6"	4 7/8	6	5		glass
GARCIA						
Conolon (fresh)						
9560	6'	2	5	1	5	
9570	7'	3	6	2	5	
9575	7'6"	3.25	6	2	6	
9580	8'	3.5	6-7	2	7	
9585	8'6"	3.75	6	2	7	
Conolon (light saltwater)						
9586	8'6"	4.15	8	2	6	
Conolon (saltwater)						
9590	9'	4.75	9-10	2	8	
Avacado Rods (fresh, saltwater)						
8237	8'	4.7	6	2	5	glass
8238	8'6"	4.5	8-9	2	6	glass
Blue Rods						
2636	7'3"	3.5	6	2	5	glass
2637	8'	4.5	6	2	4	glass
2638	8'6"	5.7	7	2	5	glass
2639	9'	5.7	8	2	6	glass
Fly Pak Rod (take-down length 19")						
N547	7'6"	3.6	6-7	5	4	glass
HARDY						
Dick Walker Rods						
Superlite	9'3"	4 1/4	8ST	2		glass
Little Lake	9'	4	7DT	2		glass
HEDDON						
Mark Wet/Dry						
8251	7'				2	
8252	7'6"				2	
8253	8'				2	
8255	8'6"				2	
8651	7'				2	
8652	7'6"				2	
8653	8'				2	
8655	8'6"				2	

specifications

Brand-Model	Length	Weight (Oz.)	Line Size	No. Pieces	No. Guides	Material
Rod of Rods (made to order)						
	7'6"					
	8'					
	8'6".					
	9'					
Mark IV						
8457	8'6".			.2		glass
8459	9'			.2		glass
Mark I						
8307	8'6".			.2		glass
8309	9'			.2		glass
Trail Blazer (spin, fly)						
7676	7'3".			.5		
Brown Pal (saltwater)						
876	8'			.2		glass
878	8'6".			.2		glass
Black Pal						
726	8'			.2		glass
728	8'6".			.2		glass
Green Pal						
526	8'			.2		
528	8'6".			.2		
Astro Pal						
626	8'			.2		
Starcast						
4885	8'			.2		glass
4887	8'6".			.2		glass
LAMIGLASS						
F702	7'	.2	.2-3			graphite
F703	7'	.2 1/8	.3-4			graphite
F704	7'	.2 1/4	.4-5			graphite
F763	7'6".	.2 1/2	.3-4			graphite
F764	7'6".	.2 3/4	.4-5			graphite
F765	7'6".	.2 7/8	.5-6			graphite
F804	8'	.3 1/4	.4-5			graphite
F805	8'	.3 1/2	.5-6			graphite
F806	8'	.3 5/8	.6-7			graphite
F865	8'6".	.3 3/4	.5-6			graphite
F866	8'6".	.3 7/8	.6-7			graphite
F867	8'6".	.4 1/8	.7-8			graphite
F906	9'	.4 1/8	.6-7			graphite
F907	9'	.4 1/4	.7-8			graphite
F908	9'	.4 5/8	.8-9			graphite
F968	9'6".	.5	.8-9			graphite
F1008	10'	.5 3/4	.8-9			graphite
F1068	10'6".	.6 9/16	.8-9			graphite
F911T	9'	.6 7/8	.11-12			graphite
F912T	9'	.7 1/4	.12-13			
LEONARD						
Graftek I Lightweight-Line Models						
1455	7'6".	.1 3/4	.4			graphite
1461	8'	.2 1/4	.5			graphite
1451	7'6".	.1 3/8	.3			graphite
1457	8'6".	.2 3/8	.4			graphite
1463	8'6".	.2 1/2	.5			graphite
1453	7'	.1 1/2	.4			graphite
1459	7'6".	.1 7/8	.5			graphite
1465	9'	.2 7/8	.5			graphite
Graftek I Medium-Weight-Line Models						
1467	7'6".	.2 3/8	.6			graphite
1473	9'	.3	.6			graphite
1479	8'	.3	.8			graphite
1469	8'	.2 3/4	.6			graphite
1475	8'	.2 7/8	.7			graphite
1481	8'6".	.3 1/4	.8			graphite
1471	8'6".	.2 7/8	.6			graphite
1477	8'6".	.3	.7			graphite
1483	9'	.3 1/2	.8			graphite
Graftek I, Heavyweight-Line Models						
1485	8'6".	.4 1/2	.9			graphite
1487	9'	.4 3/4	.9			graphite
1489	9'	.5	.10			graphite
Graftek I 5/4 Lightning Rod						
1344	5'	.3/4	.4			graphite
Catskill Series						
1125	6'	.2 7/8	.6	.2		glass
1127	7'6".	.2 3/4	.6	.2		glass
1129	8'	.3 1/4	.7			glass
1131	8'6".	.3 1/2	8			glass
1133	6'6".	.2	.4			glass
1135	7'	.2 1/4	.5			glass
Rangeley Series						
1137	7'	.2 7/8	.5			glass
1139	7'6".	.3 1/8	.6			glass
1141	8'	.3 1/2	.7			glass
1143	8'6".	.3 3/4	.7			glass
Saltwater Gear						
1167	8'6".	.4 1/2	.9	.2		glass
1169	9'	.5 1/4	.10	.2		glass
Graftek I (spin, fly outfit, spin reel and line included)						
1383	6'6".		.3	.2		graphite
Rangeley (fly, spin pack rod)						
1161	7'		.4			
OLYMPIC						
9,000 Series (fresh water)						
9170	7'	.2.6	.6-7	.2	.7	graphite
9175	7'6".	.3	.6-7	.2	8	graphite
9180	8'	.3.5	.8-9	.2	.9	graphite
9185	8'6".	.3.7	.9-10.	.2	.9	graphite
9190	9'	.4.5	.10-11.	.2	.10	graphite
7,000 Series (fresh water)						
7180	8'			.2	.7	
3,000 Series (fresh water)						
3180	8'			.2	.7	glass
3185	8'6".			.2	.7	
2,000 Series (fresh water)						
2175	7'6".			.2	.5	
2180	8'			.2	.7	
2185	8'6".			.2	.7	
2190	9'			.2	.7	
1,000 Series (fresh water)						
1180	8'			.2	.7	

specifications

ORVIS

Brand-Model	Length	Weight (Oz.)	Line Size	No. Pieces	No. Guides	Material
M9270-1	7'	1 5/8	5			graphite
M9270-11	7'	2	5			graphite
M7276-1	7'6"	1 3/4	6			graphite
M9276-11	7'6"	2 1/8	6			graphite
M9280-1	8'	1 7/8	6			graphite
M9280-11	8'	2 1/4	6			graphite
M9286-1	8'6"	2 7/8	8			graphite
M9286-3	8'6"	2 7/8	8			graphite
M9290-11	9'	4 1/4	9			graphite
M9290-1	9'	3 1/8	9			graphite

Special Function Graphite Fly Rods

Brand-Model	Length	Weight (Oz.)	Line Size	No. Pieces	No. Guides	Material
M9266-1	6'6"	1 3/8	4			graphite
M9279-1	7'9"	2 1/8	5			graphite
M9283-1	8'3"	2 1/2	7			graphite
M9287-1	8'6"	2 5/8	6			graphite
M9297-1	9'6"	3 5/8	8			graphite
M9289-1	8'9"	4	10			graphite
M9211-1	10'	4 7/8	10			graphite
M9296-1	9'6"	6 1/8	11			graphite

Fullflex A Glass Fly Rods

Brand-Model	Length	Weight (Oz.)	Line Size	No. Pieces	No. Guides	Material
M9907-1	7'	2 3/4	5	2		glass
M9912-1	7'6"	3	6	2		glass
M9918-1	8'	3 1/4	7	2		glass
M9920-1	8'6"	3 3/4	8	2		glass
M9922-1	8'6"	4 1/4	9	2		glass

Full Flex A II Glass Fly Rods

Brand-Model	Length	Weight (Oz.)	Line Size	No. Pieces	No. Guides	Material
M9908-1	7	3	5	2		glass
M9913-1	7'6"	3 1/4	6	2		glass
M9919-1	8'	3 1/2	7	2		glass
M9921-1	8'6"	4	8	2		glass

Camper Fly-Spin Rod

Brand-Model	Length	Weight (Oz.)	Line Size	No. Pieces	No. Guides	Material
M9971-1	7'	3 3/8	6	4		glass

Golden Eagle Fly Rods

Brand-Model	Length	Weight (Oz.)	Line Size	No. Pieces	No. Guides	Material
M9069-1	6'6"	1 7/8	4			glass
M9068-1	7'	2	5			glass
M9077-1	7'6"	2 3/8	6			glass
M9083-1	9'	4 3/8	6			glass
M9078-1	8'	3 3/4	7			glass
M9079-1	8'6"	4 1/4	9			glass
M9080-1	9'	6 7/8	9			glass
M9081-1	8'9"	7	11			glass

PFLUEGER

115 Series (fresh water)

Brand-Model	Length	Weight (Oz.)	Line Size	No. Pieces	No. Guides	Material
115F	8'			2	5	graphite-glass
115F	8'6"			2	5	graphite-glass

110 Series (fresh water)

Brand-Model	Length	Weight (Oz.)	Line Size	No. Pieces	No. Guides	Material
G110F	7'6"			2	5	graphite
G110F	8'			2	5	graphite
G110F	8'6"			2	5	graphite
G110F	9'			2	5	graphite

315 Series (fresh water)

Brand-Model	Length	Weight (Oz.)	Line Size	No. Pieces	No. Guides	Material
315 FY	8'			2	5	glass

515 Series (fresh water)

Brand-Model	Length	Weight (Oz.)	Line Size	No. Pieces	No. Guides	Material
515FY	8'			2	4	

SHAKESPEARE

Graflite

Brand-Model	Length	Weight (Oz.)	Line Size	No. Pieces	No. Guides	Material
GFII-FY	7'6"	1 5/8	5	2	7	graphite
GFII-FY	8'	1 6/8	6	2	7	graphite
GFII-FY	8'6"	3 7/8	8	2	7	graphite
GFII-FY	9'	4	9	2	8	graphite

Custom Pro 708's

Brand-Model	Length	Weight (Oz.)	Line Size	No. Pieces	No. Guides	Material
FY708UL	7'	3.2	5	2	5	glass
FY708	7'6"	3.4	6	2	6	glass
FY708	8'6"	4.2	8	2	7	glass

200 Series

Brand-Model	Length	Weight (Oz.)	Line Size	No. Pieces	No. Guides	Material
FY200	7'6"	3.7	6	2	6	glass
FY200	8'6"	4.5	8	2	7	glass

608 Wonderod Series

Brand-Model	Length	Weight (Oz.)	Line Size	No. Pieces	No. Guides	Material
FY608	8'	3.8	7	2	6	glass
FY608	8'6"	4	8	2	7	glass
FY608	9'	4.2	9	2	7	glass

Presidential 508 Series

Brand-Model	Length	Weight (Oz.)	Line Size	No. Pieces	No. Guides	Material
FY508	8'6"	4	8	2	7	glass

190 Maroon Series

Brand-Model	Length	Weight (Oz.)	Line Size	No. Pieces	No. Guides	Material
FY190	7'6"	3.8	6	2	5	glass
FY190	8'6"	4.5	8	2	5	glass

408 Wonderod Series

Brand-Model	Length	Weight (Oz.)	Line Size	No. Pieces	No. Guides	Material
FY408	8'6"	4.5	8	2	5	glass

170 Wonderglass Series

Brand-Model	Length	Weight (Oz.)	Line Size	No. Pieces	No. Guides	Material
FY170	8'	4.2	8	2	5	glass

160 Wonderglass Series

Brand-Model	Length	Weight (Oz.)	Line Size	No. Pieces	No. Guides	Material
FY160	8'6"	4.5	8	2	5	glass

Heavy Duty Fly Rod

Brand-Model	Length	Weight (Oz.)	Line Size	No. Pieces	No. Guides	Material
FY940	9'	6.2	11		8	glass

Take Down Pack Rods (spin or fly)

Brand-Model	Length	Weight (Oz.)	Line Size	No. Pieces	No. Guides	Material
PRC70	7'			4	4	glass

Telescoping Pack Rods

Brand-Model	Length	Weight (Oz.)	Line Size	No. Pieces	No. Guides	Material
FTP8	8'	5	7		6	

QUICK

Brand-Model	Length	Weight (Oz.)	Line Size	No. Pieces	No. Guides	Material
6176	7'6"			2		
6180	8'			2		
8186	8'6"			2		

R. L. WINSTON

Stalker Series

Brand-Model	Length	Weight (Oz.)	Line Size	No. Pieces	No. Guides	Material
	6'6"	1 2/3	DT3	2		glass
	6'6"	1 7/8	DT3, 4	2		glass
	7'	1 3/4	DT3	2		glass
	7'	2 1/8	DT3, 4	2		glass
	7'6"	1 7/8	DT3	2		glass
	7'6"	2 1/4	DT3, 4	2		glass
	8'	2 3/8	DT3	2		glass
	8'	2 5/8	DT3, 4	2		glass
	8'6"	2 7/8	DT3, 4	2		glass

Light Fly Rods

Brand-Model	Length	Weight (Oz.)	Line Size	No. Pieces	No. Guides	Material
	5'6"	1 5/8	DT4, 5	2		glass

specifications

Brand-Model	Length	Weight (Oz.)	Line Size	No. Pieces	No. Guides	Material
Backpacking Fly Rods						
	7'		DT5	3		glass
	7'6".		DT5	3		glass
	8'		DT5	3		glass
	7'6".		DT6	3		glass
	8'		DT6	3		glass
	8'6".		DT6	3		glass
	7'		DT5	4		glass
	7'6".		DT5	4		glass
	8'		DT5	4		glass
	7'6".		DT6	4		glass
	8'		DT6	4		glass
	8'6".		DT6	4		glass
	6'	1 3/4	DT4, 5	2		glass
	6'6".	2	DT4, 5	2		glass
	7'	2 1/8	DT4, 5	2		glass
	7'6".	2 1/4	DT4, 5	2		glass
Trout Rods						
	7'6".	2 3/4	DT6	2		glass
	8'	3 1/8	DT5	2		glass
	8'	3 1/2	DT6	2		glass

Brand-Model	Length	Weight (Oz.)	Line Size	No. Pieces	No. Guides	Material
	8'	3 5/8	DT7	2		glass
	8'6".	3 1/2	DT5	2		glass
	8'6".	3 7/8	DT6	2		glass
	8'6".	4	DT7	2		glass
	8'9".	4 1/8	DT7	2		glass
	9'	4	DT6	2		glass
	9'	4 1/4	DT7	2		glass
	9'3".	3 7/8	DT5	2		glass
Steelhead and Salmon						
	8'6".	4 3/8	WF8	2		glass
	8'9".	4 5/8	WF8	2		glass
	9'	4 7/8	WF9	2		glass
	9'6".	5 1/4	WF9	2		glass
	9'	5	WF10	2		glass
	9'6".	5 1/2	WF10	2		glass
	9'	5 5/8	WF11	2		glass
	9'3".	5 3/4	WF11	2		glass
	9'6".	5 7/8	WF11	2		glass
Salt Water Fly Rods						
	9'	5 5/8	WF11	2		glass
	9'	7 1/2	WF12	2		glass

F.M. CLAUDIO

For fiberglass rods contact the F.M. Claudio Rod Company, 1482 38th Avenue, San Francisco, CA 94122.

VINCE CUMMINS

For graphite and fiberglass rods contact Vince Cummins, 73 Main St., Dobbs Ferry, NY 10522.

WALTON POWELL

For graphite and fiberglass rods, contact Walton Powell, 1148 West 8th Ave., Chico, California 95926.

FLY REELS
THEY'RE NOT JUST PLACES TO STORE YOUR LINE

By Harmon Henkin

A fly reel is just a place to store your line.

Like a lot of clichés that one has a trace of the truth but not enough to matter for the practical angler. While a reel is not directly involved in the mechanical process of casting a fly — like the rod and the line — it is nonetheless an integral part of the modern fly fishing system.

The reel has come a long way since it was first described in the 17th Century by the venerated Izaak Walton, who discussed the "winch" at the base of the rod. It was a way for him to organize excess line and a big technical advancement in the sport. Up until the mid-19th Century most quality reels were brass, which produced machinery that was elegant and sturdy but also heavy and bulky. With the advent of the tapered silk line anglers needed reels with a larger capacity than those used for the older horsehair lines. A brass reel carrying 30 yards or so of silk line was still a sizable piece of hardware, even though silk was thinner than our modern synthetics.

Charles Orvis, the founder of the company bearing his name, came up with a solution in 1869. His alloy reel with a perforated spool was a development that profoundly affected the future. Although improvements have been made in the 20th Century, our modern reels are in some ways no better than old masterpieces like the Vom Hofe, the Leonard and the Hardy Perfect, which are collector's models and practical fishing reels prized by their owners. In fact the Hardy Perfect, whose solid construction and ball bearings have set standards since 1892, is considered by many veteran fly anglers the best trout and salmon reel ever built.

The angler today is faced with a wide array of reels sporting a confusion of price tags. But they all do the job. However, it's in the area of a specialized reel for specialized fly fishing tasks such as steelhead or saltwater that the choices become more difficult and the stakes steeper. One of the biggest changes recently in the tastes of fly fishermen is the emphasis on lightness. But many anglers think the lightness fetish is irrelevant because the rod is gripped in front of the reel anyway. Nevertheless, companies like Hardy with its Lightweight series and Orvis with its recently introduced CFO models have dominated the $50-plus market. That brings us to an interesting point.

How much should you spend for a fly reel? Should you spring for a high priced job for general fishing when a Pflueger Medalist, a Berkley, or one of the Heddon imports

(continued on next page)

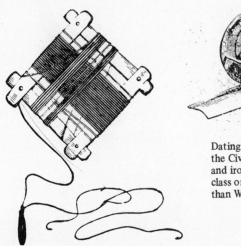

In the beginning ....
It wasn't much more
than something to wrap
a few feet of line
around.

Dating from the years of
the Civil War, this brass
and iron relic was in a
class only a little higher
than Walton's "winch."

William Mills & Son sold this
triple-multiplying, single click
fly reel in the 1890s for $13.
It featured an automatic drag
and carried 35 to 40 yards of
line. The reel is cut away to
reveal gears which multiplied
"from the center by an
entirely new and superior
principle."

In a testimonial to the
prowess of this Yawman and
Erbe automatic reel, John
N. Hills of Chicago in 1894
predicted that the automatic
"is the coming reel."

THEY'RE NOT JUST FOR STORAGE

(continued from preceding page)

will do the job? A good question with not much of an answer. It just seems that when someone spends the hundred or more dollars that is openers in the quality rod market these days they usually wind up getting a quality crafted reel to go along with it. If you want quality you'll have to pay. That seems to be life.

When you get into the specialized brackets it does require more money. Superb machines like the Bogdans, Seamasters, Fin-Nors and the like are worth the price if you're after big salt water fish. Their drags are dependable, and dependability is the name of the game for fish bigger than 50 pounds. Sure, a Hardy Perfect, Medalist or the like will do the job but when it comes to pushing and shoving the high priced stuff can be counted on.

For fishing with a No. 8 line or above, I prefer reels that multiply 2 to 1. It's far easier to retrieve the lassos that seem to accumulate with long casts and heavy line. Even for mundane trout fishing reels like the Hardy Lightweight multipliers and the British Gladding multiplier, this ratio can be quite a convenience for anglers who haven't mastered the intricacies of retrieving with their fingers.

Izaak Walton

Walton's "winch" was a big technical advancement for the sport.

For practical considerations always get a reel that not only holds the desired fly line but lots of backing too. For trout, bass and the like you'll probably never need the backing but you should never squish your fly lint onto the spool. It drastically curtails its life.

Whether your reel should have the capability for an extra spool is another subjective matter. Most modern anglers demand this feature and manufacturers have obliged. In case of accident I prefer carrying two reels and an extra spool, especially when going to out-of-the way places in Montana or on expeditions around the country. Some of the very, very best reels like the Bogdans are not equipped for extra spools. And if you get an extra spool always try it out for fit before buying. With some of the modern "tolerances" — better named "intolerances" — there is sometimes a problem, especially if the reel is older and the spool new.

The drag question, except for whales and such, is also a moot point. For big fish a drag is very desirable but the draglets put on some of the outsized reels aren't really much more than decoration. It's nice to be able to adjust the tension on your line a little for playing fish right off the reel on very light tippets, but it's not essential. Check out the general amount of tension and smoothness before you worry about drag.

A perforated click reel from the turn of the century. Made by Ideal, it weighed 4 ounces, held 35 yards of line and was cast from German silver.

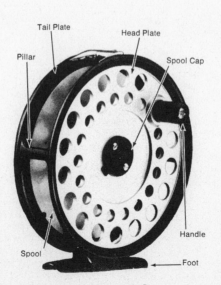

The modern perforated fly reel.

Orvis marketed the Kelso automatic reel in the early 1900s. Made from a new material — aluminum — it had enough spring to take up to 150 yards of No. 6 line. It sold for only $4.

The Hardy Perfects between 1910 and 1919 ranged from a 6¼-ounce model that sold for about $4.50 to a monster 28-ouncer that was priced at $20.

Finest Trout Reel Ever Made

The finest trout reel ever made, in my opinion, was the Hardy Perfect patented in 1890. I have never been able to damage one and they seem to improve with age. I own one that's at least fifty years old and it's slightly smoother running, if anything, than its younger cousins. This reel was discontinued several years ago and replaced by a lightweight series — perhaps to cash in on the theory that a reel that is light on the scales is more sporting because this measurement is applied to rods. One of the few smart things I have ever done was to lay in a last-minute supply of Perfects that will last me my lifetime no matter how cleanly I live.

From *Fishing the Dry Fly as a Living Insect* by Leonard M. Wright, Jr. (C) 1972 by Leonard M. Wright, Jr. Used by permission of E. P. Dutton & Co., Inc.

There's only one place for an automatic reel

When the Martin Company introduced its first automatic fly reel in the late part of the last century, there were cries of amazement. Since then, however, even the best automatics have been criticized for their lack of dependability, insufficient capacity, heaviness and so on.

But they continue to sell, finding a hard-core angling acceptance that persists over time. The new ones put out by Martin, Perrine and others are much more dependable and have a larger capacity than older models. If you're attracted to a reel that picks up slack line with a touch of the finger, go to it.

But the only place automatics have a place is in boat fishing for bass and panfish where a craft full of loose line is a discouragement. Please, oh please, don't get an automatic that winds up as you pull line off — if you hang into a lunker that shoots away with your line, it may take a skilled watchmaker to put all the springs back together again.

—H. H.

The birth of the automatic

By the Martin Company

Back in the late 1800s Herman W. Martin was a member of a group of Adirondack region anglers who took their fishing pretty seriously. For years they had been holding an informal contest to see who could land the biggest bass.

One day in the summer of 1881, Martin, a watchmaker who apparently preferred fishing to his business, hooked into a bass which he knew would place him well on the top of the list. But in playing the fish, his line got tangled up in his oar and around his feet. The giant bass made a powerful lunge and threw the hook. Martin exploded. He returned to his shop determined to develop some type of reel which would enable the fisherman to control the slack line at all times and prevent tangling — something his single action fly rod could not do.

His watchmaking experience proved to be a valuable asset in the work which followed. With a collection of clock and watch parts, Martin produced the first automatic fishing reel — a large, crude affair which bolted to the butt of the rod and weighed about three pounds. It controlled slack line by means of tension produced by winding a gear on top of the reel which compressed a large clock spring. Once the reel was properly wound, the tension could be thrown on or off by means of a long reverse lever which was also located on top of the reel.

The first reel, though very crude, actually worked, and the basic principle is still employed in modern automatic reels. Martin was issued a series of patents on these designs during the 1890s.

The first field tests weren't too successful. He soon learned that his reel was far too heavy and clumsy for actual fishing. Nevertheless, this model did retrieve slack line, and prevented it from becoming entangled. Martin decided that this idea was right and believed that if he could improve the design and eliminate some of the dead weight, he would have a reel that would increase the pleasure of thousands of fishermen.

Then Martin incorporated the results of his findings in the field into a new reel. This one was much lighter than the previous model and many of the projections which tended to snarl the line were removed. Unfortunately, this original reel has had a rough life. In 1936 the Martin factory was damaged by a disastrous fire. But in spite of the fact that Martin's second model was subjected to terrific heat it still worked and is still in operation today.

Not yet satisfied, by about 1890 Martin developed a third reel. This model was round, fastened to the reel butt with a reel seat — as do the present-day reels — and was equipped with two protruding handles for winding. These handles were soon discarded because of the tangling problem. After a few refinements in design, it became the first automatic reel to be manufactured in quantity and the first product to be offered by the Martin Company.

Herman Martin's second try at the automatic.

WHAT WE LOOKED FOR IN QUALITY

You'd think that something as simple as a single-action fly reel would be a snap to construct. Well, it ain't necessarily so.

In choosing our models we looked for those that operated smoothly even under the stress of playing a decent fish. On some cheaper models the spool can jam against the frame, causing problems.

A drag was of less importance to us than this smoothness. The most effective drag for a trout-sized fly reel is a side plate that can be palmed. Whatever drag saltwater reels have should operate easily and effectively. It shouldn't tighten up as a fish runs.

We also looked for a finish on the reel that would withstand wear and minor abuse.

DAIWA

HEDDON

top of the line

Freshwater Reels

BERKLEY SPECIALIST II. A newcomer weighing only 3½ ounces with a very interesting drag feature — a lever system whose tension is controlled by the pressure of your finger. Berkley also puts out a line of reels built on the patent of the Hardy Lightweights but they are more or less on the order of quality of the Heddon Lightweight series made in Japan. They do the job, however.

CORTLAND C. G. GRAPHITE. A gadget? A gidget? A very dependable lightweight reel? Yes, yes, yes! At 2½ ounces with a No. 5 line capacity, Cortland's newest entree is a companion to their featherlight graphite rods and is even lighter than the Hardy Lightweights. They're incredibly durable and perfect for packing. Available in two models for lines up to No. 7 and spare spools are cheap. It's an excellent choice for those twixt the Medalists and the high-priced Hardys.

DAIWA. A popular discount house reel. A Japanese import, the Daiwas are slightly strange-looking with their square base but they do the job of getting the line in and out and are quite serviceable for any number of beginning tasks.

GLADDING – SOUTH BEND. A nice functional multiplier (2.66:1 ratio) this company brings in from England at a reasonable price. It's the same reel that Cortland used to import until Gladding took over the British works — an excellent example of reel imperialism. They do the job for heavy trouting, can be switched from right to left hand use and have rapidly interchangeable spools. Gladding also markets a reasonable

FAVORITES OF THE EXPERTS

Our experts might be a lot of things but their choices in fly reels showed them to be a discriminating bunch.

Those Hardy Lightweights made in England that start out at $60 or so for the smallest were the big choice of those polled. "Simple and great. Used my Flyweight for 15 years," said one fellow who lives in the West. The most popular single model was the Princess, which takes a No. 6 line and lots of backing.

The recently resurrected Hardy Perfect, which is, from the standpoint of design and durability, the best fly reel ever made, got votes, too, especially from western anglers who don't mind the extra couple ounces of weight.

Pflueger's Medalist, the American classic, got quite a few votes, especially from the bass and panfish crowd down South. The poppers liked the simplicity, price and durability of the Medalists.

Orvis' relative newcomer, the CFO line, priced in the $60 and over range, got votes but it hasn't really been around long enough to become as popular as the Hardy Lightweights. "Best looking reel there is," said one CFO II owner.

The most popular big game fly reel was the Fin-Nor. Respondents liked its rugged construction and dependability. The new John Emery reel got one vote and has a strong saltwater future.

Scientific Angler's reels, which are companions to their system rods, also got quite a few votes from experts who liked their simplicity and English-made elegance.

SOUTH BEND

top of the line

facsimile of the Medalist, which is quite serviceable though a little loose-clicked.

HARDY LIGHTWEIGHT. This high-quality line of reels from England has come to dominate the market in high-priced models. Though the familiar refrain of, "They're not building 'em like they used to" has shadowed the Lightweights in the past couple years they're still the standard.

Among the advantages of the perforated spool reels is the lightness of the alloy from which they are constructed, the rapid interchangeability of spools and, yes, the sweet whine of the click. According to some, their disadvantages are a not-so-sturdy constitution that doesn't take to knocks and bruises very well. Also the price tag is now closing in on $60 for even the smallest No. 3 line capacity Flyweight model and $80 for a No. 9 or No. 10. The drag isn't much more than a tension adjustment but Hardy is still the reel most often found on expensive cane fly rods, especially in an era when lightness is a virtue for many anglers. The new ones have an optional right or left hand wind and a nickel silver reversible line guard.

HARDY LIGHTWEIGHT MULTIPLIERS. With a 1 2/3-to-1 gear ratio, the lightweight multipliers are great for those who want to take up line quickly but don't want a mammoth-sized reel. They are of the same good quality as the other lightweights.

HARDY PERFECT. Lots of anglers thought the Hardy Perfect, which was produced in England from 1892 until the 1960s, was the most perfectly designed reel ever made. The originals ranged in size from a tiny trouter with a diameter under 3 inches to some gargantuans for salmon that were over 5 inches. The

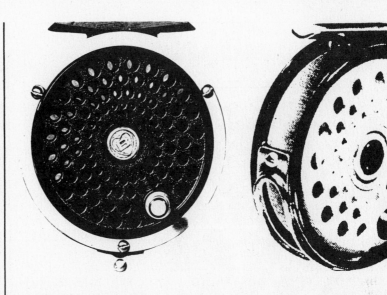

BERKLEY SPECIALIST   CORTLAND GRAPHITE

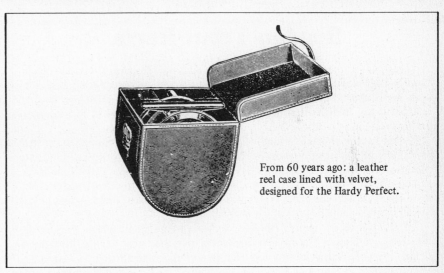

From 60 years ago: a leather reel case lined with velvet, designed for the Hardy Perfect.

HARDY LIGHTWEIGHT   HARDY PERFECT

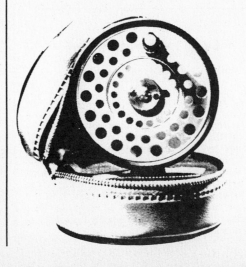

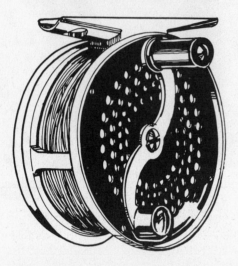

ultimate commodity

Bogdan Trout Reels

There aren't many Bogdan trout reels around, perhaps a couple dozen. Stanley Bogdan, who has made wonderful salmon and saltwater reels for decades from his Nashua, New Hampshire, machine shop, just hasn't taken the time to produce many of them despite the clamorings of anglers. He has all the orders for bigger models he can handle.

Except for the absence of the finely honed click drag, the Bogdan trout reel is basically a miniaturized version of its big classically designed brother; both are continuations of the absolute quality introduced to reel craft by Vom Hofe.

Bogdan trout reels aren't for the fly angler bitten by ultra-litis. They're in the eight-ounce class — the same as a comparably priced Hardy Perfect — and hold a No. 6 line with some but not much backing.

The Bogdan is a superbly fine-tuned piece of equipment which, barring the unforeseen, will last a lifetime and can handle even the finest tippets. It is a complementary companion for any rod from the seven-and-a-half to nine-foot range.

Perhaps if you whine and beg, Mr. Bogdan will have mercy and make one for you in the $150 price range. Though you'll probably have a long wait, you'll never need another one.

COVER-GUARD REEL CASES

A nice line of zippered reel cases available in three sizes for fly, spinning and larger saltwater reels. Padded top and bottom, the bigger model has a carrying handle. Made from vinyl. They also make a zippered rod case for up to four rods and will special-manufacture others.

Indestructible Graphite

I once watched a Cortland salesman throw one of their graphite reels across a shop as a demonstration of their construction. I said to myself, "There are many reels I'd like to do that to." But the graphites are indestructible. Or almost, anyway. For the money, graphite reels are a bargain, and extra spools are cheap enough. They are a real boon to backpackers, especially since they are unspeakably light and can hold up to the rigors of camp life. They also blend well with the equally light graphite rods now available.

—H.H.

top of the line

company lifted its eyebrows in the mid 1970s when prices for Perfects in mint condition were bringing as much as $100 on the used tackle market. They started re-tooling and the Perfect has returned.

What makes the Perfect so desirable is the smoothness produced by a set of tiny ball bearings, its sturdiness and a revolving sideplate that allows anglers to palm the spool when a big fish is running. This manual drag is something most of the small reels omit in the quest for lightness.

The revived Perfects are almost as smooth as their forebears, though some Perfect connoisseurs claim that the reels made in the early 50s were the best ever. The basic disadvantage according to those who spurn Perfects is their heaviness. But even though they can weigh half or more again than a comparable capacity lightweight, their advocates argue that since a clammy hand is placed between the top of a rod and the reel, lightness is a matter of fashion and fad. It also takes a bit more effort to change spools on the Perfect but how many times does that happen?

Anyway their price is enough to scare some anglers away.

HARDY ST. JOHN. Another popular revival that Hardy has brought back because of demand. The St. John, with its large 3 7/8-inch capacity, is a fine steelhead or salmon reel one notch or so below the Perfect. But well worth the $60 or so being asked. An extra spool in the $25 class gives this reel big fish versatility.

HEDDON LIGHTWEIGHT SERIES. If imitation is the highest form of flattery then Heddon is in love with Hardy. Except for the pale green coloration the made-in-Japan Heddons are such good replicas of the Hardys that even the spools on some models are interchangable —

MARTIN MODEL 72

top of the line

which strikes some anglers as being dangerously close to incest.

But they're good reels, especially since their price is about 20 per cent that of the reel McCoy. They're available in models ranging from 3½ ounces for a No. 6 line to a big one that weighs 5¾ ounces and takes a No. 10. At any rate, a fine, fine reel for beginning anglers and those without much pretense.

MARTIN MODEL 72. Interesting because it has a 3-to-1 retrieve ratio giving it incredibly quick line pickup. It has a pretty fair Teflon drag system and at a little over nine ounces can hold up to a WF 9 No. 1 line, and 150 yards of 10-pound Dacron backing. It also has a quick spool change mechanism which isn't bad for a multiplying fly reel. Martin also makes other very serviceable fly reels but they aren't as unique as their multipliers.

ORVIS CFO. One hundred years after Charles F. Orvis introduced the first ventilated spool reels in 1874, his descendants produced a line of expensive lightweights in his memory. They boast a truly dazzling line capacity. For instance, the CFO II, which weighs two ounces, will take an entire No. 4 line and backing. The 3½ ounce CFO IV takes a No. 8 line with backing. That's something.

Perhaps it's only a minor drawback, but some folks say the dark alloy steel — which is actually only half a frame, the spool itself making up the other half — is too fragile. Yet lots and lots of anglers have forsaken their Hardy Lightweights for the newcomer, showing how fickle fly angler affections are.

PFLUEGER MEDALIST. This is *the* American fly reel and has been for eons. More fly anglers have begun their streamside careers with this one than probably all others put togeth-

There are no weight formulas

I was nurtured in the school that believed in a reel balancing a rod. Now I'm not sure what that meant, aside from some metaphysical nonsense, like there being harmony in an angler watching a 6-pound fish snap off a 6X tippet. The old formula was that a reel should be 1½ times the weight of the rod for balance. A 4-ounce rod took a 6-ounce reel. But practically, one should operate within the bounds of common sense rather than by formulas. It must be admitted that a 10-ounce Hardy Perfect feels weird on a 2-ounce Thomas 6-footer. On such a rod, a Hardy Lightweight or Tiny Walker might feel and look better, but aside from these far-fetched examples, weight and balance are a moot point in choosing a reel. Scientific Angler's idea of balanced rods and reels is sensible, but an extra ounce more or less wouldn't change the appropriateness much, especially if it means a better-built reel. The balance problem is that both thin and chubby hands go between the rod and reel at the top of the handle, like the scales of justice. If the two parts were roughly equal in weight, then we were using a just combination, but the weight of your hand, like the weight of the law and the court, intervenes and it becomes a silly equation.

It was my interest in the relatively heavy Hardy Perfects that made me rethink the balance issue. Those delights are usually a good 2 ounces heavier than the equal-capacity lightweights that I had been using, but are much better built. Instead of a 4-ounce Princess reel I began using a 6- or 7-ounce Perfect on my Para 15 4-ounce reel — big deal. I have never really felt the difference. If you are going to make a fetish of lightness, then go ahead with the CFOs, Lightweights and the like, but don't feel sacreligious if the weightier models seem better to you. Take whatever seems right. There are no meaningful objective formulas.

From *Fly Tackle: A Guide to the Tools of the Trade* by Harmon Henkin. Copyright (C) 1976 by Harmon Henkin. Reproduced by permission of J. B. Lippincott Company.

"This is not moody work; it keeps
a man alive and stirring."
WILLIAM SCROPE

top of the line

er. In its long spell on the scene as a very dependable medium priced reel, it has come in a variety of sizes and diameters. Some large models with narrow spools are still prized for their quick retrieves by veteran steelheaders. The Medalist has also spawned a wide variety of imitations from far off oriental lands.

They're constructed from a dark aluminum alloy and are as light as everyone except the fanatics could want. They are, for the most part, convertible for either right or left handers. Like the Hardys, they have a rudimentary drag system.

RYOBI. The Ryobi is one of the few recent Japanese imports that doesn't duplicate a Hardy Lightweight. Available in sizes for either No. 5 to No. 7 line or No. 8 and No. 9, they're handsome in their own right. Extra spools are available for these smoke-gray reels. They have a ratcheted drag system that actually just regulates line tension. Not bad products at all.

SCIENTIFIC ANGLER SYSTEM. From Hardy Brothers of England. Made from the same alloy as the Lightweights, this has become quite a popular reel, especially when used in conjunction with the System rods. The System reels are numbered from 4 to 12 to correspond with the line size plus backing they hold and also to correspond with the rod that Scientific Angler puts out in each line size. With good quality workmanship — now that some early bugs have been ironed out — they are a bridge between the expensive reels like Orvis and other Hardys and the merely functional like the Pflueger Medalist.

One of the big advantages of these reels (which can sometimes be found discounted) is that the spool's outer edge can be palmed, giving the angler lots of control over a running fish.

PFLUEGER MEDALIST

SCIENTIFIC ANGLER SYSTEM

A Pflueger Testimonial

Offhand the only item of tackle that I know of offering such obvious advantages is Pflueger's Medalist reels. For reliability, take-apart ease, wearing qualities, and superiority of drag mechanism, I know of no other reel that offers so much for the money.

Are all my reels, therefore, Medalists? No, because before Medalists became readily available after the war, I had bought a couple of reliable and fairly expensive models, which are still good, and which I will probably use until they are worn out. Also, I still have the first reel I ever owned — an old brass skeleton model single action I use for dry fly fishing on my lightest rod.

From *Larger Trout for the Western Fly Fisherman* by Charles Brooks. (C) 1970 by A.S. Barnes and Co., Inc. Used by permission of A.S. Barnes and Co., Inc.

RYOBI

ORVIS CFO LINE

top of the line

The reels have a quasi-drag like those on most other trout reels. But this is more of a tension regulator — making it superior in some ways to other drags.

VALENTINE. Designed in large sizes for large angling jobs, the Valentine represents some interesting choices for the angler bothered by traditional reels. The main difference is that the handle remains stationary when a fish runs. It automatically hangs down but works like a regular reel on the retrieve, due to the planetary gearing system. The flying handle that skins knuckles and tempers doesn't exist here. It has a Teflon drag system, bronze bearings and is hewn from a gold-anodized aluminum alloy. The reel is highly corrosion proof and therefore ideal for salt water use. The drag ratio is 1.5:1. A finely made reel that comes in three sizes for the angler after big fish.

WALKER. The off-again on-again Walker fly reel is back. Without a doubt one of the prettiest reels around. Made for lines from No. 3 to No. 7, the five models, except for the little Faerie at three ounces, all have ratchet drags that are designed more for regulating line output than slowing down big fish. They come with bronze bearings, stainless steel cut gears and a fine finish. An interesting item for the committed trouter who likes aesthetics as well as fish. Not cheap, but what quality is these days?

Saltwater Reels

BOGDAN. Except that the marvels made by Stanley Bogdan in his Nashua, New Hampshire, shop are 2-to-1 multipliers and therefore not usable for world records in salt water, the Bogdans are ultimate reels.

VALENTINE

MEDALIST

How to cook trout

This is the method of the woods, and in the woods I learnt it; but having learned, I practice it at home, considering the Trout one of the most delicious morceaux, when thus cooked, in the world. It must be cooked, however, in the open air, by a wood fire kindled on the ground or by a charcoal fire in a small Boxton furnace.

Clean and scale your fish, open, clean and wash him internally; take for a one pound fish two small skewers of red cedar wood, upon each thread a piece of fat salt pork half-an-inch square; with these fasten the belly of the fish asunder, annex him by the tail to a twig of pliant wood, which suffer to bend over the fire so as to bring the fish opposite the blaze, place a large biscuit or a slice of thin dry toast under the drip of the gravy, cook quickly — for a two-pound fish, ten minutes will suffice — dish with the biscuit under him, and eat with salt and lemon-juice, or, if you please, with shrimp or lobster sauce, though I think these, for my own cheek, bad taste.

From *Fish and Fishing of the United States* (1864) by Frank Forester.

ORVIS

JOHN EMERY

mini-microscope

BUD LILLY'S TROUT PUMP

A bit much for some, this is another ultimate for the fly fishing fanatic. A revised trout stomach pump. You inject some water into the fish's stomach to put the contents in solution, then remove the liquid for examination and identification. You release the trout unharmed, but probably give it a very different perspective on life.

BUD LILLY

Bud is selling everything for the homespun entomologist, including two field guides to aquatic insects: *The Field Book of Fresh Water Life* and *How to Know the Immature Insects*. Also sells a catch box to examine insects; a mini-microscope, insect bottles, nymph seines, insect dip nets and a variety of thermometers.

top of the line

They are especially favored by salmon anglers along the East Coast. But even West Coast steelheaders who have tasted the blessings of Eastern civilization are buying more and more of them. Bogdan machines the frame and spool from a solid bar of aluminum, which means there are no pillars to loosen with time. The drag, which either clicks or stays silent, works with the flick of a side lever. The seven stations run from very light to heavy for tarpon-type work.

The 11-ounce reel on occasion can be bought with such personalized alterations as a perforated spool or an all black anodized version in place of the goldish frame and spool. All in all, a positive delight.

JOHN EMERY. A new 13½ ounce single-action big game reel that has the astonishing capacity of a WF13 No. 1 line plus 600 yards of a 30-pound test Dacron. Like the Bogdan and other fine reels, the spool and frame are made from a one-piece aluminum alloy bar.

Finished in a dark, anodized nonglare style, it has a large cork-disk drag. Like the Hardy Perfects, the reel has a ball-bearing system to ensure smooth operation and can be converted into right or left hand usage. A serious reel for special purpose anglers.

ORVIS. At slightly under $60, this single-actioned reel, with a capacity for WF11 No. 1 line and 200 yards of backing, can put you in the big leagues about as cheaply as possible. Though lacking the elegance of a Bogdan, Seamaster or Fin-Nor, the Orvis will do the job on even the biggest fish. The reel features oversized controls, a star-type drag and a selective anti-reverse that will allow a fish to run without twirling a bunch of knobs. It has a ventilated spool and is supposedly very corrosion-resistant.

top of the line

SEAMASTER. This Florida-made saltwater reel occupies the same position among the briny cognoscenti as the Bogdan does among salmon anglers — the top. Seamasters are unconditionally guaranteed and take more abuse from the vagaries of the ocean than other reels. The spools are machined from solid bar stock. The cross plates are a single piece. The claim is that 90 per cent of all world record fish over 50 pounds have been taken on Seamasters. They are also available on special order in left hand models.

SHAKESPEARE. A relatively inexpensive big game reel that boasts a capacity of 200 yards backing plus "any fly line." It has a disk drag and non-reverse feature, plus a built-in drag click. Extra spools are available. A good way to ease into the expensive world of fly casting for big saltwater species like tarpon and stripers or large freshwater species like Lake Michigan coho or steelhead.

TYCOON FIN-NOR. A cross between a Rolls-Royce and a Sherman Tank, this solid aluminum reel is offered in a variety of sizes from regular old trout to modified whale. Fin-Nor, with its gleaming gold modernity and outstanding reputation, is the reel that most anglers associate with big game fly fishing.

They have a full circle disk brake that is very smooth to operate. Their weight, which starts in the 10-ounce category for the trouter, should trouble no one except the diehard lightweight freak. Extra spools are available.

THE LAST HATCH
A FISHING MYSTERY
HARMON HENKIN

(continued from page 20)

Don't give me any more grief. Okay?"

"What do you want the phone for?"

"To call the sheriff."

"Why?"

"To tell him Halford's been murdered."

Dun let out the sort of scream they call "bloodcurdling" in detective novels and dropped the $10,000 weapon to the floor with a loud crash. Somewhere a gunsmith smiled for no apparent reason.

"My God! Why? Where?"

"Mouth of the creek."

Dun charged down the path screaming and sobbing. Paul was met at the door by a short, squat man with a big, beefy face.

"Greetings. Name's Wallace Wormer. What's with Dun?"

Paul told him. If Wormer hadn't been a typical city dweller, in fact if he hadn't been known as the Attila of Akron because of the environmental damage his coast-to-coast housing subdivisions had wreaked, we could say his face went ashen. At any rate, his complexion flashed a shade or two whiter. Paul knew by now that no one was going to help him find the phone, so he brushed past the stricken Wormer and began looking for himself.

Down a short hall, bristling with the heads and horns of departed beasts, Paul entered the main room of the house, furnished predictably with leather and wood in the image of a writer who had parlayed 12 outdoorsy novels into seven films, a minor fortune and a score of barroom brawls.

In one corner towered a vast gun cabinet stuffed like a Rockefeller Christmas stocking with the cream of fine European shotguns and custom-built American rifles. The exquisite Jerry Fischer .30-06, in fact, was used by Halford to bag three kangaroos in one afternoon — or so he claimed in his Pulitzer Prize-winning work, *Danger Comes A'Hoppin'*.

The hardwood floor was partially covered by a very ornate Navaho rug, the grey type that's so fashionable these days. Dead insects glared at Paul from their graves inside glass cabinets on the wall behind a Steinway Grand, burnished to a high gloss.

But socially, the most interesting thing about the room was the arrangement of its furniture. The sofa and the chairs were gathered around a big recliner placed in front of the fireplace. It was obvious

(continued on page 55)

GARCIA KINGFISHER

HEDDON

The Martin Automatic circa 1910.

The Martin Automatic today.

SHAKESPEARE 1826

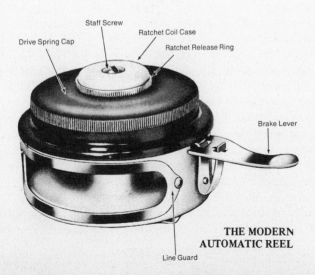

Staff Screw

Drive Spring Cap

Ratchet Coil Case

Ratchet Release Ring

Brake Lever

Line Guard

**THE MODERN
AUTOMATIC REEL**

top of the line

Automatic Reels

GARCIA KINGFISHER GK-50.
A good quality automatic fly reel that'll hold to 35 yards of No. 6 line. Anodized for corrosion proofing, it winds easily and has a trigger lock. A decent buy.

HEDDON. Heddon's Models 5 and 11 automatic reels are essentially the same model with one big difference: Model 11, which takes up to a No. 9 line, is vertical and Model 5 for up to a No. 8 is horizontal, depending on what your choice is for ease of handling. They take up lots of line with one winding, have a stainless steel line protector and have an anodized finish. The trigger folds away. Slightly over 9 ounces each.

MARTIN. Most of the Martin's many automatics have one distinct advantage: they can be taken apart with the turning of a screw. Martin made the first automatics eons ago and they still offer about the largest selection on the market. One for every taste, including some models designed not for fly rods but for bait fishing. All of the better features for automatics are found on these including free stripping, adjustable triggers and quick-acting brake.

SHAKESPEARE MODEL 1826.
The Shakespeare Model 1826 is a well-constructed automatic that has a fold-away trigger, lots of line intake with a single winding and a safety button to prevent accidental line pickup. Will do the job.

"Fishing is a delusion entirely surrounded by liars in old clothes."
DON MARQUIS

SHAKESPEARE

The true fly fisher

True fly fishermen stick to the manual single-action reel, although a good, strong brake is necessary for large saltwater gamefish. Some anglers prefer the heavy-duty variety with elaborate drag systems like those found on spinning reels. This greatly reduces the skill required to subdue big, acrobatic fish. Just set the drag and keep cranking. These reels are quite expensive, $100 to $150, and are extremely heavy. This weight is partly due to the compli-cated drag system and partly due to the built-in capacity for packing. A good guideline for buying a reel is to select a well-known brand. Get the lightest-weight model of the right capacity you need, and spend as much as your pocketbook will allow. Hardy, the Scientific Angler reels, and the Orvis CFO are all excellent.

Taken from *Fly Fishing Strategy* by Doug Swisher and Carl Richards. (C) 1975 by Doug Swisher and Carl Richards. Used by permission of Crown Publishers, Inc.

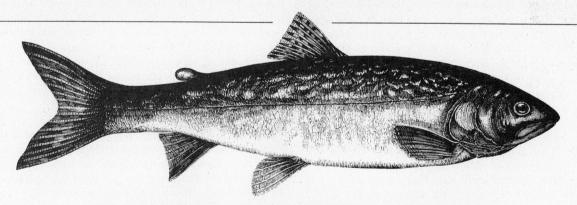

GAMEFISH: CUTTHROAT TROUT

NAMES
Mountain trout, Rocky Mountain trout, cut, native trout, Montana black-spotted trout, Lake Tahoe trout, green-back trout, winter trout, Yellowstone cutthroat. *(Salmo clarki)*

DISTRIBUTION
The cutthroat trout is found throughout the West from California to Alaska and through the Rocky Mountains.

DESCRIPTION
The cutthroat is green on the back with yellow or pink sides. Black spots cover the entire body and the underside of the lower jaw is marked with two red streaks. The coastal cut-throat is a thick fish with a large mouth. If given the chance, the cutthroat will migrate to the sea.

SIZE
Like the rainbow trout, the cutthroat varies greatly in size. Fish of up to 40 pounds have been recorded but the average is around 2 to 5 pounds.

HABITAT
The cutthroat trout favors clear, cold waters but prefers quieter habitats than the rainbow trout. It is found in slow-moving streams where it can find deep holes and hiding places near submerged debris.

FEEDING HABITS
The diet of the cutthroat consists of insects, insect larvae, small baitfish and worms. Cutthroats that migrate to the sea are usually found in brackish water or at the mouth of coastal rivers. They tend to feed on minnows, sand fleas and small crabs.

BEST FEEDING TEMPERATURE
About 47°.

TACKLE
This fish loves colorful flies on the surface or below. Small spinners and spoons do the job with an ultra-light outfit. Heavy tackle never needed in streams, almost never in lakes.

Some thoughts on steelhead and salmon tackle

By Russell Chatham

Before going into this discussion of steelhead and salmon tackle, it might be helpful to first define some conditions — the water where these fish are sought is varied. Probably 90 per cent of it, however, is large and open like the lower Eel, the tidewaters of most Oregon streams, the Dean, Kispiox and Babine. In writing this, then, I have that in mind since more intimate rivers like the North Umpqua in Oregon, the Gold on Vancouver Island, or the Stillaguamish in Washington can be handled with heavy trout tackle.

You hear a lot of trout fishermen say that short casts are more effective than long ones. This is very often true in trout fishing; it is not true in steelhead fishing. I suspect that a man always insisting upon the value of short casts is compensating for his own inability to make long ones.

I'm reminded of novelists who outspokenly disdain any connection with Hollywood until they are approached with a movie contract, then suddenly their faces are pressed against the window of Big Money along with everyone else.

If you've mastered distance casting, trout casting is very easy to adapt to. The reverse is not true because distance casting is much more difficult. The reason is easy to understand. Fly casting is a matter of line control and line speed; the farther you cast, the more each deficiency is amplified. Most trout fishermen entertain fantasies of long casts perhaps because there is a suggestion of machismo there, insofar as that concept might be applied to so gentle a pastime as angling.

All this is by way of saying that to become a steelhead and salmon fisherman you will need to learn the skills involved in the casting. And you will need appropriate tackle. The long and short of it is a 9-foot rod and No. 10 line.

You could get by, say, 30 per cent of the time with a No. 8 shooting head outfit but that doesn't make good sense unless you don't mind spending 70 per cent of your time sitting in the car.

The last time I went to British Columbia, my companion, a reasonably accomplished fly caster who had nevertheless not yet fished for steelhead or salmon, brought along a No. 8 graphite rod and a corresponding complement of shooting heads. At home on his lawn he thought he was casting about 90 feet with this stuff. That was at home with no wind, no fly, no wading and no rolling fish to unsettle his nerves. When he got out in the river three thousand miles from home and tried to show some big salmon a No. 4 comet, he failed by about 30 feet.

To be in the picture you should be able to cast 90 feet consistently while wading belly deep. You should learn to deal with wind. You should practice where you can measure your casts. And you should always use a practice fly that approximates the real thing, with a regular fishing leader. Strive to make clean casts which turn over properly.

So then, the basic general tackle is a 9-foot rod and a No. 10 shooting head. Twenty-five years ago Ted Trueblood said everything there was to say about shooting heads and anyone not using them today on big water is simply being stupid or perverse.

In the rod, the quality you will most appreciate if you are going to fish avidly, is light weight. A difference of a few ounces will become pounds at the end of a 12-hour day. In that regard, during 25 years of constant and pretty serious salmon and steelhead fishing, I only knew two men who used bamboo rods and both of them took long afternoon naps and could usually be counted upon not to be present at the time of the evening grab.

(continued on next page)

This article appeared originally in *Montana Outdoors*, July/August 1974.

A Duel with the Baker Boys

By Harmon Henkin

Boy, were they dumb!

Here they were, the Baker brothers challenging Dick and me to a fish-out and giving us our choice of water.

We met them during the winter in a sporting goods shop where we were gossiping about the latest tackle. They were both native Montanans and dyed-in-the-wool bait fishermen. Specializing in worms, Dewey, at 25 the older Baker, claimed he could outfish any fly angler anytime — especially a couple of rookies. Dick and I had tossed fur and feather around the Midwest for a few years before coming to Montana and knew better.

The argument was one of those endless disputes that keeps sportsmen out of mischief between seasons. The only place to settle it was on the field of honor, a trout stream.

Since we were new to the area, they let us choose when and where we would go at it and set up a pair of dinners as the prize. Local fly fishermen told us that the Little Blackfoot, which flows into the Clark Fork 80 miles east of Missoula, was a good place for us to go. It is a relatively small creek about 25 feet wide and resembles the famous Michigan and eastern streams we knew well. Many of its residents were brown trout and everybody knows they love flies more than anything.

There are usually good hatches on this stream in July and the water is so clear that spinning gear is generally not favored tackle. We couldn't help snickering upon discovering that the Bakers had never fished the creek before. How could we lose?

Dick and I looked elegant after climbing into our waders and hoisting on our fancy vests loaded down with enough gear to give competition to any fly shop in the country. Between us we toted a dozen rods, matching reels, floating lines, sinking lines, lines that couldn't make up their minds what they were, untold thousands of flies and an index of miscellaneous gear that would have required a computer to keep track of.

The Bakers headed downstream carrying only spinning tackle and jars of ugly worms and we took the upstream stretch. But it took us a half hour of knot tightening and leader straightening before we could get down to the serious business at hand — choosing the proper fly. We vacillated between mayfly nymphs and floating caddis imitations, finally deciding that Dick would use the dry and me the nymph.

We fished through some of the grandest looking trout water imaginable — classic pools, long runs and a smattering of rock-coated white water. We didn't get a strike.

A conference brought us to the conclusion that our nine-foot leaders weren't long enough. We tied on lighter tippets and lengthened the leaders to 12 feet. We fished another fruitless hour. We changed fly patterns and we changed fly patterns and we changed fly patterns — nothing.

It called for a change in basic strategy. I tried sinking lines and big stonefly nymphs and Dick put on some large Bucktail streamers. Nothing. We started desperately changing flies and ideas. The hours passed and still nothing. I used wet flies weighted so heavily that if they landed on a trout it would have thought it had been mugged. Dick tried dry flies so tiny a fish needed a microscope to see them.

We used short leaders, long leaders, fat leaders and thin leaders, big rods and small rods, bright flies and dull flies, tiny flies and huge flies. It didn't make any difference. Nothing worked.

We covered miles of water and never saw a fish or had a strike — an absolute fishing disaster.

The walk back to the car at dark was conducted in silence. The Baker boys were sitting on the grass behind a limit of 10 browns ranging from 1-3 pounds. They had been resting for an hour and had taken an hour off earlier to eat their lunch.

Dick and I ate crow that night and it tasted terrible.

Steelhead & salmon tackle

(continued from preceding page)

Glass fills the bill nicely and so, obviously, does graphite. The difference is price. Yes, graphite is a bit lighter, slightly faster. Whether it is $150 lighter and faster will depend on where you work and what you want others to think of you.

Not long ago I was fishing the Gualala River in California — classic water. One day I met a young man making his first try for steelhead. He had a No. 8 graphite rod and a sinking tip, weight-forward line, a combination almost perfectly calculated to insure his lack of success. He explained he'd spent all his money on the rod which he had planned to use for both trout and steelhead, and couldn't afford another special steelhead rod.

Too bad and, in fact, plainly absurd. You can buy a perfectly fine glass rod blank, a Lamiglass for instance, for $8 or $9. All the fittings might cost as much as another $5. In two very easy hours you can have a rod that nine out of ten blindfolded casters could never tell apart from a dozen others.

Any of the $15 to $25 single-action reels are also a perfectly adequate bottom line. The Pflueger Medalist is the most venerable standby of them all. Model number 1495 is just right. You in no way need a $150 Fin-Nor. If you want something in between, Scientific Anglers makes a good medium-priced reel. From there you can refine it all you want, getting into antique Hardys or handmade Bogdans.

A Scientific Angler System Reel

Cortland and Scientific Anglers both sell shooting heads. These come from the factory in standard 30-foot lengths. There are basically three kinds: the number one which sinks slowly; two, which is a fast sinker, and three, which sinks extra fast.

I would not advise skimping on the lines. They play a more important part in salmon and steelhead fishing than the rod or reel, or even the fly. The line is what holds the fly at fish level, be it lagoon, riffle or deep pool. You should have the three lines. It's far more important to buy $30 worth of fly lines than pay $90 for a rod or $50 for a reel.

If the young man at Gualala had followed this, or similar advice, he could have outfitted himself *completely* for both trout *and* steelhead, rods, reels, lines and all, for something less than half the price of his one graphite rod. He would not have squandered his time and effort on the first trip using

(continued on next page)

Some thoughts on steelhead and salmon tackle

(continued from preceding page)

tackle with which not even an expert could have hoped to catch anything. And with the money saved he could have taken another fishing trip or gone to dinner with a lady friend at Trader Vic's and come home delightfully stuporous.

There is another important item you must have: good monofilament shooting line. No matter what else you hear, nothing works like monofilament. If you use the thin diameter fly line marketed specifically for the purpose, you may as well use a three diameter line because your distance will be very much reduced. That stuff was made to humor those who object to shooting heads on some kind of moral grounds.

A new monofilament is now available which is far better than anything we had before. It's called Amnesia, sold by the Sunset Line Company. It's glass smooth and very limp. The best feature, the most important feature of this line, is that it rarely tangles. You can literally stretch any kinks out of it with your hands. It has no "memory" of coils, thus its name.

Put enough backing on the reel to fill it up, leaving enough room for a hundred feet of the shooting monofilament and the shooting head. When the monofilament starts to wear, as it does in a very

Sunset "Amnesia"

short time, throw it out and tie on another hundred feet.

Leaders may vary from six to fifteen feet and from four to twelve pound test. The variance is naturally due to the wide range of conditions you can run into.

With the flies, first avoid the mistake of being taken in by lots of complicated patterns. You need four types, all easily tied by a novice: large, small, bright, dark. Large would be fours and twos; small would be eights and tens. Bright would be silver, yellow, orange, the fluorescent materials; dark is basically black.

Fly patterns are completely irrelevant, so choose what appeals to you. These fish are never taking any particular fly other than those of the four different characteristics listed above. Beyond that, it is simply a matter of the fish biting or not, depending upon moods in no way connected with the pattern of fly.

Of course, you can get into this business on a variety of levels. The choice of rods is not simply between the $12 home-crafted model and the $800 Garrison or $200 graphite. Most people use Fenwicks, or Winstons, or Scientific Anglers — rods that sell for $80 or $90. The same applies to reels, and in different degrees, to all aspects of the equipment from waders to dark glasses, hats to raincoats.

Some items are more important than others. Some cost a lot more than others, on some the price is fixed and essential. Whether you get into the game for a nominal ante or to your ears depends entirely upon how much you can afford in relation to the quality of equipment you wish to own. The point is, common sense and knowing what you must have and what you don't really need, can get you started quite painlessly.

specifications

BRAND-MODEL	WEIGHT (OZ.)	LINE CAPACITY (YDS.)	PILLAR PLATE
BERKLEY			
1056	3.5		
550		.30 #6 + 100 backing	3 1/4"
540		.30 #6 + 50 gacking	2 7/8"
530		.30 #6 line	2 1/2"
510		.30	
500		.25 fly line or 50 braided line	
BOGDAN			
F1662	11	WF9F + 200 backing	1 3/8"-3 1/4"
F1663	13.25	WF10F + 200 backing	1 3/16"-3 3/4"
F1664	14	WF10F + 300 backing	1 3/8"-3 3/4"
CORTLAND			
CG Graphite Fly Reels			
CG1	2.5	#3-5	2 7/8"
CG2	2.75	#5-7	3 1/4"
Crown Fly Reels			
Small		WF6	3 1/4"
Medium		WF7	
CORTLAND			
CG Graphite Fly Reels			
CG1	2.5	#3-5	2 7/8"
CG2	2.75	#5-7	3 1/4"
Crown Fly Reels			
Small		WF6	3 1/4"
Medium		WF7	3 1/2"
Large		WF8	3 5/8"
DAIWA			
700 Series			
731	5.3	#7	
732	6.3	#8	
734 (salt-fresh)	7	#10	
GARCIA			
Kingfisher (single action)			
GK40	4	DT4	
GK42	4.5	#6 + 50 backing	
GK44	5	#6 + 100 backing	
Kingfisher (automatic)			
GK-50		.35 of #6	
HARDY			
Hardy Lightweight Range			
LRH Multi-plier	3.75		3 3/16"

BRAND-MODEL	WEIGHT (OZ.)	LINE CAPACITY (YDS.)	PILLAR PLATE
Feather-weight	3	.40 of DT4F	2 7/8"
Flyweight	2..38	.50 of WF4F	2 1/2"
LRH light-weight	3.75	.70 of DT4F	3 3/16"
Princess	4.75	.100 of DT5F	3 1/2"
Zenith	7.25	.180 of DT7F	1 1/8"-3 3/8"
Husky	7.25	.180 of DT7F	1 1/8"-3 3/8"
Saint Aidan	6	.180 of DT7F	3 3/4"
Perfect			3 1/8"
Perfect			3 3/8"
Perfect			3 5/8"
Saint George	7.75	.120 of DT7F	3 3/4"
Saint John	8.5	.180 of DT7F	3 7/8"
HEDDON			
Automatic reels			
11	9.4	up to #9	
5	9.1	up to #8	
Single Action			
340	5.75	up to #10	
320	4.5	up to #8	
310	4	up to #7	
300	3.5	up to #6	
755	4	up to #8	
MARTIN			
72	9.25	.35 of WF9F + 150 of backing	
70	8	.35 of WF9F + 150 of backing	
71 (salt)	9	.35 of WF9F + 200 of backing	
68	7	.35 of WF9F + 150 of backing	
67A	5.5	.35 of WF9F + 150 of backing	
MG-7	4	DT8F or WF9F	3 5/16"
60	3.5	.30 of DT6F	
61	3.75	.35 of WF8F	
62	3.5	.30 of DT6F	
63	3.75	.35 of WF8F	
64	6.25	.35 of WF9F + 150 of backing	
65	5.5	.35 of WF9F + 130 of backing	
66	5	.35 of WF9F + 130 of backing	
ORVIS			
CFO Fly Reels			
F1928-II	2	DT3F or WF4F	2 9/16"
F1695-III	3	WF6F + 50 of backing	3"
F1695-2-III	3.25	WF6F + 50 of backing	3"
F1930-IV	3.5	WF8F + 50 of backing	3 3/16"
F1932-V	4.5	WF10F + 150 of backing	3 7/16"
Battenkill Fly Reels			
F1710-III	3.75	WF5F + 100 of backing	3 1/4"
F1712-IV	4	WF7F + 125 of backing	3 5/8"

specifications

BRAND-MODEL	WEIGHT (OZ.)	LINE CAPACITY (YDS.)	PILLAR PLATE
F1714-V	5.25	WF9F + 200 of backing	3 7/8"
Madison Fly Reels			
F1618-4/5	4	WF4F or WF5F	3"
F1620-6/7	5.25	WF6F + 100 of backing	3 1/4"
F1622-8	6	WF8F + 150 of backing	3 5/8"
F1624-9	6.75	WF9F + 200 of backing	3 5/8"
Magnalite Fly Reels			
F0802 Multiplier	6.5	WF8F + 50 of backing	3 1/2"
F0804 Wide Multiplier	7	WF10F + 150 of backing	3 1/2"
Saltwater Fly Reels			
F1697	12.25	WF8F + 275 of backing	4"
F1667	12	WF11F + 333 of backing.	

PFLUEGER

1400 Series (single action)

BRAND-MODEL	WEIGHT (OZ.)	LINE CAPACITY (YDS.)	PILLAR PLATE
1492	4	25 of #7	13/16"-2 7/8"
1492½	4.5	30 of #7	1"-2 7/8"
1494	5	40 of #7	3/16"-3 1/4"
1494½	6	50 of #7	1"-3 1/4"
1495	6	50 of #7	3/16"-3 5/8"
1495½	6.75	60 of #7	1"-3 5/8"
1498 fresh/salt	6.88	80 of #7	1"-4"

Supreme (single action)

BRAND-MODEL	WEIGHT (OZ.)	LINE CAPACITY (YDS.)	PILLAR PLATE
577	10.5	any size.	
578	12.5	any size.	

Single Action

BRAND-MODEL	WEIGHT (OZ.)	LINE CAPACITY (YDS.)	PILLAR PLATE
1534	4	40 of #7	
1535	6	any size.	
576	4.5	any size.	
1554	5	#7	

Medalist Automatic

BRAND-MODEL	WEIGHT (OZ.)	LINE CAPACITY (YDS.)	PILLAR PLATE
575	8.9		

Special Purpose Trolling

BRAND-MODEL	WEIGHT (OZ.)	LINE CAPACITY (YDS.)	PILLAR PLATE
3178 Pakron	.22	400-45 lb. test monel wire	
1558 Sal-trout	14	275-15 lb. test braided nylon	

RYOBI

BRAND-MODEL	WEIGHT (OZ.)	LINE CAPACITY (YDS.)	PILLAR PLATE
444	5.7	30 of #5-#7	4/5"-3 3/5"
455	7	30 of #8 or #9	1"-4"

SCIENTIFIC ANGLER

System Fly Reels

BRAND-MODEL	WEIGHT (OZ.)	LINE CAPACITY (YDS.)	PILLAR PLATE
4	3.5	#4	3/4"-2 3/4"
5	3.75	#5	3/4"-3"
6	4.25	#6	3/4"-3 1/4"
7	4.5	#7	3/4"-3 7/16"
8	5.75	#8	3/4"-3 5/8"
9 (fresh/salt)	6.25	#9	3/4"-3 3/4"
10 (fresh/salt)	7.5	#10	15/16"-3 7/8"
11 (fresh/salt)	8	#11	15/16"-4"

SEAMASTER

BRAND-MODEL	WEIGHT (OZ.)	LINE CAPACITY (YDS.)	PILLAR PLATE
F1667	12	WF11F with 1000 of backing	

SHAKESPEARE

Automatic Fly Reels

BRAND-MODEL	WEIGHT (OZ.)	LINE CAPACITY (YDS.)	PILLAR PLATE
1826	9.4	up to #6	
1827	9.4	up to #6	
1822	8.5	up to #6	
1824	8.9	up to #6	
1837	9	up to #6	

Purist Fly Reels (single action)

BRAND-MODEL	WEIGHT (OZ.)	LINE CAPACITY (YDS.)	PILLAR PLATE
7593	4.5	up to #6	1"-2 3/16"
7594	4.88	up to #7	13/16"-2 11/16"
7595	5.63	up to #8	1"-2 11/16"
7596	5.63	up to #11	13/16"-3 1/16"
7597	6.38	up to #12	1"-3 1/16"
1898		200 of #20	

SOUTH BEND

Automatic Fly Reels

BRAND-MODEL	WEIGHT (OZ.)	LINE CAPACITY (YDS.)	PILLAR PLATE
1140 Oreno-Matic	9.5	35 of #6	
1130 Oreno-Matic	8.5	25 of #6	
1190 Oreno-Matic	9.5	35 of #6	
1180 Flat-Mounting	9	35 of #6	

Fly Reels

BRAND-MODEL	WEIGHT (OZ.)	LINE CAPACITY (YDS.)	PILLAR PLATE
1122 Finalist (single action)		35 of #5	-2 1/2"
1055 King-size gear		100	
1044 Regular gear		100	
1033 Light-weight gear		75	

TYCOON

Fin-Nor Anti Reverse Reels

BRAND-MODEL	WEIGHT (OZ.)	LINE CAPACITY (YDS.)	PILLAR PLATE
1268	10.125	30 of #9 + 200 of backing.	
1270	12.25	30 of #10 + 250 of backing	

specifications

BRAND-MODEL	WEIGHT (OZ.)	LINE CAPACITY (YDS.)	PILLAR PLATE
LEONARD			
TBS-312 Saltwater Reel			
1171	.11	WF11F + 250 of backing.	1 1/4"-3 1/2"
1174 (left hand)	. . . . . .	. . . . . .	. . . . . .
OLYMPIC			
400 Series			
440	.7.1	.50 of AFTMA L-8-F	13/16"-3.6"
450	.3.8	.40 of AFTMA L-6-F	13/16"-3.2"
460	.9.8	.70 of AFTMA WF-10-F	1"-4"
470	.5.7	.50 of AFTMA L-8-F	13/16"-3.6"
480 (auto)	.9.5	.40 of AFTMA L-6-F	. . . . . .

BRAND-MODEL	WEIGHT (OZ.)	LINE CAPACITY (YDS.)	PILLAR PLATE
QUICK			
25	.4.5	.30 + 50 of backing	1 3/16"-3 1/2"
45	.6	.30 + 50 of backing	
55	.6.5	.30 + 50 of backing	1 1/4"-3 1/2"
VALENTINE			
400	.9.5	.WF11F + 300 of backing	.-4"
375	.9	.WF9F + 200 of backing	-3 3/4"
350	.7.5	.WF7F + 150 of backing	-3 1/2"
WALKER			
77		.100	
777			-3 1/4"
778			13/16"-3 5/8"
666 (auto)	. . . . . .	. . . . . .	. . . . . .

Scientific Angler and Cortland have sewed up the line market, for better or worse, but there are alternatives

By Harmon Henkin

Scientific Angler and Cortland have dominated the quality fly line market for so long that a whole generation of anglers automatically buys one or the other without really knowing why. Their reputation is part of the oral tradition of the sport passed from veteran to rookie, year after year.

Lots of fly line brands have made runs at the market but have never really gotten anywhere, and the two brands are entrenched for better or worse.

Scientific Angler was a small outfit in Midland, Michigan, when it came up with the first really good synthetic fly line just a short couple decades ago. After the phase-out of silk during the 1950s, there was a variety of synthetic lines but none were of the standard that would make a contemporary angler happy.

The S.A. lines, dark brown and somber at first, revolutionized the sport far more than such evolutionary changes as synthetic rods or new fly discoveries. They also set off a wave of action in the tackle market. All sorts of companies, big and little, tried to produce fly lines that, like S.A.s, were buoyant, smooth-casting and long-lasting. The only one that came really close, and that took some years, was Cort-

land with the introduction of its 444 Line.

What both lines shared was a blending of those qualities which anglers wanted in a synthetic line. There were some brands that floated well but often they had far too light a density to cast well and had a tendency to drift in the air. Other brands would cast like bullets but had a tendency to sink like them, too.

Both Scientific and Cortland have their rooters. Most anglers are firmly in one camp or the other, although there are quite a few who prefer Cortland's floating lines and Scientific Angler's sinking models.

The criteria for a sinking line is exactly the same as for a floater with, of course, one difference. Instead of staying atop the water, you want it to sink at the correct rate of speed for the kind of water you're fishing. It's important to keep this in mind.

These days, you can buy anything from a complete quickly sinking line to sink tips, along with all the gradients in between. So you should put more effort into choosing a sinker than a floater where choices are limited between a weight-forward or a double taper.

It takes a little practice to

(continued on next page)

William Mills & Son said their aluminum spare line carrier "was gotten up to fill a long felt want for a safe, convenient and get-at-able way to carry salmon and tournament lines." It was sold between 1910 and 1920 for $4.50.

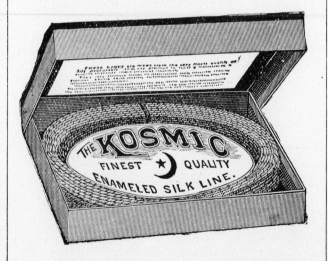

Marketed by the Wilkinson Co. in the 1890s, Kosmic line came in tapered and level models and in sizes of "D" through "G".

(continued from preceding page)

Level lines are no bargain

decide what kind of sinker you need, and the bulletins put out by the line companies are a good starting point. There are no strong guidelines to choose between weight-forward and double-tapered floaters. Most advanced anglers choose double-tapered lines for light fly fishing (No. 6 line and under) but there are exceptions to that too.

There is still a hard-core group of anglers around the country who prefer the feel of silk for light fly fishing. For these intransigents, there is now Masterline Chalkstreams from England. It may be the finest fly line on the market for light dry fly fishing. It's synthetic, but the masterlines have a delicacy some miss in Cortland and Scientific lines. Masterlines are gray, which may bother anglers weaned on more visible whites and pinks. They are more expensive, but for the angler dissatisfied with the Big Two, Chalkstreams may be an answer.

On the lower end of the price scale, Berkley's Masterlines are trying to gain a goodly share of the market. Anglers can save a few bucks on them and they are pretty good lines. Other possibilities for bargain hunters are Shakespeare and Gladding, both of which make a serviceable line.

Make sure any line you get is tapered. Level lines are no bargain. They're much harder to cast and turn over a leader with.

And just be happy it's not the 1950s when it was very difficult to find a good synthetic fly line. It's an embarassment of riches today.

THE LAST HATCH
A FISHING MYSTERY
HARMON HENKIN

(continued from page 45)

who sat where; Paul imagined how intently the sycophants must have listened while the master pronounced.

Paul couldn't find the phone so he strolled into the library, covered wall-to-wall by books obviously bought for their covers as much as their contents. Instant tradition. On one end of a monstrous teak desk sat Halford's famed angling journal, a daily record of his fishing trials, tribulations and plentiful boats that was reprinted each spring in meticulous detail by the "Fly Flinger's Journal."

He dialed the number from memory.

"Sid?"

"That you, Paul? Thought you were fishing."

"I was. You better come on out to Halford's. He's dead. Somebody gaffed him."

There was a momentary silence.

"That's a pity. I probably won't be able to fish tonight, now. See you."

Paul started to place the phone on the hook but stopped when he heard the sheriff call his name.

"Hey Paul! Paul! It wasn't you, was it?"

"No such luck, Sid."

"That's good. Who do you think it was?"

"That's your job, sheriff."

"Oh. I forgot. Bye."

He put down the phone and glanced at the Remington portable typewriter, the kind the company probably batters for writers right at the factory. There was a half-filled piece of paper tagged "Page 47" in it. The last sentence read:

> *Her alabaster thighs glistened in the diaphanous moonlight as she walked toward Abernathy, lying confidently in the dewy grass, ignoring the dangers of the wild African veldt. This was the supreme moment of her biological destiny as woman. Her heart pounded. Her ivory breasts heaved with joy as she anticipated this holy union with a man protecting his territory.*

Paul fought an urge to gag as he turned away from the typewriter. It was generally accepted in the literary world that Halford's current

(continued on page 65)

top of the line

Fly Lines

BERKLEY. Not bad at all. That's one way of looking at the comparatively inexpensive pretender to the Scientific Angler and Cortland thrones. The Berkley Specialist line, especially in the lighter double tapers and weight forwards, is a very serviceable item that casts and floats well. A distinct possibility, especially if you want to save money.

CORTLAND. Along with Scientific Anglers, Cortland 444s are considered the best on the market, among the major brands anyway. Actually in the past few years the wide variety of 444s have overtaken at least in reputation the Scientific Anglers lines, though the S.A. sinkers are considered quicker on the downtake. But these peach-colored lines are high floaters and last a long time. What more could you want. Top notch stuff, and any type your heart or rod could desire.

GLADDING. Gladding, which used to be one of the leaders of fly line production, has slipped back over the past decade but still makes a decent enough product in their Invincible line, which, like some other lines, boasts a Teflon coating for smooth running through the guides. Besides the standard tapers and weights, Gladding has saltwater tapers and tapered shooting heads as well. In sizes as light as No. 5.

GLADDING SINKING LINE. Gladding makes some very interesting specialized lines, including a pretty complete variety of fast-sinking models in weights as light as No. 5. They have a lead core. Yup, that's right. A lead core for fast, fast sink-

WHAT WE LOOKED FOR IN QUALITY

Our fly line choices were based on their ability to do the job for as long as possible. A floating line should float on top of the water, not in it, should cast easily and have an exacting tolerance of diameter and weight. Modern sinking lines should get down to where they are supposed to be with a minimum of fuss. That may sound simple but a number of lines that we tried simply didn't do the job. The ones we listed are a representation of what we believe are the leaders.

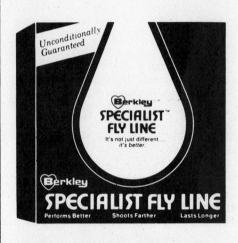

GLADDING FLY LINE SELECTION

Courtesy of McHardy's

topoftheline

ing. They also market a salmon taper line in No. 9 through No. 12 sinkers which have 200 yards of backing already spliced to the line. They're finished in a bonded plastic.

GREASED LINE ANGLER. Somehow this Portland fly shop has gotten hold of a batch of those luscious old Ashaway Fly Sport Lines in the old-system sizes of GAF, GBF and HCE. These line diameter designations correspond respectively to No. 9, No. 8 and No. 6 weight-forward lines. What makes them top drawer stuff is that they are an ultra-smooth braided combination of silk and nylon. It's a real shame that No. 4s and No. 5s aren't available, because silk is wonderful on the lightweight end of the scale. Excellent lines that are a memorable experience to use. They sink slowly unless dressed but they don't rot or mildew like other silks.

KING EIDER SILK. Those wonderful King Eider Silk fly lines aren't made any more but Norton Remmer has 100 of them for sale. Generally considered to be among the best of the smooth-casting silk lines ever made, they are probably the last you'll ever find except for a stray one getting dusty in an out-of-the-way shop.

MASTERLINE CHANCELLOR CHALKSTREAM. It just may be that this item, made by Masterline and imported by Sunset, is the best fly line in the world today. The Chalkstream has been colored a pleasant gray, unnatural to Americans weaned on pinks and whites. They are available in double tapers in weights from 4 to 8 with a very gentle taper indeed. Unlike other lines, these have to be broken in before they achieve their maximum suppleness and feel. Should be con-

MASTERLINE OXBRIDGE

MASTERLINE SINK-TIP

MASTERLINE CHANCELLOR

A few words about Masterlines

There are two things in particular you'll discover about Masterlines. One is they need to be broken in. When you first cast them, you'll find them comparatively stiff. How quickly they'll reach their maximum suppleness depends on how much they are cast. Also, the tips of Masterlines are quite fine and will break the water's surface. In relatively quiet water this poses no problem, but if you like a high floating tip in faster-moving water, the lines can be dressed with a paraffin base compound without damage. The original Mucilin is the best.

CHANCELLOR CHALKSTREAM

An old name returns

PAYNE. Gladding, which owns the Payne trademark, is marketing via its Highland Mills, N.Y., shop (where Ed, then Jim Payne built their superb reputations and rods) a top-quality fly line. They're available in double-taper, weight-forward and sink-tips and are competitively priced with Scientific Angler and Cortland. According to Gladding these lines have a Teflon coating, multiple floatation sphere and a guaranteed tolerance in the diameter of .003. Light green in color.

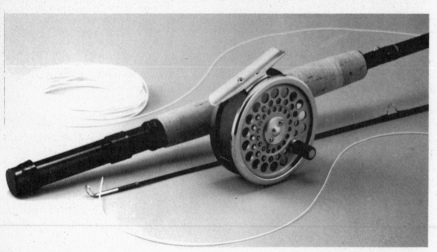

SCIENTIFIC ANGLER

LAGGIE'S LEADER STRAIGHTENER
A vest-hanging leader straightener from Laggie, it's made of leather sandwiched with rubber. Long-lasting.

Courtesy of McHardy's

top of the line

sidered, especially by light-dry-fly fanatics who want every possible advantage. Masterline also makes other lines in double taper, weight forward and sinking models at a lesser price, but none have the allure of the Chalkstream.

SCIENTIFIC ANGLER. Scientific Angler fly lines are as important to the history of fly fishing as Mr. Leonard. S.A. made the first really fine synthetic lines a couple decades ago and also pioneered the earliest special-purpose sinking lines. Quite an accomplishment for the firm that started out in Midland, Michigan. Their Air Cell Supremes, which dazzled people when they first came out, in white are still the best floaters and a step better than the plain Air Cells. Get a Supreme, well worth the extra cost involved. The various Wet Cell lines are excellent, too. S.A. has everything that sinks, including Hi-density sink tips, sinking heads, whole sinking lines and a very specialized line that goes either way depending on the dressing.

Tippets, Backing & Leaders

BERKLEY. Berkley leaders — those inexpensive ones you see everywhere — are a good buy for the money, especially since they are discounted lots of places. Available in lots of styles including a sinker and a Specialist model with a flat butt. (Berkley testers claim the flat butt helps the leader turn over in a tighter loop.) You can get them from 6 to 9 feet in a variety of tippets.

BERKLEY LEADER KITS. The Berkley Company sells saltwater-type leader-making kits that include their

top of the line

crimping pliers and spools of 20- and 30-pound test Steelon — a coated wire line — and assortments of connector sleeves. A money-saver available in a variety of styles.

BERKLEY QWIK-SINK TIPPET MATERIAL. If you have a thing about getting your tippet under water so as not to cast a revealing shadow, you might consider Berkley's Qwik-Sink Tippet Material. Available OX to 6X, it sinks quickly because of its rougher finish. Works well with small nymphs, too.

CORTLAND MICRON. Micron is the standard fly line backing. It's available in bulk or 100-yard spools. An excellent Dacron line that will do the job that backing is supposed to.

CORTLAND NYLORFI. Cortland's Nylorfi tippet material took much of the fly fishing fraternity by storm when it was introduced in 1975. Available down to 7X, it is supple, takes a knot very well and behaves well with a fly. It's the best new stuff thus far. Expensive, but a small price to pay for a spool.

GLADDING. Gladding Gladyl leaders, on the market for 15 years, are almost as old as the current era in fly fishing. Despite all the changes, lots of anglers still prefer them. Initially they were one of the most expensive leaders on the market — but that was in the days of yore. Available in 7½- and 9-foot lengths down to 6X. And spools of Gladding's Gladyl tippet material remain a favorite with some despite the new popularity among fly anglers of European monofilaments. Available from 2/5 to 7X.

GUDEBROD BACKING. Gudebrod's G-6 dacron fly line backing is available in 15, 20 or 30 pound test.

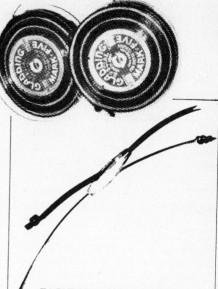

GLADDING

BERKLEY

LINE DRIER AND CHANGER

A very nice but over-priced collapsing aluminum line changer which will clamp anywhere. It can be very useful, considering the number of lines that most fly casters have around these days. Essential for drying silk lines. Available from Angler's World in New York.

EAGLE CLAW LEADER-LINK

For the angler who wants a leader-to-fly-line link, try Eagle Claw. Though few really experienced anglers like them, for the beginner, they sometimes eliminate the need to tie those arduous nail or needle knots. Sold in models for level lines, tapered lines and in fluorescent orange to signal strikes when nymphing.

"There are as good fish in the sea
as ever come out of it."
SCOTT, *Fortunes of Nigel*

A fine-diameter line, it has very little stretch, an advantage to the angler with a big fish. Will not mildew or rot. Can be stored on the reel.

ORVIS LEADER TYING KIT. One of the best on the market. Includes the obligatory instruction book with various leader formulas. The kit has 20 spools of Orvis' good leader material in diameters from .021 for butt sections down to a miniscule 7X.

Miscellany

MAXIMA MONO-SLIK. Maxima's Mono-Slik is a nifty cleaning device for both your fly or other type of cleansers. It increases casting distance on all sorts of line by lubricating the finish and removing all sorts of sediment. Works pretty well, too. To be used only before and after fishing, not during. Beware!

MUCILIN CANS & BOTTLES. Good enough for dear old dad and good enough for you. That's what anglers who scorn modern silicones and sprays say about these little bottles of old-fashioned, made-in-England Mucilin. Has a delightful little brush applicator. Works well, as do the cans of Mucilin line dressing. This waxy substance will also double for flies when rubbed between the fingers.

SEIDEL'S 600 LEADER SINK. Like the other Seidel products, the 600 leader sink is good stuff. It helps eliminate those trout-spooking shadows.

SEIDEL

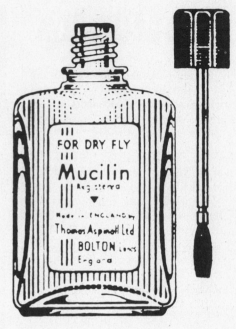

MUCILIN

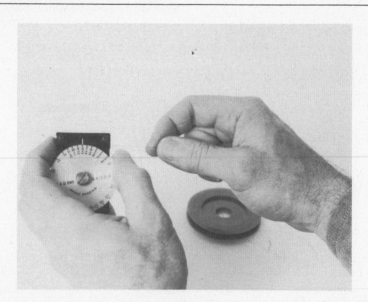

LEADER GAUGE

How often have you puzzled over what size your tippet was, and ended with a bad guess, so the blood knot came apart or the leader hinged and just wouldn't turn the fly over properly? The Leader Gauge is is an ingenious new device which lets you conveniently measure the diameter of leader tippets and butts. The calibrated range is from 0.002 inch to 0.025 inch, and it is marked in both 0.001-inch increments and X numbers. It is more accurate than a micrometer at a fifth of the price. The Leader Gauge is compact and ruggedly made from anodized aluminum. You need not hesitate to carry it on the stream. Included are calibrated shims and a tool to periodically check the calibration.

BALANCE YOUR LINE AND LEADER

Fly fishing, as the ancient Greek philosophers used to say about life in general, should be a balanced, harmonious pursuit. But despite the great variety of leader material currently available, some anglers out of habit refuse to balance their leader and fly line.

There are just a few things to remember. As a rule of thumb the butt end of your leader should be at least two-thirds the diameter of the end of your fly line. For instance, if the butt of your leader is .021 it will serve any fly line up to .027. I have found that with a weight-forward line the closer you match its diameter with your leader the smoother your fly lands. With a softer double taper, however, there is more leeway than with a weight-forward line.

Once you match up the leader and line diameter the next problem is how to attach them. These days you shouldn't bother with anything other than a very tidy nail knot or a needle knot. Also, it's best to coat the knot, just to be sure, with a glue such as Pliobond. In a pinch, Five-Minute or other kinds of epoxy work but Pliobond gives the smoothest knot coating.

Another thing: the butt section of your leader should be made from hard nylon rather than some kind of limp stuff. The butt absorbs the shock of the line and also has to turn the fly over properly, a job that soft nylons can't handle.

There are lots of leader formulas around. Most range from good to very good. However, the longer and lighter your leader, the more crucial the graduations between the diameters. With 7-foot leaders for wet fly or nymph fishing you can almost wing it by tying 18 inches of tippet material together in diameters that eyeball correctly. But for a 15-foot, 7X leader you better look over the formulas.

The other thing to be concerned about: the tippet material at the fly end should be limp. New spools of tippet material such as Cortland's Nylorfi, Orvis or Maxima measure up well though Nylorfi just might have an edge when it comes to holding a knot. — **H.H.**

GAMEFISH: TARPON

NAMES
Silver fish, silver king, sabalo, grande ecaille. *(Tarpon atlanticus)*

DISTRIBUTION
The tarpon is a fish of tropical waters. In the Atlantic, it is found as far north as Nova Scotia, but they are found in abundance off Florida, Texas and eastern Mexico.

DESCRIPTION
The color of the tarpon is usually blue-green on the back with iridescent silver sides. Large, thick scales cover the body and there is a bony plate between the branches of the lower jaw.

SIZE
The average size of the tarpon is between 30 and 60 pounds. Catches of over 100 pounds are not considered unusual.

HABITAT
The tarpon is a school fish that is usually found close to shore. They are often found in inlets, bays and river mouths. At times, they travel many miles up freshwater rivers.

FEEDING HABITS
The diet of the tarpon consists of small fish such as mullet, pinfish, and needlefish and crabs and shrimp. Early day or late evening are the times they are most active.

TACKLE
When schooled up, the tarpon is fair game for every kind of tackle, from heaviest saltwater trolling gear to light fly rods. The lighter the tackle the more sport and at times light spinning tackle with plugs will do the job perfectly. Likes big flies precisely cast since it spooks easily. Sometimes baitcasting is the best way to go.

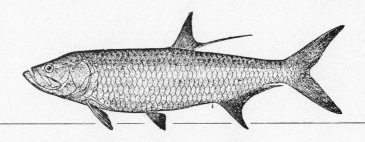

HOW TO CARE FOR FLY LINES

Modern, plastic-coated fly lines require very little extra attention to keep them in top-notch floating or sinking shape.

Floating fly lines usually are the ones that require the most care, since they are the ones most often used. The single biggest cause contributing to the tip sinking on your fly line or the fly line itself not riding as high on the water as it did when you first purchased it, is the buildup of dirt and algae. Obviously, if the bulk of your fishing is on clean, cold, trout streams, there will be less algae or dirt buildup than if your fishing is in dirtier rivers or lakes.

There are two ways in which you can remove this stuff. The first is to wash your fly line with mild soap and water. This should be done twice a year, only if you have heavy buildup on your line. Otherwise, once a year, at the end of the year when you finish fishing, is sufficient.

The other way is to use the line conditioner or cleaner product that comes packed with some fly lines or is sold by the major fly line manufacturing companies. As with the mild soap and water solution, a little bit of cleaning with these products goes a long way.

There are other contributing factors to the deterioration of a fly line. The most typical of these is chemical attack, induced by some line dressings, fly floatants, insect repellents, or contact with gasoline, such as might be found in the bottom of a boat or canoe. Avoiding any of these factors will help contribute to the life of your fly line.

Common-sense care and storage of your fly line will also help to contribute to its life. Leaving a fly line on the reel in the trunk of one's car on the back window can significantly contribute to its deterioration because of the intense heat — often more than 100 degrees in these places.

Whether we're talking about taking care of your fly line, your spinning line, your waders, or any of your other fishing gear, that little bit of extra effort at the end of each fishing trip to wipe down your rods, reels, and other tackle and put them away in the house in a safe storage place is well worth the extra effort and almost always produces longer life for your fishing tackle.

HOW THE AUTHOR ALMOST DECIDED TO TAKE UP CHESS, INSTEAD

By Harmon Henkin

I hesitated before entering the water. On opening day, a month before, I had learned that when westerners talk about high water they mean "High Water." Anglers driving up Rock Creek to begin the season in late May had been greeted with a torrent of brown water. The stream, normally about 50 feet wide and always tough to wade, had doubled its usual size and appeared as menacing as the river Styx. Any trout stupid enough to show its head would have probably been washed out to the Pacific Ocean in two minutes.

But now it looked mellow and normal. The bottom was visible and the wealth of trout-holding water looked accessible — but best accessible from the other side.

I had spent my first Montana winter talking with anyone who would stand still long enough to be questioned about fishing and reading anything with the words "Montana," "fishing" and "flies" in it. I was an "expert" and had the 10-dozen finely tied western flies for which I had scrimped and saved to prove it.

But I retreated after one step and decided that a stout staff would be added insurance for my first big wading outing. I broke off a dead limb and started out again. I would take a step, plunk down the staff and then repeat the maneuver. After 15 feet, I thought I had it made. That business about how rough western wading was seemed like nonsense. Just another 30 feet and I would start hauling in monster trout.

Then I took the big step. I plunged the stick into a hole 3 feet deeper than the surrounding water. Naturally my body followed it down and the strong current knocked me over. When I righted myself, I was heading downstream like a rudderless kayak. A few hundred yards away I could see churning white water bouncing off a boulder the size of my house. Having no desire to imitate the steel ball in a pinball machine. I frantically stuck the bamboo rod in my teeth and anxiously paddled to shore like a big beaver building a dam with precious sticks.

A few minutes later I crawled on the bank and lay there. The roaring water was a few scant yards downstream and I thanked the angler's god for my survival.

Then I felt the big pocket on my vest. It was empty. Ten dozen valuable flies were gone. They must have been floating downstream in that big plastic box, appearing to fish like a behind-the-glass-offering in an automat. They could see them at least, so they were one up on me. Maybe some lucky angler in the 20 miles of river below would go home with $60 worth of flies — pretty good, even if he got skunked.

Still stunned, I looked at my rod. Near the handle was the prettiest set of teeth marks I'd ever seen. I could have sold them to a dental college, but as a fishing rod that $150 stick was doomed. The marks made in my panic were a good 1/8-inch deep, but the marks on my soul were deeper.

I started shivering. The blue line on my water thermometer was at 51 and it looked like rain.

Waddling back to my car, I gave serious consideration to becoming a professional chess player. They never have to behave like beavers nor are their boards and pieces washed away.

This article originally appeared in *Montana Outdoors*, July/August 1974.

Expect only the best

By Harmon Henkin

Flies should be constructed by the book with only top-quality materials

Anglers have every right to expect only top-quality flies for their money. The price of good flies now hovers from 75 cents to $1 apiece; with trees, bushes and snags being what they are, a day's fishing can cost you a dozen or more. Even so, a well-balanced, well-made fly is a joy to use and even to lose.

Now for the absolute beginner who is just learning to cast, inexpensive flies, the kind made in Japan, Taiwan and the like, will do the job, though not very well. But since wind knots, snapped tippets and flies inadvertently cast into logs are an apprentice's everyday hazard, there isn't much point in forking over the money for the best. The rookie will know it's time to move up in quality when something inside tells him that his cheaper fly isn't doing the job a better one could. It's more of a feeling than a precise moment and it surely varies from angler to angler.

Other than this exception you should try to stick with the best, tied in the traditional way. Learn what a good fly is by ordering a few from very reputable tiers such as the Fly Fisherman's Bookcase, Orvis or Dan Bailey. They aren't cheap, and even though some outfits like Orvis are having some of their flies made in the Far

Orvis sold these dry flies in 1905 for $1.50 per dozen.

East, they're still very conscious of what a good fly is. But having a few representative patterns around is just a starting point, something to compare your future local acquisitions with.

The possibilities within the craft of fly tying have expanded greatly in the past few years. There are many more materials available, including an amazing increase in the quality of the hackle feathers that float dry flies. Purveyors of fine rooster necks like Hoffman and Metz, who specialize in blue dun and grizzly feathers, have made top-notch materials a commonplace where they were once rare.

The criteria for top quality remains the same. In the first place your flies should be constructed by the book. A pattern usually develops for the historical reason that it functions as an imitation of something a fish likes to

munch on. Whether it's a tiny Quill Gordon imitating the small Iron Fraudator mayfly, an early season emerger on eastern streams or a Bob Boyle shrimp for bonefish in the Florida Keys, it has a specific use and shouldn't be changed at the whim of the tier. The substitution of materials on a given pattern should have a real function or shouldn't be done at all. If it doesn't improve the fly, why do it?

In the second place, the fly should be made of the best materials. There has never been a really good case, at least in my mind, for the notion that synthetics like polypropylene make for better flies than do natural dubbed furs. Whenever possible, I prefer the real to the artificial. The highly touted polys make a tier's job easier but whether they should replace the natural materials is an entirely different question.

If someone is selling flies made from inferior materials to cut corners saving them a penny or so apiece, it's an indication of their approach to things. And this doesn't only include the hackle feathers, which should be very stiff on dries, of course, and soft but without webbing on wets and nymphs. Top quality hooks, these days, usually means

(continued on page 77)

"Ever let your hook be hanging; where you least believe it, there will be a fish in the stream."
OVID, *Ars Amatoria*

Ray's bum child
The odyssey of the Canoe Fly

By Richard Eggert

We always called it the Canoe Fly because, as near as we could tell, it was born the bum child of the proprietor of Ray's Canoe Livery in Grayling, Michigan.

Ray, who probably didn't have a last name, displayed cases of the humble little deer hair flies behind rows of gleaming aluminum canoes at his shop on the AuSable River. On a warm summer day during those early 60s you could trace the course of that celebrated river by the glitter of Ray's hired canoes. And on those muggy evenings Michigan's finest anglers would pinch off stately Adams and Cahill flies and tie on one of these wretched little deer hair bugs (as Ray called them) to cast to the burps of the river's nocturnal browns.

The Canoe Fly was far too ugly to use during the day but ideally suited for evening and night-time fishing. These businesslike Michigan fishermen knew that any hackle fly — even patterns such as Wulffs, which have a great deal of hair — would eventually become soggy or gummed up. The all-deer hair Canoe Fly, on the other hand, would dance all night no matter what happened. The AuSable angler could tie on a Canoe Fly in the Gloaming and fish 'til dawn.

As Ray tied it, the Canoe had a bound-on deer hair

body with the eye trimmed close like a muddler and a short frazzle of hair ends at the tail. The wing, the genius of the species, was tied down at the head and bristled out over the body to the bend. The Canoe Fly could bob for hours on its chunky head with its tail held aloft by the spreading deer hair wing tips.

For several years the Canoe and I drifted through Michigan's worst and best — from the Huron river above Ann Arbor to the beaver bogs of the Keweenaw Peninsula. At first I regarded the ugly misfit as an adversity fly — for bad light and hard times. Then its caddis-like configuration dawned on me and I began fishing it when the "millers," as they were called in upper Michigan, were waltzing on the bright surface of the streams.

However, the true ecumenical value of the Canoe did not occur to me until one evening in early June on the Upper Peninsula's Paint River. It was warm and heavy when two chums and I arrived at the banks of this unsung little stream. The caddis were fluttering and I tied on a Canoe to see if one of the river's brookies was in the mood. As I waded out above a bend, I noticed a small but steady rise amid a swarm of skimming caddis. I dropped the Canoe through the hovering caddis just above the rise. He took.

To my surprise, the fish was not an 8-inch brookie attempting to nip off a careless caddis, but a 14-inch brown gorged with emerging cahill duns. He, and later another brown who broke off, had

taken the Canoe as an adolescent dun.

Flushed over the consequences of my discovery, I worked my way up to a large wood jam at the foot of a long series of riffles. The caddis were still bustling above the surface but the cahills had stopped. I got out of the water to walk back to the car as the rapidly gathering dusk fell around me. But that magic evening — an evening every fisherman should have to sustain him through the dogdays of his life — was not over yet.

I suddenly realized it was not night that was shrouding the river but a thick organic cloud of flies. Green drakes. They were rising and falling in rhythm over the riffles with coupled pairs dropping down from the crowd and gently dancing just above the surface. As I stood there spellbound, I noticed a few of the enormous drakes floundering on the surface of the stream. Then more — and more. Suddenly I became conscious of the careless slashing of fish by the woodjam. And then, like an epidemic, the slashing spread throughout the hole at the bottom of the riffle.

I broke off the small Canoe I had been using and tied on a large, clumsy local imitation of a Michigan Drake (*Hexagenia limbata*). I cast the monster on a surface

(continued on next page)

The Canoe Fly's odyssey

(continued from preceding page)

frosted with spent green drakes. The fly safely ran the torpedoes several times before I finally decided the fish were more sensitive to the hex than I.

I switched to a brand-new counter-perfect Gray Wolff with large upright hair wings. This was received with an occasional slash or nudge but no takes.

The frenzy of the trout increased as the carpet of dying flies thickened and dark began to settle. I rummaged frantically through my dry boxes and finally settled on the largest Canoe I had, a dull, well chewed No. 10. Straining against the last light, I finally got it tied on and tossed it out to the top of the woodjam. A torpedoing brown took it along with a mouthful of naturals and I scurried downstream to land him.

In the next hour I landed five of the river's best, ranging from 12 to 16 inches, and lost a larger one. The Canoe had not only been accepted as a spent drake but had actually been preferred by the incensed fish. It had been an evening of revelations.

Shortly afterwards I moved to the greener waters of Western Montana with my Paul Young fly rod and Canoe Fly. The natives were amused by the skinny little 7½-foot rod but could take the fly seriously. It followed in the tradition of western caddis-like flies such as the Trude, the Goofus and the Picket Pin. It was also easy to tie once you got the knack.

(continued on next page)

THE LAST HATCH
A FISHING MYSTERY
HARMON HENKIN

(continued from page 55)

prose couldn't draw flies. His readers had deserted him faster than a nightcrawler salesman at a Trout Unlimited banquet.

He went back into the main room where a man and a woman had joined Wormer in an excited conversation. Wormer turned and pointed at him.

"That's the one who told me."

They edged toward Paul.

"The sheriff will be here soon," Paul said, holding his ground. "Nothing to do but wait."

That didn't satisfy them. They closed in for the verbal kill. The woman was easily recognizable. Alexandrea Softhackle, Halford's favorite wife. Her meteoric career in Hollywood had consisted of two R films and a sleazy hardcore X about the adventures of a nun driven wild by mysterious Rock 'n' Roll music from outer space. She was wearing those casual, pre-ordained slacks popular in suburban Los Angeles and tearfully affecting the grief she learned in "Sorrow Class" at the seven-lesson acting school Halford had shipped her to in profound desperation. The thirtyish man in skin-tight Levis next to her carried the tanned good looks people like him used to cover a multitude of defects, especially those concerned with the cerebrum. He looked at Paul with a spark of recognition.

"Don't I know you?"

"Probably not. We don't travel in the same circles."

Wormer suddenly became animated. "Wait a minute, I know him too. He's the crackpot who gave us a hard time last month at that hearing in Stevensville. The one that said we were ruining the Bitterroot Valley. Remember? He said somebody had to stop us."

They stared at Paul in horror, backed up a step and shouted in unison.

"He killed Frederick! He killed him to save that stupid creek!"

It sounded plausible, even to Paul. Everyone glared. No one seemed sure what to do next. An impasse. Then the door swung open and Dun raced in from his inspection trip, still sobbing.

"God, God, God! The best writer who ever lived is dead."

"And there's the murderer!" Wormer bellowed, pointing at Paul. Alexandrea joined the chorus with a High C of her own. Chaos had

(continued on page 84)

How to tie the Canoe Fly

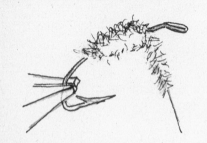

Dubbing on fur body

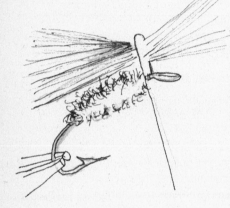

Binding on deer hair wing

Trimming deer hair from head

Finished Canoe Fly

Odyssey of the Canoe Fly

> As highly as I regard the Canoe Fly, I have no curiosity about its genealogy.

(continued from preceding page)

Fast water anglers accustomed to frequent breaks from heavy fish in heavy water could whip up a week's supply in an evening.

Montana's fish were equally enthusiastic about the immigrant Canoe, especially after Harmon Henkin and I retailored the body dressing to suit western fancy. We replaced the buoyant but scraggly bound deer hair with spun fur while retaining the unsinkable wing. The Canoe could now be offered to boisterous western fish in a variety of colors and textures to match nearly any dining occasion.

Ray, like Alfred Russel Wallace, made his humble contribution to the world and left it orphaned to float on its own.

But now there is a Darwin commercializing on Ray's genius and I am offended. In a spring 1976 catalog from one of the harder-sell mail order tackle houses there is a page of Ray's sober-looking Canoe Flies credited to this year's upstart — somebody who had nothing more to do with the development of the Canoe Fly than I to the theory of relativity.

A couple of years ago I was fishing upper Rock Creek east of Missoula, during the ebb of an extremely high spring runoff. The fish were still lying low in the dusky water and the only action was in the quiet glides along the banks. I came around a bend and there, like a ghost of my AuSable days, was an old gent slowly working a dry fly downstream. I got out of the water and walked up the bank to see how he was doing.

"Not too bad, a half dozen honest ones," he claimed.

As he reeled in I noticed the familiar flutter of a hair wing skimming the surface. I asked and felt a warm glow of fraternity when I discovered it was a Canoe with the deer hair wing replaced with about a dozen elk hair tips tied back against the shank.

I showed him my Canoe which was nearly a replica of his fly and he smiled at me.

What was Ray's last name? Neither the old fellow on Rock Creek nor I had ever bothered to find out and, I think, neither of us cared. As highly as I regard the Canoe Fly, I have no curiosity about its genealogy. Names, as the ancient Chinese taught, are only functions.

The old fellow on Rock Creek and I were content to contribute our shares to Ray's vacations in Florida, borrow some aspects of his fly and catch fish.

Ray may or may not have invented the Canoe fly. He never said and nobody ever thought to ask because in those days fly philology was

Illustrations by Richard Eggert

f interest only to scholars ch as Harold Hinsdale meadly, who actually wrote book on the descent of ies. Most anglers didn't give damn who invented a pat- rn or even who tied it as ong as it caught fish. And if a y didn't catch fish, it was estined to rot unused in felt ats that looked like bee- ives even if Charles Cotten imself tied it.

This empirical method of y selection naturally pre- luded most exhibits of reast beating and fanfare in ame designations. Flies were mply identified by a proper ame, such as Adams, endrickson or Trude, or a roper name and a generic ad- ctive such as Quill Gordon, ray Wolff, Royal Coachman r Silver Sedge. Even the bril- ant fly development of the 0s — such as the thorax pat- rns of Vince Marinaro, the rrestrials of Ed Koch or the uddlers of Dan Gapen — ere labeled with their inven- rs unsung.

In those simple days a fly as simply a fly and inventor- rs such as Ray were con- nt to sell a bunch during e summer so they could run ff to Florida for the winter ith the profits.

In the old days, 15 years go, there were only a few ex- rts around. They wrote eautiful, significant or out- ageous books or were regular ontributors to the sporting ress. We could either accept r reject what they said but e respected them because hey were our experts.

Now we buy our experts and trout flies anew each year because we are promised that they are better than last year's theory and panaceas. There are scores of new books published each year now — most of them dull and unworthy — which give us an annual crop of experts to be harvested. And each new year brings an entirely new system of flies and a lesser breed of experts who market them, to add to our fly selection frus- trations during the summer.

Yes, trout fishing has be- come big business complete with dynamic obsolescence. You can now buy anything from a trout stream estate to a tie tack from a tackle cata- log and by next year the stream will be polluted and the tack supplanted by a "tight lines fishing bolo tie." We are being sold ready-made class fashioned by finite ex- perts to make us fashionable for a season.

Fifteen years ago we used the rods our fathers had used, talked about fishing theory which had been digested by two generations before us and were content with bastard, fatherless flies. Today, rod lengths and materials change faster than we used to change flies. Ideas come and go out of fashion at a bewildering rate and flies have become as ephemeral as the naturals they are marketed to imitate. And there will probably never be another what's-his-name who will be content to invent a fly merely to supplement leases on a fleet of canoes.

Trout fishing has become big busi- ness complete with dynamic obsoles- cence.

Jorgensen Salmon Flies

Picking an ultimate fly tier is dif- ficult. It's a craft based on nuance, and the fine art of obeying laws while keeping one's individuality. Every pattern has developed the way it has for simple reasons of practicali- ty and effectiveness. Fly tying per- fection comes from an adherence to the spirit, form and function of the pattern.

It's the same limitation as that im- posed on Leonard Bernstein, who interprets, for example, Beethoven in a way that is unmistakably Beethoven but also unmistakably Leonard Bernstein.

Danish-born Poul Jorgensen, now living in Towson, Maryland, ties some of the finest traditional salmon flies ever assembled. Undoubtedly a large portion of these exquisite flies devised for the most part in 19th Century England wind up on walls rather than in the mouths of Atlantic salmon.

But wherever they land they are certainly an expression of the most refined heights of tying. The variety of furs and feathers used in Jorgensen's work make most trout patterns seem like bare hooks.

Jorgensen also ties outstanding trout flies such as cut wing patterns that work well, despite their frail ap- pearance, and are perfect for the col- lector. His flies are sometimes avail- able from the Fly Fisherman's Book- case, but don't hold your breath. He's very much in demand.

top of the line

Flies

ANGLER'S WORLD SALMON FLIES. Without a doubt the most expensive flies in the galaxy. In sizes 2 and 4 at $6 apiece and sizes 2-0 at $7.50 apiece, these flies are the ultimate, at least in price. Whether they're worth it or not is questionable, but what the hell! Available in some of the more popular patterns. Designed by 19th-Century English anglers, some of whom were gentlemen.

DAN BAILEY'S. This Livingston, Montana, shop is deservedly the best-known fly purveyor in the Rockies. Bailey has popularized such patterns as the Wulff series, the Muddler and the very effective Bucktail. He continues to create new fly patterns, such as George's Brown Stone Nymph, which has been very effective in recent years in the West. Bailey's Devil Scratchers are another unique series of moss-backed nymphs that are quite effective at times. Don't buy Western flies without looking in Bailey's catalog.

BETTS BASS POPPERS. Cork bass bugs are cheaper and last longer than the very pretty deer-haired ones. Betts has a number of interesting patterns ranging from simple panfish and small bass types like their Fire Pop and Poka Pop to more complicated ones with feathery wings like the Bullfrog Popper and Ring-Bee Popper. The Fire-Glo has a luminous finish that glows in the dark and can be "re-activated" with a flashlight. Different sizes available.

BETTS PANFISH FLIES. The Betts folks down in North Carolina make a goodly line of panfish and crappie flies for the warm-water fly

WHAT WE LOOKED FOR IN QUALITY

We looked for flies that are well-made and unique. Lots of people make respectable muddler minnows, for instance, but a Dan Bailey muddler seems to sum up western angling while a Don Gapen muddler gets back to the start of the fly. The unusual or special-purpose flies are the ones we tried to list. Every fly shop has its own regional specialties, but hopefully the flies in this chapter can be useful to anglers around the country.

BETTS BREAM GETTER

DAN BAILEY BUCKTAIL STREAMER

BETTS BASS BUG

ANGLER'S WORLD SALMON FLIES

"There are only two occasions when Americans respect privacy, especially in Presidents. Those are prayer and fishing. So that some have taken to fishing." HERBERT HOOVER, 1944

FLIES & DRESSINGS 69

FLECTOLITE MINNOW

BODMER'S BULLET HEADED MUDDLER

CASCADE TACKLE
SHAD FLY

top of the line

tosser. Ants, bees, Bream Getters, True Bee and Water Spiders are among the foam rubber and hackle patterns available. A very good variety.

BODMER'S. Bodmer's Fly Shop in Colorado Springs offers a couple of very interesting flies. They tie a bullet-headed muddler with deer hair pulled completely over it. This gives a dipping and darting action on the retrieve. They offer this pattern in regular and marabou, waded and unwaded. They also offer Colorado King caddis fly imitations, which is one of the most effective all-around Western flies ever devised.

CASCADE TACKLE COMPANY. Besides a decent enough selection of standard trout patterns and fly tying gear, the Cascade Tackle Company also provides a goodly list of specialized steelhead flies, bass bugs and shad flies, as well. They offer many of the more popular West Coast patterns and will tie on special order, too. Their shad flies are the basic Umpqua River patterns. Among their hair bass bugs are mice, frogs and the ever-popular bees.

LEN CODELLA. The Thomas & Thomas/Len Codella line is one of the few offering nymphs from Ernie Schwiebert's *Nymphs* — which only served up pictures of the naturals. Helpful to the tier puzzling over the book. These flies are sold by insect name — exact imitations, no less. Worth taking a look at.

FLECTOLITE. An interesting minnow imitation marketed by Glen L. Evans. It has a Flectolite wing, a semi-metallic shield that reflects light in somewhat the same way as Mylar. It's weighted and comes in fluorescent red/black, olive green and cerise in hook sizes No. 2, 4 and 6.

November 1976

Date Day	AM Minor	AM Major	PM Minor	PM Major	Date Day	AM Minor	AM Major	PM Minor	PM Major
1. Fri.	11:25	**5:30**	11:40	**5:55**	17. Sun.	11:30	**5:35**	11:45	**6:05**
2. Sat.	....	**6:20**	12:10	**6:45**	18. Mon.	....	**6:20**	12:20	**6:45**
3. Sun.	12:30	**7:05**	1:00	**7:30**	19. Tues.	12:30	**7:05**	1:00	**7:35**
4. Mon.	1:15	**7:45**	1:45	**8:10**	20. Wed.	1:15	**7:55**	1:50	**8:20**
5. Tues.	1:55	**8:30**	2:25	**8:50**	21. Thurs.	2:05	**8:45**	2:35	**9:10**
6. Wed.	2:40	**9:10**	3:05	**9:30**	22. Fri.	2:55	**9:35**	3:25	**10:05**
7. Thurs.	3:20	**9:45**	3:45	**10:10**	23. Sat.	3:45	**10:30**	4:20	**11:00**
8. Fri.	3:55	**10:25**	4:25	**10:50**	24. Sun.	4:40	**11:35**	5:15	....
9. Sat.	4:35	**11:10**	5:05	**11:35**	25. Mon.	5:45	**12:20**	6:20	**12:40**
10. Sun.	5:20	....	5:50	**12:05**	26. Tues.	6:55	**1:15**	7:25	**1:45**
11. Mon.	6:20	**12:30**	6:40	**12:50**	27. Wed.	8:00	**2:20**	8:30	**2:50**
12. Tues.	7:05	**1:20**	7:30	**1:45**	28. Thurs.	9:05	**3:25**	9:35	**3:50**
13. Wed.	8:00	**2:10**	8:20	**2:35**	29. Fri.	10:05	**4:20**	10:30	**4:50**
14. Thurs.	8:50	**3:00**	9:10	**3:25**	30. Sat.	11:05	**5:10**	11:20	**5:35**
15. Fri.	9:40	**3:55**	10:05	**4:20**	31. Sun.	11:50	**5:55**	....	**6:15**
16. Sat.	10:35	**4:50**	11:00	**5:15**					

© The Solunar Table

THE SOLUNAR TABLES

More than 40 years ago John Alden Knight, one of the best fly fishermen of the golden age of Eastern angling, devised these arcane little timetables for predicting the active feeding periods for both fish and game. Remarkably, they're still around (*Field & Stream* carries them every month), and lots of oldtimers still check them, perhaps just for luck. Like newspaper astrology, you can take the tables as seriously as you want — they will certainly do you no harm — and it's intriguing to see how often they are correct (some writers claim 70-75% accuracy). Neither will they take the place of knowing something about structure, temperature, and other tangibles that may well be the real facts behind the Solunar Tables. Ed Zern once said he used the Solunar Tables to fill out his income tax.

top of the line

GAPEN MUDDLER MINNOW

DON GAPEN MUDDLER MINNOW. Get a little piece of history floating or sinking. Don Gapen, who devised the infamous Muddler Minnow — which has probably accounted for more big trout than any other fly — is still selling them. The original pattern has deer hair, gray squirrel, mottled turkey wing and a flat, gold tinsel body. They're a little sparser than some of the other modern adaptations but work well. Sold from No. 1/0 to No. 12 in floaters and from No. 2 to No. 6 in weighted.

HACKLE AND TACKLE FAN WINGS. Once upon a time in the 1930s, fan wings were the end-all patterns. Their delicate matched wings are visible in rough water but ever-so-vulnerable to toothy trout. The Royal Coachman, which was the standard of the breed, and the Light Cahill are currently made in 10s and 12s. Probably the prettiest trout flies ever made. Still sold by Hackle and Tackle.

HILDEBRANDT'S SILVER DOCTOR

HILDEBRANDT'S. Hildebrandt's weighted bass flies on 1/0 and 4/0 hooks and at ¼ ounce are an old tradition that should be kept up by progressive anglers. In Oriole, Yellow Sally and Silver Doctor patterns they have been fooling bigmouths since the 19th Century, are somewhat weedless and much prettier than rubber worms.

HILDEBRANDT'S ORIOLE

When if or chance or hunger's powerful sway
Directs the roving trout this fatal way,
He greedily sucks in the twining bait,
And tugs and nibbles the fallacious meat.
Now, happy fisherman; now twitch the line!
How thy rod bends! behold, the prize is thine!
JOHN GAY, *Rural Sports.* Canto i, 1. 150.

HULA POPPER. A long-time favorite bass bug, the Fly Rod Hula Popper is as good as they get. Gurgles when the rod is jerked and twitches its legs. Many colors, of course, and lots of tradition. Sheer ecstasy from Arbogast.

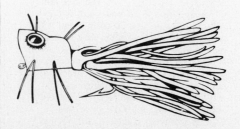

HULA POPPER

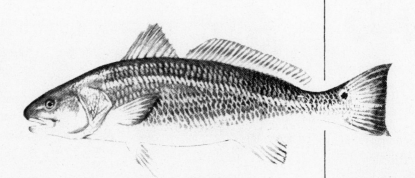

GAMEFISH: CHANNEL BASS

NAMES
Redfish, red drum, redfin, red bass, spottail.
(Sciaenops acellatus)

DISTRIBUTION
The channel bass is a fish of the Atlantic and the Gulf of Mexico. It ranges from New York to Texas.

DESCRIPTION
The channel bass, a member of the croaker family, is generally reddish or bronze all over with shadings of grey or silver. The head is long and there is a black spot at the base of the tail.

SIZE
The average size of the channel bass is between 5 and 15 pounds although fish of up to 80 pounds have been caught.

HABITAT
The channel bass is a coastal fish that is found in inlets, channels, bayous and coves. It likes to stay near the shore where it feeds on all types of bottom life.

FEEDING HABITS
The channel bass is a bottom feeder that favors shrimp, crabs, worms and small fish such as mullet. They travel in large groups.

TACKLE
The channel bass is a great favorite of medium-equipped surfcasters but is also taken by baitcasters and even fly fishermen who have stout gear. A good fighter, this fish'll take plugs of the diving sort with relish and almost anything else when it's in the mood.

BUD LILLY PHEASANT HOPPER

KEEL FLIES

top of the line

KEEL FLIES. The Keel fly, celebrated in owner Dick Pobst's book, *Fish the Impossible Places*, is a nifty idea. It is available in all manner of patterns and sizes that are tied on the reverse of the normal — upside down as it were — on flies that are constructed to be weedless. These patterns are especially practical on the Keel-tied bass bugs, steelhead flies and bucktails. They work well on anything that goes down to the snaggy depths. They're also available in small dry fly patterns and nymphs. They claim to look more natural. The bare Keel hooks are also available for those into making their own. An interesting innovation but surely not foolproof — nothing is.

KORKERS. Korkers are small panfish-type bugs that work wet or dry. They come in a variety of shapes such as Hopper, Lady, Beetle and Grub on small hooks down to No. 16. Good assortment.

BUD LILLY'S. Bud Lilly's in West Yellowstone, Montana, has developed into one of the leading Western fly shops. It offers some very interesting contemporary patterns, such as a high flying, side winding no hackle, stillborn duns, fly body dregs and all sorts of grasshoppers. A very interesting selection of flies for the angler heading West.

top of the line

ORVIS. The Orvis Company's picturesque catalog includes some of the nicest commercially tied flies, including some specialized assortments such as caddis flies a la Leonard Wright, parachute selections, terrestrials and bass bugs. Their selection of flies is staggering, enough to whet the appetite of any angler. Their prices reflect the current levels of the higher-priced market. For the instant "expert" there is a $90.35 composite of wets, dries, nymphs and streamers to impress even the spring creek crowd. Packaged in one of those gorgeous Wheatley boxes.

RALPH THE HORSE FLY. Bored with your angling partner? Take along Ralph the Horse Fly from Kegara. He probably won't be any more interesting but the No. 12 imitation might account for a few sunfish at any rate.

RANDALL'S. One of the few thought-out selections of high-country lake flies comes from Randall's. It includes such effective patterns as the Timberline, the Timberline Emerger, two caddis patterns, a California mosquito, an emergent mosquito, a Trueblood Shrimp and a Trout Shrimp plus others. Good idea.

REED MATCHED FAN WINGS. For the old-fashioned fly caster who still loves very visible, very pretty fan-winged dries, Reed sells packages of white fan wings in small and medium sizes. Every angler should try them at least once and so should every tier.

HANK ROBERTS. The most interesting flies in this Boulder, Colorado, tackle entrepreneur's line are the woven body nymphs. Roberts was into this sort of thing long before most and the assortment of deli-

A SELECTION OF FLIES FROM ORVIS

Concise directions for making a fly

Take some fine silk, of the proper colour, and wax it well with bees' wax; then hold the bend of the hook between the forefinger and thumb of the left hand, and with the right give the silk two or three turns round the shank, and fasten it; then take a small feather, of the colour you intend the fly should be, strip off some of the fibers towards the quill, and leave a sufficient quantity for the wings, holding the point of the feather between your finger and thumb; turn back most of the remaining fibres, and laying the point end of the feather upon the hook, give a few more laps round it with your silk, and fasten; then twirl the feather round the hook till all the fibers are wrapped upon it; which done, fasten and cut off the two ends of the feather; then, with dubbing of the proper colour twisted round the remaining silk, warp from the wings towards the bend of the hook, till the fly is the size required. Before the young artist tries his skill at dressing or making a fly, (suppose a green-drake), he should carefully take an artificial one to pieces, and observe how it is formed.

Thus, having learnt how to apply his materials to the hook, the knowledge how to make the may-flies is first requisite to be understood; for these flies are of so much value to the Angler, that every one who wishes to excel in Fly-fishing, should learn how to make them as soon as possible. There are several persons in London who manufacture artificial flies for sale; and among those professed fly-makers, some, for a gratuity, will instruct the Angler in the whole art and mystery of fly-making. The manufacture of the green-drake, grey-drake and stone-fly, in particular, should be well understood, as it is sometimes difficult to procure, or preserve the natural ones; and, moreover, a proficiency in the art of making these will enable any person to make a fly to any pattern, an art highly necessary, for it will often happen that Trout will refuse every fly you may have with you; and the only resource then is, to sit down and make one resembling, as much as possible, those which you may find flying about the spot.

The Angler's Guide (1814).
By Thomas Salter.

"Only the gamefish swims upstream. But the sensible fish swims down."
OGDEN NASH, *When You Say That, Smile*

FLIES & DRESSINGS 73

REED MATCHED FAN WINGS

RALPH THE HORSE FLY

HANK ROBERTS

A POPULAR SALTWATER STREAMER

top of the line

cately woven patterns are generally recognized as being very effective. They are especially interesting for Western trout fishing. Among the most effective are yellow drake, ginger quill and mayfly, though his shrimp patterns and dominos will also do the job. The weaving process makes for segmented bodies that more closely resemble the real thing.

POLLY ROSBOROUGH PATTERNS. An effective line of nymphs was developed some years back by Oregon's Polly Rosborough and written about in his booklet *Fishing the Fuzzy Bodied Nymphs*. The pamphlet is out of print but Kaufman's offers the 20 patterns in a labeled set or individually. Effective flies.

FRANK SAWYER NYMPHS FROM DERMOT WILSON. Frank Sawyer is one of England's best-known anglers and some anglers think his book, *Nymph Fishing*, is a classic. Dermot Wilson's tackle shop in England offers a goodly selection of the river keeper's favorite patterns including the Bow Tie Buzzer, Grey Goose, Pheasant Tail and Scandinavian Nymph. Good possibilities for American waters. And direct from Britain is not all that expensive a buy.

DICK SURETTE'S TANDEM STREAMER. In the old days tandem trolling flies were the standard for hanging out behind your canoe when you were after New England's landlocked salmon, lake trout and big browns after the ice went out and fish were near the surface. Dick Surette's Shop in New Hampshire ties a dozen patterns of these tandem trollers in all of the popular patterns including Barnes Special, Gray Ghost, Ballou Special and Smelt. These are good, special-duty flies.

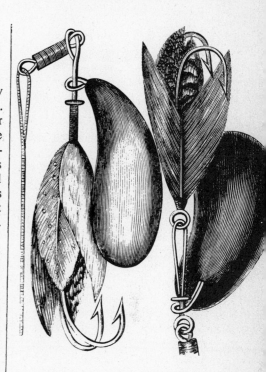

OLD TROLLING LURES

DICK SURETTE'S TANDEM STREAMER

top of the line

JIM TEENY. The Teeny nymphs — a patented fly, no less — are very reminiscent of the Pots flies tied in Missoula, Montana, some years back. Anyway, Teeny's flies, sold in a variety of colors and from sizes 10 to 2, fish best with a sinking line. The kind of simple sinking pattern that's often effective.

THUNDER RIVER FLIES. They only supply a mimeographed listing, but Thunder River Flies are quality tied and very interesting. Their Pteronarcy's tie imitates the big Western stonefly. They also offer no-hackle dries, popularized by Swisher-Richards, parachutes, spent-wings and high riders like the Wulffs and Humpy patterns.

AL TROTH. Al Troth, who was one of the better Pennsylvania tiers, is now just as good since moving to Dillon, Montana. His Troth Olive Mayfly and Brown Mayfly are productive patterns. His best-known innovative patterns include the Terrible Troth, the Rubber Legged Nymph, the Troth Salmon Fly and his elk hair caddis, one of the most effective Western patterns yet devised.

WEBER. Weber has been around for a long time, way before the current fly fishing boom has beset us with all manner of peculiar flies and bugs. Actually, Weber has been making some strange looking flies itself, for decades. Among the flies offered that aren't your average everyday ties are the Erskine life-like shiner minnow and a weedless deer hair mouse. And we can't forget Harry Big Crab, an authentic Henshall lure devised at the turn of the century by Dr. James Henshall, whose most famous

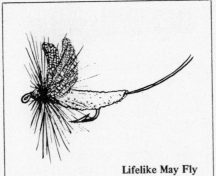

Lifelike May Fly

Handkraft Wet Fly

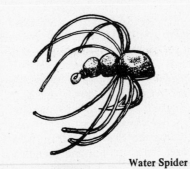

Water Spider

"Harry" Big Crab

WEBER'S FLIES

JIM TEENY NYMPH

AL TROTH OLIVE MAYFLY

FLY RETRIEVER

The Fly Retriever is a money-saving gadget that removes flies hung up on trees, bushes, telephone poles or the necks of giraffes. Used in tandem with your rod, this will retrieve many a 75-cent fly, giving you more cash to squander on other fly tackle.

quote was that "ounce for ounce and pound for pound, the black bass was the fightingest fish around." They also sell a bass fly that was popular in the good old days. Take a look at Weber.

YAKIMA BAIT COMPANY. The Egg Head lies somewhere between a bait and a fly but works on your fly rod anyway. These fluorescent flies on No. 12, No. 10 or No. 8 hooks in various colors have a head that looks like a salmon egg and a feather at the tail.

CASCADE LAKES FLOATANT

Fly Dressing

CASCADE LAKES DRY FLY FLOATANT. Cascade Lakes fly floatant is one of those new high-powered solutions applied at home under a measure of heat. It gets permanently bonded to the fly for excellent floatation for the life of the fly. Just in case, other fly dopes can be applied on top. Saves time, especially for the tier who can presoak his creations.

FLI-JELL. Fli-Jell is one of those fly floatants that has been doing the job of keeping it up for a long time. It comes in a convenient little bottle with a brush applicator. Sold through the Common Sense fly book people, it's a nice, simple product that does the job. Ditto for their Fli & Leader Sink, which is packaged the same way.

GEHRKE'S GINK. A really neat fly dressing. Neat in the slang sense, anyway. It's an odorless and colorless cream that becomes liquefied when rubbed between the fingers. Perhaps

GEHRKE'S GINK

MINIVAC VISE BASE

This vacuum base for your favorite vise may be just what you need to motivate you to tie at your office or while traveling. The Minivac Vise Base accommodates the 3/8-inch diameter post of most vises and it holds firmly to any smooth, non-porous surface without marring. The base unscrews into two parts, which makes it easy to tuck away when traveling. (It is designed for use with the Fly Tyer's Carry-All and holds all day on the Carry All's acrylic work board.) You may find it desirable to cut a few inches off the post of your vise with a hack saw so that the vise can be positioned at a comfortable height.

SEIDEL'S 800

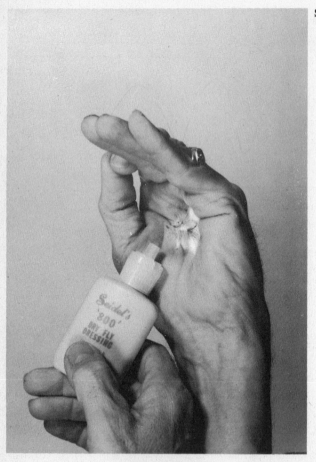

SEIDEL'S 700

top of the line

it doesn't work as quickly as the aerosol kinds, but it's better environmentally, lasts a long time and is a very fine floatant.

HIGH AND DRY. A good quality liquid fly dressing that fits into a leather holder with pin. Laggie makes this convenient rig and also sells bottles of refill.

RUSS PEAK DRESSING. Russ Peak, that wondrous glass rod creator from Pasadena, also makes an excellent line dressing. Probably the best around. Safe for plastic-coated fly line, it cleans and slicks all lines well. Very worthwhile.

SEIDEL. Seidel's 700 dry fly spray, which is packaged in a very convenient 1¼-ounce polyethylene atomizer squeeze bottle, is a very effective dry fly dope, and is more convenient to use than the bottled stuff. Yet it's not as environmentally and technically wasteful as aerosol cans. Good stuff.

SEIDEL'S DRY FLY DRESSING. Seidel's 800 dry fly dressing earns its keep. Its powdered silicone formula saves flies that have been dragged around by trout. You rub a little of the powder in your hand, dip the fly into it and it dries and waterproofs it instantly. A real lifesaver for any sensible angler.

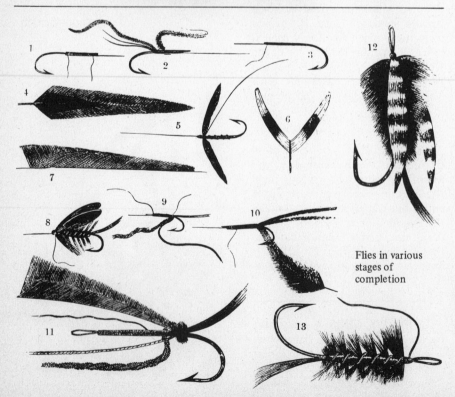

Flies in various stages of completion

KAUFMANN'S FLY SHADOW BOX

Sooner or later most fly fishers get ahold of a few patterns that either are tied by a famous tier or are just spectacular-looking. Well, put them on display in Kaufmann's Fly Shadow Box. The 8 x 10 picture-frame box comes in precut form and simply has to be stuck together. It's one of those things that you've probably wanted for years.

GAMEFISH: SEA BASS

NAMES
Black fish, black sea bass, humpback, black Will, black Harry. *(Centropristes striatus)*

DISTRIBUTION
The sea bass is an Atlantic fish that ranges from Maine to Florida. It is plentiful off Cape Cod.

DESCRIPTION
The color of the sea bass is grey to brown to bluish-black. The sides are mottled and at times appear to be covered with narrow stripes. The upper ray of the tail is elongated.

SIZE
The average size of the sea bass is between 1 and 4 pounds. Anything weighing 8 pounds or more is considered a large catch.

When artful flies the Angler would prepare,
This task of all deserves his utmost care:
Nor verse nor prose can ever teach him sell
What masters only know and practice tell;
Yet thus at large I venture to support,
Nature best followed best secures the sport:
Of flies the kinds; their seasons, and the breed,
Their shapes, their hue, with nice
    observance head:
Which most the Trout admires, and
    where obtain'd,
Experience will teach,
    or perchance some friend.

— Moses Brown

HABITAT
The sea bass is most apt to be found inshore in waters of moderate depths. They favor waters near rocky ledges, bridges, pilings or any areas near large rocks. Large sea bass are often found in much deeper waters.

FEEDING HABITS
The sea bass is a bottom feeder that eats various mollusks, squid, sea worms and small fish. Summer and fall are the times these fish are most abundant. In the south, they are active year round.

TACKLE
A stillfisher's delight, the sea bass can often be taken on light casting gear just stable enough to take the bait down to his dining room.

Expect only the best flies

(continued from page 63)

Mustads but also includes English hooks such as Alcocks. Ask your tier what kind are used. Quality materials should be used for everything from the tying thread, which can be silk or nylon depending on the pattern and the tier's inclination, to the tail materials.

The fly must be balanced, too. The hackle, wings, tail and body must be in the right proportions. Here's where those snazzy flies you ordered will help out. Pictures may be worth a thousand words but a model in the hand is worth two thousand words. Look for that same sense of balance that the Orvis, Bailey or other first-rate flies have.

Each type of fly has its own kind of balance. Experience is the ultimate determinant but books of patterns and tying can help develop your sense of fly proportion. Art Flick's little *Streamside Guide* has some excellent pictures of eastern mayfly imitations. Other newer books such as Bob Boyle's *Fly Tyer's Almanac* is good for modern patterns.

But most important of all, the fly should do its job. The ultimate judge of a pattern doesn't speak. It just swims around looking for food. After you examine a pattern for its quality and the finny arbiter agrees, you have a winner. Buy a dozen more and don't ask any questions!

Each fly has its own kind of balance.

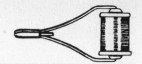

FEATHER & FUR
A GUIDE TO NATURAL MATERIALS

By Eric Leiser

Fly tying materials are the bits and pieces of feather, fur, tinsel, wool, chenille, poly and other sundries which are tied onto the shank of a hook to produce what is known as a fly. A hook is not a material. Nor are any of the tools, such as vises, bobbins, hackle pliers or dubbing needles. Waxes, threads and lacquers are not materials either, they're accessories.

With that definition out of the way, how many kinds of materials are there and what are they used for? To answer in detail would require more than a few chapters. Concepts for new uses of materials and additional materials are evolved every season. You would need a regular briefing just to keep up with the trends.

As a beginner in fly tying, there is one way to avoid some of this confusion: don't be overly concerned with most of the *manufactured* materials. Items such as tinsels, flosses, chenilles, wools, poly yarns and dubbings, mylars, and the like, are all manufactured materials. They are made by machines and sold through supply houses. They are readily identifiable. Very, very vew are of inferior quality. These materials will fall into place at the right time and you will have no trouble understanding their nature or use.

The type of materials you should be concerned with are nature's raw materials; namely, feather and fur. Of the two, feathers will give you the most trouble, especially an item called rooster neck. So let's start with that.

ROOSTER NECKS

A top-quality rooster neck is probably the most basic material necessary for the tying of flies. Especially dry flies. As its name implies, a rooster neck is the hide, with feathers attached, of a male chicken. It comes in many colors. More importantly, it comes in many grades of quality. It is the one material that can waste a hard-earned dollar if you don't know what to look for.

[1.] The neck itself should be of a good overall size, or at least have a respectable number of feathers in the proper sizes. After all, you don't want to pay $5 for a neck that will only produce a couple of dozen flies.

[2.] Before you even handle a neck, you should notice a certain lustre or shine in its color. The neck should be alive — light and bouncy.

[3.] Hold the neck in one hand and brush the fibers back and forth with the fingers of your other hand. As you push the feathers around, observe how quickly they return to their natural position. The more rapidly they jump back into place, the better the quality. This is a prime indicator of hackle stiffness in a dry fly.

[4.] Bend the neck into a curve. (Be careful with a domestic Grizzly neck, These have a thick, stiff skin and you may break them.) Poke around inside and see if there is an abnormal number of pin feathers, the feathers that have not yet fully matured. They will usually be protruding from a waxy shuck. Don't misunderstand. Some very good rooster necks have pin feathers. But be careful of ones that seem saturated with them.

(continued on next page)

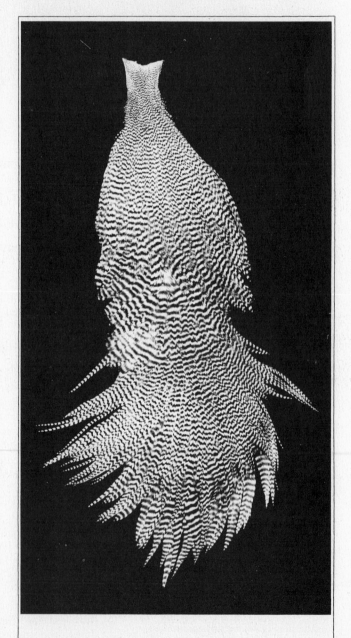

A Super Grizzly neck with saddle from Hoffman's Hackle Farm in Warrenton, Oregon. Hoffman markets his high-quality necks in three grades.

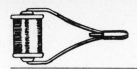
(continued from preceding page)

[5.] Check the amount of web in the hackles you are most likely to use for tying. If the web, which is the softer and denser part of the hackle feather, extends too far toward the tip of the feather, it may not tie as stiffly as you want it to. There are exceptions to this, such necks as Furnaces and Badgers. The black center, which gives these necks their name, is actually the webby portion of the feather. For some genetic reason the quality of a Badger is usually much better than that of a Furnace. Webbiness is a point to consider, but it is not crucial.

[6.] Many tiers determine the stiffness of a hackle by poking their nose or their lips with the tips of the hackle barbules. If you enjoy doing this, go to it.

[7.] I know many tiers who would not consider a rooster neck of top quality unless it tied all sizes of flies from 10 to 22. Forget it. That's a rarity. The only reason you should check for hackle size is because of the size of the fly you are going to tie. I've had excellent necks returned to me because the hackle size was too *small*. What the customer wanted was a quality neck that would tie salmon dry flies. For him, the larger the hackle, the better. Generally speaking, a neck that will tie a No. 22 will not have hackle on any of its feathers large enough to tie a No. 10 or 12. And, if it does, I doubt if you will find fibers long enough to tie a tail, in proper proportion, for that fly.

Incidentally, hackles from most of the Indian capes rarely carry a range of feather smaller than a No. 20, if that. The only time you can consistently obtain the smaller hackles is if you purchase a neck that has been bred especially for fly tying. Of course, they're much more expensive.

In addition to the neck feathers of a rooster, the saddle hackle feathers are also used. They are longer and are more slender. They're generally used for streamer flies.

Chicken feathers are used mostly for wet flies and nymphs. The hackle feathers are webby and soft.

Feather

The following is a list of other feathers commonly used in fly tying.

WOOD DUCK SIDE FEATHERS

The feathers from the sides of a male wood duck. They are lemon brown in shade and barred with a black stripe throughout. About half of the side feathers on a mature duck also have a wide black and white barring across the tip of the feather. These are not nearly as much in demand as those without the prominent wide barring. Unbarred (at the tip) lemon/brown wood duck side feathers are used for the winging of dry flies (Hendrickson, Quill Gordon, Light Cahill) and wet flies. They are also used for wing cases and legs on nymphs.

Because of the scarcity of this natural feather, mallard sides are often dyed to imitate them.

MARABOU

The soft fluffy feather obtained from a domestic white turkey. These feathers are used as is and dyed many shades for the various

(continued on next page)

Rooster Neck Colors

WHITE: as such.

CREAM: as such.

CREAM GINGER: a dark rich cream used for such patterns as the Light Cahill and Cream Variant.

GOLDEN GINGER: a buff shade, golden. A true light ginger color. Good quality is fairly rare in the natural. Many brown necks are bleached to attain this shade.

DARK GINGER: sometimes called a red game. Light brown in shade.

BROWN: as such.

COACHMAN: dark brown, rich.

DUN: in natural shades it is scarce and expensive. Most Dun necks available are of the dyed variety. The word *Dun* implies any shade of grey from light to dark, or any shade of brownish (bronze) grey from light to dark. The term *Blue Dun* will fool you. There is no blue in a natural blue dun neck. There are also very few mayflies that are colored blue. Caddis flies have none.

BLACK: natural black is almost black . . . but not quite. Check the underside of any natural black neck (or any neck for that matter) and you will see what I mean. Naturals are fairly scarce in good quality. Most available necks are of a dyed black.

GRIZZLY: one of the most necessary necks for fly tying. Also one of the most expensive. Color is grey/black with white barring. Original Grizzly capes came from the Barred Plymouth Rock rooster. This breed is now used less domestically. Extremely good Grizzly capes are available from those breeding them for fly tying.

THE VARIANTS: any rooster neck with a barring of more than one color. A ginger Grizzly is a cream or golden Ginger with Red Brown barring. A Red Grizzly is exactly the opposite. A Chinchilla is a White or Cream neck with dark barring.

CREE: also a variant, except that it is barred with three colors, usually black or grey, with light ginger and brown. It is often used as a substitute to hackle the pattern called Adams, since it attains the same effect.

BADGER: a white or cream neck with a black stripe running through the center from tip to butt.

FURNACE: a Dark Ginger or Brown neck with a black center stripe.

COCK-Y BONDHU: a Furnace neck on which the tips of the barbules are also edged in black.

(continued from preceding page)
streamer patterns. Marabou is a common material. It is utilized more and more frequently because of the natural breathing action of the fibers when a pattern containing it is fished.

DUCK QUILLS

Sometimes called duck pointer quills, these are the flight feathers taken from either a domestic (white) or a wild duck. The most used color is the natural slate grey, obtained mostly from a mallard duck. They are used for making wings on both wet and dry flies, and for wing cases on nymphs. White duck quills are used as such and dyed many shades for various patterns.

GOOSE QUILLS

The flight feathers from a domestic (white) or wild goose. Again, the most popular shade is the natural grey, which is obtained from the Canada goose. Goose wing quills are much larger than duck quills. They are more suitable for the wing cases on the larger stoneflies. The white and dyed versions are ideal for winging some of our flashy bass bugs.

MALLARD FLANK

Also called Mallard Side feathers since they do come from the sides (or flank) of a drake mallard duck. The feathers are a light pearl grey

with black barring. They are used for wings, legs and hackle as is, and are also dyed various shades, especially a brownish yellow, which is used as a wood duck imitation.

PEACOCK EYED TAIL

This is the brilliantly colored tail feather from a male Peafowl. The individual bronze/green fibers are used for the bodies of wet and dry flies, for topping and parts of wings on streamer and salmon flies and for gilling, tailing, and feeler effects on nymphs. If you require the fibers for dries or wets you will need a tail that has very wide flues. The best flues (barbules) are usually found in that area just below the "eyed" portion and three to four inches below it. The flues on a select tail are much longer than a non-select grade. If the fibers are required for winging, it is less expensive if you purchase the strung peacock herl. You

will get more fibers. The width of flue is not important.

The "eyed" portion of a peacock tail is also stripped (the flues or barbules are removed) so that the bare quill

may be used for such dry flies as the Quill Gordon and Ginger Quill.

GOLDEN PHEASANT NECK

This material is the most commonly used of all the pheasant feathers. It consists of the neck portion — called tippets — and the topknot — called the crest. The tippet feathers are orange with narrow black bars. It is used for tailing, (Royal Coachman Dry) and the winging of some salmon fly patterns.

The crest is a smooth, almost glassy fiber in texture and of a brilliant light orange shade — almost like polished gold with light bouncing from its surface. The crest is used mainly in salmon flies for tips and topping.

RINGNECK PHEASANT TAIL

Most of you are familiar with this reddish, grey/brown barred tail. It is often used to decorate hats. It is used for tailing and wing cases.

(continued on next page)

(continued from preceding page)

SILVER PHEASANT

The body feathers of this bird are white with fine black bars. It is used mostly for shoulders on streamer flies.

PARTRIDGE OR GROUSE

Much confusion surrounds the nomenclature of this feather. Our native bird, the Ruffed Grouse, is called "Partridge" by many New Englanders. The English or European Grouse was called Partridge when it was imported. (It is no longer allowed to be imported.) Forget about the name. What you want to look for is either a grey or a brown feather which is very finely barred and dotted. A good example is the March Brown Nymph.

The quality of most feather materials is generally good. What you should look for, however, is the rubbing of edges and signs of infestation. Wing quill feathers such as goose or duck should have an unbroken edge if they are to be used for winging. The left and right feathers should be fairly alike in color and size.

Infestation, caused by moth larvae, can be detected by looking for small holes or scars. Check all feathers for this type of spoilage.

OSTRICH

Available in natural white, black and grey. It is also dyed various colors. Though occasionally used for topping or winging, it's primarily used as a gilling effect on nymphs. It can be obtained in both wide and narrow flued fibers.

MOTTLED TURKEY WING QUILLS

Sometimes called Speckled Brown Turkey wing quills, these feathers have almost become a collector's item since this breed of turkey is no longer raised in the U.S. for food. The feathers can be found in the wild turkey, or an occasional show bird. The coloration, which puts them in such demand, is a light to medium dark brown with splotches of off-shades of brown, white or grey intermingled, thus creating a speckled effect. Substitutes are the rare flight feathers from a peacock and the side tail feathers from a Ringneck or Golden Pheasant.

TURKEY TAIL

Very dark brown and speckled. A few still exist but these also are gradually diminishing in supply.

Fur

When supply houses refer to Furs they usually mean the underfur of a particular animal which can be used as a dubbing to form the body of a fly. Hides are a mixture of both dubbing and tailing material, such as the guard hairs and underfur on a piece of badger skin. Tails are primarily all guard hairs and are used for tailing and winging. Here are a few of the more commonly used materials from animals.

BEAVER

Used for its underfur which is a lustrous soft light to medium grey.

MUSKRAT

A light to medium dark blue grey. Used for dubbing bodies on dry flies, wets and nymphs.

RABBIT

Available in natural grey, natural white and a variety of dyed shades. Readily water absorbent, it is used mostly in wet flies and nymphs.

SEAL FUR

Two kinds are sold. The coarse baby Hair Seal, which is available in a natural cream and many dyed colors, and the Fur Seal, which is extremely soft and brown in color.

The coarse Hair Seal is difficult to dub because of its glassy smooth texture.

BUCKTAIL

When listed, it usually refers to the tail of the Eastern White Tail Deer. Color is white on the underside and brown to black on the back. It is dyed many shades. Used primarily for winging and tailing of some dry flies, but mostly the winging of bucktail and streamer patterns.

CALF TAIL

Once a substitute for bucktail, the calf tail is now preferred because it is easier to work with and stands up better. It is not as long as bucktail. Thus, when winging is needed for large flies, such as some of the salt water patterns, bucktail is used. Color is natural white, brown, black and a variety of dyed shades.

BLACK BEAR

Guard hairs, which range on different animals from brown to black, is used for winging of bucktail and streamer patterns.

SQUIRREL TAIL

The Grey Squirrel tail is the most commonly used. It is mostly grey speckled and carries a black barring below its white tip.

Red Fox Squirrel tails are also used. They are reddish brown with a black barring near the tip. Both are used as winging on streamer type flies.

MOOSE MANE

Very fine hair fibers ranging from off white to brownish grey. Alternate fibers are used to obtain a ribbing (segmentation) effect on the bodies of dry flies.

DEER BODY HAIR

Grey to brown/grey in shade, Deer Body Hair is hollow, thus making it an excellent material for spinning onto a hook shank. In this fashion it is then trimmed to form hair bodies on dry flies, salmon patterns and bass bugs.

CARIBOU

A similar material to Deer Hair but much finer. Used for the same purpose. It is light grey to white in shade.

ANTELOPE

Again, a hair for spinning bodies. Antelope is very coarse.

POLAR BEAR

A rich lustrous creamy white hair fiber used for winging of

(continued on next page)

(continued from preceding page)

streamer-type patterns. This hair is now restricted in many states. Calf tail is used as a substitute.

PECCARY

The hair of this animal is almost not hair at all. It is coarse and stiff . . . almost brittle. It does make an excellent material for the feelers and tails on nymphs. It is brown to black in color, occasionally having white tips.

WOODCHUCK (GROUNDHOG)

Color ranges on the individual fibers from black to tannish brown, to black with a white tip. Overall color varies in different animals. Hair is easy to work with. Excellent for winging and tailing of both dry flies and streamer-type patterns.

The tail of the Woodchuck is mostly a solid brown to black, depending on the animal. Occasional tails have a salt and pepper effect in coloration.

OTTER

A coarser dubbing fur. Usually used with some of the short guard hairs mixed in with the underfur. It ranges from tan to brown.

FITCH

Soft in texture. Color ranges from a rich cream to beige.

AUSTRALIAN OPOSSUM

A deep rich, almost yellow, cream on the underside to a medium grey shade on the back. A dubbing fur easy to work with.

FOX

Red Fox ranges in shade from pale white, cream, beige to grey. Much sought after is the *urine stained* belly fur, which has a pinkish cast.

Grey Fox, while having many of the color shades of the Red, is used more often for its guard hairs, which are a finely marked grey to black with white tips.

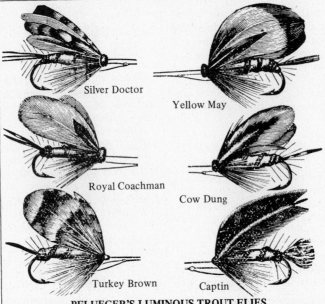

PFLUEGER'S LUMINOUS TROUT FLIES

Silver Doctor

Royal Coachman

Turkey Brown

Yellow May

Cow Dung

Captin

Pflueger sold a dozen of these iridescent flies in the 1890s for $1. They were tied from natural and treated Jungle Cock, Golden Pheasant and Wood Duck feathers. Anglers were advised to "expose luminous bait to day or artificial light before using in dark."

HARE'S MASK AND EARS, ENGLISH

This is the face mask of the true European hare. It is ginger/tan to light brown in shade. It has both soft underfur and coarse short guard hairs. Both types, the soft and the coarse, are blended together to tie the pattern, Gold Ribbed Hare's Ear, and to obtain similar effects in other patterns.

HUGUNIN BASS FLY

Tied in the 1890s, this fly was designed with wings that formed a weed guard by covering the point at the hook. They sold for $2.25 a dozen.

Natural Oils

Nature has given animals different talents and protections. There are birds which live and feed primarily on the land when they are not flying. Others such as ducks and geese, live on the water. And generally do much of their feeding in it.

Water birds, or fowl, need more protection from the cold than their land relatives. Hence, they are endowed with thick skins covered with feathers that repel water due to their oily content.

Use these properties to your own advantage in fly tying. If the feathers from water fowl are water repellent, they are excellent material for dry flies. After all, a dry fly should float. On the other hand, the feathers from a land bird absorb water fairly readily. Use them for wet flies, streamers and nymphs.

These applications will not always work, but by all means take advantage of them.

The same holds true for animals. Beaver, Muskrat and Otter live in or near water and their fur is oily. Use them, if at all possible, for your dry fly patterns. For wet flies and nymphs, try to stay with Rabbit, Mole, Raccoon, Fox and the like.

Sources

While most, if not all, the materials listed (and those not listed) are available to you from your local retailer, or your favorite mail order house, you can obtain many of them at no cost at all. If you are a hunter, save all the skins of the birds and animals you shoot, or at least their fur and plumage. If you do not hunt, ask your friends. (You can always tie a few flies for them in exchange.)

Certain animals can also be picked up along the road. Many of them are hit by cars. Depending on the state of decomposition, they can be salvaged. Your nose and eyes will tell you whether or not to start working on a carcass. Skunks have excellent fur material . . . but even I have chickened out on that animal. I prefer to purchase them.

Another place you might look is the local taxidermist, farmer or furrier. They always have scraps that you will be able to use.

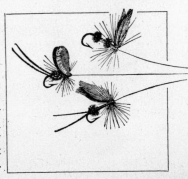

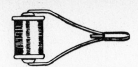

FIRESIDE ANGLER DRY FLY KIT

FIRESIDE ANGLER NYMPH AND WET FLY KIT

FIRESIDE ANGLER BUCKTAIL AND STREAMER KIT

FIRESIDE ANGLER POPPER AND HAIRBUG KIT

Kits

FIRESIDE ANGLER. Fireside Angler offers a series of kits that are probably best for the specialized beginner. There's one for dry flies, one for nymphs and wet flies, one for bucktails and streamers and one for poppers and hair bugs. They don't have the tools, but everything else needed for tying these particular kinds of flies is there. Good for starting out. They also sell kits for particular kinds of patterns such as Quill Gordons, Light Cahills, Muddler Minnows, Montana Nymphs, etc. Enough to tie two dozen of each pattern — not a real bargain financially, but a good way to gain tying expertise.

LAGGIE'S STREAMSIDE FLY-TYING KIT. Not cheap, but that's about the only flaw Laggie's Streamside Fly-Tying Kit has. Inside the custom vest-sized kit is a Croydon hand vise with leg strap mount, Matarelli whip finisher and bobbin, scissors, bobbin threader, Thompson midget pliers plus such goodies as 18 colors of dubbing, tinsel, floss, chenille, hackles and feathers. Then there are Flymaster tying threads, GlosCote head cement and Mustad hooks in all sizes. It has more stuff than many home tiers stock. What more could you want? Also available as a kit with just the tools or else as simply a leather case for those who want to add their own innards.

OLD PAL. Old Pal model TS 500, the tackle satchel, works very well as a portable fly-tying kit of a very extensive nature. It has two large sliding shelves at the top with rubber straps to hold gear in place, and eight slide-out plastic boxes for other materials. Has a key lock. Will hold an amazing amount of gear safely.

FIRESIDE ANGLER GRAB BAG

OLD PAL

"Doubt not but angling will prove to be so pleasant that it will prove to be, like a virtue, a reward to itself."
IZAAK WALTON, *The Compleat Angler*

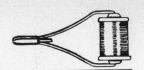

THE LAST HATCH
A FISHING MYSTERY
HARMON HENKIN

(continued from page 65)

taken over. Paul fell back on the leather couch and began thumbing through an Albanian translation of Halford's best-selling *The Rhinoceros Points The Way*, which the translator noted was given to the Albanian people as an example of the hopeless decadence of the Western World.

Two more people entered the room and the volume went up. Paul didn't notice. He was wondering if the universe really was exploding. Dun crept off into a corner and sniffled.

Then a rapidly approaching siren could be heard. The crowd fell silent. Everyone froze as the noise got louder. After what seemed eons the siren stopped and they heard a car pull into the gravel driveway. A car door opened. And slammed. Footsteps approached. The crowd stepped back. The door flew open. The sheriff. Paul smiled.

Sheriff Sid Gordon could never have gotten a part on *Police Story*. In his mid-20s, he wore old corduroys, sneakers and a faded chambray shirt bordered with embroidery. In a literal sense, his badge was tarnished. But the good citizens of Ravalli County prided themselves on knowing a bargain when they saw one. When the Vietnam Veteran with the droopy mustache, tired eyes and bushy, curly hair had offered his services for $550 a month plus a small cabin, they couldn't refuse. He was eagerly sworn in. The old sheriff had cost them $1200 a month and spent most of his time busting the sons and daughters of the community's pillars for possession of marijuana, a misdemeanor Sid conveniently overlooked. Like everyone else in the valley who hadn't dedicated their lives to making money by destroying the environment, Sid spent most of his time fishing and hunting and lying about the results at the Longbranch Saloon over pool and beer.

"You're the new sheriff?" Dun asked cautiously, breaking the communal silence.

"I ain't the Tupperware lady, mister. Now, what the Hell's going on?"

Paul could tell from the glaze around Sid's eyes that the lying last night at the Longbranch must have taken on larger-than-usual proportions. Although at times like this Sid liked to play the tough cop, the role didn't suit him.

(continued on page 100)

top of the line

Material

CHARLES BROOKS FLY-TYING MATERIALS. Bud Lilly in West Yellowstone, Montana, is packaging a selection of materials to be used in whipping up some of his friend Charlie Brooks' favorite big bozo Western patterns. Included are Black Melody and Brown Melody Yarn, Antique Gold Yarn, Brown saddles, green grizzly saddles and copper wire for getting them down deep.

BUZZ'S. Buzz's fly shop in Visalia, California, sells a very complete line of fly-tying material especially geared for the western and coastal angler. Their materials are top-notch and they've been in the business a long time.

FIRESIDE ANGLER PHEASANT SKINS. Pheasant skins are a very useful feather for many patterns, especially the more traditional ones. Fireside Anglers offers a complete selection of skins and parts of skins, including English Ring Neck, Silver Pheasant, Golden Pheasant and Lady Amherst. Good quality tying material.

FURS FROM KAUFMANN'S. One of the best selections of furs around is from Kaufmann's in Portland. They have all the common ones plus such delicacies as albino beaver, cougar, albino muskrat, lynx and marten, ermine in the process of changing coat colors and albino nutria. Sold in small patches and in assortments and mixes. Good stuff for the dubber, especially.

GUDEBROD NYMPH THREAD. Gudebrod has a carefully thought-out nymph-tying thread with an .0015 diameter. It's geared to tie like

top of the line

6/0 silk but has the strength of 3/0 nylon. Doesn't need waxing but works best in a bobbin. Comes in a dozen colors.

HERTER'S. Herter's remains one of the best places for anyone to get his tying supplies, especially the beginner. Besides the regular stuff like tying kits, their own range of tools and all sorts of necks at very low prices — including a big assortment of dyed skins — they feature specialties such as: radiant hackles, shouldering eyes for streamers, variegated chenilles, wax holders, veined fly wings, potluck assortments and on and on. They will also special-dye your feathers for you. Overwhelming.

KAUFMANN'S SEAL. One of the better body and dubbing materials is seal. Kaufmann's offers one of the best possible selections of it in 25 different colors, ranging from cream and white to purple and green-olive plus an assortment of fluorescent colors for steelhead flies or whatever.

METZ HACKLE. Buck Metz produces wonderful natural blue dun in the same league as Hoffman's grizzly feathers. They ain't cheap but Metz's feathers are as good as any in the history of fly fishing. Metz knows his chickens from genetics on up and he has developed a product that is a genuine joy and something for him to be proud of. Take a look at his and you won't be satisfied with any other blue dun neck.

MYLAR PIPING. A convenient way to tie a shiny metallic body on a streamer or muddler. Braided Mylar piping, sold by the Reed Company, is

HERTER'S GAMECOCK NECKS

HERTER'S WIGGLING DISCS

HERTER'S HALF NECKS

REED'S MYLAR PIPING

Silver Skin

Lady Amherst Skin

Golden

Ringneck Skin

Reeves Skin

KAUFMANN'S PHEASANT SKINS

top of the line

fitted onto the hook and tied on at both ends. Sold in gold or silver for all common streamer hook sizes, by the foot or in 5-foot strips.

ORVIS SPECTRABLEND. Just use your fingers to stir around this assortment of 30 fur blends and you're bound to come up with the exact shade desired. Orvis has packaged these fur blends across the spectrum to meet almost any color need. Each color comes in its own container and is replaceable. One of the last words in dubbing material for the serious tier.

SUPER GRIZZLY. Things aren't what they used to be. Well, perhaps. Our milk and bread are made of plastic, but at least we're living in a time when the best Grizzly hackle is available. The Super Grizzly necks raised by Henry Hoffman of Oregon, are without a doubt, the best ever available. Over the past 25 years, Hoffman has just about perfected the art of raising roosters for the tying vise. It isn't cheap, but there's no reason to think that the specialized knowledge that went into producing these necks and whole skins should be. The initial investment may be high, but one neck should last the average tier years. Doesn't pay to skimp.

TACKLE CRAFT. Tackle Craft's catalog lists lots of fly-tying stuff ranging from tools to feathers in most of the prominent brands. Feathers, furs, corks and threads are all offered. A solid outpouring of good stuff.

Miscellany

BENCH AND STORAGE CASE. An elegant fly-tying bench and storage case is this 9- by 15¼- by 10½-inch green-stained, white pine outfit.

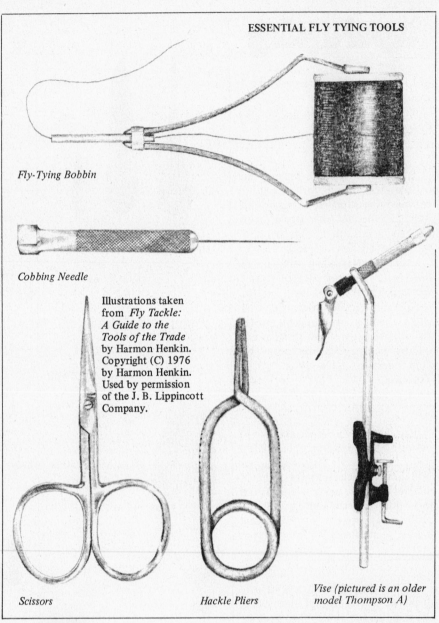

ESSENTIAL FLY TYING TOOLS

Fly-Tying Bobbin

Cobbing Needle

Illustrations taken from *Fly Tackle: A Guide to the Tools of the Trade* by Harmon Henkin. Copyright (C) 1976 by Harmon Henkin. Used by permission of the J. B. Lippincott Company.

Scissors

Hackle Pliers

Vise (pictured is an older model Thompson A)

ORVIS SPECTRABLEND

BENCH AND STORAGE CASE

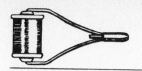

Give me mine angle,
we'll go to the river:
there,
My music playing
far off, I will betray
Tawny-finn'd fishes;
my bended hook shall
pierce
Their slimy jaws.

Shakespeare,
Antony and Cleopatra

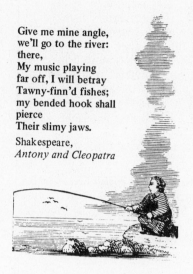

GLOSCOTE

GAMEFISH: BROWN TROUT

NAMES
Loch Leven trout, German brown trout, Von Behr trout. *(Salmo trutta)*

DISTRIBUTION
The brown trout is a native of Europe and was introduced to the United States in the late 1800s. It is now found throughout the United States except for the Deep South where the water is too warm.

DESCRIPTION
The coloring of the brown trout is usually brown or greenish-brown on the back with lighter brown sides and a creamy yellow belly. The sides, back and dorsal fins are marked with brown or black spots. These are some-times ringed with a circle of white. Sea-run brown trout are more silver in color.

SIZE
The size of the brown trout varies according to its habitat. In most streams and lakes, the average size is about 1 to 1½ pounds. In larger streams, fish of up to 8 pounds in weight can be found.

HABITAT
Although the brown trout prefers cool waters, they can stand warmer waters than most of the other trouts. The favorite habitats, much like those of the brook trout, are streams and rivers where there is an abundance of rocky ledges and deep holes. On the Atlantic coast, the brown trout has found its way into the ocean.

FEEDING HABITS
The brown trout feeds on insects, crustaceans, minnows and worms. It feeds primarily at night when it rises to the surface in search of insects. Fall is the best time to go after brown trout.

BEST FEEDING TEMPERATURE
Between 50° and 65°.

TACKLE
Except in lakes where trollers equipped with medium baitcasting stuff haul out monsters on plugs, spoons and bait, the brown is a fly rod fish par excellence. Suspicious and well-adapted to its habitat, this fish can require light lines and delicately cast flies that imitate what's going on in the stream. Rarely makes a fool of itself over a badly presented lure.

top of the line

You can work right out of it and it will hold lots and lots. Has brass-plated hardware and a transport handle. Very well thought-out. Sold by Bud Lilly's.

FLY-TIER'S CARRYALL. This is a case for the real serious portable fly tier. Made from canvas, it has two large pockets for necks, loops for your vise, four large plastic boxes for bigger things, 12 boxes for hooks, tubes for spooled materials and a workboard, toolbox and magnet for holding finished flies or whatever. A good item.

GLOSCOTE HEAD CEMENT. One of the best head cements on the market is GlosCote, which penetrates deep even into waxed threads and dries almost instantly to a very hard finish. Designed originally for industrial use. Get a bottle of thinner from GlosCote while you're at it.

MAYFLY PROPORTION CHART. That clever fellow Chauncey Lively has come up with a mayfly proportion chart that will be of lots of help, especially for the beginner. It gives wing, body and hook length for over 150 species region by region. Lots of work went into this thing, including extensive details on the tying of cut wings.

WASTE-TROL. The perfect thing for the ultra-neat tier who doesn't want to litter up the bench. It mounts underneath your vise, collects all your droppings and will swing underneath your bench. Available in a mini-size as well.

Tools

ADJUSTABLE LOOP FLY-TYING SCISSORS. These adjustable

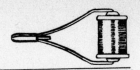

"Angling may said to be so like the mathematics that it can never be fully learnt."
IZAAK WALTON, *The Compleat Angler*

Artificial impregnation of a trout

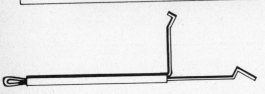

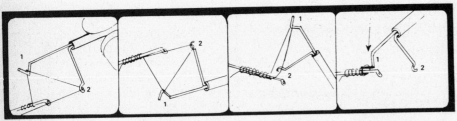

1. Loop tying thread on both "whipper" hooks and hold thread back (not too tight) along side of fly-head.

2. Rotate whipper hook No. 1 around fly-head as many times as desired, releasing additional thread as needed.

3. When fly-head is completed, move whipper hook No. 2 above fly and release from loop.

4. Pull tying thread – thus lowering whipper hook No. 1 to fly-head. Then remove.

CHARLIE'S WHIPPER

WASTE-TROL

CHASE BOBBIN

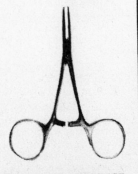

FISHERMAN'S BOOKCASE MINI-FORCEPS

top of the line

loop fly-tying scissors are a welcome product for many tiers. With their forged stainless-steel blades supposedly able to hold their sharpness for a lifetime they would be good enough. But there's more. The finger loops are adjustable for any size pinkies and even thumbs. Better than trying to force big fingers into little loops. Excellent. Available from Buzek's.

CHARLIE'S WHIPPER. Charlie Cole, dissatisfied with other whip-knot tools for finishing the heads of flies, is selling his own. Especially designed for smaller hooks down to size 28. Can be used either right or left handed.

CHASE BOBBIN. This is the first bobbin chosen by many tiers. The Chase bobbin is simple and relatively easy to use. Tension is altered with a screw on the side and it comes with thread and a threader.

D-BOONE HALF-HITCH TIER. One of the more ingenious half-hitch tiers around is from the D-Boone company. (Hmm . . . familiar sounding name!) Their cone-shaped gadget can handle half-hitch finishes on flies from No. 8 through No. 22 and down to 8/0 thread size. Works well.

FISHERMAN'S BOOKCASE MINI-FORCEPS. These mini-forceps will do a number of fly fishing-related tasks and stay out of the way when they're finished on a retractable vest pin. Good as hook removers, an emergency vise for streamside tying, an assist for tying knots and lots else. Get them from Fly Fisherman's Bookcase if you can't whine away a pair from your friendly, over-charging physician.

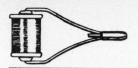
top of the line

GEORGE GRANT WEAVING POST. For those tiers into the popular woven fly patterns, Bud Lilly is selling a George Grant Weaving Post to hold your weaving threads taut to make the operation much simpler. Also available is a hackle-weaving tool. Some other George Grant weaving accessories are flat monofilaments, Tynex for weaving hackles, special pins and badger hackle.

HACKLE GUARDS. A set of three hackle guards plus a weighted string is wonderful for the beginning tier. Offered by the Fly Fisherman's Bookcase. It holds the hackle out of the way for other operations.

HAIR SHAKER. This is a scoop-like accessory designed to make evening up the tip of hair an easier chore. You place the cut hair in the scoop and tap it a few times. *Voilà!*

HAIR STACKER. Having hair problems? Try a Hair Stacker that will even out those split deer-hair ends and get them ready for tying. Handles any length hair. A good product.

HANDY BOBBIN THREADER AND CLEANING TOOL. Here's a handy tool for the tier. It quickly threads any size bobbin and also removes wax buildup from them. Available from Buzek's.

POUL JORGENSEN TROUT FLY CHARTS. Poul Jorgensen, considered by many to be America's premier fly tier, has produced with photographer Lee Boltin a series of 220 full-color photographs of trout flies along with pattern descriptions, tying instructions and additional information. They cover the spectrum of modern trout flies very well. A small investment for the tier who wants to expand horizons.

The grounde lyne rennynge.

The grounde lyne lyenge.

Fish hooks from Renaissance England

HAIR STACKER

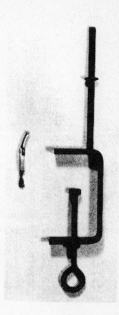

GEORGE GRANT WEAVING POST

HAIR SHAKER

HACKLE GUARDS

Dick Surette's *How To Tie Basic Flies*

Dick Surette's pamphlet, *How To Tie Basic Flies*, is just that — a 23-page fully illustrated primer that shows and tells you how to tie the various types of flies and even jigs. It's good especially for those who know nothing about the intricacies of the art.

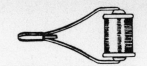

MATARELLI BOBBIN. The Materelli clip bobbin is one of the better ones on the market. It has a finely ground tip and adjustable tension. Works smoothly.

MATARELLI WHIP FINISHER. Like all of the products offered by Frank Matarelli, this whip finisher, made from all stainless steel, works for all size flies. Functions for right or left handers. A well-made product available from Buzek's.

MINI FUR BLENDER. A really nice accessory for the more advanced tier. It works on the same principle as the blender in the kitchen. It will blend any assortment of furs you want to make any shade of dubbing or body material desired. Small, simple and safe, the Mini-Blender is excellent.

SPIRALATOR. Parachute hackle flies are very visible and float well but are a little more difficult to tie than regular patterns. Well, author-tier Chauncey Lively has come out with a gadget that simplifies the tying on these helicopter-type wings. The hackle is tied around the Spirala-tor and then tied onto the shank. The wire and hook accessory can also be used for tying spent wings. Comes with detailed directions. Available from Fly Fisherman's Bookcase.

STAINLESS STEEL MIDGE WHIP FINISHER. This 3-inch midge whip finisher is ideal for the small flies favored by many anglers. Made from stainless steel the midge tier will handle larger-sized flies as well.

SUNRISE INDIA. India, which has a modest legacy of fly tying courtesy of British colonialism, is turning out a line of adequate fly-tying tools via the Sunrise India Company and available through a number of

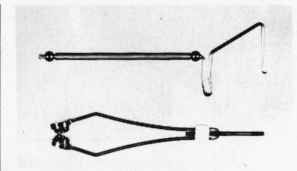

MATARELLI WHIP FINISHER & BOBBIN

SPIRALATOR

MINI FUR BLENDER

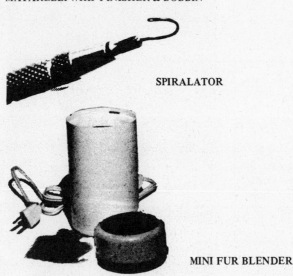

GAMEFISH: BLACK BULLHEAD

NAMES
Bullhead, yellow-belly bullhead, stinger, Northern bullhead. *(Ictalurus melas)*

DISTRIBUTION
One of the more widely distributed members of the bullhead family, the black bullhead is commonly found in a range from southern Canada west to the Rocky Mountains and South to Texas.

DESCRIPTION
The black bullhead is a heavy-set fish of dark green to black coloring on the back with a yellow or yellowish green belly. The base of the tail is usually light in color. The chin barbels are dark grey or black and the black bullhead is not mottled in color.

SIZE
A small fish, the black bullhead rarely attains a weight of more than 1 pound.

HABITAT
The black bullhead is most often found in ponds, sluggish rivers and muddy lakes. It prefers warm, shallow water although it is an extremely versatile fish and can be found in all types of environments.

FEEDING HABITS
The black bullhead will eat anything it can get in its mouth from small crustaceans to small fish and frogs. It is an active night feeder that often travels in large schools.

TACKLE
Worms and the bullhead go together like hamburgers and catsup and are probably more nutritious. Use light spinning rigs and still-fishing poles with wigglers attached, though other small baits work as well, sometimes. A fine beginner's fish.

A CHECKLIST OF FLY TYING TOOLS

HACKLE GAUGE

Being able to select the right size hackle for your dry flies is pretty important, and unless you have a lot of experience and can pick them from the cape and estimate their size at a glance, you will need a small hackle gauge.

The one I use is a homemade affair consisting of a thin piece of aluminum sheet, 1 x 4 inches. One end is tapered so that it will fit in the jaws of the vise, and on the other end is a small spur that serves as a guiding post for the hackle stem. The measuring scale is a small piece of cardboard glued to the aluminum with the lower edge snug up against the guidepost. To make the fiber-length guidelines on the board, lay the hook on the cardboard with the shank against the guidepost, and make a mark on the card at a position equal to 1½ to 2 times the hook gap, measuring from the guidepost. Now draw a line across the board, making sure to leave enough room at one end for the hook-size number. Make several such lines by using the various size hooks used most often for dressing your flies. You can bend the aluminum forward toward you after it is placed in the vise to get a comfortable work angle.

To use the gauge, hold the hackle by each end and lay it on the board with the middle portion of the stem against the guidepost. Pull the hackle ends lightly toward you and the fibers will angle up on the board so the length can be determined.

MEASURING CARDS

Since I often use fly wings that are cut from whole feathers, I made a set of cards with the different wing lengths marked off with a pencil line across a small 1½ x 3-inch piece of cardboard. The wing lengths are set off from the narrow edge of the card and identified by the name of the fly for which it is used. Lay the feather on the board and line the lower fibers up with the pencil line. Trim the excess feather along the cardboard edge and you have the proper wing length.

CALIPER

A small caliper marked with both millimeters and inches is a helpful tool when working with artificials that require exactness in pro-

(continued on next page)

CROYDON VISE

sources in this country. Hackle pliers, scissors, vises and a modified hemostat are among the featured products. Okay stuff.

DICK SURETTE'S FLY-TYING INDEX. A good idea for the fly tier is Dick Surette's index pages of patterns. Each of the large variety of color-illustrated pages contains a history of the pattern, what it imitates and when it is most effective. Also listed are tying materials and basic instructions. Not the best guide for the beginner but plenty detailed for the advanced tier.

THOMAS & THOMAS. About the best tools on the market are these T & T Lifetime models. They aren't as cheap as some but include everything you need, ranging from standard and midge bobbins, floss bobbins, brass dubbing needle, brass half-hitch tools, scissors, standard and midge hackle pliers and a whip-finishing tool. They are also put up in kit form for those who want one of everything — and who doesn't?

WISS QUICK-CLIP SPEED CUTTERS. The Wiss Quick-Clip Speed Cutters are a boon to the tier who does lots of work with hair flies. They are worn on the ring finger of the cutting hand and can be turned inside the palm when not used. Replaceable blades are available and they make short work of your irresistible or bass bug.

Vises

CROYDON VISE. The last word for the streamside tier is the Croydon hand vise. It takes a little getting used to but is the best around. Holds tight any size hook and is convenient for instant hatch-matching in your lap.

top of the line

LEONARD CATSKILL. A new and fancy vise designed after the model used by noted terrestrial innovator Vince Marinaro. The Catskill can be adjusted to four different positions — 30°, 60°, 90° and completely vertical. Will take almost any size hook. Simplicity itself. As an added bonus it has a drill bit adapter that lets you screw it into a log for streamside tying.

LEONARD FLYBODY. A special-purpose instrument for the specialized angler. It's used to tie flies on those elongated flybody mayfly hooks. The shaft rotates to allow the oversized hook to be worked on while clamped in the very small vise jaws. A streamside adapter in the form of a drill bit is available at an extra cost.

ORVIS VISE. As befits the snazzy Vermont-based company, Orvis markets the highest priced vise in the land. It's a seriously built item, tough looking and functional. It has a rotating jaw designed for the lazy to wrap with or just to check out your creation. Will take any size hook from No. 1/0 to No. 28 and you can raise the jaw to 8 inches above your tying table. They have replacement parts in

the unlikely case that the vise needs them.

VENIARD MIDGE, NO. 5. Despite claims that this or that vise takes all hook sizes, a model designed for a particular size range usually works out better. This is true for midge flies especially. Veniard's of England makes their No. 5 vise strictly for the purpose of taking hooks in the No. 28 range. Finely finished and quite lightweight, the vise has a thread button built into the base for convenience.

THOMPSON A. Fads and fashions in vises come and go but the Thompson A and its refined brother the "Ultra" remain. Though there have been recent claims that Thompson isn't making them like they used to, the Thompson vises were known and still are for having firm gripping jaws that would take any size hook. They also have adjustable heights. The "Ultra" has some refinements over the original, including adjustability for collet angle and greater support for the collet itself. Both allow for rapid work, which helps give them a commercial reputation.

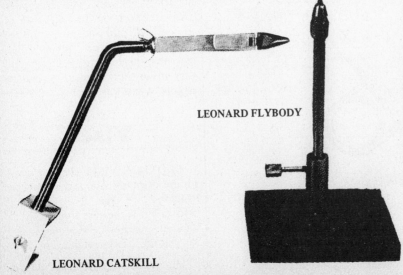

LEONARD FLYBODY

LEONARD CATSKILL

TOOLS

(continued from preceding page)

portion. They can be purchased in many sizes, but I like the small ones that take up less space on the table.

SMALL FUNNEL

To align the hair after it is cut from the skin, you can hardly beat a small funnel with a container in which it can be shook and rattled around until the hair is even. When ready, the hairs can be pushed through the narrow end where you can grasp them before they get disarranged. This setup is not found in the catalogue from Abercrombie and Fitch, but your local dime store carries funnels in various sizes, and the base can be a glass, cup, or other common object found around most households. My funnel is shown in action in the section on tying caddis adults.

QUILL SECTION EQUALIZER

This tool is designed to enable the flydresser to cut two wing quill sections that are exactly the same size. It is not available commercially as a unit but can be made very easily by trimming a paper clip to form the legs and inserting the piece in the end of an X-Acto knife handle. The longer leg will serve as a guide held along the edge of the quill fibers, while the other is inserted in the wing quill and drawn out through the feather, separating a particular width of quill section. The legs can be adjusted in or out, depending on the size wings you are making.

FUR BLENDER

It may seem like a luxury to buy a special piece of machinery to blend fur unless you need a lot of it, but believe me, it is the best investment you can make next to the vise. The small electric grinders used in Europe for grinding coffee beans are excellent for fur blending, as was first discovered by an Italian fly-tyer from Pittsburgh named Tony Marasco. With a small blender you can mix fur in just seconds, and chop wool and other yarns that are so hard to pull apart.

X-ACTO SAW

This tool is rarely used in fly-tying unless you make bass bugs, but I have found it extremely useful for roughing up the dubbing when dressing the special nymphs in this book. They come in different sizes which can all be used provided they are the fine-toothed variety. Shortly after giving a demonstration of this type of dubbing at a club meeting I saw someone use a hacksaw blade, but they are too rough, particularly for making smaller nymphs.

TOENAIL CLIPPERS
(Wing Cutters)

I have seen a number of different wing cutters in action, but none can beat an ordinary pair

(continued on next page)

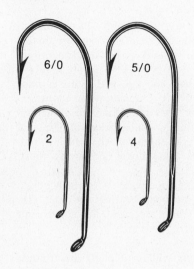

MUSTAD

HERTER'S

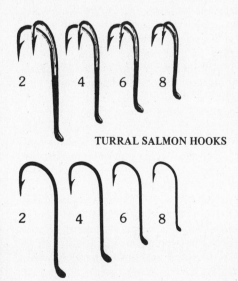

TURRAL SALMON HOOKS

TURRAL WET FLY HOOKS

top of the line

Hooks

EAGLE CLAW. Eagle Claw produces one of the more popular hooks for West Coast steelhead patterns. This heavy wire hook with a sproat bend is available in sizes No. 2 through No. 8. A very sturdy hook that is quite well made.

HERTER'S HOOKS. Bored with Mustads? Try Herter's tying hooks, available in all the popular styles and sizes. They sell them for mayfly ties, nymphs and wet flies, bass bugs, salmon flies and streamers. Barbless hooks, too. Reasonably priced as things go these days.

MUSTAD. For better or worse Mustad has come to totally dominate the quality fly-tying hook market. These Norwegian-made products have taken over as English and American manufacturers have gradually withdrawn from the field. This is not to say that it isn't possible to get other hooks, but anglers feel Mustads are plenty good enough for most tying tasks. They are available in all sizes down to No. 28 for standard tying and in varieties for nymphs, streamers, bucktails, single and double salmon flies, saltwater hooks or whatever else you want.

TURRAL HOOKS. For those epicurean souls jaded with mere Mustads there are now Turral hooks forged in English angling heartlands. Not cheap but very high quality, they are geared more for the tying specialist who is willing, for instance, to cough up $20 for 100 double salmon wet fly hooks. Turrals are also available in dry fly, wet fly, nymph/wet fly and streamer models. Maybe worth it if you really need it — like lots of other angling stuff.

ultimate commodity

actual size

No. 32 hooks

If you're into ultimates, and few fanatic fly fishermen don't go through that phase, get some No. 32s from Fly Fisherman's Bookcase. These gold-plated beauties, about half the size of a No. 28, are eyeless so they have to be snelled or glued onto your tippet materials. Somebody will catch a fish on one sooner or later so you might as well try to tie a Jock Scott on yours now.

TOOLS

(continued from preceding page)

of large toenail clippers. Dr. Scholl's "Nail Clip" is very good and can be purchased at almost any drugstore. I should like to emphasize the importance of getting one that will make a clean cut without tearing the fibers on the feather. I had to purchase four or five before finding one that did the job and would cut a perfect curve. Needless to say, such "rare tools" must be kept in the safe when not in use, or worn around the neck on a string like a medallion.

STREAMSIDE TYING KIT

I can't even begin to explain how important this little jewel has been to me over the years. A real lifesaver! After I wrote an article about it in *Trout Magazine* it was suggested that I market it for the benefit of my fellow anglers, which has since been done. It can be purchased from Fly Fisherman's Bookcase Tackle Service, Route 9A, Croton-on-Hudson, N.Y. 10520. It is supplied with tools, including a Croydon vise, and mounting bracket, plus half a dozen fur selections and tying thread. A small brochure explains how to pack it and what essential materials to carry on the stream.

Taken from *Modern Fly Dressings for the Practical Angler* by Poul Jorgensen. (C) 1976 by Poul Jorgensen. Used by permission of Winchester Press.

Fly boxes:
Plastic is good but there's plenty more

By Harmon Henkin

(above) Orvis marketed this metal case in the early 1900s for 35 cents each. (below) "The Levison" was patented in 1886 and sold by William Mills & Son, who claimed it was "the perfect fly book." It was 7½ inches long and held each fly separately with a spring-and-slot mechanism.

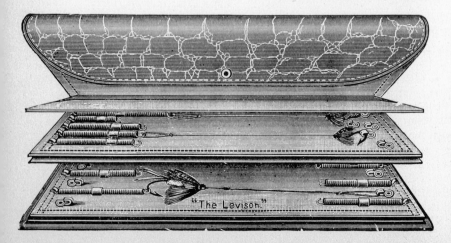

Soft plastic fly boxes are by an overwhelming majority the choice of most anglers looking for a place to stick their favorite and not-so-favorite flies.

A decade ago the soft plastic boxes once made by the Dewitt Company were almost extinct. Then everyone started making or marketing them in every combination of size and shape. Other than slight variations such as bottom coatings, these boxes are pretty much alike.

But there is a good reason for their popularity. They are inexpensive. They are practically unbreakable. They are light and convenient. What more could you want?

Plenty.

Some anglers willing to plunk down much more money get one of those wonderful Wheatley boxes. Available in a multitude of styles and usually made from aluminum alloys, these boxes and wet fly cases are ultimates. The most desired and desirable Wheatleys are the famed dry fly models cased in an alloy. Each compartment in the 6-, 12-, 16- and 32-compartment versions has its own transparent lid. They're heavy and bulky, but they protect your prime dries very, very well.

Other brands of boxes have specialized uses. Scientific Angler's Fly File, made of soft plastic, is good for large nymphs and especially saltwater flies. They hold the patterns tightly and have nothing to rust or mold.

The other popular type of fly box is actually a fly book marketed for lo these many years by the Common Sense people. Their best model is one that's a combination wet-dry box. It has a soft plastic box with eight sections with a number of replaceable envelopes for wets. It's all surrounded by a leather or leather substitute wallet. Common Sense also makes an assortment of leader wallets and streamer books that are good.

Fly wallets, which were a mainstay for subsurface flies in England for decades, are making a comeback in this country. With sheepskin, felt or synthetic pages, some are remarkably ornate. Fine ones can also be ordered from your local leather crafter.

The standard for a fly case should be whether it can carry your flies without damaging them. This is a simple advantage of soft plastic boxes but sometimes it is so difficult to get flies onto the clips of others that they aren't worthwhile. Try them out before buying. It should be a simple matter to get flies in and out of the box.

That's about all there is to choosing a case. The rest is a matter of taste and budget.

top of the line

Fly Books

COMMON SENSE. The Common Sense line of fly books has been around for a long time. At one time, they could be found in lots of hardware store nooks and crannies as well as sporting goods stores. Their most unique product is the combination wet-dry wallets, which consist of a soft plastic box encased in a leather or imitation-leather wallet. These books also have envelopes for wet flies. Common Sense also makes leader wallets, simple wet fly and nymph books and a variety of streamer books. Can be had in most models with the real thing — leather or pigskin — or plastic. Very nice accessories for the fly angler.

KAUFMANN'S. A very elegant leather fly book for wets and streamers handcrafted by Bill McMillian and sold by Kaufmann's. It has a leather strap and buckle and is offered with sheepskin inside and with or without felt inserts. Finely made.

LEONARD FLY BOOK. The Leonard fly book is made of top-grain cowhide with six heavy felt pages to take up to 50 flies. An old-fashioned way of carrying wet flies, nymphs and streamers, but still one of the best. Designed to lie flat inside a vest. Pages are replaceable.

REED'S FLY BOOK. Reed makes an old-fashioned wet fly and nymph book in the looseleaf style that works as well as any of the modern ones. They come with either imitation or real leather covers and six white-felt leaves that help dry the used flies and make for easy hooking and unhooking. The pages fit into

WHAT WE LOOKED FOR IN QUALITY

A fly box should hold flies. Right? Well, that was our major consideration in judging this category. Of course, nobody really needs anything but a plastic box. Yet such delicacies as the Wheatleys and the Common Sense Books certainly have their place. We fully admit that whim and fancy played a part in our evaluation of fly boxes. So there.

COMMON SENSE

KAUFMANN'S

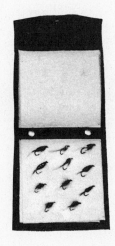

LEONARD

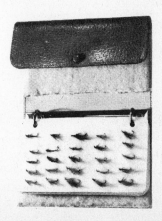

REED

top of the line

the ring binding. Extra pages are available, including lamb's wool pages for bigger flies. Measuring 7 inches by 4¼ inches, it holds more than 150 flies.

Fly Boxes

FLY-SAFE. Another really good box for big flies. With 72 stainless-steel clips in an aluminum shell, this kit holds the flies in such a way that they dry quickly. A little bothersome for really small flies, like midges, however.

GODDARD FLY FISHING CASE. Dermot Wilson offers the Goddard Fly Fishing Case, a one-of-a-kind gray plastic case perfect for the fly caster on a lake or in a boat. The 12- by 10- by 4-inch case has room for reels and other gear in the main section. The lid opens up to hold hundreds of flies in the foam and there are other compartments for leaders and whatever tools you carry. Get organized. A reasonable buy from England.

MARTIN. The Martin Fly-Safe box with 72 clips that will hold flies from 16 to 1/0 upright is a good way to go. It's made from anodized aluminum and is especially good for nymphs and streamers.

ORVIS WORKHORSE. Soft plastic boxes in a variety of shapes and sizes for just carrying flies in a practical way. They are just about unbreakable and very light in vest or pocket.

PERRINE NO. 91. A reasonably priced box with a transparent lid covering ten deep compartments for

FLY-SAFE

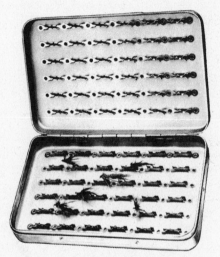

MARTIN FLY-SAFE

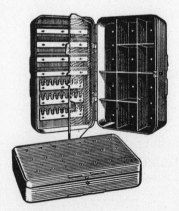

PERRINE NO. 91

Wheatley Fly Boxes

These English-made boxes with their individual compartments and individual lids are an ultimate. Though the new ones aren't made with the unerring tolerances of those of a few years back they sure do the job of being the best dry fly holders. Prices can get astronomical for the very elegant ones. For instance the dazzling 32-compartment box retails for around $60, the price of a very decent cane rod 15 years ago.

They are available in a variety of styles and compartment numbers ranging from 6 to 32. Some models have clips in the lid for wets and others have foam for placing flies that have been fished. As the commercial says, sooner or later you'll probably own a Wheatley.

PERRINE NO. 98

WHEATLEY BLACK SEAL

dries. It also has four coil clips for streamers and big flies and 30 clips for nymphs, etc.

PERRINE MODEL 98. The newest of Perrine's line of ventilated Perrine boxes — model 98 — has a molded polypropylene insert that clips in as many as 100 flies, wet or dry, in an upright position. Good for bigger flies. Keeps them dry and visible.

RICHARDSON'S. The Richardson fly box, which used to be known as the Fye fly box, is an excellent choice for the angler who takes lots of patterns but doesn't like vests. It's a multi-level aluminum box available in 2-, 3-, 4- or 5- tray models. It's worn on the chest and holds more flies than you can imagine. Also available with an attachment to hold a small flashlight and dry fly dope. One of the compartments can be reserved for tippets or whatever else you haul around. Ingenious boxes for the advanced fly caster.

WHEATLEY BLACK SEAL. A less expensive Wheatley dry fly box without the elegance of the individualized compartment models. It has a single transparent lid covering the 16 compartments. There is a foam pad in the lid for wets.

Miscellany

CHATILLON SCALES. Chatillon scales are among the neatest of the fishing accessories. Available in either 6, 12, 25 or 50-pound capacities, these brass spring scales are truly elegant, and have been around for a long time. Accurate enough and sturdily built.

HARDY TELESCOPIC FISH TAILER

Hardy's telescopic Fish Tailer is a nice way to beach large fish like salmon when such manuevers are possible. Weighing only 7¾ ounces and folding down to 32 inches, it forms a bow which can be slipped underneath the fish when extended. Typical high-quality Hardy stuff.

CHATILLON SCALES

top of the line

FRENCH CLIP. Sold by lots of the better catalog houses, this French Clip is the best way to carry your lightweight trout net if you prefer to use it detached from a lanyard. The positive action jaws release only under direct pressure. Works fine.

FRENCH CLIP

SEAWAY MUSETTE BAGS. Seaway sells an interesting budget line of cotton or nylon musette bags in a variety of colors. They make a fine over-the-shoulder carrying kit bag for the angler not happy with tackle boxes or vests. Side pockets for little things and a large main pocket for bigger things. Altogether a worthwhile product.

SEAWAY MUSETTE BAG

ORVIS TAC-L-PAK

DERMOT WILSON'S SENIOR BAG. The English still favor keeping their fishing gear in canvas-type bags rather than vests or tackle boxes. Dermot Wilson's shop carries some wonderful items such as the Senior Bag, made for him in England. It's 16 by 12 inches, large enough for everything and anything. It has compartments on the front and rings for knives or whatever. Lots of other styles and sizes offered. Very well made.

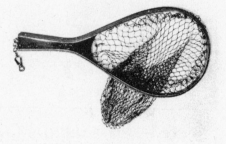

CASCADE LAKES

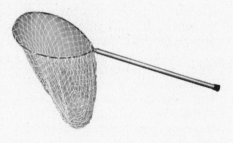

BEAN

Nets

L. L. BEAN. Bean's Collapsible Landing Net is one of the more convenient around for use with bigger boats. It has a 29-inch handle and the bow measures 16 inches by 18 inches. Has a 30-inch nylon net and it weighs only 15 ounces. The net wraps around the folded bow.

CASCADE LAKES. This company produces a nice series of very lightweight nets designed in both

ORVIS TAC-L-PAK

Another Orvis instant look-like-an-expert outfit. This one is equipped with leaders, angler's clip, leader conditioner, fly spray, Dry-N-Float, fly threader, plus selections of dry flies, wet flies, nymphs and all the others necessary to pass as an expert. More of a gift idea for the novice than what one gets into through the normal routes.

top of the line

teardrop and regular shapes. Made from various woods, including ash, cherry and mahogany, they are no chore to haul around on the back of your vest. Cascade also makes a very glamorous boat net with an 18-inch handle made from ash edged with cherry. Not many elegant boat nets around, but this one will make you the envy of your next bass tournament! Very good products.

ED CUMMINGS. Ed Cummings produces a complete line of nets geared mostly for the boat angler. Available in a variety of sizes with such optional features as telescoping handle. These nets, which will float when dunked, are a good buy. He also makes smaller models for the trout angler.

FIRESIDE ANGLER. Fireside Angler offers a decent wooden trout-landing net at a very reasonable price, something that's getting rarer. This one has a 10-inch wide by 14-inch long hoop holding up a 22-inch deep cotton net. An 18-inch lanyard is attached to the end.

INSTA-NET. A very convenient gadget. This net folds into a 5 by 5 inch leather holster on your belt. When you grab the handle, the spring steel frame untwists. It's not that hard to get back into the holster, either. Draw, partner. Available from Bud Lilly.

MOODUS ANGLER'S TOOL

One of those convenient tools that more fly anglers should carry. It works as a fly threader on dark evenings and aids in tying barrel knots, clinch knots, nail knots and needle knots as well. Only 4 inches long and ½ ounce. Well-made and functional. Dan Bailey's distributes them.

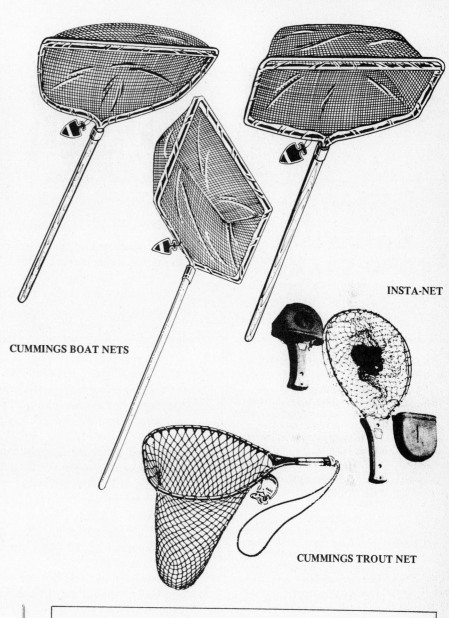

CUMMINGS BOAT NETS

INSTA-NET

CUMMINGS TROUT NET

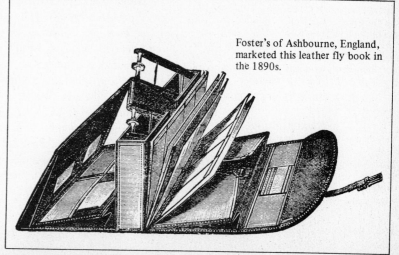

Foster's of Ashbourne, England, marketed this leather fly book in the 1890s.

GAMEFISH: COHO SALMON

NAMES
Silver salmon, hooknose. *(Oncorhynchus kisutch)*

DISTRIBUTION
The coho salmon is silver blue with silver sides, the upper sides of which are sprinkled with small, dark spots. During spawning, the males take on a reddish cast and in freshwater the fish turns quite dark.

SIZE
The average size of the coho salmon is around 6 to 10 pounds, although they do range as large as 30 pounds.

HABITAT
Like most salmon, the coho is a saltwater fish that ventures into fresh water during spawning season. They favor large rivers near the sea and bay areas. Puget Sound is one place where the coho is found in abundance.

FEEDING HABITS
The coho feeds primarily on baitfish, such as herring, and small crustaceans. Although they do not generally feed in freshwater, the coho usually stays close to the surface and therefore presents an excellent opportunity for the angler. They strike readily at artificial flies and fight enthusiastically. The best season for coho salmon is during the fall runs.

BEST FEEDING TEMPERATURE
Between 59° and 54°.

TACKLE
Fishing for the silver has been in great flux lately because of their introduction to the Great Lakes. Caught on all sorts of gear these days, mostly medium to heavy. Fly rods, bait-casting rods, spinning tackle and trolling gear work at various times.

THE LAST HATCH
A FISHING MYSTERY
HARMON HENKIN

(continued from page 84)

"Like I said on the phone, somebody took very serious objection to Halford and skewered him," Paul said.

"Hmmmm. Anything else?"

"Not really. I was fishing the Hole and he floated by, dragging a gaff with his neck."

Wormer grew impatient and cut into the conversation. "You're wasting your time, sheriff. He did it." Heads bobbed in agreement.

"Who are you, fella?"

"Wallace Wormer, land developer."

"Yeah, you were at that hearing last month. Thought I'd split a stitch when the Commissioner asked you whether you thought trout were worth anything and you said yes but they didn't sell as well as sardines."

Paul and the sheriff laughed but no one else saw anything funny. Wormer started to object but Sid cut him off.

"Look, dude, you don't say nothing unless I ask, understand? We don't cotton to no city slickers coming out here and telling us how to run things. Got it?"

That Sid had moved out six months before from Philadelphia didn't seem important to the proceedings. At any rate, the crowd had been bullied into silence.

"Now Paul, here, he told me he didn't kill Halford and I usually believe him. Of course that alleged 6-pound brown he said he caught last week at Tucker's Crossing on a Quill Gordon was a lie. But that's something else. Anyway, you folks the only ones around?"

Dun had calmed down enough to talk rationally. "No . . . sir." He hesitated since he wasn't quite sure whether he should address the scroungy constable with respect or arrogance. "There are these people plus four others somewhere on the place. A Belle Parmachene, her husband Edward Hewitt, Mr. Halford's angling companion Bernie Schielbacht, and another guest, um, a Miss Julie Berners."

They heard another siren.

"Well, me and Paul are going to mosey down to the creek to look things over." He pointed to Dun. "You go out and find the rest of this crew and don't let nobody leave, understand? I got the best tracking dogs in ten counties just waiting for work."

That his dogs were a pair of old Chesapeakes barely able on a clear

(continued on page 110)

FLY TACKLE FOR WESTERN FISHING

By Charles E. Brooks

In fly casting, whether north or south, east or west, you cast the *line* and you fish the *line*. In both cases the fly just goes along for the ride and the leader's supposed function is to promote better delivery of the fly while deceiving the fish into thinking that fly and line have no connection. So, fly fishing, wherever, starts with the proper line.

I splice my own fly lines because no manufacturer makes lines that exactly suit me. But lines have improved so much that my excuse is getting pretty lame. You can get a fly line nowadays that will do just about anything you want it to do.

My advice always is to buy the best line you can afford, even if you have to scrimp on the rest of your tackle. And to be completely equipped for all kinds of fly fishing in western waters, you need five kinds of fly lines: a double taper floating line, one with a 10-foot Hi-D sinktip; and a slow sinking, fast sinking and Hi-D line, each of which has a 30-foot sinking head, but floating shooting and running portions. All except the floater should be weight-forward types. Of course, if you confine your fishing to one type of water, or to one small stream, use any line that suits you.

What size? Out here in the wide open spaces, with big rivers and gale-force winds, at least a No. 7 and a No. 8 is better, especially if you use big nymphs and streamers. I prefer Scientific Anglers' lines because they are closer to those that I build myself, but any major brand that does what you want it to is fine. Scientific Anglers offers more kinds and types, however.

The purpose of the rod is to get the line out and the fish in. Give me an 8- or 8½-foot glass rod of good quality and medium price and I'm happy. I want it to handle a No. 8 line, and I'll equip it or have it equipped with foulproof spinning guides for ease in casting and shooting the line. Snake guides have been with us, unimproved, for about 100 years. Their demise is long overdue. As far as length, you can cast with less effort and *fish* the fly better with a longer rod (within reason) than you can a shorter one, other factors being equal. And this is true whether you are Lee Wulff, Arnold Gingrich, Doug Swisher or Joe Blow.

In a reel I want a simple design, quick take-apart single action with an adjustable drag, a click and perforated side plates. I want it large enough to carry a 30-foot No. 8 shooting head, 50 feet of floating shooting-running line and 50 yards of 20-pound test backing and still have a ½-inch clearance under the pillars. I don't want to be bothered looking at my reel while reeling in a large trout to see if the line is going to jam. So, I use a Pflueger Medalist 1495. It's the most reel for the money.

Leaders? For big nymphs in deep fast runs, short and stout. Six feet, 1X is as long and as fine as I'll go, and after a few fly changes I'm down to four feet, 0X which works better. For my slow and fast sinking lines, I'll go 7½ feet, 3X; no longer or finer and often shorter and heavier. For dry fly fishing, suit yourself. But Charles Ritz, one of the world's great fly fishers, fishes the dry fly on chalk streams with a 9-foot, 1X leader, or in very special cases, 2X. I think Charlie would do fine out here if he just knew how to handle a big, weighted stonefly nymph on a Hi-D line, and I could teach him that in ten minutes.

Illustrations taken from *Fly Tackle: A Guide to the Tools of the Trade* by Harmon Henkin. Copyright (C) 1976 by Harmon Henkin. Used by permission of the J. B. Lippincott Company.

HOW TO MAKE STREAMSIDE REPAIRS

By Richard Eggert

The easiest way to avoid streamside problems with tackle is to buy well-made equipment suited to your purposes and take care of it. But no matter how sturdy your tackle is or how careful you are with it, accidents do happen. And a broken rod, jammed reel or severed line can completely ruin a fishing trip.

Most tackle mishaps can be at least temporarily repaired with a simple, lightweight kit of materials and tools. The kit should include: a small tube of Pliobond cement, a stick of fast-reacting ferrule cement, a roll of waterproofed fabric patch, a small spool of nylon thread, a chunk of beeswax, a needle, a candle stub, a pair of spare guides, an oversized tip-top and a small screwdriver. All this stuff will fit neatly into a Bull Durham cigarette bag or a plastic cigarette box. For long trips such as hikes into mountain lakes, a couple tubes of epoxy cement could come in handy, but they are messy and will require another package.

The most common tackle disaster is a broken rod joint. However, with a hollow fiberglass rod, the fracture usually looks worse than it is. If it's a clean break, find a hardwood or green and healthy softwood stick of about the same diameter as the inside of the rod at the break. Cut the stick to about four inches in length and whittle the ends down so they will fit snugly into both ends of the fracture. Two inches of the stick should just barely fit into the upper portion of the break; the other two inches will be somewhat looser in the bottom section (the taper of the rod makes it impossible to get a really good fit). Generously apply Pliobond on the inside of the shank above and below the fracture and smear the glue over the entire surface of the stick. Wait five minutes, then jam the stick into the upper portion and gently force on the lower portion of the rod. Make sure that the splinters from the

break match when the rod goes together. Splint the rod with another stick wrapped to the outside with thread and let it set for an hour.

After the glue has set, remove the outside binding and wrap the fracture tightly with thread. Paint a coat of Pliobond over the wrap and let it set for another hour. It should be ready to fish but don't put too much stress on the mend because it's only slightly stronger than the stick.

If the rod breaks close to the top, it's impossible to internally support the fracture due to the narrow inside diameter. The only feasible emergency repair is to glue and wrap the oversize tip-top to the break.

A broken reel seat or reel ring is easily fixed by binding the reel foot to the handle cork (or whatever is left) with waxed thread.

Ferrules are the weak link in the flow of a rod. They seem to have an uncanny way of failing when you can least afford it. Metal ferrules are particularly annoying because they are supported entirely by glue at both connections with the shank. It's always wise before leaving on a long angling trip to check the windings at the ferrules for shriveled threads or splintered varnish.

But even with this precaution, it's not unusual to pick up a rattle or send a rod section sailing across the stream when the glue fails. If this happens, stop fishing immediately. Never try jamming the loose ferrule back on the shank. The wobbly metal end can splinter the rod joint in a few casts.

Remove the ferrule entirely. If it's just rattling and refuses to pull off, apply heat with the candle and gently pull it out. Scrape off the old glue on both the shank and the inside of the ferrule. Reseat the ferrule on the shank and try to wiggle it. If it seats firmly, remove it and apply Pliobond to both connecting surfaces. Wait five min-

This repairing outfit marketed in the early 1900s by Orvis contained most everything you'll need in a modern kit: wax, ferrule cement, varnish, brush, rod rings, keepers, ring tips, thread, needles, file, screwdriver, scissors and pocket oiler. It sold for $1.50.

(continued on page 104)

GAMEFISH: WHITE CRAPPIE

NAMES
Silver crappie, papermouth, strawberry bass, calico bass, bachelor, grass bass, speckled perch. *(Pomoxis annularis)*

DISTRIBUTION
The white crappie is found throughout the Great Lakes region, south into the Mississippi Valley, and in the southeastern part of the United States. It has also been extensively stocked in other areas.

DESCRIPTION
The white crappie is dark olive on the back with lighter sides. Dark marks form vertical lines on the sides of the body. The white crappie has a slightly arched back and 6 spines in the dorsal fin.

SIZE
Although there have been reports of white crappies weighing up to 5 pounds, the average is about ½ to 1 pound.

HABITAT
The white crappie is a fish of warm, weedy waters. It prefers large lakes and streams, ponds and cypress bayous. It likes to hide near sunken logs and weedbeds.

FEEDING HABITS
The crappie feeds primarily on gizzard shad and other small baitfish. They will also eat worms, crustaceans and insects. The white crappie can be found near the shallows come evening.

BEST FEEDING TEMPERATURE
Between 65° and 75°.

TACKLE
A school of white crappie will hit almost anything cast from light or ultra-light spinning rigs. Flies at times and stillfishing with live minnows is often the ticket. Jigs work well when deep.

Ed Garrison: the "amateur" builder

By Hoagy Carmichael, Jr.

Edmond Everett Garrison liked to think of himself as an "amateur" rod maker. And in the purest sense of the word, he was. He carried a full-time job as an engineer in New York City and did all of his rod making in the evenings and on the weekends. But it is estimated that in his lifetime he was able to produce some 700 exquisite rods.

"Garry" was born in Yonkers, New York, in 1893. After graduating from Union College in Syracuse he was interested in rod building by his friend, Dr. George Holden, who had written a guide called *The Idyle of the Split Bamboo.* Garry's education and work in engineering aided him greatly in later years as he developed his own rod tapers and experimented with new materials and the design of equipment.

To him the strength of the rod itself and its components was of prime importance. In the mid 1940s he began using the dark, wine-colored resorcinol resin glues which were 100 per cent waterproof and boilproof. The glue, when dry, left a dark line in the bamboo as it permeated the fibers. To many this was unsightly, but to Garry it was the best glue available and the mark of a rod that could withstand almost anything.

He also made his own aluminum cases out of tubing that was considerably thicker than any used by other makers. He had seen the good rods of several friends crushed by automobiles; although it was time-consuming to machine the end caps and fit the cases, he did so in the interest of strength. Garry often said that he considered himself a rod designer first and then, "because nobody else wanted to build them this way," a rod builder second.

Garry's interest in mechanical things also influenced other aspects of his rods. After toying with the desirability of the four, five, and six strip design he concluded the hexagon was the strongest and yet most practical geometric design for a bamboo rod.

Next, he began to think through the most logical displacement of the nodes — the weakest part, in terms of tensile strength, of each strip. His answer to the problem was novel and yet taken from the experiments done by the Ford Motor Company with the six-cylinder engine. In arriving at the final node displacement, he reordered the six strips, staggering the nodes equidistantly, to conform to the firing order of the six-cylinder engine — 1, 5, 3, 6, 2, 4. By doing so he got the desired effect, arranging the nodes (pistons) to gain the most (least) amount of strength (vibration).

Garry's work gives hope to other people interested in building bamboo fly rods. He developed a method of hand-planing his strips that allowed him to hold tolerances to within .001 inch, without the use of expensive beveling and milling machines. And he was able to make most of his own tools and small machines — the gluing binder, heat-treater and varnishing machine. He had to buy only one machine, a lathe, and some of the needed accessories.

The details of Garry's innovative techniques can be found in his book, *A Master's Guide to Building a Bamboo Fly Rod.*

HIS RODS COULD WITH~STAND ALMOST ANYTHING

The Trade

By Harmon Henkin

It took me years to get it away from the old man.

The rod had collected cobwebs in his attic for a long time. He was of the old long-rod school of fly fishermen — and the six-foot cane stick wasn't exactly his ideal, especially in trout-poor Maryland. He had won it in some sort of contest in the 1940s. It had never even carried a line. I first saw it in 1963 when I got into fly fishing. The old man was an expert tier, especially of streamers, and sold them for a piddling quarter apiece complete with genuine junglecock. He was the suspicious sort, having once been burned by being too open. The local newspaper had run a feature on his wondrous creations and how he sold them in his spare time to pick up loose change. The charmers from the Internal Revenue Office in Baltimore had visited him the next day demanding an account of his unregistered income. So he was justifiably suspicious. He wanted payment in cash and all that.

In the midst of a discussion about fly rods, in which I was lauding the qualities of bamboo (even though I had never owned a wood rod), he went upstairs and brought down this fine old Heddon. It dazzled me. I wanted it. But my impoverished offerings didn't bat his eye.

He put it away.

Every time I went over for flies or

idle angling chatter I tried to pry the rod away. I went away to school in Michigan but visited Baltimore often during breaks. On one of those occasions I had lots of spare cash from some minor writing job or another so I went off on my pilgrimage to the old man again. I plied him with trout fishing anecdotes of northern Michigan, which seemed to me at the time to be a wilderness — at least compared to Maryland.

He was a sharp fellow and knew where these trout tales were heading — to the Heddon. It was by now a fixation with me. I had never cast it but knew instinctively that it was perfection. The old man's heart warmed a bit, especially after finding out that I was finally willing to cough up $50. That was a steep price for a cane rod in those days but I gladly paid him and rushed back to Michigan.

But before I even had a chance to try it out during that wet spring, I met Richard Eggert, an incipient tackle fanatic as least as wild as me. We met on a small lake near school on a day that we were supposed to be cramming for

finals. We started talking about angling and its accouterments as time drifted by.

At dark we were back in my stuffy apartment where I was showing him my tackle. To make things worse we discovered that we loved to trade gear. Things didn't really get perking until he saw the little Heddon. His reaction was the same as mine had been.

No. Of course I didn't want to get rid of it. I hadn't even tried it. The potlatch began.

It started simply enough but Dick kept adding things to his offer. By early in the a.m., it was wild and woolly. We needed a piece of paper to keep track of all the minor goodies he was throwing in. Then there came the proverbial straw. A sleeping bag. The last one I had owned was a piece of what I considered rightfully part of my Marine Corps mustering-out pay. But a black bear in Yellowstone had thought it obnoxious and had torn it apart two years before when I was hitching through.

That did it. I reluctantly agreed. The long-sought-after rod was Dick's.

At sunrise Dick rushed to a nearby stream to try it out. It broke in half. It must have been structurally weak. Dick's glorious two-piecer was now a three-piecer.

He called me up with the news. I was half glad it was out of my life. My sorrow over trading it had been fierce.

It's been over ten years now and Dick and I are neighbors in Montana. And, yes, we still trade tackle like maniacs. But whenever we're about to close a deal, Dick gets that funny look in his eye. Suspicion.

He still thinks I knew the Heddon was a goner.

(continued from page 102)

STREAMSIDE REPAIRS

utes and reseat it by pushing it against a hard object such as a tree.

If the ferrule is loose or wobbly when you seat it dry, you're going to have to tighten the connection. Glue the shank joint and lay crossed pieces of thread lengthwise over the end of the section. This will act as both a filler and a shock absorber. If the ferrule still does not set snugly, wrap the rod end until the ferrule barely clears the first

winds. Apply glue over the threads and the inside of the ferrule, then drive it home.

Fly reels are sturdy and generally so simple that they're practically indestructible. Spinning and bait reels, on the other hand, rely on a lot of gearing and fragile parts and are subject to sudden malfunctions. The only way to correct a break or a jam, other than carrying spare parts, is to

(continued on page 109)

"... you will search far to find a fisherman to admit that a taste for fishing, like a taste for liquor, must be governed lest it come to possess its possessor." **SPARSE GREY HACKLE**

TACKLE BUILDING, MAINTENANCE & REPAIR 105

top of the line

Guides

FUJI

AETNA FOULPROOF. The Gudebrod Company is selling these guides and tip-tops for every kind of rod imaginable. They traditionally have been considered very good, especially for fly rods, when distance is what you're after. Much larger than snake guides, they flex with the rod. Designed for all practical purposes, they're at least as good as today's vaunted ceramic guides.

AETNA

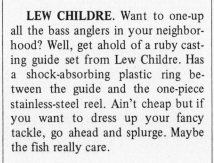

CHILDRE

LEW CHILDRE. Want to one-up all the bass anglers in your neighborhood? Well, get ahold of a ruby casting guide set from Lew Childre. Has a shock-absorbing plastic ring between the guide and the one-piece stainless-steel reel. Ain't cheap but if you want to dress up your fancy tackle, go ahead and splurge. Maybe the fish really care.

FUJI. Another interesting idea from the Fuji Speed-Stick people is a folding series of guides designed to make spinning rods more portable. Stainless steel, it folds flat. Such guides were commonplace in the 19th Century, proving once again the cyclic nature of things.

MILDRUM. Mildrum is one of those companies that has been around making quality items for a long time. Their guides and tip-tops are available for every sort of rod and are good quality. They have recently put out a line of ceramic guides that are favored by many anglers enamored of the new technology. They also make some excellent roller guides and double rollers for the big game freak.

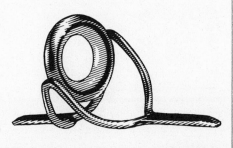

MILDRUM

FENWICK ROD BUILDER'S HANDBOOK

Fenwick's *Rod Builder's Handbook and Blank Catalog* is a good starting point for the rod-making amateur. Lots of blanks for sale plus detailed step-by-step instructions for spinning rod construction and some information on other rods for casting, surf spinning, salmon/steelhead and fly fishing. Also descriptions on how to make the popular diamond wraps.

top of the line

PUCCI. Manufactured in Italy, these guides are made of hard chrome steel. They're extremely lightweight — a set of seven for spinning weighs less than a quarter of an ounce. Long lasting. Should be considered by the serious ultra-light rod builder.

PUCCI GLADIATOR. The Pucci Company is importing from Europe a line of top-quality roller guides and tip-tops made from anodized aluminum with animated nylon bearings. Available in ranges for rods up to 20-pound test and also for unlimited test lines under IGFA standards. Good materials.

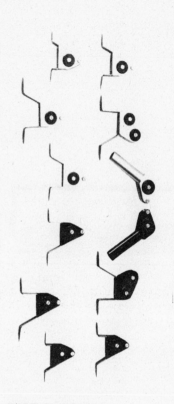

PUCCI GLADIATOR

Materials

GENE BULLARD. Gene Bullard Custom Rods, in good old Dallas, sells a wide variety of glass and graphite blanks as well as all the other features necessary for building your own sticks. Nice selection of rods, grips and handles.

DALE CLEMENS. Dale Clemens, who has written an extensive book on the subject, is running a shop in Allentown, Pennsylvania, that has everything you need to build your own rod in either glass or graphite. With both Lamiglass and Fenwick graphite and glass blanks plus a large variety of accessories ranging from walnut fly-reel seats — an absolute delight — to magnugrip locking spinning reel rings to Fuji stainless-steel reel seats. He also sells flies, rod holders, walnut hosels and butt caps, burnt cork and walnut trim rings and prefinished handles. Quite a shop.

COREN'S. Coren's in Chicago sells a very good variety of rod-build-

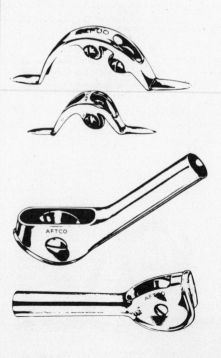

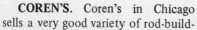

top of the line

ing materials. You have your choice of Fenwick, Browning or Lew Childre's speed stick rod blanks as well as featherweight rawhide blanks. They sell a big variety of guides, ferrules and custom rod kits as well.

J. LEE CUDDY ASSOCIATES. J. Lee Cuddy Associates provides an excellent service for the rod builder, especially those putting together saltwater or heavy freshwater tackle. They sell Lamiglass glass and graphite blanks, Fisher graphite blanks and one of their own making. They also sell a complete line of guides, tiptops and reel seats and finishing equipment such as varnish, winding checks and wrappings. Everything you need to put together a top-quality rod and save yourself money.

HILLE'S. Hille's may not boast the most beautiful catalog of rod building supplies but it sure has one of the most complete. They have their own brand graphite rod kits and blanks, a multitude of glass blanks and every sort of construction aid and accessory you could want. An excellent assortment of stuff for the home builder and the home tier.

MIKE REIDEL'S BAMBOO BLANKS. Mike Reidel has begun selling sets of bamboo blanks with hand-lapped ferrules and two tips. Guaranteed for a year. They range from a 6½ footer for a No. 4 line with dry fly action to an 8½ footer for No. 8 with a parabolic power action. Not cheap but neither are finished bamboo rods or, for that matter, are loaves of bread. He'll also provide the hardware and repair your damaged rods. Strictly a low-key sidelight for him.

SCOTT POWR PLY KITS. If you're not ready to move up to the

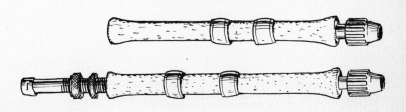

SPINNING AND FLY ROD HANDLES FROM HILLE'S

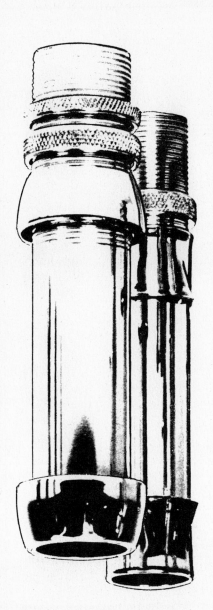

CUDDY

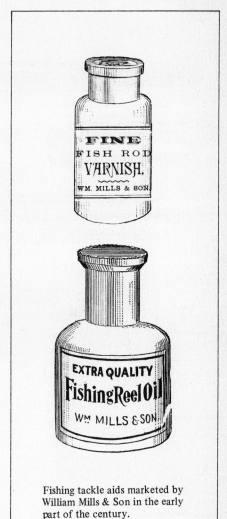

Fishing tackle aids marketed by William Mills & Son in the early part of the century.

Fiberglass Rod Making
By Don McLain

Don McLain's 89-page booklet is another one of the recent little publications about rod making, a subject that has become very popular. Fully illustrated, it goes into all the basics of various kinds of rods from steelhead to fly and into detail about things like ferruling the blank, guide wrapping, rod repair and rod refinishing. A good starting place.

"Inch for inch and pound for pound, that gamest fish that swims."
JAMES A. HENSHALL, *Book of the Black Bass*

top of the line

advanced intricacies of fiberglass rod building, you might get started with a Scott Powr Ply Kit. The rods are essentially complete, except for winding thread and varnish. Very nice glass fly rods. A whole bunch of models are available from 7 feet to 9 feet, 3 inches. Not cheap but good products for anglers who want a smooth-casting rod that can be completed at home. Available from Fireside Angler.

SHAKESPEARE GRAPHITE BLANKS. The Shakespeare Company, which is one of the pioneers of graphite, sells Howald process graphite blanks and Howald process fiberglass blanks for the custom builder. These blanks are double-built with a continual spiral fiber. They are available from Shakespeare in a variety of sizes for just about every type of angler.

SCHOFF'S. A good source for the amateur rod builder for all kinds of supplies, including Lamiglass, graphite and fiberglass blanks, hordes of reel seats and handles, guides, etc. In short, everything to build your own. The Kent, Washington, outfit, which also has fly tying equipment, features Fuji ceramic guides, very popular among the technologically oriented anglers.

3M GRAPHITE BLANKS. The 3M Company, which owns Scientific Angler and Phillipson among other diversified concerns, is now marketing their own graphite blanks. They have an internal metal ferrule and are available in line sizes from No. 4 to No. 11 in a brownish finish. We've waited for them a long time. They have a lifetime warranty.

ROD HANDLES
AND CORK
FROM SCHOFF'S

FUJI GUIDES FROM SCHOFF'S

top of the line

THOMPSON ROD WINDER. The last word for the home rod builder is a rod winder from the Thompson people, who have been building such equipment for a long time. The winder clamps onto your bench and holds the spool of nylon or silk at an adjustable tension leaving both hands free. A good product.

VARMAC. The Varmac manufacturing company of L. A. produces a line of what they call rod jewelry. They make such things as ceramic guides with aluminum oxide, carboloy guides (which used to be so popular), snake guides and more or less standard spinning rod guides. They also make aluminum reel seats for any sort of fishing as well as chrome-plated solid brass reel seats for heavy duty use, and are a very fine quality. Also other rod handles and miscellaneous.

IKE'S FLY SHOP. Ike's Fly Shop has gotten ahold of some reasonably priced bamboo blanks from 5½ to 9½ feet long, available in either natural color or burnished. All are two pieces except the single-piece 5½-footer. These blanks have a hand-made serrated ferrule. English birch or rosewood reel seats are also available. A fine way for the home builder to get into the intricacies of rod building.

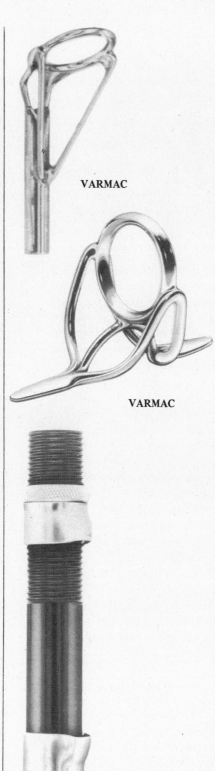

VARMAC

VARMAC

VARMAC

STREAMSIDE REPAIRS

(continued from page 104)

know your tackle well enough to catch problems before you begin fishing.

Conversely; spinning and bait lines are simple — remedying a break is no problem. Fly lines, however, are perhaps the most critical part of the equipment and a broken or peeled line could be a disaster. If you use a double-tapered line, simply reverse the taper on the reel so that the injured portion is not used. A broken taper on a weight forward, however, leaves you with only a thin running line to drive your fly.

To mend a broken synthetic-coated fly-line, scrape the coating off the core for about one inch on either side of the break. Smear the two exposed cores with Pliobond and cement them together side by side. Wax a piece of thread, wrap the exposed cores with it and coat the wrapping with Pliobond. The splice will create a perceptible lump in the line but will probably outlast the coating.

Wader punctures can be permanently mended with a patch made from the waterproofed nylon in your kit and Pliobond. After bonding the patch to the hole (from the inside of the wader if possible) coat it with more Pliobond.

Pliobond can also be used as a head cement on fraying flies, touch-up varnish on rods, to rebind the coating on a fly line and to repair any waterproof equipment such as tents and raincoats.

Wax is handy to re-whip flies, tighten loose male-female ferrule connections (especially on glass-to-glass ferrules) and to add friction to a reel (helpful if a fly spool becomes loose in its bearing or you break a click-cog).

The needle and thread can mend rips in clothing or waterproofs. The thread alone can wrap a new guide on a rod and repair unstrung flies. The needle alone can be used for tying nail knots in the line-leader connection or knots in leaders.

Melt-on ferrule cement provides a fast although brittle bond for just about anything that breaks.

These few materials and tools, along with a good understanding of how your tackle functions, can keep you fishing through just about any minor tragedy.

(continued from page 100)

day to find a wounded goose didn't matter either. Everyone seemed impressed. Paul got up and joined the sheriff walking out the door. An ambulance from the County Seat at Hamilton was parking in the driveway in front of a couple silver Mercedes, a Volvo station wagon and a vintage Beetle. The drivers ambled out and almost came to attention when they saw Sid.

"You boys bring your stretcher and get on down to the river with us."

"Your accent is getting atrocious, Sid," Paul said when they were on the path. "Those *Gunsmoke* re-runs are frying your brain."

"Well, damn, Paul. Who would respect me if they knew I was one of the first men to graduate from Vassar? My mother and her stupid school loyalty."

Trout were rising everywhere on the meandering creek, which is known in England as a chalkstream. It was lined with watercress and other aquatic vegetation — an ideal trout habitat the 19th Century British originators of fly fishing would have swooned over. Insects abounded and hatches occurred almost daily year-round. Since all the water originated in a large gurgling spring a mile upstream there was no muddy, early-season runoff or rapid temperature changes. Halford had picked up an angling paradise for peanuts.

There were two paths running along the bank, one right by the edge and another ten feet back. Expert anglers favored the second one since any untoward vibration on the bank was enough to spook the bigger fish. Paul and Sid took the back path almost instinctively.

"Wish we were fishing, Paul."

"Halford never let anyone except his putrid circle of friends in here. What a waste. He posted the whole thing the day he bought it."

Sid nodded. "You know, there's gonna be lots of trouble over this murder. Not that the bastard didn't deserve it. Christ! A trailer court here? What a load of crap. Can't believe he needed the money that bad."

"Yeah, it's going to be a bad stink — wow! . . . look at that brown!"

They stopped and stared goggle-eyed at a 4-pound trout rising lazily to gorge itself on a large yellow mayfly.

(continued on page 112)

GAMEFISH: BROOK TROUT

NAMES
Eastern brook trout, speckled trout, speck, squaretail, brookie. *(Salvelinus fontinalis)*

DISTRIBUTION
The brook trout was originally found only in the eastern part of the American continent from southern Canada into Georgia. Due to its transplantation, it is now found in almost all of the northwestern states. Native brookies, however, are disappearing due to the pressures of civilization and pollution.

DESCRIPTION
Actually a member of the Char family, the brook trout is perhaps America's best loved game fish. It is an active fish of dark green or brown coloring on the back with vermicular markings and numerous yellow and red spots on the sides, each encircled by a ring of light blue. The belly is white except during spawning when the belly of the male turns pink or red in hue. The tail is almost square in shape.

SIZE
The size of the brook trout depends on where it lives. In larger lakes, catches of up to 14 pounds have been recorded but usually a brook trout will not weigh more than 2 to 5 pounds. In small streams, a fish weighing ½ pound will be a normal catch.

HABITAT
The brook trout prefers clear, cold, fast-moving streams and creeks. It tends to seek out deep pools where it can lie close to the bottom. They can also be found in clear, cold lakes.

FEEDING HABITS
Insects, insect larvae and small crustaceans comprise the bulk of the brook trout's diet. They do, however, eat other fish, including baitfish and minnows.

BEST FEEDING TEMPERATURE
Between 50° and 65°.

TACKLE
Unless it's in deep lakes, a light fly outfit with colorful wets or dries or hatch-matching flies will be the ticket. Ultra-light fly outfits with small spinners or spoons or tiny Flatfish can also work quite well. It's really a fly rod fish, however.

HOW TO AVOID BURNS
ON THE BULLISH USED CANE MARKET

By Richard Eggert

The used bamboo rod trade has not made it on the commodity board of the New York Stock Exchange but it's one of the few gambles that show a consistently high return on any angler's investment.

Rods that sold for $150 two years ago are going for $250 and more today. Like all limited resources, bamboo rods appreciate with the loss of the artisan. Ev Garrison's rare sticks shot up 200 to 300 per cent in value following his death.

Used cane is one of the few bullish markets around — complete with sacred cows, slaughterhouses, beef watering and bum calves. Although there is no reason to believe that genuine rods from several makers will not continue to increase in value, it is possible to get burned on a phony or an overpriced original.

In fact, the demand for used cane fly rods far exceeds the supply and the prices for the best rods are so high that the vacuum naturally invites fakes. Like Navajo jewelry, Western art and Tiffany lamps, fine vintage fly rods are being forged by clever craftsmen.

A cane fly rod is a comparatively simple tool, and the differences between a Jim Payne (perhaps the best and most consistently valued rod ever made) and the good but second-rate Heddons are so minute that even experts would have a difficult time distinguishing a well-dressed fake. Heddon canes looked very much like Paynes; remounted with Payne hardware and colors, a $50 Heddon could easily be confused with a $600 Payne.

The marketplace for used fly rods also creates a situation ripe for large-scale fakery. The prospective used-rod buyer can't go to his local antique store to take his pick of second-hand Leonards — he must correspond with one of a handful of used-rod brokers. Most of these brokers are reasonably honest and relatively knowledgeable, but fakes or doctored originals have gotten by them. The mail order customer can be hung up for months exchanging suspicious or unsatisfactory rods through the slow and precarious mails.

If a phony is good enough to fool both the broker and the investor, chances are it will be good enough to fool a prospective customer when the owner decides to cash in on his investment. But for the angler buying a used cane rod to fish with, a fake will prove expensive. Paynes, for instance, are valuable not only because they are exquisitely pretty, but also because of their famous functionality and durability. A phony Payne, no matter how elegant, will not cast or last like a genuine one.

What protection does the prospective buyer have then?

There is probably no way of being absolutely sure the gleaming wand that came in the morning mail is genuine. But you can eliminate most of the outright fakes and white elephants by knowing what to expect in a vintage rod, something about second-hand rod condition and as much as possible about the maker and his style.

Collectors and investors have their own reasons for buying a used cane rod but the prospective bamboo fisher should examine his motives and needs carefully.

The prospective cane angler should decide what to expect of his new rod: what size and weight to buy. About the only functional advantage (and a fairly obscure one at that) of bamboo over synthetics is the personality of better cane rods. An 8-foot five or six line glass rod will cast as far as efficiently for most anglers as the greatest bamboo ever built. But each bamboo rod has its own personality and each model is cast into a character role. For instance, the famous Leonard 50df is cool and patient and will do just about everything for the caster but tie on the fly. Jim Payne's celebrated 200, another 8-foot, five or six line rod, is much quicker and more demanding but gives the fisherman more volition in the cast. The same could be said of Leonard's modified 50 "Hunt" and the Thomas dry fly action 8-footer. These are dominant rod actions which have their own pace and style which the angler must conform to.

With Paul H. Young's fabulous Perfectionist 7½ footer, on the other hand, the fisherman must do all the work. The

(continued on next page)

AVOID USED BAMBOO BURNS

(continued from preceding page)

rod is just a passive lever. Most of Young's "P" designated rods and the parabolic rods of other makers are also designed to accent the angler's strengths and weaknesses.

The next step is finding a selection of rods. Persons living in the general New York-New England area are within casting distance of most of the cane rod brokers. With the prospect of spending from $250 to as much as $1,000 for a new rod, it might be a good idea to spend some time and gas looking over the pick. Provincial anglers are going to have to shop by mail. (There are, however, some good brokers west of the Hudson.) Examine the descriptions carefully. Most brokers seem to be relatively honest about the physical condition of a rod but don't fall for the common line that a 2-inch short mid or 3-inch short tip will "fish beautifully."

If you can examine the rod — all mail order brokers offer a return privilege — check the cane first and check it carefully. If it's been "refinished like new," look at it even more carefully with a magnifying glass.

Make sure the sections of the rod stack up evenly. Most American makers cut all sections exactly even. Some British rods have slightly longer or shorter tips. The "butt biased" design is characterized by a much longer tip.

Run your thumbnail along each seam from end to end watching for "glue lines," discolorations along the seam (some makers such as Garrison and Phillipson used glues which stained the cane along the seam) and "open joints" — places where the strips have separated.

While you're at it, look for cracks or fractures in the flat surface of the strips. They're often found at the nodes.

Put the rod together and sight down it. Is it straight? An even "set" or curve is no big deal, but it should be reflected in the price. If, however, it shows *sharp* sets (probably at the fer-

(continued on page 121)

THE LAST HATCH
A FISHING MYSTERY
HARMON HENKIN

(continued from page 110)

"I could have nailed him with one cast using a light Cahill," Sid declared.

Paul gave him a double-take.

"The way you handle a fly rod?"

"You insulting a law officer, boy?"

"No. Insulting a hack angler."

"Well, you should be more considerate. Halford's an important man. Everybody in the world knew who he was. There's going to be reporters, TV people and the rest. And they'll all expect me to find out who did it."

"Just use your police science skills and forensic laboratory resources."

"What the Hell you talking about? I majored in poetry and was a cook in the Army. The city council didn't care. What did you major in?"

"Ichthyology."

The sheriff looked at him glumly.

"Fish, huh? No wonder."

They approached the fence that marked the outer edge of Halford's property. A small brown caddis fly was fluttering above the creek laying its eggs. Trout probably prefer the taste of mayflies but wouldn't turn down a caddis if offered, as more and more anglers had been discovering. They climbed through the wire and Sid snagged his shirt momentarily on a barb. The vibrations carried into the water and alarmed some trout, which hesitated in their incessant munching.

"What am I going to do, Paul? I don't want to go back to graduate school in Philadelphia. What a drag. I'm having a good time out here."

"Is it too late for you to enroll in the Famous Policemen's School?"

The body was where Paul had left it. For a moment Paul suffered a bout of pure paranoia in which he feared he had imagined the whole thing. He looked Halford over carefully for the first time. Other than seeing him occasionally in town, on TV talk shows or on book jackets, Paul had never given him more than a once-over. He was wearing his traditional bushjacket, the one he wore when he wasn't sporting his Northwoods Parka. What was he, about 55? Trimmed mustache and a Vandyke beard. His usual sneer was unchanged even by death. He had on a pair of Leonard fishing pants and Russell leather wading shoes with felt bottoms for gripping slippery rocks. Nothing but the top

(continued on page 126)

ELEGANT ANTIQUES ARE NOT PRACTICAL

By Harmon Henkin

It's gotten out of hand. The price of used rods like Paynes, Garrisons, Dickersons and others is out of line, considering their worth as practical fishing tools. In fact, for most part these elegant antiques are simply not that good for the modern angler. At least not good enough to warrant a $500-plus price tag.

Now this isn't to say there aren't solid reasons why an angler might really want the organic feel of a highly specialized cane rod. They certainly have a sensitivity and delicacy not available in even the best glass rods. But angling fashions and trends are a reality, for reasons of snobbishness and because new and advanced strategies develop. We have just witnessed and shaped a decade of incredibly rapid tactical changes in fly fishing. Nymph and emerger fishing has become refined to a degree not possible 25 years ago and new lines have made distance casting possible for all anglers.

When the great rod makers like Payne and Garrison — and they were the greatest — were building their creations, much of the sport revolved around dry fly fishing with flies in the No. 12 to No. 16 range that imitated the common Eastern hatches. The masters' rods were primarily designed for this task and performed their duties wonderfully.

But it's a different game now. Fly fishing is more versatile, less dogmatic. And most of the finest bamboo rods I've seen are not as good for modern fly fishing as a well-made production glass rod, not to mention a fine modern cane rod by Winston, Thomas and Thomas, Orvis or the like. These rods are designed for contemporary conditions.

The problem with almost all vintage rods is that they are either very tippy, which makes for line overloading and a difficulty in controlling free-floating nymphs, or they have very soft wet fly actions, which are simply ridiculous to handle. Some of the short Paynes and Garrisons were stiff "rug beaters" and very, very few of their models had the rich uniform action favored by most anglers today. There are exceptions to this generalization, of course, but you can't be sure that just because a rod is a master's it's good.

The ferrules of modern rods aren't as finely made, aren't finished as delicately and don't have the overall workmanship of the classics but they're better rods for the angler who fishes everything from midges to weighted nymphs with synthetic fly lines.

The reasons that prices have soared for the masters' rods are complex but center around supply and demand, elitism and the perpetual search for a viable tradition in this society. Regardless of the reasons, the market has become a used rod dealer's delight. As the prices of the classics soar, they drag the tab for lesser used rods along with them.

So what it boils down to is that if you want a rod to wave in your friends' faces get a Payne or Garrison or their kin. If you want a versatile fly casting rod, don't.

> The problem with vintage rods is that they're either too tippy or they have very soft actions.

GOOD REASONS TO COLLECT TACKLE

By Mary K. Shepard

A simple case of love.

An American angler writing in 1884 in the *New York Spirit of the Times* extolled his new, two-butted general rod in terms so glowing one might think he was describing a new mistress. "Look at the silvery tippings of those butts," he wrote. "Gaze upon the graceful form of those joints. See the oily smoothness of those guides!"

Well, in the past 92 years times have changed some. Extinct is the much favored general rod, a preponderous affair with multiple, interchangeable joints, and at least one of the two butts hollowed to store spare tips. No longer do rods weigh up to three pounds. Snake guides replace the old ring and keeper guides. Yet, one thing has remained constant: an angler's passion for fishing rods.

Ask ten fishers why all the fervor over rods and you'll get ten different answers. And really the why is not important. The fact is: anglers feel a close, personal attachment to their rods — they warm to the look and feel of a favored one, excite to the touch of a new, untried one. On this basis alone one collects rods.

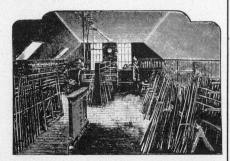

Some become students.

Most people get only casually involved in angling history. Often they simply want to know something about their grandfather's memorabilia. Or possibly learn enough to buy the correct vintage reel to display with grandfather's rod.

But there are those who become so deeply involved and curious about angling history that they become students. The student of rods has an insatiable appetite. He wants a rod of every type, a general, the Henshall black bass rod, the striper, the fly rod. Too, he must have at least one rod by every maker, John Conroy, the Welches, Pritchards, Landman, Wheeler, Leonard and so on.

A kind of peace.

In England, where tradition prevails and preservation is the challenge, the Walton-Cotton fishing house, built in the late 1600s, continues its vigil overlooking the Dove River. Multitudes of anglers visit this area every year, and many report that while at this ancient, hallowed site, where Walton, Cotton and countless unknown others have trod and fished, they were drawn back through the centuries to a rare tranquillity.

Well, today's world and what will happen tomorrow are uncertain, unsettling. But what happened yesterday is done. One does not lie awake and worry over the Great Depression of 1876. Many, therefore, collect old rods as a relief from today's tensions. In handling a century old rod, identifying with its place in time, one enjoys the same kind of peace that's found at the Walton-Cotton house.

Rod building is an art.

There is a story making the rounds that a rod maker so successfully learned to fit together the six strips of bamboo, his rods showed no visible glue lines. This made his customers unhappy because they liked to see seam lines, a natural part of the rod. The rod maker, therefore, had to backtrack, and again make the joints visible.

I don't believe this tale, but it does bring up a point: the craftsmanship and artistry involved in rod building. In fact some feel the fine rod builder has the same skill, sensitivity, and perspective as an artist or sculptor. Therefore, as some want oil paintings or sculptures, others want rods.

Money.

Money is involved in rod collecting, and anyone who has been in the field for any length of time has seen prices double and triple. For example, five years ago an H. L. Leonard rod of the 1920 period could be had for $50 or less. Now they're going for $150 and upwards. Many people, therefore, feeling prices will continue to climb, are buying rods as an investment.

top of the line

Second Hand Cane

By Richard Eggert

DICKINSON. Another Detroit rod, somewhat more elegant than Young's but more traditional in engineering. Darkened cane is normally spiral-noded, similar to Paynes.

EDWARDS. Billy Edwards was another Leonard breakaway who started making good quality six-strip cane rods in coastal Connecticut. These rods, sometimes marketed under the Bristol label, are usually random-noded, darkened cane with a swelled butt. The hardware and finish were extremely well done and they are a good buy at $150 if you can find one that suits your needs.

Gene Edwards, the son of Billy, took the edges off the business when he inherited it at mid-century and took two corners off the cane. His four sided "quadrate" rods are unmistakable and good fishers for those who like to push their tackle. They tend to fetch a bit more than the six strippers, about $200.

ENGLISH RODS. English rods are fairly common on brokers' lists and in general they are good quality and good buys. Hardys, the most famous and abundant, generally sell from $150 to $200.

Most Hardys are extremely well-built, well-appointed rods (although some later models show a discernible drop in overall quality). Most Hardy rods, however, were designed for English angling and English tastes — Americans have a hard time getting used to them. Exceptions are the Deluxe and Marvels, which were specifically designed for American use, and the Jubilee and Fairchilds, which adapt well to the colonies. Stay away from early steel-centered rods, however.

Hardys are made of light, English-noded cane without a butt swell.

Most other English rods such as Farlow, Constable, Sharpe (which is now making impregnated blanks for several American firms), Sealy and the elegant Ogden Smith, are similarly built but generally cheaper.

GARRISON. The clean, unscratched and unstained cane of a Garrison was made with two nodes opposing each other all the way up the rod. This technique was also used by Young and E. C. Powell but they darkened the cane. A unique feature of Garrisons is the "mirrored" tips. Both tips were cut from the same culms of cane and glued together exactly the same way, which is one of the reasons Garrisons are perhaps the most desirable rods today. These rods are usually not swelled at the handle and are normally clear-wrapped at the guides. Garrisons also have very distinct glue lines showing all the way up the rod.

GILLUMS. Pinky Gillum, a close friend and sometime associate of Jim Payne, made a handful of very valuable Payne look-alikes under his own name. Gillum is known for his fanatical standards in cane — Ev Garrison once said that he found some of his best bamboo rummaging around in Gillum's discards.

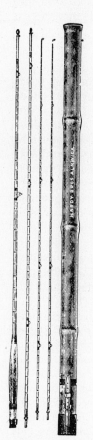

A Hardy 3-piece Palakona with two tips, designed between 1910 and 1919 for S.W. Fairchild.

A Collapsible butt spear was fitted into Hardy Brothers' rods in the early part of the century.

"The pleasant'st angling is to see the fish
cut with her golden oars the silver stream,
And greedily devour the treacherous bait."
SHAKESPEARE, *Much Ado About Nothing*

top of the line

GRANGER. Granger slid through the peculiar evolution of making a lot of rods with a number of different names on them, then having other firms make rods with his name on them. In the 20s and 30s Granger made several models of his own good quality rods as well as shop rods for L. L. Bean, Abercrombie & Fitch, FL & A and others. The shop was then taken over by Wright & McGill who continued to make lesser quality Granger rods — usually marked Wright-McGill and Granger.

Most of the Denver-made rod models were hard and tough for western fishing but Granger also produced some really delightful light actions. The three-piece eight-foot light is like a laid-back Leonard 50df, casting the tightest and gentlest five line imaginable.

Granger cane was identical to Leonard but darkened. Ferrules were fine quality "punched," made from one piece of nickel silver. Reel seats started out as delicate slide-band on silver, later evolving into a heavy, ugly screw caning device. But they're still among the best second hand buys, selling from $100 to $150 for originals and $50 to $100 for Wright McGills.

HAWES. Hiram Hawes was a son-in-law and associate of Hiram Leonard until he broke away in the early 1900s to make rods under his own shingle in those rich Hudson River Highlands near Leonard and Payne. His rods were exquisitely over-crafted Leonards but they are so rare they can hardly be regarded as fishable second hand rods.

HEDDON. The James Heddon shop at Dowagiac, Michigan, has made a lot of respectable tackle in its long history, including exquisite bait rods and very good fly rods. Heddon, like Granger, made rods for several retailers as well as a range of grades under its own name.

The better grades of Heddons sold for as much as Leonards in the 30s and still fetch fairly extravagant prices. Lesser grades were lesser.

Many anglers can't adjust to Heddon actions, which tend to be extremely fast-tipped in dry-fly models and unmanageably whippy in wet-fly rods.

However, Heddons are usually quite presentable with a fine finish over darkened, butt-swelled, spiral-noded cane. Ferrules ranged from barely adequate to jewelry-quality silver, as did the reel seat hardware.

LEONARD. Hiram Leonard and his descendants have probably made more fine rods than any other shop. Leonard began making Calcutta cane rods in Bangor, Maine, in the 1870s and the shop, which subsequently moved to Central Valley, New York, has ever since been making rods at various prices. There were probably hundreds of thousands made and tens of thousands are still in use. And Leonard, due to a succession of really brilliant marketers and designers such as Arthur Mills, of the William Mills & Son store in New York, produced virtually hundreds of usable modern designs.

Leonards were considered easily good enough for the likes of English master G. E. M. Skues and America's favorite sons — Theodore Gordon and George LaBranche — and at times during their long history were altogether as good as Paynes. The current used value of a Leonard is about half that of a comparable Payne which, together with the greater variety of Leonards, most brokers offer, makes them a really good buy in a first-rate rod.

Leonard caning is distinctive and

Leonard won gold medals for its split bamboo rods at an international exhibition in 1883.

(continued on next page)

top of the line

difficult to doctor. From about the turn of the century, the shop used the so-called "English" noding system. They cut three strips for each rod section from two different culns and lined them up so that strips from different culns were adjacent. The result is a section with three nodes on alternating flats at one point of the section spaced by several inches with another series of alternating nodes. The system absolutely ensures against two nodes being located side by side and creates uniform loading along the length of the section. Payne and some other rod builders objected to this method because it concentrated the three noded stress points. But a lot of very fine rod makers used it including Granger, Phillipson, Hardy and most English makers, and even Thomas on their better rods.

Leonard, along with Thomas, Granger and Phillipson, built swells into the butt just ahead of the handle to break off the action. The later three normally, but not always, darkened their cane, while Leonards were usually left pale blond. Some Leonards, such as the rare Hunt trout and salmon rods, have stained bamboo.

Leonard hardware was as well-crafted as anybody's although not as dandy as some. The ferrules were always pinned (in the barrel of the male and halfway through the rod tube on the female) and the reel seats or butt caps and handle rings were cleverly pinned in the knerled rim.

ORVIS. The Orvis Company of Manchester, Vermont, is probably the best known maker of bamboo rods in the U.S. today. Orvis has produced and marketed thousands of rods every year for the past couple of

decades under a succession of marketing-oriented managers. The engineering is stout but unimaginative and the finish is a dour but durable Bakelite impregnation. Some say older Orvises are O.K.

It is a common axiom among bamboo aficionados that everybody's first cane is an Orvis, their second a real bamboo rod. And this old saw is certainly reflected in the secondhand lists. There are more Orvis rods available than all others put together. They tend to hold some value though — from $100 to $150 — so unless bricklike durability is more important than finesse, they are not a good secondhand buy.

PAYNE. Jim Payne and his father Ed made what many, including the late Ev Garrison, considered the finest rods in the world. Garrison said Jim Payne had "micrometers for fingers. He could feel a thousandth of an inch difference." Unburdened with the clumsy micrometer, Payne could turn out incredibly fine rods at an amazing pace — one per day for every man working in his Highland Mills, New York, shop. It is estimated that there were between 15,000 and 20,000 Paynes made which, assuming normal attrition minus the durability factor, means that there are probably about 5,000 existing today in fishable condition.

Both Paynes used the simple yet effective spiral noding system which assured that at no point in the length of a rod were there two nodes. Payne eyeballed the sections for even distribution of nodes and came up with rods that seldom set — and broke only with abuse. Unfortunately, many lesser makers used the same system and even imitated Payne's flame-darkened cane. This means there are Heddons, Montagues, South Bends

(continued on next page)

A split bamboo rod produced by Orvis in the early 1900s.

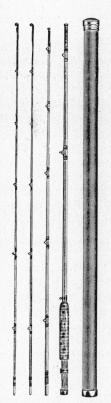

Payne produced this 3-piece fly rod with an extra tip in the 1920s for $50. It was built of dark bamboo and came with an extra tip.

top of the line

(continued from preceding page)

and other factory rods all of which can be a Payne in the butt, mid and tip.

Paynes normally have a gentle swelling of the cane at the handle to break the action and this can sometimes separate the Paynes from the aches. Also look for the jewelry-like Payne hardware, including almost invisible pins in the reel seat (or butt cap) and the ferrules.

PHILLIPSON. Granger look-alikes by a Granger shophand. Good rods and good buys at Granger prices.

POWELLS. E. C. and son Walton Powell made and are still making functional quality rods in the California Bay Area. The Powells have had a cadre of devotees who claim that the tempering process in their rods produces the crispest and most durable cane. Their dark cane rods are glued similarly to Youngs and some have a hollowing process.

For plain but eminently functional rods, they are a good buy at $100 to $150.

THOMAS. Fred Thomas, along with Ed Payne, was originally a Leonard rodbuilder in Bangor who broke off to start his own shop. The shop made Leonard-appearing but stouter rods from about 1895 to about 1955. During those 60-odd years they made thousands of fine quality rods.

Unlike most other fine makers, Thomas offered three or more grades of rods. The Brown Tone series was the top of the line followed by the famous Special and the less extravagant Dirigo. The higher grades had English noding with a swelled butt while the Dirigo had a more random node pattern. The Brown Tone was stained very dark while the Special and Dirigo had a deep heat-tempered color. Fittings and hardware were fine and very Leonard-like.

The price of Thomas rods differs modestly from broker to broker. Specials and Brown Tones generally cost about the same as Leonards with some sellers undercutting by as much as $100, while others ask from $50 to $100 more for a high grade Thomas than for a comparable Leonard.

THOMAS & THOMAS. A new firm which grew out of the Montague-fertilized soil of Springfield, Mass. They make a variety of rods from modestly expensive to modestly exorbitant. But they look good and seem to be developing a following. Too early for many to appear on the used-rod lists though.

USLAN. Nat Uslan has been making five-sided cane rods for a long time. First in upstate New York, then in Florida. They are remarkably tough, hard-casting rods with a good finish and excellent appointments. Uslans are the only five-sided rods likely to appear on brokers' lists so a detailed description is not necessary.

If the engineering works, Uslans are tremendous buys. Prices range from $100 to $130 used and they are a lot of rod for that kind of money.

WINSTON. San Francisco rods famous for their light weight and snappy actions. Lew Stoner (the second part of the Win-stone acronym) developed a fluted-hollow construction technique which cleverly eliminated the middle pith in bamboo sections while retaining the deep glue surface. They were hot stuff in casting tour-

(continued on next page)

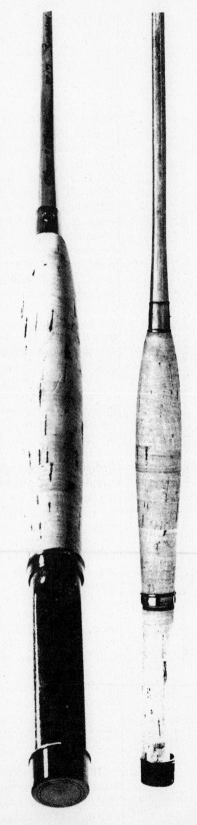

THOMAS & THOMAS

The modern fly rod

The modern dry-fly rod is such a very perfect piece of mechanism that it is almost a sacrilege to use with it any imperfect tackle; and yet it seems to me that offence is being daily committed. For this reason an attempt is here made to show that the reel has not followed the progress of the rod, but has rather, in some respects, retrogressed. In this attempt it is necessary to consider first, along certain lines, the mechanics of a single-handed rod.

A single-handed rod is one which can be comfortably manipulated by one hand. Thus used, the power that can be applied to it is the turning power of the wrist, which I have found to be about equivalent to a force of six pounds acting at a distance of one foot. It will, of course, vary somewhat with the individual. The result of the application of this power will not always be the same, but depend on how it is applied. First, proof will be given that, when playing a fish, less strain can be put on a fishing line when the rod is held vertically, than when it is held at an angle to the horizon. In order to simplify this proof, the rod will, in the first place, be assumed to be perfectly rigid.

Fly Fishing, Some New Arts and Mysteries
(1915).
By John Cecil Mottram.

top of the line

(continued from preceding page)

naments until the advent of glass and have a considerable following as fishers.

Most Winstons are noded in the English pattern, have light cane and lack the swell at the butt. Nicely finished with bronze-machined ferrules and reel seat hardware. Secondhand they run from $150 to $250 depending on model.

PAUL YOUNG. Young died in 1959 leaving some remarkable machinery and bizarre designs to his sons and apprentice rod maker Bob Sommers. Young's early rod designs were nice-but-conventional; however, his later offerings were almost revolutionary. He modified the so-called parabolic design by compounding or "denting" his tapers and came up with a series of extremely powerful, light-line rods.

Appropriately made in Detroit, these "P" designated Young rods tend to accelerate power like a V-8. But watch them on the curves. They want to throw high, open loops and are inclined to collapse into the lower butt when playing large fish. Young "P" rods are an amazing tool but not for everybody. Yet there are enough people seeking them as an angling panacea that they are hard to find. Midges, Martha Maries, Driggs and Perfectionists are seldom seen on secondhand lists and they are dear when found.

Young's cane is very distinctive and nearly impossible to forge. The surface is flame-tempered with mottled black, brown and amber tones. He noded most of his rods with two nodes opposing one another in a spiral up the section.

Young often put aluminum ferrules on his lightweight rods, a practice that has been abandoned by his successors. Better specimens have super Z silver ferrules. Reel seat hardware is normally simple yet efficient aluminum or punched silver.

GAMEFISH: LAKE TROUT

NAMES
Mackinaw, togue, Great Lakes trout, salmon trout, grey trout, laker, forktail. *(Salvelinus namaycush)*

DISTRIBUTION
The lake trout is found throughout Canada and the Northern United States. It is found in the lakes of New England, New York and the Great Lakes region. It is also found in some lakes in the West.

DESCRIPTION
The lake trout is a member of the char family and is the largest of the trouts. It is grey or grey-blue in color with light, irregular spots scattered over the head and sides. The lower fins are edged with white. The tail is deeply forked.

SIZE
The size of the lake trout varies according to its habitat. In some lakes, catches average about 5 pounds and in others about 20 pounds. Specimens of over 100 pounds have been recorded.

HABITAT
The lake trout prefers large, cold lakes of deep water. It seeks out deep waters most of the time but can be found near the shallows in the spring and fall months.

FEEDING HABITS
The lake trout feeds primarily on smaller fish such as smelt or cisco and whitefish. It is generally not considered a popular game fish because of its preference for deep water.

BEST FEEDING TEMPERATURE
Between 40° and 55°.

TACKLE
Except for early spring when they come up to chase minnows, imitating plugs and even flies, the lake trout occupies the deeper waters of big lakes. Trolling gear sometimes heavy enough to handle wire line with small spoons or plugs does it. Occasionally deep-working jigs are effective.

LEONARD ROD CASES

Leonard's heavy-duty rod cases with brass fittings are available through the company for two- or three-piece rods of any size. Just tell them whether you want one for a two-piece or three-piecer and if you have an extra tip. They also sell their fine poplin bags separately, too. About the sturdiest case you can buy.

A gold medal awarded to Leonard Rods at a competition held in 1880 in Berlin.

A new name in old rods

PAYNE ROD COMPANY. The reborn Payne Rod Company in Highland Mills, N.Y., is one of the latest entries in the used cane rod field. They have lots of Jim Payne's rods, plus a goodly selection of other brands, reels and other goodies. Not cheap but another place to look for that special tackle antique. They also take trades on the new Payne, which is being fashioned by Leo Decker and Walt Carpenter.

top of the line

Dealers in used cane rods

Used cane rods are like love: they're where you find them.

There are only a few places that have lots of used cane, but more and more tackle shops will have some around. With the price of good rods going higher more anglers want to trade in the old before buying the new.

There are some disadvantages and advantages in buying them from a non-dealer. On the debit side, a large dealer will have ready access to a rod company to make the necessary repairs on a trade-in. If they get top-quality rods that just need refinishing that's what will usually happen. They bring lots more money that way. A reputable dealer will also have a strong fix on the rod's history and its potentialities for fishing or collecting. But they do get top dollar and the roof is getting mighty high.

On the other side of the ledger, your local dealer will often not expect to get the prices listed by the exclusive secondhand establishments.

Often they will be willing to dicker, especially once you establish that you are roughly as knowledgeable as they are. No reason to pay list price on anything except perhaps an especially choice cane rod.

Big dealers can wring top dollar because they know who is looking for that one special model. People will buy or collect most anything.

CLASSIC RODS. Martin J. Keane was one of the pioneer secondhand rod dealers and has a reputation as a rod historian. His Classic Rods, based in Bridgewater, Connecticut, often has a princely inventory of vintage rods of historical interest as well as more practical modernish cane. Always willing to buy or trade, he is a good source when you're hankering after a particular rod.

HERITAGE ROD AND REEL. Run by Mrs. Mary Kefover Shepard, Heritage is a wonderful place to look for vintage fishing tackle. Mrs. Shepard is as knowledgeable on the topic as they come and will often have real delights from angling's past for sale. She can also tell you the background of tackle and likes to buy, sell and trade. An excellent source for the collector and connoisseur. She sometimes has fine contemporary cane rods as well.

H. L. LEONARD STORE. The H. L. Leonard store is located in New York's Central Valley, original nesting place for Hiram Leonard and his 19th Century shop, where the American bamboo rod really got started. Anyway, the store features a large list of used rods, as well as reels and the miscellaneous. Ron Kusse, who runs the store, is fairly knowledgeable about that kind of thing. He mails out lists of rods every few months.

THOMAS & THOMAS. Len Codella is now operating out of the Thomas & Thomas rod company selling the secondhand bamboo rods that he accumulates. Len is a solid person to deal with and, as much as possible, you get what you pay for. Len also has at times a good selection of fly reels and other vintage equipment. He will also arrange trades of your "junkie" old bamboo rods for brand-spanking-new Thomas & Thomas goodies, if that's your delight.

ANTON UDWARY, JR. From an unlikely nest at Spartanburg, South Carolina, Udwary has been part of the secondhand rod market for quite a while. He usually has at least a few interesting rods around.

HOW TO AVOID BURNS ON THE USED CANE MARKET

(continued from page 112)

rule) better watch out: it probably means either a slipped glue seam or a covered external crack or internal fracture.

While you have it together, flick the rod sharply. Hear any clicks or feel any rattles? This is probably a sign of loose ferrules. Check the windings at the ferrule-cane connection for frazzled thread and the metal-to-metal connection for snugness. If the ferrules are sound, it could mean something is drastically wrong with the cane.

Look over the windings and the varnish (and don't forget to check wear on metal guides and cracks in agate guides and tips). A rod can always be rewrapped and varnished but it will cost dearly (about $100), and that should make a good haggling point with the broker.

Actually, it's probably wise to seek rods that show some cosmetic wear. Not only can a recent refinishing hide faults in a genuine rod but more often it will conceal a beggar in gentleman's clothing. A Payne with alligatored (crystallized) varnish and missing guides is bound to be a Payne while a shiny "like new" Payne could easily be a fake or a doctored original. In fact, it is a good rule for us all to avoid recently refinished rods entirely, so maybe brokers would stop shipping off the weary and orphaned to the factory and nipping the customer for the price of the shine. The only existing broker I know that doesn't fiddle with the finish is Classic Gun and Reel in Livingston, Montana.

(continued on next page)

How cross-fishing was practiced in Nineteenth-Century Britain

In the North of England, two-handed or cross-fishing is practised for Salmon, Trout, and also for Jack and Pike, though this method of fishing is but little practised elsewhere. Indeed, it can hardly be called fair fishing; and, as such, it is generally forbid by the proprietors of private waters, who seldom deny a sportsman a day's angling, under fair restrictions. This two-handed Snap-fishing for Jack and Pike is practised in the following manner: — take about forty or fifty yards of strong cord, sash, or jack line, and fasten each end to poles about seven or eight feet long; and on each pole fasten a large winch that will hold fifty yards of the strongest platted silk trolling-line; in the middle of the strong line (which is fastened to the poles) tie on a small brass or wooden pulley; then draw the trolling line from the wenches, and pass it through the pulley; now, bait a snap-hook or hooks with a full-sized bait-fish, and fix it to the trolling-line, and all is ready to commence two-handed Snap-fishing. The parties managing the poles proceed directly opposite each other, on the banks of rivers or other waters, and drop their baited hooks in places where they expect to find fish; and when they feel a bite, one strikes very smartly, and his companion then lowers or otherways manages his pole, so as to give him any or every assistance while killing and getting the Jack or Pike on shore. When the gorgehook is used in this way of fishing, it is then proper to have two pulleys fastened to the thick cord, near the centre of it, at about a yard apart; because, when one Angler feels a run, the other should immediately keep all still while the Fish pouches: this cannot be so well done when both lines pass through one pulley; and the Troller knows that if Jack or Pike are not well on the feed, they will throw or drop the bait from the least check or alarm; if there be only one pulley, then only one line should be used. In some places, the country people get a strong small rope or clothes line, and tie one or more snap-baited hooks to it, and take hold one at each end of the rope, and walk opposite each other, on the banks of small rivers and ponds, letting the baited

(continued on next page)

FLY ROD HANDLE STYLES

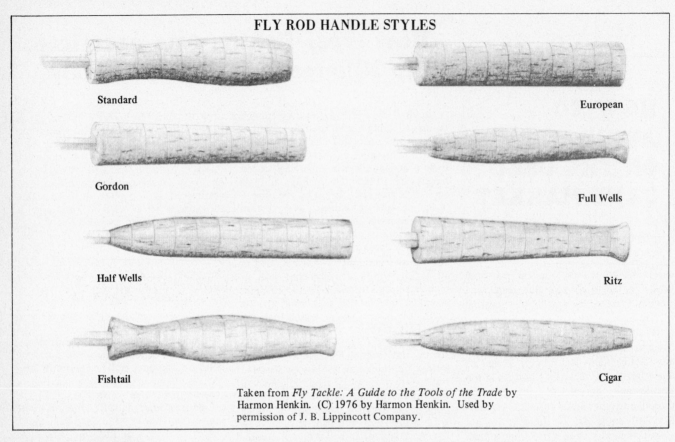

Standard

European

Gordon

Full Wells

Half Wells

Ritz

Fishtail

Cigar

Taken from *Fly Tackle: A Guide to the Tools of the Trade* by
Harmon Henkin. (C) 1976 by Harmon Henkin. Used by
permission of J. B. Lippincott Company.

THE CANE MARKET

(continued from preceding page)

If you stick to wounded or poorly dressed cane, you have less chance of getting stuck with a phony, and you can always have it reconditioned or finished later.

What are the benchmarks of good rods? Every good maker signed his craft. Most of them stamped their name and logos on the end cap or metal of a reel seat. Some, such as Young, Garrison and Phillipson, printed their name and the rod model on the butt section above the grip. But just because Garrison's name is printed on the cane doesn't necessarily mean the rod is a Garrison. The list in this chapter identifies the hard-to-fabricate benchmarks of several great makers.

The used rod market tends to fluctuate wildly on arbitrary internal and external stimuli. A few years ago, for instance, Thomas rods jumped from a cruising price of about $200 to $300 and even $400. The market tetered for half a year, then returned to about $200. I suspect that somebody had a bunch to get rid of so they artificially watered their prices — sparking an inflationary chain reaction.

The point is: the prospective bamboo fisher is probably better off setting his sights on a distinct function (say, an 8-foot, No. 5 line, easy casting rod) rather than a maker, because the price could multiply while you're seeking a suitable specimen.

HOW CROSS-FISHING WAS PRACTICED

(continued from preceding page)

hooks drag in the water, until they feel a bite; the one strikes and immediately drags the Jack on shore, the other person slacks the line he holds, while his companion is so doing.

Various other ways are practised for taking Jack and Pike, by night lines, trimmers, etc.; but such methods are justly reprobated by the true Angler who exercises his skill and art for amusement more than profit; therefore, I shall say but very little on this part of the subject. The trimmers mostly used in lakes, meers, broads, pools, and large ponds, are taken up from a boat; if the place be not too broad, you may get them with the drag hooks, or with a large stone, fastened to plenty of strong cord, being thrown over the trimmer line: these trimmers are made of strong thin hempen cord, with a hook tied to brass wire (but gimp is better) and wound on a large piece of flat cork, about five or six inches in diameter, with a groove to admit the line: the hook is baited with a Gudgeon, Roach, or some small Fish; you then draw as much line out as admits the bait to hang about a foot from the bottom. There is a small slit in the cork, that you pass the line in, to prevent it unwinding: as soon as the Jack or Pike seizes the bait, the line loosens, and runs from the groove of the cork free, and allows the Fish to retire to his haunt, and pouch at leisure.

The Angler's Guide (1814).
By Thomas Salter.

BUY USED TACKLE
IT'S FUN AND SAVES YOU MONEY

By Harmon Henkin

This is a firsthand society.

Except for antiques (whatever they are), maybe fine firearms, vintage sports cars and cane fly rods made by the departed masters of the craft, buying something brand-spanking new is considered a badge of honor. It's as if we fear disapproval if all our possessions don't come in fancy wrappers. ("What's the matter, buddy? Couldn't afford a new reel?") We have to cloak our second-hand purchases with the label "collector's items" to give them authenticity.

Many of us would rather have *new* junk rather than quality second hand. It's a shame, too. There are bargains to be found, especially in fishing tackle, which in many cases hasn't had much hard use.

A number of the best equipped and most knowledgeable anglers I know have never bought a new rod or reel. All it takes to find good second-hand tackle is common sense and an eye practiced to look for quality.

Bamboo fly rods, which can develop ailments beyond the capabilities of most anglers to heal, are one danger area, however. The cane rod you find for $25 in a second hand or junk store that has to be refinished by one of the better custom shops will cost you perhaps $125 before it's over. It takes experience to detect structural weakness in cane, to check the glue lines to make sure they aren't parting or to decide whether the click you hear is from a ferrule that simply needs rewrapping — re-seating, a more complicated job. If there aren't any cane fanatics in your neighborhood, you'll have to pay your money and take your chances.

But with other tackle it's an easy job. Glass rods are usually as good as they feel and look. The ferrules should fit easily, seat deeply and make no noise when flexing. Minor problems like missing guides or loose reel seats are easy to repair at home. Even if the rod has fewer guides than the recommended minimum of one per foot, a re-wrapping job is a minor inconvenience.

Reels is as good as they feels, so to speak. If they work smoothly after the drag is tested you've got a sound piece of machinery. One of the big problems with spinning reels, especially the cheaper ones, is the tendency for the drag to tighten up as a fish takes out line. Grab a few handfuls and tug, checking the pressure. It should work smoothly and evenly. The better reels of all sorts, the ones that stay on the market basically unchanged year after year, remain repairable. Parts are either available from the factory or from repair stations around the country. You might want to check up on that.

Get all the second-hand lures and flies you can find. Every angler knows that a lure is more effective once it loses its virginity. Second-hand lures can usually be found for nickels and dimes and some of the older models have actions as modern as any available today.

Second-hand fly lines pose a different problem since their weight is sometimes in question. I have bought No. 6 lines that turned out to be No. 8s and vice versa. A gram scale can guide you. Check the finish on the line to make sure it's smooth and never pay more than half retail for one regardless of its condition since the better fly line companies will warranty their new lines, a protection not available for used lines.

Waders and other rubber goods are a stickier problem since they can't be tested before buying and slight flaws can make for major inconveniences. Take your chances or buy new.

All in all, purchasing used tackle cannot only save money — it's fun. And if enough people buy recycled gear perhaps some of the tackle manufacturers will begin making equipment that lasts longer and wears better.

BOOKS ARE A BASIC FLY FISHING ACCESSORY

You can't own them all, so discretion is the better part of greed

By Harmon Henkin

Fly fishing is the most specialized and technical of all angling; the depth and breadth of its literature mirror this sophistication. Yet many anglers, refusing to view books as a real accessory to their fishing, build their library in the most haphazard way.

Over the centuries as casting a fly developed into a very distinct branch of angling so did its literature. Since the late 19th Century most of the important additions to the sport have come from works devoted solely to fly fishing. With exceptions, such as Ray Bergman's immortal *Trout*, few fly anglers want much to do with any book that even has a trace of lures or, heaven forbid, bait in it. That Bergman could write a book crucial to any fly fisherman who broaches the subject of garden hackle is a credit to Bergman more than anything else.

But that book was written during the 1930s and nothing else like it has come down the pike. Since the renaissance of fly fishing during the 1960s there has been a great abundance of works on this and that relatively minor aspect of the sport. It's very difficult or impossible for anyone to own them all. So discretion, as they say, is the better part of greed.

It's safe to break down books into various categories. In one grouping would be the historical works of interest, in the next the anecdotal works and the "literature" of fly fishing and lastly and most important to the majority of anglers are the various sorts of how-to works.

If you believe you can't know where you're going unless you know where

She started it all off. Proving that fishing is not a total bastion of male chauvinism, Dame Juliana Berners produced the first work on the sport back in the 15th Century.

The delightful *Treatyse on Fysshynge wyth an Angle* not only tells you such essentials as how to make rods and baits but also delves into a lofty morality in defense of fishing.

(continued on page 144)

A Visit to Roderick Haig-Brown

By Thomas McGuane

National Film Board of Canada photograph

"A man more interested in the whole kingdom of nature than holding water and hot spots."

For many who have seen angling as the symptom of a way of living, rather than a series of mechanical procedures, the writing of Roderick Haig-Brown has served as scripture. And in a sport with an ample but often abysmal literature of easy heroism and quasi-technical advice, the reader turns to Haig-Brown with the same general sensation he would have when the oxygen mask drops into his lap upon what is referred to on commercial aircraft as "a sudden loss of cabin pressure."

For one thing, at the center of each of his works is the conviction that the world will not cease its circumnavigation of the sun if no one goes fishing again. Fishing for Haig-Brown is sublimely without function; and therefore, in its explication, without the perpetually wearying assumption that the angler is *sui generis* really hot stuff.

Haig-Brown is a famous fisherman in an era when famous fishermen scramble to name flies and knots after themselves with a self-aggrandizing ardor unknown since the Borgia popes. Anyone who has sat in on the bad-mouth sessions at fly shops and guides' docks will welcome the serene observations of a man more interested in fish than fishing; and more interested in the whole kingdom of nature than holding water and hot spots.

There is scarcely an angler so avid that he doesn't spend most of his time not angling; much of the time because of the inclemency of the weather or the demands of work or the inferiority of actuality to fantasy, he pursues his sport in what is called "the armchair." There are any number of armchair anglers who do not own armchairs. These are harmless creatures whose minds have beaten out everything else for the control of things; and for them the theory of the sport lies heavily upon the sport itself. In the end, they find themselves prisoners of the harmless-looking armchair, though the armchair may in the long run turn out to be a little spot they know with a go-go dancer whose parts tremble like molded fruit medleys.

Others use the armchair, sometimes an actual armchair, selectively to read and to think; and at such times, if they are anglers, they are susceptible to the guidance of men who have written about this peerless sport which affects the world's fortunes not at all. For them there is no better place to turn than to the writing of Roderick Haig-Brown.

That much has been clear for some time; Haig-Brown's prominence in this fugitive literature is seldom doubted. His great series *Fisherman's Spring, Summer, Fall* and *Winter* is an integral part of the shelf of every angler who thinks about what he is doing. *Measure of the Year, Return to the River,* and *The Western Angler* amplify that great series and lead the angler to increasingly broad preoccupations within his sport, until he shares with Haig-Brown a continuity of perceptions from the tying of small brilliant flies to the immeasurable and celestial movements of fish in migration. Finally, he treats the way the angler holds his fishing grounds in trust; because I suppose before anything else Haig-Brown is a conservationist — and not, I was to learn, one of the everlastingly whining, walking-wounded of the ecology movement.

He lives in Campbell River, British Columbia; and one summer I decided to pay him a visit, not, I hasten to admit without some trepidation. Sportsman, magistrate, English prose

(continued on page 130)

THE LAST HATCH
A FISHING MYSTERY
HARMON HENKIN

(continued from page 112)

brands would do for Halford. The wound from the gaff wasn't bleeding. Those kinds of gashes seldom do when the heart stops beating.

The ambulance crew, which had been tagging behind Sid and Paul, caught up. Sid was trying to suppress nausea. He wasn't used to death, except that of fish and deer. He walked around the body peering for clues. He poked and prodded and searched and even got up the courage to touch the gaff. Nothing.

Paul looked back into the creek. The brown trout, which didn't give a damn about murders or detective novels, had come back to their feeding station and were taking small midges again. Sid's eyes perked up when he saw them. Paul noticed his greed and tried to get him back on the job.

"Sid, why don't you have these guys take the body over to the coroner in Hamilton for a complete autopsy?"

Sid waved to the ambulance attendants, who had been trying to skip rocks in the river. "Take this body over to Doc in town and get him to do a real careful check over everything. Watch how you handle Halford, too, or you boys will be back at the Dairy Queen. Understand?"

They nodded and one of them stepped forward. "Excuse me, sheriff, but don't you think you oughta take some pictures or dust for fingerprints or something? Like on *Kojak?*"

"This ain't *Kojak*, dimwit. What am I gonna do? Dust the sand? Now get going."

With an exaggerated strain made to impress Sid, they picked up Halford, loaded him into the stretcher and trudged off up the path toward the ambulance.

Sid sat down glumly on the beach and kicked at the ground.

"Now what?"

"I think we should find out where he was killed," Paul suggested. "Somewhere along the creek, for sure. Nobody would have dragged him far. He was too big for that. Maybe we'll find something interesting there. Let's walk up different sides of the bank, okay?"

"Hell of an idea, Paul. You wade across the creek. As a law officer I have to look neat at all times."

Paul glared at him, but jumped waist-deep into the 52° water. Though there wasn't much current, the thick vegetation made it rough

(continued on page 146)

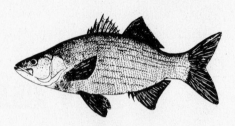

GAMEFISH: WHITE BASS

NAMES
Stripped Bass, Silver Bass, streak, Bar Fish, Stripper. *(Roccus Chrysops)*

DISTRIBUTION
The White Bass is widely distributed throughout the southern states, and into the Mississippi River Valley and Eastern Texas. It is also found in the Great Lakes and through the St. Lawrence River System.

DESCRIPTION
Along with its cousin, the Yellow Bass, the White Bass is a freshwater member of the Sea-Bass family. It is a small fish of silver coloring with yellowish overtones. Thin, brown unbroken stripes run laterally along the sides. One of its more distinctive features is a projecting lower jaw.

SIZE
The White Bass averages between 1 and 2 pounds rarely reaching a maximum of over 5 pounds.

HABITAT
While Bass usually travel in schools and favor large, clear lakes and slow-moving rivers and streams, they can often be found in deep, open water with rocky or gravel bottoms. Preferred locations include areas of turbulent water at the foot of dams and locks.

FEEDING HABITS
Small gizzard shad and other baitfish are the favorite choices of the White Bass, although they will feed on insects, worms and small crustaceans. They are most active in the early morning and evening and on overcast days. Large schools often feed on the surface.

BEST FEEDING TEMPERATURE
Between 65 and 75 degrees.

TACKLE
This fish rarely requires anything more than light spinning gear though medium fly outfits with streamers work well sometimes. Good with small jigs, spoons or spinners. Baitfishing is sometimes effective and even stillfishing.

"To become an expert angler one must either consistently catch more and bigger fish than others or else write a book on the sport. The writing is much easier."
ANON.

FLY FISHING BOOKS 127

DRY-FLY FISHING
f.m. halford

See page 131 for a review

Atlantic Salmon Flies & Fishing

JOSEPH D. BATES, JR.

top of the line

American Nymph Fly Tying Manual
By Randall Kaufmann

Randall Kaufmann, the owner of Kaufmann's Fly Shop in Oregon, has put together a soft-backed guide for the American nymph tier that's as complete and practical as they come. Over 200 patterns are listed with colored illustrations. Also plenty of material on tying materials and nymph collecting. Good for advanced as well as beginning tiers.

Published by: Salmon Trout Steelheader (Portland, Oregon). **Price:** $7.50.

The Atlantic Salmon
By Lee Wulff

One of the most important books about the world of the salmon. It explains everything the angler needs to pursue this magnificent fish including tackle, tactics and techniques as well as the beast's life cycle. A very complete work and a must for anyone heading for the coastal streams.

Published by: A. S. Barnes. **Price:** $12.

Atlantic Salmon Flies & Fishing
By Joe Bates

This is a complete treatment of the patterns most effective for the Atlantic salmon, including both the traditional and newer hair-wing varieties. It also includes tackle and techniques for the fish but its real value is in the descriptions of patterns and the 100 color illustrations that accompany them.

Published by: Stackpole. **Price:** $14.95.

Book of Trout Flies
By Preston Jennings

Preston Jennings' *Book* was one of the pioneering works of stream identification in this country. It has lots of solid information for today's an-

American Nymph
Fly Tying Manual

By Randall Kaufmann

the
CURTIS
CREEK
MANIFESTO

A Fully Illustrated Guide to the Strategy, Finesse, Tactics and Paraphernalia of Fly Fishing

WRITTEN AND ILLUSTRATED BY
SHERIDAN ANDERSON

See page 130 for a review

— THE SNEAKY ART OF APPROACH

THE FLY CAN BE ATTACHED TO THE KEEPER RING OR LEFT TRAILING IN THE WATER. IF POSSIBLE, REEL-OUT THE CORRECT AMOUNT OF LINE SO YOU WON'T NEED MORE THAN ONE FALSE-CAST.

THE UPSTREAM CRAWL

·ORIGINATED BY THE MARQUIS DE SADE IN FEBRUARY OF 1764·

THE ART OF STALKING IS ALMOST UNKNOWN IN THE U.S.A., YET IT IS THE MOST EFFECTIVE TACTIC IN FLY FISHING. PERHAPS THIS OVERSIGHT IS DUE TO SOME VAGUE PURITANICAL CONCEPT THAT EQUATES KNEELING, STOOPING, AND CRAWLING WITH SELF-ABASEMENT UNLESS CONFINED TO THE PEW. THE MEDIA HAS ALSO UNWITTINGLY REINFORCED THIS CONDITIONING — I DON'T RECALL EVER SEEING THE COVER OF A FISHING GAZETTE DEPICTING AN ANGLER ON HIS KNEES, MUCH LESS CRAWLING.

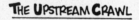

STAY LOW AND TRY AND KEEP A BUSH, TREE, OR ROCK BETWEEN YOU AND THE FISH.

NO QUICK MOVEMENTS! ADVANCE SLOWLY TO THE SPOT FROM WHICH YOU INTEND TO CAST.

IF POSSIBLE, STAY IN THE SHADOWS & DON'T BRANDISH THAT ROD UNTIL READY TO CAST.

THE BEGINNER WILL LEARN STALKING BEST BY FISHING FROM SHORE WHENEVER POSSIBLE. NOVICE ANGLERS RELY TOO HEAVILY ON WADERS AND HIP-BOOTS.

AN EXPERT SNEAK WILL EXERT CONSIDERABLE PHYSICAL AND MENTAL ENERGY TO THE ART. HE WILL TAKE TIME TO PLAN THE APPROACH TO EACH HOLDING STATION — TO HIM, THE WATER BECOMES A GLORIOUS, SHIMMERING THREE-DIMENSIONAL CHESSBOARD, A GAME TO BE MASTERED THRU SKILL, DILIGENCE, AND IMAGINATION.

This and the illustrations on pages 129 and 141 taken from *The Curtis Creek Manifesto* by Sheridan Anderson. (C) 1976 by Sheridan Anderson. Used by permission of Salmon Trout Steelheader.

See page 130 for a review

top of the line

gler and serves as a sourcebook for modern angling entomologists such as Ernie Schwiebert and Swisher-Richards. Important.

Published by: Crown. **Price:** $7.50.

Building a Bamboo Fly Rod: A Master's Guide
By Everett Garrison with Hoagy Carmichael

Building a Bamboo Fly Rod is in many ways like the prospect of owning one; what seems at first a luxury one can fish without soon becomes a necessity — or at least an indulgence well worth skipping meals and other "necessities" to acquire. As many anglers discover the hard way, once you succumb to the charms of bamboo, the prospects are really limited only by your tackle budget and the other earthly considerations that keep us all from angling heaven. *Building a Bamboo Fly Rod* opens up a whole new dimension of cane mania. Should you want to carry your enthusiasm for *Arundinaria amabilis* (roughly translated, "the lovely bamboo") to the point of acquiring the skills and equipment necessary to become a rod maker, you will find a patient guide and angling's finest standard in rod maker Everett Garrison.

But the idea of selecting and splitting cane and using mathematical formulas for figuring rod tapers shouldn't scare the bamboo newcomer from using Garrison's book to attempt simple repairs like rewinding guides (it's still advisable to practice on other rods before you try it on your bamboo), or for making rod accessories like an aluminum carrying case or modifying your reel seat. Beyond that, there is another satisfaction in having this book at hand in terms of understanding the rod maker's art, even if it is strictly as a voyeur.

Building a Bamboo Rod is also a

top of the line

unique angling document; it's something more than a collaboration, and in fact Everett Garrison died while the work was still being organized, which was perhaps even greater impetus for Hoagy Carmichael to carry the book through as a privately printed edition which matches the standards of the Garrison rod in its own way. The anecdotal material that Carmichael has recorded of Garrison at work is itself enough to keep the observer interested, and the book carries a live sense of building bamboo rods that will only increase the value of the ones you own — or dream about.

Available through Fly Fisherman's Bookcase.

The Caddis and the Angler
By Larry Solomon and Eric Leiser

Fly fishing's emphasis on the mayfly hatches is uncovered for the tradition that it is in this book, which might be compared in every way to *Selective Trout*. For ironically, as the number of fly fishing and fly tying books on the Ephemera increases, the number of insects in the streams seems to be decreasing, making the importance of Trichoptera, the caddis flies, fully the other half of angling life in most areas. *The Caddis and the Angler* is not the first book to talk about the caddis flies or list their imitations (caddis pupa patterns have been used by successful and unwitting anglers for many years). It is a one-volume guide to all the scattered techniques — and some startling new ideas from entomological research — that anglers need to know to fish caddis hatches across the country. The emergence charts and other identification keys can be used to start straight through 50-plus patterns of caddis flies in *The Caddis and the Angler*. A handsome book.
Published by: Stackpole. **Price:** $13.95.

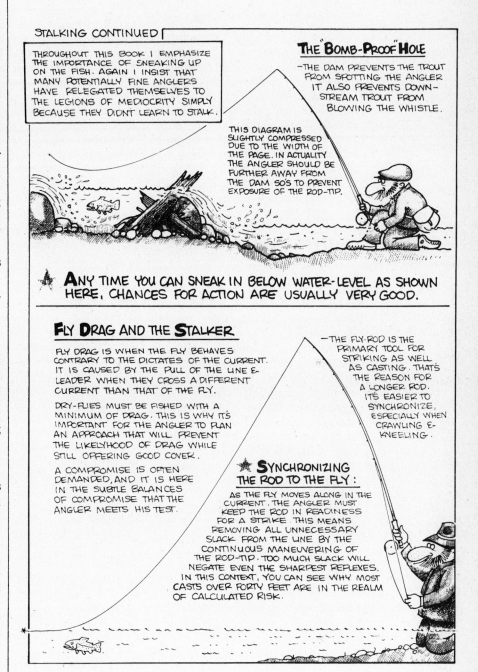

The Curtis Creek Manifesto
See page 130 for a review

top of the line

The Challenge of the Trout
By Gary LaFontaine

This is a specialized, informative book, slightly marred by its over-prosey Schwiebertesque qualities. LaFontaine, who is a field editor for *Fly Fisherman*, tells what he has learned about advanced fly fishing around the country — and it is considerable. Most interesting parts are about caddis flies. Worth reading.

Published by: Mountain Press (Missoula, Montana). **Price:** $12.95.

The Curtis Creek Manifesto
By Sheridan Anderson

Every beginning fly fisher should be issued along with rod, reel, line and leader a copy of this wonderful angling comic book. Angling comic book, you ask? That's right. The 47-page fully illustrated booklet is without a doubt the best basic primer of fly fishing around. It won't replace any of the other sourcebooks, but as a place to get the first rush of questions answered, the *Manifesto* can't be equaled. Anderson has an ironic sense of humor and knows that of which he speaks. An antidote to the stuffiness infecting much angling literature.

Published by: Salmon Trout Steelheader. **Price:** $2.95.

The Dry Fly and Fast Water
The Salmon and the Dry Fly
By George LaBranche

Two of the classic American fly fishing books now reprinted and compiled into one volume. Written around the turn of the century, these works are the first systematic formulation of adapting the Halford dry fly techniques to American waters. Some authorities consider *The Dry Fly* to be the most nearly perfect fishing book ever written.

Published by: Abercrombie & Fitch. **Price:** $2.95.

Roderick Haig-Brown

(continued from page 125)

stylist of weight, Haig-Brown seems artfully contrived to make me feel in need of a haircut and refurbished credentials. I wanted to withdraw my two novels from publication and extirpate the bad words, reduce the number of compliant ladies by as much as 96 per cent. The arbitrary appearance in my last novel of Frederick's of Hollywood brassieres weighed darkly upon my conscience. I was heading for northern Vancouver Island where I felt sure that short work is made of fuzzy-minded vanguardist creeps. The essential schizophrenia of my life was being put to the test; it was rather like discovering that the cuisine is not up to scratch in most communes.

As I winged my way north, the Rockies, in my present mood, unrolled themselves beneath me like skin trouble. A drunk boarded the plane in Spokane and chose the seat next to me. He wore a shiny FBI drip-dry DeLuxo summer suit and a pair of armadillo cowboy boots. He told me he couldn't fly sober and that since he was doing emergency heart surgery in Seattle that afternoon, he didn't have time to drive.

"At three o'clock," he explained, "I'm going to thwack open a guy's heart and I'm already half in the bag. I may have to farm this mother out. I'm totaled." He leaned over to look out the window. "Aw hell," he said, "I'll end up doing it. It's my dedication. Think about this: when the hero of Kafka's *Metamorphosis* wakes up and discovers that he has been transformed into a giant beetle, the first thing he does is call the office and tell his boss he's going to be delayed. Where are you headed?"

I explained about my trip. As a reply, I suppose, my seatmate told me he had seen matadors in the Mexico City Plaza de Toros fighting a giant Coca Cola bottle as it blew around the arena in the wind; ultimately it was drawn from the ring behind two horses and to resonant *olés*, just like a recently dispatched bull. "Tell that to your buddy Haig-Brown. He's a writer. He'll like that story."

My schizophrenia, my need of a haircut, the patch on my pants, my chipped tooth — all formerly coiled like a well-fed cobra — now began to move restlessly about far from the snake-charmer of self-confidence. Haig-Brown seemed to loom in the northern fastness while I was being coached to tell him a story about a Coke bottle in a Mexican bullring. I felt entirely off on the wrong foot.

At this point, my companion confessed that he was not a doctor. He was an inventor. He had invented an aluminum ring that you put over the exhaust pipe of your automobile; stretched across the aluminum ring was a piece of cheesecloth. It was an antipollution device. It had been patented in twelve states. "If you can come in with $20,000," he said, "I can let you have half the action when we go public."

"Well, I don't know . . ."

"I've got a friend who sold ten million smackers' worth of phony stock and got a slap on the wrist from the Securities

(continued on next page)

"All men are equal before fish."
HERBERT HOOVER, 1951

FLY FISHING BOOKS 131

Dry-Fly Fishing
By F. M. Halford

This was the book that really started the whole sport. First published in 1889 — but surprisingly modern — this first work on surface fly fishing revolutionized the sport so quickly that it became angling dogma in England a couple decades after its publication. Although a rather stuffy writer, Halford explains in great detail the techniques he developed for British chalk streams.
Published by: Barry Shurlock & Co. **Price:** $14.95.

The Essential Fly Tier
By J. Edson Leonard

If you know your way around a vise already, and you're ready to expand into saltwater flies and the finer points of tying, this new Edson Leonard book will be an able guide. The line drawings of flies (including some step-by-step sequences) are luscious and there's a foldout color plate. The sheer variety of patterns and the intelligent text — for the accomplished tier — makes it a worthwhile addition to the fly tying collection as an all-around exercise book. Beginners, however, will feel a little lost in the dearth of photographs. A good second-tying-year book.
Published by: Prentice-Hall. **Price:** $12.95.

Fisherman's Fall,
Fisherman's Winter,
Fisherman's Spring,
Fisherman's Summer
By Roderick Haig-Brown

Without a doubt Roderick Haig-Brown is the master angling writer of this century and Nick Lyons did all fishers a big service by getting Crown Press to reissue some of Haig-Brown's better-known works. These reprints represent the peak of angling literature, full of information flaw-

Roderick Haig-Brown

(continued from preceding page)

Commission. This is free enterprise, pal. Get in or get out."

"I just don't see how I . . ."

"How about your friend Haig-Brown? Maybe he can buy in. Maybe he can stake you and the two of you can split the action. What say?"

In Vancouver, I spent a long layover waiting for the small plane to take us to Campbell River. There were a number of people whose small luggage suggested a weekend trip to Vancouver, an enormously muscular girl in hot pants and a number of loggers. At one point, I looked up from the book I was reading to see a familiar face. It was Roderick Haig-Brown, lost in conversation with the ordinary people around me, many of whom seemed to know him.

I introduced myself and we flew north together, Haig-Brown describing the country of mountain ranges and fjordlike inlets beneath us with great specificity. Everything we saw reminded him of something he knew, and despite his modesty as a storyteller (and he is a meticulous listener), I was reminded of his two great strengths as a writer: his command of anecdote and his ability to reason.

I told him about the surgeon-inventor with whom I'd flown to Seattle. His chin dropped to his chest and he laughed convulsively. I began to be able to see him.

Haig-Brown is British-born and somehow looks it. Though the great share of his life has been spent as a Canadian, you are reminded of the "county" English for whom culture and sport are not mutually exclusive. To say that he is a youthful sixty-three, suggests nothing to those who know him; he is neither sixty-three nor, it would seem, any other age. He is rather tall, strong and thin. He is bald on the top of his head and the prelate's band of hair that he retains sticks out behind like a merganser in profile. His eyes are intent and clear and so suggest seriousness that it is perpetually surprising how quickly he laughs. He has a keen appreciation of genuine wit; but he will accept whatever is going. He relished *Mister Hulot's Holiday*.

By the time we approached Campbell River, Haig-Brown was at my urging describing his origin as a lay-magistrate in the British Columbian courts. "Well, my predecessor as magistrate was a teetotaler and didn't drive an automobile; and he was hard on the loggers and fishermen who were my friends."

We landed on the edge of the forest. Haig-Brown's wife, Ann, met us in a car that said on its bumper:

LET'S BLOW UP THE WORLD.
WE'LL START WITH AMCHITKA.

Both Haig-Browns, I was to see, had a firm sense of Canadian nationalism, a sense of belonging to a distinct political and cultural entity, that seems so fresh among Canadians today as to be something of a discovery both for them and for Americans who see it. The inherent optimism is in some ways painful for an American in the 1970s. But to a man like Haig-Brown whose formal judicial district is some 10,000 square miles, mostly wil-

(continued on next page)

lessly rendered. No angler can be complete without reading Haig-Brown. They tell of the cycles of rivers and the anglers who fish them, and he is remarkably attuned to the moods of nature and man.

Published by: Crown. **Price:** $7.50.

Fishing the Dry Fly as a Living Insect
By Leonard M. Wright, Jr.

One of the most important and better written of modern fly fishing books, although it has never had the circulation it rightfully deserves. It was the first book to deal with the caddis fly as a serious alternative to imitations of our declining mayfly population and it was also the first book to challenge the prevailing short rod orthodoxy.

Published by: Dutton. **Price:** $6.95.

Fly Casting with Lefty Kreh

A solid contribution to the difficult task of teaching casting via a book. But Kreh, who is an accomplished angler, manages to do the job as best as possible with a series of concise photos. The step-by-step approach is a masterpiece of its kind and can help the casting of any fisher no matter what level of proficiency.

Published by: J. B. Lippincott. **Price:** $8.95.

A Fly Fisher's Life
By Charles Ritz

This is an intriguing book by the hotelier and master angler who is the sole major representative of the French angling tradition to become well known in America. Ritz's *Life* is a combination of reminiscences and highly technical analyses of such things as fly rod action and casting. Ritz has been a highly important figure for fly fishermen, even those

Roderick Haig-Brown

(continued from preceding page)

derness, it would be difficult not to be touched by the optimism of a frontier.

The Haig-Browns headed home, caught up in their own talk, while I waited for my rented car. Later Ann Haig-Brown would ask me quite ingenuously, "Isn't Roddy wonderful?"

I was raised 2 miles from Canada; but this seemed to be the interior. Most of my trip from Vancouver to Campbell River had been over grizzly country; yet I had seen some of the ugliest clear-cut logging in those noble ranges. The woman who brought me my car had moved to Campbell River from the Yukon. My spirits rose. How did she like Campbell River? Very well, she replied, but the shopping plaza in the Yukon was better. I wondered if she would have the same chance to marvel at decimation's speed as we'd had at home.

From the largest seaplane base in North America, poised to survey the roadless country around us, to the hockey hints in the newspaper and the handsome moored salmon boats with names like *Skeena Cloud* and *Departure Bay* (despite the odd pleasure boat with *Costa Lotsa* on its transom), I felt I was in another country.

During my week of visiting Roderick Haig-Brown, at some inconvenience to his intensely filled schedule, I began to see that I had little chance of discovering that precise suppurating *angst*, that dismal or craven psychosis that is so indispensable to the author of short biographies.

I had fantasized a good deal about Haig-Brown's life; angler, frontiersman and man of letters, he seemed to have wrestled a utopian situation for himself. It was with some shock that I perceived his immersion in the core problems of our difficult portion of the 20th Century.

I knew that his work with the Pacific Salmon Commission represented an almost symbolically tortuous struggle for balanced use of a powerful resource among explosive political forces. But the hours I spent in his court did as much as anything to disabuse me of any cheerful notions that Haig-Brown's clarity as a writer was the product of a well-larded sinecure.

A man was brought before him for reckless and drunken driving. The man allowed that he did not feel he was "speeding too awful much." His speed was established by the arresting officer as something like 300 per cent of the limit. The officer mentioned that the man had been impaired by drink; he described the man's spectacular condition. "I wasn't all that impaired." A numerical figure from the Breatholizer test was quoted, one which suggested saturation. The accused had heard these numbers against himself before. He reiterated doggedly that he hadn't been "impaired that awful much," and gave up.

A young logger and his girl friend who had run out on a hotel bill appeared before Haig-Brown. What did he do, Haig-Brown inquired, referring to the specifics of the young man's profession. Boomed and set chokers. Haig-Brown nodded; he

(continued on next page)

top of the line

who have never heard his name, and this book has gone through more editions than almost any other modern fly fishing book.

Published by: Crown. **Price:** $7.50.

Fly Fishing Heresies
By Leonard M. Wright

In this book Wright continues doing what he does best: breaking trails for other anglers to follow. *Fishing the Dry Fly as a Living Insect*, one of the most important fly fishing works of the last few decades, rediscovered and popularized not only caddis fly fishing but also the long rods that are fashionable today. *Heresies* covers many aspects of technique and tackle that probably will become tomorrow's gospel. He's a fine writer with a clear concise style and should be read as one of the modern masters of the game.

Published by: Winchester. **Price:** $8.95.

Fly Fishing in Salt Water
By Lefty Kreh

The basic guide for a growing sport. Kreh is truly a master angler. This book deals with all the problems that make briny fly casting seem so difficult for so many anglers. Covers everything from tackle and species to knots and boats as well as patterns, fighting the fish, tides and on and on. Top-drawer stuff.

Published by: Crown. **Price:** $9.95.

Fly-Rodding for Bass
By A. D. Livingston

A. D. Livingston has become a major source of bass fishing information. In *Fly-Rodding for Bass* he has compiled a full guide to the most exciting way to catch them. He covers everything from the tackle and techniques

Roderick Haig·Brown

(continued from preceding page)

had been a logger too, one who had blown up his inherited Jeffries shotgun trying to make fireworks in camp on New Year's Eve.

"You are addicted to heroin, aren't you?" Haig-Brown asked the sturdy young man. The logger replied that he was; so was his girl friend. He had always lived between here and Powell River, had only had eight dollars the last time he got out of jail, and so on. He and his girl friend wanted to help each other get on the methadone program. He thought their chances of doing so were reduced if he went to jail.

The prosecutor wanted a jail sentence. Haig-Brown released the young man on promise of restitution to the hotel keeper and adjourned to his chambers, where his mongrel dog slept in front of the desk. I noted that the prosecutor was anxious for something stiffer; and Haig-Brown remarked that the prosecutor thought the logger was not being sincere with the court. I asked him what he thought about the young logger. "He's probably conning me," Haig-Brown said, then added with admiration, "but he's a marvelous talker, isn't he?" We talked on until I discovered what is an essential axiom to Haig-Brown in his practice (he is frequently accused of leniency): a magistrate who risks an accused man's liberty risks his own honor.

Haig-Brown feels himself in the presence of the potentially ridiculous at all times. He does not seem to feel that his position as magistrate or as Chancellor of the University of Victoria separates him by nature from the people who come before his court. And when he talks about the scheme to dam the Fraser River and wipe out the major run of Pacific salmon, a toothy smile forms around the stem of his pipe and he says, "Bastards!" as though to discover that his opponents cannot resist the temptation to be ridiculous.

After court one day, Haig-Brown and I stopped to buy some wine. While he shopped, I wandered through the store and discovered some curious booze called (I think) Woodpecker Juice. I brought it up to the cash register to show Haig-Brown. "Bring it." He grinned. "We'll take it home and try it."

We spent a number of evenings in his study and library, where I prodded him to talk about himself. He would stand with one foot tipped forward like a cavalier in an English painting, knocking his pipe on his heel from time to time, trying to talk about other than himself: his children, Thomas Hardy, whom he knew as a child, his literary heroes like Richard Jeffries and Henry Fielding, the great Indians of the Pacific Northwest.

Eventually my persistence led him to sketch things in: his schooling at Charterhouse, his attempts to get into the then shrinking Colonial Service, his emigration to Canada, his experience during World War II as a major in the Canadian Army on loan to the Mounted Police, a post which took him over the entire country — "The making of a Canadian," said his wife — his life as a logger, angler, conservationist, university administrator and writer. As I saw him, standing amid an Edwardian expanse

(continued on page 144)

See page 133 for a review

See page 133 for a review

top of the line

to reading the water and the biological habits of his quarry. This is a solid book and *the* basic text.
Published by: Lippincott. **Price:** $8.95.

Fly Tackle: A Guide to the Tools of the Trade
By Harmon Henkin

OK, you've made it through your first season of fly fishing, and you're still convinced there's something in it for you. You're starting to hang around the fringes of fly tackle shop conversations where you hear words like "parabolic," "multiplier," "impregnated" and a thousand other vaguely mechanical terms that keep cropping up in tackle descriptions in catalogs and books. What to do — give up and go back to plunking bait? Quit your job and go back to fly fishing school? Here's hope and guidance, and a good bit more. Harmon Henkin has put together a long-overdue book (as endorsements from Leonard Wright, Lefty Kreh and others note) about fly fishing tackle that is both practical and elevating.

Perhaps no other group of fishermen is so tackle-conscious as flycasters, and to top off the profusion of new gadgetry and fishing technology, there is a strong school of old-line tackle traditions to contend with in choosing and using fly tackle — not to mention debating it. *Fly Tackle* avoids both the factionalism of old vs. modern, and the false diplomacy (Henkin names names) that characterizes so much of our outdoors writing these days. Henkin has created a very readable and nearly complete angler's guide to rods, reels and accessories that will delight the tackle junkie and save the newcomer lots of embarrassment in the fly shop and perhaps a bad investment. To top it all off, the endsheets and interior of *Fly Tackle* are decorated with luscious drawings by

top of the line

Jeff Johnson that will have you urging Henkin to write faster so you can get to the next one. Before you buy your second rod — or your first — get this Henkin fellow's book; it will stay on your bookshelf as you progress from Fenwick to Payne, and give you nearly as much pleasure as both.

Published by: Lippincott. **Price:** $9.95.

The Fly-Tyer's Almanac
By Robert H. Boyle and Dave Whitlock

Dave Whitlock and Robert Boyle have put together a very helpful volume for the more advanced or intermediate tier looking for a good place to learn the new patterns for salt- and freshwater fishing. There are pictures of wondrous imitations of such things as midges, leeches, minnows, shrimp and flies for steelhead and bass. Beautifully illustrated.

Published by: Crown. **Price:** $10.

Fly-Tying Materials
By Eric Leiser

The basic text on the subject, this book covers everything from the mundane to the esoteric and features such things as photo-dying, an advanced technique with widespread application. Leiser also covers the laws regulating importing and exporting feathers, offers a full-color spread on neck colors and explains how to preserve perishable tying materials. A must book for the serious tier.

Published by: Crown. **Price:** $7.50.

Hatches
By Al Caucci and Bob Nastasi

This book is a continuation of the work of such people as Art Flick, Ernie Schwiebert and Swisher-Richards. It tells the angler almost everything necessary to handle the major hatches on North American trout streams. Finely illustrated and

See page 132 for a review

simply written, it's an important work for serious anglers.

Published by: Comparahatch. **Price:** $15.95.

Fly Fishing Strategy
By Doug Swisher and Carl Richards

This is the dynamic duo's second volume, a fairly distant runner-up to their *Selective Trout* that still has some new things to say to fly fishers and tyers, too. There's a lot of casting technique here that calls for dedicated practice, and a few discoveries about the hatches that make it worthwhile for the serious angler.

Published by: Crown. **Price: $10.**

In the Ring of the Rise
By Vincent Marinaro

Marinaro, the lord of limestoners, carries his powers of observation to new heights—or rather, depths—in a very interesting analysis of the patterns and behaviors of rising trout. Some remarkable photographs and a mathematical proof of his theories about the rise forms are reminiscent of Newton and his apple and may have a like effect on fly fishing, at least to advanced wading scientists. Lots of fine-and-far-off fishing with a modern master and absorbing talk about flies and tackle. Well worth owning for the serious angler.

Published by: Crown. **Price:** $12.95.

Dressing Flies for Fresh & Salt Water
Modern Fly Dressings
for the Practical Angler
By Poul Jorgensen

In the flood of general interest fly-tying books that have appeared in the last decade, Jorgensen's work stands out for his sensible and still masterly approach to the art. *Modern Fly Dressings* is in many ways an update of the author's excellent first book, but the two together are a solid two-volume tying library worth owning. Jorgensen shows his master's hand in the selection of ties that are beautiful and functional. The first

FISHERMAN'S SPRING

RODERICK L. HAIG-BROWN

One of our finest nature writers—on the art and joy of early-season fishing

FISHERMAN'S SUMMER

"Not since Izaak Walton has there been a writer who can describe the joys of fishing as does Haig-Brown!"

volume is somewhat easier to follow visually than *Modern Fly Dressings,* but the latter contains some good caddis ties that the proficient tyer will want to get into before the next season.

Published by: Winchester. **Prices:** $12.95, $15.00.

A Modern Dry Fly Code
By Vince Marinaro

A Modern Dry Fly Code was first released a couple of decades ago as a limited edition that soon commanded exorbitant prices secondhand. It was the first book to deal with terrestrials in a systematic way. Since its re-issue by Crown, it has become a staple work on modern fly fishing. No angler's education is complete without it.

Published by: Crown. **Price:** $10.

New Streamside Guide
By Art Flick

Art Flick's book was the first of Nick Lyons' reprints at Crown Publishers and the one that ushered in the modern renaissance of the literature of the sport. Though it doesn't have universal application — it's directed toward fishing upstate New York rivers — its methodology has universal application. The *Streamside Guide* is the source for much of our modern hatch-matching inspiration and has been for years.

Published by: Crown. **Price:** $4.95.

Nymph Fishing
for Chalk Stream Trout
Minor Tactics of the Trout Stream
By G. E. M. Skues

Skues is to nymph fishing what F. M. Halford is to the dry fly. These two English contemporaries from their turn-of-the-century vantage points developed the two branches of the sport almost single-handedly. Skues' classics have been reprinted together. *Nymph Fishing* was originally issued in 1910 and with its sub-surface advocacy caused great anxiety among

"When one has fished a water season after season for five years, then its friendship is a great and living thing."
WILLIAM CAINE

FLY FISHING BOOKS 137

top of the line

the floating fly dogmatists. *Minor Tactics* came out in 1939 after the controversy had been settled to accommodate both sides. Fine books.

Published by: A & C Black. **Price:** $7.95.

Nymph Fishing for Larger Trout
By Charles Brooks

Charlie Brooks has a unique position among trout writers. From his West Yellowstone, Montana, home he has developed a large body of theoretical information on fishing for big trout with heavy tackle. In a simple writing style he details the techniques he has learned for using big flies and has come as close to systematizing western big water trout fishing as anyone. A solid work whose importance will certainly grow.

Published by: Crown. **Price:** $9.95.

Nymphs
By Ernie Schwiebert

The only flaw in this excellent work is the lack of illustrations of the artificials that Schweibert describes. Otherwise a detailed text and some breathtaking illustrations of the naturals continue the matching techniques Schwiebert developed in *Matching the Hatch.* Like the earlier work this is a true classic and important for any serious trout angler.

Published by: Winchester. **Price:** $12.95.

Professional Fly Tying,
Spinning and Tackle Making Manual
By George Leonard Herter

Well, what can you say about Herter's massive, wonderfully chaotic tome? The title goes on and on and so does the book, which covers lots of practical and weird things about tackle making. It can carry you through a hard winter's doldrums single-handedly. Unabashedly funny

ERNEST SCHWIEBERT

NYMPHS

A COMPLETE GUIDE TO NATURALS AND IMITATIONS

By the author of *Matching the Hatch*

Charles E. Brooks
NYMPH FISHING
FOR LARGER TROUT
Illustrated by Dave Whitlock

top of the line

in places, too. George Leonard Herter strikes again!

Published by: Herter's. **Price:** $4.39.

Reservoir and Lake Flies
By John Veniard

John Veniard, one of England's best-known fly crafters, has put together in one place much of what the British have learned about fly patterns for what they call still-water angling. This recent development over there has produced its own styles, tackle and techniques and some of it would be useful for Americans seeking trout in our own impoundments. Plenty of patterns and finely illustrated.

Published by: St. Martin's Press. **Price:** $17.50.

Secrets of Fishing the Nymph
By Ed Sisty

An odd little book by veteran western fly fisherman Ed Sisty (he also did the cartoonlike drawings for his booklet) that has a few interesting theories about nymph fishing to offer, not the least of which is "smelling them out" — Sisty claims you can smell schooled fish, which perhaps you can in unpolluted western streams. Well worth a dollar, if you're unacquainted with the basics of nymphing and don't want to part with the price of the several books on the subject. A short course, but a practical one.

Published by: Ed Sisty's Streamside Adventures (3751 Inca St., Denver, CO 80211). **Price:** $1.

Selective Trout
By Doug Swisher and Carl Richards

Though *Selective Trout* does not have the universal application that some anglers believe, it's still a very important book. It deals with the authors' mayfly and nymph imita-

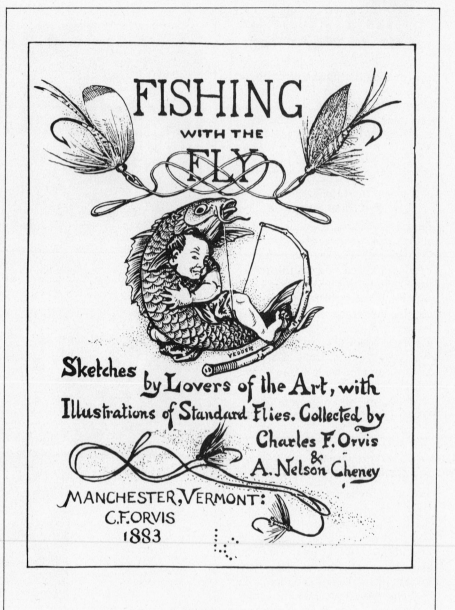

FISHING WITH THE FLY

Sketches by Lovers of the Art, with Illustrations of Standard Flies. Collected by Charles F. Orvis & A. Nelson Cheney

MANCHESTER, VERMONT: C.F. ORVIS 1883

AVOID BULKY FLIES

The great point, then, in fly-dressing, is to make the artificial fly resemble the natural insect in shape, and the great characteristic of all river insects is extreme lightness and neatness of form. Our great objection to the flies in common use is, that they are much too bushy; so much so, that there are few flies to be got in the tackle-shops which we could use with any degree of confidence in clear water. Every possible advantage is in favour of a lightly-dressed fly; it is more like a natural insect; it falls lighter on the water, and every angler knows the importance of making his fly fall gently, and there being less material about it, the artificial nature of that material is not so easily detected; and also, as the hook is not so much covered with feathers, there is a much better chance of hooking a trout when it rises. We wish to impress very strongly upon the reader the necessity of avoiding bulky flies.

The Practical Angler (1857).
By W. C. Stewart.

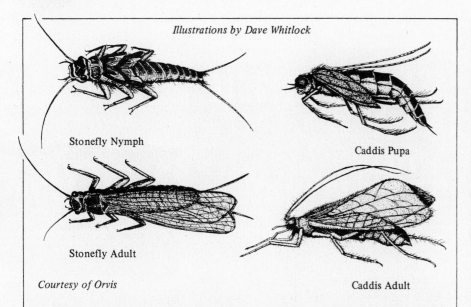

Illustrations by Dave Whitlock

Stonefly Nymph

Caddis Pupa

Stonefly Adult

Caddis Adult

Courtesy of Orvis

ENTOMOLOGY & THE FLY TYER

Close working knowledge of their streams is the fly fisherman's stock-in-trade, and for the fly tyers among them there exists a rich source of information about under-water insect life in the papers and journals of the entomologists. This is a species-by-species affair, and titles like *The Caddis Flies or Trichoptera of Illinois* may make you cringe but the value of the work of these scientists is hard to appreciate unless you try to find it elsewhere. Nonetheless, it is hard to translate their studies into fishing information, and this material is for dedicated anglers and tyers only.

One recent tying book has already made the vital connection between fly tying and entomology, *The Fly Tyer's Almanac* by Bob Boyle and Dave Whitlock (Crown). It contains a very useful listing of out-of-print book services and specialists in entomological books and papers, as well as a glossary of entomological terms, mostly for caddis and odonata (dragonflies and damsel flies) and some extracts that perfectly illustrate the point. The Dover two-volume paperback, *Insects,* by David Sharp ($10), is a good grounding in entomology, even though it only goes down as far as families. Volume 2

features the most aquatic insect material.

Here are a few places you may want to investigate for further reading; ask for a catalog on your subject interest:

Entomological Reprint Specialists
P.O. Box 77224
Dockweiler Station
Los Angeles, California 90007

Kraus Periodicals
Route 100
Millwood, New Jersey 10546

Henry Tripp
92-06 Jamaica Avenue
Woodhaven, New York 11421

E. W. Classey Ltd.
Park Road, Fraington
Oxon, SN7
England

Boyle lists several others in *The Fly Tyer's Almanac,* but unless you already have a specific book or paper in mind, you'd do well to start with these catalogs to see if you really want to take this avenue to improve your fly tying and angling. It might seem that the laboratory approach takes the fun out of a Sunday afternoon's fishing, but in actuality it adds something to the whole art of angling — often a 4-pounder on the end of a line. **—J. H.**

tions and their new hackle patterns. Very well illustrated.
Published by: Crown. **Price:** $10.

The Soft-Hackled Fly
By Sylvester Nemes

A pleasant little book in which the soft-hackle fly (as opposed to the properly stiff, bouncy hackle of traditional flies) is resurrected from angling obscurity. The soft-hackled fly is basically a wet fly tie that Nemes traces back to Dame Juliana and beyond, claiming all the way that it is the best new old fly since the Quill Gordon. It's easy to see how that might be true, since the soft-hackled fly could easily be taken for an emerger that is no longer a nymph or pupa, but not yet a dun. Pete Hidy had this tantalizing intermediate stage in mind in his edition of Leisenring's *The Art of Tying the Wet Fly,* but *The Soft-Hackled Fly* makes a bit more sense of it.
Published by: Chatham Press. **Price:** $4.95 paperback, $7.95 cloth.

Steelhead Fly Fishing and Flies
By Trey Combs

An excellent primer of the sport written in a very simple, clear way. Combs describes a year-round approach to these ocean-run rainbows that grow to enormous size. The history and illustrations of the most popular fly patterns are very valuable. Should be a hardback for the money, but that's modern life.
Published by: Salmon Trout Steelheader. **Price:** $9.

Streamer Fly Tying and Fishing
By Joseph D. Bates, Jr.

Another member of Bates' series of informative books. He tells as much as is known about the intricacies of streamer flies including their history, development, use and the patterns that are most effective. Streamer

See page 139 for a review

top of the line

fishing is an often neglected part of the education of a fly fisher but it's a deadly and fun way to catch big fish.

Published by: Stackpole. **Price:** $8.95.

Tactics on Trout
By Ray Ovington

A good book for the intermediate angler who wants to know the ins and outs of reading the water — probably the most difficult single thing to learn. As far as is possible, the illustrations in this work (which dominate it) transmit the information well. Unless you've hired a veteran angler to tell you patiently where trout are lying, read this one.

Published by: Knopf. **Price:** $10.95.

Tie a Fly, Catch a Trout
By S. R. Slaymaker II

Three of the grand old gentlemen of angling, Charlie Fox (foreword), George Harvey (tying instructions and drawings) and Sam Slaymaker (editor), combine their talents and experience to bring together one of the best beginner's guides to fly tying to date. Like all manuals, this one suffers from one inevitable drawback: It's easier and more fun to learn fly tying from someone else. And even in this book there could be more photographs of the steps along each tie. The title makes it sound easy, but those who've already been out on the stream know better. Still, a good guide for the enthusiastic beginner, since the author relates the specific ties to fishing situations.

Published by: Harper & Row. **Price:** $8.95.

Trout
By Ray Bergman

Ray Bergman's *Trout* is the classic American work on that fish. Despite

See page 135 for a review

The Trout Fisherman's Bible in its third edition, with new material by Edward C. Janes on recent developments in trout rods, reels, flies, lures, and other tackle

"Bait the hook well; this fish will bite."
SHAKESPEARE, *Much Ado About Nothing*

FLY FISHING BOOKS 141

top of the line

claims of the importance of other books, the new edition of the 1930s volume remains as basically relevant as ever to the angler who wants to know trout fishing from a position not rigidly defined by orthodoxy. Edward Janes wrote some interesting appendix material for this edition, mostly about changes in tackle. Bergman in a plain style covers what there is to cover with cant. Your angling education can't be complete without this book.

Published by: Knopf. **Price:** $15.

Trout Fishing
By Joe Brooks

Trout Fishing was not only the finest book among the many good ones Joe Brooks wrote but also the best single primer on the sport, especially for the westerner. Brooks covered everything from the history of angling to its modern tackle, the species of trout, the modern strategies and the intricacies of casting. Wonderfully illustrated with lots of color and line drawings.

Published by: Harper & Row. **Price:** $10.

Trout Fishing
A Basic Guide to Dry-Fly Fishing
By Charley Dickey and Fred Moses

The subtitle of this paperback is what's important: it's a bargain guide to dry fly techniques and tackle that stands up well against the other higher-priced general fly fishing guides. The special emphasis on the aesthetics and thrills of the dry fly will be welcome to the most knowledgeable angler, who may find a few tricks of the trade here that he's missed in Swisher, Schwiebert, et al. Nothing is taken for granted, on the other hand, and those who've learned to cast and are ready for a season of specialization could do well with this book as a guide.

Published by: Oxmoor House. **Price:** $2.95.

top of the line

Art Flick's Master Fly-Tying Guide
By Art Flick

Art Flick, the guy who started the fly fishing book revival, is the starting pitcher in this 1974 all-star team of master tyers, including Helen Shaw, Lefty Kreh covering saltwater patterns, Swisher and Richards in the outfield, Ed Koch on terrestrials, and a good dozen assorted other ties that make this book the learner's best friend. It's well illustrated and a great buy in the paperback edition. A good workbook for second-year tyers.

Published by: Crown. **Price:** $10 hardcover, $5.95 paperback.

How To Tie Freshwater Flies
By Kenneth E. Bay

Learning to tie, even more than the other angling skills, is best accomplished by personal instruction and lots of individual practice. But the Bay book, which focuses primarily on individual tying steps rather than particular ties, is the next best thing. Part of that can be attributed to Matty Vinciguerra's remarkable photography, and to plain good planning. Enough complete ties to satisfy the beginner's urge to complete a first fly—wet, dry, or nymph—and lots of good advice.

Published by: Winchester. **Price:** $10.

Fly Fishing for Trout:
A Guide for Adult Beginners
By Richard Talleur

If you've just given up hope of converting the heathen baitcaster by sermon, try giving him—or her—this beginner's guide for grown-ups. Its chattiness may put off the knowledgeable angler, but Talleur does convey a genuine enthusiasm that has to rub off on anyone who's at least curious. A full course from whybother to tying basics, ending on a note of trouting ethics, and laced with good, simple advice.

Published by: Winchester. **Price:** $10.

A THINKING MAN'S GUIDE TO TROUT ANGLING

Fishing the Dry Fly as a Living Insect

AN UNORTHODOX METHOD

LEONARD M. WRIGHT, JR.

See page 132 for a review

top of the line

Trout Flies
By Richard Salmon

A truly elegant addition to the book and tying material collection of serious anglers is the limited edition of *Trout Flies* by Richard Salmon. There are only 589 copies of this book. It includes the actual furs, feathers and tinsels used by the author in tying the classic trout patterns he describes in Spencerian script prose. There are line drawings as well as descriptions of the flies. Leonard is marketing this fine, step-by-step tying aid.

Trout Madness
By Robert Traver

Written in the early 1960s, this was one of the books that ushered in the current rage in fly fishing. Traver, who is actually retired Michigan Supreme Court Judge John Voelker, is certainly one of the least pretentious and most enjoyable of all fishing writers. *Trout Madness* is a series of humorous essays on or hymns of joy to various aspects of the sport. After you finish this one, read his *Trout Magic*, an equal delight.

Published by: St. Martin's Press. **Price:** $8.95.

A Trout and Salmon Fisherman For Seventy-Five Years
By Edward Hewitt

Hewitt, who fished into his 90th year, has two ordinary lifetimes astream. In his inimitable, though a bit stodgy, style, he has a lot to say. Must reading for a history of the sport from the turn of the century to its midpoint and the beginning of the modern era.

Published by: Fly Fisherman's Bookcase. **Price:** $1.25.

Robert H. Boyle and Dave Whitlock

The Fly-Tyer's Almanac

A PRACTICAL, FULLY ILLUSTRATED GUIDE TO THE LATEST ADVANCES AND DEVELOPMENTS IN FLY TYING, INCLUDING MORE THAN 20 PROVEN PATTERNS FOR FRESH- AND SALTWATER, DESCRIBED BY THEIR CREATORS—NEW MATERIALS, TOOLS, AND TECHNIQUES—PROFILES OF FAMOUS TYERS—HELPFUL SCIENTIFIC STUDIES—AND MUCH MORE

See page 135 for a review

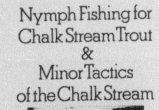

Nymph Fishing for Chalk Stream Trout & Minor Tactics of the Chalk Stream

G E M Skues

See page 136 for a review

"We have two literatures of fishing, one of retirement to old meadows, the other of going out to new waters."
JOHN McDONALD

FLY FISHING BOOKS **143**

THE Experienc'd Angler: or Angling Improved.

Sold by Rich Marriott in St Dunstans Churchyard
Vaughan sculp

Trout Fishin'
by Joe Brooks

SELECTIVE TROUT
A DRAMATICALLY NEW AND SCIENTIFIC APPROACH TO TROUT FISHING ON EASTERN AND WESTERN RIVERS
by
DOUG SWISHER and CARL RICHARDS
Introduction by JOE BROOKS

See page 141 for a review

See page 138 for a review

top of the line

The Trout and the Stream
By Charles Brooks

The second of Brooks' trilogy on fishing for western trout. It deals with the world of trout in running water from an ecological perspective. He offers his favorite patterns and angling techniques as well as dealing with stream conservation and tackle. A fine source for the western or vacationing fisher.

Published by: Crown. **Price:** $7.95.

Western Trout Fly Tying Manual
By Jack Dennis

This is one of those regional books that has caught on all over the country. Dennis deals with the intricacies of putting together western flies. He makes especially clear the nuances of handling deer hair. Finely illustrated. A very popular book in the mountain states.

Published by: Snake River. **Price:** $6.95.

The Year of the Angler
By Steve Raymond

Steve Raymond's book, which owes something to Ernie Schwiebert's stylistic approach, tells about his journey to rivers through the seasons. Also like the writings of Roderick Haig-Brown, this is an enjoyable book for the angler who doesn't have to be force-fed information on how to catch lunkers.

Published by: Winchester. **Price:** $10.

Roderick Haig-Brown

(continued from page 133)

of well-bound books, sipping brandy and wearing a cowboy belt buckle with a bighorn ram on it, the gift of the Alberta Fish and Game Department, I began to be able to visualize that powerful amalgamation and coherence it takes to make a successful frontiersman. In Haig-Brown, a Western Canadian with roots in Thomas Hardy's England, I imagined I saw an exemplary instance of the genre.

He had just made his first trip back to his place of origin in England, wandering around the streams he had fished and the places of his childhood unseen in forty years. I wondered how it had been.

"It was like being psychoanalyzed," he said.

Such a life does not make sentimentalists.

As this book was going to press, Roderick Haig-Brown passed away. If one person could be said to sum up all the best aspects of angling in this century, it was he. A dedicated environmentalist, a superb writer and a knowledgeable angler, he will surely be missed. And he will never be replaced.
—H.H.

Books are a basic fly fishing accessory

(continued from page 124)

you've been, as an angler you have an obligation to take a look at a couple of the classics. The truth be known, few people have really ever read even the world-famous *Compleat Angler* by Izaak Walton. It takes some time to get used to the heavy-handed prose of the old masters but once you do it's worthwhile. (Okay, okay, if you can't manage all of the *Compleat Angler*, at least try Cotton's fly-fishing section that appeared starting with the fifth edition.)

Another possibility is Dame Juliana Berners' *Treatyse on Fysshynge wyth an Angle*, written in the late 15th Century and the first angling book on record. She even supplied us with fly patterns.

There are plenty of others buried in the past but if you want to get at the immediate roots of fly fishing try the 19th Century and important authors like W. C. Stewart and Alfred Ronalds.

If you don't want to delve too heavily into the past you might settle for the late Arnold Gingrich's *The Fishing in Print*, which has a number of full ex-cerpts from our forebears and a good history as well.

The anecdotes and literature of the sport may not sell as well as the how-to books but can be more lasting and enjoyable. In this century Roderick Haig-Brown, Robert Voelker and Nick Lyons are among the foremost practitioners of angling as a microcosm of life. If you get any info on catching fish from their books or the many others like them it's incidental but you'll certainly feel better about life as well as fishing. Their love of the sport is infectious but sometimes only the more reflective anglers are stricken.

The how-to books can baffle the beginner with their sheer number and complexity but actually they are very simple to handle. In the first place you have the general books, things like the aforementioned *Trout*, Joe Brooks' *Trout Fishing* or any of the introductory works. One or two of these will suffice.

After these introductions, the how-to books become more definite. Important volumes like Len Wright's masterful *Fishing the Dry Fly as a Living Insect*, a work on caddis-fly fishing, or the Swisher-Richards tome *Selective Trout*, deal with a particular kind of trout fishing that can be practiced around the country. The same would hold true for works like Charlie Brooks' series *Bigger Trout for the Western Fly Fisherman*, *The Trout and the Stream* and *Nymph Fishing for Larger Trout*, which are geared for the western angler.

What kind of fishing do you do? Where do you do it? These are the kinds of questions that you have to answer in buying a book as well as a rod. If you can't fish after dark then Jim Bashline's *Night Fishing for Trout* won't do you much good.

A glance through the table of contents of a book or skimming it in a tackle shop will reveal whether it's the book for you.

But you shouldn't let the thousands and thousands of titles of angling books scare you away. Get excited instead. As Karl Marx said, ignorance never solved anything. That goes double for fly fishing!

TACKLE
FOR SPINNING, BAITCASTING, TROLLING & RELATED TECHNIQUES

 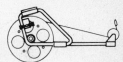

"North American sportsmen, even in this polluted age, are still blessed with a great variety of high quality fishing."
ERWIN BAUER

OPEN-FACED REELS 145

HOW TO BUY
A FRESHWATER SPINNING REEL

The cheapest and most expensive reels are not the worst and the best

By Lefty Kreh

Certain requirements are vital in the proper selection of a freshwater spinning reel, and other factors are either relatively unimportant or just window dressing.

There are several types of freshwater fishing where the spinning reel is best used, and they range from ultra-light rigs with 1- to 4-pound test lines to muskie outfits that demand stout lines and heavy lures.

Basically, however, freshwater spinning requirements fall into two general categories: ultra-light and medium tackle.

The ultra-light tackle would demand the use of lines testing from 1 to 4 pounds, and lures that are rarely more than ¼ ounce.

Such outfits are specially designed and the reels for this work are actually unsatisfactory for medium-size spinning, even though many anglers insist on using them for such work.

Ultra-light reels are used with soft rods to take trout, shad, bluegills and other panfish. Because the lures are so tiny and light (1/32 to ¼ ounce) the very thinnest lines should be employed.

Manufacturers will generally agree that their ultra-light reels are designed for lines **not to exceed 4 pounds test.** This is an extremely important fact

Although its revolving spool disqualifies it as a forerunner of the modern open-faced spinning reel, this 1926 experiment produced by the W. C. Manufacturing Co. may have given inventors tinkering with the open spool idea some lessons.

overlooked by many freshwater spin fishermen.

Nylon monofilament is the standard for spinning work. Nylon has a factor chemists call "memory," meaning that the nylon tends to remain in the position in which it was last stored. Heavier lines have greater memory than thinner lines.

Memory becomes very important so far as matching the proper diameter of line to the size of a spinning reel spool.

The true ultra-light spinning reel is smaller than the conventional medium size one. Since very thin, light lines to 4

pounds are used on these reels, little or no memory problems occur.

However, a spool with an outside diameter of less than 2¼ inches should never have line of more than 4-pound test on it. Too many anglers use 6-, 8- even 10-pound test on ultra-light reels. This is incorrect; the manufacturer did not design the reels for such lines, and the angler will suffer casting problems.

If you want to use 6 or more pound test line for spinning, use the conventional medium-size spool.

Ultra-light reels also need a small spool for another reason. The starting drag on any reel (that amount of pressure required to get the spool to begin slipping) is about twice the running drag. And, the larger the surface of the individual drag washers, the greater the starting drag generally is.

Thus anglers using 2- to 4-pound test lines will need a reel with a very light starting drag — and manufacturers have accommodated them by making small spools with tiny washers.

For perhaps 90 per cent of all spin fishing in this country, the standard medium-size reel seen in most tackle stores is the best selection.

But even here some judgments must be made. Color in all freshwater spinning reels is relatively unimportant, al-

(continued on next page)

HOW TO BUY A SPINNING REEL

(continued from preceding page)

though dark colors retain more heat in hotter climates and can be a bit uncomfortable to handle.

Finish is only a minor consideration and most reels have a finish that will hold up under freshwater angling.

Weight is somewhat important. Some of the best-designed reels are a bit on the heavy side, and weight requirements are dependent upon the strength of the angler. What is heavy for one person may be fairly light for another. Proper weight must be decided by the individual. But, be aware of this factor when looking over one you may consider buying.

A spool that is very wide holds considerably more line — usually more than is required or needed in fresh water. But wide spools can also be a liability. In order for the wire bail to swing easily around the spool and trap the line so you can retrieve the lure, it must of necessity be very large on wide spools.

Almost always when a bail refuses to close it is because it has been bent. The wider the spool, the larger the bail and the greater the chance it will get damaged and malfunction.

Light wire bails bend easier than heavier ones, and should be a factor to consider in purchasing a reel.

How easily a reel turns is also important. On a fishing trip you'll turn a handle for hours. A reel that is rough or difficult to turn can spoil a fishing trip. Check this out, remembering that sometimes even two reels of the same make and model will turn differently.

The handle of a reel may seem like a trivial consideration — until you hold it for several hours. Generally, the flattened types are more comfortable than round ones.

The cheapest and highest-priced reels are almost always not the worst and best. Generally a careful look at the above points will allow you to select an excellent reel for your freshwater fishing.

THE LAST HATCH
A FISHING MYSTERY
HARMON HENKIN

(continued from page 126)

going. Paul heaved himself up on the bank and paused for a moment to shake off the effects of the water. He looked across at Sid, who was staring at him with more than his usual alertness.

"Hate to say this, buddy, but despite what I told them back at the house you're the best suspect I have."

"I'm the only suspect you have. I'm like that squawfish you caught in the Clark Fork a couple weeks ago when you went back to town and told everyone you weren't skunked."

"Yeah. But you had a motive. Everyone knows you hated him for wanting to cut the creek up into plots."

"Look, Sid, I grew up on a little dirt farm down the valley. My father put my first fishing rod in my hands on this creek. When Halford got the place and kept me and everyone else off, sure I was mad. But I didn't do anything . . . at least not until he started up with that slug Wormer. But fighting him in court and at hearings is as far as I went. Sure, when we lost I was burned up enough to think about killing him. But if thinking like that is a crime we'd all be in jail."

"You had the time to kill him, too."

"But I didn't do it."

"Paul, it doesn't look real good. As Plotinus said, 'The circumstances dictate the person.' "

"But Plotinus isn't part of a jury of my peers. So we'll have to find the real killer, as they say."

"How?"

"I never tried it before. But it's probably just like figuring out what fly to use to trick a trout. I can't believe detectives are smarter than just-folks."

"Probably the reverse is true."

"Right. When you get to a strange river there are always hints about what the fish will hit. You look at hatching insects, the temperature of the water, the kind of creek bottom and the time of the year. You have to use your eyes. Put all that data together, come up with the right pattern and toss the fly out. If you're right, you'll have a fish on."

"What if you're wrong?"

"Then you have to go and get more information. Are the trout feeding on the bottom or near the top? Are they taking hatching insects on

(continued on page 169)

"At the outset, the fact should be recognized that the community of fishermen constitute a separate class or subrace among the inhabitants of the earth." GROVER CLEVELAND

OPEN-FACED REELS 147

ROUGHFISHING: A GENTLE ART

By Harmon Henkin

In England they take these things more seriously.

Over here the image conjured up by the term roughfishing is of someone too lazy — or too intelligent — to work like decent folks from 9 to 5, of someone lounging on an idyllic river bank waiting for a carp, catfish or the like to sample an atrocious-looking hunk of bait.

But in Europe, where the cliched trout angler is outnumbered many times over by fishermen seeking tench, dace, chub, eels and the omnipresent carp, roughfishing is known to be as difficult as any type of angling.

And, alas, as our water conditions deteriorate, there will be more and more anglers with the glum option of either roughfish or no fish at all.

Tackle for this sort of angling can be summed up in one word: gentle. The act of

tossing a doughball, nightcrawler, cut bait or the like requires a fine touch. Abrasive impact of bait with water can mean nothing at the end of the line. Bare hooks catch few fish, as Confucius said.

The best outfits are open-faced spinning reels attached to long, limber rods. A seven, eight or even longer rod is the favorite of English anglers. The rods should not be tippy, which makes for a rougher landing than those sticks which respond down to their butt. Bait rods are usually "heaved" rather than cast so the longer rod is better.

Open-faced reels are better than their closed-mouth kinfolk because of the way roughfish approach bait — gingerly and suspiciously. Carp don't hit doughballs the way bass hit surface plugs, to say the least. Once you cast out, flip the bail open and allow the fish to take out all the line it wants. Though you can do the same thing with a closed-faced reel, things work simpler with open-faced ones. More control.

Make your monofilament as light as possible. Unless you are after big bozo carp or channel catfish or angling turbulent spots like dam tailwaters or mighty rivers, your line shouldn't be above No. 6. And you'll be more successful if it's No. 4 or less.

Your hooks should be small as well. Since you can't prevent these fish from swallowing the bait anyway, it's simpler to go with models such as Eagle Claw baithooks in sizes under No. 8.

Split shot, whenever possible, works more efficiently than larger sinkers. It can be added in tiny increments to get the bait down on the bottom where it belongs yet not stick it in the mud. Roughfish can be very sensitive to weight.

My favorite Maryland carp outfit when I was a roughfishing maniac consisted of an old converted 8½-foot Montague bamboo rod on which I put a spinning reel seat and large guides. I used an Alcedo Micron with No. 2 Dupont Stren and in most still waters no weight at all. It was deadly and represented an almost ideal outfit.

A SPINNING REEL PRIMER

A spinning reel is a simplified casting machine in that the line, pulled by the lure or bait, merely unfurls from the reel's stationary spool. Since the spool does not revolve there is little friction, minimum possibility of backlash; smooth, long casts with light lures are routine.

Spinning reels have anti-reverse locks, which prevent the crank handle from turning backward. The anti-reverse lock is useful when playing hooked fish, and when trolling or still fishing since it will prevent line from paying out except against the tension of the pre-set drag.

Spinning reels are designed to be used chiefly with monofilament line. The reels are mounted under the rod, which keeps the cast line from slapping against the rod.

Spinning reels have three kinds of line pick-up mechanisms: bail, manual and automatic. The bail type, which is most popular, is a wire ring with a roller which catches the line and circles the spool when the handle is turned. thus re-spooling the line. The bail must be flipped downward, or "opened" by the angler to free the line prior to casting.

Spinning reels with manual pick-ups have no bail but, instead, a simple roller mounted on the spool housing. The angler uses the tip of his forefinger to lift line from the roller and free it for a cast, replacing line to the roller the same way to pick up and retrieve line.

Automatic pick-ups are small, curved metal "arms" on the spool housing which catch and secure the line.

To cast, the fisherman lifts line from the re-spool line, the handle is cranked forward and the miniature pick-up automatically contacts and spools the line.

Most spinning reels have the handle mounted on the left side, which means that the right-handed caster casts with his right hand and then retrieves with his left. A left-handed caster will cast with his left, switch the rod to his right hand, and crank the reel with his left hand.

To give fishermen the opportunity to handle a spinning rod any way they like, some reels are offered in either right- or left-hand models; some are so built that the handle is interchangeable and can be mounted on either the left or right side.

A quick, easy spool release is important. Many spinning reels have a depressible button on the spool face which, when pressed, instantly releases the spool.

(continued on page 159)

Know your reel before you cast

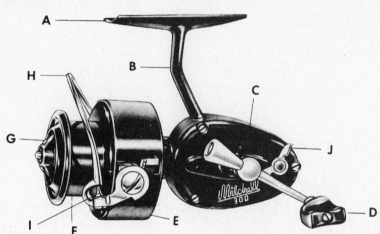

Much can be learned by observing the different fishing reels, their parts, and their functions. There are certain features which are desirable in each reel; there are certain parts which must be made properly, and located properly, if they are going to be useful. Casting with the reels is indeed important, but it is another step, a step which should take place only *after* a study has been made of the mechanics of an individual reel and the application of the mechanics to the individual reel. Learn about your reel first, and good casting will come more naturally.

(A) Reel foot. This is the part of the spinning reel which attaches to the rod. This part should be slim and streamlined so it will fit into the reel seat, yet strong enough to support th[e] reel.

(B) Reel stem. This is the connection b[e-]tween the reel foot and the gear box. It shoul[d] be long enough to keep the reel away from th[e] fisherman's hand, thus keeping him from bar[k-]ing his knuckles.

(C) Housing (gear box). This part of the re[el] contains most of the mechanism which cause[s] the reel to operate. Herein lie the gears, slide[s] and shafts which cause the rotating head [to] turn, the spool to move in and out, and s[o] forth. Half of the housing can be removed, pe[r-]mitting inspection and lubrication of the gear[s.] The removable portion is called the cover plat[e.]

(D) Handle. This handle is turned while r[e-]trieving line or fighting fish. While a foldi[ng] handle is unimportant during actual fishing, it [is] desirable as a storage aid. Just make sure th[e] handle knob is large enough and comfortab[le] enough to prevent the hand from tiring.

(E) Rotating head (winding cup). This pa[rt] revolves as the handle is turned and, since oth[er] mechanisms are mounted on it, it should b[e] counterweighted for perfect balance. Check t[he] balance of the rotating head by turning the ha[n-]dle and looking for wobble. Remember, a sm[all]

GAMEFISH: SMALLMOUTH

NAMES
Black Bass, Bronze Bass, Black Perch, Brown Bass, Gold Bass, Little Bass, Bronze Back, Tiger Bass. *(Micropterus dolemieui)*

DISTRIBUTION
Like the Largemouth Bass, the Smallmouth is found not only throughout the continental United States, but also in Mexico and Canada. It is indigenous to the Great Lakes region, New England, and the area from Georgia west to the Mississippi River Valley.

DESCRIPTION
The Smallmouth is reputed to be the most worthwhile of game fish due to its excellent fighting strength and feisty nature. Lighter in coloring than the Largemouth, it tends towards greenish-bronze on the back, shading into light green or brown with an off-white underside. Darker, vertical stripes mark the sides. The dorsal fin is only slightly notched and appears to run continuously along the top. The jaw joint of the Smallmouth does not extend beyond the end of the eye and cleek scales range from 12 to 17 rows.

SIZE
The average weight of the Smallmouth Bass is between 1 and 3 pounds. Anything over 5 pounds is considered an unusually large catch.

HABITAT
The Smallmouth Bass is found in cold, clear lakes and rapidly flowing streams. It tends to seek out deep pools near the foot of rapids and prefers areas close to submerged rocks and gravel beds. In lakes, it is often found near drop-offs, rocky ledges, or shoals; areas where they can lie close to protective growth.

FEEDING HABITS
Smallmouth Bass prefer to feed in early morning but they can be taken at almost any time of the day. Although somewhat particular in its feeding habits, the Smallmouth Bass will eat anything from small fish to mayflies. Favorite foods include crayfish and hellgrammites.

BEST FEEDING TEMPERATURE
Between 60 and 70 degrees.

TACKLE
Standard equipment for the tough smallmouth, when it's not at trolling depths, is medium-weight spinning or casting gear with spoons, spinners and medium-running plugs. In moving waters the smallmouth is prime prey for the flyfisher with an 8-foot rod and streamers or big nymphs.

Oh the brave Fisher's life,
It is the best of any,
'Tis full of pleasure, void of strife,
And 'tis belov'd of many:
    Other joys Are but toys;
    Only this Lawful is,
    For our skill Breeds no ill,
But content and pleasure.
IZAAK   WALTON

mount of wobble will appear in all reels.

(F) The spool. The spool of the spinning reel should have sufficient capacity to contain enough line for your fishing conditions. If your fishing calls for more than that amount of line, then you're going to need a larger reel. If ever, there is a question concerning the size of the spool, it is always better to get one with a larger capacity, since the capacity can always be decreased. On the other hand, if you first buy a reel with a small-capacity spool, there is nothing that can be done. As a general rule, most spinning reels will hold more than enough light spinning line. Observe the forward lip of the spool. This is the part of the spool that the line rushes against during the cast. This forward lip should be smooth and well rounded.

(G) The drag adjustment. This is a friction clutch mechanism which allows the spool to turn as line is drawn from it. The drag works only while fighting a fish and has nothing to do with casting or retrieving. Yet, fighting a fish is vital to the sport and a good reel will have a smooth drag. If the fisherman plans to exchange spools from time to time, and most fishermen do, it is desirable to have the simplest and least complicated drag mechanism available. Check the drag by removing the spool from the reel. If the drag is built into the spool, and the spool comes off the reel in a single unit, it is highly satisfactory. If, however, in removing the spool it is necessary to disassem-

ble a number of parts, and since these parts can be lost while you're fishing, it is best to avoid such a drag setup.

Another part of the drag (or you can call it a part of the spool) is the click (not illustrated). In a spinning-reel spool, there is a special mechanism that serves to warn the fisherman *when the spool is turning*. This click is nothing more than a noise-maker or signal. It serves several important purposes, and the clicking noise should be clear and audible.

(H) Bail pickup. This mechanism is swung out of the way while casting. It does absolutely nothing during the cast. At the end of the cast, however, a turn of the handle flips the bail over the front of the reel, thus capturing the line. Once the line is captured, the revolutions of the rotating head wind the line onto the spool.

(I) Pickup friction guide. Since fishing line rubbing against a piece of metal will eventually wear a groove into it, this part should be exceedingly hard. It should be positioned so the line rubs on it always. While rollers are frequently used as pickup friction guides, they are satisfactory only while they actually roll. A roller that fails to function because of dirt is far less valuable than a stationary friction guide made hard enough to resist line wear.

(J) Antireverse. This serves only to keep the handle from turning backward; thus, while fighting a fish, the fisherman can have his left hand free. The antireverse is generally left in

the "off" position so it is inoperative during normal casting and retrieving. It is an aid in fighting the fish, and that's when it should be used.

The antireverse serves an additional purpose, and that is for the new fisherman. A new fisherman who turns the handle of a spinning reel in the wrong direction is asking for disaster. This simple step can result in a tremendous tangle of line. The beginner might well engage the antireverse during his first few days of practice. With the antireverse engaged, it is impossible to turn the handle in the wrong direction.

Conveniently located, close to the handle, the antireverse should be engaged only while the fisherman is holding the handle. If it is necessary to let go of the handle in order to engage the antireverse, then reject the reel. As soon as you let go of the handle, it will start to spin backward, and engaging the antireverse at this time is sure to result in stripped gears.

(K) Manual pickup. Some reels are made as manual pickup reels while others have a manual pickup attachment which can be used in place of the full bail pickup. This mechanism is called a manual pickup because the line must be picked up by the fisherman.

From *Fishing Tackle and Techniques* by Dick Wolff. (C) 1961 by Dick Wolff. Used by permission of E. P. Dutton & Company.

Old reels work just as well

By Harmon Henkin

Recently a friend who is just beginning to fish watched as I rummaged around in the morass of assorted things in my garage.

An ancient Bache-Brown spinning reel turned up. The tarnished 25-year-old fellow was the first spinning reel I had ever owned. I put it aside one day when the handle fell off. The friend looked it over carefully, amazed at its age and manual half-bail.

He needed an all-around reel. Could he have it?

My first instinct was to defer on sentimental grounds. But then, looking around at the mounds of sentimentality, that didn't seem like a firm reason. So I explained the utterly simple mechanism. Just lift the slim bail handle, cast and replace the handle to retrieve. Nothing easier.

"But modern reels are so much better," I argued.

"Why?"

"They have ball bearings. They're smaller. They have automatic bails. All the latest gadgetry."

"Does that really make a difference?"

"The new ones have Teflon drags and

stuff."

"This drag seems smooth."

"It was a great drag. Never slipped."

"Are the new ones really any better?"

"Ah. Umm. Well, you see . . . just take the reel. It's as good as you'll ever need. Send it back to White Plains and get the handle redone."

He seemed happy as he left with it. I pondered my reaction.

Are the new ones really better than the classics? Probably not better than the average angler would ever need. We don't buy Ferraris because they handle better than Chevies. We buy them for other, more metaphysical reasons. The same goes for fishing tackle.

You might as well get the best reel for the money, one that has all the latest deluxe features.

But that doesn't mean they're better. That's a different quality entirely.

top of the line

WHAT WE LOOKED FOR IN QUALITY

The general quality of spinning reels has greatly increased over the past few years. In a very competitive market the junkers are becoming more isolated and can be more easily avoided.

This competition made it rather difficult to compile the following list of leading products. On one hand we delved into those new high-quality reels such as the Olympics and Daiwas that have taken over much of the market but we were also impressed with old favorites that remain high-quality items such as the Quicks, Mitchells and Brettons.

On the most practical level, those excellent reels from the 50s and 60s are still excellent reels. Many anglers who own vintage spinning outfits are still happy with them. So despite revolutionary changes, the criteria of workability remain the same. What we sought in the reels listed were models that would simply do the job of catching fish. Fancy innovations have not, we hope, clouded our judgment.

Perhaps the most important consideration was the smoothness of the drag. Line should go out with a running fish evenly and without increasing tension. Another thing we took note of was whether the line has a tendency to get wrapped up on the central pillar of the reel. Other standards were corrosion resistance, the accessibility of the drag, sturdiness of the bail and overall construction.

BERKLEY 604

BERKLEY CASTAMATIC. Progress? Well, anyway, the Castamatic has a fingertip lever that opens the bail for casting. They advertise that you'll never have to feel around for the line again, scarcely one of the major problems facing the Western World. High quality with such features as positive drag adjustments knob, stainless-steel ball bearings, machine-cut helical gears and rolling line guide. An interesting piece of equipment.

BERKLEY 604. The Berkley model 604 ultra-light spinning reel offers the company's cam-operated bail system. The reel is designed to go with the para-metric spinning rods line. It has a 3.6:1 retrieve ratio, a side plate that's removable with the twist of a coin and an antifoul drag knob.

BRETTON. The old Martin Company, famed for its automatic fly reels, is now importing these respected French reels. They rank along with Quick, Alcedo and Record as the best made in Europe. Brettons are simple, classically designed reels available in sizes from ultra-light to light saltwater. Very dependable.

BROWNING. A readily available line of reels produced by the gunmaker. While not up to the standards of the company's fine shotguns and pistols, these medium-priced, good quality reels range from an ultra-lightish 8-ouncer with a fast retrieve to a 15-ouncer that's good for steelhead and light saltwater work.

FAVORITES OF THE EXPERTS

The Mitchell 300 series of reels offered by Garcia remains the most popular open-faced spinning reel line despite the recent market advances and technological innovations made by the Japanese.

"I've used them for years and am quite satisfied," said one Southern spinfishing fanatic. "I can depend on them," said another.

Other reels chosen by our unofficial panel of experts around the country were the Zebco Cardinal – another finely tuned model – Quicks and the Penn 700 series. Some other experts preferred the Shakespeare's top of the line reels. Interestingly, in the Northeast there was more than a smattering of support for Orvis' European imports despite a lack of national advertising. Word of mouth gets around, too. There was a strong cry from one writer for the Alcedo Micron. "I don't care what anyone else says. That's the best reel."

BROWNING

top of the line

DAIWA GOLD LINE. One of the best values on the market in open-faced, skirted spool spinning reels. The days when *made in Japan* was a term of derision are gone; quality even touches products not used abundantly over there like sport fishing tackle. In sizes ranging from ultra-light to heavy-duty for salt water, the reel has features like a crank in right- or left-handed retrieve, stainless-steel ball-bearings, a skirted spool mechanism to keep line from getting entangled in the gears and a six-piece drag system. Enough said. They also make a special very deluxe series of open-facers called the SS (gulp) Series with a big teak handle, a black satin body and other ritzy goodies.

EAGLE CLAW MEDITERRANE-AN. A carefully crafted line of open-faced spinning reels with all the newly incorporated features of the breed including a fast spool release, a heavy-duty bail pickup, ball bearing head and an adjustable friction drag. These "Neapolitan specials" are available from ultra-light to heavy saltwater with gear ratios ranging from a zingy 5.5 to 1 on the 6-ounce ultra light to a respectable 3.5 to 1 on the 21-ounce briny model. Considered one of the better practical reels available.

FEURER BROTHERS. This is an obscure old spinning reel manufacturer that deserves more recognition. Among the quality items this White Plains, New York, firm markets is the classic Bache Brown, around almost continually since the late 1940s when the field was pretty empty. The 9-ounce model featuring a finger-controlled antireverse is simplicity itself. I still have one that is more than 25 years old. Feurer sells a variety of other open-facers including the larger Spinster and the Mastereel. Worth trying to find.

BERKLEY CASTAMATIC

BRETTON

BASS PRO SHOP BAGS
A convenient way to carry your favorite reels around. They come with Velcro fasteners. Just slip the reel into the vinyl bag and away you go.

DAIWA GOLD LINE

EAGLE CLAW MEDITERRANEAN

FEURER BROTHERS

Workhorses: the Shakespeare 2052,
the Daiwa 2500 and the Zebco Cardinal 4.

THREE GOOD REELS FOR WESTERN TROUT

By Norman Strung

Three reels are my workhorses for trout fishing out West: the Shakespeare 2052, the Diawa 2500 and Zebco's Cardinal 4.

The Shakespeare 2052 is a smooth-operating, well-engineered reel with a reliable drag system. I've used this relative lightweight (7½ ounces) in pursuit of modest-sized, small-stream trout for several years now. The reel has suffered no major breakdowns and is still running quietly, an indication of a precise gearing system.

The drag deserves special note, in that this reel is essentially one-half of my ultra-light combination. Granted, 7½ ounces is a little heavy by Eastern standards, but I've acquired the Western taste for

SHAKESPEARE 2052

bigness. At any rate, I normally load the reel with two- to three-pound test line, according to water conditions, and have caught trout up to 4½ pounds with it. The drag has never malfunctioned — when you're dealing with

two-pound limits, that's a critical factor.

The reel is not, however, without fault. The worst one is that the pickup has a release position that coincides with the position I seem to want to cock it in most often, and there are times when I must make several attempts at locking the bail open before casting. This can be a powerful frustration when a swirl appears within lure range. Two other minor matters: the line tends to build up toward the front of the reel spool when you gather a fresh refill direct from a manufacturer's spool (as opposed to new spooling via sporting goods store machines), and Shakespeare is not a terribly popular brand. If the reel ever breaks down, I suspect it will prove difficult to find replacement parts locally.

There is beauty in simplicity, and that accounts for my endorsement of Daiwa's 2500, my heavyweight reel (15½ ounces) for steelhead and lake trout when they move into shallows.

The pickup on these reels is an inertia-triggered mechanism that is highly resistant to gumming and binding, and its design is such that there is no cog in the cocking device to break. The eccentric mechanism works directly off the main gear, so there are minimal parts within the body, and the reel can be quickly

(continued on next page)

top of the line

HEDDON. Featuring a multiple drag and a ball-bearing system for smoothness, Heddons are readily available. Often discounted, they'll do the job.

HEDDON CLASSICS. This line of reels is regarded as the first one to the barricades in the open-faced minirevolution. With models ranging from ultra-light to heavy saltwater, there are an extra-long handle, anodized outer parts, Teflon-coated line roller and all-ball-bearing construction. They boast a "magnum" (that's a favorite spinning word these days!) drag with a smooth, wide range. They don't brag about their weight but they are comparable to other similar model reels.

HERTER'S. The Herter's line is modestly priced in sizes from ultra-light with a 4 to 1 gear ratio, to a heavy saltwater model with a 3.5 to 1 gear ratio. They have a ball bearing mounted gear system, a die-cast aluminum case that's corrosion resistant and a brass pinion gear. They also have a stainless-steel bail. Well worth considering, regardless of who the real manufacturer is.

KENCOR. Kencor's entry in the better open-faced reel field consists of three models ranging from an ultra-light 10-ouncer to a medium to heavy saltwater reel at 21 ounces. They have a skirted spool, which helps keep monofilament from getting snagged up, as well as features found on more expensive reels such as ball-bearings, anti-corrosion finish, a manual or automatic bail system and right- or left-handed retrieve. They are nice-looking reels and a good value, especially for the aspiring serious spinner. Kencor also manufactures a lesser-priced line of reels that are a good buy for the beginner or those outgrowing close-faced models.

"Angling: incessant expectation, and perpetual disappointment."
ARTHUR YOUNG, *Travels in France*

OPEN-FACED REELS 153

top of the line

HEDDON CLASSIC

LEONARD. Ultra-light and lightweight spinning reels are new items from this venerable bamboo rod company, which is just beginning to spread out again after slacking off in the 1960s. Priced in the $30 range, they aren't for everyone, but their quality and claimed resistance to corrosion from salt water make them desirable to the serious spinner or brand-name-conscious dilettante.

MITCHELL 300

MITCHELL REEL FIELD REPAIR KIT

For owners of the popular Mitchell 300, 302 and 402 spinning reels the company sells a field repair kit which contains almost all of the parts that might need instant replacement plus gadgets for taking your reel apart. One kit is for the 300 and another one is marketed for the other two. Can be a trip saver.

MITCHELL 300. As the Garcia company likes to boast, the Mitchell 300 sold for $27 a quarter century ago and can be bought for less than that today. This reel is a longtime standard and one of the first to grab a major share of the market when the sport was introduced to this country. Whether it's a better reel today — as Garcia boasts — is another matter. It now has a Teflon drag, oilite bushings, a one-piece bail and a tungsten carbide line guide. They are widely available and there are many places to get them repaired. Despite everything that has happened in the spinning reel market, the Mitchell remains one of the most popular items.

THREE GOOD REELS

(continued from preceding page)

changed to left-hand operation in the field. While these limited parts minimize the chance for malfunction, the resulting tolerances are not exactly up to NASA standards, and unless you pack the body with cup grease (which stiffens in cold weather steelheading), the reel sounds like a coffee grinder.

One-piece parts have not been spared in the drag. Several Teflon washers and a spring-loaded pressure plate

2500C — 1 steel ball bearing

DAIWA 2500

ensure a smooth, even pull. The reliability of this drag has had some tough testing too; I've also used it for snook and snapper in salt water.

One other welcome feature on this reel is a high-speed retrieve (4:1 ratio). Steelhead, especially, are lightning fast, and should they come toward you, this rapid retrieve feature at least gives you a fighting chance to keep slack out of your line. Another small feature that anglers will greatly appreciate is a readily accessible tab on the skirted spool that will accept the tag end of your line, holding it firmly in place without snap clips or rubber bands.

Of all the reels I've tested and used for trout fishing, one of the newest has become the reel I use most often. Zebco's Cardinal 4 (11 ounces) incorporates nearly every pleasant feature I've found scattered across the sea

(continued on next page)

top of the line

MITCHELL 308

MITCHELL 308 AND 408. Like the Mitchell 300 and the 314, the 308 and 408 ultra-light reels are longtime American favorites. They remain a couple of the best-selling lightweights. The 308 has a 4.6:1 retrieve and the 408 has a very rapid 5.5:1 ratio. Now equipped with ball bearings for ease of operation, these reels make it remarkably easy to switch spools. The 408 has a chromed rotating spool guide and the 308 has a tungsten carbide guide for maximum performance. Also available in left-hand retrieve. Pretty good buys, for the ultra-light buff.

MITCHELL 408

THREE GOOD REELS FOR WESTERN TROUT
(continued from preceding page)

of today's brands. The line spool snaps on and off with the push of a button so you can change line weights fast, the throat is comparatively wide for maximum casting range, and the reel is well balanced and velvet quiet. The Cardinal's most innovative feature is a drag control located on the butt end of the reel housing. It's easy to reach when you're fighting a fish full of line-peeling energy, and it's even calibrated to line strengths, though I suspect the device can't be depended upon to deliver hairsplitting accuracy. My only reluctance to brand this one best is that I've worked with it for only a season-and-a-half now, so I really can't comment on its durability, which to some extent is a personal value. I don't feel the burning need to get every new gadget on the market, then replace it with the next new gadget. I'd much rather develop an intimate knowledge of, and close association with, a superior piece of machinery, using it long and using it well.

The rods I prefer for most of my trout fishing are distinctive — they're parabolic. The "omni," "universal," or "fast tip" rod was built for the fisherman who wanted one rod for everything. Their

light tip and fast tapering, stout butt allow for light action (and weights) at the tip, and enough backbone down the shaft of the rod to handle heavy pike. When it comes to most trout fishing, I don't want or need that universality. I prefer a soft action rod

ZEBCO CARDINAL 4

that bends to the corks and is sensitive to every nibble and strike.

These rods are admittedly hard to come by. Most of the major makers are on the fast-tip bandwagon. One option is to buy a 7-foot glass, 5- or 6-weight fly-rod blank and build a spinning rod onto the shaft. Herter's catalog features one of the best soft spinning rod blanks in kit form that I've run across (No. RB60J) but Herter's over-all quality has gone downhill so fast in the past two years that I hesitate to predict what you might end

(continued on next page)

LEONARD

top of the line

OLYMPIC. This Japanese import is so highly rated that it's giving American manufacturers fits. It has captured enough of the market over the past few years in terms of quality and percentage that U.S. companies are planning revenge, a definite bonus for fishermen. Top of the line Olympic is the Seiki 940 which has everything you want including a very fast 5.1:1 gear ratio, sealed ball-bearing pinion gear, stainless-steel spool and fancy bushing gear. The whole case is made from extra-light aluminum. At 11.6 ounces and with a capacity of 270 yards, the 940 is a fine all-around freshwater reel. There are lots of other Olympics deserving a further look by anglers once they realize that the Japanese are really hip to spin fishing, and no longer merely imitators of American products.

OLYMPIC

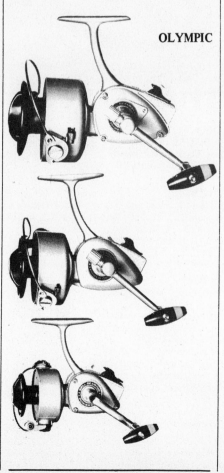

Three good reels

(continued from preceding page)

up with in the future. Of the few ready-made rods I've encountered, Leonard's 7-footer is my runaway favorite.

Should you not agree with my choice of parabolic shafts, my second choice would be a 6½- to 7-foot omni shaft, capable of handling ¼- to 3/8-ounce lures. Note, however, that my choice of length is predicated upon burly Western rivers. For spinning on smaller Eastern streams, you might want a shorter shaft. Brands of universal rods I have used and liked include Zebco, Diawa and Garcia's top-of-the-line models, in that order of preference.

One convention I strongly oppose on every commercial rod I've found is the size of the butt guide. I am a believer in a butt guide that is only slightly smaller in diameter than the size of the spool on your reel, and whenever time and desire are coincidental, I remove the second guide from the top on a new rod, move every other guide up a step, and install a larger guide in the butt position.

Yes, I'm aware that "exhaustive tests" have proven that a larger butt guide makes no difference in casting or performance, but tests or no, that larger guide makes a perceivable difference to me in both reach and feel. The only explanation I ever received for this feature not being offered at least as an option on rods was that it would cause packaging problems. And when it comes to those tests, I'm reminded that established scientific fact has proven inconclusively that bumblebees can't fly . . . . yet they do so very nicely.

Down and back at day dawn,
  Tramp from lake to lake,
Washing brain and heart clean
  Every step we take.
Leave to Robert Browning
  Beggars, fleas, and vines;
Leave to mournful Ruskin
  Popish Apennines,
Dirty stones of Venice,
  And his gas lamps seven,
We've the stones of Snowdon
  And the lamps of heaven.

CHARLES KINGSLEY
Letters and Memories
Aug., 1856.

top of the line

OLYMPIC A-M. One of the most interesting of Olympic's series of skirted spool spinning reels is their Model No. 4. Ultra-light, with a gear ratio of 4.5 to 1, it isn't that much bigger than a pack of cigarettes. It, and its bigger kin, have a small skirted spool that absolutely forbids line snagging. Well worth their cost. Also available in slightly different models in sizes up to heavy saltwater use.

ORVIS. This maker of fine bamboo rods also imports a line of quality spinning reels from Europe ranging from ultra-light to heavy-duty. The 6½-ounce lightweight is geared for use with No. 2 monofilament and lures in the 1/16-ounce category. Among the more expensive reels in their class, they are well constructed and designed for use on waters like bonefish flats, where a variety of reel sizes are required for a variety of tough fish. Well worth investigating, especially the 6-ounce manual retrieve bail model, one of the few manuals still available. The big reels have stainless-steel bearings constructed to beat the meanest briniest conditions.

PFLUEGER. Another one of the old, respected American makers of fishing tackle. Pfluegers are everywhere. These sturdily constructed reels are available from ultra-light to salt water. Repairs are easy to arrange. Like some other companies, Pflueger offers skirted models, which prevent line jams.

PFLUEGER 640. Best known for its Medalist fly reel, Pflueger has become a leader in the production of fine spinning reels, as well. Though all of their well-designed equipment is rated high by open-faced addicts, the 640 Ball Bearing series is rated tops. Available in standard sizes and capacities, the 640 can be had with a stainless-steel bail and line roller and a very high-speed retrieve ratio of 5.2:1.

BASS FISHING: OPEN-FACED VS. BAITCASTING REELS

Open-faced, underslung spinning reels are a lot of fun, and I use them often, especially in open water. But, as I have already explained, they are not as accurate as baitcasting reels. They do, however, permit more distance, and they will handle lures as light as 1/16 ounce if they are properly spooled with the right weight line.

One advantage — at least to me — is that many open-faced spinning reels have interchangeable spools that can be switched in seconds. (My baitcasting reels also have interchangeable spools that can be switched in seconds. (My baitcasting reels also have interspools ready: one loaded with 20-pound monofilament, one with 14-pound, and one with 8-pound. (But the 20-pound stuff doesn't work too well and tends to spring off the spool in coils, causing bird's nests.)

The drags on open-faced spinning reels are generally good. One can override the drag by fingering the line as it comes off the spool, but this method is not as easy or as natural as thumbing the spool on a baitcasting reel.

From *Fishing for Bass: Modern Tactics and Tackle* by A. D. Livingston. Copyright (C) 1974 by A. D. Livingston. Reprinted by permission of J. B. Lippincott Company.

GAMEFISH: LARGEMOUTH

NAMES
Green Trout, Bigmouth Bass, Straw Bass, Oswego Bass, Green Bass, Black Bass, Bayou Bass, Moss Bass, Lake Bass. *(Micropterus Salmoides)*

DISTRIBUTION
The largemouth bass is found in every area in the Continental United States, as far south as Mexico and through Southern Canada into the Great Lakes System. It is native to the Eastern United States and has been widely stocked throughout the rest of the country.

DESCRIPTION
The coloring of the largemouth bass ranges from dark or olive green on the back, to varying shades of brownish green on the sides, with a whitish underside. The coloration does, however, vary according to surroundings. In clearer waters, the fish tend towards lighter coloring. A thin black band runs horizontally along the side from the head to the tail. The dorsal fin is deeply notched and appears as two separate fins. The end of the upper jaw joint of the largemouth extends beyond the eye and cleek scales range from 9 to 12 rows.

SIZE
Largemouth bass usually average 1 to 2 pounds. In the North, they seldom reach over 8 pounds, and in the south, 12 pounds is the maximum.

FEEDING HABITS
The largemouth bass is not particular about its diet; it will eat almost anything from minnows to frogs, mice, and ducklings. They are voracious feeders and will generally strike at any offering. Early morning and evening are prime times for catching these fish.

HABITAT
Slow-moving streams and still, shallow lakes are the preferred environment of the largemouth bass. The warmer the water, the better they bite and they can generally be found near submerged logs or brush, weed-beds and grasses. Muddy bottoms with thick protective growth are their favorite haunts.

TACKLE
The largemouth, which has been receiving so much attention from anglers lately, is still a sucker for all sorts of plugs, luscious rubber goods such as worms and spoons and spinners. Heavyish line is necessary when they're in the lettuce but at other times a heavy-duty fly rod casting big bass bugs or flies is the ticket for maximum fun. Gear varies widely from place to place.

top of the line

QUICK MICROLITE. Though some claim it has been dated by recent technical developments, it is one of the standby performers in the ultra-light field. This 8.5-ounce reel has been around for a long time. It features a ball-bearing main shaft drive, self-lubricating handle bearings, a stainless-steel bail and a distinctive anticorrosion finish. Though not as well known as some of its American counterparts, this European import is a high-quality item. And for those so disposed, Quick offers some larger models up to saltwater sizes.

RECORD. These Swiss-made reels exude quality. Record was one of the first companies to export reels to this country when spinning made its debut after World War II. Records, which are middleweights designed for freshwater use, have an unusual and very functional drag located in the rear of the housing. Another feature is a stud that can convert the reel to manual bail retrieve — something serious spin anglers find very desirable. Records are hard to find but worth searching for.

RYOBI. One of the newer of the better Japanese-imported skirted spinning reels is the slick, space-age Ryobi with ball-bearing innards, ceramic line retriever and corrosion-resistant finish. They're available in sizes from 10 to 20 ounces and line capacities to match. Called "Powerful," they've got neat writing and gauges on the side. Very distinctive.

SHAKESPEARE. Starting from the top with the President line down to the lesser quality 2300 Series, Shakespeare offers a lot for the money. They've been in the spinning business for a long time and always seem to be able to take advantage of tackle developments. Anything you need and easy to repair.

ORVIS

KENCOR

OLYMPIC H-M

"There's no taking trout with dry breeches."
CERVANTES, *Don Quixote*

top of the line

SOUTH BEND CLASSICS. This model line is tops among the new breed of spinners. In fact, some claim that the classics carried most of the design features of the best of today's reels long before the others were around, such as all-ball-bearing construction, anticorrosion finish, a design that eliminates snagged monofilament and an extra-strong handle. They are easy to get, in sizes ranging from ultra-light to heavy salt water. Among mass line reels, South Bend is probably the best bet.

ZEBCO. This is a rarity among tackle companies, one whose quality has dramatically improved over the past few years. After starting out primarily as a maker of questionable close-faced reels, it is now heavier into the tackle game and is selling its Cardinal reels, well designed and made with a numbered drag system set on the bottom of the housing. It also sells a variety of other models ranging from ultra-light to saltwater size which are simple to repair and very functional.

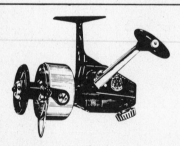

ZEBCO CARDINAL. The Cardinal is thought of as a top reel in its class. It has all of the necessary model sizes and features including ball-bearing drive, corrosion-resistant body, stainless-steel worm gear and a handy, calibrated drag on the bottom of the reel. It's a good buy for the becoming-serious spinner. Zebco has improved itself by leaps and bounds since the days when its cheap closed-faced reels were its main offering. The Cardinal reflects this change of heart.

PFLUEGER

RECORD

QUICK MICROLITE

ultimate commodity

Fin-Nor

With handcrafted components, full circle disc drag and an automatic pickup finger — a safe alternative to the full bail — the Fin-Nor line for heavy freshwater to heavy saltwater spinning reels is the closest to the ultimate commodity in this field we can find. This is a no-nonsense line of reel for any spinning function, except ultra-light. The only drawbacks to these pieces of machinery are their weight — excessive for those raised on standard American or Japanese fare — and a gaudy gold color. But after a Fin-Nor there's nowhere else to go. It's the last reel you'll ever have to own. However, the extra spools cost around $25, more than the price of many other spinning reels themselves. Only serious anglers need apply.

SPEED GEARS

Just like your car, you can now speed up your Garcia Ambassadeur or Daiwa Millionaire reel. You can buy speed gears made of cold rolled steel and half-hard brass. Tell the Coren Rod & Reel Service people what model the gears are to be used on and they'll send you the stuff to transform your reel into a 4.8-to-1 retrieve.

The advantages of the manual retrieve

Even though many anglers consider them *passé*, you might think about getting a manual return for your next spinning reel.

When the first commercial spinning reels were introduced in this country shortly after World War II they were mostly manual retrieve models. The early Bache Browns and Mitchell manuals were incredibly well-constructed and smooth-operating pieces of equipment.

But like the automatic transmission in cars, the American fetish for machinery dominated and the automatic spinning reel came to "own" the market.

The advantages of the manual are its simplicity and design. After casting you simply bring the halfbail back with your forefinger and begin the retrieve. There is very little to go wrong and those horrendous monofilament "bird's nests," which can occur when the automatic bail begins to chew up line, don't exist.

In a word: they are dependable and can be lighter than the same capacity automatic, a factor for the ultra-light compulsive. The fine little Orvis is one of the few manuals still available.

And who knows, like the four-on-the-floor revival in cars we may all again be shifting to retrieve in our spin fishing.

—H. H.

Ball bearings: an old idea

Sound ideas last, regardless of fad or fashion.

Take for instance the ball bearings that tackle companies are boosting as the latest idea for smooth functioning in reels. They claim this technical development allows for high-quality mechanical operation in spinning, baitcasting and even a few spincasting reels. And they're right.

But there's more to the story. Ball bearings aren't by any stretch of the imagination a modern development. When England's renowned Hardy Brothers marketed their Perfect fly reel as early as 1892, it featured a whole set of ball bearings. Many fly tackle experts consider the Perfect, which came in a variety of sizes ranging from trout to big salmon, the smoothest-operating and best-constructed reel ever made. The company produced them from the 1890s to the mid 1960s, stopped for a few years and then started up again in 1975 when the prices for used Perfects soared above $100 for mint models.

Other quality fly reels such as the Fin-Nor line of heavy freshwater and saltwater models adapted the ball bearing idea. But it has taken a long time for the big companies to pick up on the idea. Nothing wrong with that, but they shouldn't claim that an idea more than three generations old is brand new. **H.H.**

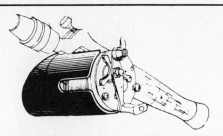

Draw, partner. Your baitcasting outfit, that is. This quick-draw gadget can be mounted on your boat, though it would probably work in a car as well. Will take your bait casting rod and reel, then at the first sign of trouble, you can be casting faster than a flash.

A Primer

(continued from page 147)

Other designs require the spool knob to be screwed counter-clockwise to be released.

Interchangeable spools provide the advantage of changing lines conveniently — from a light line to heavier line, for example, or to replace a worn or lost line.

The drags on most spinning reels are pressure discs located on the face of the line spool. Some reels, however, have drag adjustment knobs at the back or bottom of the reel. The best drags are easy to reach, reliable and smooth with no "catches" or hesitation.

American Fishing
Tackle Manufacturers
Association

ultimate commodity

Daiwa Minicast

The Daiwa Minicast is the answer to a poacher's dream! It's a 5-piece, 5-foot glass rod with one of those high-quality ultra-light Daiwa open-faced reels imbedded in a Dura-cork handle. There are other rod lengths available in the series with the same glass-to-glass ferrules, epoxy finish and stainless steel ringed guides but the 5-piecer is an especially neat outfit. Although it's perfect for the backpacker or traveler, it's designed for a maximum of No. 6 mono and therefore is not an all-around outfit. It is, however, the best of its type and sure to spawn imitators. Very handsome. Extra spools available for the ball-bearing equipped reel.

PEQUEA "WATCH-DOG" ROD GUARD

Ever want to hold the line from your spinning reel taut but still keep the bail open? Well, Pequea's Watch Dog Rod Guard will let you. Made from non-corrosive materials, the clip-spring combination will let a nibbling fish take and run. Handy.

ultimate commodity

Alcedo Micron

Despite an uncertain marketing future and the great technical advances of Japanese reels like Daiwa and Olympic, the Italian-made Alcedo

Micron remains the best of the ultra-light reels, according to many hard-core experts. It's an unassuming reel but very solidly made and features a smooth running drag that seldom fails. The extra spools slip on very easily and line hangup behind the bail was pretty much eliminated years before it was an area of concern for other makers. The anti-reverse button is oversized and conveniently located. Alcedo will be the one ultra-light that can last you the rest of your life. Even if they are no longer imported, there are still plenty of them around in supply houses and better stores. Get one before the collectors discover the joy of owning this fine piece of machinery.

Tom Mann's *Methods for Catching Bass*

Tom Mann, one of the bass tournament hot-shots, has put together a 108-page manual on bass fishing that includes most of the modern techniques. Illustrated and published by the Bass Anglers Sportsman's Society (BASS), it has lots of information especially helpful for those below the Mason-Dixon Line.

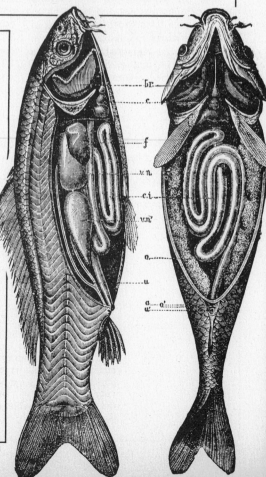

specifications

BRAND-MODEL	WEIGHT (OZ.)	GEAR RATIOS	LINE (YD.) CAPACITY	DRAG
BERKLEY				
725	.12	.4.2:1	.330, 8 lb.	
612	.12	.3.6:1	.250, 8 lb.	
Castamatic	.13	.3.7:1	.225, 8 lb.	
4201	.13	.4.5:1	.375, 8 lb.	
420ALX		.3.2:1	.8 lb. or 10 lb.	
604	.10	.3.6:1	.200, 4 lb.	
446	.10	.4.1:1	.275, 6 lb.	disc
435	.10	.4.1:1	.200, 4 lb.	disc
412	.12	.3.3:1	.250, 8 lb.	
680	.16	.3.6:1	.250, 17 lb.	disc
810	.16	.4:1	.225, 17 lb.	disc
BRETTON				
Martin Bretton 600 Sets				
620 (with rod)		.4.8:1	.200, 6 lb.	adjustable
630 (with rod)			.150, 8 lb.	adjustable
Bretton Spinning Reels				
104	.9	.5:1	.200, 4 lb.	disc
400P	.11	.3.8:1	.200, 6 lb.	
400M	.11	.3.8:1	.300, 8 lb.	disc
804SRM	.11	.4.75:1	.300, 8 lb.	disc
807	.12	.4:1	.175, 20 lb.	disc
207A	.10		.200, 6 lb.	
BROWNING				
Spin'r-8 1330	.8	.4.2:1	.385, 2 lb.	disc
Spin'r-12 5330	.12	.4.1:1	.485, 4 lb.	disc
DAIWA				
Gold Series				
GS-1	.8	.5.4:1	.200, 4 lb.	disc
GS-2	.16	.4.9:1	.500, 6 lb.	disc
Silver Series				
1000C	.7.7	.5.4:1	.200, 4 lb.	disc
1300C	.11	.4.9:1	.270, 6 lb.	disc
Bronze Series				
B130	.10	.3.7:1	.270, 6 lb.	disc
B250	.16.5	.4.1:1	.350, 10 lb.	disc
R/L Series				
7150HRL	.8	.5.4:1	.410, 4 lb.	disc
7450 HRL	.13	.4.1:1	.430, 8 lb.	disc
400 Series				
401	.7	.3.2:1	.270, 4 lb.	adjustable
402	.8.5	.3.2:1	.270, 4 lb.	adjustable
Minispin System (reel built onto rod)		.4.4:1	.100, 4 lb.	disc
Minimite system (reel with matching 2-piece rod)	.6.3	.4.4:1	.110, 4 lb.	disc
EAGLE CLAW				
Blue Pacific				
1125	.8	.4.5:1	.200, 4 lb.	disc
1225	.9.5	.4.5:1	.200, 8 lb.	disc
1325	.16	.4.5:1	.250, 12 lb.	disc
1425	.22	.4.2:1	.275, 15 lb.	disc
125	.8.5	.4.1:1	.170, 6 lb.	disc
225	.10	.3.4:1	.130, 10 lb.	disc
325	.13.5	.3.6:1	.220, 12 lb.	disc
425	.16.5	.3.5:1	.250, 15 lb.	disc
FEURER BROTHERS				
FB417	.9.6	.3.44:1	.240, 6 lb.	expansion
F410	.9	.3.44:1	.240, 6 lb.	expansion
F414	.10	.3.44:1	.240, 6 lb.	expansion
FB430		.3.39:1	.240, 6 lb.	
FB412 (large spool)	.12	.3.44:1	.200, 8 lb.	
FB412			.140, 8 lb.	
GARCIA				
Mitchell				
300 (with arbor)	.11.25	.3.7:1	.200, 4 lb.	disc
300 (without arbor)	.11.25	.3.7:1	.325, 8 lb.	disc
301 (left-hand with arbor)	.11.25	.3.7:1	.200, 4 lb.	disc
301 (left hand without arbor)	.11.25	.3.7:1	.325, 8 lb.	disc
300C (with arbor)	.11.25	.3.7:1	.200, 4 lb.	disc
300C (without arbor)	.11.25	.3.7:1	.325, 8 lb.	disc
301C (left hand with arbor)	.11.25	.3.7:1	.200, 4 lb.	disc
301C (left hand without arbor)	.11.25	.3.7:1	.325, 8 lb.	disc
300DL (with arbor)	.11.25	.3.7:1	.200, 4 lb.	disc
300DL (without arbor)	.11.25	.3.7:1	.325, 8 lb.	disc
301DL (left hand with arbor)	.11.25	.3.7:1	.200, 4 lb.	disc
301 DL (left hand without arbor)	.11.25	.3.7:1	.325, 8 lb.	disc
308 (with arbor)	.7.4	.4.6:1	.200, 2 lb.	disc
308 (without arbor)	.7.4	.4.6:1	.300, 4 lb.	disc
309 (left hand with arbor)	.7.4	.4.6:1	.200, 2 lb.	disc
309 (left hand without arbor)	.7.4	.4.6:1	.300, 4 lb.	disc
408 (with arbor)	.7.8	.5.5:1	.200, 2 lb.	disc
408 (without arbor)	.7.8	.5.5:1	.300, 4 lb.	disc

specifications

BRAND-MODEL	WEIGHT (OZ.)	GEAR RATIOS	LINE (YD.) CAPACITY	DRAG
409 (left hand with arbor)	7.8	5.5:1	200, 2 lb	disc
409 (left hand without arbor)	7.8	5.5:1	300, 4 lb	disc
410 (with arbor)	11.5	4.8:1	200, 4 lb	disc
410 (without arbor)	11.5	4.8:1	325, 8 lb	disc
411 (left hand with arbor)	11.5	4.8:1	200, 4 lb	disc
411 (left hand without arbor)	11.5	4.8:1	325, 8 lb	disc
410DL (with arbor)	11.5	4.8:1	200, 4 lb	disc
410DL (without arbor)	11.5	4.8:1	325, 8 lb	disc
330 (with arbor)	11.3	3.7:1	200, 4 lb	disc
330 (without arbor)	11.3	3.7:1	325, 8 lb	disc
331 (left hand with arbor)	11.3	3.7:1	200, 4 lb	disc
331 (left hand without arbor)	11.3	3.7:1	325, 8 lb	disc
440 (with arbor)	11.8	4.8:1	200, 4 lb	disc
440 (without arbor)	11.8	4.8:1	325, 8 lb	disc
441 (left hand with arbor)	11.8	4.8:1	200, 4 lb	disc
441 (left hand without arbor)	11.8	4.8:1	325, 8 lb	disc
206	10	4.4:1	225, 6 lb	disc
207 (left hand)	10	4.4:1	225, 6 lb	disc
204	6.25	3.8:1	200, 4 lb	disc
205 (left hand)	6.25	3.8:1	200, 4 lb	disc
320	9.9	3.6:1	200, 6 lb	disc

Kingfisher

GK-22	9	4:1	300, 4 lb	
GK-24	12.5	4:1	300, 8 lb	
GK-26	15.75	4:1	325, 15 lb	
GK-10	8.5	3.8:1	225, 8 lb	
GK-12	12	3.8:1	325, 15 lb	

HEDDON

283	16	4.5:1	200, 15 lb	disc
282	13.5	4.5:1	200, 8 lb	disc
281	9	4.5:1	100, 6 lb	disc
212	15		200, 15 lb	
222	12		200, 8 lb	multiple disc
238	10		200, 6 lb	
204	7		80, 6 lb	
205	12.5	4.5:1	200, 8 lb	
215	6		175, 6 lb	
248	13	4:1	200, 10 lb	disc
233	8	4:1	200, 6 lb	disc
277	18	4:1	200, 15 lb	disc

HERTER

Professional Spinning Reels

910	8.5	4.1:1	170, 6 lb	disc

BRAND-MODEL	WEIGHT (OZ.)	GEAR RATIOS	LINE (YD.) CAPACITY	DRAG
920 (fresh, salt)	10	3.4:1	130, 10 lb	disc
930	13.5	3.6:1	220, 12 lb	disc
940	16.5	3.5:1	250, 15 lb	disc

Imported German-made 109A Spinning Reel

RH9D (fresh, salt)	11	3.3:1	100, 10 lb	

Ball Bearing Spinning Reel

640-P		4:1	200, 10 lb	disc

KENCOR

Spinit Skirted Spool Reels

725AA	10	4.2:1	200, 4 lb	disc
745AA	14.5	4:1	275, 12 lb	disc

Spinit Standard Reels

510	6.25	3.2:1	200, 8 lb	disc
520	10	3.8:1	250, 8 lb	disc
640	13	3.6:1	250, 12 lb	disc
610	9	4:1	220, 6 lb	disc
614	9.5	4:1	220, 6 lb	disc
616	10	4:1	220, 6 lb	disc
642	12.5	3.8:1	250, 12 lb	disc
646	13	3.8:1	250, 12 lb	disc

LEONARD

Ultralight 1234	8	4.56:1	300, 2 lb	
Lightweight 1235	11	5:1	350, 4 lb	

OLYMPIC

H M Series

1	13.1	5.1:1	315, 8 lb	disc
2	12	5.1:1	440, 4 lb	disc
3	11	5.1:1	350, 4 lb	disc
4	8.1	4.6:1	240, 4 lb	disc
1/0	13.6	5.2:1	400, 8 lb	disc
Auto 2	24.7	5.1:1 and 2.83:1	280, 15 lb	disc

Spark Series

1500VO	13.9	3.82:1	185, 10 lb	disc
1800 VO	15.5	4.5:1	230, 10 lb	disc
2000 VO	15.9	4.5:1	260, 10 lb	disc
3200 VO	19	4.5:1	245, 15 lb	disc
3100	8.8	3.36:1	260, 8 lb	disc
3120	12.2	3.64:1	310, 8 lb	disc
3180	16.2	4.3:1	250, 12 lb	disc
3150	14.5	4.0	220, 10 lb	disc
Seiko 940	11.6	5.13:1	270, 10 lb	disc

No. 500 Series

540	20	4.5:1	240, 20 lb	disc
530	15.3	4.5:1	200, 15 lb	disc
520	13.1	4.1:1	180, 8 lb	disc
510	9.9	4.7:1	160, 6 lb	disc

No. 2000 Series

2200	8.5	3.31:1	200, 8 lb	
2100	6.5	3.18:1	180, 8 lb	
2000	5.9	3.18:1	180, 8 lb	
2600	13.2	3.66:1	200, 15 lb	
2400	11.5	3.35:1	200, 10 lb	

"Nightcrawlers make good pets. They're clean. They're not harmful. All they need is a little care."
GEORGE SRODA

OPEN-FACED REELS 163

specifications

BRAND-MODEL	WEIGHT (OZ.)	GEAR RATIOS	LINE (YD.) CAPACITY	DRAG
ORVIS				
Orvis 50A				
F1627	6.5	.5:1	.250, 2 lb.	
1628 (51A left hand)	6.5	.5:1	.250	
Orvis 100A				
F1632	.10	.3.65:1	.400, 4 lb.	
F1633 (101A left hand)				
Orvis 100SS				
F1650	.10	.4.8:1	.400, 4 lb.	
F1651 (101SS left hand)				
Orvis 150S				
F1652	.13		.340, 8 lb.	
F1653 (151S left-hand)				
Orvis Ultra-Light Manual 50A				
F1646	6	.5:1	.250, 2 lb.	
PENN				
Ultrasport 714		.5.1:1	.200, 6 lb.	
Ultralight 716	8.5	.5.1:1	.225, 4 lb.	multi
706 Manual Pickup		.3.8:1	.300, 20 lb.	Penn
707 (left hand)		.3.8:1	.300, 20 lb.	Penn
Spinfisher				
720	9.5	.4:1	.300, 4 lb.	teflon
722	9.75	.5:1	.300, 4 lb.	teflon
712			.135, 12 lb.	multi disc
704	.21	.3.8:1	.450, 10 lb.	teflon
705 (with right-hand wind)	.21	.3.8:1	.450, 10 lb.	teflon
710		.3.6:1	.200, 12 lb.	
711 (with right-hand wind)		.3.6:1	.200, 12 lb.	
PFLUEGER				
800 Series				
822	8.75	.5.2:1	.190, 6 lb.	multi disc
827	.14	.4.2:1	.220, 8 lb.	multi disc
829	.17	.4.2:1	.360, 10 lb.	multi disc
600 Series				
640	9	.5.2:1	.170, 6 lb.	
646	9.3	.5.2:1	.330, 6 lb.	
641	.12	.4:1	.180, 8 lb.	
642	.17	.4:1	.270, 15 lb.	
400 Series				
422	9	.3.2:1	.180, 6 lb.	multi disc
427	.11	.3.2:1	.240, 8 lb.	multi disc
429	.18	.3.4:1	.250, 15 lb.	multi disc
300 Series				
322	8	.3.2:1	.180, 6 lb.	multi disc
327	.10	.3.8:1	.240, 8 lb.	
200 Series				
222	8	.3.2:1	.180, 6 lb.	multi disc
227	.10	.3.8:1	.240, 8 lb.	multi disc
QUICK				
Microlite 11 O-N	8.5	.4.75:1	.200, 6 lb.	
220N	.11	.3.55:1	.250, 8 lb.	
330 O-N Finessa	.11.5	.3.55:1	.225, 12 lb.	
331-N Fast Retrieve (left-right conversion)	12.8	.4.68:1	.225, 16 lb.	
RECORD				
21	8	.3.5:1	.175, 6 lb.	
50B	.10	.3:1	.200, 8 lb.	
400	.11	.3:1	.200, 8 lb.	
50A	.10	.3:1	.200, 8 lb.	
50N	.10	.3:1	.200, 8 lb.	
RYOBI				
Powerful DX Series				
DX-5	.20.1	.4.3:1	.251, 22 lb.	
DX-4	.16.8	.4.5:1	.218, 19 lb.	
DX-3	.12.4	.4.3:1	.164, 14 lb.	
DX-2	.10.1	.4.3:1	.240, 9 lb.	
DX-1	7.6	.4.75:1	.159, 9 lb.	
Powerful Series				
5	.26.6	.4.3:1	.280, 28 lb.	
4	.23.4	.4.3:1	.270, 22 lb.	
3	.19.5	.4.3:1	.280, 17 lb.	
2	.16	.4.7:1	.270, 14 lb.	
1	.11.4	.3.8:1	.229, 14 lb.	
Powerful GL Series				
GL-6	.27.9	.3.07:1	.185, 43 lb.	
GL-5	.26.7	.3.07:1	.280, 28 lb.	
GL-4	.23.5	.3.2:1	.270, 22 lb.	
Catcher Series				
4	.22.6	.4.3:1	.250, 22 lb.	
3	.18.5	.4.5:1	.260, 17 lb.	
2	.15.5	.3.8:1	.270, 14 lb.	
1	.13.9	.3.8:1	.273, 14 lb.	
0	.8.3	.3.8:1	.190, 11 lb.	
SHAKESPEARE				
President II				
2800		.4.7:1	.150, 6 lb.	disc
2810		.3.7:1	.300, 12 lb.	disc
2840		.3.2:1	.300, 12 lb.	disc

specifications

BRAND-MODEL	WEIGHT (OZ.)	GEAR RATIOS	LINE (YD.) CAPACITY	DRAG
2860			.250, 20 lb.	disc
2400 Series				
2400		.5.2:1	.180, 6 lb.	disc
2410		.4.5:1	.270, 8 lb.	disc
2430		.4.2:1	.300, 10 lb.	disc
2450				
Marina Green Reels				
2200 II		.5.2:1	.170, 6 lb.	disc
2200 LH		.5.2:1	.170, 6 lb.	disc
2210 II		.3.7:1	.180, 8 lb.	disc
2210LH		.3.7:1	.180, 8 lb.	disc
2230 II		.4:1	.240, 10 lb.	disc
2240 II		.4:1	.260, 12 lb.	disc
2240 LH		.4:1	.260, 12 lb.	disc
2500 Ball Bearing Reels				
2500		.4:1	.200, 6 lb.	disc
2510		.3.8:1	.200, 8 lb.	disc
2540		.3.5:1	.250, 12 lb.	disc
2300 Series				
2300		.3:1	.150, 8 lb.	disc
2301			.200, 6 lb.	disc
2302 RL		.3.9:1	.150, 8 lb.	disc
2310		.3.3:1	.200, 8 lb.	disc

SOUTH BEND

BRAND-MODEL	WEIGHT (OZ.)	GEAR RATIOS	LINE (YD.) CAPACITY	DRAG
800 Series				
870		.3.5:1	.250, 15 lb.	disc
840		.3.5:1	.250, 8 lb.	disc
820		.4.2:1	.200, 4 lb.	disc
Classic Reels				
935		.3.7:1	.265, 10 lb.	magnum

BRAND-MODEL	WEIGHT (OZ.)	GEAR RATIOS	LINE (YD.) CAPACITY	DRAG
930		.3.7:1	.250, 8 lb.	magnum
925		.4.75:1	20, 6 lb.	magnum
700 Series				
730-A		.3.5:1	.225, 8 lb.	disc
725		.4.2:1	.200, 4 lb.	disc
Gladding 2202			.185, 8 lb.	disc
830		.3.75:1	.8 lb.-15 lb.	disc
600 Series Maroon Reels				
630			.190, 8 lb.	
600			.200, 6 lb.	disc

ZEBCO

BRAND-MODEL	WEIGHT (OZ.)	GEAR RATIOS	LINE (YD.) CAPACITY	DRAG
Cardinal Reels				
3	7.5	.5:1	.178, 4 lb.	disc
4	10.7	.5:1	.200, 8 lb.	disc
6	14.3	.3.5:1	.230, 12 lb.	disc
7	14.65	.3.5:1	.220, 17 lb.	disc
7X	14.8	.5:1	.220, 17 lb.	disc
Ball Bearing Reels				
65XB	13.5	.4.3:1	.170, 14 lb.	disc
Interchangeable Handle Reels				
45XBL	5.75	.4.3:1	.250, 6 lb.	disc
77XBL	13.5	.3.4:1	.170, 14 lb.	disc
39XBL	13.4	.3.4:1	.220, 8 lb.	disc
37XRL	12.3	.3.4:1	.200, 8 lb.	disc
40XRL	5.75	.4.3:1	.250, 6 lb.	disc
35XRL	12.3	.3.4:1	.170, 8 lb.	
15XRL	9.5	.3.4:1	.130, 8 lb.	disc
20XR	8.5	.3.3:1	.160, 8 lb.	disc
11XR	6.75	.3.2:1	.130, 8 lb.	disc

LAMIGLASS

For information, write: Lamiglass, Dept. FF, Box 148, Woodland, Washington 98674.

Push buttons have come a long way

By Harmon Henkin

If imitation is the highest form of flattery then the new order of spincasting reels are flatterers of the highest order.

In years past the push buttons were in many ways the black sheep of the reel family. Though there were decent enough models on the market, manufacturers lavished special care on open-faced spinners and baitcasting members of the family, leaving spincasters to fend for themselves.

It was a byword among most anglers that spincasting was an offshoot for beginners and kids and that anything they could do open-faced reels and baitcasters could do better. It was generally figured that the people interested in spincasting, the newest of the casting forms, were either rookies or the types who didn't have a lot to spend on equipment.

But times and tastes have changed. There is a generation of anglers on the scene now which grew up with a spincasting outfit in their hands and they see no real reason to change. They've read the arguments against them but still aren't about to change their taste in tackle. And they don't want junk.

Much of the recent innovation in spincasting reels is actually spinoff technology from other forms of angling. Ball bearings, easily set drags, alloy line guides and corrosion-resistant finishes all come from spinning and baitcasting.

There is now lots and lots of competition among manufacturers for the hefty spincasting dollar. Even the lower end of this market has seen an increase in quality, but to really take advantage you have to get something like Zebco, Garcia, Heddon or other top-of-the-line gear.

If you choose spincasting as the way to go, however, you'll have to accept its built-in limitations. For example, you'll never have the line control and therefore the accuracy possible with open-faced or baitcasting reels. You can have enough control for almost all practical casting but there are limits to what you can do with monofilament streaming from a hole atop a metal container.

Ditto with drag performance. Some spincasters have good ones but not the great ones possible with other tackle. Another restriction that bothers seekers of big fish is line capacity, almost always much smaller than with open-faced reels.

Such is life, however, and if the ease of casting appeals to you, get the best available.

THE MODERN SPINCASTING REEL

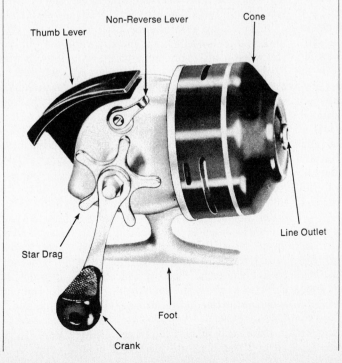

HOW TO CARE FOR FISHING REELS

By C. Boyd Pfeiffer

Fishing reels vary greatly in appearance, but all need the same care. They need to be kept clean, dry when not in use, well lubricated and free of dirt, grit or sand. With the extremes of weather and water conditions, this may seem to be a pretty tall order for any angler. For the saltwater angler coping with salt corrosion, it may seem impossible.

Proper care begins when the reel is taken out of the box the first time and filled with line. Follow the manufacturer's directions and keep the tools and lubricants that come with the reel. File the instruction booklet for later use and to order spare parts if needed.

Keep the reel in a reel bag or a dry tackle box until the moment of fishing. When fishing, keep all reels off the ground to keep sand and dirt out. The oil film that sometimes covers reels after a little use collects dirt.

If fishing from the bank, use a forked stick to hold the rod and reel up off the ground. If fishing from a boat, use rod holders to keep them up off the deck and away from any grime. If fishing from the surf, use sand spikes or beach-buggy rod holders.

After fishing, store the reel carefully until you get home. Once home, dry the reel, wipe it off to remove any dirt, and lubricate free moving parts lightly. On casting reels, grease the pawl and level wind, and oil the handles. On spinning reels, oil the roller bearing, the bail hinges and the handle. Lightly oil the handle and spool shaft on fly reels.

More extensive care after each fishing trip is required by the saltwater angler. The salt spray in the air will not come off with a simple wiping or soaking in water. For best results, immerse the reel for a few minutes in lukewarm water. Shake out any water from fly reels and casting reels and from behind the spool on spinning reels. Wipe dry with a clean cloth, oil as above and spray lightly with a demoisturizing agent such as WD-40, CRC, or P-38.

Once each season, follow the manufacturer's instruction sheet and completely dismantle the reel, clean, lubricate and reassemble. Before beginning, get the necessary reel tools or the right size screwdrivers and wrenches. Use a muffin tin, egg container, plastic utility box or some similar compartmented box in which to place each part as it is removed from the reel. This will make reassembling easier.

Clean each part in a solvent or kerosene to remove all old grease, oil and grime. (Use care if using kerosene or inflammable cleaning solvents, since they are dangerous and their vapors harmful. If these are necessary, use outside only.)

Clean one part at a time, replacing it in the box to keep it in order. Clean any plastic parts such as reel handles in soapy water, since solvents frequently react with and destroy plastics.

Once all parts are clean, replace them in order, lubricating with grease or oil. Be sure to follow the manufacturer's instructions. With this kind of care any reel used in fresh or salt water will continue to work and look like new for years.

Lessons from a Victorian poacher

As I began with Fish poaching, let me Finish with this Sport. In Daventry there are two large Reservoirs containing very Large fish – Pike, Carp, Roach, Perch, Tench. I have never caught any other sort.

One reservoir is the property of Edward Burton, the other of Major Clarke. I have never known either of these Gentlemen to summons a man in my time although many men trespassed there in search of fish. But you don't find men today like some sixty years ago. Major Clarke kept a Coachman of the name of Jim Kent. He was a big, powerful man and played the part of Keeper. He had Rabbets and Pheasants but I never saw Hares there although since leaving home, I have been there many times. I usually went at night – when living in Northampton – and used the Long Net with others. We carried many a Bag of Rabbets away. We would take them to Weedon and then walk about five miles, sell our stuff at Buckley Warf to a man who would retail them, and then come back home again with sometimes the best part of a quid each.

Sometimes we made more than this, sometimes nothing. If the weather proved Bad we had our Journey for nothing. You may wonder how we captured the Fish. First we would go to the Canal and catch small Bait and set Dead Lines for Pike. Put twenty or thirty in and you would not have to wait long before you had one. The Keeper would set a net called Tramel at a certain time of the year when the Pike were on the Run. I hardly knew what the term meant, but this net would be s t about fifty yards from the Tale End or Shallow Part about twelve foot deep, and among the weeds. This net might be twenty yards in Length and was twelve Feet deep, held up by large flat corks. When fish were in these corks would move.

How did we get the fish out? Well, where there's a will, there's a way. To swim to the net would be dangerous because of the weeds – and I have seen several drown in Daventry Reservoir through swimming in weeds – especially when they were out of sight. If ever you get among weeds, turn at once on your Back and float over them. Don't forget this.

You may get into strange water and find weeds just when you think all is safe.

We bought a Ball of String at sixpence, tied a Stone on the End and also a Pot Hook and threw it over the net and pulled it out. Once in this way we brought in three Large Gold coloured Tench and several Pike. To get the net in again, thread the line through Double, pull it in and draw the line out and no one will be any the wiser.

How did the net kill or catch the fish? I should like you to know all about it for it might prove useful to you someday. One day when you have a lot of Spare Time and a Spare Bob or two, instead of going and Sitting in a Pub and Drinking – what Robs you of manliness – go and buy some thing and make a net as I have done; then when bad times come use it against the Class that caused the Bad Times.

These nets are called Single Walling and Double Walling. If the net was twelve feet deep, that portion that kills in twenty feet, you should do well. If you had Double Walling, you would have another net in larger mesh. When the fish are dashing about amongst the weeds, they go through the Large Mesh, strike the small, and then tumble through the large to lie helpless. It does not matter which side they strike if there is Double Walling, but if there is only single walling, they would only be caught one way. It is going through the Large mesh into the Small that does them. Then they hang down Helpless.

(Although this book was first published in 1961, Hawker, born in 1836, wrote these memoirs at the turn of the century.)

From *James Hawker's Journal: A Victorian Poacher*, edited by Garth Christian (1961). PP. 106-108. Reprinted by permission of Oxford University Press.

GAMEFISH: GOLDEN TROUT

NAMES
Volcano Creek trout, Sierra trout, Volcano trout *(Salmo Aguabonito)*

DISTRIBUTION
The golden trout was originally found in an extremely small range in the high Sierras and in Volcano Creek, California. It has since been transplanted throughout the West.

DESCRIPTION
The golden trout is considered the most beautiful of all trout. It is olive on the back with golden yellow sides and a yellow-white belly. Along the sides a red band, which is marked by dark oval spots, runs from head to tail. Small black spots mark the upper sides and fins. Another crimson stripe runs along the belly.

SIZE
The golden trout is a small fish that usually averages about 1 pound. In larger lakes it may reach 5 pounds.

HABITAT
The golden trout is only found in extremely high altitudes from 9,000 to 12,000 feet and is therefore a fairly inaccessible game fish. It will only live in very cold, clear water. In both creeks and lakes it favors deep holes and areas near rocky shores.

FEEDING HABITS
The diet of the golden trout consists of minute insects, insect larvae and small crustaceans. It is a difficult fish to catch. Summer is the best time to try.

TACKLE
This high country fish is best sought by backpackers equipped with the tiniest available ultra-light spinning gear with bait (a shame) or tiny spinners. But the best way whether in lakes or creeks is with small bright-colored flies, wet or dry, cast from a shortish pack rod.

The anatomy of the close-faced reel

(A) The nose cone serves chiefly to confine or cover the pickup mechanism and the spool. The interior should be smooth and well machined, and it should be readily removable. A positive locking mechanism should hold it in place, and there must be ample room to allow the line to fly off the spool. A retrieved fishing line will pick up water. Water confined inside the reel cover will reduce casting distance. A good spincasting reel will have some means for letting the water drain.

(B) The orifice is a small hole in the nose cone through which the line passes while casting and retrieving. This should be more than a simple hole, for it is subject to a tremendous amount of line wear. Rather than a hole, it should have an extremely hard and very smooth metallic insert.

(C) The spool of the spin-casting reel does not necessarily oscillate as it does on a spinning reel. However, if a nonoscillating spool is in the reel, it must be quite narrow to ensure good line spooling. An oscillating spool can be much wider and have much more line capacity. There is nothing wrong with a non-oscillating spool as long as it is narrow enough to control the line.

(D) The handle should be easy to grip.

(E) The reel foot must be sturdy and rather close to the body of the reel. Since the spincasting reel is designed for use with a rod having an offset bait-casting handle, it must be tapered to fit snugly in the offset handle locking reel seat.

(F) The push-button or trigger is the mechanism which controls the line during the cast. Since this mechanism will be used constantly, and since it is directly responsible for casting accuracy, it must be large, and conveniently lo-

cated. The wise fisherman, interested in a spincasting outfit, will mount the reel onto a rod and make sure that his thumb rests on the push-button without reaching or straining.

(G) The adjustable drag. Since the spool is built inside the cover, a drag built in front of the spool as in the conventional spinning reel, would be inaccessible. Therefore, on all spincasting reels, the adjustable drag is located elsewhere.

Illustrated here is a star wheel adjustment, which has proved to be convenient and accessible. This type of drag adjustment has been used and approved, for many, many years by the salt-water fishermen. It is, without a doubt, one of the finest and most convenient ways to regulate a drag.

(H) The housing. The housing of the spincasting reel serves no purpose other than to enclose the gear mechanism. It can be almost any shape, and the only thing to look for is a durable and rustproof finish.

(J) The winding cup. This is the part which is similar to the rotating head of the spinning reel. **Line passes over it while retrieving or fighting a fish.** Since line rubs against this mechanism 50 per cent of your fishing day, it must be extremely hard. To cut down on line wear, the surfaces must be highly polished and beautifully machined.

(K) The line pickup. This pin functions in the same way as the full bail or manual pickup of the spinning reel. When it is extended, the line is hooked by it and then wound around the spool. It therefore must be extremely smooth and, if anything, even harder than the winding

GAMEFISH: SUNAPEE TROUT

NAMES
Sunapee golden trout, golden trout, white trout. *(Salvelinus aureolus)*

DISTRIBUTION
The Sunapee trout was originally found in the lakes of Vermont, New Hampshire and Maine. Its most famous habitat is Sunapee Lake in New Hampshire.

DESCRIPTION
The Sunapee is a member of the char family

and is related to the Arctic char. Its coloring is dark olive or blue on the back with pink or white spots on the sides. The lower fins are colored red or orange with a white border.

SIZE
At one time, specimens weighing up to 10 pounds were not uncommon but today the average Sunapee is around 2 pounds.

HABITAT
The Sunapee prefers the large cold lakes of

New England. They are usually found in deep water but move into the shallows in the fall and spring.

FEEDING HABITS
These fish feed primarily on smelt.

TACKLE
This deep diver is usually a victim of adroit trollers with lightish gear — small spoons and spinners or even flies. When in the shallows in the spring it will take a variety of near surface baits.

cup. If the fishing line is going to wear a groove in any part of a spin-casting reel, it will first wear a groove in the pickup pin. Tungsten carbide is an ideal material for it is one of the hardest metals known to man. When the reel is in the casting position, with the button depressed, this pickup pin should be retracted flush with the winding cup. Any extension at this time could cause line-catching and other troubles.

Some of the better reels have two pickup pins. A pickup pin located on each side of the winding cup helps to balance this part so it will rotate more smoothly. But — more important — the two pins divide the amount of line wear on this part in half. The law of averages says that the line will be picked up one time on one pin, and the next time on the other. Thus there is less line wear on either pin.

(L) The rubber cushion. This is located on the face of the winding cup and serves two purposes. When the push button is depressed, thus retracting the pickup pin, the line would flow from the spool unless a means were provided for holding it. So, when the push button is pressed, the winding cup moves forward and keeps it from flying off the spool *during* the cast. The cushion serves to protect the line during this operation. Were there no rubber cushion on a spin-casting reel, the metal winding cup would press against the hard nose cone with the line in between. This would certainly injure a fishing line. The second purpose for the rubber cushion is to protect the line at the end of the cast.

From *Fishing Tackle and Techniques* by Dick Wolff. (C) 1961 by Dick Wolff. Used by permission of E. P. Dutton & Company.

The first men that our Saviour dear
Did choose to wait upon Him here,
Blest fishers were; and fish the last
Food was, that He on earth did taste:
I therefore strive to follow those,
Whom He to follow Him hath chose.

IZAAK WALTON
*The Compleat Angler:
The Angler's Song*

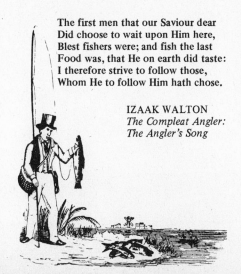

THE LAST HATCH
A FISHING MYSTERY
HARMON HENKIN

(continued from page 146)

the bottom or near the top? Are they taking hatching insects on the surface or are they nymphing near the bed? If you don't put the right signs together, you get skunked."

"Paul, you trying to say there's only one way to skin a trout?"

"Right. If you were a big city cop —"

"Which I would never be."

"If you were, you'd have lots of police specialists to help you. There'd be technical equipment to analyze everything. Lots of manpower to ask lots of questions. Worse came to worse you could even beat the right answers out of people."

"But I'm not. I'm the only cop around. Anyway, all that high-powered stuff would be like fishing with dynamite."

"Right. So all you have is your powers of observation. Your knowledge of the eco-system of the social stream and your mental fly rod."

He started up his side of the bank vehemently but as he began searching his side there was an occasional "Lordy, look at that hawg."

Then Paul stopped and walked to the brush a few yards from the bank. He picked up some sticks and tossed them into the creek at various points across its width. When they floated from sight he eased himself back into the stream and waded across gingerly.

"Halford had to be killed over here."

"Why?"

"Just look at the current. It's consistent over the whole width until it gets down to that last bend before it hits the pool. He came drifting by me on this side. So somebody either killed him over here or they got him on the other side and pushed him across the current. That wouldn't make any sense."

"Suppose the murderer caught him in the middle of the creek and nailed him there."

"That's not logical. Whatever I thought of Halford, he was a very good fly angler. Now any fly fisherman worth his salt wouldn't fish the creek by wading. That soft bottom and flat surface would make waves and mud for 20 yards. The creek's only 30 feet wide and it's got a grassy bank you can cast from without hanging up on trees and bushes. That's why there are those two paths. He would have been fishing from the bank like he always did."

(continued on page 188)

top of the line

WHAT WE LOOKED FOR IN QUALITY

Close-faced spinning reels, which have become the most popular way for many of America's 20 million or so anglers to catch fish, are — to put it bluntly — in a lot of cases just junk.

Many expert anglers consider spincasting a beginner's game that lacks the control and finesse offered by baitcasting or open-faced tackle. Manufacturers often agree, not giving much attention to the spincasting gear they market.

But there are exceptions, usually in reels that imitate the quality characteristics of tackle demanding more skill than the mere pressing of a button. They sport such features as ball bearings, smooth functioning drags and an overall construction that offers at least some corrosion resistance.

Among those we considered the best on the market were Zebco's XL33, which had all the above. But here again we could not consider spincasting as anything much more than a tool of the casual or rookie angler. Even so, consumers should demand quality in whatever they purchase.

DAIWA MINICAST. The most interesting of the Daiwa spincasting reels, of which there is a full line, is the new Minicast matching rod and reel. This 4½-foot ultra-light rod is matched with a tiny 5.3 ounce close-faced reel that's only 3¼ inches long but has a large handle and a 4:1 retrieve ratio. The good quality reel can be bought with a rod in either one, two or even five sections for ultimate portability. The perfect outfit for the casual angler looking for something to haul around in a pack or a car. The 600 spincaster, the top of their line, has almost all the best close-faced features, including an oscillating spool system, which feeds the line evenly.

DAIWA 5400 R-L. One of the better heavy duty spincasting reels around. This quality reel, with ceramic pick-up pin, oscillating spool retrieve, is advertised as being okay for saltwater use. But heed this warning: closed faces have too many recesses — which encourage saline buildup. We really can't recommend them for saltwater use. Even the best of them.

DAIWA MINICAST

DAIWA 600

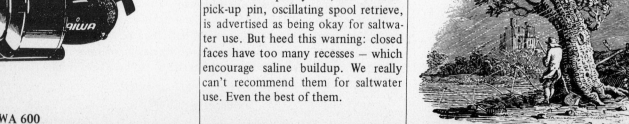

top of the line

EAGLE CLAW EC88B

GARCIA ABUMATIC

DAIWA 600. Daiwa's excellent 600 spincasting reel has all the features of the breed, including a chrome-plated pickup pin, big grip, dark finish, foul-proof oscillating spool retrieve and a big button line release for casting ease. Daiwa also makes lots of other close-faced reels but this one is the top of their line.

EAGLE CLAW EC88B. The top of the line EC88B spincaster has all the better features of the best of the breed, including ball-bearing drive, interchangeable right or left hand retrieve and a full circle drag system. Everything you could want in a close-faced reel. Other models not so deluxe are also available.

EAGLE CLAW 88B. The 88B is one of the better close-faced reels around. Incorporating some of the better features of open-faced reels in its construction, it has four ball bearings, right or left hand interchangeable retrieve and a corrosion-proof design. Worth looking into.

GARCIA ABUMATIC. The Abu-matic line, along with Zebco, dominates the better close-faced reel market. The Abu-matic 270 line has ball bearing drag, a rubber cushion for the line and positive drive retrieve. These reels have been around for a long time now and have improved technically over the years. Garcia makes lots of models including some very low priced ones but the top of the line is where you should be looking unless you want a dollar-and-cents bargain.

CLOSE-FACED REELS FOR BASS FISHING

The larger reels, such as the big Zebco's, are quite adequate for bass fishing, especially in open water where pinpoint accuracy is not usually required. In addition to being easy to cast with, the better ones are virtually foul-proof. They don't have the backlash problem of bait-casting reels; nor are they as prone to bird's nests as the open-faced spinning reels, provided they are spooled with the right line. Still, they are just not accurate enough for the all-around bass fisherman, although I suppose some people do develop some proficiency with them.

I've recently been using a True Temper Uni-Spin rod-and-reel combination. Essentially, it combines the qualities of the open-faced, underslung spinning reel with the ease of the spincast reels. In other words, it's a push-button underslung outfit, with the release button extending up through the rod handle.

The reel has a unique drag system, which allows the pickup cup to revolve, instead of the spool, when the drag is working. Thus, you can turn the handle without twisting the line. The drag system also exerts a constant pressure regardless of how much line is on the reel. The reel seats into the rod, so that one has to purchase the whole outfit. It comes with three interchangeable rod tips in light, medium, and heavy action.

A spokesman from True Temper said that Uni-Spin was designed to make all other fishing systems obsolete. Well, I like the outfit, and it could possibly replace my spinning and spincast reels, but I think I'll keep my bait-casting outfit for a while longer. And my fly rod.

From *Fishing for Bass: Modern Tactics and Tackle* by A. D. Livingston. Copyright (c) 1974 by A. D. Livingston. Reprinted by permission of J. B. Lippincott Company.

top of the line

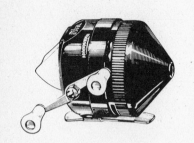

ZEBCO REELS

OLYMPIC

HEDDON MODEL 190. The 190 is a spincasting reel designed to handle big fish. For those so inclined, it will take monofilament from 6 to 30 pounds test. Has machine cut gears, stainless steel main shaft, carbide pick-up pin and a neoprene ring on the flier for more dependable line control when tossing heavier weights. A spincaster for bigger jobs.

JOHNSON GUIDES. The dependable guides have been snazzed up this year. They now come in a sexy black finish with the traditional ball bearing retrieve. Oscillating spool, Teflon-coated gears, stainless steel line guide and other goodies. Model 165 comes with 125 yards of 14-pound test Stren and the lighter Model 155 is sold with 85 yards of 12-pound test Stren. With star drags, they're some of the better built reels.

MARTIN MODEL 270. With a star drag, a capacity of 100 yards of 15 pound test and an oscillating spool, the Martin 270 is one of the better reels around for medium heavy duty work.

OLYMPIC 100. Another one of the good products from Olympic is their 100 spin series casting reel. Available in a wide range of sizes. They have a star drag on most models (that could be larger), brass cut pinion gear and stainless steel rotor.

PFLUEGER 541 AND 543. Pflueger's models 541 and 543 are a pair of adequate close-faced reels produced especially for the serious beginner. They both have star drags and the 543 has a positive ceramic pickup pin assembly. Reels to consider.

JOHNSON GUIDE

MARTIN 270

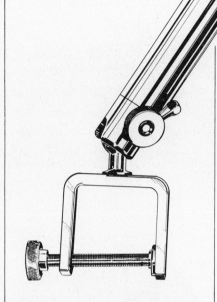

ANGLER'S PAL ROD HOLDER

Angler's Pal is offering a pair of rod holders that are available in either 7¾ or 10 inches and in either permanent or clamp-mount models. They can also be had in either aluminum or steel models. They give you a full hemisphere of possible locking positions and come apart for storage by turning a single screw.

Of books and covers

Pete could be a very secretive angler.

And so he didn't say anything when he happened to run across that very pretty lake in the Eastern part of Maryland. He just went back there and started fishing by himself.

An old man sat on a hill and watched him intently.

Pete tried every angling trick he knew. Nothing. He even dug up some nightcrawlers and patiently sat while they crawled around on the bottom.

Finally the old man walked down and came over.

"Can I ask you a question, sonny?"

"Sure."

"How come you fishing in the sulphur pit?"

It was the acid runoff from a neighboring coal mine. Pete put on fresh monofilament when he went home. And he never went back.

You can't tell a book by its cover. Heh-heh.

—H.H.

top of the line

SHAKESPEARE 1810. The Shakespeare 1810 Deluxe Spin Wondereel, like other Shakespeare products, is a very acceptable item at the top end of the close-faced market. Wondereels of all sorts — spinning, baitcasting and spincasting — have been around long enough to eliminate most of the bugs. This model has a level wind, a big capacity, lever non-reverse, chromed roller pickup and most of the other better features, though not all.

SOUTH BEND BASSIN' MAN. The South Bend Bassin' Man is designed for the close-faced fan who hasn't progressed to baitcasting for lunker bass. It's one of the better reels made — with double ball bearing drive, twin steel pickup pins and oscillating spool for level winding of monofilament. The spool has a chenille wiper to prevent line wraparound. It has a very adequate 3.5:1 retrieve ratio, a star drag and a large capacity for 150 yards of 15-pound test line. Everything you'll need and then some.

TRUE TEMPER UNI-SPIN. The Uni-Spin line is a very acceptable bunch of models for medium fresh water to heavy duty use including salt water. Big handles, big button line release, a convenient drag set system and a decent line capacity make this a dependable performer.

ZEBCO. How many of today's berserko anglers started off with one of these discount house close-faced rod 'n' reel combos? Plenty for sure. Close-faced combos have been Zebco's bread and butter. A simple outfit, Zebco is available in various price and weight ranges that almost anyone can learn to handle very quickly without denting budgets. They're still a fine way to get a kid into fishing and can be bought almost anywhere in the civilized(?) world. Some combos even carry lures thrown in with the purchase price. A real artifact of current Americana.

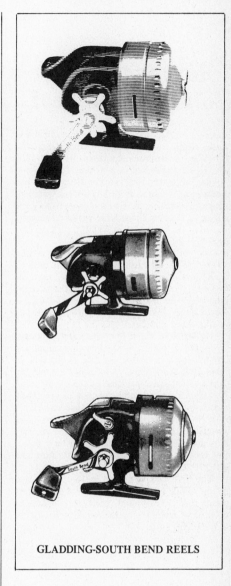

GLADDING-SOUTH BEND REELS

SOUTH BEND BASSIN' MAN

How we got the close-faced reel

Some tackle, like people, at least claims to spring from humble origins. Take the closed face reel, for example. Its inventor, R. D. Hull, says it was conceived in a Rotan, Texas, supermarket in 1945. Hull, so the story goes, was working at the time as an $85-a-week watch repairman, spending his free time spin fishing and trying to clear up the trouble with his backlash. One day he happened to watch a package boy peel cord off a fixed spool.

"All of a sudden it hit me," HUll recalls. "The trouble with fishing reels was the use of a drum. When the drum revolved faster than the line played out, the line snarled. But what if the line were attached to a fixed spool? Backlash would be impossible, wouldn't it? I decided to go home and find out."

He tinkered for a few years and produced 15 workable prototypes, somewhere along the line adding a cover for the face of the reel. In 1948 Hull approached Zebco, then a small producer of explosive devices for the oil industry. He asked for a job and presented his yet-unpatented product. The initial response was "What is it?" It looked like a beer can with holes punched in the ends. Or, as some anglers were later to call it, "a pencil sharpener on a pole." But Zebco looked again, liked the idea and hired Hull on the spot.

The first reels were sold in May, 1949. Hull is now a vice president in charge of product research and development, and Zebco claims its total sales from his brainchild have hit better than 70,000 units.

JIFFY BLOOD KNOT TIER

A handy gadget for those needing such things. Comes with directions.

top of the line

ZEBCO CARDINAL. The Cardinal is thought of as a top reel in its class. It has all of the necessary model sizes and features including ball-bearing drive, corrosion-resistant body, stainless steel worm gear and a handy, calibrated drag on the bottom of the reel. It's a good buy for the becoming-serious spinner. Zebco has improved itself by leaps and bounds since the days when its cheap close-faced reels were its main offering. The Cardinal reflects this change of heart.

ZEBCO 113 OMEGA. A poacher's delight. It's palm-sized and weighs only a little more than 4 ounces. It has a gear ratio of 4:1 and comes equipped with 65 yards of 6-pound test Stren, enough for small spincasting chores. The reel features a stainless steel cover, selective anti-reverse and is well made. Perfect for the traveling or backpacking spincaster.

ZEBCO 33XBL. This is the company that invented the close-faced spinning reel and still dominates the market, especially with its super-abundant line of lower priced reels, which are smartly outfitted in low-priced outfits. The rod, reel and line combinations are bought most often by absolute beginners or kids.

But Zebco also produces one of the best close-faced reels available. The 33XBL comes equipped with a very smooth functioning drag and ball bearings, just like the better open-faced models preferred by more advanced anglers. It isn't as cheap as the "bargains" you can find but if you haven't switched to baitcasting or open-faced it's a reel to look at long and hard. Other features on the 33XBL include dual ceramic line pickup pins, an easily replaceable spool and stainless steel worm gears and covers. It also features a wide range drag and a 3:1 drag ratio.

ZEBCO 33XBL

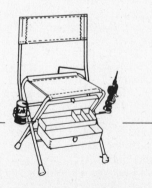

AMCO FISHING CHAIR

The ultimate for the lazy angler is the Amco fishing chair, a folder that you can pop out anywhere. It has a rod holder on the side and a tackle box underneath. Will also convert into a camp chair or camp stool.

NOTES ON THE PUSH-BUTTON REEL

The main components of a standard spin-casting or "push-button" reel are the body or gear housing, nose cone (front cover), foot, push-button (trigger or thumb release), drag adjustment knob, handle and anti-reverse.

All spin-casting reels are similar in their basic operation. The monofilament line is stored on a stationary spool contained within a nose cone, and is released for the cast when the push-button is depressed to withdraw the spool's pick-up pin(s) from line-holding position. On the cast, the freed line is pulled by the lure (or bait) off the spool through a hole in the nose cone.

A forward turn of the reel handle returns the pin(s) to the line pick-up position, and continued turning of the handle causes them to rotate around the spool and thus re-spool the line.

There is some short delay in pick-up of the line on spin-casting reels having only one pin; surer and quicker line retrieve is possible with reels which have more than one.

Since a spin-casting reel's pick-up pin(s) work constantly, they should be well-made of hard material, not unduly subject to wear or breakage. A faulty or broken pin makes a spin-casting reel inoperative.

The push-button of a spin-casting reel should be shaped and located for casting comfort. Most manufacturers build reels with push-buttons on top, and these are most popular, but some reels have release buttons on the side.

The majority of spin-casting reels have single-knob handles; some have double knobs. Other than comfort, handle design contributes little to a reel's performance so, as with type of push-buttons, single or double handles is a matter of personal preference.

As with spinning reels, some spin-casting reels are available with cranks on either the left or right side of the reel and some have handles that are interchangeable. These factors are important to the fisherman who will cast with his left hand and retrieve with his right.

Anti-reverse mechanisms are useful, preventing handles from turning backwards. Some reels have built-in, permanent anti-reverses; others are engaged by levers. The latter models should have the levers located out-of-the-way yet easy to reach.

All quality spin-casting reels have quickly adjustable drags with a wide range of tensions. "Star" drags, mounted on the handle are popular, but some reels have drag knobs top-mounted for handling ease. Other drags are adjusted by turning nose-cone rings.

One of the most important considerations in selecting a spin-casting reel is that it properly fit the rod to be used. All spin-casting reels will not mount well on all bait-casting or spin-casting rods. It is wise to test the reel on the rod to be used to be certain it is held securely in the reel seat and at a comfortable height.

American Fishing Tackle Manufacturers Association

specifications

BRAND-MODEL	WEIGHT (OZ.)	GEAR RATIOS	LINE (YD.) CAPACITY	DRAG
DAIWA				
Silvercast Series				
208 RL	8.1	4.1:1	105, 6 lb.	dial
210 RL	9.1	4.1:1	100, 8 lb.	dial
212 RL	11.1	4.1:1	160, 8 lb.	dial
Popular Spincast Reels				
2100	6	2.1:1	125, 4 lb.	star
2200	6.3	2.3:1	125, 4 lb.	star
9300	7	2.5:1	125, 4 lb.	dial
24	10	3.1:1	100, 10 lb.	star
28	12	3.1:1	130, 10 lb.	star
Minicast Gold System (reel with matching lightweight rod)				
MG1-59	5.8	4.1:1	85, 4 lb.	dial on thumb wheel
MG1-438	5.8	4.1:1	85, 4 lb.	dial on thumb wheel
Minicast System (reel with matching lightweight rod)				
MC1-438	5.3	4.1:1	85, 4 lb.	dial
MC1-59	5.3	4.1:1	85, 4 lb.	dial
EAGLE CLAW				
38B			250, 4 lb.	full circle
Blue Pacific				
102				star
103				star
104				star
GARCIA				
ABU 330	13	3.1:1	150, 10 lb.	with extra drag brake
ABU 350	13.5	3.1:1	175, 10 lb.	with extra drag brake
ABU 270	12	3:1	185, 12 lb.	disc
ABU 290	13	3:1	200, 12 lb.	disc
ABU 170	11	3:1	185, 12 lb.	star
ABU 150	11	3:1	185, 10 lb.	pre-set coin adjustable
ABU 120	9	3:1	250, 8 lb.	pre-set coin adjustable
Kingfisher Series				
GK-34	8.5	3.5:1	175, 8 lb.	star
GK-32	8	2.7:1	150, 6 lb.	dial
HEDDON				
190	14		30, 6 lb.	power
185	11	4:1	100, 10 lb.	
152	10		100, 8 lb.	star
112	7		100, 6 lb.	star
JOHNSON				
Guide 165			122, 14 lb.	internal and star
Guide 155			87, 12 lb.	internal and star
Sabra 130B			108, 17 lb.	
710, 710B			102, 10 lb.	disc
The Convertibles (for spinning or spincasting rods)				
Century 100B			187, 4 lb.	multiple shoe
Citation 110B			207, 8 lb.	multiple shoe
Laker II 140C		3:1	187, 4 lb.	
088, 088A		3:1	80, 10 lb.	star
Skipper 125		3:1	80, 10 lb.	
MARTIN				
500	9		100, 8 lb.	star
700	9		100, 8 lb.	star
220	6		80, 6 lb.	star
OLYMPIC				
Olympet				
1000		4.25:1	98, 4 lb.	
1000DX		4.25:1	98, 4 lb.	
No. 100 Series				
100	7.6	2.7:1	75, 10 lb.	star
115	8.3	2.7:1	95, 10 lb.	star
120	9	3.5:1	110, 8 lb.	star
125	9.1	3.5:1	130, 8 lb.	star
130	11.5	3.5:1	165, 8 lb.	star
No. 300 Series				
310	7.5	2.65:1	80, 8 lb.	star
311	7.6	2.75:1	80, 8 lb.	star
312	8	3:1	90, 10 lb.	star
175	5.6	2.75:1	90, 8 lb.	star
PFLUEGER				
500 Series				
543	8	3.5:1		star
541				star
SHAKESPEARE				
Pushbutton Reels				
1700II		4:1		star
7500		4:1	100, 8 lb.	star

"Many fish bite if you got the right bait."
BLACK AMERICAN FOLKLORE

CLOSE-FACED REELS 177

specifications

BRAND-MODEL	WEIGHT (OZ.)	GEAR RATIOS	LINE (YD.) CAPACITY	DRAG
1767II (comes with 100 yds. 8 lb. line)		.4:1	70, 12 lb.	star
1766II		.4:1	100, 12 lb.	star
7504 (fresh-salt)		.4:1	85, 20 lb.	star
7503		.4:1	90, 8 lb.	star
998			85, 8 lb.	star
Level Wind Reels				
1777		.4:1	120, 10 lb.	micro
1778		.4:1	120, 10 lb.	micro
1797		.4:1	100, 12 lb.	micro
1810		.4:1	190, 8 lb.	micro
1756			145, 8 lb.	

BRAND-MODEL	WEIGHT (OZ.)	GEAR RATIOS	LINE (YD.) CAPACITY	DRAG
633			100, 10 lb.	
636			17 lb.	
638			17 lb.	
66 (fresh-salt)			15 lb.	

SOUTH BEND

BRAND-MODEL	WEIGHT (OZ.)	GEAR RATIOS	LINE (YD.) CAPACITY	DRAG
Thumber 135			100, 8 lb.	star
Bassin Man 195		3.5:1	150, 15 lb.	star
165			100, 8 lb.	star
125			100, 8 lb.	star
40			100, 8 lb.	friction spool
30-A			100, 8 lb.	

TRUE TEMPER
Uni-Spin

BRAND-MODEL	WEIGHT (OZ.)	GEAR RATIOS	LINE (YD.) CAPACITY	DRAG
63			100, 10 lb.	

ZEBCO
Omega Series

BRAND-MODEL	WEIGHT (OZ.)	GEAR RATIOS	LINE (YD.) CAPACITY	DRAG
113	4	4.1:1	65, 6 lb.	disc
1	11.25	3:1	105, 14 lb.	star
909	9		100, 10 lb.	disc
33XBL	10.5		100, 10 lb.	
Zebco 33	8		100, 10 lb.	internal expanding

800 Series

BRAND-MODEL	WEIGHT (OZ.)	GEAR RATIOS	LINE (YD.) CAPACITY	DRAG
808 (fresh-salt)	.13		100, 20 lb.	delrin
888 (fresh-salt)	.13.5		100, 20 lb.	star
800	9		50, 14 lb.	disc
802	9		50, 14 lb.	disc/star
700	8		80, 20 lb.	
600	7.5		75, 10 lb.	
404 (fresh-salt)	7.5		75, 15 lb.	ratchet
202	6		70, 10 lb.	ratchet
76	4		50, 8 lb.	star
77 (permanently mounted on a 50" glass rod)	8		40, 6 lb.	ratchet

THE FINE POINTS
Drag, capacity, ball bearings and retrieve

By Harmon Henkin

The one significant difference between baitcasting reels and all other types is that the mechanism of the reel itself is crucial in casting. The reels used for fly casting, spinning, trolling, etc. — are used to store line and aid in retrieve and fighting fish.

You can cast as far with an atrocious spinning reel as with the best model on the market but that isn't true with baitcasting reels. So in looking at equipment you must examine what kind of casting you will be doing as well as what kind of fish you will be fighting and how much line you will need.

This isn't as rough a process as it once was. A few decades back it took an incredibly educated thumb to smoothly handle a multiplying reel (as they were called in the 19th Century) without causing that horror of horrors — the infamous bird's nests. Today most of the better models on the market — Shakespeares, Ambassadeurs, Heddons, Daiwas, etc. — come with free spools that disengage the gear mechanism when casting. They also come with incredibly fine-tuned drags that can be adjusted to the exact weight of the lure or bait being cast. If the drag mechanism that regulates the spool tension is too tight then casting is a practical impossibility. But — and a big but — if the mechanism is too loose the spool will override the outgoing drag tension and the line will snarl.

So look for a fine, turnable drag. However, if you don't cast light lures very far you might forego the freespool mechanisms. They're convenient but not essential. Many fine old-time baitcasters who couldn't afford them or didn't want to spend the extra bucks never really missed them.

Smoothness, with or without the freespool mechanism, is the key to the operation of baitcasting reels. Other features to consider are ball bearings, which also aid smooth operation, a corrosion-resistant finish to add seasons to its life and a level wind that's in perfect sync with the handle. It should allow the retrieved line to get back on the spool evenly if your next cast is to be successful.

Of course you must consider line capacity but that's a personal preference. The bigger the fish and the rougher the watery terrain the larger the capacity should be. That's simple enough.

Retrieve is another factor these days. Consider what kind of fishing you're going to do. If it's fast retrieve, top water stuff you might be satisfied with a retrieve in the 4-to-1 neighborhood. Some of the more popular reels such as the Ambassadeurs, Quicks and Daiwas can be converted to a faster retrieve with the relatively inexpensive addition of a gear.

Other minor features to consider are the accessibility of the various buttons and dials, such as the drag and free spool, and handle size as well. Bigger handles (which sometimes can be bought as options) are handy when playing big fish.

William Mills sold the "Intrinsic" baitcasting reel for $15 in the first part of the century. The spool and handle were made of aluminum and the plates and bars were cast from German silver.

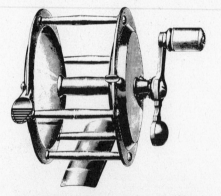

The "Henshall-Van Antwerp" black bass reel was sold by Thomas H. Chubb in the 1890s for $15. "It is a perfectly symmetrical reel," Dr. J. A. Henshall claimed at the time in his book *More About the Black Bass*, "the end plates being struck up so as to form, with the spool plates, a concavity at each end, in one of which is placed the gearing, and the adjustable click and automatic drag in the other."

Heddon called its "Auto-Spooler" reel a "radical departure in self-spooling reels." It sold in 1923 for $18.

THE ESSENTIAL BAITCASTING REEL

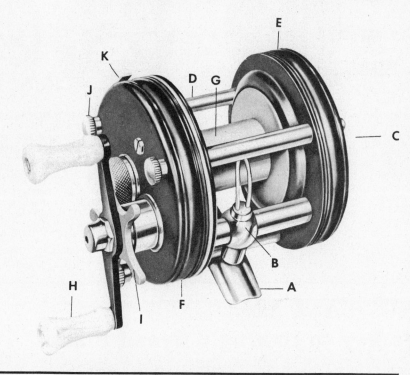

As a general rule the bait-casting outfit requires considerably more skill than does the spinning or spin-casting outfit. However, since the thumb of the casting hand is in direct contact with the flow of the line, an educated thumb can control the line to a fraction of an inch.

(A) Reel foot. This should be a flat and sturdy piece of metal for it serves to hold the reel on the rod. This material should be flat for it is desirable to have the bait-casting reel as close to the rod as possible. It should also be adequately long, to lock into the bait-casting rod you plan to buy. Since there are so many different locking mechanisms on all different fishing rods, it is a good idea to try the reel before buying.

(B) Level wind. This part should be made of extremely hard material, for the line passes through it both in casting and retrieving. This part moves back and forth across the front of the spool as the spool turns. Thus the line is wound onto the spool in a level fashion.

(C) Adjustable casting drag. This part is located in the center of the left side plate and generally appears as a knurled knob. It can be tightened or loosened as casting requirements change. This part creates friction on the spool, and the amount of friction is important. A pointer or indicator on this part to remember the setting is most desirable.

(D) Reel pillars. These parts separate and support the reel frame. Good chrome plating is desirable.

(E) Left side plate. It serves as part of the frame, and also encloses the mechanism on the left side of the reel.

(F) Right side plate. Also supports the frame and covers the drive gears and free spool mechanism.

(G) Reel spool. The spool of bait-casting reels should be sturdy enough to withstand the strain of monofilament line, and it should have sufficient capacity to hold enough line for fishing needs. This part should be just as light as possible, made from aluminum, or even magnesium.

(H) Reel handle knob. The reel handle knob should be large and comfortable, to give a sure grip even when the fisherman is tired.

(I) Star drag. The star drag should be as small as possible, yet the drag should be extremely smooth.

(J) Quick takedown screws. The purpose of these three screws is to enable the fisherman to disassemble part of his reel to facilitate cleaning and oiling. All bait-casting reels do not have this feature, although it is very desirable. However, the absence of the quick takedown system will not affect the casting one way or the other.

(K) Free spool lever. This disengages the gear mechanism and allows the spool to turn without moving the handle.

From *Fishing Tackle and Techniques* by Dick Wolff. (C) 1961 by Dick Wolff. Used by permission of E. P. Dutton & Company.

GAMEFISH: THE SHAD

NAMES
Common Coastal Shad, White Shad, Jack Atlantic Shad. *(Alosa sapidissma)*

DISTRIBUTION
The American shad is found in the coastal rivers from St. John's in Florida to the Gulf of the St. Lawrence. In the mid-1800s it was introduced to the Pacific Coast and now inhabits a range from southern California to Alaska.

DESCRIPTION
The American Shad is a member of the Herring family. It is a long, compact fish of blue-green coloring with silvery sides. Areas of indistinct spots cover the shoulders and gill covers.

SIZE
The American Shad averages between 3 and 6 pounds, the female generally being the heavier. Catches from 8 to 15 pounds are not considered unusual.

HABITAT
The American Shad is a saltwater fish that only ventures into fresh water during spawning season, which lasts from the months of January to May depending on the location. Coastal rivers well known for Shad runs include the Susquehanna, the St. John, the Delaware, the Potomac, the Connecticut, the St. Lawrence and the Russian River in California.

FEEDING HABITS
In salt water, the American Shad feeds primarily on plankton. While spawning it rarely eats at all. It is, however, considered an excellent game fish due to its tendency to hit artificial lures.

BEST FEEDING TEMPERATURE
Between 55 and 65 degrees.

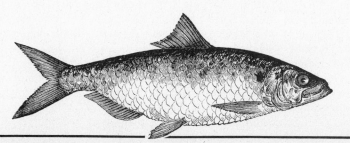

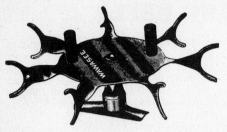

The "Wawasee Reel," marketed in the 1920s by the Creek Chub Bait Company, had no gears and weighed only 4 ounces. It cost only $3.50.

The "Huffman Attachment" was used in 1912 to clamp a baitcasting reel on most kinds of rods and cane poles. Made of German silver; sold by Abbey & Imbrie for $1.

William Mills & Son sold the quadruple "Manhattan Take-a-Part" reel in the early 1900s for $3.25. It held 80 yards of line, was nickel-plated and featured an adjustable click.

RUSS CHATHAM REVEALS ALL:
Vegetables are the key to fishing's Grand Slam

Dear Mr. Chatham:

One recent evening down at our local tavern, a friend told me that canned corn made good fish bait. Is this true? Any help you can give me on this subject will be appreciated.

Henry (Hank) Applebaum
Lincoln Center, Kansas

Dear Mr. Applebaum:

Yes, I can confirm that canned corn kernels may be used as bait. They make good chum too. And since your question lies a bit outside my main field of interest, I'd like to accompany my reply with a suggestion that you address a similar query to Homer Circle (a fishing editor, not a group of ball players with four baggers to their credit, as Ed Zern once thought).

The use of corn is familiar to all writers. We use it most frequently to dupe weakminded editors or strafe innocent laymen. In these cases its use is probably best described as chum, though occasionally a sucker is actually caught.

You are not the first to be confounded by corn. During the late forties I used to read a comic book called Colonel Corn. I was ten years old before I realized the word Colonel wasn't pronounced like it was spelled. So you see, I was had by corn at an early age.

But to move along to your question. Corn makes fine bait, having many advantages over other conventional types. In the Rocky Mountains, for example, fishing for whitefish is a popular winter sport. Maggots are the favored bait. Some of the locals save rotting carcasses and during thaws probe the festering depths to get enough of the white larvae for a day's fishing.

In very cold weather the maggots are held in the mouth to keep them from freezing. Hold them long enough and you can create your own hatch. (But that's another story.) I ask you, would you rather have a mouthful of writhing maggots freshly dug from a skunk's stinking spleen, or a teaspoon of Green Giant Niblets?

Which brings us to the use of succotash in lakes where there are more than one kind of fish. Say you want to go for the *Grand Slam*. That is to say, catch four kinds of fish at once. Succotash is your answer.

Weekend fishermen may be satisfied with a canned product but this will never do for the very avid. For one thing, the traditional recipe calls only for corn, lima beans and string beans. As the home run simile implies, four baits are required, and here, carrots get the nod.

During tournaments where the competition can get pretty stiff, hard-core anglers lightly salt and simmer fresh ingredi-

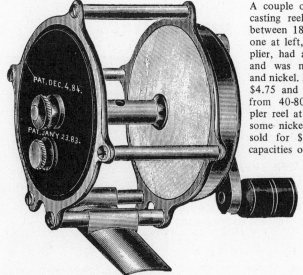

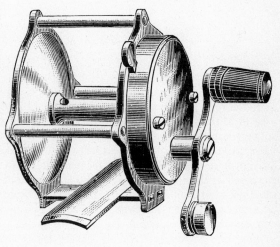

A couple of early Orvis bait-casting reels made sometime between 1883 and 1892. The one at left, the "Gem" multiplier, had an adjustable click and was made from rubber and nickel. It sold for $4.25 to $4.75 and came in capacities from 40-80 yards. The simpler reel at right was made of some nickel-plated metal and sold for $1.10 to $1.25 in capacities of 40 to 100 yards.

...ts, but frozen or canned veg-ables can be used in a pinch. ...ost consider the actual bait ...r less important than the ter-...inal tackle.

Start with your lima bean. ...t off one end and carefully ...sh it out slightly with a ba-...'s silver egg spoon. Using ...ht green size A Nymo ...read, tie the lima (it should ...a nice plump one) to a num-...r six popper hook.

Next comes your carrot. ...ere is where those who use ...esh vegies score a real plus. ...aving the carrot raw (or ...oiled only enough to make it ...st slightly flexible) put a hole ...rough it lengthwise with an ...e pick or similar tool. Slip a ...n-foot piece of twelve-pound ...ader material through the ...le and tie to it a number one ...eble hook.

On separate leaders and ...oks (Eagle Claw bait barb ...pes are best) impale your ...ing bean and your corn ker-...l, leaving the leaders random-...long.

Rig the four baits on a stif-...h boat rod as follows. First ...t your string bean on a ...elve-foot dropper. Six feet

behind that tie your corn hook on a three-foot dropper. At the end of the line itself (which may be braided dacron or monofilament of at least eigh-teen-pound test) attach a swiv-el. To the swivel tie your pre-pared lima on a four-foot leader. Trickiest of all is the carrot: its leader must be ex-actly eight feet long, affixed to the main line precisely one foot behind the twelve-foot string bean dropper.

Now you need a float. Any kind sufficient to main-tain the surface will do. It should be fastened to the main line at the swivel. The last time I tied up this outfit I used a cork from a bottle of Riche-bourg '63 which I drank during rigging up.

Now you're ready to go fishing. Take your boat out to the middle of the lake (the middle is as good a place to start as any). Carefully lower the four baits over the side, avoiding tangles. Keeping your eye on the float, row slowly away to a distance of about fif-ty feet.

Your lima bean, if it was properly prepared, should be

barely visible four feet behind the float. The corn, carrot and string bean will be hanging straight down from the line on their droppers, the latter, hope-fully, on or near the bottom.

Now you must wait. Your first strike comes on the string bean, probably a carp or suck-er, though you hope for the catfish necessary to begin the *Grand Slam* correctly (aficiona-dos dip the string bean in a mixture of warm pork fat and ox blood to improve their luck in attracting Mr. Whiskers).

When you have a bite, set the hook. Put the rod in a holder or other secure place and begin rowing steadily to-ward shore. The corn kernel will dart erratically, irresistible to a nice fat crappie or bluegill. Either of these beasts will hook themselves.

As you continue on, the struggles of the bream will at-tract a pike. Remember, your carrot is on an eight-foot drop-per which should allow it to wobble within a foot or so of the struggling sunfish. The pike will hit the carrot first, think-ing it is another small fish.

As you near the shore, the

struggles of the three captives will cause the lima to pop along the surface much like a baby frog. A bass will take it in shallow water.

Beach the boat and reel in your *Grand Slam*. There is no official recognition available from the Field & Stream con-test, but it should be reward enough to know that only a small handful of anglers, large-ly in the British Isles, have ever accomplished this difficult feat.

One final point: the use of corn, other vegetables, and even dairy products provides an advantage for the elderly on fixed incomes, the poverty-stricken, and anyone else otherwise disenfranchised since they may purchase their fish bait with U.S.D.A. Food Stamps.

Tight lines!

Russell D. Chatham

(Editor's Note: We regret that demands on the editor's time do not permit longer, more de-tailed answers.)

Collectors are hungry for the multipliers

By Mary K. Shepard

There is no question that the most sophisticated bit of 19th Century fishing tackle was the four-multiplying reel used in bait/plug casting. In its earliest and simplest design — without level wind or anti-backlash devices — it was also the most difficult piece of tackle to learn to use. If the angler had not developed a so-called "educated" thumb to control the speed of the spool, backlashes and bird's nests caused by the spool overrunning and snarling the line were an every-cast occurrence. Many an otherwise gifted angler gave up and forever condemned baitcasting. But with the growing interest in America's angling heritage, the casting reel is enjoying a newfound reputation. It is, in fact, the most eagerly sought item of all of angling's memorabilia — with prices corresponding to the demand, and sometimes being astronomically high.

The origin of the multiplying reel is cloudy. Dr. James A. Henshall in the revised editions of the *Book of the Black Bass*, published in 1904 and 1923, repeatedly argued that it was an American invention. He credited George Snyder of Paris, Kentucky, with building in 1810 for his own use the first multiplier. Snyder was a jeweler by trade, a bass angler by choice.

No one has ever disputed that Snyder was the first American to build a multiplier. However, the English were building and recommending them during the American Revolution — which was many years before Snyder. For example, in Smith's *True Art of Angling*, published in London in 1770, there appeared an advertisement for multiplying reels by the London tackle maker Onesimus Ustonson. In 1787, Best, a British angling author, advised in his *Concise Treatise* using the multiplying reel for salmon fishing.

Historically, wealthy southern gentlemen maintained very close ties with England. They imported from the mother country almost all their furniture, clothes, china, etc.; and this included fishing tackle and angling literature. Under these circumstances it is easy to believe that Snyder was aware of the multiplier before making his first.

Today many collectors are reverting to an old term and indiscriminately calling all multipliers "Kentucky" reels. The term "Kentucky" for the quadruple multiplier was coined

*Photo above by Warren Shepard
and Mary Kefover Shepard*

after the middle of the 1800s to distinguish it from the 2:1 ratio reel used on the East Coast for striped bass fishing; this latter was often called the "New York" reel. As originally applied, however, the term Kentucky also meant a work of art. Built by hand on foot-treadled lathes, the reel was slowly, meticulously turned out of solid brass, later German silver. Some have claimed that seven reels per month was the output of the earliest smiths. At any rate, every Kentucky reel is a baitcasting reel, but not every baitcasting reel is a Kentucky.

Two F. F. Meek & J. F. Meek quad reels from 1845 photographed with an 8-foot 3-inch Varney Henshall rod from 1890

Besides George Snyder, the more famous Kentucky reel makers were: J. W. Hardman, Benjamin C. Milam, Benjamin F. Meek, M. J. L. Sage, and George W. Gayle, all of Kentucky. Makers in later years were William H. Talbot of Missouri and J. A. Coxe of California. Shakespeare, Heddon and South Bend also made some reels that can qualify as "Kentucky."

The used tackle market has never been tested on reels made by Snyder, Hardman or Sage. That is, none have ever come up for sale. Therefore, no price can definitely be set; but one can guess that at auction the bidding on a marked Snyder would start at $1,500. The price on Gayle reels will vary extremely. Gayle cheapened his product, eventually selling some reels for 25 cents. A fine early Gayle is worth a lot; the later, two-bit model, not much.

Early reels made while J. F. Meek worked with his brother, and marked, "J. F. and B. F. Meek," bring a premium. Even the Meek reels made after 1916 — when Horton Manufacturing Co. of Bristol, Connecticut, purchased the Meek company — fetch in the $100 neighborhood.

Reels inscribed B. C. Milam, and no "Son" with the marking also are early and demand a good price.

Meek reels made in 1905. Both were cast from German silver and came with extra spools of silver or aluminum. They each sold for $26. For another $6 you could get yourself a Meek with jeweled pivot bearings.

top of the line

WHAT WE LOOKED FOR IN QUALITY

Baitcasting reels have been around for a long time but it's been only recently that they've gotten markedly smoother.

Most of the good old multipliers, even from before the turn of the century, were very functional pieces of machinery. And they'll still work very well today in the hands of anyone who knows baitcasting.

What the modern reels feature is smoother-functioning drags (often star drags), free spools that are very accessible, highly corrosion-resistant finishes, the ability to cast very light lures and efficient level winds.

Baitcasting has recently become much more popular and simpler. Even a novice quickly comes to appreciate how much accuracy and delicacy are available with modern equipment.

In examining the plethora of baitcasting reels on the market we zeroed in on qualities like the functioning of the drag, simplicity of operation, finish, mechanical reliability and smoothness.

But this gadget-enthralled culture of ours has a tendency to overdo things, some baitcasting reels being prime examples. Some of them carry more gimmicks and junk than the angler really needs. Remember that even some very simple reels will do the job — and a simple, well-made reel will last longer than a cluttered competitor reel made just as well. The more there is to go wrong, the more that will go wrong.

Get what you need, nothing more.

DAIWA MILLIONAIRE. A fancy, perhaps overdressed baitcasting reel that's still functionally excellent. It comes in a variety of capacities with star drags (almost mandatory these days), ball bearings, calibrated bearing brakes and oversized handles. Free spool, of course, these reels have lots of stainless-steel parts and a special system to allow you to set the brake tension according to the weight of the plug you are casting. Everything you'll need in a well-made package and then some.

HEDDON 3200. This free spool baitcasting reel is another of the modern outpourings caused, at least philosophically, by the rapid growth of tournament bass angling. Everything frees up when the clutch is hit including the level wind, an impressive if not actually necessary extra. Like the other better reels the 3200 has ball bearings in its innards, centrifugal star drag system, big bozo handle and a calibrated spool tension system. This is one of those reels that make baitcasting almost as easy as spinning was. Some changes are progressive!

LEW'S SHIMANO SPEED SPOOL. This is a very fine, rather specialized baitcasting reel designed with the black bass in mind. It weighs only 10 ounces and has a hand-fitted shape that's more streamlined than other baitcasters. Stainless steel ball bearings, a 4.4-to-1 gear ratio, a star drag, a free spool and a centrifugal speed control brake to control backlash. It also has an eyed line guide and very oversized handles. One of the most interesting reels around.

FAVORITES OF THE EXPERTS

In the category of baitcasting reels there were no great surprises — our polled experts chose the Garcia Ambassadeur line almost two to one over other available models. Garcia, which has advertised Ambassadeurs very heavily over the past decade, has reaped the reward. They are generally considered an excellent and functional piece of equipment. "There's nothing as smooth as the Ambassadeur," replied one writer who is a bass aficionado.

But the longtime favorite — the Pflueger Supreme — also has its partisans. "Still the best," says one. Among the other reels receiving some votes were Shakespeare and Mitchell. There was also support for the Daiwa Millionaire series of baitcasters but not as much as we would have suspected considering the design, quality and heavy exposure of these models. We had a sense, however, that among the experts the Daiwa would become more and more popular as baitcasting reels are used more by top money winners to take tournament bass.

DAIWA MILLIONAIRE

MITCHELL 5000

It's come to this. Oversized Hog Handler handles for your Garcia Ambassadeur reel. Available in various anodized colors. Gives you that customized look. Helps make you the best-dressed in your local tournament.

BOONE HAND LINE SPINNING REEL

The Boone Bait Company wants to get us back to our roots with their Hand Line Spinning Reel. Line is spun off with an overhead tossing motion and retrieved onto the spool. Advances hand line fishing almost to the stage of the development of the fishing reel! Lots of angling and non-angling uses.

top of the line

MITCHELL 5000 SERIES. Before the current baitcasting revival, the Ambassadeur 5000 family was the only serious contender for the top reel spot. But now this group is just one of the better items in a much bigger field. The Garcia baitcasters are available with every sort of desired feature, including ball bearings, star drags, quick retrieves, big capacities, mechanical breaks (to set lure weight) and any other thing your angling heart desires. The Ambassadeur is available from the ultra-light 1750 to sizes for casting and water trolling.

OLYMPIC 7700. The Olympic Company, which has become a major force in the spinning reel market, has now edged its way into the baitcasting field with its 7700 and other models. Has a free spool mechanism, ball bearings, a very delicate drag and one of those ever-so-popular big handles. An interesting possibility.

RYOBI ADVENTURER 40. Is the Ryobi a serious baitcasting reel or a gimmick for kids? Maybe a little of both. The tiny reel weighs in at only 3.2 ounces — and that's small. The palm-sized, bright-red caster has no level wind but it does have an adjustable drag, an anti-reverse and a click. Its 4:1 gear ratio does allow adequate casting, especially for the angler with thumb educated well enough to manage without a level wind. It has metal bushing and will hold over 200 yards of 8-pound test line. Nice to wave around or to keep in your pocket or box as a spare for emergencies. A unique item.

Izaak Walton's Carp Recipe

But first, I will tell you how to make this Carp, that is so curious to be caught, so curious a dish of meat as shall make him worth all your labor and patience. And though it is not without some trouble and charges, yet it will recompense both. Take a Carp — alive if possible; scour him, and rub him clean with water and salt, but scale him not; then open him, and put him with his blood and liver, which you must save when you open him, into a small pot or kettle; then take sweet marjoram, thyme, or parsley, of each a handful; a sprig of rosemary, and mother-of-savory; bind them into two or three small bundles, and put them to your carp, with four or five whole onions, twenty pickled oysters, and three anchovies. Then pour upon your Carp as much claret wine as will only cover him; and season your claret well with salt, cloves and mace, and the rind of oranges and lemons. That done, cover your pot, and set it on a quick fire till it be sufficiently boiled. Then take out the Carp, and lay it with the broth into the dish, and pour upon it a quarter of a pound of the best fresh butter, melted and beaten with a half-a-dozen spoonsful of the broth, the yolks of two or three eggs, and some of the herbs shred; garnish your dish with lemons, and so serve it up, and much good to you.

Fish and Fishing (1864).
By Frank Forester.

LEW'S SHIMANO SPEEL SPOOL

"From his dark haunt beneath the tangled roots
Of pendent trees the monarch of the brook,
Behoves you then to ply your finest art."
THOMSON, *The Seasons*

BAITCASTING REELS 185

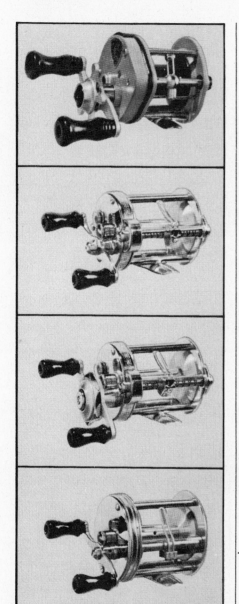

top of the line

PENN LEVELMATIC. This is a new series in the middle range of baitcasting sizes. Available in two models with slightly different handle arrangements, Penn, which has been making top-quality salt water reels for decades, says its centrifugal spool "eliminates drag." We've all heard that one before, but nonetheless, it sure is good quality and has such features as a free spool that works with a sideways flick of a button. Comes with a 4:1 gear ratio. All in all, a nice reel.

PFLUEGER SUPREME. The top name, eons before the current bass fishing-inspired baitcasting craze began, is still around. In fact, many of the very popular Pflueger casters are still being made, adapting to technical changes but still keeping their integrity. The Supremes (not the singing group, Clyde), the Akron and the beginner's Trump are still being produced. The 610-B, favored by serious casters, now has ball bearings, stainless-steel outers, power handle and free spool. The old Supremes, if you can find one, are still very usable. Either way Pflueger Supremes — at the top of the line — and the Akron and Trump are all a fine value.

QUICK CHAMPION. This series of baitcasting reels is a fine new addition to the Quick line. The No. 800 with free spool operation and a multiple disc drag (coated with asbestos to minimize heat), like the other three models, has a smooth-operating star

drag. The 700 and 700S, smaller versions of the 800 and 800B, are very lightweight — under nine ounces. The 700 and 800Bs have high-speed gear ratios of 4:65 to 1. Handsome-looking devils, too.

OVERLAND CRIMPER PLIERS

Multi-purpose crimper pliers. Overland's fairly well-made, 4½-inch all-purpose tool will work in a pinch as a pliers, crimper, wrench, vise, straightener, cutter, disgorger and hook puller. Other than warmth and understanding, what else does the angler need?

PENN LEVELMATIC

QUICK CHAMPION

PFLUEGER
(from top to bottom)
Supreme, 1893L Akron,
1895 Akron, Trump and
1913 Pflueger

SHAKESPEARE 1980. This free-spool casting reel, labeled the President II, boasts that it has "all the features demanded by serious anglers." It probably does. Such as: the now *de rigueur* star drag, plunger-operated free spool, the omnipresent ball bearings, centrifugal braking mechanism and that dark color that everyone knows means "serious angler at work." Such reels are undoubtedly easier to handle for anglers not schooled in the "bird's nest" trial and error method that took years to master. Oh yeah. It has a big handle for hauling in whoppers. An excellent reel.

SHAKESPEARE 1973a. With its now rarish direct drive and very narrow spool, this is a fine baitcasting reel and one favored by tournament casters. It weighs only 5.5 ounces. It has stainless steel bearings, nylon gears and bronze bushings. A no-nonsense reel for the angler who doesn't necessarily accept change for change's sake. A serious piece of lightweight machinery for the serious minded.

Baitcasters: bargains for collectors

Perhaps the most promising area to look for bargains in secondhand tackle is baitcasting reels.

Despite reams of PR flack, the baitcasting reel hasn't improved technically in half and maybe even a full century. The crafted Meeks, Heddons and Shakespeares of years ago are the equal of anything on today's market and some of the old tournament casting free-spool reels are superior.

This is not to say that there aren't good reels available to baitcasters today but bargain hunters would do better with older models. Many of the casting reels bought today aren't used much except for jobs too heavy for open- or close-faced spinning reels. Therefore they're often in like-new condition.

—H.H.

THE TOOTHSAVER

Cabela's is offering this neat gadget that fits on Garcia, Daiwa and Quick reels. It attaches on a rear screw and is useful in cutting lines or knots — hence has the name Tooth Saver. Made from stainless steel, it will work on either braided or monofilament lines. Very convenient, especially considering what dental bills are these days.

Estimating Fish Weights

Here's a quick and easy method for estimating fish weights. All you need is something to measure the fish's length and girth. A tape measure is ideal but if you don't have one handy, a dollar bill is 6¼ inches long and a king-size cigarette is about 3¼ inches long.

For fish shaped like bass, perch and walleyes, the weight equals the length times the girth squared, divided by 800. For example, if your smallmouth bass is 21 inches long and 15 inches around, the girth squared is 225, times the length is 4725. Dividing 4725 by 800 gives you 5.91 lb. or about 5 lb., 14½ oz. For fish shaped like northern pike, trout and barracuda, you simply divide by 900 instead of 800.

This is a relatively accurate method, but it will not take the place of good scales. If the estimated weight comes close to a record or even gets close to being exceptional for that species in that area, carefully preserve it by keeping it wet and cool and get it to the nearest official scales as quickly as possible. It just might be the fish of a lifetime.

WEBER REEL GREASE

If you're going out on an extended trip, carry a tube of this Weber reel grease. Provides excellent protection against salt and fresh water incursions.

When the wind is in the east,
Then the fishes bite the least;
When the wind is in the west,
Then the fishes bite the best;
When the wind is in the north,
Then the fishes do come forth;
When the wind is in the south,
It blows the bait in the fish's mouth.

UNKNOWN, *Old Rhyme.*

A primer on baitcasting reels

In its simplest form, a bait-casting reel comprises inter-locking gears, hubs, side plates, screws, nuts, a handle and a "foot" (stand) by which it is secured to a rod handle. When a cast is made, the momentum of the lure (or bait) pulls line from the reel by rotating the spool; line is re-spooled when the angler turns the reel handle.

Simply designed bait-casting reels are best suited to still-fishing or light trolling — fishing that does not require casting. If casting is to be done, better quality bait-casting reels are preferred since they give almost complete trouble-free casting performance.

Most bait-casting reels have brakes, level winds, anti-backlash devices, free-spool arrangements and adjustable drags.

The level-wind on a reel is a guide which, when the reel's handle is turned, moves back-and-forth to re-spool line evenly on the spool. Level-winds may be of varying shapes and sizes, but all serve the same purpose — controlling and spooling line evenly.

Manufacturers have different names for anti-backlash devices they build into their reels, but all perform the same basic function: slowing the reel spool during the cast. Many bait casting reels have "centrifugal" brakes to control the spool. This "braking" of the swiftly turning reel spool prevents annoying line tangles called "backlashes" or "over-runs." The amount of pressure or brak-

ing exerted by an anti-backlash mechanism is knob-adjustable, and should be varied according to the weight of the lure or bait cast.

Most modern bait-casting reels are "free-spool" type, and some "total free-spool." Free-spool means that a clutch-like system disengages everything during the cast except the level-wind, reduces friction, and allows smoother, longer casts.

A reel with total free-spool also disengages the level-wind, which remains stationary on the cast and further reduces friction, while only the spool turns to pay out line. By turning the handle of a free-spool or total free-spool reel, the clutch automatically re-engages gears to begin the retrieve.

Drags on bait-casting reels apply tension to the spool so that the line will pay out under pressure. The amount of pressure or "drag" is adjustable by turning a knurled knob or "star" drag control. Drags are valuable in fighting strong fish and in trolling.

The fisherman who will do serious bait-casting should buy the best reel he can afford. The best-built, best-designed reels are the more expensive models; casting ease and efficiency are in direct proportion to the quality of the reel.

American Fishing Tackle Manufacturers Association

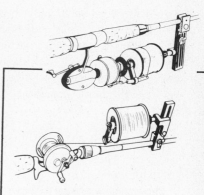

THE LINEMINDER

The Lineminder is a useful gadget for the hardcore spinner or baitcaster who buys spinning or casting line in bulk spools. Taking up to quarter-pound spools, the Lineminder clamps on to the end of the rod, ensuring an even intake of line. The adjustable rubber clutch ensures proper tension and eliminates berserko zig-zagging of line. Saves money in the long run; not expensive in the short run.

THE LAST HATCH
A FISHING MYSTERY
HARMON HENKIN

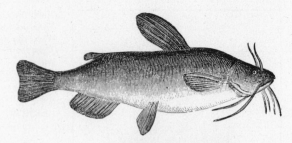

GAMEFISH:
CHANNEL CATFISH

(continued from page 169)

"Your reasoning is inexorable, as they said in Humanities 104. Let us proceed, Sherlock."

They continued up the bank for several hundred yards to a point where a small stand of cottonwoods blocked off the view of the house. Rosehips and wild strawberries surrounded a little hollow in the trees.

"This looks like the perfect place to murder someone, Sid."

The sheriff was already pawing the grass anxiously.

"Yeah. He got it here. Bloodstains."

There was a flattened area roughly the size of Halford marking the spot. The vague outline wasn't as moist as the surrounding ground. A Dan Bailey trout leader and a large Royal Coachman lay in the middle of the impression.

"No rod or gear, Paul. What happened to them? He was going fishing, wasn't he?"

"That's the feeling I got from Dun."

Paul dropped to one knee near the outline. "Somebody's been here since the murder. Look at these prints. The grass is popping back up where Halford fell but it's still pressed against the track."

"Did *you* go to the Famous Policeman's School?"

"No. This is just simple elk tracking. You have to know how long ago the beasts went through an area. But I can't make much sense of the tracks in this stuff. They're too vague. And besides, too many people from the house have been wandering around here the last few days."

"Well, this track is new, right?"

"Yeah. I thought for a minute it could have been Dun. But he would have taken the back trail when he ran down here to look at Halford. I just don't know."

They made widening circles around the track, covering the whole clearing and a bit of the brush.

"Well, one thing for sure, Sid. There wasn't a struggle. No signs of that. It must have been someone he knew."

"Could have crept up behind him."

"No, not from the angle the gaff hit. Couldn't get to that point coming up from behind. He must have been talking to the killer and got plopped."

(continued on page 201)

NAMES
Great Lakes Catfish, Fiddler, Spotted Cat, Silver Catfish. *(Icatalurus punctatus)*

DISTRIBUTION
The Channel Catfish is found from southern Canada and the Great Lakes region south into the Mississippi River System, the Gulf states and Mexico. It has been introduced almost everywhere in the United States and stocking has been most prevalent in southern California and the Midwestern states.

DESCRIPTION
The Channel Catfish is a smooth-skinned fish of silver or blue-gray coloring with silver sides and a white belly. Small, dusky spots cover the sides and other distinctive features include long snout whiskers, which facilitate feeding, and a deeply notched tail.

SIZE
The average weight of the Channel Catfish is between 1 and 6 pounds. Anything over 10 pounds is considered unusual.

HABITAT
The Channel Catfish is an extremely versatile fish and is found in environments of all sorts, from farm ponds to large, rapidly-moving rivers. It prefers cleaner water than most other members of the Catfish family and is usually found in wide, clear rivers or lakes with sandy or rocky bottoms.

FEEDING HABITS
Just about anything edible can be considered a part of the Channel Catfish diet. It is a voracious eater and will eat both aquatic growth and all forms of fish life. Like all Catfish, it is primarily a night feeder.

BEST FEEDING TEMPERATURE
Between 70 and 75 degrees.

TACKLE
The channel cat can be a tackle-busting brute at certain times and places but it can also be a finicky nibbler of cut baits, dough balls and corn attached to the heavy gear required to fish rough waters for rough fish. It'll even take artificials at times but the spinners and spoons it hits are not the mainstay of this bait eater. A 10-pound test line on a baitcasting outfit is good.

"Simon Peter saith unto them, I go a fishing. They say unto him, We also go with thee."
New Testament: John

specifications

BRAND-MODEL	WEIGHT (OZ.)	GEAR RATIOS	LINE (YD.) CAPACITY	DRAG
LEW CHILDRE				
Speed Spool				star
DAIWA				
Millionare Series				
3H	10.5	5:1	225, 10-lb.	star
5H	11.9	5:1	225, 10 lb.	star
GARCIA				
Ambassadeur				
7000	17.5	4:1	275, 20 lb.	star
8600	15.4	4.2:1	375, 20 lb.	star
9000	15.4	4.2:1/2.5:1	375, 20 lb.	star
10,000 CA	16.1	4.2:1/2.5:1	500, 20 lb.	star
5600 C	10.8	4.7:1	300, 10 lb.	star
6600C	13	4.7:1	375, 10 lb.	star
2500C		4.7:1		star
500 C (fast retrieve)	10.3	4.7:1	300, 10 lb.	star
5500 (fast retrieve)	8.5	4.7:1	300, 10 lb.	star
5000	8.5	3.6:1	175, 12 lb.	star
5000B	8.5	3.6:1	225, 12 lb.	star
5000D	8.5	3.6:1	100, 20 lb.	star
5000C	10.7	3.6:1	225, 12 lb.	star
50001C	10.7	3.6:1	225, 12 lb.	star
6000 (large capacity)	9.7	3.6:1	250, 10 lb.	star
6000C (large capacity)	12.5	3.6:1	375, 10 lb.	star
6500 (large capacity)		4.7:1		star
6500C (large capacity)		4.7:1		star
Kingfisher (trolling, bottom fishing)				
GK-60	14	3:1	300, 15 lb.	star
GK-61	18.5	3:1	425, 20 lb.	star
GK-62	19.5	3:1	450, 20 lb.	star
GK-64	24	3:1	425, 30 lb.	star
GK-72	24	2.75:1	425, 30 lb.	star
GK-74	30	2.75:1	550, 30 lb.	star
HEDDON				
3200		4.1:1		star
Trolling Reels (salt or fresh)				
409	20	3:1	300, 20 lb.	star
499	14	3:1	250, 15 lb.	star
445	20	3:1	300, 20 lb.	star
450	19	3:1	200, 36 lb.	
422	22	2.5:1	300, 30 lb.	star
421	18	3:1	240, 30 lb.	star

BRAND-MODEL	WEIGHT (OZ.)	GEAR RATIOS	LINE (YD.) CAPACITY	DRAG
OLYMPIC				
6600	10.4	4:1	180, 10 lb.	star
7700	10.8	4:1	245, 10 lb.	star
700 Series				
707	4.4	3:1	100, 12 lb.	
720A	6.	3.3:1	100, 15 lb.	
727	5.7	3.8:1	100, 15 lb.	
737	5.6	3.8:1	100, 15 lb.	
PENN				
Levelmatic				
910	11	4:1	175, 12 lb.	centrifugal spool
920	11	4:1	175, 12 lb.	centrifugal spool
930	11.63	4:1	225, 12 lb.	centrifugal spool
940	11.63	4:1	225, 12 lb.	centrifugal spool
Monofil Level Wind Reels				
9 Series				
9F	11	3:1	225, 15 lb.	star
9MF	12	3:1	275, 15 lb.	star
109 Series				
109F	11	3.75:1	225, 15 lb.	star
109MF	12	3.75:1	275, 15 lb.	star
209 Series				
209F	18.5	3:1	300, 20 lb.	star
209MF	19.5	3:1	350, 20 lb.	star
Super Peer				
309M	26	3:1	300, 36 lb.	star
Level Line				
350	19	3:1	175, 36 lb.	
350M	20	3:1	225, 36 lb.	
Jigmaster				
500		4:1	200, 36 lb.	star
550M		4:1	300, 36 lb.	star
501		4:1	350, 12 lb.	star
501M		4:1	500, 12 lb.	star
500L			275, 36 lb.	brake lining
Baymaster				
180F	12		200, 20 lb.	
180MF	12.5		250, 20 lb.	
185MF	12		250, 20 lb.	
Beachmaster				
155	14		175, 36 lb.	star
160	13		150, 36 lb.	star
155M	16		225, 36 lb.	star
160M	14.5		200, 36 lb.	star
Delmar				
285	17	2.3:1	200, 36 lb.	star
285M	18	2.3:1	250, 36 lb.	star

specifications

BRAND-MODEL	WEIGHT (OZ.)	GEAR RATIOS	LINE (YD.) CAPACITY	DRAG
Seaboy				
85	.16	.2.3:1	.200, 36 lb.	star
Sea Scamp 78	.10		.150, 36 lb.	
Sea Hawk 77	.9		.125, 36 lb.	
PFLUEGER				
Supreme				
610-B	.9		.200, 15 lb.	star
611-B	.8.7		.130, 15 lb.	star
Baitcasting Reels				
1893L	.7.75	.4:1	.175, 15 lb.	star
1943	.7.88	.4:1	.175, 15 lb.	
1983	.5.6	.3.5:1	.100, 15 lb.	
1895		.4:1		star
1913	.4	.4:1	.100, 15 lb.	
QUICK				
Champion Series (fresh, light salt)				
700	.8.4	.3.65:1	.250, 12 lb.	star

BRAND-MODEL	WEIGHT (OZ.)	GEAR RATIOS	LINE (YD.) CAPACITY	DRAG
800	.11	.3.65:1	.275, 15 lb.	star
700B				star
	.11	.4.65:1	.275, 15 lb.	star
RYOBI				
Adventure Series				
SD-101	.34.4	.3.4:1	.655, 33 lb.	star
SD-103	.31.6	.3.4:1	.405, 33 lb.	star
40	.3.2	.4.1:1	.196, 9 lb.	
SHAKESPEARE				
President II				
1980		.5:1		star
1906	.5		.100, 15 lb.	
1973A	.5.5		.50, 12.5 lb.	
1924	.9		.100, 15 lb.	star
599	.3.9		.125, 12.5 lb.	
1950	.8.7		.100, 15 lb.	
1950S	.9.4		.100, 15 lb.	star

SPINNING RODS:
STICK WITH ESTABLISHED BRANDS AND AVOID GIMMICKS

By Harmon Henkin

Today's spinning rods are more specialized than could have been imagined even a decade ago.

When spinning reels first made their commercial appearance in this country after WWII, the accompanying rods were broken down into three categories: light, medium and heavy. Unlike early glass fly rods, some of the early spinning rods were excellent especially those produced by Shakespeare, Silaflex and Heddon. Their reel seats held an open-faced reel tightly, and they had wide guides to allow the monofilament line to uncurl gently and an action neither too fast nor too slow.

Some of the early bamboo spinning rods by Orvis, Payne and other top makers remain the best ever made for basic spinning.

But today's spinners are more specialized. They will usually want a rod for a particular range of line or even for a particular type of lure fishing. There are many rods sold for worm fishing, jigging, top water plug casting or heaving bait. However, if you haven't progressed into one of those sorts of specialties stick with buying a rod for the range of line you use most often.

As far as action goes, as in all kinds of rods, get a medium action rod unless you have a special use in mind. For instance, a rod with an action that goes almost into the handle is favored by some anglers who baitfish a lot. They believe these rods cast more gently. At the other extreme there are some, most especially ultra-lighters, who like a tippy rod for lots of pinpoint casts with tiny spinners and plugs. But if you're that specialized already you don't have any reason to read this. You know exactly what you want.

Graphite or glass? A good question without a good answer. Graphite can make life lighter for the angler. You can cast a little further and you will spend quite a bit more money. That's all that can be said for sure. The decision is up to you. Some people like the feel of them in casting and fighting a fish and others hate them. Consult a psychologist for the reasons.

Get big guides, of course, but whether they should be the new ceramic types or made of a traditional metal alloy kind is another unanswerable. Some claim the ceramics add distance to your cast and last longer and others say no. It's not crucial, however.

Reel seats should hold a reel. Simple. On an ultra-light rod get two metal rings on an all-cork handle. That's the lightest and it holds tight on a decent rod. The bigger the fish, the heavier the reel and the bigger the rod, the sturdier the reel seat should be. The double-locking types are very good in the heavyweight category.

And actually that's about all there is to know. Stick with an established brand. Watch out for gimmicks and you can't go too wrong.

Look for a rod with medium action, big guides and a sturdy reel seat.

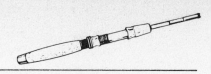

"If fishing interferes with your business, give up your business."
SPARSE GREY HACKLE

MEMOIRS OF A TACKLE JUNKIE

By Harmon Henkin

Whenever the urge to accumulate fishing tackle seizes me, I remember back to that weekend 10 years ago and the itch seems anticlimactic.

Richard Eggert and I were your regular semi-impoverished college students. But instead of spending our spare coins on booze, drugs and sex, we were fixated on the higher realms of fishing tackle. Endless hours of abstract debate were frittered on the relative merits of Paul Young fly rods vs. Orvis, or whether the Hardy Lightweight reels were superior to the old St. George's. The discussions were abstract since our tackle at the time consisted of regular production rods and reels and the quasi-grotesque flies we were learning to tie.

On the weekend in question we were visiting a classmate in Grand Rapids, Michigan — now enshrined as the home of Gerald Ford. We had spent Saturday visiting all of the sporting goods shops listed in the yellow pages, pawing over the monotonous tackle they contained. It was all new stuff with new prices — nothing very exciting.

So there we were back at his house nursing a beer and watching the last quarter of a basketball game. It was late afternoon. A commercial came on. Our friend turned his head.

"If you guys like old tackle, you should have been here a few months ago. There was a store called Baisch's. Been here for 50 years. Tons of stuff."

Our heads jerked around. Our voices trembled.

"It's not there anymore?"

"No. the old man just died. They're selling everything off."

We might not have broken the land speed record getting downtown in Dick's 59 VW, but we were close runners-up.

Baisch's was an old store front, hidden in the downtown decay. Social derelicts on society's margins were the prime occupants.

It was 4:45 — 15 minutes before closing — when we rushed inside. The place was unbelievable; I thought a time machine had transported us back to an earlier time. The store must have been one of the biggest in the Midwest in its heyday. And even two days into the closeout sale the long narrow shelves, towering to the top of the high ceiling, were packed with tackle, guns, skates, baseball bats and on and on.

Now you have to remember that in 1965 tackle collectors were an unknown breed. Fly fishing and baitcasting hadn't entered their current renaissance and the small minority who still practiced these occult activities were mostly contented with mass-produced equipment. But for us, after years of catalog mulling, the mounds of gear were a fairyland. All of the

historic brand names of the 20th Century were there and to make things even more unreal, everything was dirt cheap.

The owner hadn't changed the original prices. For instance, our dreamed-about Hardy reels from England were marked at under $20, the price they must have been in the 1940s. And . . . and to make things even wilder the two men handling the closeout for the estate had marked everything off an additional 50 per cent.

We spent the last 15 minutes in complete shock, too stunned to even buy a single box of fine fly tying hooks from England at a dime! At 5 P.M. on the button, we were sternly ushered from paradise, our pleas falling on deaf ears. Suppose the world ended before the store reopened on Monday? Disaster! The men didn't care. They were going home.

From Saturday afternoon to Monday morning we were consumed by a mania the likes of which hadn't been seen since Alexander decided to conquer the world. We devised a buying game plan and made endless phone calls to raise money.

ME.
Hi. Is this Susan Smith?
THEM.
Yes.
ME.
Well. My name is Harmon Henkin. I sat next to you in 11th grade civics class and I'm wondering if you would

(continued on page 204)

"I shall stay him no longer than to wish . . . if he be an honest angler, the east wind may never blow when he goes a fishing."
IZAAK WALTON *The Compleat Angler*

SPINNING RODS 193

HOW TO CARE FOR FISHING RODS

By C. Boyd Pfeiffer

If a reel drag is set properly, no fish can break a fishing rod. Home and car doors can, and are responsible for most fishing rod damage. But rod care involves more than just avoiding such obvious rod breakers.

Most fishing rods come in cloth bags and/or rod cases, and should be carried in them at all times when not fishing. Assemble rods carefully, first making sure that the ferrules are clean and free of grease and oil. Line up the guides before tightening the ferrules.

Avoid hitting the rod against any sharp object. Such a hit may break or bend guides, or even worse, can bruise the glass of the rod blank. Such a bruise may not break the rod initially, but the damage to the glass can spread, causing the rod to break months or even years later.

Guides are particularly susceptible to breakage, with agate and tungsten carbide the most fragile. Chromed stainless steel and ceramic guides are tougher, but still should be treated with care.

Rods can also be broken in the field by carrying them through the woods with the rod tip forward. The rod tip catches on a limb and snaps. To prevent this, carry rods handle first. The guides and line still may catch on twigs, but not with the same disastrous results. Keep rods off the ground. The dirt and grime won't do the damage that they do on reels but rods become "lost" in the grass and are easily stepped on. Similarly, keep rods arranged orderly or in rod racks when boat fishing. This also keeps them from being stepped on, or sticking out from the hull and running afoul of pilings and other boats when docking.

Most rods require little more than a thorough wiping off after a fishing trip to keep them clean. Saltwater rods will require a more thorough washing and wiping to keep saltwater corosion off the guides, reel seat, metal ferrule and any other metal parts.

Each season, go over the rod carefully to check for wear and any damage that can be corrected. The thread wrappings that hold guides on are most susceptible to wear and fraying. One way to prevent this is to seasonally give each thread wrapping an additional coat of varnish, or better still, one of the new epoxy rod finishes such as Diamond One Coat or Gudebrod's Hard 'n Fast.

If a guide wrapping does start to unravel, remove it, and rewrap the guide or take it to a competent tackle repair shop for the job.

Check tip tops and ferrules for looseness. Remove and replace with ferrule cement if necessary. Aside from such simple yearly checks there is not much that can go wrong with fishing rods, except for the obvious care required in handling a fragile, flexible and expensive stick.

A new epoxy rod finish

top of the line

WHAT WE LOOKED FOR IN QUALITY

Action, fittings and ferrules. That was the general standard applied to spinning rods.

Thankfully, the general quality of spinning rods has increased over the past few years. Almost all of the rods we examined had enough guides and did not have those awful tinny ferrules that used to plague inexpensive rods. They've now been replaced by the saner glass-to-glass ferrules pioneered by Fenwick.

Also, very few of the rods considered had the very weak tip – strong butt syndrome that was perfect for beating rugs but little else, especially casting lures. For general use a spinning rod should be even-actioned and smooth casting.

There is a large variety of actions available. You can afford to be picky about the feel you need for your kind of fishing. All of the rods listed seem to us to be fitted well with balanced reel seats, handles and wrappings. Some were a bit too gaudy for our tastes – but that's a matter of opinion.

All in all we found it easy and "safe" to pick a spinning rod.

BERKLEY PARAMETRICS. The Berkley parametric series, especially the ultra-light models, are some of the better spinning rods around. Though the Cherrywood and Buccaneer lines, which are lower priced, are also good, for appearance and nice casting, the parametric is tops. At 5½ feet, it has an all-cork grip, anodized aluminum reel seat, stainless steel ferrules and a pleasant mahogany finish. Definitely worth considering.

BROWNING. An interesting piece of fluff is the tiny 4½-foot, 2-ounce spinning rod from the famed gunmaker of the same name. While not packing the wallop of a Browning 9mm, the one-piece rod is designed for lines up to No. 4 and will correctly handle lures to 3/16 ounce. As befits such a lightweight, it has an all-cork reel seat with metal rings and only three guides (four might be better, however). But if you're bitten by the ultra-light mania bug, this may comfort you.

DAIWA. This mass-marketing company manufactures a wide but perhaps overdressed series of line for the spin fishermen. Its VP series, atop the line, boasts of stainless steel ringed guides, royal purple wrappings and dark corked handle with reel seat sturdily made from aluminum and double locking. There are also other series of rods made down to the 1500 series, less expensive but still functional.

FENWICK. This company, which started pumping quality back into mass-produced fishing tackle some time ago after things had gotten pretty tacky, still produces a single line of simple, very functional spinning rods. Fenwick's stuff is made for almost

DAIWA

FENWICK

top of the line

every conceivable purpose. The glass ferrules it helped pioneer still guarantee good-actioned rods. Unlike other companies, it does not market different series of rods in various price ranges — a blessing to the angling consumer (or writer) faced with a bewildering array of choices. Suffice it to say that Fenwick's rods are available for any purpose and are well worth the price.

FENWICK "THE LONG ONES." Designed basically for steelhead fishing, these rods at 8 feet 3 inches and 9 feet come in light and medium light action. They work well in lots of spinning situations where a longer rod will give increased sensitivity (there are more of these situations than most shorter rod people are aware of). These two-piecers have hard chromed, braced spinning guides, cork grips and double locking aluminum reel seats.

GARCIA. This big-selling company still produces a large number of spinning rods, though not as many as a few years ago when they were almost impossible to tell apart even if you knew the color coding system. Garcia's Deluxe series features a fine little 5-foot ultra-light glass rod aimed at line from 1 to 6 pounds. The company still makes a fast-tapered rod perfect for spoons and spinners in the lightweight range. It also makes a fairly complete lesser line. The best of this bunch is the "Avocado" series.

HEDDON. This old Dowagiac, Michigan, company now offers a very complete line of glass spinning rods ranging from the more mundane Lucky 13 (named after one of their popular plugs) and the Starcast to the rather expensive Mark V, which features an elegant walnut handle top. The Mark Vs are available in different actions and come in 6½-, 6¾- and 7-foot sizes with stainless steel wire-wrap guides and carbide guides and

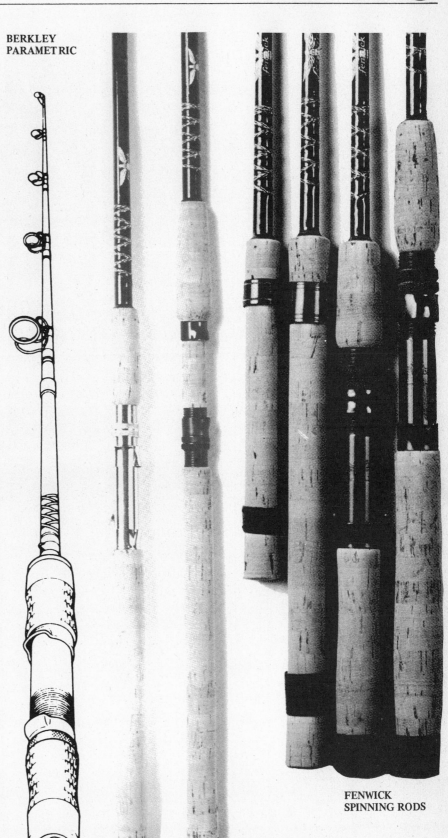

BERKLEY PARAMETRIC

FENWICK SPINNING RODS

FENWICK "THE LONG ONES"

"This dish of meat is too good for any but anglers, or very honest men."
IZAAK WALTON, *The Compleat Angler*

top of the line

tip-tops. Heddon also offers a worm spinning rod with all ceramic guides to cut down friction.

HEDDON ROD OF RODS. This deluxe model keeps a long-time company tradition of individually crafted tackle in a mass-production line. In the old days of wood, Heddon produced some fine fly rods. This rod, with its ultra-high-quality cork, 00 extra-fine silk-ette, hand-rubbed finish and walnut inlays among other things, keeps things going. They've learned a lot in 77 years of production and this rod is one of the things that shows it. The Rod of Rods comes in 6½- and 7-foot spinners and 7½-, 8-, 8½- and 9-foot fly rod models, all with a wood grain finish covering the high-class glass blank. One of the more interesting items around, especially for spin fanatics.

HERTER'S. The Herter's line of spinning rods offers a variety of handles, including some with built-in reel seats, an adjustable sliding reel seat that fits anywhere on the handle (once a very popular style) and a smaller adjustable reel seat. These rods, one of the few lines on the market with instant purchaseable extra tips, are two-piece with adequate guides and a butt cap button — a detail that makes sense when you want to put your rod down. Available from 5 feet to 7 in ultra-light and regular action. They also offer some other interesting open-faced rods.

LAMIGLASS. Lamiglass was one of the first entries in the rapidly changing graphite rod field with a line of models designed with the aid of a computer. They now market some 115 rods and blanks. Their spinning rods are available in standard casting models as well as specialized versions for the caster of mooching and worms. They are well-put-up rods that use to maximum ad-

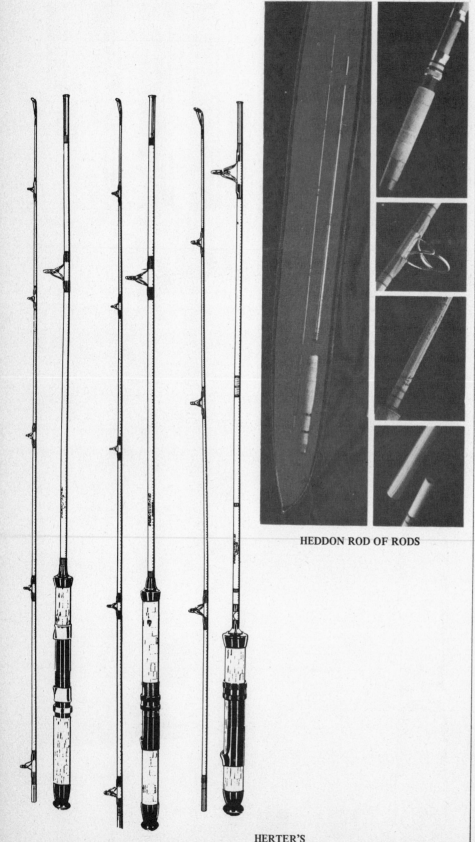

HEDDON ROD OF RODS

HERTER'S

vantage the power inherent in graphite. The Kent, Washington, outfit — which makes blanks for other companies as well as their own rods — has something for every spinfisher, baitcaster and fly flipper.

LEONARD CATSKILL. Elegant and expensive glass rods, the Leonard Catskill series is put up with the customary grace of this ancient tackle company. With lure casting and balance in mind, they are designed in sizes from 5½ to 7 feet.

LEONARD GRAPHITE. Leonard, which has jumped into graphite with great abandon, is selling four spinning models ranging from 5 to 6½ feet. They are ideal for ultra- and lightweight lure fishing. The six-and-a-halfer can also be converted to ultra-light fly fishing with a No. 3 line — an item not designed for the rookie fly caster. Good rods for open-faced reels if you're into spinning far enough to justify the price tag.

OLYMPIC GRAPHITE. The Olympic line of carbon fiber (read graphite) spinners is an interesting low-priced series with 5½-, 6½-, 8½-, and 11-foot models. With Mildrum and/or Fuji ceramic guides, anodized reel seats and classic wrappings, these are very suitable rods — especially for those who want to try out graphite without making the major expenditure that some other brands require.

QUICK FINESSA. The Quick Company, which doesn't mess around with needless change, has been producing this line of rods for a long time. Like their open-faced spinning reels, these rods are available from ultra-light to light saltwater. They come in sizes

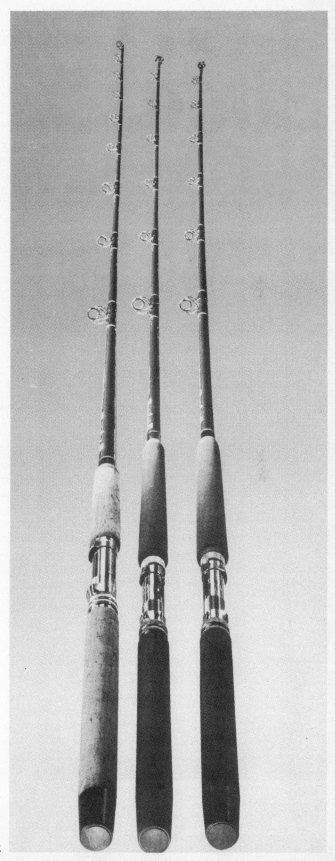

OLYMPIC GRAPHITE

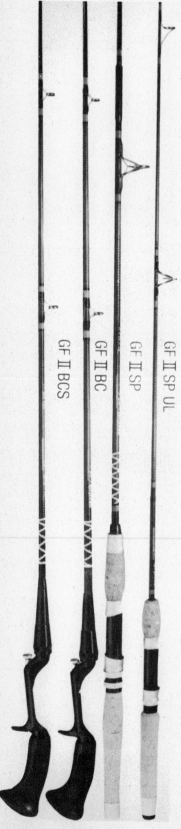

top of the line

from 5½ to 7 feet and carry an adequate number of Quick's Polygon guides.

SHAKESPEARE GRAPHITE. Shakespeare, which came out early with a top-quality graphite rod under their Graflite brand, makes some of the more functional of these space-age wonders. They are currently marketing a 5-foot ultra-light and a standard 6½-foot model. Both rods have stainless steel guides, are one piece and have anodized aluminum reel seats. Among the most responsive of all the graphites.

SHAKESPEARE WONDERODS. They've been around since, well, since before Ernie Schwiebert became a fly angler. They are still very reasonably priced and come in a wide variety of sizes and styles for every sort of spinning chore. Wonderods are marked by their distinctive white hue and colored wrappings matched to the model price line. The first and probably second rod for many an angler, they still maintain their high quality and functionality. Shakespeare's softish actioned ultra-light rod remains one of the best around for any spin angler regardless of station or skill.

SOUTH BEND SOLID GLASS. For some purposes, like tossing nightcrawlers, solid glass rods still seem to have the edge over tubular glass for some anglers. South Bend continues to market a few solid rods among the inexpensive end of their line for those still inclined. Though the rods could use a few more guides, that's not much to change. Available in a couple of two-piece, 6-foot models and a "Rainbow" ultra-light rod that is 5 feet long with only (gulp) two guides. These are usually thought of as beginner's rods but they have their place in the specialist's tackle collection.

SHAKESPEARE GRAPHITE

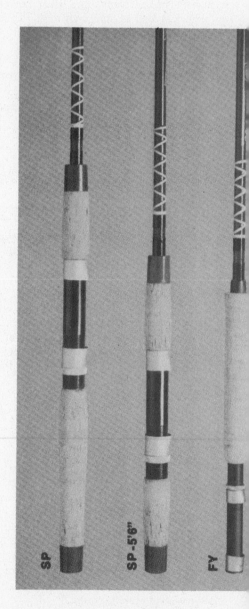

SHAKESPEARE WONDERODS

top of the line

ZEBCO PRO STAFF. The most interesting line of Zebco spinning rods, available in a range of weights and sizes for a variety of angling tasks. These rods have burnt cork handles and a flared butt reminiscent of the old rubber butts of surf rods. With ferrules protected by full wrapping and an anodized aluminum reel seat, they deserve their spot as head of the Zebco family.

G-96 SPORTSMAN'S TOOL

The Jet-Aer Corporation is marketing one of those very nice all-around tools the spinner-baitcaster finds so much use for. Like a pliers, this one works as a sinker crimper, hook remover, fish skinner, vise, straightener, wrench or cutter. Hardy little devil. A good addition to any tackle box.

DIAL-A-CATCH

Not quite automated, but what the hell. It's called Dial-A-Catch. It's a fishing wheel and it tells you how, when and where to catch 51 species of freshwater fish. It also tells you what lure or fly to use, what bait, what hook flies and what natural feeding conditions fish like.

GARCIA

ZEBCO PRO STAFF

HARDY CAR TOP ROD CLAMP

A car top rod carrier that clamps onto the gutter of your vehicle is often quite handy, especially for those cruising western rivers. Hardy Brothers sells such things lined with sponge rubber to protect the rod. They fit most cars.

CONSIDER ACTION IN YOUR SPINNING ROD, TOO

Though action is usually an important consideration of anglers purchasing a fly rod, spin fishermen are usually content with the obligatory wiggle and flick in the shop, analogous to kicking the tire on a prospective car. But the action of a spinning rod should be related to its task in just the same way as fly tackle.

When spinning rods were first marketed in this country in the late 1940's shortly after the introduction of what the English call fixed spool reels, they were mainly made of solid glass. Makers of fine cane rods also marketed a few and those hard-core spinners lucky enough to find bamboo rods crafted by Payne, Leonard, Pezon & Michel and others have quite the thing. But they are rare, though Orvis still makes fine impregnated spinning rods.

Most of the early American spin fishermen were content or had to be content with real bozo rods not suited for much except bait fishing. They were heavy and slow but they could heave a worm or minnow relatively gently. These old solid glass rods, wherever they can be found, still work well for various live and semi-live bait.

The lure caster had to wait for the hollow-state development of glass, which facilitated rods suited for precise angling chores.

My own preference in spinning rod action is as follows: *The heavier the gear and the longer the required cast, the slower the rod should be.*

With ultra-light tackle and tiny lures (No. 2 and No. 4 pound test — lures under 1/16th ounce) I prefer very tippy rods. It seems to me that the fast-actioned rods allow for the short, precise casts for which ultra-light gear is designed. Tippy rods make for greater control on casts roughly within 40 feet or so.

At the other extreme — for spinning surf gear— I like a limber rod that works down into the handle with an action described in fly rods as semi-parabolic. These rods seem to have the power to deliver long casts without having to put lots of strain on either the rod or the caster.

By Harmon Henkin

In the middle of these extremes I go for what is labeled progressive action; that is, the whole rod works in casting but the tip absorbs most of the work.

Beware of rods which don't have a continuous action flow. In these models there are a strong butt and a weakish tip but very little connecting them, which makes for awkward casting. The other 'bad' rods are those either so stiff or so weak that little control or accuracy can be had.

But of course, after these flaws are avoided, choice is a matter of the angler's preference. Just try to think about the kind of fishing you do and get a matching rod.

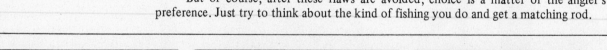

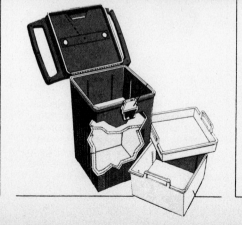

OLD PAL TACKLE SEAT

This is a very interesting idea — a combination tackle box, seat and insulated cooler. What else could the angler want? It has two movable trays for lures and other tackle and an insulated lower section that will keep food and drinks cold or hot for hours. Perfect for ice fishermen. Has a broad base that won't sink easily on the ice. Lots of other uses for this ingenious piece of gear.

FEATHERWEIGHT

The Featherweight Company is marketing a Foamlite line of rod handles as replacements for cork. Easily installed on your spinning rod, these soft grips, equipped with anodized aluminum reel seats, will make your rod the best-dressed in the neighborhood. Featherweight also makes a complete line of handles, butt ferrules and good quality size-matic ferrules for glass and graphite rods. They also market ceramic guides and lots of other things for the builder.

"All is fish, that cometh to net."
JOHN HAYWOOD, *Proverbs*

SPINNING RODS 201

THE LAST HATCH
A FISHING MYSTERY
HARMON HENKIN

(continued from page 188)

"God, this is like casting blind. Might as well go back to the house and question the folks." He tugged glumly at his mustache and plodded along behind Paul.

The group was assembled around the bar in the main room talking softly as they walked in. Their numbers had expanded. Paul walked up to a young woman sitting in a chair away from the group. Wearing the obligatory Levis and poplin shirt, she was browsing through a copy of Halford's *Trutta Fruity: An Angler's Reminiscences*. She was obviously bored.

"Hi, Julie."

"What are you doing here? Come for the wake?"

"Had the same question for you."

"Just visiting for the day." Paul smiled as she blushed and turned away slightly. "I met Halford in town yesterday and, uh, he invited me out."

"I was fishing down at the mouth of the creek when he floated by."

"I can't find it in myself to describe it as a horrible thing."

"Me neither."

"Sid figure out who did it?"

"The general consensus around here is that I'm the prime suspect."

"Can't believe it. That's much too practical an act for you. Besides, you only murder fish."

"As friendly as ever."

"We aren't college sweethearts anymore. No reason to be nice."

"That's your fault, not mine."

"I think of it as an act of maturity."

They glared at each other until the sheriff held up his hand for attention.

"Now one at a time, from left to right, I want your names and addresses and what you're doing here."

Everyone sat down in the semi-circle of chairs clustered around the bar. Sid stood in front of the bar, looking severe and dedicated — two adjectives rarely used to describe him.

"You first, Dun."

The little man got up slowly and glanced around nervously at the others.

(continued on page 218)

GAMEFISH: BLUE CATFISH

NAMES
Forktail cat, great blue cat, chucklehead cat. *(Ictalurus furcatus)*

DISTRIBUTION
The blue catfish is found primarily in the Mississippi River system although it is also distributed from southern Canada and the Great Lakes southward into Mexico.

DESCRIPTION
The largest member of the catfish family, the blue has a blue or blue-grey back with silver-blue sides and a white belly. Its small mouth has a projecting upper jaw. The blue can be distinguished from the channel catfish by the number of rays on its anal fin; it has 30 to 36 compared to 24 to 30 on the channel.

SIZE
Although the average size of the blue is about 5 pounds, catches of up to 100 pounds have been reported. In some waters, fish weighing 15 to 30 pounds are not uncommon.

HABITAT
The blue catfish also prefers cleaner water than most of its cousins and is most often found in large, clear lakes and wide, slow-moving rivers. Reservoirs and large impoundments below dams are favored locations.

FEEDING HABITS
Like most catfish, the blue will eat almost anything. It is a bottom feeder and a scavenger, dining primarily at night.

BEST FEEDING TEMPERATURE
Between 70° and 75°.

TACKLE
All sorts of baits, doughballs and slimy concoctions heaved out by medium or heavy baitcasting or spinning rigs are often required for this bozo. It takes some finesse at the terminal end of the line at times, but brute force is usually advised.

Notes on American spinning rods

From *Secret Fresh and Salt Water Tricks of the World's 50 Best Professional Fishermen* by George Leonard Herter and Jacques P. Herter. Available from Herter's, Inc., Waseca, Minnesota.

American fresh-water spinning rods are usually made seven to seven and one-half feet long. Grips run from 12 to 14 inches long, and the rod runs down through the full length of the grip on all good spinning rods. The grip is made long so that you can shift your reel to any desired place, thereby to balance the rod with the lure you are casting. For light-weight lures your reel should be more toward the butt end of the grip and for heavy lures more toward the front of the grip. The action of a spinning rod should be made with the same general principles as the action on a dry-fly rod. Any of the dry-fly-rod principles will produce a satisfactory spinning rod. A spinning rod should never be a whippy, soft rod. If you take the specifications for any good eight-foot dry-fly rod and cut off six inches at either end, you will have a good light spinning rod.

Spinning rods weighing from four to five ounces are the most popular in America. Such rods will cast lures from 1/8 to 3/8 of an ounce.

A spinning rod of 5½ to 6½ ounces should be used on lures of ½ ounce to 3/4 ounce.

The guides on a spinning rod are of the utmost importance. In fact, if the guides are not of the correct sizes the rod will not cast at all (or very poorly) no matter how well the rod is made. Never use conventional snake guides on a spinning rod. Use guides that are held well away from the rod by their supports. Good solid metal Sheffield spinning guides or Guild Quality side support spinning guides are excellent for use on either bamboo or fiberglass rods. The butt guide on a spinning rod must be an all-metal guide made just for spinning rods to assure the fact that you will get near maximum performance from the rod. This butt guide should be at least 11/16 inch in diameter for maximum results. It cannot be a heavy standard salt-water guide or it will add too much weight to the rod. If your butt guide is too small, you cannot cast well enough with a spinning rod to merit using one. If you buy your spinning rod in a kit form you should receive complete instructions for assembly that will include correct guide spacing for that particular rod.

If you are new at spinning, be sure to watch the pound test of the line you use. Spinning successfully cannot be done with heavy lines. The lighter the line you use for spinning, the better spinning rods perform.

ultimate commodity
Orvis bamboo spinning rods

Call it arrogance, elitism or just plain tradition but these Orvis impregnated spinning rods with their walloping big prices certainly shame the rest of the field. Nothing fancy and available in sizes from five to seven foot, they are the remnants of a once-flourishing bamboo spinning rod business that peaked in the decade after the Second World War. Once great rodmakers like Jim Payne and Thomas even made them. These Orvises keep things going if just a little ways. Their advantages? Simple: they have the solid feel and sensitivity that no artificial has yet reached and their high quality ferrules, simple reel bands and elegance make them still the standard.

THE FISH IS ULTIMATELY MORE IMPORTANT THAN THE TACKLE

By Harmon Henkin

His name was Dean Holmes and his little shop was behind his Crooked Lake, Michigan, home.

Dean brandished the kind of profound fanaticism that characterizes most of the interesting rodmakers I have met. When he cornered you in his shop full of rod blanks hanging from the ceiling, handles in varying degrees of completion and other mounds of rod-making paraphernalia you were in for a long stay.

But I was very anxious that day. My ultimate ultra-light spinning rod was supposed to be finished. It was to be five feet long, made from good tonkin cane and weighing a minuscule 1.5 ounces. I had been heading toward this extreme for years, sampling all of the production ultra-lights from the cheapest discount-house junk to the Orvis cane models. But my extremism had come to the fore the day I asked Dean for the lightest practical rod he could make.

His answer after months of tinkering was the beautiful rod he placed in my hand. He wasn't half as excited about it as I was since his own mania was towards glass fly and spinning rods with a strange wooden dampener in the bottom, rods which though theoretically sound never achieved for me the practical soundness of their builder.

I flicked the rod a couple times. It was everything I had hoped for. I paid him, thanked him profusely and headed for a small river near his northern Michigan place. No time for lectures on rod dynamics that day. I wanted some action.

The gentle flow of the river camouflaged the fact that there were some nice smallmouths in the water. I put on a 1/32-ounce leadheaded jig and cast out to the weeds. Nothing. But the rod was a joy. It handled the tiny lure perfectly and its delicacy was so subtle that it made the small Alceda Micron reel seem like a winch. To Hell with what everyone said. The lighter the better was going to be my motto. I probably could unload all my other rods.

But then reality struck. From a weed patch a smallmouth bass about four pounds charged the lure. It was the biggest smallmouth I have ever had a shot at. It bit the tiny jig like a Labrador nipping a grasshopper.

I set the hook, or tried to set the hook. The fish went berserk. The rod bent over ominously. The biggest fish vs. the finest rod. The rod didn't stand a chance. In fear for it, I aimed it at the smallmouth, which pulled the two pound test till it snapped.

After the beast swam away, I sat down on the bank and looked at the rod. It was the end of my ultra-light fanaticism. I learned one thing: the fish, ultimately, is far more important than the tackle used to catch it.

HERTER'S ENGLISH SPINNING ROD BUTTS

Having a rubber butt at the end of your rod simply makes sense. It protects the bottom of your rod when you put it on the ground. Or you, when you're playing a large fish. Of course most of the nation that invented tailfins on cars uses streamlined rod butts. But these rubber butts are a good idea.

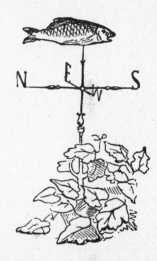

AIRLITE PLASTICS

The Airlite Plastic Company is still producing those basic outfits, now made of plastic, that were the source of many a kid's first fishing thrills. Wrapped around a hand-held winder, they have 18-foot monofilament or green dacron line, either a No. 6 or No. 4 Kirby hook, a piece of split shot and, sure, a bobber. Good for cane poling or just sentimentally thinking of youth.

ROD CADDY ROD CASES

The Rod Caddy cases have been around for a long time. They have models constructed of either plastic or fiber in diameters big enough to hold 8 or 10 rods at a time, down to cases for single rods. These telescoping models, available in a range of colors, will give good protection against the miseries that can beset rods.

The blank is the heart of the rod

There is one basic axiom in buying a rod, regardless of whether it's designed for spinning, baitcasting or fly fishing, or made of bamboo, graphite or glass:

A fishpole ain't no better than the blank it's built around.

A staggering number of companies produce rods, but there's a much more limited number of companies making the blanks that go into them. For instance, there are several high priced fly rod outfits working with bamboo that sell glass rods. These companies put on fancy reel seats, windings and guides but their blanks are the same inexpensive ones on rods selling for a third as much. If you like the deluxe fittings on a put-up rod, that's your prerogative. But don't believe they make the rod something it isn't.

The same is very true with graphite. Companies like Lamiglass and Fisher are making the blanks for any number of the graphites you see sold these days under private labels. You can't tell much from advertising copy.

If you look through the catalogs, you can see the repetition. If you like the action of a particular rod but don't like the uptown price tag, search for the identical action in a cheaper rod or buy the blank and either put it up yourself or pay someone to do it.

The blank is the heart of the rod and no glossy finish is going to change that.   —H.H.

GAMEFISH: RED SNAPPER

NAMES

Pensacola red snapper. *(Lutjanus blackfordi)*

DISTRIBUTION

The red snapper is found on the Atlantic coast and is abundant in the Gulf of Mexico.

DESCRIPTION

The red snapper is bright red all over with a black spot on each side. There are nine rays on the anal fin and the pectoral fin is long.

SIZE

The red snapper runs from 5 to 30 pounds. It reaches about 2 to 2½ feet in length.

HABITAT

The red snapper is not considered an important game fish due to its preference for extremely deep waters. It is often found close to rocks.

FEEDING HABITS

The red snapper feeds on small fish and crustaceans. It is most often taken by commercial fishermen.

TACKLE

This fish takes spoons or jigs regularly. Light to medium casting or spinning tackle is all that's required. Most often sought by bait trollers or party boat types, it is also taken on artificials.

MEMOIRS OF A TACKLE JUNKIE

(continued from page 192)

loan me $100 to buy some neat fishing tackle?

THEM.

Click!

But despite rebuffs we managed to raise a few hundred dollars by the time the doors opened. We were there an hour early, forgetting such trivia as university finals and family obligations.

And now the rub. If we knew then what we know now . . . .

We ignored the $10 Granger fly rods now valued by second-hand dealers at over $150 because they were three-piecers, not the two-piece models that were the fashion then. We ignored brand-new Hardy Perfects at a few bucks apiece because they were too heavy. (I recently bought a used Hardy Perfect with an extra spool for $125 – gulp.)

And so it went. We loaded down for some strange reason on scads of olde English wet flies at pennies apiece, flies that still litter my collection unused. There were also myriads of fly boxes ranging from lovely Wheatleys to strange English salmon boxes that somehow had wound up in Grand Rapids — which at that time only had salmon in cans. We picked up a few lightweight Hardy reels and some old-time baitcasting reels of fine quality which have increased many times over in value. But most of the cash we squandered went for the most trivial accessories.

That day and in the next few weeks — until everything had been sold or auctioned off — we filled our apartments with stuff from Baisch's. The old man's inventory still lives with us.

In the cyclic way that history operates, we currently fish with Hardy Perfects, three-piece rods and the other sorts of equipment that were memories from a bygone angling era but are the rage again. As has been said of Paris, the more fishing changes the more it remains the same.

> "The fishermen could perhaps be bought for less than the fish."
> UVENAL, *Satires*

specifications

Brand-Model	Length	Lure (oz.) Weight	No. Pieces	No. Guides	Material
BERKLEY					
Para/Metric					
P30	6' 6"	1/8-3/4	2	5	
P30	7'	1/8-3/4	2	5	
Cherrywood					
C30	6' 6"	3/16-1/2	2	4	
C30	7'	3/16-1/2	2	4	
C32	6' 6"	1/8-3/4	2	4	
C32	7'	1/8-3/4	2	4	
Buccaneer					
B30	6' 6"	1/8-3/8	2	4	
B30	7'	1/8-3/8	2	4	
Para/Metric					
P21	5' 6"	1/16-3/8	2	4	
Cherrywood					
C21	5'	1/16-3/8	2	3	
C21	5' 6"	1/16-3/8	2	4	
C26	5' 9"	1/8-3/4	2	4	
Buccaneer					
B21	5' 6"	1/16-3/8	2	3	
Boat Rods					
B70	6'		1	3	
B70	7'		1	4	
B70	8'		1	4	
B74	6' 6"		1	3	
B75	7' 6"		2	4	
B72	6'		1	3	
B60	7'	3/8-3/4	1	4	
B62	7'	3/8-3/4	1	4	
B73	6'		1	3	
B73	7'		1	4	
Steelhead Rods					
P94	8'	3/8-3/4	2	8	
C94	8'	3/8-3/4	2	6	
B94	8'	3/8-3/4	2	5	
Mooching Rods					
P91	8' 6"		2	4	
BROWNING					
STD Rods					
032906	6'	1/16-1/2	2	5	glass
032915	6' 6"	1/8-1	2	5	glass
332904	4' 6"	1/20-1/4	1	3	glass
332955	5' 6"	1/20-3/8	2	5	glass
332905	6'	1/16-1/2	2	5	glass
332906	6'	1/16-1/2	2	5	glass
332910 (fresh, salt)	6'	1/4-1 3/4	2	5	glass
332912	5' 6"	5/8-3 3/8	1	5	glass
332914 (pack rod)	6' 6"	1/16-1/2	5	5	glass
332915	6' 6"	1/8-1	2	5	glass
332970	7'	3/16-1	2	5	glass
332971 (pack rod)	7'	1/16-1/2	5	6	glass
332990	9'	1/16-1 1/2	2	7	glass

Brand-Model	Length	Lure (oz.) Weight	No. Pieces	No. Guides	Material
142961 (fresh, salt)	7' 1½"	1/4-4	2	6	glass
142957 (fresh, salt)	6' 9"	3/8-4	1	6	glass
DAIWA					
Alpine Pack Rods					
3051	6' 6"		6	5	glass
3052 (spin and fly)	6' 6"		6	5	glass
3053 (and fly, spincast)	6' 6"		7	5	glass
VIP Rods					
19	5'		2	5	glass
10	5' 6"		2	5	glass
11	6'		2	5	glass
12	6' 6"		2	6	glass
13	7'		2	6	glass
32	6' 6"		2	6	glass
83	7'		2	6	glass
Regal					
5019	5'		2	5	glass
5310	5' 6"		2	5	glass
5012	6' 6"		2	6	glass
5013	7'		2	6	glass
5312	6' 6"		2	5	glass
5312	7'		2	6	glass
5312D	6' 6"		2	5	glass
5313D	6' 6"		2	6	glass
5312	6' 6"		2	5	glass
1500 Series					
1510	5' 6"		2	4	glass
1511	6'		2	5	glass
1512	6' 6"		2	5	glass
1513	7'		2	5	glass
1582	6' 6"		2	5	glass
1583	7'		2	5	glass
1300 Series					
1310	5' 6"		2	4	glass
1312	6' 6"		2	5	glass
1313	7'		2	5	glass
1324	7' 6"		2	5	glass
1325	8'		2	5	glass
1327	9'		2	5	glass
1000 Series					
1019	5'		2	4	glass
1012	6' 6"		2	5	glass
1013	7'		2	5	glass
Special Promotion Rods					
212	6' 3"		2		glass
Minispin System					
MS38 (built-in reel)	4' 6"		2	5	
MS59	5'		5	5	
Minimite System					
MM18 (with reel)	4' 6"		2	5	glass

specifications

Brand-Model	Length	Lure (oz.) Weight	No. Pieces	No. Guides	Material
FENWICK					
HMG Spinning Rods					
G-145	4' 6"	1/16-1/4	1		graphite
GFS-55	5' 6"	1/16-1/4	2		graphite
GFS-64	6' 6"	1/8-3/8	2		graphite
GFS-70	7'	1/4-1/2	2		graphite
GFS-83	8' 3"	1/4-5/8	2		graphite
GFS-83C	8' 3"	1/4-5/8	2		graphite
GFS-87	8' 9"	3/8-1	2		graphite
GFS-87C	8' 9"	3/8-1	2		graphite
G-953	5' 3"	1/8-5/8	1		graphite
GPLS-65	6' 6"	1/4-5/8	2		graphite
GPLS-66	6' 6"	1/2-1	2		graphite
Voyageur Rods					
FS67-4	5' 9"	1/16-3/8			glass
FS65-4	6' 6"	1/8-3/8			glass
FS70-4	7'	1/8-1/2			glass
PLS70-4 (fresh, salt)	7'	1/8-5/8			glass
SF74-4 (fly, spin)	7'	1/8-3/8			glass
SF75-5 (fly, spin)	7' 6"	1/8-3/8			glass
Fiberglass Spinning Rods					
140	4' 6"	1/16-1/4	1		glass
FS50	5'	1/16-1/4	2		glass
FS55	5' 6"	1/16-1/4	2		glass
FS60	6'	1/16-1/4	2		glass
FS61	6'	1/16-1/4	2		glass
FS64	6' 6"	1/8-3/8	2		glass
FS65	6' 6"	1/4-1/2	2		glass
FS70	7'	1/4-1/2	2		glass
FS75	7' 6"	1/4-1/2	2		glass
PLS60	6'	1/4-1/2	2		glass
PLS61	6'	3/8-5/8	2		glass
PLS65	6' 6"	1/4-5/8	2		glass
PLS70	7'	1/4-5/8	2		glass
Heavy Action Lunkersticks					
PLS66	6' 6"	1/2-1	2		glass
PLS72	7'	1/2-1	2		glass
953	5' 3"	1/8-5/8	1		glass
960	6'	1/2-1	1		glass
965	6' 6"	1/2-1	1		glass
Long Ones					
FS79	7' 9"	1/4-5/8	2		glass
FS83	8' 3"	1/4-5/8	2		glass
PLS75	7' 6"	1/4-5/8	2		glass
FS80	8'	3/8-1	2		glass
FS85	8' 6"	3/8-1	2		glass
FS90	9'	3/8-1	2		glass
FS86	8' 6"	5/8-1 1/2	2		glass
FS88 (fresh, salt)	8' 6"	5/8-1 1/2	2		glass
GARCIA					
Mitchell					
7121	5'	1/16-1/4	2	4	glass
7132	5' 6"	1/8-1/2	2	4	glass

Brand-Model	Length	Lure (oz.) Weight	No. Pieces	No. Guides	Material
7135	6' 6"	1/4-1/2	2	5	glass
7133	7'	1/4-1/2	2	5	glass
7122	6' 6"	3/8-3/4	2	5	glass
7123	7'	3/8-1	2	5	glass
7124	5' 6"	1/4-1/3	1	4	glass
7125	6'	3/8-1 1/4	1	4	glass
7126	6' 6"	1/4-3/4	2	5	glass
Brown Rods					
2500	5'	1/6-1/4	2	4	
B501	5' 6"	1/8-1/2	2	4	
2503	6'	1/16-1/4	2	4	
2502	6'	1/4-5/8	2	4	
2508	6' 6"	1/4-1/2	2	5	
2510	7'	1/4-1/2	2	5	
2512	6' 6"	3/8-3/4	2	5	
2513	7'	3/8-1	2	5	
2506	9'	5/8-1	2	5	
2509	7'	1/2-1 1/2	1	7	
D503	4' 6"	1/8-3/8	1	4	
B526	6' 3"	1 3/4-6	2	6	
Spin Pak Rod					
N546	6'	1/4-1/2	4	5	
Combo Spin-Fly Pak Rod					
N548	7'	1/4-1/2	4	6	
Avocado Rods					
8200	4' 6"	1/16-1/4	1	4	glass
8202	5'	1/8-1/2	1	4	glass
8201	5' 6"	1/8-1/2	2	4	glass
8208	6' 6"	1/4-1/2	2	5	glass
8210	7'	1/4-1/2	2	5	glass
8212	6' 6"	3/8-3/4	2	5	glass
8207	7'	1/4-3/4	1	5	glass
8206	7'	5/8-1	2	5	glass
8217	5' 6"	3/8-3/4	2	5	glass
8216	6'	3/8-3/4	1	6	glass
Blue Rods					
2601	5'	1/16-1/4	2	4	glass
B601	5' 6"	1/8-1/2	2	4	glass
2604	6' 6"	1/4-1/2	2	4	glass
2609	6' 6"	1/4-5/8	2	4	glass
2610	7'	1/4-1/2	2	4	glass
2605	7'	1/4-1/2	2	4	glass
2606	7'	3/8-3/4	2	4	glass
2650	8'	5/8-1 1/4	2	5	glass
King Fisher Outfits					
GK-6 (with reel, rod, line)					
GK-10 (with reel, rod, line)					
GK-12 (with reel, rod, line)					
HEDDON					
Ceramic Mark Rods					
7662	5' 7"	1/4-5/8	1		glass
7663	6' 3"	1/4-5/8	1		glass
7664	6' 6"	1/4-5/8	2		glass

specifications

Brand-Model	Length	Lure (oz.) Weight	No. Pieces	No. Guides	Material
Mark V Rods					
7562	6' 6"	1/4-5/8	2		glass
7564	7'		2		glass
7574	6' 9"	1/4-5/8	2		glass
Mark IV					
7512	6' 6"	1/4-5/8	2		glass
7552	6' 6"	1/4-5/8	2		glass
7554	7'	1/4-5/8	2		glass
7555	7'	1/4-5/8	2		glass
Pro-Weight Mark Rods					
7420	5' 3"	1/8-3/8	2		glass
7423	6' 7"	1/4-1/2	2		glass
7424	6' 9"		2		glass
Stainless Wire Mark					
7241	6'	1/4-1/2	2		glass
7242	6' 6"	1/4-5/8	2		glass
7246	6' 9"	1/4-5/8	2		glass
Rod of Rods (made to order)					
	6' 6"				
	7'				
Golden Mark					
7640	5'	1/16-1/4	2		glass
7642	6' 6"	1/4-5/8	2		glass
7643	6'	1/4-1/2	2		glass
7644	7'	1/4-5/8	2		glass
7646	6' 9"	1/4-5/8	2		glass
Mark II					
7372	6' 6"	1/4-5/8	2		glass
7374	7'	1/4-5/8	2		glass
7376	6' 9"	1/4-5/8	2		glass
Mark I					
7250	5'	1/8-3/8	2		glass
7302	6' 6"	1/4-5/8	2		glass
7304	7'	1/4-5/8	2		glass
7306	6' 9"	1/4-5/8	2		glass
Mark Brute					
7408	5' 3"	1/4-5/8	1		glass
7410	5' 7"	1/4-5/8	1		glass
Mark Special Purpose					
7404	6' 9"	5/8-1	2		glass
7411	6'11"	1/4-1/2	2		glass
7444	6' 3"	3/8-1	2		glass
7450	5'	1/16-1/4	2		glass
7545	6' 3"	3/8-1	2		glass
Silver Mark					
9902	7' 6"		1		glass
9908	8' 6"		2		glass
9909	9'		2		glass
9912	9'		2		glass
Brown Pal					
845	6'		2		glass
846	6' 6"		2		glass
848	7'		2		glass
Black Pal					
716	6' 6"		2		glass
718	7'		2		glass

Brand-Model	Length	Lure (oz.) Weight	No. Pieces	No. Guides	Material
720	5' 6"		2		glass
Green Pall					
516	6' 6"		2		
518	7'		2		
Astro Pal					
616	6' 5"		2		
618	7'		2		
620	5' 6"		2		
Starcast					
3771	6'		2		solid glass
3772	6'		2		solid glass
4663	6' 6"		2		glass
4665	7'		2		glass
Lucky 13					
3670	6'		2		solid glass
3671	6'		2		solid glass
4565	6' 9"		2		glass
4566	6' 9"		2		glass

LEONARD

Brand-Model	Length	Lure (oz.) Weight	No. Pieces	No. Guides	Material
Graftek I					
1375	5'	1/16-3/16	1		graphite
1376	5' 6"	1/16-3/16	2		graphite
1379	6'	1/8-1/4	2		graphite
1381 (fly, spin)	6' 6"	1/8-1/4	2		graphite
Catskill Spinning Rods					
1147	5' 6"	to 1/4	2		
1149	6'	to 1/4	2		
1151	7'	to 1/2	2		
Rangeley					
1153	5' 6"	to 1/4	2		glass
1155	6'	to 1/4	2		glass
1157	6' 6"	to 3/8	2		glass
1159	7'	to 1/2	2		glass
1161 (fly, spin pack)	7'		4		

MAGNUFLEX

Brand-Model	Length	Lure (oz.) Weight	No. Pieces	No. Guides	Material
Series 100	6'6"-11'6"		1 or 2		
Series 200	6'6"-11'6"		1 or 2		
Series 300	6'6"-9'		1 or 2		
Series 400	6'6"-9'		1 or 2		

OLYMPIC

Brand-Model	Length	Lure (oz.) Weight	No. Pieces	No. Guides	Material
900 Series					
9055	5' 6"		2	4	carbon fiber reinforced plastic
9065	6' 6"		2	5	carbon fiber reinforced plastic

specifications

Brand-Model	Length	Lure (oz.) Weight	No. Pieces	No. Guides	Material
8000 Series					
8060MF (worm)	6'		1	5	
8065MF (worm)	6' 6"		1	5	
7000 Series					
7055	5' 6"		2	4	
7065	6' 6"		2	4	
7070	7'		2	5	
3000 Series					
3055	5' 6"		2	4	glass
3065	6' 6"		2	4	glass
3070	7'		2	5	graphite
3055-FG	5' 6"		2	4	glass
3065-FG	6' 6"		2	4	glass
3070-FG	7'		2	5	glass
3065-IS (live bait)	6' 6"		1	5	glass
3070-IS (live bait)	7'		1	5	glass
3065-ILB (live bait)	6' 6"		1	8	glass
3070-ILB (live bait)	7'		1	9	glass
3070-ILBC (live bait)	7'		1	9	glass
2000 Series					
2050	5'		2	3	
2055	5' 6"		2	4	
2060	6'		2	4	
2065	6' 6"		2	4	
2070	7'		2	5	
2075	7' 6"		2	5	
2570X (spin, fly combo)	7'		4	5	
2065PR	6' 6"		2	4	
Telescopic Rods					
560-T	6'		6	3	
563-T	6' 6"		6	3	
570-T	7'		6	3	
2093	9'			3	
2103	10'			3	
2114	11'			4	
123	12'			3	
143	14'			3	
163	16'			4	
1000 Series					
1065	6' 6"		2	4	
1070	7'		2	5	

PFLUEGER

Brand-Model	Length	Lure (oz.) Weight	No. Pieces	No. Guides	Material
115 Series					
115S	5'		2	4	glass
115S	6' 6"		2	5	glass
155S	7'		2	5	glass
115SP	5' 6"		1	4	glass
G110 Series					
G110S	5'		2	4	graphite
G110S	6' 6"		2	5	graphite
315 Series					
315SP	5'		2	4	
315SP	6' 6"		2	5	
315SP	7'		2	5	
415 Series					
415SP	5'		2	4	
415SP	6' 6"		2	4	
415SP	7'		2	4	
415PB	6'		2	4	
515 Series					
515SP	5'		2	4	
515SP	6' 6"		2	4	

QUICK

Brand-Model	Length	Lure (oz.) Weight	No. Pieces	No. Guides	Material
Finessa Rods					
6055	5' 6"		1		
6060	6'		2		
6066	6' 6"		2		
6071	7'		2		
6056	5' 6"		2		
6056R	5' 6"				
6065	6' 6"		2		
6065R	6' 6"		2		
6070	7'		2		
6070R	7'		2		
6080	8'		2		
6080R	8'		2		
CS60	6'		1		
CS70	7'		1		
FS65	6' 6"		1		
FS70	7'		1		

SHAKESPEARE

Brand-Model	Length	Lure (oz.) Weight	No. Pieces	No. Guides	Material
Graflite Rods					
GFIISP UL	5'			4	graphite
GFIISP	6' 6"			5	graphite
Custom Pro 708's					
SP708XL	5' 6"	1/16-1/4	2	4	glass
SP708XL	6'	1/16-1/4	2	4	glass
SP708	6' 6"	1/8-3/8	2	5	glass
SP708	7'	1/8-3/8	2	5	glass
200 Series					
SP200	5' 6"	1/4-5/8	1	5	glass
SP200	6' 6"	1/8-3/8	1	5	glass
SP200	7'	1/8-3/8	1	5	glass
608 Wonderod Series					
SP608	6' 6"	1/8-3/8	2	5	glass
SP608M	6' 9"	1/4-1/2	2	5	glass
SP608	7'	1/8-3/8	2	5	glass
Presidential 508 Series					
SP508UL	5'	1/16-1/4	2	4	glass
SP508	6' 6"	1/8-3/8	2	5	glass
SP 508	7'	1/8-3/8	2	5	glass
SP508SL	7'	1/8-3/8	2	5	glass

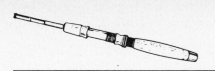

specifications

Brand-Model	Length	Lure (oz.) Weight	No. Pieces	No. Guides	Material
190 Maroon Series					
SP190L	.5'	.1/16-1/4	.1	.5	glass
SP190	.6' 6"	.1/8-3/8	.2	.5	glass
SP190	.7'	.1/8-3/8	.2	.5	glass
408 Wonderod Series					
SP408UL	.5'	.1/16-1/4	.1	.4	glass
SP408	.6' 6"	.1/8-3/8	.2	.4	glass
SP408	.7'	.1/8-3/8	.2	.4	glass
170 Series					
SP170L	.5'	.1/16-1/4	.1	.4	glass
SP170	.6' 6"	.1/8-3/8	.2	.4	glass
160 Series					
SP160L	.5'	.1/16-1/4	.1	.3	glass
SP160	.6' 6"	.1/8-3/8	.2	.3	glass
60 Series					
SP60	.5' 6"	.1/8-3/8	.2	.3	
Solid Glass 11's					
SP11	.5' 6"	.1/8-3/8	.2	.2	glass
Heavy Duty					
SP860	.8' 6"	.1/4-5/8		.7	
Close-Faced Spinning Rod					
SP905	.7'	.1/8-3/8	.2	.4	
Downrigger Spinning Rod (fresh, salt)					
SP940	.9'	.various		.7	glass
Telescopic Pocket Rod					
SP900	.6'	.1/8-3/8		.2	
Jet Set Pack Rod (spin, spincast, baitcast or fly)					
SP999	.7'	.1/8-3/8	.7	.4	
Pack Rods					
PRS66 (take-down)	.6' 6"	.1/8-3/8	.4	.4	glass
PRC70 (fly, spin take-down)	.7'	.1/8-3/8	.4	.4	glass
STP6 (tele-scoping)	.6'	.1/8-3/8		.3	
STP7 (tele-scoping)	.7'	.1/8-3/8		.4	
TP-12 (telescoping Wonderpoles)	.12'			.3	
TP-16 (tele-scoping)	.16'			.4	
TP-20 (tele-scoping)	.20'			.5	
Bigwater Rods					
BWS617 (fresh, salt)	.7'		.1	.7	glass

SOUTH BEND

Brand-Model	Length	Lure (oz.) Weight	No. Pieces	No. Guides	Material
Classic IV					
C1-246-866	.6' 6"				glass
D1-246-970	.7'				glass
B1-246-150	.5'				glass
Classic III					
C1-242-050	.5'		.2		glass
D1-242-866	.6' 6"		.2		glass
1-242-970	.7'		.2		glass
Classic I					
B1-236-866	.6' 6"		.2		glass
C1-236-966	.6' 6"		.2		glass
D1-236-970	.7'		.2		glass
Bassin' Man Rods					
D1-332-966	.6' 6"		.1	.5	glass
All-Carbide Guide Series					
1-224-868	.6' 8"		.2	.4	glass
Outdoorsman					
1-232-050	.5'			.4	
1-232-056	.5' 6"			.4	
1-232-266	.6' 6"				
1-232-270	.7'				
Forester					
B1-230-866	.6' 6"		.2	.4	glass
1-230-250	.5'				glass
White Knight					
B1-228-266	.6' 6"		.2		glass
1-228-270	.7'		.2		glass
Rainbow Rods					
1-334-050	.5'				glass
1-220-000	.6' 6"		.2		glass
1-220-266	.6' 6"				
Spinning Tubular Rod Riot (a variety of brand names, sold together)					
Gladding A	.6'				glass
Horrocks-Ibbotson B	.6'				glass
U.S. Fiberglass C	.6'				glass
Bass-Oveno	.6'				glass
South Bend E	.6'				glass
Quality Solid Fiberglass Rods					
1-212-260	.6'		.2		solid glass
1-204-260	.6'		.2		solid glass
Solid Rainbow Rods					
1-206-000 (assortment of 12)	.6'		.2		solid glass
1-206-260					solid glass
1-306-050	.5'				solid glass
Pack Rods					
1-624-660 (fly, spin)	.6'		.6		glass
1-624-260	.6'		.6		glass
1-624-360	.6'		.6		glass
Camper's Fishing Kit					
4-300-610 (with reel)				.3	

ZEBCO

Brand-Model	Length	Lure (oz.) Weight	No. Pieces	No. Guides	Material
Pro-Staff Rods					
PS19	.5'		.1	.4	glass
PS20	.5' 6"		.2	.4	glass

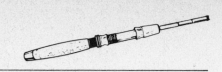

specifications

Brand-Model	Length	Lure (oz.) Weight	No. Pieces	No. Guides	Material
PS21	6' 6"		2	5	glass
PS22	6' 6"		2	5	glass
PS24	7'		2	5	glass
PS71	7'		1	5	glass
PS72	7'		2	5	glass
Sundowner Rods					
7550	7' 6"		2	5	glass
7500	7'		2	5	glass
7450	7'		2	4	glass
7400	6' 6"		2	4	glass
7190	5' 9"		1	4	glass
7050	5' 6"		2	4	glass

Brand-Model	Length	Lure (oz.) Weight	No. Pieces	No. Guides	Material
Centennial Rods					
7301	6' 6"		2	4	glass
7101	6'		2	3	glass
7090	5' 9"		1	4	glass
7051	5' 6"		2	4	glass
Pack Rods					
7054	5' 6"		4	3	glass
4443	4' 10"		3	3	glass
Zebco Rods					
4440	5' 4"		2	3	glass
4470	6'		2	3	glass

For information about Lamiglass Spinning Rods, write Lamiglass, Dept. FF, Box 148, Woodland, Washington 98674.

Spincasters are finally taken seriously

By Harmon Henkin

Spincasting is now being taken seriously by manufacturers and as a result anglers have a wide choice of not only reels but rods as well.

A few years ago most of the spincasting rods were chintzy things either found in discount house tackle sets or hand-me-downs from a line of baitcasting rods that a manufacturer didn't know what to do with.

But times change and with them equipment. Since there are quite a few serious spincasters there are now quite a few excellent quality reels and specially designed rods.

Though spincasting rods are first kinfolk to baitcasters there is at least one fundamental difference: while plug casters might have lots of use for a very tippy stick to go along with their little free spool baitcasting reel, that isn't the ideal rod for the spincaster. It is important to have a rod that has a slower action more in tune with the relatively awkward procedure of holding line in preparation for spincasting. For the fingers to work in harmony with the rod and reel the rod should bend fairly deep and be powerful enough to pick up and magnify the momentum of the cast.

It's very possible to get such a rod since every type is currently available. Most are still basically baitcasters but some have special reel seats to facilitate close-faced reels.

Whether you're after graphite or glass the characteristics of a spincaster are generally the same for any quality rod. There should be enough guides to ease the line through without slap. It doesn't seem crucial if the guides are made of one of the ceramics or a steel alloy as long as they're hard. For spincasting, guides can be pretty small and still work.

The rod should be joined with glass-to-glass or graphite-to-graphite ferrules. Many of these rods are one piece but any rod over 4 feet should be two pieces unless you have a very specific reason for a single unit. Any decent rod feels fine with two sections.

The reel seat should not only screw down tightly, it should screw down tightly on your particular reel. You can add tape or other fillers but that's asking for trouble in the long run.

There are hundreds of options in finishes available. You can get whatever you want. And you have nothing to lose but your hand-me-downs.

Some pointers
on the homemade baitcasting rod

From *Secret Fresh and Salt Water Tricks
of the World's 50 Best Professional
Fishermen* by George Leonard Herter
and Jacques P. Herter. Available from
Herter's, Inc., Waseca, Minnesota.

At one time, bait casting rods were considered strictly fresh water rods. This, however, is no longer true. A great many salt water fish are commonly taken on these rods, and expert fishermen think nothing of catching tarpon on them.

There are a few important points to be brought out relative to the making of bait casting rods that were not covered under the making of fly rods.

Although the illustration does not show one, bait casting rods can be made with the front grip built up on the "bamboo" of the rod itself on such rods as No. 3. In such cases, the front grip can be made by wrapping the area just ahead of the reel seat with heavy linen cord or fishing line, or by gluing cork rings onto the bamboo and sanding them to shape.

By far the most popular types of bait casting rods today are numbers 1 and 2 in the illustration. One piece bait casting rods with no detachable grip or butt are also very popular among those who have means conveniently to carry them. Rod number 3 is an obsolete type, as the ferrule in the center weakens the rod and also destroys much of its action. Rod number 4 is also an obsolete type. It has the female ferrule protruding slightly which is a disadvantage instead of an advantage.

Regardless of what type of bait casting rod you make, use a reel seat that has a finger hook on it. The finger hook is not necessary (as it once was) to hold your reel onto the rod. It is necessary so that you can hold onto the rod firmly. Nothing takes the place of this finger hook. Many well known rod makers build expensive split-bamboo casting rods without these finger hooks. This is a bad error, and I have heard them criticized for it on many occasions. If you cannot secure a reel seat for bait casting rods which has a finger hook, make one from spring-tempered stainless steel wire or something similar.

The offset grip is most common.

Most bait casting rods are made with double grips, as the large percentage of casters prefer them this way. For the man that "palms" the reel in his hand, the front grip is not necessary, and for him the single grip rod is preferable. Such casters, however, are far in the minority.

The offset type of detachable grip or butt has become very popular in late years and is now by far the most widely used.

To make the grip or butt on such rod types as number 2, the following method, or a version of it, is used. Take a section of glued up bamboo strips or a piece of aluminum tubing as long as the total butt or grip, minus the length of the empty socket of the female ferrule. Then fit and glue your female ferrule to the end of the bamboo joint or metal tube with Silhower ferrule cement. Pin the female ferrule to the bamboo or tubing in addition to gluing it. Then glue a grip check tightly around the end of the female ferrule and glue cork rings right up against the grip check to form the front grip. Now glue on a wooden sleeve over which you will fit your reel seat. Then glue and pin the reel seat onto the wooden sleeve. Now glue on your cork rings for the rear cork grip. Shape your cork grips as you desire them. If you have used a bamboo section to build your butt, it should have a little metal collar around the rear end. Screw an aluminum washer below the rear grip. The metal collar on the end of the bamboo section will prevent it from splitting and will hold your screw tightly in place. If you have used metal tubing, glue a wooden plug into the end and screw the washer fastening screw into the wooden plug.

The illustration shows a bait casting rod with a 50 inch tip. It has three guides sizes 9/32, 7/32 and 5/32. This is the conventional number of guides for this length of tip.

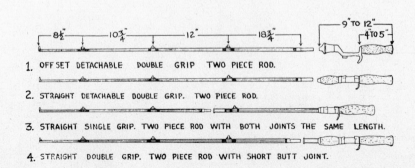

1. OFFSET DETACHABLE DOUBLE GRIP TWO PIECE ROD.

2. STRAIGHT DETACHABLE DOUBLE GRIP. TWO PIECE ROD.

3. STRAIGHT SINGLE GRIP. TWO PIECE ROD WITH BOTH JOINTS THE SAME LENGTH.

4. STRAIGHT DOUBLE GRIP. TWO PIECE ROD WITH SHORT BUTT JOINT.

top of the line

WHAT WE LOOKED FOR IN QUALITY

There have been many dramatic changes in baitcasting rods in the past few years, especially in their action.

Baitcasting rods, which are often used interchangeably with close-faced spinning reels, have different responsibilities than in the past, when their prime job was plug casting. There are now many rods designed for jigging, spoon fishing and especially that most effective bass angling tactic – rubber worming.

But the areas of quality remain the same, despite the introduction of graphite. The rods which interested us the most had a good, consistent action, sensitivity, well-built reel seats and sturdy construction. Whether the rods had ceramic or tungsten carbide guides didn't seem as important to us as the overall quality.

Unless you're a specialist looking for a special function item, your baitcasting rod should have an action that works deep down rather than a weak-tipped model, which has limited application. Its ferrules should have an abundance of guides. It should also be balanced and its fittings should blend in with the entire rod.

In looking over the possibilities for spincasting rods we came up with one sad conclusion: these rods – mostly designed and marketed for the beginning angler – showed a remarkable degree of sameness.

It was very difficult to weed through the mass of rods available and come up with many of outstanding merit. Many of the rods are overdressed; that is, they are garishly wrapped to catch the eye of the beginning angler rather than to serve any truly functional purpose.

We have tried to list those with at least a little special ability but it was not an easy task.

If you are serious about spincasting, something that many anglers think is a contradiction in terms, try out a baitcasting rod. They will do the same job and are available in scores more variety of action and quality.

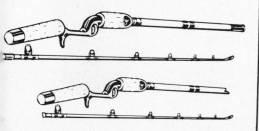

EAGLE CLAW

DAIWA VP. The top Daiwa line, the VPs, includes an obligatory 6 foot, two-piece spincaster with all the features of the line including its diamond double wrap (royal purple no less), stainless steel ringed guides, aluminum double locking reel seat and dura-cork handle. About as good a rod as you can get. Daiwa also produces other lower-level spincasting rods.

EAGLE CLAW. Cashing in on the specialization of lure fishing, Eagle Claw markets a line of rubber worm rods for casting and spincasting or spinning. In models ranging from 5½ to 7 feet, these rods have either ceramic or carbide guides and tip-tops and there are even two ultra-light spinning-worm rods designed for line as light as No. 4 though they will take mono up to No. 10. The ultra-lighters are 5-foot, 4-inch one-piecers with either type of guide plus an anodized, fixed aluminum reel seat. The spincasters and baitcasters are designed for lines from 10- to 20-pound test. A good line of rods.

EAGLE CLAW GRAPHITE. Eagle Claw's entry in the burgeoning graphite rod field is named after their famed Granger label. Their four baitcasting/spincasting five-and-a-half foot models are available in actions from ultra-light to high power and with a choice of double offset or straight handles. All ceramic guides and tip-top, contour shaped grip and Eagle Claw mini-ferrule built up from the blank. These one-piece rods will do the job for the angler who likes the increased sensitivity of graphite.

FAVORITES OF THE EXPERTS

Fenwick baitcasting rods, available in a widening variety of models, were the overwhelming favorite of our polled experts around the country. "Best for saltwater," said one. Others who chose Fenwick were also impressed by their saltwater applications.

Other rods chosen by experts in a field becoming overcrowded by brand names were the specialized tournament type bass rods, the Lew Childre's Speed Sticks, Garcia's top-of-the-line models, Wright-McGills and Berkleys. There was a scattering of votes for a few other rods as well but nothing resembling a developing pattern among them has emerged from our non-scientific survey of writers around the country. Lots of respondents were partial to custom rods they made up themselves or had friends build, considering that the only way to get exactly what they wanted.

DAIWA

"The fish adores the bait."
GEORGE HERBERT, *Jacula Prudentum*

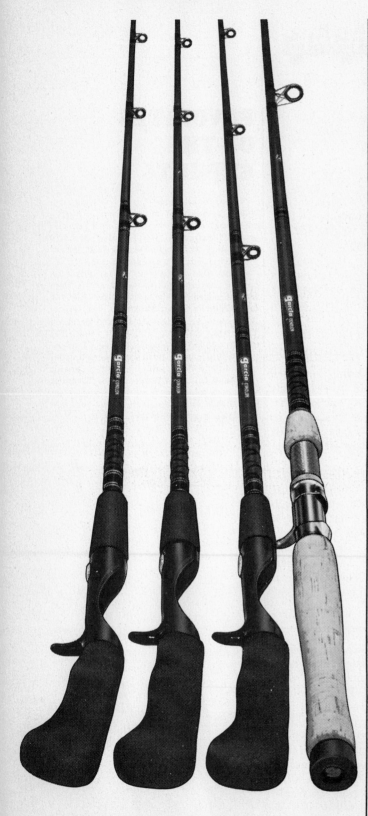

top of the line

FENWICK. Fenwick's popping and deep jigging rods are something worth considering by the serious baitcaster or spincaster. In both two- and one-piece models, ranging in length from 6 feet, 2 inches to 7 feet, they are geared for the various weighted bucktails and jigs that bring in the big bass, muskie and Flats type fishes. These are heavyweight rods, weighing from slightly over 6 ounces to 9 ounces, with a 10 inch rear grip. Boasting the characteristic finger holder and usual Fenwick quality, they're good stuff. Available for various line tests and lure weights.

FENWICK LUNKERSTIK. This line was designed for the serious baitcaster. Available in Fenwick glass as well as five graphite models, they come in lengths from 6½ feet with light action to a 5½ footer with extra power action. All models have ceramic guides and tip-tops and a big butt cap for dig-in comfort. They have aluminum butt ferrules held in place by a plastic sleeve. This allows for a variety of handle options. Fine for the bass or pike angler. The extra expense for graphite, as opposed to glass, is pretty much subjective, though some claim that graphite is much more sensitive.

GARCIA. The deluxe 6½ foot spincasting rod is another good one, especially since it has all-ceramic guides to cut friction and ensuing line wear. Two-piece with internal ferrule, it sits high in the ranks of spincasting rods. Garcia also has other spincasting rods but their difference from the baitcasters is blurred.

GARCIA AMBASSADEUR. Garcia has begun producing a line of baitcasting and popping rods dubbed after their famed Ambassadeur reels. These companion rods come in sizes from five to six feet in a variety of actions, plus a seven foot popping rod with the traditional finger rest. The rods come equipped with the now fashionable

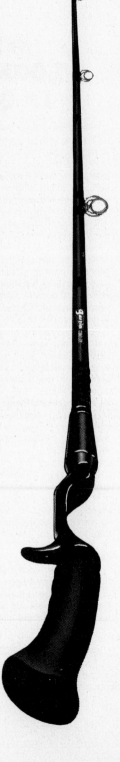

GARCIA
AMBASSADEUR

GARCIA

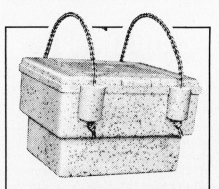

PLASTILITE MINNOW BUCKET

Need a minnow bucket? Well, look at the Plastilites. Foam with metal handles, the lid is capped and can be tied down. They really do a job in keeping minnows alive in summer or winter. They can be used as a beverage container as well. Various models ranging from three to ten quart capacity.

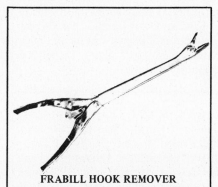

FRABILL HOOK REMOVER

Frabill's "E-Z out" hook remover is sort of a long-nosed pliers with a positive hand grip control. The jaws are serrated to hold hooks firmly for easy removal.

top of the line

ceramic guides and sturdy dark reel seat and handle. Garcia croons about its beauty but that, of course, is in the eye of the beholder.

HEDDON MARK V SERIES. Another superabundant spincasting line, this one features three models, a 6½ footer and two six footers with differing action. All three are more than enough for their angling function. Genuine walnut inlays make them stand out from other production rods. Features like carbide guides, stainless steel wire wrappings and Heddon's Sizamatic ferrules give them more than a mere touch of quality. Heddon makes some other lines but the most interesting is the Mark V Special Purpose rods for spincasters, which are broken down into function such as a crappie jigging brush rod, a worm action, a walleye bottom action and an extra-powerful action. Now they're making some sense!

HERTER'S. A cleanly designed, very functional variety of rods for the baitcaster. These reasonably priced models are available in all of the popular styles and models for both baitcasting and spincasting, including offset handles and thumb rests. As a special bonus some of the models are available with a very oversized eight-inch handle. Despite Herter's reputation as an imitator, their rods are very well worth considering.

KEYSTONE ALL-AMERICAN SPINCAST OUTFIT. Keystone's solemn Bicentennial outpouring from Japan is red, white and blue — and designed, we hope, for children. The tricolored equipment comes with everything the kid bait angler will need. At least this equipment will probably be cheaper after 1976.

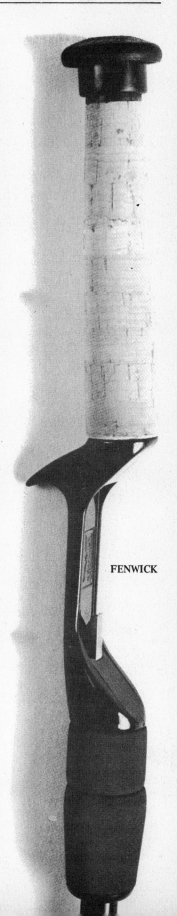

FENWICK

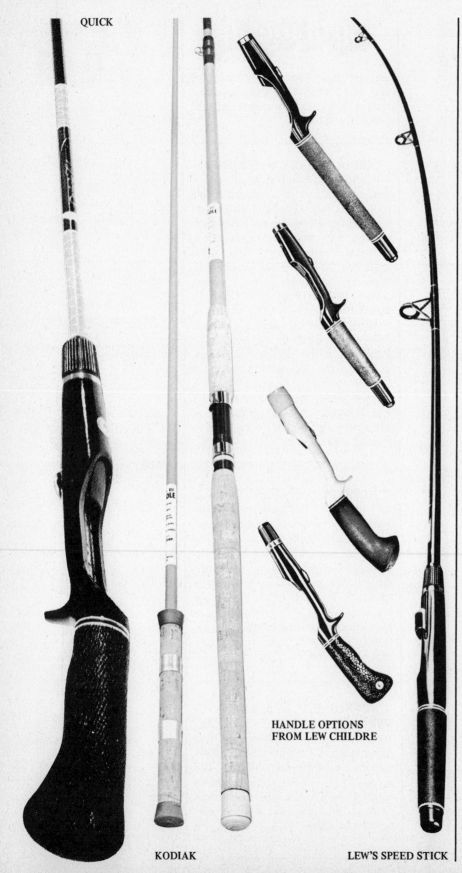

QUICK

HANDLE OPTIONS
FROM LEW CHILDRE

KODIAK

LEW'S SPEED STICK

top of the line

KODIAK. For the technologically inspired still-fisherman who wants to switch from a bamboo pole, Kodiak makes Flip Poles, which can be extended from 10 to 20 feet in length, depending on the model, with merely a flip of the wrist. Made of fiberglass, of course. They even make a fancier model with guides, one with a cork handle and one with a reel seat. The last word in meditative fishing or advanced stump jigging.

LEW'S SPEED STICK. A line of one-piece baitcasting or even spincasting rods designed to efficiently capitalize on modern bass fishing techniques. These rods are available in a 5 foot 8 inch size long range and deep bait use; a 5½ footer for medium short and shallow range, and another 5½ footer for medium long range and medium deep baits. With its "high performance" bass handle and deep black and pearl epoxy finish, it's part of the attempt to make the art of fishing a science.

QUICK. Quick's entry into the rapidly expanding graphite rod market is a 5½ and 6 foot casting model that boasts a 97 per cent true graphite base. With offset handle and aluminum oxide guide, these one-piece rods are designed to accompany Quick's baitcasting reels. The graphite blanks are detachable for those with differing tastes in handles. Overt function for the pair is worm and/or plug casting and both have medium stiff action as befits a graphite.

RAY SCOTT. Ray Scott's Outhouse is selling a line of specialized sticks used to take a lot of largemouths. Available in actions from light to heavy, these rods are in the 5½ foot range, have ceramic type guides, Fuji handles and solidly constructed reel seats. They are designed for plug casting, worming and spinnerbait angling, but except for the fanatic, they'll do

"They say a fish should swim thrice . . . first it should swim in the sea . . . then it should swim in butter, and at last, sirrah, it should swim in good claret." SWIFT, *Polite Conversation*

top of the line

as all-purpose rods. Also available in a couple of spinning models, a medium- and light-action version, they have the same features as the baitcasters.

RAY SCOTT GRAPHITE. Ray Scott's Bass Angler's Sportsman's Society is marketing this relatively inexpensive 100 per cent graphite baitcasting rod through its Outhouse retail outlet. It comes in two five-and-a-half-foot models with Fuji handles for either medium all-purpose action in lure weights from ¼ to 7/8 ounce (quite a range) or medium-heavy action for worming. It has ceramic guides and is very cleanly put up. Also available in the Mini-Stix, a five foot, 3 incher. But it's not an ultra-light, the usual action for a rod this size. This one has medium action for lures from 1/8 to ½ ounce, a set of ceramic guides and an all-cork handle. A good buy.

SHAKESPEARE 200 SERIES. Features a convenient pistol-grip, a clean finish and, depending on the size, five or six aluminum oxide guides. The 200s are made from Shakespeare's Wonderglass blank which has been performing for a long time.

SKYLINE. One of the comers in the graphite field is the outpourings of Skyline Industries. In the medium-priced range, these graphites, especially the eight baitcasting models, are making a stir. Featuring four 5½-foot rods with extra-light, light, medium and heavy action, a 6-foot light action, a two-piece 7-footer for popping and a baitcasting 8½-footer for steelhead.

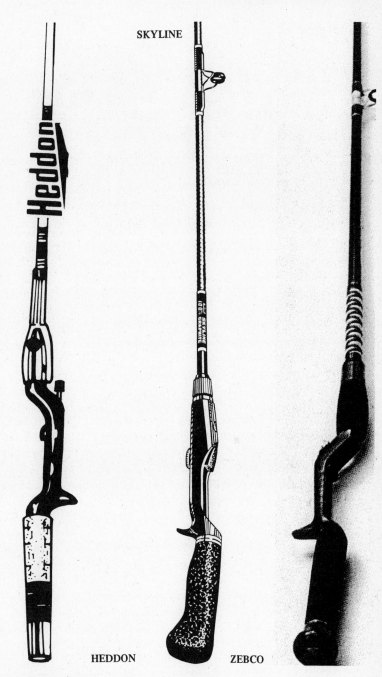

SKYLINE

HEDDON   ZEBCO

SHAKESPEARE 200 SERIES

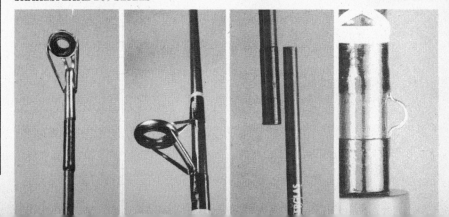

THE LAST HATCH
A FISHING MYSTERY
HARMON HENKIN

(continued from page 201)

"My name is Alexander Dun, Mr. Halford's secretary for 20 years. I live here in the summer and in Key West for the winter."

"Wallace Wormer. Akron, Ohio. I am — I mean was — Halford's business partner in a little development we were planning. Came out here to arrange the last details."

Paul jumped up from the arm of Julie's chair.

"You mean you haven't signed the papers yet? The Nature Conservancy still has a chance to buy it up!"

Wormer gazed away. Sid shook his finger at Paul.

"Now you just sit back down, partner. I'm handling this. You next, lady."

"Alexandrea Softhackle. Hollywood, California. That's on the Coast. The West Coast. Actress, mostly movies. You may have seen me in *The Rutabaga That Ate Newark*. Frederick and I used to be husband and wife. We're still good friends, mutual consent and all that. I was just on my annual summer visit here for a few days." She smiled at the crowd as if expecting applause and sat down glumly when none arrived.

The man beside her patted her arm, then stood up and twirled to face the sheriff.

"Tups Indespensable. Model and entertainer. I live, well, here and there. I'm Miss Softhackle's escort for her holiday." He fell back into his seat.

"You did good, honey," Alexandrea whispered.

A fortyish woman in a soft cotton dress rose.

"Belle Parmachene Hewitt. Palo Alto, California. Housewife — but I did have a promising career as a poet before I married Mr. Hewitt. We were just visiting our friend, Mr. Halford."

A distinguished, grey-templed man, a good ten years her senior, was next. He looked down disdainfully at the others and addressed the sheriff. "My name is Edward Hewitt. I'm a gentleman, full-time, and reside in Palo Alto."

Belle smiled at him as he sat down but he ignored her.

"Bernie Schielbacht's my name. World-renowned angler. People watch every time I cast. You may have read my book, *Matching the Hitch*. Sold trillions of 'em. It's about married fishermen. Oh, I'm from Rutgers, New Jersey."

Nobody seemed particularly interested, so he retreated back to the bar as Julie got up.

(continued on page 222)

Wrapped in heavy-duty nylon coated with epoxy. Plenty of ceramic guides. They also make a selection of fly rods and spinners, too. Worth looking at.

SOUTH BEND CLASSIC IV. The top of the line Classic IV spincast rod is one of the best at the usual length of six foot. With ceramic-type speed guides, soft burnt cork handles, die-cast aluminum handles and double wraps this may be more rod than most spincasters will even want to own. The others in the South Bend line aren't as elegant but are just as functional.

STILLFISH. Back to basics for the youngster and those panfishers who look on the sport as an adjunct to meditating on the secrets of the universe from the bank. The Stillfish Tot rod and the other Stillfish rods are in the 2½- to 3-foot class and come with a reel built into the handle. Unlike other rods, the Stillfish models feed the line through the rod, minimizing the chance of botching things up. They come equipped with 15 pound monofilament that's easier for inexperienced hands to handle. Good for simple stillfishing.

ZEBCO PRO-STAFF. As could be expected, Zebco, the company which started the whole spincast boom, produces not only one of the best reels but also some top rods. The Pro-Staff series of rods from 5 to 6½ feet long also come in a variety of actions designed for rubber worm fishing or general medium weight chores. These rods have convenient butt caps, double wrapped braided windings, ceramic type guides of aluminum oxide and burnt cork handles. They are almost too much for the poor spincaster to bear!

A touch of class
By Harmon Henkin

My world came crashing down that warm summer afternoon.

It was 1950, most likely, and as usual I was fishing for carp in murky Lake Roland, a three mile hike along the railroad tracks from my parent's Baltimore row house.

I thought I was king of the Lake. Two years of hard work, a lot for a ten-year-old, had given me a mastery of my Ocean City Baitcasting reel, which I equipped with cuttyhunk No. 12 and an Eagle Claw No. 12 snelled hook. With a doughball cooked from one of the exotic recipes available in books from the Enoch Pratt Library and a quarter-ounce sinker, I could cast 50 feet with ease. None of the other kids could toss their lines that far and I was usually rewarded with the biggest and most numerous catches of the carp which seemed to mill around at that distance. It was a source of pride, my first real sense of achievement, and paled such illusory accomplishments as schoolwork.

That the carp were rough fish — sought in undesirable waters by fishermen considered by more socially advantaged anglers to share their quarry's personality-- hadn't entered my sense of reality. I could never figure out why the outdoors magazines didn't devote more space to the carp I found so strong and wary. I put it down to whim rather than social or economic class.

My burlap bag was almost filled with fish ranging from two to five pounds that I would sell to Black construction workers for a dime apiece. Then the fancy sports car pulled into the parking lot atop the small dam. Now I know it was an MG-TD. Then it

was simply the most wondrous piece of machinery I had ever seen.

The fellow driving it was perfect. I can still remember his wool crew-neck sweater, short blond hair and classic features. He's probably a lawyer today.

Friendly enough, he explained that he was a student at Johns Hopkins, that fancy university across town where nobody in my neighborhood

(continued on next page)

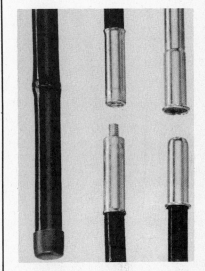

FRABILL CANE POLES

These cane poles, available with either slip or screw tape ferrules, in 10, 12, 14 and 16 foot lengths, are Frabill's contribution to bankside fishing and still fishing. These two and three piece rods, finished in dark brown with high gloss lacquer, have butt tip protectors and hand-wound tip-top guides. Also available in kit form. An elegant way to get back to basics.

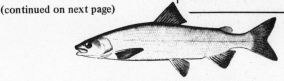

GAMEFISH:
ROCKY MOUNTAIN WHITEFISH

NAMES
Mountain Whitefish, Montana Whitefish, Mountain Herring, Pea Nose. (Prosopium Williamsoni)

DISTRIBUTION
The Rocky Mountain Whitefish is found on the western slope of the Rocky Mountains from Colorado to Canada. It has also been found in the coastal states of Oregon and Washington.

DESCRIPTION
The coloring of the Rocky Mountain Whitefish ranges from greenish or bluish silver on the back to silver on the sides with a white underbelly. There are no distinctive markings. Due to its over-sized dorsal fin, this fish is frequently mistaken for a Grayling.

SIZE
Rocky Mountain Whitefish range from 1 to 2 pounds in size with a maximum of 4 to 5 pounds.

HABITAT
Clear, fast-moving streams or deep mountain lakes are the favored environments of the Rocky Mountain Whitefish. They generally prefer the same waters as mountain trout and will often be found in depths up to 100 feet.

FEEDING HABITS
Insects and insect larvae compose the bulk of the Rocky Mountain Whitefishes' diet, but it will also feed on plankton, worms and small fish. Although they are primarily bottom feeders, in the evening they will frequently rise to the surface in search of flies and other insects.

TACKLE
The lake whitefish is usually way, way down like the lake trout, but isn't as voracious a feeder. Small jigs on spinning outfits will sometimes work but grubs and other live baits are more often the answer.

Fishing was never the same again

(continued from preceding page)

ever went. It could have been on Mars.

He wanted to fish, catch a bass in particular. There were rumored to be a few bass in Lake Roland, relics of an ancient, cleaner day, but they could have been Loch Ness monsters as far as my techniques were concerned. I explained all this to him in my best deferential manner. He'd give it a try, though.

From the tiny trunk of the car he removed the first spinning outfit I'd ever seen in person. And was it ever glorious. After 25 years I can still picture that light bamboo spinning rod with matching Swiss-made Record Reel crammed with six pound test line. It seemed like the crown of Western Civilization. Everything the magazines had said about spinning tackle, then just beginning to be seen in this country, was true, even though their price then was prohibitive.

He carefully threaded the line through numerous guides. Then he took a tiny spinner, probably a sixteenth ounce, from a plastic box full of the small hardware and lures that used to be called fly rod sized, and put it on.

As he walked along the familiar path, pausing every so often to carelessly flick the rod tip and send the lure out a good hundred feet, I followed. It was overwhelming to watch him cast further and with a much lighter weight than anything I'd thought possible. My once-proud baitcasting outfit seemed to take on the aura of a monkey wrench. The more I watched, the worse I felt.

But he didn't get a hit. After a while he sat down and asked if I would like to try the outfit. He might as well have asked if I wanted to drive his MG. I dropped the baitcasting stuff and took the spinning rod. It was a magic moment. I just stared, not having the vaguest idea how to cast.

He patiently showed me how to flick the manual bail out of the way, hold the line with the forefinger and cast. It was a religious experience, though today I realize how much more difficult it is to handle baitcasting gear well than spinning tackle. My first serious cast traveled further than my two years of journeyman baitcasting had ever allowed. The tiny Flatfish hit the water with a discreet plop rather than the vulgar splash of the doughball rig. I made a few more casts, hypnotized by the process.

Then he got up and reclaimed his rod. We walked back toward the dam. There were a few carp sunning themselves about 75 feet away. Scarcely breaking stride he tossed the plug a few feet over the biggest fish and gave the rod a sharp twitch. The fish was snagged. The line zinged out but the smooth drag did its job. The carp was landed within minutes. It weighed about five pounds. He picked it up, and after removing the hook from its gill plate, tossed it into the bushes.

I couldn't believe it.

"Why?"

"They're just trash fish, kid."

He turned and climbed into the MG, gunned the engine, waved and drove away.

It was never the same again.

GAMEFISH: BLUE MARLIN

NAMES
Cuban black marlin. *(Makaira nigricans)*

DISTRIBUTION
The blue marlin is found in both the Atlantic and Pacific oceans. It is most prevalent in the warm waters of the Caribbean, especially the areas around Cuba, Puerto Rico and Florida.

DESCRIPTION
The blue marlin is a heavy-set fish of dark blue in color on the back shading into silver on the sides and belly. The sides are sometimes marked by dark vertical bars. The dorsal and anal fins are dark blue or purple and the colors will intensify while fighting the hook.

SIZE
Although they have been known to reach weights of over 700 pounds, the blue marlin averages about 200 to 400 pounds.

HABITAT
The blue marlin is a fish of deep, open waters. It can often be found feeding on the surface.

FEEDING HABITS
The diet of the blue marlin consists of those fish abundant in its range. These include mackerel, mullet, tuna and bluefish. They also eat squid.

TACKLE
This top-notch fighter is almost always trolled with teasers and then enticed to hit whole mullet or other kinds of bait fish. It usually takes very heavy tackle to do the job and lots of backing to wait out the reel-stripping runs.

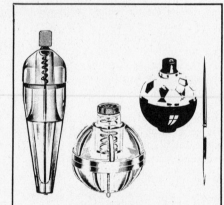

PLASTILITE FLOATS

Floats are really intriguing things and the Plastilite Corporation people certainly have a big variety of them. They range from a reflec-ta-bob which has a multi surface top portion with chrome-like finish that reflects available light, to more traditional types of bobbers such as the delicate hand fish floats that tip up when a fish hits. They respond to delicate pressure. They also sell natural porcupine quill floats which are the most delicate responders of all. Many other varieties as well.

PLASTILITE SPINNING BUBBLES

For the spinning rod adept who likes to cast flies, the Plastilite people make a number of spinning bubbles that are used to give the weight needed to cast a dry or other fly. They also make a bubble which can be partially or totally filled with water to give you more weight.

Create ultimate tackle by building your own

By C. Boyd Pfeiffer

Tackle cost savings of one-half to a third, the fun of an off-season fishing hobby and being able to design equipment to your own needs and specifications — these are the three big pluses of making your own tackle.

Unfortunately, most anglers are unaware that most of the tackle available in stores can be easily made at home with a few simple tools. Spinners, plugs, soft plastic worms, bucktails, jigs and all kinds of fishing rods can be assembled successfully by anyone who ever threw together a model airplane.

Spinners and spoons involve only the assembling of component parts and making an eye to hold the hook. Plugs can be rigged from plastic parts or carved from blocks of wood. Inexpensive molds and simple molding techniques will produce plastic worms and lead bucktails and jigs. Even rod building requires only care in assembly plus a little practice in making a guide wrap. To make matters even simpler, kits are available for almost all these tackle projects. For most kinds of tackle — including rods — tools and work procedures can be improvised.

SPINNERS

The loose parts come in kits or can be ordered separately from a number of mail order houses. The guts of the lure are small shafts of wire, on which you can string a variety of spinner blades, bodies and beads to create tackle store look-alikes or your own custom designs. Use pliers to turn an eye in the end of the wire and put a hook on the eye before completing the wrap. Cut off the loose ends of wire and you've got yourself a spinner. You can make any of the popular models now available for about 25 cents, using quantity-ordered parts. But if you prefer to start on a small scale, Netcraft, Worth, Weber and Nifty all offer good spinner kits from $3.95 to $6.95.

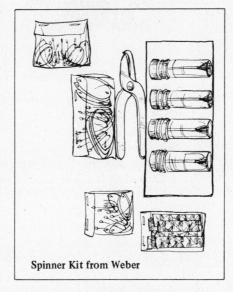

Spinner Kit from Weber

SPOONS

The blade and hook are assembled with a split ring, many sizes of which are available in tackle stores. Another split ring on the forward eye of the blade makes a ready-to-use or ready-to-paint spoon. For the experimenter, soft sheet metal can be cut and hammered into shape for spoon blades. If you buy component parts, you can produce a dozen spoons for as little as $4. Weber, Netcraft and Herter's offer a full line of spoon parts and some nice small-scale kits for about $5.

LEAD-WEIGHT LURES

Bucktails, jigs, sinkers and other lead-weight lures can be cast in aluminum molds, a simple and safe technique you can do in your kitchen. Commercial molds are readily available in tackle stores and jobbers' catalogs. A melting pot and a ladle (about a $5 investment), hooks and finishing materials — fur, feathers, thread and paint — is all you need. Heat the metal until it takes on a purple or golden color, place the hooks into the mold and close it, then pour the lead. Remove the casting, clean the

lead head and paint it with a coat of white.

Place it in a vise, wrap thread around the collar, then wrap the fur or feathers in place. Tie off with half hitches and paint the head with a second coat of enamel.

Sinkers can be cast even more simply, since there are no hooks and no finishing procedures. If you gather free lead from old tire weights, for example, you can bring in a good bucktail or jig for as low as 10 cents. Ament and Do-It make especially good bucktail molds. If you prefer not to deal with hot metal, you can order pre-formed bucktail heads and finishing materials, including paints, from almost any of the major suppliers. The Worth Company and Tack-L-Tyers both offer jig-making kits through tackle stores for about $7. Herb's Hairjig Kit from Netcraft is an especially good jig mold outfit for about $10; it allows you to seat the tail material into the mold, eliminating one tying step.

RODS

All types of fiberglass rods can be assembled from rod components. Preformed handles make it easy to glue on the butt section, but you can go as far as sanding down a cork grip from ½-inch rings. Likewise, most blanks come with ferrules already in place, but you can build your own, including glass-to-glass models. You'll have to file the guides, tape them in place for proper spacing and wrap them down (a handy skill to acquire for other rod repairs). Guides are available from all the major suppliers in sets of four or five for $1.50 to $5. Thread wrappings, which should be protected with an epoxy finish, are needed at the tip-top, at each ferrule and just above the handle. If you're willing to in-

(continued on next page)

BUILD YOUR OWN TACKLE

(continued from preceding page)

vest a little time, you can actually duplicate rods of several major manufacturers from their own blanks. In many ways, you can improve on a good thing by adding high-quality handles and guides to mass-produced products. Many of the names in the rod component business will be familiar — Fenwick, Herter's, Orvis, Leonard, to name a few.

Building your own rod is really the ultimate in personalized tackle. With a little forethought, you can put together a custom rod that's built exactly for the kind of fish, waters and lures you want it to match. You can make a good 6½-foot spinning rod for about $10; about $25 will put in your hands a custom rod that would cost you twice that much from the manufacturer. Herter's, Hille, Reed Tackle and Angler's Pro Shop all have good kits to suit your brand of fishing. Featherweight Products carries a complete line of handle components and a handle kit is a good investment if you're planning more than one rod, or you want to practice your winding skills by making repairs on other rods.

With components and a little imagination, you can create the ultimate in custom nets, reel seats, boat rods and almost anything your tackle box tells you you need — but can't afford. Obviously, making your own tackle does require an investment in time, materials and a little practice. But the rewards in dollar savings and sheer fishing satisfaction are well worth a few winter evenings in the basement. There's a special thrill that comes with hooking a bass on a home-made plug with a rod you built yourself.

And as you become more familiar with tackle, new ideas or refinements of your store-bought stuff will start to suggest themselves. Making your own tackle will give you a better idea of what's effective. Also, knowing that you're using a lure that only cost you 25 cents instead of a dollar makes plying those snaggy, fish-infested waters more attractive. In short, building your own tackle will make you a better and more accomplished angler.

THE LAST HATCH
A FISHING MYSTERY
HARMON HENKIN

(continued from page 218)

"Julie Berners. I live in Stevensville. Just visiting for the day."

Alexandrea and Tups looked at each other and snickered. The sheriff fixed a baleful glare on them.

"What's bothering you two? This ain't no TV show."

"Nothing, officer." They put on their best serious, respectful masks.

"I don't understand all this questioning," Dun interrupted, pointing at Paul. "He's the one who did it. Do your duty, sheriff."

Sid paused and scratched his head.

"As Limy, the Elder, said: 'Justice is not served by lies or slander.' " Everyone stared. Hewitt snorted.

Paul grinned and stood up. "Before this attempted Star Court gets out of hand, let's deal with Dun's accusation. I'm tired of people pointing fingers at me. Halford was killed with a gaff, right?"

A couple of people nodded gravely and the rest were silent.

"A saltwater gaff, wasn't it, Mr. Dun?"

He agreed and Paul continued.

"The kind used to land big fish like tarpon, barracuda or sharks?"

Dun kept nodding.

"Well, the only sharks around here are land sharks, right, Mr. Wormer?"

Wormer turned away and mumbled.

"So we can assume that the gaff belonged to a saltwater angler like Halford. Did he own an Abercrombie & Fitch gaff?"

"Yes, it was his gaff. He used it on hundreds of big fish. To think it was turned on him. Irony of ironies." Tears were forming again.

"So the only way I could have gotten 'the murder weapon,' as they like to say, was by walking in the house, probably today, and searching until I found it. Then I would have had to comb the grounds until I found Halford. Why wouldn't I just bring a knife or a gun or, in Halford's case, a big rat trap? It would have been simpler than trying to avoid being seen by a mob like this. Did anyone see me?"

Nobody responded. Sid stepped forward.

"Seems to me we can assume that it was one of this crowd who did it."

Dun had become thoughtful. "The gaff was always stored in the corner of the den and everyone here knew that. It was in plain sight."

(continued on page 224)

CHOOSING TACKLE FOR PANFISH

By David Richey

Panfish are the smallest tribe of gamefish but the thrill of catching them appeals to anglers of all age and wage classes. Lots of youngsters cut their fishing teeth on bluegills while oldtimers often revert to their childhood as the lure of these tasty little beasts begins teasing them again.

The simplest rig for catching panfish is the old-fashioned cane pole. Good poles are rather difficult to obtain today since much of the cane is of inferior grade. Select a straight piece 10 to 15 feet in length and as free of nodules and scars as possible. A good cane pole will last for many years if stored either in an upright manner or lying flat so the cane is not bent during storage.

Braided dacron fishing line with a monofilament leader is all the line an angler needs with a cane pole. Most people use 15 or 20 dacron and a six or eight foot length of 6- to 10-pound mono for a leader. The line is wound clockwise around the tip of the rod and unrolled as more depth and line are called for.

An alternative to the cane pole is the new telescoping rod-reel combination manufactured by the Stillfish Corporation in Toledo, Ohio. A small but effective reel and line are stored in the butt section of the rod, which comes in various lengths to cope with specialized panfishing problems. I've used several models personally and can recommend them highly.

Although there is a breed of panfishing experts that refrain from using bobbers, the average fisherman after bluegills, sunfish, perch, etc., will normally use one. I much prefer using quill bobbers since they are very sensitive to the light nibble of panfish.

Much panfishing is done with natural bait such as earthworms, nightcrawlers, crickets, grasshoppers and other insects. I prefer a light wire Eagle Claw hook in sizes 10 through 14. A long shank model is perfect and facilitates easy removal from undersized fish.

Spinfishermen can have a field day casting tiny lures or jigs to panfish. Select a light or ultra-light spinning reel such as a Mitchell 300 or a Shakespeare 2052 and team this with a light-action spinning rod in the 6 to 7½ foot class. Spool on either 2- or 4-pound test line for a sporty combination.

STILLFISH ROD

I prefer casting the smallest Mepps or C. P. Swing spinners I can find. Occasionally a white Uncle Josh flyrod strip of porkrind will let you cast further — and lure more strikes.

When bluegills go deep I'll often drift with the wind and jig with Gapen's smallest Pinky jigs tipped with a cricket or grasshopper. This is a deadly method.

Flyfishing has to be the number one method of taking sunfish. I prefer a 6 to 7½ foot flyrod, a matching reel and level flyline. Tapered lines aren't needed and constitute an unnecessary expense. Keep it simple and use a six foot leader of 4- or 6-pound mono. This will be satisfactory for casting up to 40 feet. I prefer either a white or orange Scientific Anglers or Shakespeare flyline. Buy a floating model.

Gapen of Big Lake, Minnesota, offers a wide range of small flies ideally suited for bluegill fishing. Burke Fishing Lures of Traverse City, Michigan, has a vast array of plastic hoppers, crickets, wigglers and other small lures that will appeal to both the panfish and the fisherman. Whatever you buy, however, keep it on the small side because panfish have dainty mouths.

A wire mesh live basket is handy for keeping the fish alive while in the water. The flavor of panfish can be kept at its peak by keeping the fish cold. I buy a 10-pound block of ice and place it in my Coleman cooler. The fish are still firm and fresh when it comes time to clean them in the evening. Coolers take up very little space in the boat and also keep sandwiches and drinks cold.

One last piece of advice: I never scale panfish; it's simply too much bother. I fillet them in the same way as larger gamefish. Normark Corporation of Mineapolis offers a dandy FNF-4 "Fish 'N Fillet" knife designed strictly for small fish. The four-inch blade is just right for quick, easy filleting.

Panfish tackle is simple and easy to buy. Just be sure to gear your purchases toward the lighter range of tackle.

GAMEFISH: BLUEFIN TUNA

NAMES
Horse mackerel, bluefin, tuna, tunny. *(Thunnus thynnus)*

DISTRIBUTION
The bluefin tuna is found in waters throughout the world and in all kinds of temperature zones. In the Atlantic, it is found as far north as Hamilton Inlet, Labrador, and as far south as Cuba. In the Pacific, it is common in the waters off Catalina Island, California.

DESCRIPTION
The bluefin tuna is dark on the back, the color ranging from greenish blue to dark blue, with iridescent silver sides and a white belly. The pectoral fins are very short and all of the fins are dark in color. The bluefin has a thick, bulky body and a small head.

SIZE
The bluefin tuna has been known to reach over 900 pounds in weight, but the average is around 50 to 100 pounds.

HABITAT
The bluefin tuna is an open-water fish that travels in large schools. Schools of smaller bluefins sometimes show up quite close to shore. The bluefin will travel great distances in search of food.

FEEDING HABITS
The bluefin tuna feeds primarily on other fish although they also eat squid and crustaceans.

BEST FEEDING TEMPERATURE
About 73°.

TACKLE
One of the most desirable of all the big game fish, the bluefin is usually caught on substantial trolling equipment and live bait, but sometimes large jigs do the trick. It takes a well-equipped boat and gear that won't freeze up under the pressure.

THE LAST HATCH
A FISHING MYSTERY
HARMON HENKIN

(continued from page 222)

Wormer wanted revenge. "Yeah, well that alibi might impress some of you but not me. We'll see if a jury believes it."

"All right, Wormer, this is the clincher. Where's the kitchen?"

Dun pointed south. Everyone followed Paul and gathered around him in Halford's kitchen, which looked like the set of *The Galloping Gourmet.*

"What time was dinner over today, Dun?"

"At 1, exactly. I remember because Mr. Halford had a phone call to make at that time and was anxious to be punctual."

"So he couldn't have left the house before 1."

"That's correct."

"And I found the body at 1:45. I was at the house at 2 calling the sheriff. Right, Sid?"

"Right."

"The current in the creek runs about one mile per hour. We've done a lot of research — that's a fact. We found the spot where he was killed, about a half mile from the mouth of the creek. That means he had a 30-minute float trip. So if we knew he was on the phone at 1 and dead at the mouth of the creek 45 minutes later, he had to have been killed between, say, 1:10 and 1:15. That's counting the 10- or 15-minute walk to the spot where he was offed."

Wormer was squirming again. "What's all this got to do with the price of beans, mister? You could have killed him at 1 o'clock, 15 minutes later or whenever."

"No I couldn't have. I was fishing then."

"Says who?"

"My witness."

"Your witness!" everyone cried almost in unison.

Sid's mouth had dropped to an uncharacteristic low. "What witness, Paul? Why didn't you say something before?"

Paul reached into the creel pocket at the back of his Orvis vest and pulled out a 15-inch rainbow trout.

"Sounds like a fishy story to me," Tups cried as Alexandrea squealed with laughter. "Ain't he a card?"

"That fish got a watch?" Wormer asked.

"He has a biological watch."

(continued on page 232)

"He has well fished and caught a frog."
JOHN HEYWOOD, *Proverbs*

BAITCASTING & SPINCASTING RODS **225**

specifications

Brand Model	Length	Lure (oz.) Weight	No. Pieces	No. Guides	Material
DAIWA					
Alpine Pack Rod (spin, spincast, fly)					
3053	6' 6"		7	5	glass
VIP Rods					
31P	6'		2	6	glass
91DP	6'		2	6	glass
60DP	5' 6"		1	6	glass
61DP	6'		1	7	glass
50DP	5' 6"		1	6	glass
51DP	6'		1	7	glass
Regal Series					
5031P	6'		2	6	glass
5330P	5' 6"		2	6	glass
5430P	5' 6"		1	6	glass
5430DP	5' 6"		1	6	glass
5331P	6'		2	6	glass
5331DP	6'		2	6	glass
5431DP	6'		1	6	glass
5431DP	6'		1	6	glass
5100-8	8'		2	6	glass
5100-8½	8' 6"		2	6	glass
1500 Series					
1591P	6'		2	5	glass
1531P	6'		2	5	glass
1300 Series					
1331P	6'		2	5	glass
1340P	5' 6"		1	5	glass
1000 Series					
1031	6'		2	5	glass
Special Promotion Rod					
231	6'		2		
Minicast Gold					
MG1-59	5'		5		
MG1-438	4' 6"		2		
Minispin System					
MC1-438	4' 6"		1		glass
MC1-59	5'		5		glass
MC1-38	4' 6"		2		glass
EAGLE CLAW					
Granger Graphite Blue Diamond Rods					
GC55FL	5' 6"			5	graphite
GC55UL	5' 6"			5	graphite
Water Seal Rods					
WC50LC	5'		2	5	glass
WC55LC	5' 6"		2	5	glass
WC55MC	5' 6"		2	5	glass
WC55PC	5' 6"		2	5	glass
Granger Heavy Duty Series					
C8765	6' 6"		1	5	glass
8765	6' 6"		1	5	glass
C8770	7'		1	5	glass
8770	7'		1	5	glass
M8770J	7'		2	5	glass
CMBNWT74	7' 4"		2	4	glass
MBNWT74	7' 4"		2	4	glass
CMDF	8' 6"		2		glass
MDF	8' 6"		2	6	glass
MC8485	8' 6"		2	6	glass
M8485	8' 6"		2	6	glass
MC8485TR	8' 6"		2	6	glass
M8485TR	8' 6"		2	6	glass
CMA9SH	9'		2	6	glass
MA95H				6	glass
Power Light Series					
CMPLC8	8'		2	6	glass
MPLC8	8'		2	6	glass
MPLC8½	8' 6"		2	6	glass
CMPLMC10	10'		2	7	glass
MPLMC10	10'		2	7	glass
MPLLC82	8' 2"		2	6	glass
CMPLT8	8'		2	5	glass
MPLT8	8'		2	5	glass
Featherlight Series					
MLWC6	6'		2	4	glass
MLWC6½	6' 6"		2	4	glass
Trailmaster (pack rods)					
M4TMC	6' 6"		4	5	glass
VM4TMC	6' 6"		4	5	glass
M6TMC	6' 6"		6	5	glass
VM6TMC	6' 6"		6	5	glass
1-VM8TM	5'		5	5	glass
2-VM8TM	5'		5	5	glass
Sweetheart Series					
CM2RC6	6'		2	6	glass
M2RC6	6'		2	6	glass
CM2RC6½	6' 6"		2	6	glass
M2RC6½	6' 6"		2	6	glass
Pro Worm Series					
CPWR5½	5' 6"		1	5	glass
CPWR6	6'		1	5	glass
CPWR6½	6' 6"		1	5	glass
CPBC5½	5' 6"		1	5	glass
CPBC6	6'		1	5	glass
CPWRB4½	4' 6"		1	5	glass
CPWRB5	5'		1	5	glass
CPWRB5½	5' 6"		1	5	glass
Deluxe Series					
CDHC5½	5' 6"		1	5	glass
CDHC6	6'		1	5	glass
DHC5½	5' 6"		1	5	glass
DHC6	6'		1	5	glass
MDRC6	6'		2	6	glass
MDRC6½	6' 6"		2	6	glass
MDRC7	7'		2	6	glass
MDRC6½	6' 6"		2	6	glass
CDHCB4	4' 6"		1	4	glass
CDHCB5	5'		1	4	glass
CB55W5½	5' 6"		1	5	glass
CB60W6	6'		1	5	glass

specifications

Champion Series

Brand Model	Length	Lure (oz.) Weight	No. Pieces	No. Guides	Material
MGCJM6	6'		.2	.4	glass
CMGCJM6	6'		.2	.4	glass
MGCJM6½	6' 6"		.2	.4	glass
CMGCJM6½	6' 6"		.2	.4	glass
MTR6½	6' 6"		.2	.3	glass
CMTR6½	6' 6"		.2	.3	glass
MTR7	6' 6"		.2	.4	glass
CMTR7	7'		.2	.4	glass
MTR7	7'		.2	.4	glass
CMTR7½	7' 6"		.2	.4	glass
MTR8	7' 6"		.2	.4	glass
CMTR8	8'		.2	.4	glass
MTR8	8'		.2	.4	glass
MTRL7	7'		.2	.4	glass
MTRT7	7'		.2	.4	glass

Favorite Series

Brand Model	Length	Lure (oz.) Weight	No. Pieces	No. Guides	Material
M2360MRC	6'		.2	.4	glass
CMB2360MRC	6'		.2	.4	glass
M2365MRC	6' 6"		.2	.4	glass
CMB2365MRC	6' 6"		.2	.4	glass
MB2360M	6'		.2	.4	glass
CMB2360M	6'		.2	.4	glass
MB2365M	6' 6"		.2	.4	glass
CMB2365M	6' 6"		.2	.4	glass
MBFLX6½	6' 6"		.2	.5	glass
CMBFLX6½	6' 6"		.2	.5	glass
MBFLX7	7'		.2	.5	glass
CMBFLX7	7'		.2	.5	glass

Denco Series

Brand Model	Length	Lure (oz.) Weight	No. Pieces	No. Guides	Material
MB1360	6'		.2		glass
MB1365	6' 6"		.2		glass
MB1355M	5' 6"		.2		glass
CMB1355M	5' 6"		.2		glass
MB1360M	6'		.2		glass
CMB1360M	6'		.2		glass
MB1365M	6' 6"		.2		glass
CMB1365M	6' 6"		.2		glass
B1355W	5' 6"		.1		glass
CB1355W	5' 6"		.1		glass
B1360W	6'		.1		glass
CB1360W	6'		.1		glass
MB1360X	6'		.2		glass
CMB1360X	6'		.1		glass
MFLC	6'		.2		glass
DTR	7' 6"		.1		glass

Tom Mann Signature Rods

Brand Model	Length	Lure (oz.) Weight	No. Pieces	No. Guides	Material
CTMC5½	5' 6"		.1	.4	glass

Granger Professional Action Rods

Brand Model	Length	Lure (oz.) Weight	No. Pieces	No. Guides	Material
MCGPLC84	8' 4"		.2	.6	glass
MCGPC82	8' 2"		.2	.6	glass

Telescopic Rods

Brand Model	Length	Lure (oz.) Weight	No. Pieces	No. Guides	Material
TEC-6	6'				glass

Solid Glass Rods

Brand Model	Length	Lure (oz.) Weight	No. Pieces	No. Guides	Material
NR5	5'		.2		solid glass
NR5½	5' 6"		.2		solid glass
NR6	6'		.2		solid glass
CH5	5'		.2	.4	solid glass
CH5½	5' 6"		.2	.4	solid glass
CH6	6'		.2	.4	solid glass
TY4½	4' 6"				solid glass
TY5	5'				solid glass
TY5½	5' 6"				solid glass
RR4½	4' 6"				solid glass
RR5	5'				solid glass
RR5½	5' 6"				solid glass

FENWICK

HMG Graphite Casting Rods

Brand Model	Length	Lure (oz.) Weight	No. Pieces	No. Guides	Material
GFC-554	5' 6"	.3/8-3/4	1		graphite
GFC-555	5' 6"	.1/2-1	.1		graphite
GFC-605	6'	.1/2-1	.1		graphite
GFC-556	5' 6"	.5/8-1 1/4	.1		graphite
GFC-557	5' 6"	.5/8-1 5/8	.1		graphite

HMG Inshore and Live Bait Rods

Brand Model	Length	Lure (oz.) Weight	No. Pieces	No. Guides	Material
GJB-65C	6' 6"	.1/2-2	.1		graphite

The Long Ones

Brand Model	Length	Lure (oz.) Weight	No. Pieces	No. Guides	Material
FS110	9'	.3/8-3/4	.2		glass
FS79C	7' 9"	.1/4-5/8	.2		glass
FS83C	8' 3"	.1/4-5/8	.2		glass
FS80C	8'	.3/8-1	.2		glass
FS85C	8' 6"	.3/8-1	.2		glass
FS88C	8' 6"	.5/8-1 1/2	.2		glass
FS89C	8'10"	.1-2 1/2			glass

Popping, Musky and Deep Jigging Rods

Brand Model	Length	Lure (oz.) Weight	No. Pieces	No. Guides	Material
PLP56	5' 6"	.1-3	.2		

Lunkerstik Rods

Brand Model	Length	Lure (oz.) Weight	No. Pieces	No. Guides	Material
FC60	6'	.1/4-5/8	.2		glass
FC65	6' 6"	.3/8-5/8	.2		glass
1155	5' 6"	.3/8-3/4	.1		glass
1160	6'	.3/8-3/4	.1		glass
PLC60	6'	.1/2-1	.2		glass
1450	5'	.1/2-1	.1		glass
1455	5' 6"	.1/2-1	.1		glass
1460	6'	.1/2-1	.1		glass
1465	6' 6"	.1/2-1	.1		glass
1456	5' 6"	.5/8-1 1/4	.1		glass
1461	6'	.5/8-1 1/4	.1		glass
1457	5' 6"	.5/8-1 5/8	.1		glass

Flippin' Stick

Brand Model	Length	Lure (oz.) Weight	No. Pieces	No. Guides	Material
775	7' 6"	.3/8-2	.1		glass

GARCIA

Ambassadeur

Brand Model	Length	Lure (oz.) Weight	No. Pieces	No. Guides	Material
8300C	5'	.1/2-1	.1	.5	glass
8315	5'	.1/2-1	.1	.5	glass
8316	5' 6"	.1/2-1	.1	.6	glass
8317	5' 6"	.5/8-1 1/4	.1	.6	glass
8318	5' 6"	.5/8-1 1/2	.1	.6	glass

"Here comes the trout that must be caught with tickling."
SHAKESPEARE, *Twelfth Night*

specifications

Brand Model	Length	Lure (oz.) Weight	No. Pieces	No. Guides	Material
8327	5' 6"	.5/8-1 1/4	1	6	glass
8319	6'	.1/2-1	1	6	glass
8321	6'	.5/8-1 1/4	1	6	glass
8322	6'	.3/8-1	1	6	glass
8326	6'	.5/8-1 1/4	1	6	glass
8324	6' 6"	.1/2-1	2	6	glass
Brown Rods					
2524	6'	.1/4-5/8	1	5	glass
2522	6' 6"	.1/4-5/8	2	5	glass
2526	6' 6"	.3/8-5/8	2	5	glass
2529	5' 8"	.3/8-3/4	1	4	glass
B529	5' 8"	.3/8-3/4	2	4	glass
B521	5' 6"	.1/2-1	1	4	glass
B523	5' 6"	.1-3	1	3	glass
B520	5' 6"	.1 3/4-6	2	4	glass
Avocado Rods					
8226	6' 6"	.3/8-5/8	2	5	glass
8225	6'	.1/2-1	1	5	glass
8229	5' 8"	.3/8-3/4	1	4	glass
8220	5' 6"	.1 3/4-6	1	4	glass
Blue Rods					
2622	6'	.1/4-1/2	2	4	glass
2621	6' 6"	.1/4-5/8	2	5	glass
2628	6'	.1/4-5/8	2	4	glass
2629	5' 8"	.1/4-5/8	1	4	glass

HEDDON

Brand Model	Length	Lure (oz.) Weight	No. Pieces	No. Guides	Material
New Ceramic Mark Rods					
6101	5' 6"	.3/8-5/8			
6105	6'	.3/8-5/8			
6110	5' 6"	.3/8-5/8			
6115	5' 6"	.3/8-1			
6120	6'	.3/8-1			
Mark V					
6318	6'	.3/8-5/8	1		
6319	6'	.3/8-1	1		
6322	5' 6"	.3/8-1	1		
6923	6'	.3/8-5/8	2		
6916	6' 6"	.3/8-5/8	2		
6926	6'	.3/8-5/8	2		
Mark IV					
6305	5' 6"	.3/8-5/8	1		glass
6308	6'	.3/8-5/8	1		glass
6309	6'	.3/8-1	1		glass
6903	6'	.3/8-5/8	2		glass
6904	6'	.1/4-5/8	2		glass
6906	6' 6"	.3/8-5/8	2		glass
6907	6' 6"	.1/4-5/8	2		glass
6909	7'	.3/8-5/8	2		glass
Pro-Weight Mark					
6225	5' 6"	.3/8-5/8	1		
6781	5' 3"	.1/8-3/8	2		
6783	6'	.1/4-5/8	2		
6786	6' 6"	.1/4-5/8	2		
Stainless Wire Mark					
6244	6'	.3/8-5/8	1		glass

Brand-Model	Length	Lure (oz.) Weight	No. Pieces	No. Guides	Material
6248	6'	.3/8-5/8	1		glass
6743	6'	.3/8-5/8	2		glass
6744	6'	.3/8-5/8	2		glass
6746	6' 6"	.3/8-5/8	2		glass
6749	7'	.1/2-1	2		glass
Golden Mark					
6444	6'	.3/8-5/8			glass
6446	6' 6"	.3/8-5/8			glass
Mark II					
6205	5' 6"	.3/8-5/8	1		glass
6208	6'	.3/8-5/8	1		glass
6803	6'	.3/8-5/8	2		glass
6806	6' 6"	.3/8-5/8	2		glass
Mark I					
6154	6'	.3/8-5/8	1		glass
6155	5' 6"	.3/8-5/8	1		glass
6158	6'	.3/8-5/8	1		glass
6753	6'	.3/8-5/8	2		glass
6755	6'	.1/2-1	2		glass
6756	6' 6"	.3/8-5/8	2		glass
Mark Brute					
6270	5' 6"	.3/8-1	1		glass
6271	6'	.3/8-1	1		glass
6272	5'10"	.5/8-2	1		
Trail Blazer					
6450	6'			4	glass
Mark Special Purpose					
5123	5'	.5/8-2	1		glass
6273	5'	.5/8-2	1		glass
6276	5' 6"	.5/8-2	1		glass
6277	5' 6"	.3/8-1	1		glass
6279	6'11"	.2-8	1		glass
6280	8'		2		glass
6299	7'	.1/2-1	1		glass
3330	2' 6"	.2			glass
6275	5' 8"	.3/8-1	2		glass
6298	7'	.1/2-1	2		glass
6575	5' 8"	.3/8-1	2		glass
6799	7'	.3/8-7/8			glass

HERTER'S

Brand-Model	Length	Lure (oz.) Weight	No. Pieces	No. Guides	Material
RBCOHO	6' 6"		1	5	glass
RK9L7	6' 6"			4	solid glass
800D	6'	.1/4-1	1	4	glass
700D	5' 6"	.1/4-1	1	4	glass
Perfection 100 Series					
100HE	5' 6"	.to 5/8	1	4	glass
101HE	6'	.to 1/2	2	4	glass
102HE	6' 6"	.to 1/2	2	4	glass
Mark 500 Series					
M500	6' 6"	.to 3/8	2	5	glass
M501	6'	.to 3/8	2	5	glass
Graphite Carbon Filament Rods					
RB6G82	5'10"	.to 1/8	1	6	graphite

specifications

Brand-Model	Length	Lure (oz.) Weight	No. Pieces	No. Guides	Material
RB6G83	5'10"	to 3/8	1	6	graphite
RB6G84	5'10"	to 5/8	1	6	graphite
Heavy Duty Musky and Trolling Rod					
107M	5' 2"	1-3	1	4	
Hollow Glass Casting and Trolling Rods					
RB6Y3C	6'	to 1/2	1	5	glass
RB6Y4C	6'	to 5/8	1	5	glass
Fast Taper Power Butt Hollow Glass Spin Casting Rods					
RH9LPB3	6'	to 5/8	2	5	glass
RH9LPB4	6' 6"	to 5/8	2	5	glass
Grand Deluxe Hollow Glass Spin Casting Rods					
RSC2	6'		2	5	glass
Double Wall Reinforced Hollow Glass Worm Rods					
BC201D	5' 6"	1/8-	1	5	glass
SC2020	6'	1/8-	1	5	glass
Hollow Spun Glass Traveler-Pack Trip-Suitcase-Compact Spincasting Rods					
RPSC6	6'	to 5/8	5	3	glass
Fast Taper Power Butt Finished Hollow Glass Casting Rods					
RB6CPB	5' 6"	to 3/4	1	4	glass
RB6DPB	5' 6"	to 3/4	1	4	glass
4-In-One Grand Deluxe All-Purpose Rods					
108P	6' 2"	3/8	7		glass
Guide Series 5-Piece Travel Pak Rods					
700HE	5'10"		5		
KEYSTONE					
All-American Spincast Outfit					
3715 (with reel)	5'		2		
Solid Glass Rods					
900	5'		1	2	solid glass
902C	5'		1	2	solid glass
902	5'		1	2	solid glass
945	5'		1	2	solid glass
903	5'		1	2	solid glass
056	5'		1	2	solid glass
129	5'		1	3	solid glass
451	5' 3"		1	2	solid glass
053	5' 3"		1	2	solid glass
452	5' 6"		1	3	solid glass
055A	5' 6"		1	3	solid glass
919B	5' 6"		2	2	solid glass
919	5' 6"		2	2	solid glass
453	5' 6"		2	2	solid glass
054	5' 6"		2	2	solid glass
946	5' 6"		2	2	solid glass
943B	5' 6"		2	3	solid glass
943	5' 6"		2	3	solid glass
138G	5' 6"		2	3	solid glass
951B	6' 2"		2	3	solid glass
Solid Glass Special Purpose Rods					
355	2'		1	1	solid glass
355B	2'		1	1	solid glass
381	2' 6"		1	1	solid glass
097	3'		1	2	solid glass
052A	3' 6"		1	2	solid glass
450	4'		1	2	solid glass
112	4' 6"		1	2	solid glass
314A	5' 3"		1	3	solid glass
113	5' 6"		1	3	solid glass
Deluxe Matched Shaft Series					
444	5' 6"		1	3	solid glass
967J	5' 6"		2	3	solid glass
967K	6'		2	3	solid glass
1976	5' 6"		2	3	solid glass
Hipster Spincast Rod and Reel Combos					
3717 (with reel)	2'				
3716 (with reel)	2'				
Elite Promotional Series Tubular Rods					
610	6'		2	3	glass
KODIAK					
8000 Series					
8101	6'		2	4	glass
8401	5' 6"		1	4	
Specialty Action Rods					
3601-C	8'		2	8	
4000 Series					
4000	5' 6"		1	4	glass
4101	6'-6'6"		2	4	glass
Fresh Water Solid Glass					
30	2' 6"		1	2	solid glass
36	3'		1	2	solid glass
90	3'		1	1	solid glass
95	4' 6"		1	2	solid glass
100	5'		1	2	solid glass
110	5' 6"		2	2	solid glass
115	5'-5'6"		1	3	solid glass
135	5'		1	2	solid glass
Special Purpose Rods					
2410	5' 6"		1	4	glass
2415	6'		1	5	glass
2418	5' 8"		1	5	glass
2411	5' 6"		1	4	glass
2412	6'		1	4	glass
2413	5' 6"		1	4	glass
2420	5' 6"		1	4	glass
4000	5' 6"		1	4	glass
E-Z Pack Rods					
3140	6' 6"		4	4	glass
Flip Poles					
5010RSC	10'		2	2	glass
5016RSC	16'		4	3	

specifications

Brand-Model	Length	Lure (oz.) Weight	No. Pieces	No. Guides	Material
LEW CHILDRE					
Speed Sticks					
1L-16HO	6'	.1/8-1/2	.1		glass
1-152HO	5' 2"	.3/8-5/8	.1		glass
1-156HO	5' 6"	.3/8-5/8	.1		glass
1-159HO	5' 9"	.3/8-5/8	.1		glass
1-16HO	6'	.3/8-5/8	.1		glass
4-156HO	5' 6"	.3/8-1	.1		glass
4-16HO	6'	.3/8-1	.1		glass
6-158HO	6'	.1/2-1 1/4	.1		glass
6-16HO	6'	.1/2-1 1/4	.1		glass
IL-26HO	5' 9"		.2		glass
1-259HO	5' 9"		.2		glass
1-26HO	6'		.2		glass
4-26HO	6'		.2		glass
6-258HO	5' 8"		.2		glass
6-26HO	6'		.2		glass
Telescopic Speed Stick					
IL-T59	5' 9"				glass
1-T59	5' 9"				glass
4-T59	5' 9"				glass
6-T59	5' 9"				glass
QUICK					
Champion Graphite Rods					
GRF56	5' 6"		.1		graphite
GRF60	6'		.1		graphite
Champion Casting Rods					
FC60			.1		
FC58	5' 9"				
FC59	5' 9"		.1		
RAY SCOTT					
100% Graphite Rods					
25BO	5' 6"	.1/4-7/8			graphite
25AO	5' 6"				graphite
Ray Scott Rods					
2040	5'6½"		.1		glass
2070	5'7¼"		.1		glass
2050	5' 9"		.1		glass
2090	5'7½"		.1		glass
SHAKESPEARE					
Graflite Rods					
GFIIBC	5' 8"			.5	graphite
GFIIBCS	5' 8"			.5	graphite
Custom Pro 708					
BC708	5' 6"	.3/8-5/8		.5	glass
BC708	6'	.3/8-5/8		.5	glass

Brand-Model	Length	Lure (oz.) Weight	No. Pieces	No. Guides	Material
200 Series					
BC200	5' 6"	.3/8-5/8	.1	.5	glass
BC200	6'	.3/8-5/8	.1	.5	glass
PB200	6'	.1/8-3/8		.5	glass
PB200	6' 6"	.1/8-3/8		.6	glass
608 Wonderod Series					
PB608	6'	.1/8-3/8		.5	glass
PB608	6' 6"	.1/8-3/8		.6	glass
Presidential 508 Series					
BC508	5' 6"	.3/8-5/8	.1	.5	glass
PB508	6'	.1/8-3/8	.2	.5	glass
PB508M	6'	.1/4-5/8	.2	.5	glass
PB508	6' 6"	.1/8-3/8	.2	.5	glass
190 Maroon Series					
BC190	5' 6"	.3/8-5/8	.1	.5	glass
BC190	6'	.3/8-5/8	.1	.5	glass
PB190	6'	.1/8-3/8	.2	.5	glass
PB190	6' 6"	.1/8-3/8	.2	.5	glass
408 Wonderod Series					
PB408	6'	.1/8-3/8	.2	.4	glass
PB408	6'	.1/8-3/8	.2	.4	glass
170 Wonder Glass Series					
BC170	5' 6"	.3/8-5/8	.1	.4	glass
PB170	6'	.1/8-3/8	.2	.4	glass
PB170	6' 6"	.1/8-3/8	.2	.4	glass
160 Wonderglass Series					
BC160M	5' 6"	.3/8-5/8	.1	.3	glass
PB160	6'	.1/8-3/8	.2	.3	glass
60 Series					
BC60	5' 6"	.3/8-5/8	.1	.3	solid glass
PB60	5' 6"	.1/8-3/8	.2	.3	solid glass
11 Series					
BC11	3'	.1/4-3/4		.1	solid glass
BC11	4'	.1/4-3/4		.2	solid glass
BC11	5'	.3/8-5/8		.2	solid glass
PB11	5' 6"	.1/8-3/8	.2	.2	solid glass
Jetset Pack Rods					
SD999	7'	.1/8-3/8	.7	.4	
SKYLINE					
SKC5512	5' 6"	.3/8-1 3/4	.1		graphite
SKC5508	5' 6"	.1/4-1 5/8	.1		graphite
SKC5504	5' 6"	.1/4-3/4	.1		graphite
SKC5502	5' 6"	.1/4-3/8	.1		graphite
SKC6004	6'	.1/4-3/4	.1		graphite
SKH8505	8' 6"	.1/4-1 3/4			graphite
SOUTH BEND					
Classic IV					
A1-146-860	6'				glass

"Still he fishes that catches one."
THOMAS FULLER, *Gnomologia*

specifications

Brand-Model	Length	Lure (oz.) Weight	No. Pieces	No. Guides	Material
Classic III					
A1-042-460	6'		1		glass
B1-142-860	6'		2	5	glass
1-142-460	6'		2	5	glass
Classic I					
A1-136-860	6'		2	4	glass
Bassin' Man Rods					
A1-032-461	6'		1	5	glass
1-032-561	6'		1	5	glass
B1-042-461	6'		1	5	glass
1-042-561	6'		1	5	glass
1-060-557	5' 6"		1	6	glass
C1-060-561	6'		1	6	glass
All Carbide Guide Series					
1-024-456	5' 6"		1	4	glass
1-024-460	6'		1	4	glass
1-124-860	6'		2	4	glass
Outdoorsman					
1-132-260	6'		2	5	glass
1-132-266	6' 6"		2	5	glass
Forester					
A1-130-860	6'				glass
White Knight					
A1-128-260	6'		2	4	glass
Tubular Rainbow Rods (assortment of 12 rods)					
1-120-000	6'				glass
Spincast Tubular Rod Riot (variety of brand names sold together)					
Gladding A.	6'				glass
Horrocks-Ibbotson B	6'				glass
U.S. Fiber-glass C	6'				glass
Bass-Oreno D	6'				glass
South Bend E	6'				glass
Solid Fiberglass Rods					
1-112-260	6'		2	3	solid glass
1-004-250	5'		1		solid glass
1-104-256	5' 6"		2		solid glass
Solid Rainbow Rods (assortment of 12 rods)					
1-106-000	5' 9"		2		solid glass

STILLFISH

Pan Fish Rod/Reel

Brand-Model	Length	Lure (oz.) Weight	No. Pieces	No. Guides	Material
208	8'		2		styrene

Brand-Model	Length	Lure (oz.) Weight	No. Pieces	No. Guides	Material
210	.10'		2		styrene
312	.12'		3		styrene
314	.14'		3		styrene
418	.18'		4		styrene
Tot Rod					
204	4'		2		styrene
Ice Fishing Rod/Reel					
1226	2' 4"		2		styrene
1232	2' 8"		2		styrene
1248	4'		1		styrene
ZEBCO					
Pro Staff Rods					
PS10	6'		2	5	glass
PS12	6' 6"		2	5	glass
PS30	5'		1	4	glass
PS32	5' 6"		1	5	glass
PS34	6'		1	5	glass
Sundowner Rods					
6300	6'		2	5	glass
6200	6'		2	5	glass
6150	5' 6"		1	5	glass
8900	7'		2	5	glass
8816	5' 6"		1	5	glass
8810	6'		1	5	glass
Centennial					
8800	6'		2	4	glass
6100	6'		2	4	glass
8509	5' 9"		2	3	glass
8965	6' 6"		2	4	glass
8406	5' 6"		2	3	glass
8400	5' 6"		1	3	glass
4060	5' 6"		2	3	glass
Pack Rods					
6104	6'		4	4	glass
4064	6'		4	3	glass
Zebco Rods					
4044	5'		2	2	glass
4040	5' 6"		2	3	glass
4020	5'		2	2	glass
4076	4' 6"		1	2	glass
4077	4' 6"		2	2	glass
4002	2' 6"		1		glass

CHOOSING
A SURF ROD

The challenges no longer center necessarily around distance

By Mark Sosin

There was a time when almost every surf angler muscled up to the crashing breakers with a long hand-fitted, Calcutta rod in his hands and a reel attached a comfortable distance above the butt with hose clamps. Today, the sophisticated angler recognizes that the challenges of the beachfront are not necessarily centered around distance, although that can be a factor.

Each stretch of coastline is different and has its own requirements. Veterans have learned that there is no single rod that can handle all assignments and the alternative is to either compromise or own several rods depending on how seriously you intend to pursue the sport.

The first step in selecting any rod is to carefully analyze the waters you intend to fish. In some spots, the prime requirements are to reach across a bar and drop a bait or lure in the slough on the far side. That may require distance casting and, at times, a difference of 10 or 20 feet can spell the fine line between fish and failure.

In other waters, many newcomers over-cast their quarry, believing erroneously that they must cross the ocean when the fish are really hugging the rocks or prowling the sizzling foam just behind

where the waves are breaking. Lighter and shorter rods are the answer when you are faced with less distance and the need for more precision in the casting.

After checking out the waters, you'll know if you need a long rod or a medium length such as an 8- or 8½-footer. Some of the big sticks average 10½ to 11½ or even 12 feet. Consider that if you are baitfishing and intend to push the rod in a sand spike, you may want at least a 10-footer to keep the line above the waves and prevent the bait from washing shoreward.

Regardless of the type of

fishing you will do, a good surf rod has a comfortable grip and distance between the butt and the reel so that you can grasp it without stretching or without feeling cramped. Look closely at the hardware and make sure it will resist corrosion. The combination of sand and salt water can be murderous on components. If you plan to use spinning, the gathering guide should be large enough to accept the coils of line coming off the spool of the spinning reel. Some old-timers insist on a first guide as large as 72mm. There must also be enough guides to cast well and to fight a fish. Rig the rod up and have someone hold it while you put pressure on the line. Make sure it follows the contour of the rod. If it moves at sharp angles, there aren't enough guides to carry the line or the placement is wrong.

The next consideration is to check to see that the rod can easily handle the weight lures or sinkers you will be casting. Hang various weights on the tip-top of the rod and it shouldn't take long to determine whether you can snap cast or if you have to lob the offering. Lob casting is going to cost you distance and it's not the way to go.

If you're a beginner, count

(continued on page 233)

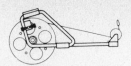

THE LAST HATCH
A FISHING MYSTERY
HARMON HENKIN

(continued from page 224)

Paul laid the fish on a hardwood cutting board by the sink and removed his thin-bladed Case pocket knife. He put a precise slice down its stomach from its gills to the tail, reached inside for a handful of innards and laid them on the cutting board.

Tups looked away. Belle gave forth little shrieks of mock horror.

"This is the craziest thing I've ever seen," Wormer said.

Paul ignored them and laid the stomach casing on a white paper towel. "Now, as most hard-core fly fishermen know, the stomach of a trout is the best record of his eating habits. You look in there, find out what he's been eating and duplicate with artificial flies his favorite food."

Schielbacht had finally found something to say. "I fully agree with all of that. In my monumental study of trout feeding habits, *Nymphettes*, I say that very thing. Of course, I said it better."

Paul looked at him impatiently. "Well, come over here, Schielbacht, and tell me what you see."

Schielbacht glanced at a couple of fully intact specimens Paul had culled from a little pile of insect remains. "The fish was feeding on *Tricorythodes*. Hatching *Tricorythodes* spinners. Common every day at this time of year."

"But when do they emerge from the larval nymph stage to the adult stage, when we fish them with dry flies?"

"Early afternoon. From about 1 o'clock until 3."

"Exactly. Today they came out at exactly 1:15 and I can get every fisherman for miles along the river to corroborate that."

Belle Parmachene spoke up. "But why couldn't the fish have eaten them yesterday?"

"They would have been completely digested by now," Schielbacht said. "But obviously they aren't, dear lady."

"Right," Paul said. "And the only time this trout could have been feeding on them was after 1:15 today — when the murder was taking place half a mile away."

Wormer was still unsatisfied. "But why couldn't you have murdered him, thrown him in the creek, run down to the mouth, caught the fish and 'discovered' the body?"

"My other witness will take care of that."

"Oh, God," Tups moaned as Paul reached into his creel for another trout. "Here we go again."

(continued on page 237)

GAMEFISH: DOLPHIN

NAMES
Dorado, bull dolphin, mahimahi, Dourade. *(Coryphaena hippurus)*

DISTRIBUTION
In the Atlantic ocean, the dolphin is found from Brazil to New England. They are usually found near the Gulf Stream and are abundant from the Carolinas to Texas. In the Pacific, they are found as far north as Oregon.

DESCRIPTION
The dolphin is a spectacular fish that varies in color. It is usually a combination of green, yellow, purple and blue. The back is generally blue and purple and the lower sides green and yellow. Silvery-blue spots are scattered over the entire body. The forehead is high and blunt and the tail deeply forked.

SIZE
Although dolphins may reach weights of over 60 pounds, the average is between 5 and 20 pounds.

HABITAT
The dolphin is generally a school fish that is found in deep water. They are usually found on the surface and leap from the water in pursuit of prey.

FEEDING HABITS
The diet of the dolphin consists of all types of fish and crustaceans. Their favorite food is flying fish which they love to pursue.

BEST FEEDING TEMPERATURE
About 75°.

TACKLE
A great fish when caught on a plug-casting outfit, this spectacular fighter is most often taken by trollers. But when it's in the mood, it will hit most any plug or even a big fly.

"Angling is somewhat like poetry, men are to be born so."
IZAAK WALTON, *The Compleat Angler*

TROLLING, SURF-CASTING & DEEP-SEA TACKLE
233

CHOOSING A SURF ROD

(continued from page 231)

the number of guides plus the tip-top on several rods and you'll get an idea of the average. Better rods generally have more guides and finer quality guides. The new aluminum oxide or ceramic guides cost more, but they increase line wear and make casting a bit easier. Quality reel seats and grips also add to the cost and are usually tip-offs to good products.

Graphite is just starting to gain acceptance along the surf as a rod-building material. Its lighter weight and higher modulus or stiffness offer unheralded fishing opportunities and it will no doubt become the tool of the veteran angler very shortly. Because it is lighter than glass, manufacturers can make longer surf rods than ever before. The stiffness and shorter power stroke enable the user to cast greater distances with the same effort and this is also magnified by the increased rod length.

From a fishing standpoint, graphite offers sensitivity and feel that have never been enjoyed before. You actually catch more fish because you can feel what's happening at the end of the line better than you ever did.

It's a lot more fun and more meaningful to choose a surf rod now than it used to be when the choices were limited. Start with the rod that meets your basic needs and then expand your arsenal when your experience tells you that the time is right.

BRIGHT-PATTERSON

GAMEFISH: YELLOW PERCH

NAMES
Ringed perch, striped perch, jack perch. *(Perca flavescens)*

DISTRIBUTION
The yellow perch was originally found from southern Canada to the Carolinas and south into Missouri and Kansas. It has been extensively stocked throughout the rest of the United States.

DESCRIPTION
The yellow perch is dark green or bronze on the back, with yellow sides and a white belly. The sides are marked with six to eight dark olive green bands. The back is slightly humped.

SIZE
The average weight of the yellow perch is about ½ to 1 pound. They rarely reach a weight of more than 4 pounds.

HABITAT
Large lakes and rivers are the favored environments of the yellow perch although they will be found in all types of lakes and streams. They prefer deep, clear waters with sandy or gravel bottoms. In the summer, they tend to hide in deep holes although at times they might be found near shorelines and weedbeds.

FEEDING HABITS
The yellow perch eats a variety of foods from insects, small minnows and crustaceans to frogs and grubs. They are a school fish that is most active during the spring.

BEST FEEDING TEMPERATURE
Between 60° and 75°.

TACKLE
Lots of light baitfishing fun. Use light open- and close-faced spinning outfits. Will also take flies, especially when it's on its early season spawning run. Likes small spinners and jigs, too.

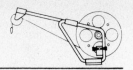

WHAT TO LOOK FOR IN A GOOD SALTWATER REEL
It must have a good, smooth drag, a fast retrieve and a roller that rolls

By Lefty Kreh

Perhaps the most important part of a saltwater spinning outfit is the reel. If it fails to function, the trophy will be lost. And the more prized the fish, generally, the more demand is made upon the reel.

Naturally, lines must be strong enough for the chore, but it is the reel where mechanical functioning is crucial. In saltwater fishing there are two vital areas. The reel must have a good, smooth drag, and the roller should roll.

In addition, a third point is often desirable — a high rate of speed for the retrieve.

The fragile nylon monofilament line that is pulled rapidly from a spinning reel when a fish tries to escape has to travel up, around and over a roller. If that roller doesn't move smoothly, the line grates against it, causing heat damage — often meaning the fish will be lost.

If the roller spins freely, the line moves over it smoothly with almost no problems.

You can easily check the roller on a reel you plan to buy. Take along a ten-inch piece of monofilament of the approximate strength you intend to use. Slip it under the roller and seesaw it back and forth under slight pressure. If the roller doesn't spin easily when it's new, chances are it won't function well when salt and dirt have worked into its innards.

Almost all spinning reels with good rollers will have a bushing between the outside of the axle shaft and the interior of the roller. These bushings are often made of Teflon or a material that will retain oil. Incidentally, never grease a roller — the stuff is too thick and will often prevent the roller from turning.

The second important factor is the drag. A drag that starts poorly, or releases line in lurches, will pop the line on a fast-running fish. Curiously, some of the most expensive reels have relatively poor drags. But you can also check the drag in the store to get a fair idea of its performance.

Take along some monofilament — an old spool of line from another reel works fine. Wind 15 or 20 feet of line from the supply spool onto the reel.

Now tighten the drag a bit, slip the line under the roller and hold the reel aloft by the end of the line. Carefully adjust the drag until the weight of the reel causes the drag to slip.

A good drag will allow the reel to slowly and smoothly descend. Poor drags will generally let it slip in jerks or lurches, even sometimes requiring that you bounce the reel to get the drag to release.

The finish on a salt water reel is extremely important. A good anodized one is best. It's tougher than a rubber tire and requires almost no care. A good baked-on epoxy finish is also excellent. Cheap spray-painted jobs will come off, and frequently break loose from the spool, making the surface too rough for lighter lines.

The bail on a saltwater spinning reel must be strong. Most reels used in salt water are carried on a boat and such outfits get banged around enough to make bent bails a common accident. In fact, many anglers prefer manual bails, since they roll better and are less subject to malfunction.

The quick-change spools, designed with an adjustable drag independent of the reel (to remove you simply depress a button) are a great advantage in saltwater angling. Many times a saltwater trophy will strip off considerable line, then break it. The greatly reduced amount of line on the spool makes casting more difficult. And, if you want to get back to fishing quickly, changing spools and re-setting drags can be a chore.

If you use quick-change spools, you can pop one off and the other on in an instant. Pre-setting the drags means you know exactly how much drag you have. All you need do is run the line from the substitute spool through the guides, attach the lure and cast.

A high rate of retrieve is vital in a lot of saltwater fishing situations. This is especially true when manipulating many types of surface lures, where a hasty retrieve increases the number of strikes.

Thus, high-speed gears can offer a distinct advantage. While it has apparently not occurred to the manufacturers, you can often convert your reel to high speed by adapting a reel handle considerably shorter than the existing one. It doesn't take much insight to see that you can turn a shorter handle more times in a short period of time than you could a longer model.

In any case, when purchasing a reel, you may want to consider whether you can adapt the model under consideration to a shorter handle for high speed work.

If the rate of retrieve is acceptable, the finish is good, the bail holds up, the drag works well, and the roller operates smoothly, you've got a good reel for almost any saltwater battle.

Great Lakes Trout & Salmon Tackle
Recommendations for rods, reels, downriggers, oxygen meters, lures and more

By David Richey

Tackle needed to handle burly Great Lakes trout and salmon must be well built, serviceable and capable of withstanding heavy pressures and plenty of strain.

The guts of any rod and reel combination suitable for open water fishing is the precision-built reel with a strong, reliable drag system and a rod built to take the punishment meted out by big fish.

Most trolling for coho, chinook, browns, steelhead and lake trout on Lakes Michigan, Superior, Huron, Erie and Ontario is done with the so-called "baitcasting" rods and reels. Many professional charter boat and private fishermen prefer Garcia's Ambassadeur 6000 series reels for deepwater trolling. This reel features a freespool mechanism and a sure, positive drag, both of which are essential when dealing with fish that often scale up to 35 pounds.

I prefer to couple an Ambassadeur 6000 with a Garcia 2525A baitcasting rod. Line testing from 10 to 25 pounds can effectively be used with this combination.

Spinning rods and reels also have a place in the Great Lakes scheme of things. But they are most often used early in the season when the fish are still relatively small. A quality Mitchell 300 reel coupled with a 7½ to 8½ foot rod is deadly medicine for early season trout and salmon. Light mono, in the six to ten pound class, is sufficient for smaller fish.

Most trolling in the Lakes is done with the aid of downriggers. These large devices enable fishermen to set their

GARCIA 6000

lines at a controlled depth. A heavy 7 to 12 pound weight, often called a cannonball, is attached to wire line on the downrigger, which can be hand-controlled or activated by electronics. In either case, the lure is released behind the trolling boat for a certain distance and then attached to a release clip on the downrigger line. The downrigger is then lowered to the desired depth and when a fish strikes, the line pulls free of the clip and the fisherman plays his fish on a weight-free line.

Downriggers vary greatly in price and there are many good models available. Some of the better ones I've used are Plath, Riviera, Big Jon and Penn. Factors that add to the final price are such things as small digital counters, electric motors, temperature sensitive probes and movable arms. They're available for mounting on the stern or on the gunwales.

One piece of equipment Great Lakes fishermen should always carry aboard

is some type of oxygen-temperature meter. I've tried several and find Garcia's OTP 8500 meter to be the finest on the market. It quickly tells the temperature and oxygen content of the water — important information for trollers.

Although many trout and salmon trollers use downriggers, a large percentage opt for the time-honored method of "chugging" with wire line rigs. Wire line rods, reels and lines are much cheaper to assemble than downriggers and their necessary paraphernalia.

One of the finest wire line rods on the market is Shakespeare's SS203 in a six foot length. I like to couple a Penn 49 reel to this rod and spool on Shakespeare or Sevenstrand 20 or 30 pound wire line. A very satisfactory combination.

Many fishermen use braided Dacron for trolling. The positive non-stretch factor and durability give it the nod over mono. Gudebrod, Garcia and Shakespeare all make quality braided Dacron. For those anglers addicted to monofilament, I'd suggest a top grade of line like Berkley's Trilene XL, Shakespeare's Super 7000 or Garcia's Royal Bonnyl.

Lures for the Great Lakes are a completely different story. A chapter could be set aside for them alone. I've found the following lures and/or dodger-fly combinations to be very successful at all times of the year.

One of the most productive dodger-trolling fly combinations is the Michigan Rattlure in green, blue or yellow behind an O sized Les Davis Herring Dodger.

(continued on next page)

"'Tis an affair of luck."
HENRY VAN DYKE, *Fisherman's Luck*

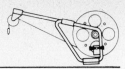

RIVIERA DOWNRIGGER

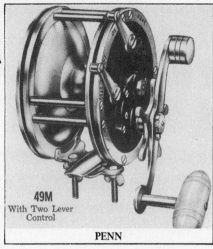

49M
With Two Lever Control

PENN

A Guide to Great Lakes Tackle

(continued from preceding page)

Dodgers are available in chrome, chartreuse, pink, red, chrome and brass and other colors. Many fishermen doctor their dodgers with Prism tape for extra flash at greater depths. These trolling flies are available from Custom Flies in Clio, Michigan.

Other deadly lures include the Flatfish, Tadpolly, Fire Plug, Krocadile, Bayou Special, Manistee Wobbler, Mepps spinners, Sagamore Spoon, Sugar Spoon, Thin Devle, Devle Dog, Little Cleo, Rapala, Dardevle, Flutter Spoons and Andy Reekers.

Many anglers tend to think of Great Lakes trout and salmon fishing as only an open water sport. Not so. Some of the best fishing each year comes during the spring, fall and winter months as big, broad-shouldered salmon and trout nose upstream to spawn. Steelhead spawn primarily in the spring while salmon, browns and lake trout spawn during fall and early winter months. A few steelhead spawn in the fall which makes for a potpourri of fishing excitement.

The tackle needed to handle these fish in rivers is a different breed from that used on open water. Rivers are generally swift, shallow and snag-infested. It takes a gutsy rod to turn a big fish from certain freedom.

Fly fishing for these salmonids is my bag and I often use a Shakespeare 1898 fly reel and an 8½-foot FY940 fly rod.

(continued on next page)

GAMEFISH: CODFISH

NAMES
Atlantic codfish, cod. *(Gadus morhua)*

DISTRIBUTION
The codfish ranges from Greenland south to Cape Hatteras. It is most plentiful off New England and Canada.

DESCRIPTION
The cod is a stocky fish of grey or brown on the back with light grey or white on the sides and belly. The cod also appears to have another phase when its coloring ranges from yellow to reddish brown. The sides are marked with dark spots. It has a long chin barbel and the appearance of being pot-bellied.

SIZE
The average cod weighs between 4 and 10 pounds. Fish of up to 60 pounds are not considered uncommon.

HABITAT
The cod prefers deep, cold waters. They are a migratory fish that travel north and south in schools. Occasionally they are found feeding on the surface.

FEEDING HABITS
The cod is a voracious feeder whose favorite foods include herring, crustaceans, crabs, clams and snails. They are bottom feeders.

TACKLE
Most angling for cod is done with various cut baits tossed or drifted to the ocean bottom. Use medium gear stout enough to handle the outsized sinkers sometimes necessary to get down through rough seas.

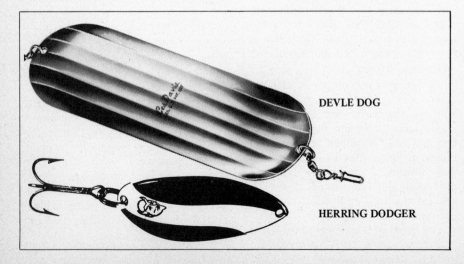

DEVLE DOG

HERRING DODGER

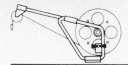

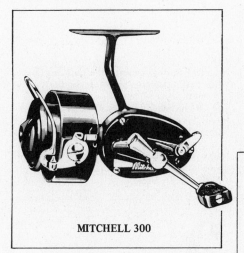

MITCHELL 300

Great Lakes

(continued from preceding page)

A fly line in the weight forward size of 7 to 11 is suitable when used with a rod in the 7½ to 8½ foot lengths. A rod should be sturdy enough to be able to apply heavy pressure to turn rampaging fish as they charge up or downstream.

Fly reels should have a reliable drag system and be capable of holding at least 100 yards of 20 pound test braided Dacron. My fly fishing is normally done with a four-foot piece of level 10 or 12 pound test mono. Spawning trout and salmon are not as leader-conscious as normal stream trout.

Medium-action spinning tackle is fine for spring and fall trout and salmon fishing. I use a Mitchell 300 reel with a Garcia rod in the 7½ to 8½ foot lengths. I prefer a rod with a heavy butt section and a fairly limber tip. This allows me to pressure a fish when need be but still enables me to feel bottom with whatever lure I'm using. Reels should have a smooth, non-stick drag and a fast retrieve.

Some fishing is done from boats as anglers work Flatfish or Tadpollys deep into holes where trout or salmon are resting. This calls for a Garcia Ambassadeur 6000 reel and the same type of ultra-long baitcasting stick as used for downrigger fishing. The longer rods enable the fisherman to set the hook with

(continued on page 239)

THE LAST HATCH
A FISHING MYSTERY
HARMON HENKIN

(continued from page 232)

After Paul had opened him and done another stomach dissection, Schielbacht instantly noticed the difference.

"You caught this fish a few minutes earlier than the other one. That's obvious. This one had been feeding on *Pteronarcy's* nymphs, the big black salmon fly larva in the middle there. There's not a trace of little *Tricorythodes*. This fish was probably caught at 1 o'clock, if what you said about the exact time of the hatch is true. Some of these larva, as you can see, have not yet succumbed to the processes of digestion. But no *Tricorythodes*, which trout love above many things. I wrote about that in *Remembrances of Rivers Crossed*."

"What's all this bug talk mean?" Wormer demanded.

"Simple, Wormer," explained Sid. "It means that Paul had to be on the creek at around 1 to catch the second trout and after 1:15 to catch the other one. So he couldn't have been a half mile away murdering Halford."

"Vindication," Paul snapped, looking at Julie. "And you always said my fishing was a waste."

"Wouldn't just being with someone have been a simpler alibi? Only you could use a trout," she snapped back.

Sid was ecstatic. "Paul, that was brilliant. As Aristotle said, 'The mind leaps while the body walks.' Now just tell us who did it and I can go fishing."

"I haven't the vaguest idea."

Everyone seemed disappointed, but Sid couldn't pass up the opportunity for melodrama. "Well, I intend to continue this investigation until we find the murderer if it takes us clear through moose season."

"Sheriff," Alexandrea said, pointing at Julie, "I think you should ask that girl a few questions." Tups put his arm around the older woman and nodded.

Julie flushed. "Sid, I don't know what the aging star of stage, screen and boudoir is talking about."

"Oh you don't, don't you, Miss?" Alexandrea said. "I wouldn't make any loose bedroom cracks if I were you. You were going to meet Frederick down on the creek after lunch. We all heard you say so."

Gossip-mongers all, the whole group became immediately interested.

"What's she talking about, Julie?" Paul asked.

"I don't know," she answered curtly.

(continued on page 241)

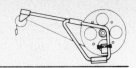

WHAT WE LOOKED FOR IN QUALITY

Besides the general qualification of good construction, trolling and saltwater gear should be extra-tough and simple to operate. Since the big and the deep are often synonymous, anglers don't have time for finicky gear. Everything on this equipment is designed simply and functionally. No frills, thank you.

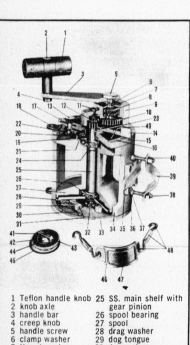

1 Teflon handle knob	25 SS. main shelf with
2 knob axle	gear pinion
3 handle bar	26 spool bearing
4 creep knob	27 spool
5 handle screw	28 drag washer
6 clamp washer	29 dog tongue
7 thrust washer	30 dog spring
8 handle bearing	31 dog
9 bridge assembly	32 shelf bearing
10 main gear	33 left side plate
11 adjusting screw	34 main housing
12 shelf bearing	35 reel stand
13 click button	36 stand screw
14 eccentric cam lever	37 rod clamp screw
15 right side plate	38 rod clamp screw
16 post screw	39 rod clamp
17 click adjuster	40 rod clamp screw
18 harness lug	41 adjusting screw
19 click	42 dial
20 click tongue	43 wing nut
21 eccentric cam	44 adjuster head
22 click spring	45 threader adjuster
23 SS. main shelf with	46 leather spacer
great pinion	47 rod brace
24 spool bearing	48 rod brace

PUCCI GLADIATOR

top of the line

Reels

GLADIATOR. Made in Italy, the Gladiator Reels, imported by Pucci, are sold in 2½-0, 4-0, 6-0, 9-0 and 12-0 sizes. They have four sets of ball bearings, a calibrated drag for exacting pressure, a marvelously large handle and are built up from solid aluminum. The three smaller models have a 3:1 gear ratio and the bigger pair have ratios of 2½:1. Top-quality stuff popular in Europe.

HARDY SILEX. The Hardy Silex has been around since 1896 and remains a favorite among equipment-conscious English trollers after big salmon or pike. It is a superb piece of gear and very simple. It has an exposed polished rim which can be palmed when casting or used as a hand brake. Better than anything else in its class.

HEDDON. The Heddon line of trolling reels for salt or heavy duty freshwater are well-made and able to do the job. Models 409, 499 and 445 are freespool. All six Heddon trollers are equipped with large star drags, have large capacities without much extra weight and are sturdily constructed. While Heddon is primarily known for lighter weight equipment, these are very adequate for the job.

KENCOR. The Kencor line of Drum trolling reels are a good value. They range in size from model 810 with a capacity of almost 300 yards of 25-pound test to the Model 950, their granddaddy, which holds 350 yards of 40-pound test mono or 450 yards of 30-pound dacron. The reels are stainless steel, free spool, have oil ports, oversized handles and anti-backlash mechanisms. All in all they have the features usually associated

In genial Spring, beneath the quiv'ring shade,
When cooling vapours breathe along the mead,
The patient fisher takes his silent stand,
Intent, his angle trembling in his hand:
With looks unmov'd, he hopes the scaly breed,
And eyes the dancing cork and bending reed.
POPE, *Windsor Forest*, 1. 135.

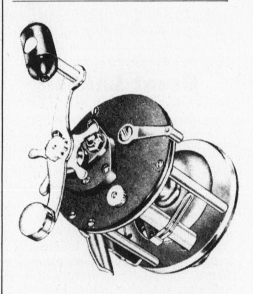

HEDDON

HARDY SILEX

top of the line

with more expensive brands and are available in any size the aspiring big game angler — salt or fresh — will need.

MITCHELL 600. The Mitchell 600 series of trolling-casting reels are reasonably priced machinery that will do the job. With such features as a free spool, indexed star drag to allow you to replace exact tension quickly, self enclosed lubricating parts and oversized handles. The 622 and 624 are basically trolling reels (no handle counterbalances) and the 600A and the 600AP are made for casting. Good line capacity and very good corrosion proof casings on all models. One to seriously consider.

PENN SEA SCAMP. An inexpensive, serviceable reel for the troller. No frills on the 10-ounce reel but it does have an antireverse and takes 150 yards of No. 36 nylon. Has a decent-sized handle and will do the basic job especially for the youngster or beginner.

PENN INTERNATIONALS. This old, respected name in salt water reels has come out with a line of deluxe models called the International. They're available in sizes from 2½/0 to a gargantuan 10/0 with a capacity of 1200 yards of 1200 pound test line. Cleanly designed, with a lever-controlled drag for easy setting, ball bearings, stainless steel one-piece pinion and spool shaft and brass rod clamps — among other things. The models are matched to IFGA line classes for the record seeker. Well-made products. Penn also continues to produce their Senator line of salt water reels as well as the other lines which have given them a solid, enduring reputation. Their time-tested equipment is the choice of many dedicated salt water buffs who don't like mechanical errors or frills.

A Guide to Great Lakes Tackle

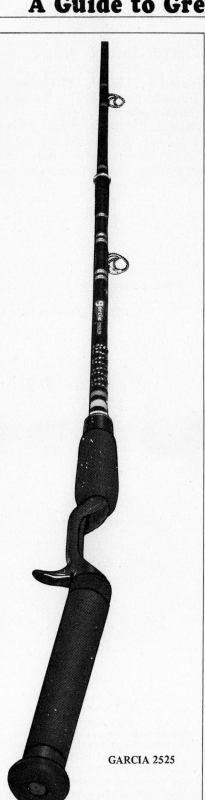

GARCIA 2525

(continued from page 237)

50 to 75 yards of line and still exert some control over a wild fish.

There are many different lure types used for river fishing but the all-time favorites would be the Flatfish, Tadpolly, Mepps spinner, Okie Drifter, Heddon Deep Diving River Runt Spook, River Runt, Little Dig and a variety of flies such as the Orange or Red P. M. Special, Babine Special, Platte River Special, Betsie Special, Richey's Platte River Pink and Dr. Rex. Live baits for trout and steelhead include spawn bag, wigglers (larvae of the mayfly), minnows, nightcrawlers, garden worms and hellgrammites.

Since much of the spawning run fishing is done strictly by wading, a quality pair of waders is necessary to keep your backside dry. I use a pair of Marathon rubber chest waders with felt soles. They have served the purpose for me wherever I've gone. Smooth rocks, clay, ledge rocks, large boulders and the like are taken in stride.

One piece of equipment I heartily recommend for the wading fisherman is a Stearns life preserver. I own one of their fishing vest models and it offers a certain peace of mind while wading. It also affords plenty of small pocket space for those odds and ends most fishermen carry on the river.

Landing nets are commonly used on both the open expanses of the Great Lakes and also on tributary streams where trout and salmon come to spawn. For lake fishing I prefer a Grizzly or Ed Cummings landing net made from linear striated polyethylene mesh. This type of bag is not subject to mildew and will not rot like cotton nets. I prefer a net with a six foot handle for Great Lakes fishing and one with an 18 inch handle for close-in work on a stream.

Choosing tackle for Great Lakes trout and salmon is a bit like choosing a husband or wife. It can be done quite easily, but you have to live with the results. Choose equipment wisely with a thought to the tackle's eventual use and you shouldn't go wrong.

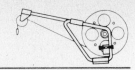

top of the line

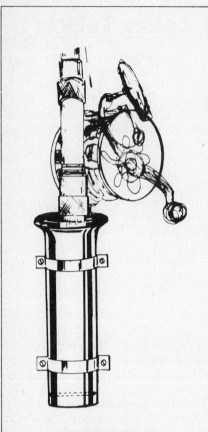

CAPT. JOE MENNEN'S ROD HOLSTER

Capt. Joe Mennen has a Hands-Free Fishing Rod Holster that's a convenient accessory for the angler who wants to haul a big fish out of the water or who's fishing in a place where the rod can't be put down. Made of PVC plastic, it has a weatherproof strap and buckle and can be attached to you, a pole or a piling, leaving both your hands free.

PFLUEGER. The Pflueger Sal-Trout and Pakron are trolling reels adapted to wire line. They've been around for a long time. Not that reels this simple have any bugs to iron out. Anyway, the Pakron, at 22 ounces and a capacity for 400 yards of 45-pound test monel wire, is the bigger of the pair. The Sal-Trout weighs in at 14 ounces and will take 275 yards of 45-pound monel. The Pakron's handle is attached to the spool. The Sal-Trout's handle comes out from the spool frame. Good basic stuff.

MITCHELL 600

PFLUEGER REELS

MAC-JAC

The Mac-Jac company of Muskegon has come up with a line of clever accessories designed for the troller who wants complete control. Their down-rigger will release baits at pre-selected depths for the right temperature. Mac-Jac also sells the rod holder, cocoon-ball weight and a release that snaps off when a fish hits. These component parts are sold separately but work very well together.

Where the puddle is shallow the weakfish
   stay
To drift along with the current's flow;
To take the tide as it moves each day
With the idle ripples that come and go.
GRANTLAND RICE, *Ballade of the Gamefish.*

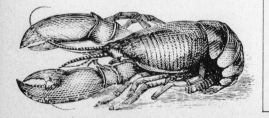

"And ete the olde fisshe,
and leve the yonge,
Though't they moore towgh be
upon the tongue."

Piers of Fulham

THE LAST HATCH
A FISHING MYSTERY
HARMON HENKIN

(continued from page 237)

"Well, I can explain it for you, young man," Alexandrea said. "Frederick had seen her around town a few times and was . . . interested. He invited her out for the weekend." Her voice turned feline and conspiratorial. "Everyone knew about Frederick's weakness for pretty little things. He liked to say that next to pan-fried cutthroat he liked country-fried fillies best."

Tups and Dun tittered.

"Hush up!" Sid bellowed. "Get on with the story."

"Anyway. Despite all her airs, she's no innocent. Why, I bet she took sex education in school."

"And probably failed," Paul said quietly.

"As I was saying," Alexandrea gushed, "our little groupie knew the score but came out this morning anyway. At lunch Frederick invited her to his room at four for some . . . entertainment. She got on her high horse and yelled that he was a filthy old man and that she'd just as soon coil up with a rattlesnake. He just laughed and said that after her diet of McDonald's hamburgers it was about time she tried steak. Frederick never meant any harm with that kind of repartee. It was just part of his charm. But she got madder and said she'd see him dead before he'd lay a hand on her. Then he said he was going to fish the mouth of the creek and if she'd care to meet him, he'd care to have her. She stormed out of the room and said she might see him there but not for the reason he thought. That's the last we saw of her until Andrew brought her back to the house."

"That's right," Dun chimed. "When I found Miss Julie she was climbing in her Volkswagen."

"What about all this, Julie?" Sid asked.

"It's all more or less true. But I didn't have killing in mind. I went down to the pool thinking to push him in. The stinking rat —"

"Don't speak badly of the dead, dear," Belle chirped.

"He was dead years ago. Anyway, I wanted to tell him exactly what I thought of him. And I wanted to take one last look at this place before it turned into a trailer court. I went to the pool, couldn't find him and took a long walk to cool off. Dun found me as I was going home."

"I guess that does it, sheriff," Schielbacht said, standing. "Can we go now? I'm supposed to fish Henry's Fork tonight at West Yellowstone

(continued on page 255)

Rods

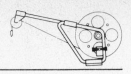

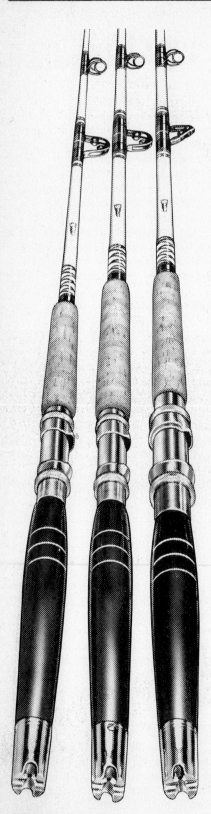

top of the line

IFGA 20, 30 and 40 pound categories. The Big Gamers can be had from IGFA 12-pound class to IGFA 130-pound class and are equipped up to 30 pounds with AFTCo double roller stripping guides and five other AFTCo roller guides. From 50 pounds upward the rods have Mildrum roller guides. All models have detachable butts and a machined reel seat.

GARCIA CONOLONS. The Garcia Conolon line of saltwater rods, named after the earliest and most reputable of American glass rod makers, represents the top of their line. The saltwater spinners range in size from 7 feet, 3 inch medium light rods for lightish casting to 11 feet, 8 inches for surfing around. The spinning rods have stainless steel guides — though not enough of them — and ceramic tip tops. The Conolons also come in conventional saltwater models from 8 feet to 10 feet, 9 inches for lines up to 50-pound test.

GARCIA SKIPPER'S SPECIAL. This line represents Garcia's collaboration with the renowned Conolon Company (the glass blank makers). They're medium and heavy-action saltwater spinning rods available from 6 feet, 8 inches to 8 feet for lines from 12 to 40 pounds and an assortment of actions. They have Varmac brass reel seats with double locks, neoprene handles and foregrips and enough guides.

HARDY MARK II TOURNEY SURFCASTER. Hardy Brothers, once thought of solely as a source of fly-casting tackle, is actually a good provider of saltwater stuff, including some excellent surf rods. There are three models of Mark II Tourney Surfcasters: the 2-4 at 11 feet for anglers who cast less than 4 ounces; a 4-6 at 11 feet, 9 inches for intermediate weights, a 12¼-footer and a 6-9 for anglers who cast in that ounce

GARCIA
BIG GAME SERIES
RODS

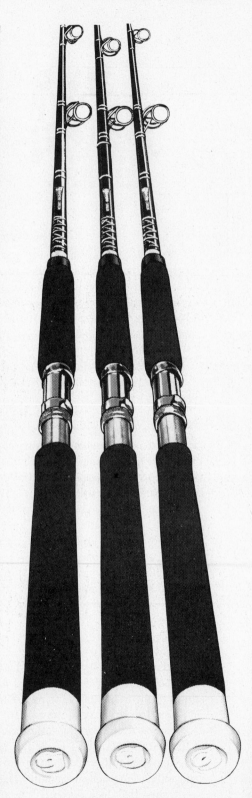

GARCIA SKIPPER'S SPECIAL

top of the line

range. These are well-put-up rods with detachable ring butts, hollow glass spigot ferrules and stainless steel fittings with snap-on sliding reel seats. Nice rods, like the other Hardy saltwater casters.

KENCOR. A serviceable, budget-priced line of surf rods is available from the Kencor company. Available in 10-, 9-, and 12½-foot models. They put out a line of steelhead rods, as well, with smaller stripper guides but in the same sizes. These are nicely put-up rods that will suffice, especially for the novice.

KODIAK. A reasonably priced saltwater boat rod is the Kodiak, made up in northern Michigan. Available in 6-, 6 1/2- and 7-foot lengths, some of the models have detachable wood handles for carrying convenience, chromed brass reel seats and stainless guides. A 7½-foot spinning boat rod is also available. It has spiral wire guides and a wood foregrip. Okay buys for the neophyte.

KODIAK REGULATION TACKLE. If you plan to break a big-game saltwater record but don't have much money, you might get started with a Kodiak Regulation Tackle rod. It comes with brass-chrome locking reel seats, a universal gimbal for holding the rod up mechanically and five heavy-duty Aftco roller guides. Available in all the major classes from 30-pound test through 130-pound plus unlimited.

KODIAK SPINNERS. Another one of the good rod buys from Kodiak is their line of saltwater spinners and salmon-steelhead rods. The saltwater spinners range from 8 to 11 feet, have fast tapers and soft tips, which are helpful in casting bait. They have stainless steel guides, anodized aluminum reel seats and come in two pieces. The salmon-steelhead models range from 7 to 8½ feet and,

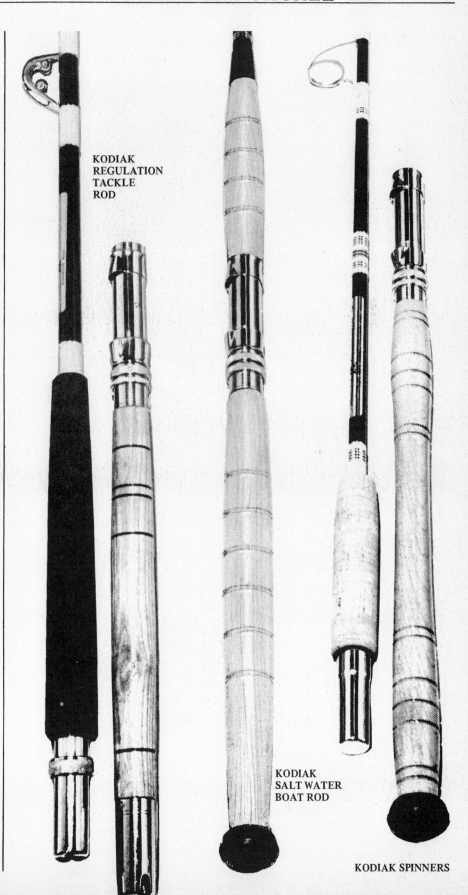

KODIAK REGULATION TACKLE ROD

KODIAK SALT WATER BOAT ROD

KODIAK SPINNERS

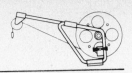

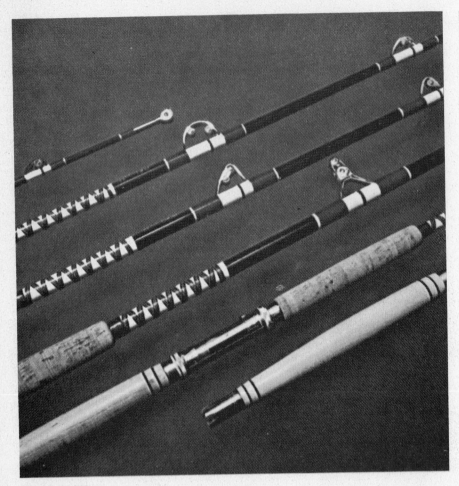

MAGNUFLEX

Tide Timer

Marine Model

HAMMACHER-SCHLEMMER TIDE TIMER

Hammacher-Schlemmer is offering a very nice tide timer that tells the number of hours to the next high or low tide on the Atlantic coast. Available in a home model or a smaller brass marine model for your boat. Wall or free-standing mounts available, too. Works on a "C" battery.

top of the line

except for two models with casting guides, the others are put up much like the saltwater spinners. A minor investment that works.

***

MAGNUFLEX. Magnuflex's trolling rods, made in Miami where they know about such things, is a line of three 6½ foot rods made from very solid glass blanks. Very elegant. Model T130 has good quality mildrum guides and an Aftco roller tip while the other two models have Aftco guides. The Deluxe model, T100, has heavy duty guides and all have detachable butts. They are also available to handle IFGA line categories from 20 to 130 pound test line. A very decent rod for the heavy duty saltwater buff.

***

POMPANETTE. Serious ocean rods for the serious angler. At prices that begin over $150 and range up to $450 for a curved butt rod in the 130-pound line category, they aren't anyone's beginning tackle choice. All models, from the six-pound spinner (geared for the flats, etc.) to the monster sizes, have anodized aluminum butts, hardy wrappings and heavy duty reel seats. All except the 6-pound test model have roller guides and roller tips. Dream on!

***

SOUTH BEND. South Bend produces a reasonably priced (for this type of rod) line of IFGA specified rods for heavy duty saltwater use in 20-30, 30-50 and 50-80 pound test line categories. These rods are equipped with quality AFTCo roller guides, double-locking reel seat, chrome-plated butt, hardwood handle and cork foregrip. One to be considered by the budget-minded Captain Ahab type. Better ones available but not in this range.

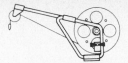
top of the line

SOUTH BEND — HARNELL.
South Bend is now marketing the
famed Harnell "double built" (which
Cross bamboo fly rods used to boast
about long ago). These rods hold
more world records with the International Game Fish Association than
any other brand. Depending on the
class, which goes all the way from 20
pounds to the 130-pound unlimited
class, they bear either AFTCo or Mildrum roller guides. They have lock-
top reel seats, Neuvo foregrips and
black-and-white stained handles plus
stainless steel guides — natch. Something for the serious saltwater angler
wishing to see his or her name on the
angling hall of fame marquee. South
Bend also markets some other Harnell heavy duty trolling tackle for
any big-game angling purpose.

SURF ROD BELT

Cabela's sells a nice, heavy leather rod
belt to hold your surf rod in place. Saves
body indentation and the styrene cup is
unaffected by salt. Well-made.

THERMAL FINDER

Well, here's an interesting accessory for
the confirmed troller. It's like an inverted kite designed for use with boats
trolling at 3 mph or less and with the
thinnest diameter line possible. The
Thermal Finder will dive, directed by its
thermostat, to the depth that your
chosen quarry feels most at home. It
works with a sensor spring that responds
to temperature change by adjusting its
control vanes. Well worth a try.

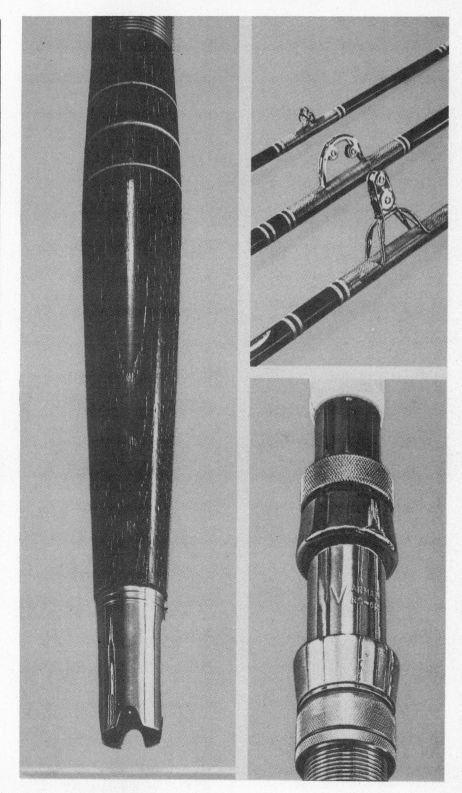

POMPANETTE

SOUTH BEND-HARNELL

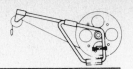

THE OFFSHORE ROD

Because of the cost of blue water trolling, don't cut corners

By Mark Sosin

Blue water trollers have favored a basic rod design for many years and, season after season, it tends to serve their needs. Standardization came through the International Game Fish Association (IGFA) in the form of line test classifications for record purposes and also in specific rules that say the tip of the rod cannot be less than 50 inches and the butt may not exceed 27 inches from a point directly beneath the center of the reel.

Almost every fisherman learns very quickly that it takes a certain rod action to properly handle a given breaking strength of line, so rods have been created to conform to the IGFA pound-test classes of 6, 12, 20, 30, 50, 80 and 130. In fact, the rods are actually referred to as a 30-pound rod, a 50-pound rod, etc. You must remember, however, that the manufacturer is merely trying to tell you that he thinks the rod will withstand the rigors of that test line.

When you get down to basics, you will find that the action that one maker labels as 30-pound test, another would call 50-pound. That's one way of competing on a price basis. Within any class, there are a number of different actions and some custom rod builders make two or three models labeled a light, medium, and heavy action.

The cost in a trolling rod is centered around the type of reel seat, the number of guides and their quality and the material from which the butt is made. A well-constructed trolling rod will be made from a first-class blank, wrapped with top-grade roller guides (at least five) and a roller tip-top. The reel seat will be machined instead of having the hoods stamped and the butt will be aluminum or fiberglass. A wooden butt is not as strong, will take a beating in a rod holder, and could expand or contract based on the amount of moisture in the air.

It pays to buy a good rod and not cut corners. Offshore fishing is simply too expensive to take chances on tackle failure and the fish are going to be larger than you'll find in most bays and estuaries so the tackle is going to be put to the test. Unless you intend to fish for giant tuna, big marlin, sharks, or swordfish (assuming you can find a swordfish for which to fish), consider a 30-pound outfit as standard. It will handle everything from sailfish and white marlin to dolphin and whatever else you might find at sea. Veteran fishermen can do wonders with a 30-pound outfit against the huskiest denizens and, in a pinch, you can slug it out, too.

Most fishermen want to overgun and they don't reap the maximum pleasure from the fish they do hook. On a 30-pound rig, you'll get your money's worth and it's fun to fish. Depending on your skill, you can also go lighter as you gain experience if you choose to do so.

For the biggest fish, you'll be fishing 80-pound or 130-pound tackle. Fifty-pound is a good mid-range for medium-

(continued on next page)

Tackle tips for the saltwater angler

By Nelson Bryant

Nearly 45 years ago when my father took me on my first surf fishing expedition — the prey was bluefish, the place Martha's Vineyard Island, Massachusetts — more than half of the men on the beach were devotees of the heave-and-haul technique.

Coiling the heavy tarred line on the beach just above the wash of the waves, those old-timers slung their six- and eight-ounce lead jigs an incredible distance to sea, or so it seemed to a lad of nine.

I tried heaving and hauling myself at that time but I was too small to get much zip into the heave and taking pity on me my father made me a Calcutta bamboo rod — the entire cane, as it grew in the forest, was used — and to it he lashed a revolving spool reel, it might

(continued on page 248)

The Edward vom Hofe & Company's "Universal Star" reel for tarpon, tuna and other saltwater beasts. Handmade, it sold in 1919 for $57.50 to $75 for line capacities of between 300 and 500 yards.

THE OFFSHORE ROD

(continued from preceding page)

sized marlin, tuna, and sharks. If you owned a 30-pound outfit and an 80, you could fish almost anywhere for any species and hope to compete.

Study the rod carefully before you buy and especially the action. It will seem stout to you if you're not familiar with this type of tackle and you'll think that it can lift a cabin cruiser off the bottom, but don't let that fool you. Some of the rod actions are too soft to troll a big enough bait or to set the hook when you drop back on a strike. Without power, you're going to be at a disadvantage in pumping a fish up from the depths or pulling it toward you from several hundred yards away.

Graphite is slowly making inroads into this type of tackle, because it offers lightness not found in glass. It is a stiffer material as well and that means you can fight a fish better because the rod has a quicker response and doesn't travel as far as glass to generate the same power. This also helps in setting the hook.

Even if you don't own your own boat, it makes sense to buy your own offshore rods and take good care of them. Too often, boat owners or charter skippers are careless about their tackle combinations and it could cost you the fish of a lifetime.

Tom Martin Creek

I walked down one morning from Steelhead, following the Klamath River that was high and murky and had the intelligence of a dinosaur. Tom Martin Creek was a small creek with cold, clear water and poured out of a canyon and through a culvert under the highway and then into the Klamath.

I dropped a fly in a small pool just below where the creek flowed out of the culvert and took a nine-inch trout. It was a good-looking fish and fought all over the top of the pool.

Even though the creek was very small and poured out of a steep brushy canyon filled with poison oak, I decided to follow the creek up a ways because I liked the feel and motion of the creek.

I liked the name, too.

Tom Martin Creek.

It's good to name creeks after people and then later to follow them for a while seeing what they have to offer, what they know and have made of themselves.

But that creek turned out to be a real son-of-a-bitch. I had to fight it all the God-damn way: brush, poison oak and hardly any good places to fish, and sometimes the canyon was so narrow the creek poured out like water from a faucet. Sometimes it was so bad that it just left me standing there, not knowing which way to jump.

You had to be a plumber to fish that creek.

After that first trout I was alone in there. But I didn't know it until later.

"Tom Martin Creek" excerpted from *Trout Fishing in America* by Richard Brautigan.   ©1976 by Richard Brautigan. Reprinted by permission of DELACORTE PRESS/SEYMOUR LAWRENCE.

SQUID BAG

Abercrombie and Fitch offers a surf squid bag made from heavy duty canvas with metal inserts. It has ten compartments for large casting lures, and six outside compartments for whatever. Comes with a shoulder strap for easy carriage.

FATHOM MASTER

This is another one of those basic aids to the hard-core troller who wants to be able to control the depth his bait or lure is chugging along at. The Fathom Master has the same sort of drag-bait control system as a Penn reel and when used with Fathomtrol weights enables the angler to get down to the level of his quarry. Well-made from non-corrosive parts, it works fine in salt or fresh water.

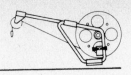

SALTWATER TACKLE

(continued from page 246)

have been a trolling reel by Vom Hofe. I could cast about 55 yards with that outfit and that was usually enough.

After World War II, the spinning outfit and the four-wheeled drive vehicle joined to create an incredible boom in surf fishing that shows no sign of abating. The Jeep, and similar vehicles that followed it, enabled men to cover a stretch of beach in minutes where a similar trek on foot would have taken hours. And when you walked two miles down the beach to a favorite hole or a salt pond opening, you had to limit your catch to what you could carry back. You could always tell whether a striper fisherman had been successful in those days, for the tails of fish over 20 pounds left drag marks in the sand.

The spinning rig — which most surf anglers use today in preference to the conventional or revolving spool rig — enables a beginner to learn how to cast well enough to catch fish in a single afternoon. The conventional reel — with which greater distance is possible with the heavier lures — takes a good deal of practice to master, especially when night fishing.

Whether conventional or spinning, the beginning surf angler would do well to start with a rod about 9 feet long rated for 20-pound test line. The reel should be able to hold 250 yards of that line.

If you have to travel to reach your fishing, you might want to invest in a two-piece rod. Garcia is producing a superb line, called Custom Deluxe, of two-piece conventional and spinning surf rods. The two-piece rod, of course, can be locked inside the average automobile and is easier to handle when traveling by airplane.

Whatever rod you get, don't skimp on cost and make sure that the tip-top and at least the next two guides on down toward the butt are of some

Don't skimp on the cost of the rod and make sure the tip-top and guides are of a super-hard material.

GARCIA CUSTOM DELUXE
CONVENTIONAL AND
SPINNING SURF RODS

(continued on next page)

SALTWATER TACKLE

(continued from preceding page)

super-hard material so that the line won't cut grooves in them.

Monofilament line may be used with conventional gear, but some anglers prefer braided Dacron.

Many rods presumably designed for surf fishing are too short from butt to reel. A rule of thumb for this length is to pick a rod with a butt as long as your shirt sleeve. And if the butt is a little long, it makes no difference, because you simply tuck the extra length between your legs when reeling in. This same 20-pound outfit should be able to handle lures from an ounce and a half to four ounces.

Penn and Garcia make excellent conventional and spinning reels for surf fishing, and the top of the Daiwa line is also very good.

There are dozens of lures available for the person seeking striped bass or blues, but a basic surf fishing assortment would include jigs of various sizes, such as those made by Hopkins and Kastmaster, a good number of surface swimming plugs (for big stripers), popping plugs (mostly for blues, but sometimes for stripers) and sub-surface swimmers and darters. Lupo, Atom and Gibbs are brands to look for in plugs.

The popping plug, which is retrieved at high speed as it is jerked, or

PENN'S 704 SALTWATER REEL

"popped" along the surface of the water is easiest to handle with a spinning reel because it retrieves faster than most conventional reels. One can get a sore wrist from retrieving poppers with a revolving spool reel, but there are some being manufactured that offer a faster takeup than did their predecessors.

Avoid bargain monofilament lines, but remember that just because a line of a certain pound test may be as strong as a line of heavier diameter, it is not necessarily better. Small-diameter lines cast farther, but a nick or an abrasion in them results in proportionately greater weakening.

DIAL-A-CRICKET

Stop your crickets from escaping and ditto for grasshoppers with this Dial-A-Cricket. Load it with the insects, then turn the lid and one bug at a time comes out. Has a tote strap for carrying ease. The plastic unit will float for two minutes. Convenient.

SEA SKEE

The Sea Skee is a useful accessory for the troller who wants to keep his offering away from the boat. The movement of the current and the wake keeps the Skee — and your lure — away from the boat and out in the water where it belongs. It's designed to work in seas up to five feet. You fill it with water of varying quantities depending on the type of tackle you use it with. Can be worked on either port or starboard sides.

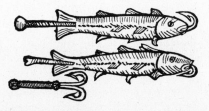

Methods of preparing a bait in 19th-Century Britain: the double and single hook.

GAMEFISH: YELLOWFIN TUNA

NAMES
Allison tuna, California yellowfin tuna. *(Thunnus albacares)*

DISTRIBUTION
The yellowfin tuna is found in waters throughout the world. In the Pacific, it is found all along the coast of California and Mexico. In the Atlantic, it is found as far north as New Jersey.

DESCRIPTION
The yellowfin tuna is dark or steel blue on the back with silver sides. The fins are yellowish in color and at times an indistinct yellow band runs from the head to the tail. The pectoral fins are longer than those of the bluefin tuna.

SIZE
The yellowfin tuna is smaller than the bluefin tuna. It usually averages less than 100 pounds and seldom reaches a weight of over 500 pounds.

HABITAT
Like the bluefin tuna, the yellowfin is a fish of open waters. It does, however, prefer a warmer range. The yellowfin is considered a Pacific fish and does not seem to migrate as much as the bluefin.

FEEDING HABITS
The diet of the yellowfin tuna is much the same as the bluefin tuna. They feed on all varieties of fish and squid.

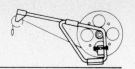

specifications

REELS

BRAND-MODEL	WEIGHT (OZ.)	GEAR RATIOS	LINE (YD.) CAPACITY	DRAG
GLADIATOR				
Big Game Fishing Reels				
2½/0			800, 20 lb.	
4/0			700, 30 lb.	
6/0			650, 50 lb.	
9/0			750, 80 lb.	
12/0			800, 130 lb.	
HARDY				
Silex			150, 18 lb.	
Longstone			400, 20 lb.	adjustable
HEDDON				
Trolling Reels (salt or fresh)				
409	.20	3:1	300, 20 lb.	star
499	.14	3:1	250, 15 lb.	star
445	.20	3:1	300, 20 lb.	star
450	.19	3:1	200, 36 lb.	
422	.22	2.5:1	300, 30 lb.	star
421	.18	3:1	240, 30 lb.	star·
KENCOR				
Drum Trolling Reels				
810	.12	3:1	390, 15 lb.	disc
810M	.13.5	3:1	280, 25 lb.	disc
810MF	.12.5	3:1	280, 25 lb.	disc
820	.12	3:1	400, 25 lb.	disc
820M	.15	3:1	410, 25 lb.	disc
820MF	.14	3:1	410, 25 lb.	disc
840M	.22	3.2:1	450, 30 lb.	disc
844M	.23	3.2:1	240, 30 lb.	disc
940	.26.5	3:1	350, 40 lb.	disc
830MH		.5:1	390, 30 lb.	disc
830M		.5:1		disc
950	.27	3.5:1	350, 40 lb.	disc
800		.5:1		disc
110	.12.5	3:1	300, 12 lb.	disc
110M	.13	3:1	320, 12 lb.	disc
130M	.17	3:1	380, 25 lb.	disc
140M	.18	3:1	420, 25 lb.	disc
160M	.22	3:1	400, 30 lb.	disc
PENN				
International (game fishing)				
20		3.5:1	1200, 12 lb.	full floating disc
30		3.5:1	800, 20 lb.	
50		3:1	600, 50 lb.	
80		2.7:1	750, 80 lb.	
80W		2.7:1	950, 80 lb.	
130		1.6:1	1200, 80 lb.	

BRAND-MODEL	WEIGHT (OZ.)	GEAR RATIOS	LINE (YD.) CAPACITY	DRAG
130H		2.1:1	1200, 80 lb.	
Senator Reels (light tackle)				
110 1/0	.18	3:1	275, 20 lb.	penn
111 2/0	.22	2.25:1	425, 20 lb.	
112 3/0	.26	2.25:1	375, 30 lb.	
Special Senators (game fish)				
112H 3/0	.25	3.7:1	375, 30 lb.	multiple brake lining discs
113H 4/0	.34	3.25:1	575, 30 lb.	
114H 6/0	.52	2.8:1	525, 50 lb.	
Senator Reels (big game)				
4/0	.30	2:1	800, 20 lb.	brake lining discs
6/0	.48	2.1:1	1050, 20 lb.	
9/0	.64	2.5:1	1075, 30 lb.	
10/0	.100	2:1	675, 80 lb.	
12/0	.110	2:1	780, 80 lb.	
14/0	.162	1.6:1	750, 130 lb.	
16/0	.174	1.6:1	950, 130 lb.	
Super Mariners (for wire, lead core, nylon, dacron lines)				
49	.29	3.5:1	250, 30 lb.	star (or free spool)
49M	.32	3.5:1	350, 30 lb.	star
149	.24.5	2.1:1	250, 30 lb.	star
349	.37	2.33:1	350, 30 lb.	star
349H	.37	3.25:1	350, 30 lb.	star
349HC	.37	3.25:1	350, 30 lb.	star
Long Beach Reels (deep sea, bay bottom)				
60	.19.5	2.5:1	250, 36 lb.	star
65	.20.5	2.5:1	300, 36 lb.	star
66	.26	2.5:1	300, 36 lb.	star
67	.27	2.5:1	250, 50 lb.	star
68	.29	2.5:1	300, 50 lb.	star
Monofil Level Wind Reels				
9S	.11	3:1	225, 15 lb.	star
9MS	.12	3:1	275, 15 lb.	star
109S	.11	3.75:1	225, 15 lb.	star
109MS	.12	3.75:1	275, 15 lb.	star
209S	.18.5	3:1	300, 20 lb.	star
209MS	.19.5	3:1	350, 20 lb.	star
Super Peer (ocean trolling, bottom fishing, fresh water game fishing)				
309M	.26	3:1	300, 36 lb.	star
Jigmaster				
500L			275, 36 lb.	brake lining drag
Squidders (tournament)				
140	.17.5	3.33:1	325, 20 lb.	
145	.16.5	3.33:1	275, 20 lb.	
146	.16	3.33:1	250, 12 lb.	
140M	.18	3.33:1	400, 20 lb.	
145M	.17	3.33:1	325, 20 lb.	
146M	.16.5	3.33:1	350, 12 lb.	
Surfmaster (squidding, pier, bridge, jetty fishing)				
100	.16	3:1	125, 36 lb.	star
150	.17.5	3:1	150, 36 lb.	star

specifications

BRAND-MODEL	WEIGHT (OZ.)	GEAR RATIOS	LINE (YD.) CAPACITY	DRAG
200	18	3:1	175, 36 lb.	star
250	20	3:1	250, 36 lb.	star
100M	17	3:1	150, 36 lb.	star
150M	18	3:1	200, 36 lb.	star
200M	19.5	3:1	225, 36 lb.	star
250M	22.5	3:1	300, 36 lb.	star
Silver Beach (surf and bottom fishing)				
99	22.5	3:1	200, 36 lb.	star
Baymaster (light tackle)				
180S	12		200, 10 lb.	
180MS	12.5		250, 20 lb.	
Beachmaster (all-around fishing)				
155	14		175, 36 lb.	star
160	13		150, 36 lb.	star
155M	16		225, 36 lb.	star
160M	14.5		200, 36 lb.	star
Delmar (all-around fishing)				
285	17	2.3:1	200, 36 lb.	star
285M	18	2.3:1	250, 36 lb.	star
Sea Boy (all-around fishing)				
85	16	2.3:1	200, 36 lb.	star
Sea Scamp (fresh-salt)				
78	10		150, 36 lb.	
Sea Hawk (fresh-salt)				
77	9		125, 36 lb.	

PFLUEGER

2800 Series

		4.7:1	250, 12 lb.	star

RYOBI

Adventure Series

SD-101	34.4	3.4:1	655, 33 lb.	star
SD-103	31.6	3.4:1	405, 33 lb.	star
40	3.2	4.1:1	196, 9 lb.	

RODS

Brand-Model	Length	Lure Weight	No. Pieces	No. Guides	Material
ABERCROMBIE & FITCH					
A & F Graphite Boat Rods					
20-046	5' 6"				graphite
20-047	5' 8"				graphite
20-048	5' 8"				graphite
20-049	5' 8"				graphite
A & F Graphite Big Game Trolling Rods					
20-003 (class 20)					graphite
20-004 (class 30)					graphite
20-005 (class 50)					graphite
20-006 (class 80)					graphite
A & F Graphite Surf Rods					
20-007	9'	¾-2			graphite
20-002	10' 6"	1-3			graphite
20-001	11' 6"	2-4			graphite
DAIWA					
TTW Series					
102	6' 6"		1		glass
200	6' 9"		1		glass
500	8'		1		glass
VIP Rods					
23	7'		2	8	glass
24	7' 6"		2	8	glass
25	8'		2	9	glass
730	7'		1	6	glass
Surf Sticks					
621-11	11'		3	4	glass
621-13	13'		3	4	glass
621-15	15'		4	5	glass
S-11	10' 6"		2	5	glass
S-12	11' 6"		2	5	glass
S-13	12' 6"		2	5	glass
Surf Spin Rods					
708DX	8'		2	5	glass
709DX	9'		2	5	glass
710DX	10'		2	5	glass
809DX	9'		2	5	glass
810DX	10'		2	5	glass
811DX	11' 6"		2	5	glass
813DX	13'		2	6	glass
Regal					
5313	7'		2	6	glass
5312D	6' 6"		2	5	glass
5313D	7'		2	6	glass
5323	7'		2	6	glass
5324	7' 6"		2	5	glass
5325	8'		2	4	glass
5329	10'		2	4	glass
5423	7'		1	5	glass
5463	7'		1	6	glass
5622	6' 6"		1	5	glass
5623	7'		1	4	glass
5624	7' 6"		1	4	glass
1500 Series					
1553	7'		1	6	glass
1523	7'		2	7	glass
1524	7' 6"		2	8	glass
1525	8'		2	8	glass
1595	8'		2	5	glass
1597	9'		2	5	glass
1599	10'		2	5	glass
1571	6'		1	5	glass
1572	6' 6"		1	5	glass
1573	7'		1	5	glass
1571RT	6'		1	5	glass
1572RT	6' 6"		1	5	glass

specifications

1000 Series

Brand-Model	Length	Lure Weight	No. Pieces	No. Guides	Material
1027	9'		2	5	glass

GARCIA

Mitchell Rods

Brand-Model	Length	Lure Weight	No. Pieces	No. Guides	Material
7107	7'	½-1½	1	5	glass
7136	7' 6"	¾-2	2	6	glass

Custom Deluxe Rods

Brand-Model	Length	Lure Weight	No. Pieces	No. Guides	Material
2142	7' 3"	.5/8-1 1/4	2	5	glass
2148	8'	.1-4	2	4	glass
2150	9'	.2½-8	2	4	glass
2157	10'	.2-6	2	5	glass
2155	10' 9"	.4-10	2	5	glass
2168	11' 8"	.3-8	2	5	glass

Skipper Special

Brand-Model	Length	Lure Weight	No. Pieces	No. Guides	Material
B573	6' 4"	.1-2½	1	5	glass
B574	6'10"	.1-3	1	6	glass
B572	6'10"	.1-2½		6	glass
B575	7'	.1½-4	1	6	glass
B577	7'	.¾-4	1	7	glass
B570	7'		1	5	glass

Big Game Trolling Rods

Brand-Model	Length	Lure Weight	No. Pieces	No. Guides	Material
R590 (class 12)				5	
R596 (class 20)				5	
R597 (class 30)				5	
R598 (class 50)				4	
R599 (class 80)				4	
R595 (class 130)				4	
WR570 (class 50)				4	

Wire Line Trolling Rods

Brand-Model	Length	Lure Weight	No. Pieces	No. Guides	Material
2566	6'		1	4	
2565	6' 8"		1	5	

Brown Rods

Brand-Model	Length	Lure Weight	No. Pieces	No. Guides	Material
2551	8'	½-2½	2	5	glass
2552	8' 6"	½-2½	2	5	glass
2572	9'	½-1	2	6	glass
2559	7' 8"	.3-5	1	5	glass
2571	9'	.1-4	2	7	glass
2553	9' 6"	.1-4	2	6	glass
2554	10'	.1-4½	2	7	glass
2573	11' 4"	.2-5	2	8	glass

Avocado Rods

Brand-Model	Length	Lure Weight	No. Pieces	No. Guides	Material
8267	8'	½-1¼	2	5	glass
8252	8' 6"	½=2½	2	5	glass
8271	9'	.1-4	2	6	glass
8254	10'	.1-3	2	7	glass
8255	7' 6"	½-4	2	6	glass
8293	6' 6"	.1¾-3½	1	4	glass

Blue Rods

Brand-Model	Length	Lure Weight	No. Pieces	No. Guides	Material
2656	7' 9"	.1-3	2	5	glass
2651	8' 6"	½-1½	2	5	glass
2653	7' 5"	.1-4	1	4	glass
2652	9'	.1-3	2	5	glass
2655	9' 6"	.1-3	2	6	glass
2654	10'	.1-4½	2	6	glass

Black Rods

Brand-Model	Length	Lure Weight	No. Pieces	No. Guides	Material
2877	5' 6"	.3¾-3½	1	3	solid glass
2876	6' 1"	.3¾-3½	1	3	solid glass
2888	7' 5"	.1-3	1	4	solid glass

HARDY

Brand-Model	Length	Lure Weight	No. Pieces	No. Guides	Material
Coastmaster	9'			2	glass

Saltwater Boat Rods (IGFA class)

Brand-Model	Length	Lure Weight	No. Pieces	No. Guides	Material
12 lb. extra light tip	7'		2	2	glass
20 lb. very light tip	7'		2	2	glass
30 lb. light tip	7'		2	2	glass
50 lb. medium tip	7'		2	2	glass
80 lb. heavy tip	7'		2	2	glass

Saltwater De-Luxe (made to special order for 12, 20, 30, 50 and 80 lb. IGFA class lines)

Mk. II Tourney Surfcasters

Brand-Model	Length	Lure Weight	No. Pieces	No. Guides	Material
	11'	.2-4	2		glass
	11' 9"	.4-6	2		glass
	12' 3"	.6-9	2		glass

Victor Surfcaster

Brand-Model	Length	Lure Weight	No. Pieces	No. Guides	Material
	12'	.3-6	2		glass

KENCOR

Longcast Surf Rods

Brand-Model	Length	Lure Weight	No. Pieces	No. Guides	Material
9H	9'		2		glass
10H	10'		2		glass
12XH	12' 5"		2		glass
209H	9'		2		glass
210H	10'		2		glass
212XH	12' 5"		2		glass

Longcast Three-Piece Rods

Brand-Model	Length	Lure Weight	No. Pieces	No. Guides	Material
311	11'		3		glass
313	13'		3		glass
315	15'		3		glass

KODIAC

Salt Water

Brand-Model	Length	Lure Weight	No. Pieces	No. Guides	Material
150	6'-6'6"		1	3	solid glass
160	7'-7'6"		1	4	solid glass
175	6'		1	3	solid glass
180	6' 6"		1	4	solid glass
185	6'		1	2	solid glass
190	6' 6"		1	3	solid glass

Tubular Saltwater Boat Rods

Brand-Model	Length	Lure Weight	No. Pieces	No. Guides	Material
3860	5' 6"		1	3	glass
3862	6' 6"		1	3	glass
3864	6'		1		glass
3865	6'		1		glass
3868	8'		1	5	glass

Regulation Tackle Rods

Brand-Model	Length	Lure Weight	No. Pieces	No. Guides	Material
3870 (class 30)	6' 6"			5	

specifications

Brand-Model	Length	Lure Weight	No. Pieces	No. Guides	Material
3875 (class 50)	6' 6"			.5	
3880 (class 80)	6' 6"			.5	
3885 (class 130)	6' 9"			.5	
3890 (class unlimited)	6' 9"			.5	

Salmon, Steelhead and Light Saltwater Rods

Brand-Model	Length	Lure Weight	No. Pieces	No. Guides	Material
3915C	8'		.2	.5	
3917C	8' 6"		.2	.5	

8000 Series

Brand-Model	Length	Lure Weight	No. Pieces	No. Guides	Material
8915	8'			.5	glass

Saltwater Solid Glass

Brand-Model	Length	Lure Weight	No. Pieces	No. Guides	Material
170	7' 6"		.1	.4	solid glass

Fast-Taper Saltwater Rods (with soft tip action)

Brand-Model	Length	Lure Weight	No. Pieces	No. Guides	Material
3940	8'		.2	.5	
3950	8'		.2	.6	
3951	8'		.2	.6	
3952	9'		.2	.6	
3953	9' 6"		.2	.6	
3954	.10'		.2	.6	
3955	.10' 6"		.2	.6	
3956	.11'		.2	.6	

Salmon, Steelhead and Light Saltwater Rod

Brand-Model	Length	Lure Weight	No. Pieces	No. Guides	Material
3700	7'		.1	.4	
3710	7'		.2	.4	
3720	7' 6"		.1	.4	
3815	7' 6"		.2	.4	
3915	8'		.2	.5	
3917	8' 6"		.2	.5	

MAGNUFLEX

Boat Rod Series 100

Brand-Model	Length	Lure Weight	No. Pieces	No. Guides	Material
	.5'-7'2"		.1		solid glass

Boat Rod Series 100

Brand-Model	Length	Lure Weight	No. Pieces	No. Guides	Material
	.5'-7'2"		.1		solid glass

Trolling Rods

Brand-Model	Length	Lure Weight	No. Pieces	No. Guides	Material
T130	6' 6"		.1		solid glass
T12	6' 6"		.1		solid glass
T58	6' 6"		.1		solid glass

Deluxe Trolling Rod Series T100

Brand-Model	Length	Lure Weight	No. Pieces	No. Guides	Material
	6' 6"		.1		solid glass

Series T20-30-50-80

Brand-Model	Length	Lure Weight	No. Pieces	No. Guides	Material
	6' 6"		.1		solid glass

IGFA Series

Brand-Model	Length	Lure Weight	No. Pieces	No. Guides	Material
Built to IGFA specifications.					glass

POMPANETTE

Brand-Model	Length	Lure Weight	No. Pieces	No. Guides	Material
30-lb. casting rod					
50-lb. casting rod					
80-lb. curved butt casting rod					
130-lb. curved butt casting rod					
6 lb. spinning rod					
12 lb. spinning rod					
20 lb. spinning rod					

SOUTH BEND

Classic IV

Brand-Model	Length	Lure Weight	No. Pieces	No. Guides	Material
C1-246-866	6' 6"				glass
D1-246-970	7'				

Classic III

Brand-Model	Length	Lure Weight	No. Pieces	No. Guides	Material
F1-243-870	7'		.2		glass
1-243-876	7' 6"		.2		glass
1-243-880	8'		.2		glass
1-243-890	9'		.2		glass

White Knight

Brand-Model	Length	Lure Weight	No. Pieces	No. Guides	Material
D1-229-370	7'			.4	glass
1-229-376	7' 6"			.4	glass
1-229-380	8'			.4	glass
1-229-390	9'			.5	glass

Outdoorsman Rods

Brand-Model	Length	Lure Weight	No. Pieces	No. Guides	Material
D1-833-276	7' 6"		.1	.4	glass
1-233-466	6' 6"		.2		glass
E1-233-470	7'		.2		glass
F1-233-480	8'		.2		glass
1-233-490	9'		.2		glass
G1-233-410	.10'		.2		glass
1-233-411	.11'		.2		glass
H1-233-870	7'		.2		glass
1-233-876	7' 6"		.2		glass
I1-233-880	8'		.2		glass

Forester

Brand-Model	Length	Lure Weight	No. Pieces	No. Guides	Material
J1-811-366	6' 6"			.4	solid glass
K-1-811-370	7'			.4	solid glass

Salt Water Specials

Brand-Model	Length	Lure Weight	No. Pieces	No. Guides	Material
1-233-380	8'		.2		
1-233-390	9'		.2		
1-233-310	.10'		.2		
1-223-446	5' 6"		.2		solid glass
1-223-460	6' 6"		.2		solid glass

Harnell Spinning and Surf Rods

Brand-Model	Length	Lure Weight	No. Pieces	No. Guides	Material
1-267-380	8'		.2	.5	glass
1-267-390	9'		.2	.5	glass
1-267-310	.10'		.2	.6	glass
1-267-490	9'		.2	.5	glass
1-267-410	.10'		.2	.6	glass
1-267=412	.12'		.2	.6	glass

From hole cutters to sunglasses
Gear Up for Ice Fishing with Quality

By David Richey

The name of the game is quality. Inferior, shoddy ice fishing equipment will simply not withstand the rigors of cold arctic winds and freezing temperatures.

My personal recommendation for an ice hole cutter is the Jiffy Power Ice Auger. These gas-powered augers come with blades big enough to cut a six- to nine-inch hole. The larger size is for big fish such as large northern pike and lake trout.

Smaller, less expensive augers are manufactured by Nor-Mark. I especially enjoy using their Fin-Bore II, which I find adequate in situations where the ice isn't too thick.

Fishing rods are a personal choice but two basic types are commonly used — the jigging type stick in which the line is merely wound around pegs on the handle, and the more conventional rod-reel in which the line can be reeled in whenever a fish strikes.

A popular jigging stick is manufactured by Bay De Noc Lure Co. in Gladstone, Michigan. Nor-Mark's "Thrumming" or "Teho 3" rod-reel combination will cover the range from panfish to big pike.

Monofilament line is important for ice fishermen because the colder temperatures will cause cheap line to become brittle and break. I advocate using quality line such as Garcia's Royal Bonnyl, Shakespeare's Super 7000 or Berkley's Trilene.

Tipups are underwater reels used extensively in the north for such toothy fish as northern pike, walleyes, muskellunge, lake and brown

When the ice settles in for the winter on the Great Lakes it really settles in. Using an ice-locked cargo ship as a windbreak this angler is seeking trout, perch, pike and whatever else he can interest in his minnows.

trout. A vast array of tipups have flooded the market in recent years but the key to purchasing these things is again to buy quality. Look for tipups with large line spools, a good spring-steel spring and a flag that isn't going to blow off in the first mean nor'easter. Avoid tipups with chintzy looking cross-arms, flimsy flags and tiny spools. They will cost you more fish than they can possibly save you in terms of dollars.

Ice strainers or minnow strainers can be purchased at any bait dealer but insist on those made from metal and always purchase one with a long handle. It prevents wet hands. Cotton strainers will not last through two fishing trips.

Minnow buckets are essential for anglers going after minnow-eating fish such as walleyes and pike. A quality container such as the Frabilite Minnow Bucket, manufactured by Frabill Manufac-

turing Company of Milwaukee, will serve an ice angler for many years.

Here are a few lures I've found to be tremendously successful wherever they are used: Swedish Pimples, Jigging Rapalas, Rapala Pilkkis, Do-Jiggers, Eppinger's Devle Dogs, Little Cleos, Russian Spoons, Barracuda jigs and Gapen's Pinky jigs.

Smaller jigs and spoons can be sweetened with natural bait such as meal worms, wax worms, corn borers, elmwood grubs, wigglers or small pieces of fish.

Cold weather protection from the elements is important. I prefer wearing a top grade of underwear, such as that made by Browning or Hanes, and cover that with a good wool shirt such as Pendleton or Woolrich. I wear an eight ounce RefrigiWear snowmobile suit made in Inwood, New York. This serves as an effective windbreak and keeps me warm in subzero temperatures. A pair of Sorel boots with one or two pairs of wool socks keeps my feet toasty warm. Dedicated ice-fishermen should carry two or three pairs of cotton gloves. And for my head, I prefer a wool stocking cap.

Never forget a good pair of sunglasses. I use CoolRay sunglasses because they prevent the nagging headache long hours of squinting into the glare of sun on snow and ice can cause. Polarized glasses are always the best buy.

Gearing up for ice fishing is easy as long as you remember to purchase the best money can afford and follow at least a few of these brand name tips.

GAMEFISH: KOKANEE SALMON

NAMES
Blueback, little red fish, Kennerly's salmon, landlocked sockeye, silver trout, silversides, kickaninny, redfish. *(Oncorhynchus nerka)*

DISTRIBUTION
The kokanee is a small, landlocked member of the salmon family and is considered a form of the sockeye salmon. It is silver in color with a blue or green back. During spawning, the male turns bright red in color. The kokanee resembles a trout in shape.

SIZE
Although the Kokanee have been known to reach the size of 4 pounds or more, they average about a pound in weight.

HABITAT
The Kokanee is found in both large and small lakes throughout its range. It spawns in shallows with gravel bottoms in the lakes and small streams.

FEEDING HABITS
The diet of the Kokanee consists of small crustaceans and plankton.

BEST FEEDING TEMPERATURE
About 50°.

TACKLE
This smallish salmon, which has been transplanted to lots of deep cold lakes around the West, falls victim to a medium trolling outfit with wire line and small spoons or bait that will get down to it.

THE LAST HATCH
A FISHING MYSTERY
HARMON HENKIN

(continued from page 241)

with Congressman Raucus. The green drake hatch is on and hundreds of anglers are anxious to watch me perform."

Sid motioned him back to his chair with a wave.

Paul tried to defend her. "It's true that Julie always wanted to see Halford's place. She told me that lots of times when we were an item."

"A marked-down item," Julie said.

Sid pondered the situation. "I know you and Julie were kinda close once. You just might back her up. As Plotinus said, 'In things of the heart, the mind takes second place.'"

"Sure we were close. But that was once," Paul observed sadly. "As Halford would have said, she and I fish different rivers now."

"Yours was too polluted," Julie said.

"Only for those with the wrong bait," Paul shot back.

They glared at each other as only an ex-couple can do.

"Oh, Lord," Dun moaned. "The incomparable Frederick Halford has just shed his mortal coil and you people stand around bickering. I, Andrew Dun, am the only one to show the proper respect."

No one had an appropriate answer. They were silent as Dun wandered over to the alcove where Halford stored his fishing gear in the best traditions of a conspicuous consumer. Dun picked an Orvis fly rod, a Hardy Perfect reel and a French angler's bag off an antique table and stepped toward Halford's rod rack, filled with the elegant cane creations of Leonard, Payne, Garrison and the others who made up the pantheon of the finest rod craftsmen who ever lived. Sid looked at the one empty spot in the 12-rod rack and at the nine-foot, six-ounce stick that Dun lovingly caressed.

"Where in the Hell did you get that gear, Dun?" he shouted.

"Why, down at the creek. They were lying on the ground by some blood spots."

"Didn't you know that was the scene of the murder?"

"Of course, but I —"

"No buts about it. I oughta arrest you for tampering with the evidence. You probably destroyed something crucial."

"I'm sorry. I just didn't think about it, sir. This equipment belonged to Mr. Halford, and there it was, just strewn about the grass. He was such a perfectionist about tackle. The absolutely correct gear for every endeavor. I just felt compelled to return it to its proper place."

(continued on page 260)

top of the line

WHAT WE LOOKED FOR IN QUALITY

The conditions requiring ice fishing gear are never optimal. Therefore, the equipment should be simplicity itself — no hidden knobs to find while wearing heavy gloves. Everything except the line and the lures should be oversized and easy to get at. That's what we searched for in our choices.

DICKEY. A simple ice fishing rod, marketed in two lightweight models, one 28 inches and one 38 inches overall. A heavy action model for bass, etc., is 38 inches. It has a cork hook holder on the side, adjustable drag on the reel and comes with lure, monofilament and jigging lure ready to go when the ice is cut. Has a hardwood handle.

DICKEY ICE ROD SAVER. The Dickey Ice Rod Saver is a tenite-bodied, fiberglass-legged stand for your rod, to keep it off the ice. It covers the hole and will attach to any rod.

DICKEY PIMPLE POLE. The folks at Dickey are marketing a 15-inch ice fishing rod designed for jigging or bobbing small lures. The "All Purpose Pimple Rod" can be used up to 200 feet underwater, has a hardwood handle, built-in reel with a simple drag and a cork hook holder in the handle. Functional.

FRABILL. Frabill makes two nice models of ice skimmer to scoop the bits and pieces that form in your entree to the underwater world. The best one is probably their model 4516, which has a red handle for easy visibility.

HAMMACHER-SCHLEMMER'S TRI-POD CHAIR. Keep off the ice with this nice light folding chair from Hammacher Schlemmer. Made from aluminum, it folds up to become a walking stick for getting across slippery ice and then converts into a 3-legged seat. Good for stillfishing, too.

HERTER'S ICE FISHING KIT. Herter's Ice Fishing Kit has everything the beginner needs and then some. You get an ice fishing rod and

HAPPY DEHOOKER

"Not touched by human hands" could be the slogan of this new "happy dehooker." Can remove even treble hooks one at a time just by snapping the dehooker guide into the line at any point and following it down past the leader to the hook. Fish supposedly pop off. Available in three sizes.

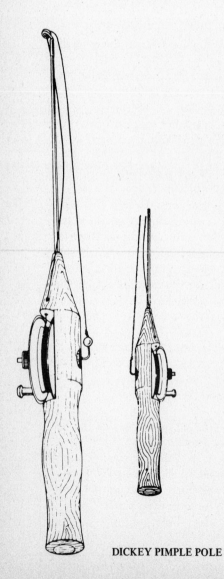

DICKEY PIMPLE POLE

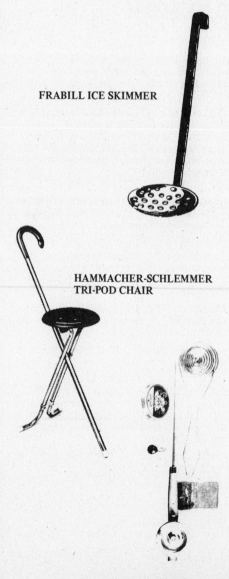

FRABILL ICE SKIMMER

HAMMACHER-SCHLEMMER TRI-POD CHAIR

HERTER'S ICE FISHING KIT

top of the line

NOR-MARK COMBO

reel equipped with their own 4-pound test monofilament and a depth finder plus sinkers, a bobber and a small assortment of flies.

HERTER'S TIP-UP. Herter's, which serves ice anglers pretty well, has a non-freeze tripod-type tip-up with an adjustable guide. There is a trigger setting that indicates whether the fish is moving or stationary. The flag indicator is fluorescent and the all-metal tip-up is wind-proof and folds down when not used. Not legal in all states!

JIFFY ICE SKIMMER. The Jiffy Ice Skimmer, in 6- and 4¾-inch diameter sizes, works simply and well in keeping the angling hole clear. It has a flat bottom and a simple tap will rid it of its burden. Necessary for the ice angler.

MUSTAD. From Norway, where they know about ice, the Mustad Hook Company is selling a line of quality ice augers. It has a straight cutting edge which makes sharpening quite easy. Replacement blades are available and Mustad sells them in 6- and 8-inch diameters with standard, deluxe and imported handles.

NOR-MARK COMBO. The Nor-Mark Teho 3 rod-and-reel ice-fishing combo, designed for heavy-duty angling, is only 19 inches long but has a double tip for feeling light strikes and fighting big fish. It has a large built-in reel, convenient grip and a depth meter. Well conceived piece of gear for the serious angler.

SCOTTY. The Scotty people put out a line of gear that's useful for the ice fisherman in his frozen vigil. Using melted snow and a heating unit, their hand warmer, body warm-

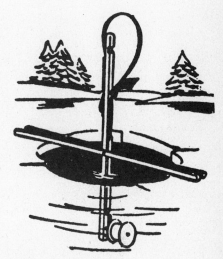

HERTER'S TIP-UP

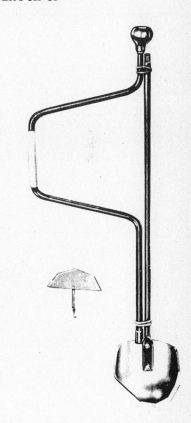

MUSTAD ICE AUGER

HERTER'S ICE FISHING SPEARS

"Canst thou draw out leviathan with a hook?"
JOB, *Old Testament*

top of the line

er and heating pad will generate a comfortable 140°- to 150°- temperature for 5 or 6 hours. Each unit will heat for 50 hours until a refill unit is needed. They work fine.

SNABB. The Mora knife people in Sweden make a top-quality ice auger with blade diameters ranging from 4 to 8 inches. They come with aluminum blade guards. Leather guards are available at slightly extra. Replacement blades and handles are also available. They are sold in a variety of handle styles and have a baked enamel finish. Another good one.

STILLFISH. A simple outfit for those frigid ice-fishing days. The Stillfish outfit feeds 6-pound monofilament through the rod rather than carrying it on the outside. They're available in a variety of sizes from a little over two feet to four. The tubular tip removes ice from the line on retrieve and has a 5-inch cork grip for easy handling with gloves. Colored black and white for snow contrast. A good ice-fishing rig.

STILLFISH

HERTER'S WINTER FISHING BOBBERS

You don't have to move Herter's bobber to change the depth of your bait. The line slides right through any of the four sizes. Made of Dylite with a fluorescent ring.

Notes on the ice auger

First of all, you need an efficient tool for cutting a hole in the ice. You have several choices.

1. Ice chisel or spud. This is a steel chisel with a steel handle about 5 feet long. The best spuds are heavy, with a chisel blade about 1½ inches wide. You should keep a loop of rope tied to the upper end of the handle and keep the rope around your wrist in case you let the spud go into the water.

2. Ice auger. The Swedish ice auger has a shovel-like, sharpened blade which cuts the hole as you rotate the auger. The Lake Mille Lacs ice auger works on the same principle as an auger bit, cleaning the hole as you turn the bit. The Ice Master auger re-

moves a solid, round core of ice. All are efficient ways of drilling holes.

3. If you want to invest a considerable amount of money, you can get power units for your ice auger — either electric motors which run off your car battery or gas-powered engines. These are a real pleasure to use, but they are expensive.

From *America's Favorite Fishing* by F. Philip Rice. (C) 1964 by F. Philip Rice. Used by permission of Outdoor Life Books.

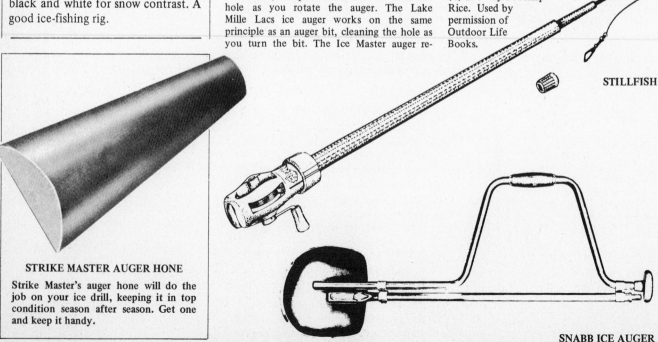

STILLFISH

STRIKE MASTER AUGER HONE

Strike Master's auger hone will do the job on your ice drill, keeping it in top condition season after season. Get one and keep it handy.

SNABB ICE AUGER

LURE LOVERS RISE THROUGH THREE STAGES

By Lefty Kreh

I believe there are three stages of fishermen: The first has just entered the sport, has a small tackle box with a few lures, and is asking everyone questions.

When he enters the second stage he has many, many lures, knows it all (usually won't tell anyone about his fishing techniques or places) and won't listen to anyone.

The third stage is an angler who will listen to anybody, asks many questions, shares his knowledge willingly, has a minimum of tackle and a very few lures that will catch fish for him under almost all conditions.

If you want to select the proper spinning and plug lures, obviously, the best method is to find a third stage angler to guide you. That's tough to do, but it's the very best way.

The complete caster will have a few lures that work from the top to the bottom. That's to say, he will have some that appeal to fish lying deep, some for the mid-depths, and a few that work just under or on the surface.

Fortunately, in salt water, the choice seems to be more easily made than in fresh. Perhaps that's because in most salt water situations the fish are more voracious, and the waters are generally less cluttered by obstructions.

For almost every salt water fishing situation, a few tucktail jigs in white and yellow (in sizes from ¼ to 1 ounce) will take fish. Other colors will work, but white and yellow will do the job better most of the time.

One or two swimming plugs

that resemble baitfish, like the Sea Bee or the Rebel, are also needed.

Finally, a lure that gurgles and pops as it is swiftly retrieved across the surface — imitating a baitfish — will make many predator species slash at it.

In southern and tropical seas, a chugger type plug, one of wood, with a scooped face that pops loudly on the surface when the rod tip is violently jerked, is a decided asset.

Oddly enough, it is in fresh water that the proper choice of lures becomes difficult. There's such a variety of conditions that lures must be somewhat matched to both these conditions and various species sought.

But I can make some generalities that will help.

Trout prefer small flashy things, like tiny spoons and spinners. And small, shiny or flashy imitations of bait fish, plugs like the Rapala, are also very effective.

Largemouth bass almost always prefer a different wiggle to a lure than does the smallmouth. The largemouth prefers a lure that rocks slowly back and forth as it swims; while the smallmouth wants a smaller lure sporting a hasty wiggle as it swims.

Pike go for wobbling spoons, and muskies want something big to chew on, whether it's a spoon or a plug.

A river makes demands too.

William Mills & Son marketed the "Celebrated Phantom Minnow" in the 1890s. It was made of silk coated with rubber. The 5½-inch model cost $1.15.

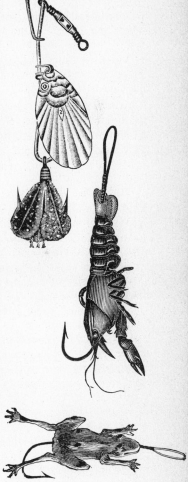

(Top) Pflueger's luminous bass spoon from the 1890s cost two bits and glowed in the dark. (Middle and bottom) A soft rubber crawfish patented in 1878 and a soft rubber frog. Both were sold by William Mills & Son in the 1890s.

(continued on next page)

LURE LOVERS RISE THROUGH THREE STAGES

(continued from preceding page)

Some surface lures, such as the Crazy Crawler or Jitterbug, often don't work well on a fast current. The swift water upsets the delicate balance of the lure, making precise manipulation difficult.

For such fishing, surface plugs with propellers are often much more effective.

On the other hand, these two plugs can be deadly when played on the slack current of a lake. And, if you fish at night, many experts feel the constant sound of the Jitterbug makes it a good target for fish.

Weed-filled waters simply demand lures that will not tangle or foul when retrieved. Two lures are now standard for such work: the Johnson Silver Minnow style, where a wobbling spoon is dressed with a wire weed guard; and the new bass spinnerbaits, protected from tangling by a V-shaped wire guard.

Color of the spoons seems unimportant for most fishing. And often the spoon is worked on top of the weeds, slinking along to draw strikes.

Underwater, bass spinnerbait colors seem to rank in this order of preference: chartreuse, black and white.

In very clear waters an extremely bright, flashy lure of silver may frighten off fish; while one of copper or gold is often extremely effective. Also, in dirty or discolored water, a very dark or black lure is more easily seen by the fish.

The size of a lure is often vital. This is especially true if you're after trophy fish. In bass fishing, for example, you can use small lures that appeal to a great number of small bass. But most trophy bass are taken on larger lures. This holds true for most species.

The method used to select good lures is complex, but you don't need a lot of lures. Select only a small number of the best type for your particular fishing task.

THE LAST HATCH
A FISHING MYSTERY
HARMON HENKIN

(continued from page 255)

"Anyone else around when you got there?"

"No, sir. Just the blood, an impression in the grass and the tackle."

"It's probably all right, Sid," Paul said. "I really don't think there were any vital clues messed up. Whoever gaffed Halford did it quickly and shoved him over the edge. No fuss, no muss."

"Look, sheriff," Schielbacht said, standing again. "She's obviously guilty."

The others nodded in agreement.

"You better mind your manners or by the time you get back over to the Henry's Fork they'll be trolling for suckers. Sit down. You too, Dun."

Schielbacht looked horrified but he did as he was told.

"I think I should arrest her, Paul," Sid whispered. "It doesn't look good."

Julie overheard him. "This is unreal, absolutely unreal. Here's my friend and an ex-weekend roommate conspiring to send me up the river. How about asking me if I'm guilty? Whatever happened to trust?"

Sid looked sheepish but Paul ignored Julie's outburst and kept his attention on the rod rack.

"Come here, Dun."

Halford's Man Friday approached the pinko hippie who had suddenly become a figure of respect in his life.

"Dun, what kind of rod was Halford using today?"

"Why, I thought every angler could recognize that one. An impregnated bamboo made in Manchester, Vermont, by Orvis. Quite expensive."

"Yeah, I know all that. But what kind of Orvis?"

"A Shooting Star. Quite a stout piece of timber, as Mr. Halford used to remark."

"A big rod for big flies and big fish. Most of them are used in salt water for steelhead fresh from their run to the ocean."

"That's correct."

"And it has limited freshwater use."

"Also correct."

"That is obviously not the kind of rod that an expert like Halford or even a quasi-knowledgeable angler of any sort would take on a spring

(continued on page 277)

NO LURE CAN REPLACE SKILL

THE SUCCESS OF SOME TACKLE IS A MATHEMATICAL PROBABILITY

Fishing, especially bass fishing, has become commercialized in the past few years to a degree never imagined before.

As a result of big money bass tourneys, it's difficult to pick up a sporting magazine without seeing some smiling winner beaming out at you holding a stringer of largemouths in one hand and his favorite rod, reel or lure in the other.

It's a manufacturer's dream come true.

And as a result of these endorsements many anglers eagerly scan the pages looking for the product that will bring them instant angling enlightenment.

I hate to be a cynic but it ain't necessarily true. A mathematician friend who happens to be an angling fanatic was looking over some of my catalogs a few days ago and sneering, the kind of look that mathematicians often get.

"Why, they never even consider possibility and random selection," he muttered at me.

"Heh?"

"Some of those lures are used more often than others in places where there are more bass by people who are better fishermen than the average grouping of anglers. That's why they break more records and catch more fish. That's all there is to it."

He painstakingly explained what he meant.

It is in the interest of manufacturers to make their products available for well-known anglers, usually gratis or at cost. It is in the interest of anglers to accept them. It is also true that some of the better-known tourney anglers are marketing their own products.

This isn't to say that you can't catch your limit on Skunk Lake up the road with a Feeley-Eel just like the Mohammed Ali of bass fishing uses. But not necessarily. In fact, there is on the scale of probability more likelihood that the

highly skilled, knowledgeable anglers who fish for money would catch more fish on a clothespin with treble hooks than dunkers like us would with the best lures on the market.

Of course all lures aren't created equally but none of them replaces skill.

The baits, lines, rods and reels that usually appear on the money winners' lists might just do so because of the frequency that they are used.

And as the mathematician added, "You pays your money and you takes your chances." —H.H.

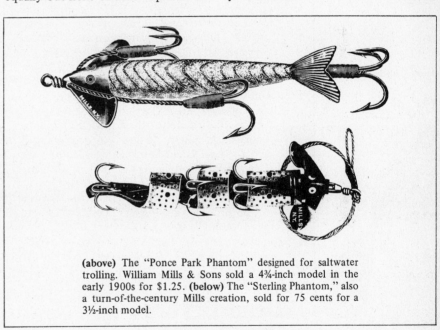

(above) The "Ponce Park Phantom" designed for saltwater trolling. William Mills & Sons sold a 4¾-inch model in the early 1900s for $1.25. (below) The "Sterling Phantom," also a turn-of-the-century Mills creation, sold for 75 cents for a 3½-inch model.

SPOONS ARE GREAT BAITS

Probably the oldest of present-day artificial lures, the spoon is said to have derived from the experience of a well-known and respected tackle manufacturer who was an enthusiastic fisherman. While fishing the angler accidentally dropped a soup spoon over the side of his boat. As it fluttered down through the dark water, he witnessed the golden flash of a huge pike as it seized the spoon. Inspiration struck and an idea took shape. If pike will seize a flashing object, perhaps in mistake for a minnow, might it not be possible to attract them with an *artificial* minnow?

Quickly the angler cut the handle from a

second spoon, using only the dish-shaped portion. To this he attached a treble hook – the world's first metal spoon or wobbler lure – and it worked! Indeed it worked so well that a company was formed to market this new artificial bait for pike and pickerel.

Today's spoons are far advanced in design from the original soup-spoon lure. Forged in almost every conceivable shape, they are fabricated in a wide range of finishes. One of the better known is the *Dardevle*, a red and

(continued on page 271)

top of the line

WHAT WE LOOKED FOR IN QUALITY

We didn't care how well a lure was constructed as long as it did a good job catching fish. Sound cynical? Well, maybe that's the only way to pick your way through the morass of lures on the market. How well a lure was made doesn't seem to have that much to do with its performance. Economics doesn't seem to be a factor either, though everyone loves a bargain. So, we just tried to isolate the most functional lures and list them.

Test with a slow retrieve

When spinning was in its early heyday some 20 years ago most of the savvy anglers favored European spinner lures over American ones.

The early favorites were French models such as the Abu-Reflex and Mepps and the Italian Panther Martin. Besides the variety, these spinners had a strong advantage — you could retrieve them very slowly and the blades would still turn quickly and evenly.

For lots of fishing an even-paced return was a marked improvement over the hectic, crazed retrieve of the first American spinners. And in those days lots of spinners that looked perfect with fast retrieves turned into torpedoes on slow returns.

Spinners are effective because of the flash that comes from the revolving blade. Without that you don't have much. There have been lots of improvements over the last decade, but the real test is still performance on a slow retrieve.

P.S.: When all is said and done, please attach the spinner directly to your line. No snaps or swivels. They mess up the action. Thanks. —H.H.

ARBO-GASTER

BIG JIM

Deep Divers

ARBO-GASTER. The Arbo-Gaster, a deep diver from Arbogast, is one of the classic deep-diving lures still on the market. Good for trolling or casting with a wide lip that helps keep it snagless and a Hula Skirt to keep it proper. Good stuff.

BIG JIM. One of the better crank-type baits, sold in either standard or iridescent colors. A classically shaped lure, it can be zipped under the water or bounced in along the surface. From Bass Pro Shops.

BOMBER BAIT COMPANY. Bomber diving lures have been around for a long time. There are five series of them including a slow sinker for 4-6 foot subsurface work, one that goes down to 7 feet, another down to 12 feet and a 4½-incher that will submerge to 15 feet for casters and down to 30 feet for trollers. Midget sizes also available in a big array of color styles. A good performer.

CREEK CHUB MOUSE. Another classic from Creek Chub is their mouse. It dives deep wagging its tail or can stay near the surface. A tackle box must.

FLATFISH. The Flatfish has caught lots and lots of fish. This classic American lure is available in 38 colors and from 1 to 6 inches with variations in hook arrangement. It's among the easiest to use and most effective lures ever made. The tiniest model can be used in fly casting and you can troll the big ones in the ocean. Most models are available in wood or plastic. But stick with the wood for old time's sake. A great lure. Made by Helin.

GUDEBROD BASSPIRIN. A solid performer, the easy-swimming Basspirin from

FLATFISH

CREEK CHUB MOUSE

"The apostolic occupation of trafficking in fish."
SYDNEY SMITH, *Third letter to Archdeacon Singleton*

LURES 263

top of the line

Gudebrod has been around for some years. It floats at rest and dives below on the retrieve. Twelve colors and 1/8-, 3/8- and ½-ouncers available.

HELLBENDER. The Hellbender by Whopper Stopper was one of the earliest deep-diving floaters on the market. Available for diving to 35, 25 or 15 feet. Many colors and from ½- to 7/8-ounce. Good trollers.

MANN'S RAZOR BACK. Another good deep diving lure is Mann's Razor Back, available in ½-ounce. Lots of colors, including translucent. And a built-in rattle. From Bass Pro Shops.

BILL NORMAN'S LITTLE SCOOPER. A very fine deep-diving lure with a built-in rattle and minnow-type finishes. Stays where it is when you stop retrieving.

ZARA SPOOK. Heddon's Zara Spook has been around for 25 years or so and it still rests on the surface, dives some when you jerk the line and catches the Hell out of bass in freshwater and stripers and their kin in salt. It weighs ¾ ounce and is 4¼ inches long.

Ice Lures

GAPEN'S. Don Gapen up in Big Lake, Minnesota — where they understand the term ice fishing — has a pretty good line of ice bugs, including Crappie Slim, Ice Ants, Anteater and a half-dozen other patterns.

SWEDISH ICE JIGGER. Al's Swedish Ice Jigger is a basic through-the-ice lure. It's nickel and weighs 3/8 ounce with a fluorescent tail teaser for murky water. Just hook on your favorite bait and jig it.

Plugs

BAYOU BOOGIE. The Bayou Boogie, in 1/3-, ¾-, ½- and ¼-ounce models, was one of the original vibrating lures. Will run at any depth. Versatile.

CISCO KID. The Midget Cisco Kid is one of the solid performers in the bass field and has been for years. Nothing flashy or gimmicky — it just catches fish. Ciscos are available in a freshwater 3/8-ounce size and in saltwater models at ¼ and ½ ounces. Jointed ones, too. Various colors. An 8½-inch, 3 5/8-ounce troller is made for big-time fishing.

CREEK CHUB WIGGLE FISH. The Creek Chub Wiggle Fish accounted for the world record largemouth of 22 pounds, 4 ounces in 1932. It's still being made at ¾ ounce. How can you not have one or two in your tackle box?

LAZY IKE. Since 1938, when the first Lazy Ike was whittled out of wood, this has been a standard for largemouth and pike anglers. It's 3½ inches long and weighs 5/8-ounce. Other models available, too.

MANN'S LITTLE GEORGE. Mann's Little George, available in ¼-, ½-, ¾- and 1-ounce sizes and in lots of color combinations, is one of the biggest sellers among the new-wave, bass-type lures. Tourney basser Tom Mann's plug has a spinner blade at the rear. His company has sold more than 5 million of them.

PIKIE MINNOW. The Creek Chub Pikie Minnow is and has been one of the standard bass fishing plugs. From 1/8 to 3½ ounces, the Pikie has accounted for many many fish over the years.

ROCKY JUNIOR. The Rocky Junior from Harrison Industries was one of the earliest truly ultra-light plugs at 1/16 ounce. Jointed and available in lots of colors, it has a No. 14 treble hook. Especially effective for chain pickerel.

SOSY BAITFISH. The Sosy is an effective soft-segmented body lure in sizes from 1/8 ounce to 2¾ ounces in many colors that can do a lot of twisting and turning at the end of your line. Also sold as an animated eel.

SPENCE SCOUT. One of the hottest lures down South these days is the shallow-running Spence Scout. Made of wood and weighing 3/8 ounce in lots of color schemes, the Scout is a basic imitating lure. That it should be so effective and

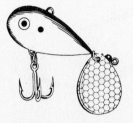

LITTLE GEORGE

ZARA SPOOK

WIGGLE FISH

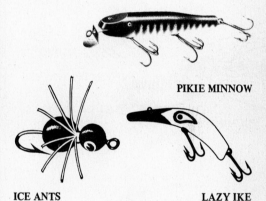

PIKIE MINNOW

ICE ANTS   LAZY IKE

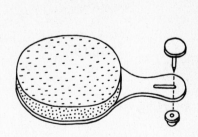

TOTE-A-LURE

Tote-a-Lure is a handy way to cart around small poppers, flies and even spinners. It's a 3-inch diameter sponge pad that fastens onto a button on any piece of clothing. You can use it to haul around a few poppers and leave the bulk in your tackle box. Convenient.

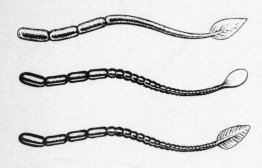

CORDELL WORMS

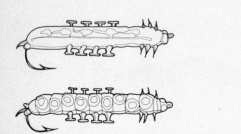

BURKE INSECTS

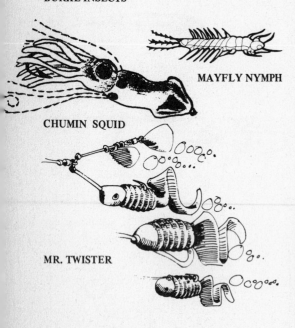

CHUMIN SQUID

MAYFLY NYMPH

MR. TWISTER

TEXAS SMALL WORM

popular these days may herald a return to the good old simple days of bass fishing — but it's doubtful.

VIVIF. The Vivif was one of the first European spinning lures imported to this country in the 1950s. Made from soft rubber and originally distributed by Garcia, the Vivif is made by Harrison Industries out of a new soft material in weights of 1/6, 1/3 and 2½ ounces. Lots of colors.

Rubber Goods

BEETLE II. The Knight Beetle II in 1/16-, 1/8- and ¼-ounce packages is an effective bait. Replaceable beetles available. Comes with a dangling spinner. From Knight.

BURKE INSECTS, NYMPHS AND LARVA. There are some who believe in soft molded insects, nymphs and larva by Burke. They're sure life-like and available in everything from crayfish, crickets and grubs to spiders, caddis flies and stonefly nymphs. Ice fishing possibilities, too.

CATCH-EM-QUICK. Catch-Em-Quick markets 45 different-colored floating rubber worms available in various 4-, 6- and 8-inch models. Plenty for the most fussy angler.

CHUMIN SQUID. Science comes to fishing with the 4-inch Chumin Squid by the Applied Oceanographic Corporation. It's a rubber-legged squid available in 1-ounce or 1½-ounce models in white, clear, pink and black. Put in a freeze-dried squid pellet for instant chum and start trolling, casting or stillfishing. Mostly for saltwater, but who knows? The squid body is replaceable. Fascinating literature can be had from the company. The only lure with a bibliography! Is it a wave of the future?

CORDELL. Rubber worms may be just rubber worms but the Cordell variety is one of the better lines. Coming in a standard assortment of colors including the pencil style, tattletail style, switchtail style and grubbies, too. A worm spoon is available from Cordell, too.

DELONG. History has caught up with DeLong Lures — the unique rubber worms they were peddling a few decades ago are now everyday things. They have them in a variety of colors including naturals, solids, spots and stripes and Color Glo. One of the first and still one of the best.

FLEX-SNAKES. Burke Fishing lures markets a 20-inch Flex Snake that will catch lunker bass or will frighten away bill collectors, but not necessarily in that order. Also available in more civilized 8-inch sizes in coral, diamondback or black. Pick your poison.

KEGARA'S WEEDLESS PLASTIC SNAKE. Outgrown worms? Get Kegara's Weedless Plastic Snake. It's 10 inches long and purple, black or pale green. Threaded on a 6/0 weedless hook.

LAZY IKE RUBBER WORM STUFF. Sounds disgusting but it might help your catch: Lazy Ike has begun marketing Ooze cheese and Bloody Bait, which are injected into a rigged 2- or 3-inch plastic worm. Vent holes allow the stuff to ooze out for chum-like fishing. Supposedly for trout or catfish. Don't think about it, just use it if you need it.

MANN'S JELLY WORM. Tourney superstar Tom Mann is now putting out a line of floating rubber worms in 15 flavors. Well, anyway, these jelly-flavored delights come in such taste treats as pineapple, watermelon and peach. If they can do it with feminine hygiene products, why not with rubber worms?

MR. TWISTER. Mr. Twister seems to be where it's at or at least where it's all going for bass fishermen. All their products have little curlicues on the tail for that bass-inciting action that's now so widely imitated. Available for crappies and other fish, too. A very important series of items for the warm-water angler. Whether it's worms, lizards, eels, grubs or whatever for salt or fresh water, Mr. Twister's got it.

SUPERFROG. Bill Plummer's Superfrog has been around for a couple decades. These weedless, leg-kicking, big-eyed frogs can even climb over logs. Made from one of those new soft materials. Sold by Harrison Industries.

TEXAS SMALL WORMS

The ultimate rubber worm is sold by M-F Manufacturing Company. It's 5 feet long and weighs 8½ pounds. Gross out your neighborhood bass tournament experts — catch Moby Dick.

top of the line

Spinners

B & B SPINNER BAIT. The B & B Tackle Company offers a dazzling array of spinner baits for the bass angler. Tandem and single-bladed in various colors with different kinds of skirts, as well. They also have grub-tailed spinner baits for bream and crappie. Anything your little heart could desire in one of these hot new items.

BEETLE SPIN. The Beetle Spin is a combination spinner bait and rubber worm from Bass Buster. Head-aching assortment of hot colors and in sizes from 1/32 to ¼ ounce. A chrome blade on the spinner. Also in twister models.

CANADIAN DEVON. Herter's version of the famed English Devon Minnows, one of the earliest commercial salmon lures. Has a 1-inch body and No. 4 trebles. Will spin excruciatingly slowly when retrieved.

DARDEVLE SPINNER. Another piece of history brought back by the old Lou Eppinger Dardevle Company is the J. T. Blue Fluted Spinner, originated in 1840. It was first produced in Whitehall, N.Y., and was one of the first metal trolling lures. The spinner is available in 1/0, 2/0 and 3/0 and in all the myriad of Dardevle colors. Can be had in bucktail or feathered like the original. Get one for old time's sake.

HAWAIIAN WIGGLER. The Arbogast Hawaiian Wiggler was one of the predecessors of today's fashionable spinner baits and is still effective. It's semi-weedless and has been adapted to a straight spinner bait called the Tournament Hawaiian Wiggler.

HILDEBRANDT. Hildebrandt has been making spinners since the turn of the century and still makes such now offbeat but effective things as a June Bug Spinner, Idaho Spinner, Colorados, Jig spinners and Willow Leafs. Top stuff and they make lots of spinner baits, too.

MEPPS. No doubt about it. "Mepps" and "spinners" have been almost synonymous since the 1950s when these French-made products were first marketed in this country. The Mepps Anglia, available in a variety of sizes, remains the standard for spinner fishing. Now available with frills like rubber minnows, colorful blades, etc. The squirrel-tail Mepps and the plain gold or silver remain as good as ever.

MEPPS SINGLE HOOKS. Single-hook spinners like Mepps are much superior to treble hook models because you can release fish with a great deal more ease, both to you and the fish. Mepps long-bladed spinners with and without skirts are available with single hooks. Very effective lures. Get them.

MONTI. A fine line of spinners and small spoons for the serious light or ultra-light lover. Especially good for trout or smallmouth, these Swiss-made lures in sizes from 1/10- to ¾-ounce work very well. Among the better European models. They deserve to be more popular.

NIPIGON COCKATOUSH PANFISH SPINNER. The Nipigon Cockatoush Panfish Spinner, slightly smaller than its name, is a spinner-woolly worm duo effective as a basic lure for kids after sunnies or as a more sophisticated spinner lure. Nickel or gold, it comes with a No. 6 hook.

BILL NORMAN SPINNER BAIT. The Bill Norman Spinner Bait has a 5/0 hook, nylon skirt and long-enough shaft to help make it weedless. It also works near the surface for versatility. Use with pork rind, too.

PADUCAH TACKLE COMPANY. The Floozy Spinner Bait presented by the Paducah Tackle Company is one of the New Wave lures. It features a Nasty, a multi-faceted rubber type skirt that's very effective. Colors and sizes available for this bass tourney generation lure.

PANTHER MARTIN. The Panther Martin, along with Mepps, is one of the most effective spinners ever made. Originally an Italian, it has attracted a coterie of sophisticated spin anglers almost from its debut in this country in the early 1960s. Perfect for ultra-light fishing in the 1/32-ounce models and for bigger things in the half-ouncers. Top stuff. Revolves at a very slow retrieve speed. Many varieties, color schemes and weights. Distributed by Harrison Industries.

PRESCOTT JIG SPINNER. Like magic, a Jig Spinner from Prescott will convert your jig of any type into a spinner bait, which is more effective than a jig alone. Lots of finishes on the blade including fluorescent and different sized blades, too.

RUFUS JR. JIG FLY. This idea by Kegara is another one that's been around for a long time. The Rufus Jr. Jig Fly is tied 18 inches behind any deep-running plug. The plug is retrieved quickly in jerks. Sometimes works.

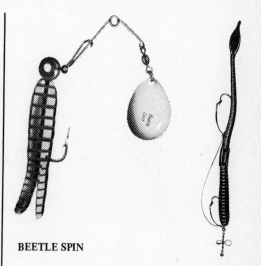

BEETLE SPIN

JELLY WORM

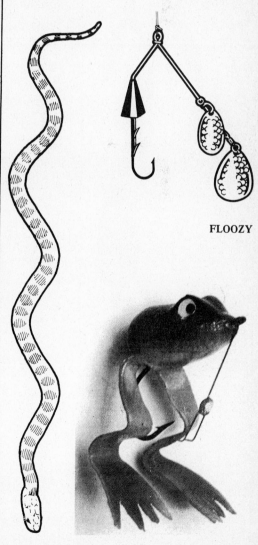

FLOOZY

FLEX-SNAKE

SUPERFROG

WEEDLESS BAIT CO.

RATTLE SPOON

YELLOWSTONE SPOON

WOOLLY BULLY

WOOLLY BULLY. Tom Mann of bass fishing fame produces one of the more solid spinner baits. The Woolly Bully has skirted or rubber bodies and one or two spinners. Various sizes and colors.

Spoons

TONY ACCETTA. Tony Accetta Pet Spoons have been a saltwater mainstay for a long time. Loved around the Chesapeake Bay, they come in nine models plus some with weed guards and others with yellow feathers and various finishes. Excellent in salt or fresh water.

AQUARIUS. The ½-ounce, 3-inch Aquarius is one of those super spoons that comes around every so often. It's made in gold, silver and chrome but that's just openers. To get color variation just mark it with a permanent marker, which can be taken off with nail polish remover. It has a cup in front to reflect light and make a commotion. Loads of fun.

AL'S GOLDFISH LURE. Al's Goldfish Lure has been spooning around for a long time in gold, copper and nickel. It's also available in the Rembrandt variation with wildly dashed-on color for the aesthetic angler after fish with good taste. Other interesting spoons from Al, too.

CHARGER SPOON. A good trolling spoon in lots of colors with weights from 1/8-ounce to 2 full ounces. Good casters from Charger Lures, owned by Lake Products.

DANCER. The Dancer is an oscillating flasher that dives for trout and salmon while trolling. Will work down to 150 feet and is made from nickel-plated brass.

DARDEVLE. The Dardevle is as American as bass tournaments but has been around a lot longer. Actually, the famous red-and-white spoons were named after the Marines in the First World War. Now available in scads of colors and every size for every task, Dardevles, in their varying blade styles, are a mandatory lure, especially for the Midwestern or Western angler. Lots of imitations but the originals are stamped with little devil's heads.

DIAMOND JIGS. Good saltwater jigging spoons from the Bead Chain Company. They weigh from 1 to 8 ounces and reflect light from a number of points. Stripers, tuna, sea bass and halibut are among its customers.

KAMLOOPER. The Kamlooper Spoon, with its raised, jagged rib, comes in sizes from 1/8- to ¾-ounce in various color patterns. Interesting-looking to anglers and fish as well. A good performer from Acme.

LUHR JENSEN'S KROCODILE. Luhr Jensen's Krocodile has been making fishy waves for a long time. Available with prism reflecting panels, various hammered-metal finishes or flat ones, this curved-body lure comes in weights from 1/6 ounce to 7 full ounces.

POINT DEFIANCE. Les Davis' Point Defiance Spoon in four sizes and five colors is designed to be used with bait such as strips of fish or pork rind, which don't affect its action. Single hook.

RATTLE SPOON. A spoon with two tiny baby spoons hanging from the bottom — that's one way of describing Marathon's brass Rattle Spoon. Different sizes. They work.

ANDY REEKER SPOON. Andy Reeker Lures, now owned by Grizzly, Inc., have been around for more than a half-century and are a Pacific Coast favorite. Lots of sizes and colors good for salmon, especially. Well-thought-out spoon.

SAGAMORE TROLLING SPOON. Among the more interesting lure resurrections is Dardevle's re-issue of Julio T. Buel's first patented trolling spoon from the 1830s. The lure of its day, it now has a very thin blade and comes in ¼-, 3/8- and 13/32-ounce weights. Get one and become a part of history.

SENECA. The Seneca Company puts out a fine line of spoons, especially in the smaller range. The Yellowstone, Wob-L-Rite and Side Winder are effective especially for pike. The light and ultra-light freak should stock up on a few of them.

SUR-KATCH. Famed Michigan Muskie guide Homer LeBlanc helped design the Sur-Katch, a spoon available in a dozen colors and four sizes. It has tiny spoonlets on the side to increase action and a wide lip for more wobbling. Stainless steel. Made by the Drifter Tackle Company.

WEEDLESS BAIT COMPANY. If you're going into the lettuce after 'em, get yourself some of these good old spoons from the Weedless Bait Company. A striking fish trips the hook guard out of the way and bingo, you got your fish. In a variety of styles and sizes plus a plug with

KAMLOOPER

SAGAMORE

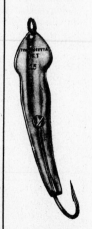

ACETTA

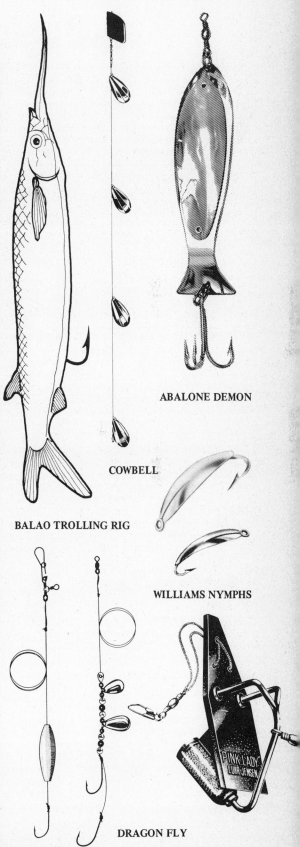

top of the line

the same hook-release mechanism. Such things are always a compromise since nothing is totally weedless — but sometimes these things are really a necessity.

WILLIAMS FISHING TACKLE NYMPH. One of the last words for ultra-light spin fishers is imported from Canada. They market a small nymph, a large one and a shad nymph that weigh 1/40-ounce. Available with silver- or gold-mirror blades. Williams also markets lots of other nice spoons.

WORTH DEMON SPOONS. Around since the 1930s, the Worth Demon Spoons are as effective as ever. This line of minnow-shaped models includes nickel-plated, solid brass Abalone Demon and Water Demon. Good performers, especially in the upper Midwest.

Trolling & Salt

BALAO TROLLING RIG. The Balao trolling rig put out by Burke is a good way to go in the salt. The 12-inch-long Balao imitation is threaded onto an 8/0 stainless hook with a stainless chain.

COWBELLS. Les Davis makes a pretty complete line of trolling attractors in the Cowbell series. His Flex-Trolls, consisting of four or so (depending on the model) spinning blades and a red plastic rudder are very effective for lots of fish ranging from lake trout to Pacific salmon. A big range of sizes.

DRAGON FLY SHAD RIG. A good trolling outfit for shad, crappie, bass or anything else deep down. It consists of a simple lead body and bucktail shad dart and a small, curved Shadspoon. Works well together with a nickel or gold spoon. A few color variations for the dart are also available.

KONAHEAD. Fenwick's Konahead series of lures do double-duty as teasers. When trolled at 6 to 12 knots they surface and dive just like a baitfish. Available with various colored skirts and heads. Some of the larger models have transparent heads with inserts and eyes. A fine series of lures.

LUHR JENSEN DIVING SINKERS. Luhr Jensen has two types of diving sinkers for the troller. The Dolphin, which has an automatic resetting mechanism, and

the Pink Lady. Three models of each are available for trolling in the 50-, 85- and 120-foot range. They work well.

MARTIN TEASER. For enticing the big saltwater buggers into hitting, the Martin Company puts out an 11-inch teaser in assorted color combos.

MEPPS GIANT KILLER. The Mepps Giant Killer, available in sizes as large as 4/0 hooks, is an excellent product, like all the Mepps stuff. It comes in 1-ounce weights plain or bucktailed or with a rubber minnow at 1½ ounces. Lots of blade colors available. Good for heavy-duty casting or trolling.

MISTER TWISTER EEL. Mr. Twister has a couple of well-rigged eels, measuring 9 and 7 inches on 6/0 cadmium Mustad hooks. Lots of colors and a twitchy tail. They also have an 11-inch eel with a face plate for more action. All are good things.

NEEDLEFISH. The single-color, single-weight Needlefish floating plug from the Boone Bait Company doesn't need much variety. It catches plenty of spotted weakfish as it is. Weighs in at ½ ounce and sinks very slowly. Boone suggests you retrieve slowly and even let it lie still in the water at times.

NO ALIBI BUCKTAIL JIGS. No Alibi's line of bucktail Special Jigs are designed for stripers but will catch a great many other saltwater fish as well. Sizes 3/0 and 5/0 in 5/16- and 7/16-ounce weights available. Many other types of jigs and bucktails available, too.

NO ALIBI EELS. No Alibi Eels are a staple for the saltwater angler, especially those after stripers and blue fish. Available in lots of colors and sizes with nylon tails. Distinctive red eye for fishy recognition.

PSYCHOHOX AND PSYCHOBEAD. Fenwick is marketing these two very competently designed marlin lures. The Psychohox is for moderate trolling (5 to 10 knots) and the second is for fast trolling (8 to 18 knots). The Hox has an 8/0 hook and the Bead has a 10/0. Different color combinations are available. Both work very well.

SALTY BOOGIE. Whopper Stopper's Salty Boogie at 3 ounces is designed for surf casting and trolling and for stripers, blues, tarpon and other big beasts. Effective.

ABALONE DEMON

COWBELL

BALAO TROLLING RIG

WILLIAMS NYMPHS

DRAGON FLY

top of the line

SANDEEL. The 6-plus-inch Sandeel from Nebco, in silver, green, red and gold, imitates a common surf creature. So does the Red Gill, which has become popular off European coasts. Lots of salty fish love these 3/8- and ¾-ounce soft baits. Using 5/0 and 7/0 English Seeley hooks, they're worth adding to your tackle box.

THE SUNDANCE. The Sundance, a large teaser offered in orange, blue or chartreuse by the Boone Bait Company, has an interesting feature: eight glass mirror strips along the sides that give off a fish-enticing reflection supposedly so enthralling to billfish that you'll have to buy replacement strips real soon. Nicely made.

TEASERLURE. A good line of teaser baits from PBI of Ft. Lauderdale. Two of the Teaserlures, the Rainbow models, are able to change body color and all are available pre-rigged if desired. From 9 to 15 inches, they'll bring fish to your ocean trolling boat. Many colors.

WIG-WAG SALT WATER JIG. The Burke Company has a line of saltwater Wig-Wag soft lures with jig heads. Models for bonefish and deep water jigging.

WORDEN'S SPIN 'N' GLO. The Spin 'N' Glo, an outgrowth of the original Cherry Bobber steelhead lure, has been a favorite Pacific Northwest salmon and steelhead lure for years. Lots of fluorescent colors but who knows what they represent. They sure do catch fish, though. Worden's also has a very complete range of other steelhead lures.

Surface Lures

CRIPPLED KILLER. The Phillips Crippled Killer is a solid surface performer. With its fore and aft blades it makes lots of commotion charging through the water.

DALTON SPECIAL. The Dalton Special was originated by P. P. Dalton back in 1930 and continues fooling bass with its rear spinner, which jerks around when the plug is twitched. Comes in many colors from 1/5 to 3/5 ounces, from 2 to 4 inches long. Available from Marine Metal Products.

DEVIL'S HORSE. A good bass surface plug. Available in lots of colors and with silver propellers at both ends. Distributed by Bass Pro Shops.

DIAMOND RATTLER. Jim Strader's lure company in Havana, Florida, produces the Diamond Rattler, a 5/8-ounce plug with a sound chamber that rattles on retrieve. Some models have electromagnetic swirl finishes bordering on the psychedelic. A very effective item with spinners on both ends. Shakes, rattles and rolls.

FISHCAKE. Though the Helin Fishcake has never gained the popularity or reputation of its brother the Flatfish, it's a dependable top water bass performer. Available in a ¼-ounce spinning model or 3/8- and 5/8-ounce casters. Lots of colors.

GAINES POPPING BUGS. The Gaines Popping Bugs, made from cork rather than modern synthetics, are good ones. They come in a variety of patterns in hook sizes from No. 6 to No. 12 and in lots of colors. Rubber legs add to their charm. Big panfish and bass love to munch them when water conditions are right.

GILMORE'S. If you go for the real thing — wooden plugs — then take a look at Gilmore's Hoodlers and Jumpers — 4-inch, ½-ounce plugs propellered at either or both ends. Available in lots of colors, they create quite a commotion.

HULA POPPER. The Hula Popper is a classic bass surface plug that's probably more fun to fish than any other bass lure. Cast it out, let it sit for 30 seconds or so then chug it in and listen to it gurgle. A tiny, tiny 1/32-ounce to a wave-forming 5/8 ounce. Top stuff for a long time.

JITTERBUG. One of the classic surface plugs. With a wide gurgle-causing lip in all sorts of colors and available in weights of 1/8, ¼, 3/8, 5/8 ounces and a bonzo 1¼-ounce muskie model. Bass still dance to its tune. Much more fun to fish than most modern lures.

RAPALA. The first of the New Wave lures. It caused an incredible stir when it was first imported from Finland. There was a big feature story in *Life* magazine and they were practically unobtainable. In fact, the balsa wood minnow imitation with its lifelike action was rented out, with a hefty deposit, at a few southern big bass resort lakes. It's still an excellent lure, especially the floating Rapala. But it's now available in sinking and jointed versions and even a jigging model. Get one.

REBEL MINNOW. The Rebel Minnow was the first generation of Rapala-type

FLOATING MINNOW

GAINES POPPING BUGS

HULA POPPER

REBEL MINNOW

WIG-WAG

RATTLEWORM

top of the line

lures to hit the market when the original Finnish balsa wood minnows were so popular they were unobtainable in many places. Well, most of the derivatives have disappeared, but the Rebel Minnow has stayed around catching lots of fish. Their floaters, in lots of size and color variations, remain the most popular but the sinkers and intermediates work well, too.

SHAKESPEARE. Swimming Mouse, Mister 13, Slim Jim and on and on. Artifacts of the great baitcasting renaissance. Shakespeare, always a big name in the thumbing form of angling, has resurrected seven of its all-time favorite plugs from whatever Heaven old-time baitcasting lures go to. Five of the plugs, available in weights ranging from ¼ to ¾ ounce in a variety of colors, are even made of wood, that substance that used to grow in forests before the practice of plastic farming caught on. Wooden lures have a very good action and these deserve a trial by even the most hypermodern of anglers.

Miscellany

AL'S GOLDFISH SHAD DARTS. Shad Darts are one of the basic lures. With a painted lead body and a dash of bucktail they will catch almost anything in fresh or salt water that has fins and swims. The standard 1/8-inch model in red and yellow or red and white is especially effective for shad or crappie.

PAUL BUNYAN. The Paul Bunyan "66" from Prescott is a regular performer among the spinner-fly set. The casting C-66 at 3/8 ounce is available with a variety of feathery patterns on its 1/0 hook, as is the spinning S-66 at ¼ ounce and the ultra light J-66 at 1/8 ounce.

BOONE BAIT COMPANY. The Boone Bait Company makes an excellent variety of shad jigs that work on just about every species of fresh- and smallish saltwater species. The little lead-headed-bucktailed lures come in sizes from 1/8 to a full ounce and lots of colors. With salt or freshwater hooks in the smaller sizes, Boone makes lots of other good jigs as well.

D.D.T. The D.D.T. from Tubby Tackle is an attempt to blend lots of modern trends in bass fishing. It has twin rattles, a soft rubber tail that squiggles and a big lip that takes it down deep. A good lure in lots of colors, it weighs ½ ounce.

GAINES HAIR BASS BUGS. The Gaines line of bass hair bugs are excellent American-made deer-hair poppers and bugs. It includes the Stream Cleaner, which works on top as well as underneath the water and comes with split shot attached. The Fuzz Bug, a mousey Mr. Whiskers and a Bush Bug might even scare up some large browns after dark.

GAPEN MUDDLER. One of the few lures to originate from fly fishing. Gapen's sells these weighted muddler minnows in both yellow and the original brown in ¼-ounce models. Excellent.

JIG-A-DO. The Jig-a-Do, a streamer jig originated by Stan Lievense, a Michigan biologist, is a very effective lure for any sort of fish. Its scoop makes for an interesting action. Quarter and 3/8-ounce models in colors based on streamer patterns like Mickey Finn and Muddler Minnow. Jig-a-Do worms and ells are also marketed.

MIKE, THE FISHERMAN'S LURE. Mike, the Fisherman's Lure, is one of those versatile items that used to be very popular. Depending on where you tie the line, it can be either a deep diver or a shallow swimmer; add a sinker, a bait or BBs and you have a bottom groper, a smell bait or a sound bait. Intriguing.

RAINBOWLURE. A color-changing lure? That's the latest development from PBI. Available in floaters and sinkers, the Rainbowlure has been designed for fresh- and saltwater angling. Looks like it's clear, but it isn't.

RATTLEWORM HEADS. If you'd like Eine Kleine Worma Music, get a Rattleworm head from Strader. Attaches above the hook and makes Texas-rigged worms more weedless. In blacks, blues, reds and purples in ¼- and ½-ounce models that sound off on retrieve.

SATURN BOBBER-LURE. The Saturn Bobber-Lure is a bobber designed for casting and releasing a bait to any depth. Works with No. 2 to No. 10 test monofilament and can be used for trolling as a streamer fly or bait adjunct. Versatile for top-to-bottom use.

STINGRAY TROLLING SINKER. Designed hydrodynamically like a stingray, this trolling sinker skims the bottom precisely, yet offers little water resistance. A good idea and available from 1/3 to 5¼ ounces.

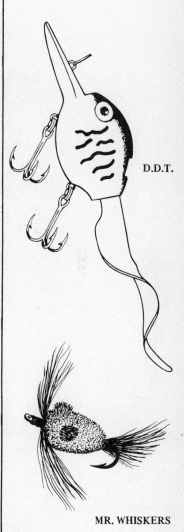

D.D.T.

MR. WHISKERS

LUSTER-LURE LURTAPE

Want to change colors in the middle of spooning? Well, get some strips of Lurtape, which comes in colors across the spectrum. Just put it on your spoon and maybe it'll change your luck. Available in prism models and for night casting, as well. Packaged various ways.

top of the line

TRAILER LURES. Fin Baits makes a line of Trailer Lures that can increase your catch. Made of marabou in various colors and sizes, they attach to the rear of your plug, spoon or spinner or can even be used alone or with bait attached.

UGLY BUG. The Ugly Bug by Gapen's is an effective spinning lure fished like a jig. It represents crayfish and the big hellgrammite found in Midwestern lakes. Different colors and weights from 1/16- to ½-ounce. Good for trout, too.

WIGGLE SPIN. P.T.'s Wiggle Spin is a combination spinner bait with a rubber skirt or plastic worm included with each lure. Use them all together. Silver or copper blades and loads of colors.

Z-PLUG. Zebco, which is just starting to move in a big way into the lure field, has just come out with the Z-Plug, a 3/8-ounce model with an internal sound chamber. Available with a lip for shallow, medium or deep fishing. Twelve colors for this newcomer.

Make Your Own

CABELA WORM MOLDS. Cabela sells a number of worm-making molds for whirl-tail and standard varieties. You can get injectors for pouring the liquid plastic, which they also sell, dyes of all tones and scents to sweeten things up. They also sell whirl-a-mander and split lizard for those exotically inclined.

HERTER'S LURE KITS. Herter's sure sells a lot of lure-making stuff. Almost anything you could want and then a lot more, including products that are really unique. Molds for all kinds of rubber worms, ranging from a 1¼-inch to 9½-inch in all kinds of styles. Lizards, crayfish and frogs, too. They also have the components for most types of spinners, spoons and plugs. Paints, eyes, swivels. It's all just too much for words. Get the catalog and get to work.

LAKELAND INDUSTRIES. Lakeland Industries offers a pretty good selection of components for building up your own spinners and related lures. Available in styles like the Colorado and Indiana as well as the Mepps type, Lakeland has the required beads, hooks and wires. Can save a lot of cash.

LURE-CRAFT. Lure-Craft's catalog is kinda the Encyclopedia Britannica of rubber worm literature. With special pouring pans, phosphorescent-colored dyes, flitter flakes, pages and pages of molds, jig hooks, regular hooks, spinner blades and whatever else you could possibly want. Too much for words, even in this book.

LURE-CRAFT DISPENSING POT. Here is the final word in worm-making gear. Lure-Craft's professional dispensing pot gives you absolute control over pouring consistency by simple thumb manipulation, bubble elimination through its needle valve, an adjustable heat control, a non-tip stand with a 60-foot control and, to add joy to your life, the whole thing is self-cleaning. It's all lightweight, too.

SHARKEY JOG HEADS. "Interesting looking" is the safest way to describe Reed's Sharkey Jog Heads. Available in ¼-, 1/3- and ½-ounce models in 1/0, 2/0 and 3/0 hook sizes. They have tooth mouths and raised eyes. A fish hitting one of your productions could probably plead self-defense.

WORTH JIG TYING KIT. A simple way to save money and pursue a hobby that'll keep you off the streets. It has 24 jig heads of various weights and styles, various bucktails and marabous plus nylon thread, cement, wax and a small vise.

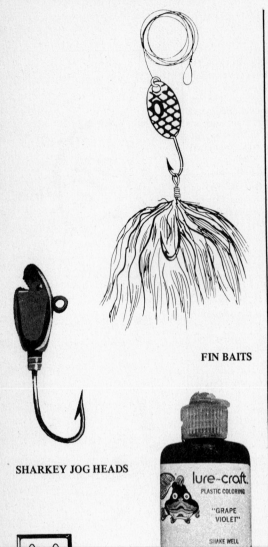

FIN BAITS

SHARKEY JOG HEADS

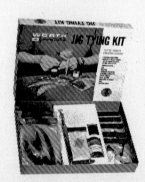

LURE-CRAFT

CABELA WORM MOLDS

WORTH JIG TYING KIT

LUHR JENSEN HOOK BONNETS

Hook bonnets are a safe way to transport lures through situations where fingers or whatever can get caught on them. They're plastic caps that simply snap on and remain till unsnapped. Carry your lures in your shirt pockets with Hook Bonnets.

SPOONS ARE GREAT BAITS

(continued from page 261)

white enameled spoon which has become one of the classics for the pike family of fishes.

Another, the famous Johnson Silver Minnow, is a highly polished silver spoon, fitted with a wire to guard the hook against weeds and snags. And there are many others.

There are spoons equipped with a revolving spinner blade at their fronts; colored feathers and hair, such as bucktail, have been dressed on the treble hooks or tied to single hooks on the spoons; and some are equipped with glass beads. When each of these attachments is produced in a wide variety of spoon finishes — silver, gold, hammered effect, and enamels of every possible shade — the total number of variations approaches infinity. In addition, the general shape or contour of the spoons varies from that of a willow leaf to that of a typical shoehorn.

It is the shape of the blade that gives the lure its erratic, darting, diving action in the water. This peculiar action, together with the lure's bright glitter, creates such a realistic impression of a darting minnow in a sunlit pool that game fish when feeding rarely hesitate to pursue and strike at this illusion.

The early models of these lures were made in rather large sizes, usually in the 5/8-ounce neighborhood. Only in recent years, since the dawn of spinning and spin-casting methods of angling, have the spoons become miniature in size. These lightweights range from a mere 1/16 to ¼-ounce. These too are made in practically every imaginable shape and color combination.

Fundamentally, then, the wobbler spoon is a blade of metal, usually following somewhat an oval or shoe-spoon shape in outline, dished or cupped to supply planning surfaces, so it will dart and wobble in the water as retrieved. The depth of the dishing, the position in which it occurs, combined with its outline is what determines the action. The more pronounced the dishing, the wider will be the darting or wobbling motion.

As mentioned, there are apparently two factors that cause fish to hit these lures. The first is the movement or action. The second is the finish. Late scientific tests show that game fish respond to certain colors and are able to distinguish them as well or nearly as well as humans can. The red and white "shoe-spoon" lure certainly is attractive to the pike family as evidenced by the great popularity of this lure.

Experience also indicates that right at the top in finish for spoons is the silver, gold, or bronze surface and more recently the gunmetal (black) finish. Generally, even though there is an enamel finish in some color combinations on one side, the other side is of polished metal. It would indicate that the predominant feature in attracting fish is action plus color and the erratic flashing of reflected light, so suggestive of the minnow's shiny scales.

The selection of such a lure should therefore be based on the possible action it will have in the water. The finish should be secondary. Included in the tackle box should be a few of the weedless variety for use in the brush-filled and weed-choked coves and bays.

The wobbler spoon has top rating as a lure, either casting, spinning, or trolling, for any of the pike family: muskies, northerns, and pickerel. In early spring it is also a fine walleye lure. Those of medium size take bass as do the very small sizes for panfish (perch, rock, bass), and frequently trout. There is a growing use of the medium-size wobbler in fishing deep holes in trout streams and in trout lakes. The large and extra large sizes are used to a great extent for salt-water game fish, such as blues and striped bass.

Some of the most experimenting and persistent anglers say that if they could take only one lure astream, they would select one of the simple wobbler spoons. Unmistakably, spoons are excellent baits, but I personally would not overemphasize these and minimize the baits in the other groups.

Taken from *Fishing Tackle and Gear* revised by Don Shiner. (C) 1950 by Stackpole and Heck, Inc. (C) 1962 by The Stackpole Company. Used by permission of Stackpole Books.

THE ULTIMATE HORRORS: FLASHERS AND DODGERS

Even the informed and skillful use of herring has not proved enough to produce satisfactory catches, so many fishermen have chosen to inflict upon themselves an ultimate horror — the "flasher" or "attractor" or "dodger." This is an enormous piece of bright metal, sometimes as much as eighteen inches long by three or four inches wide, shaped more or less like a spoon. It is attached to the line a few feet above the lure or bait and in this position is dragged through the water. Its primary purpose is to send a bright flash to a considerable distance through the water and so draw the salmon over to investigate. In the course of his investigations he is likely to come upon the lure or herring that is trailing behind and take appropriate action. A secondary purpose may be to impart some subtly different action to the lure or bait. Some fishermen believe that the flasher suggests another feeding salmon in action and so stimulates the competitive instincts of the real fish, some feel that it looks like herring or other feed, some that it gets its results simply by suggesting some sort of underwater activity.

Flashers are ugly, clumsy and awkward to fish with. They put a heavy drag on a rod and call for a heavy tension on the reel. They get in the way in the last stages, when a fish is being brought to the net and, most serious of all, they grossly inhibit the activity of the fish when it is hooked. A good-sized flasher dampens the speed and efforts of a ten- or fifteen-pound fish to feebleness and renders a five-pounder practically powerless. It is logical to assume that no fisherman in his right mind is going to ruin his sport in this way unless he feels that he must to get any results at all. And it is certain that flashers do, under some conditions, make the difference between catching fish and not catching them. Twenty years ago they were practically unknown; today they are used most of the time by a great many fishermen.

Taken from *Fisherman's Fall* by Roderick L. Haig-Brown. (C) 1975 by Roderick L. Haig-Brown. Used by permission of Crown Publishers, Inc.

"All that are lovers of virtue, and dare
trust in His providence, and be quiet,
and go a-angling."
IZAAK WALTON, *The Compleat Angler*

HOW TO RECONDITION
AND CARE FOR LURES

By C. Boyd Pfeiffer

Fortunately, modern lures require little in the way of care; but with the price of all artificial baits constantly escalating, it makes sense to give lures the minimal attention that will do a lot to prolong their lives and fish-catching ability.

The best care for lures is proper storage. Keep plugs, spoons, spinners, worms, bucktails and jigs separately in tackle boxes or in lure boxes. The large multi-tray tackle boxes, like the Plano 777, suited for the lure size and fishing, are the best insurance. For airline travel, store lures in single-tray polypropylene boxes and pack in suitcases, so they won't bounce around as they would in a checked tackle box.

Separate lures by type in trays or in tackle box to make it easy to find the right type when you're actually fishing. If your fishing requires several tackle boxes, consider outfitting one for each type of angling, stocked with the proper lures and marked. Listing the contents on the outside — even in a general way — will save time and trouble.

While most plugs today are made of plastic, metal spoons and spinners, and hooks on all lures, will rust if not properly cared for. To prevent this, open your tackle box or lure tray after each fishing trip to air out the box and to dry the lures. If the lures are very wet, or if the box was kept open in a rainstorm, remove all the lures and dry them on a workbench or kitchen table. This is also important for bucktails and jigs, with their feather and fur skirts, to prevent mildew and to prevent any hook rust from discoloring the materials.

Saltwater lures require additional care: always wash them in fresh water after use. The best way to do this is to separate lures used during a day's fishing, and keep them separate until reaching home, where they can be washed and dried properly.

The soft plastic lures — spinner bait tails, worms, plastic minnows, grub tails and some saltwater lures — *must* be separated from hard plastic plugs. The contact will generally not hurt the soft lures, but the plasticizers in the soft lures will dissolve the hard plastics, eat into them or harm the surface colors and pigments. These same soft plastics will also eat into some older tackle boxes, so store soft plastics in plastic bags, or in lure compartments by themselves or in tackle boxes labeled "worm-proof."

Most lures require little care to keep them looking new, but spinner blades and metal plated spoons may tarnish in time. To care for them carry a piece of steel wool or crocus cloth or, in an emergency, use sand or cigarette ashes to polish the lures for more fish-attracting reflection.

But in spite of the best care, lures do become worn and require repair or recycling. Plugs generally have durable plastic finishes today, but both they and older wooden plugs can be refinished in new colors. Remove the hardware, including all hook hangers and metal bills, drive a thin nail into a hook hanger hole to hold the lure and spray paint with a base coat of white. To spray a scale finish on a plug, use mesh net held in an embroidery ring pressed against the side of the plug. Spray the back of the plug with a dark color to create a realistic look and finish with a durable spray, dipped clear varnish or epoxy finish. Replace the hardware and you have a new plug for future trips.

Similarly, save spinners and spoons that become de-

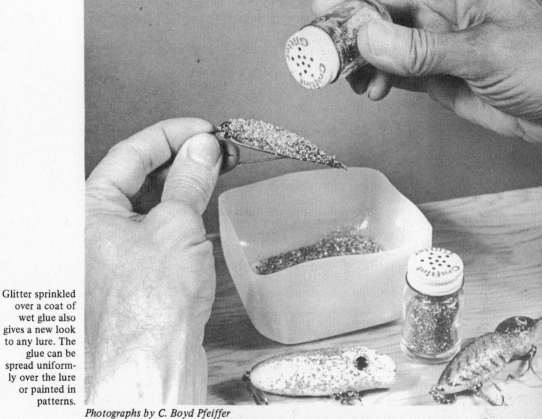

Glitter sprinkled over a coat of wet glue also gives a new look to any lure. The glue can be spread uniformly over the lure or painted in patterns.

Photographs by C. Boyd Pfeiffer

fective. Use the parts to make new spinners or spoons. Examine a typical spinner to see how the parts are assembled and then rebuild your spinners on new wire shafts with an eye twisted in one end with needle-nose pliers. Add the clevis and blade, body or beads and bend in another eye to hold the hook to complete the spinner. Spoons are simple since a few split rings make it easy to join hooks to repainted spoon blades. Use Worth Split Ring Pliers to open the split rings.

Bucktails suffer most by loosing their fur tails, especially when used for toothy saltwater fish. To refinish them, cut off all the old windings and fur, clean the bucktail head and repaint. Usually solid colors are best, and spraying or dipping both work well. Then get some bucktail fur from a deer hunter or tackle shop, a spool of nylon fly tying thread and tie on a new tail, using fly tying techniques.

The basics involve wrapping the thread on the hook shank, tying down the tail, clipping excess tail material in front of the wrap and finishing the wrap with several half hitches. Secure with a

(continued on next page)

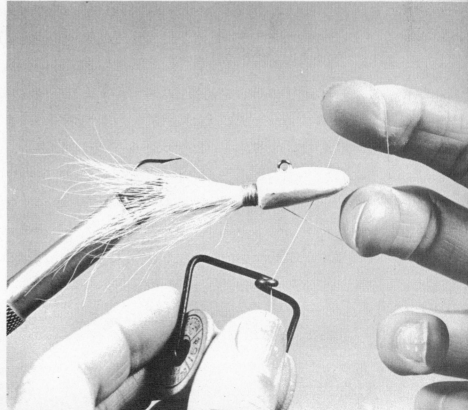

Bucktails can be refinished by cutting off the tail material, repainting the head and adding tail material as in this photo.

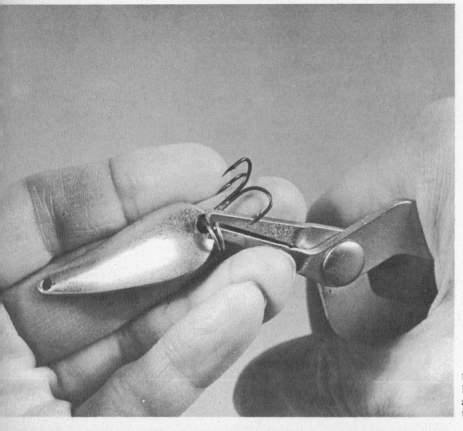

Use Worth Split Ring Pliers to add new hooks to spoon blades.

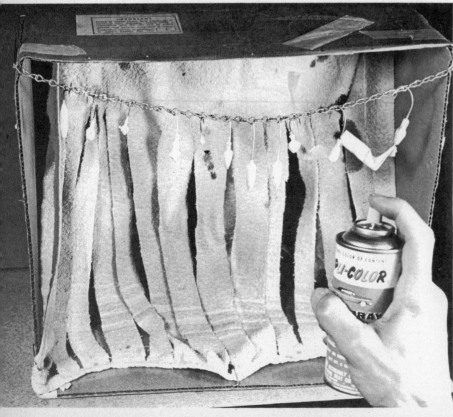

Spray paint a base coat of white on lures, spoons, and bucktail heads by hanging them up from chain or pipe strap in a cardboard box and spraying with an aerosol can. The strips of cloth in the back of the box prevent the spray paint from bouncing out of the box.

HOW TO RECONDITION LURES

(continued from preceding page)

coat of paint or epoxy rod finish.

Save old, chewed-up soft plastic lures and worms. In some cases it's possible to cut off the good parts of these lures and rejoin them by melting the cut ends with a cigarette lighter or alcohol lamp and rejoining the cut ends while the plastic is still molten. Old chewed-up soft plastic lures can also be used in worm making kits such as those by M-F and Super Sport, available in tackle and mail order stores.

In some cases it is not necessary to disassemble lures to give them a new look. Plugs, large head bucktails, spinner blades and spoons can be spruced up with the addition of colored reflective tape such as Luhr Jensen Prism Lite or Weber Flashback tape.

Glitter in many colors is available in most variety and craft stores and can be added over a base of glue in patterns or a solid coat. Other lure repairs, refurbishing and recycling can be done with lure making kits and lure materials available in tackle stores or from fishing tackle mail order houses that advertise in the outdoor magazines.

A final tip: sharpen every hook on your lures even when the lures are new. A good check for hook sharpness is to drag the point of the hook lightly across your thumb nail. If the hook point digs in, it is sharp; if it slides, it is too dull to hook fish properly.

Sharpen your lures by using a file such as the Red Devil No. 15 file or the Nicholson Rotary Mower File. The latter is coarser and faster cutting, but both work well. Sharpen the hook so that the point is triangulated, with two flat sides coming to a sharp edge running from point to barb. Finish by flattening the outer edge of the point to make the point triangular in cross section.

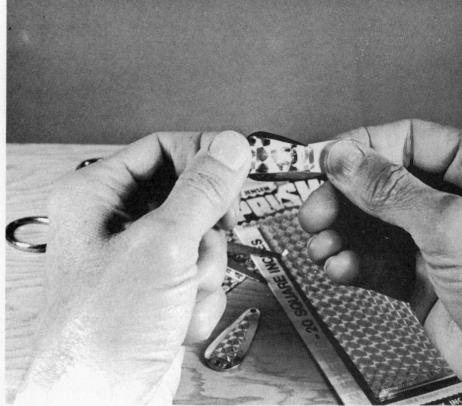

Reflective tape in many colors will add a new look to spoons, spinner blades, and plugs. It has an adhesive backing.

Old plastic worms that have been chewed up by fish can be remelted over a low flame and made into new lures with molds available from plastic worm kit suppliers.

The inventor reveals all
A history of the Dardevle

By Lou Eppinger

The discovery of the Dardevle was not an accident. It was the result of many years of experimentation. The object was to create a swimming lure that the fisherman could cast without continuous backlashing. At that period, 1907-1910, there were no artificial lures with action. The Wilson Wobbler was produced later. To my knowledge the first action lure produced, however, had only a slight wiggle, and due to its bulk was difficult to cast, especially for the beginner, for whom it produced many backlashes and headaches.

Shakespeare's Level Wind reel was an improvement, but too expensive for the budding baitcasters. The best reels, Meek & Talbot, were too fast, and only an expert could cast with them without continuous backlashing. Wooden plugs were too bulky and too light, and could not be cast into the wind without the resultant backlash. Therefore a lure that

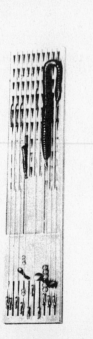

LURE CADDIE

A convenient little accessory for the boating angler is the Lure Caddie, a cord-lined tray to keep your most-used lures just a reach away. Lures are hooked into it. Will attach to the side of your boat with suction cups or can be screwed on.

would cut through the air and wind and also have action was the answer.

Up to 1916 I had produced many different types of shapes and weights. Some with turned-down noses dived to six feet with a wiggle so active it almost shook the rod out of one's hand. During this period I had the assistance of such men as John B. Thompson (Ozark Ripley) and others. We caught brook trout 4 to 5 pounds on the Nipigon, walleyes on the Black and Ottawa Rivers in Quebec and genuine eastern pickerel on lakes adjoining the Ottawa vicinity of Waltham, Quebec. Ozark also used the Dardevle in the streams of the Ozarks, where he was a native.

Late in 1916 or early 1917 we were satisfied that the present shape of the Dardevle was the answer. Any beginner could cast them, they were easy to control as to depth, wiggled slowly on slow reeling and fast with fast reeling.

In those days whippy light casting rods were unknown to most fishermen, or too high-priced for the majority. Tubular, sectional steel rods, were the vogue: Bristol, Rainbow, Luckie, Union Hardware, Samson. Lengths 3 feet 3½ feet and 4 feet mostly and used about as we did with Mud Balls at the end of a stout switch. A lure had to be heavy and yet not sink too rapidly. Heddon's 5 Gang 150 Series were mostly used. The 3 Gang 100 Series were too light, and few of them were sold. Therefore you can readily appreciate why the baitcaster went for the Dardevle, depth controlled by raising or lowering the rod aided by fast or slow reeling.

However, the average fishermen pay little attention to the finesse of handling the lure. They just cast it out and reel it in, and often with a fish on the end of the line.

We have never publicized it, but we sure ran into a lot of trouble during the early period of manufacturing. Lures were returned because they would not wiggle. It required quite some time to discover that the metal was to blame. We naturally purchased metal easy to obtain or lower in price. Also the enamel would not hold and would not take a brilliant polish. Some would warp after aging and just a slight warp, especially in the nose, would cause the lure to rise to the top of the water. Therefore our metal must have a certain consistency. Our supplier specially rolls all our metals, which must be ordered at least one year in advance. The price of metals has quadrupled since the early days, but our prices remain about the same as in the olden days. Naturally our profits have been greatly reduced. Fortunately, our sales have increased, which of course helps out a lot. No doubt you can readily appreciate that there is a lot more

to producing Dardevles than just stamping and painting.

The Lure was originally introduced in our retail store in 1917 and 1918, and believe me it required a lot of selling to get 75 cents for that piece of iron, as one dealer quoted it.

My good friend Jack Macy, then Western advertising manager of *Field and Stream*, Chicago office, prepared my advertising. 1918: the first advertisement full page headed "It Took Me Six Years to Find Out About This Bait." I owe a lot to Jack Macy for preparing my entire first year's advertising — slogans and all. The Lure was named after the Marines, called Devil Dogs by the Germans, and Dare Devils by the Allies. The Marines were sure making a name for themselves. "DARDEVLE" was misspelled as a sop to clergymen who objected to the word Devil being shown in print. Anyone, everyone pronounces it "Dare Devil."

CA/90 LURE SCENT

There are lots of anglers who believe in this kind of thing, so the CA/90 company puts out a solution which will kill the human scent on lures. Called "lure pure," which is advertised as nonpolluting, it supposedly removes all organic odors. Just squirt it. Comes in a 4-ounce container.

GAMEFISH: STRIPED BASS

NAMES
Striper, rockfish, greenhead, rock, streaked bass, squidhound. *(Roccus saxatilis)*

DISTRIBUTION
The striped bass is found from the St. Lawrence seaway south to the Gulf of Mexico. In the Pacific, it ranges from the Columbia river to Los Angeles.

DESCRIPTION
The striped bass is an anadromous fish that's dark green or brown on the back with silver or brassy sides. Seven or eight horizontal stripes mark the sides. The dorsal fins are separated.

SIZE
The striped bass averages 3 to 10 pounds although fish of up to 25 pounds are not considered unusual.

HABITAT
Although the striped is a saltwater fish that migrates into fresh water to spawn, it spends most of its time inshore near inlets, tidal flats and river mouths where the water is primarily brackish. In some areas, they go inland in the winter and out to sea in the warmer months. They run in schools.

FEEDING HABITS
The striped bass feeds on a great variety of fish. They will eat flounder, mullet, herring, crabs and shrimp. The warmer months are the times they are most active.

TACKLE
Another fish that is sought with all sorts of tackle. Since its size range varies so much at times it just takes light spinning gear or a large streamer cast from a fly rod. At other times bait-wielding trollers have a chance. Likes big plugs chugging near the surface.

THE LAST HATCH
A FISHING MYSTERY
HARMON HENKIN

(continued from page 260)

creek. That No. 8-weight line would hit the water like a bomb. It'd scare every trout for miles. Wouldn't he fish the spring creek with a rod like this 7-foot Thomas?"

"He usually did, but I fail to see what you're getting at."

"Was there a fly attached to the line when you found the rod?"

"Yes, a Muddler Minnow."

Paul nodded and with a pleased smile walked around the room slowly, obviously savoring the fact that everyone else was totally confused. He paused at the 16-by-20 photo of Halford landing a white marlin off the coast of Cuba. A younger Alexandrea was beaming at him from the stern of the outrigger.

"I don't think Halford was really going to fish the spring creek today. I think he was going to fish the big pool in the river. Muddlers work very well on that pool. He wrote about some of the big rainbows he caught there in *The Catfish Never Meows*."

Sid picked up on the thread. "You're saying that Halford lied to Julie. He wasn't really going down to the creek but on his way to the river got caught by the murderer."

"Wait a minute," Wormer said. "Halford didn't want the girl to know where he was going? I thought he was still interested in a piece of . . . conversation?"

"He may usually have been interested in Julie as a plaything but he seemed a lot more interested in someone or a group of someones not finding out where he was going."

"Then why bring the big rod," Schielbacht whined. "Somebody might have been able to figure that out."

"That's simple," Paul responded. "He wasn't thinking about fishing when he left. He was thinking about who he was going to meet. He just picked up the rod as a prop and his instincts made him pick the right rod for his rendezvous spot."

"Ah," Sid said. "So even if Julie had wanted to murder him she would have gone to the mouth of the creek and been forced to wait for him to come downstream."

Julie looked a little bit more relaxed. "Sigh. My heroes. Regular fly fishing Sherlock Holmes. Where's the coke, honey?"

Sid gave her a dirty look. "Another prime suspect down the drain. Who's next?"

(continued on page 284)

Spend the extra money
Monofilament is crucial

By Harmon Henkin

Why should an angler spend extra money for an expensive monofilament spinning line when one can be grabbed off the shelf in the same pound test for a quarter the price?

Lots of reasons. As simple as it might look in print, the line is a crucial part of your basic angling outfit; this is something some fishers won't admit to themselves even though they fork over minor fortunes for rods, reels and lures.

Better lines like Stren, Berkley Trilene and the European imports such as Maxima have lots of basic advantages over the cheaper types. In the first place a top quality line will almost always be the real pound test it says on the spool. And it will be uniform, as well. Inexpensive lines have the unnerving habit of varying strength along their lengths — a No. 10 line can be No. 6 in some places and No. 12 in others. This can affect your chances of breaking a world record since a sample of the line must be submitted for pound test verification with your record application. It can also affect your chances of landing a decent fish.

In the next place, nylon is affected by sunlight and to a lesser degree by exposure to the air. The better nylons are less bothered by the elements but freshness is a desirable quality in all of them.

Another factor to consider in choosing a nylon spinning or casting line is stretch. If mono doesn't have enough stretch to absorb the shock of a fish jerking hard at the other end it is more liable to break. But this shock-absorbing quality is a two-way proposition. If there is too much stretch the angler will have a limited amount of control in fighting the fish. Here again the better lines have a stretch factor of somewhere under 10 per cent, which is desirable. The quality control of less expensive monos is often more erratic and here again the better models give you added quality.

The better lines will also take a knot better with less slippage and a higher percentage of knot strength retained.

Many of the more affluent anglers who pamper themselves will buy new lines every week or so for added protection against minor abrasions that can affect line strength. This may be an indulgence but it can pay off, especially with light pound test lines where subtle variations in performance can mean the difference between good fish and no fish.

Lots of good lines are available these days in all sorts of shades. Whether color is really a factor among discriminating fish is a question without a firm answer as yet. Sure, fish see colors but whether they associate the dark colors, the light colors or any of the hues in between with danger is another question. There are some excellent anglers who feel that line should be as transparent as possible and others who don't care.

But all experienced fishers do feel that a good mono is a worthwhile investment.

Hardy Brothers claimed in the early 1900s that its "Cerolene" line dressing was "the most perfect preparation for spinning and dry fly lines." Anglers were advised to soak their silk lines in melted Cerolene for half an hour and to wipe away the excess with a cloth to keep the lines "pliant and in good order."

"You will find that river water speaks different words to a fisherman than lake water."
SID GORDON

LINES & LEADERS **279**

FROM WASHINGTON IRVING'S SKETCH BOOK: THE ANGLER

It is said that many an unlucky urchin is induced to run away from his family and betake himself to a seafaring life from reading the history of Robinson Crusoe; and I suspect that, in like manner, many of those worthy gentlemen who are given to haunt the sides of pastoral streams with anglerods in hand, may trace the origin of their passion to the seductive pages of honest Izaak Walton. I recollect studying his *Compleat Angler* several years since, in company with a knot of friends in America, and, moreover, that we were all completely bitten with the angling mania. It was early in the year, but as soon as the weather was auspicious, and that the spring began to melt into the verge of summer, we took rod in hand and sallied into the country as stark mad as was ever Don Quixote from reading books of chivalry.

One of our party had equaled the Don in the fulness of his equipments; being attired cap-a-pie for the enterprise. He wore a broad-skirted fustian coat, perplexed with half a hundred pockets; a pair of stout shoes and leathern gaiters; a basket slung on one side for fish; a patent rod; a landing net, and a score of other inconveniences only to be found in the true angler's armory. Thus harnessed for the field, he was as great a matter of stare and wonderment among the country folk, who had never seen a regular angler, as was the steel-clad hero of La Mancha among the goatherds of the Sierra Morena. Our first essay was along a mountain brook, among the highlands of the Hudson -- a most unfortunate place for the execution of those piscatory tactics which had been invented along the velvet margins of quiet English rivulets. It was one of those wild streams that lavish, among our romantic solitudes, unheeded beauties enough to fill the sketch-book of a hunter of the picturesque. Sometimes it would leap down rocky shelves, making small cascades, over which the trees threw their broad balancing sprays, and long nameless weeds hung in fringes from the impending banks, dripping with diamond drops. Sometimes it would brawl and fret along a ravine in the matted shade of a forest, filling it with murmurs, and, after this termagant career, would steal forth into open day with the most placid demure face imaginable; as I have seen some pestilent shrew of a housewife, after filling her home with uproar and ill-humor, come dimpling out of doors, smiling upon all the world.

How smoothly would this vagrant brook glide, at such times, through some bosom of green meadowland among the mountains; where the quiet was only interrupted by the occasional tinkling of a bell from the lazy cattle among the clover, or the sound of a woodcutter's ax from the neighboring forest.

For my part, I was always a bungler at all kinds of sport that required either patience or adroitness, and had not angled above half an hour before I had completely "satisfied the sentiment," and convinced myself of the truth of Izaak Walton's opinion, that angling is something like poetry -- a man must be born to it. I hooked myself instead of the fish; tangled my line in every tree; lost my bait; broke my rod; until I gave up the attempt in despair and passed the day under the trees reading old Izaak; satisfied that it was his fascinating vein of honest simplicity and rural feeling that had bewitched me, and not the passion for angling. My companions, however, were more persevering in their delusion. I have them at this moment before my eyes, stealing along the border of the brook, where it lay open to the day, or was merely fringed by shrubs and bushes. I see the bittern rising with hollow scream as they break in upon his rarely-invaded haunt; the kingfisher watching them suspiciously from his dry tree, that overhangs the deep black millpond in the gorge of the hills; the tortoise letting himself slip sidewise from off the stone or log on which he is sunning himself, and the panic-struck frog plumping in headlong as they approach and spreading an alarm throughout the watery world around.

I recollect, also, that, after toiling and watching and creeping about for the greater part of a day, with scarcely any success, in spite of all our admirable apparatus, a lubberly country urchin came down from the hills with a rod made from the branch of a tree; a few yards of twine; and, as heaven shall help me! I believe a crooked pin for a hook, baited with a vile earth-worm -- and in half an hour caught more fish than we had nibbles throughout the day.

But above all, I recollect the "good, honest, wholesome, hungry" repast which we made under a beech-tree just by a spring of pure sweet water that stole out of the side of a hill; and how, when it was over, one of the party read old Izaak Walton's scene with the milkmaid, while I lay on the grass and built castles in a bright pile of clouds, until I fell asleep.

A WORD ABOUT LINES

A few years ago, the most popular lines were made from Irish or Belgian linen; braided or twisted, it was known as "cuttyhunk." Linen lines were graded according to thread numbers from 3 to 72; thread strength, three pounds, wet, a 54-thread line testing at 162 pounds. These lines and designations are still used in tournament fishing. Today, most lines are braided nylon or dacron while some, including the spincasters, prefer monofilament. Braided nylon lines are rated to pound test, but not according to threads; they are available in spools of 50 to 100 yards, in boxes of from two to six spools. In the same sizes they come packed up to 1200 yards and in a variety of colors. Monofilament lines run from 6 to 50-pound test for saltwater fishing.

Wire lines of stainless steel, bronze-copper and other corrosive-proof metals are used with Monel, the present favorite for deep offshore trolling. Made in twist, braid and some fabricovered lead-core versions, they range in strength from five to 85 pounds.

Taken from *Introduction to Bait Fishing* by Ray Ovington. (C) 1971 by Ray Ovington. Used by permission of Stackpole Books.

top of the line

AMNESIA. The Sunset Line Company has been around for a long time but its new Amnesia monofilament is considered a great leap forward by many steelhead and saltwater flyfishers. The big advantage of Amnesia is that, as its name implies, it forgets. Most other mono has the disconcerting habit of remembering how it's coiled. But Amnesia can be stretched between two hands and it stays stretched. This is important for shooting head fishing where coils cause drag. Available in the most common pound tests.

ANDE MONOFILAMENT. As record-breaking becomes a more serious saltwater avocation, monofilament has become more serious, too. One of the better examples of this is Ande line, available in pound tests of 6, 12, 20, 30, 50, 80 or 130. It has already been used to break 48 world records of varying sorts and consequences. Ande is a soft line that stays put and is critically manufactured to avoid both "soft" or "hard" spots that would disquality a would-be record holder. Sold in clear, pink, gunmetal and tournament green in ¼-, ½-, 1-, 2- and 6-pound spools.

BERKLEY SEASTRAND 49'ER TROLLING LINE. This is a tough line for tough jobs. It has 49 strands of stainless steel line twisted for more strength. Available in 300- and 1000-foot spools in tests from 60 to 600 pounds. They also offer a seven-strand Steelon Trolling line and Seastrand regular trolling line, which is made with seven stainless steel strands but is uncoated.

Amnesia is easy to use.

Amnesia is a fine example of how significant product improvement can come about by chance. Amnesia was originally sold to one of Sunset Line and Twine's industrial customers and happened to be seen by one of the Company's fly fishing friends. At the time, he happened to be on his way to the Klamath River in Oregon and asked to take some with him to experiment. He found it worked perfectly for him, handed out samples to several of his friends, and started a word-of-mouth campaign that ultimately resulted in California dealers demanding that the Company make the shooting line available.

Amnesia is easy to use: you simply strip off the amount you intend to shoot and stretch it with your hands. The stretch takes out all the coil, and it will lie limp for the rest of the day's fishing. It doesn't have the memory of regular monofilament. It fishes beautifully. It's round and doesn't plane in the water the way flat monofilaments will; it easily picks up from the water and it shoots beautifully. While it was designed as a practical fishing product, tournament distance casters have started using Amnesia because it does shoot so well. —H.H.

"For the great majority of trout anglers, a day's fishing means a few hours on the river sandwiched between two long and exhausting drives."
LEONARD WRIGHT

LINES & LEADERS 281

top of the line

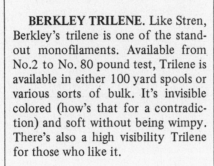

BERKLEY TRILENE. Like Stren, Berkley's trilene is one of the standout monofilaments. Available from No.2 to No. 80 pound test, Trilene is available in either 100 yard spools or various sorts of bulk. It's invisible colored (how's that for a contradiction) and soft without being wimpy. There's also a high visibility Trilene for those who like it.

BEVIN-WILCOX. The Bevin-Wilcox Line Company of Connecticut makes a pretty thorough variety of lines for baitcasting, squidding and assorted uses. They are made of braided nylon and dacron. They also produce a deep trolling lead-core line in a variety of weights. Just about anything you'll need for heavy-duty work. Available in small or bulk spools.

Of all the sports and pastimes
  That happen in the year,
To Angling there are none, sure,
  That ever can compare.
        Then to Angle we will go.

We do not break our legs or arms,
  As Huntsmen often do,
For when that we are Angling
  No danger can ensue.
        Then to Angle we will go.

Cards and dice are courtly games,
  Then let them laugh who win,
There's innocence in Angling,
  But gaming is a sin.
        Then to Angle we will go.

From Songs of the Chace

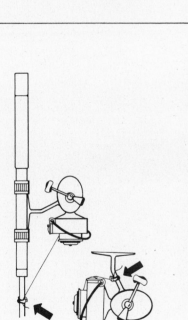

REEL ASSIST

Reel Assists are handy little products made in Wyoming to help keep your spinning and baitcasting line out of trouble. It clips on either your reel or rod and holds your line out of the way. Can fit onto the shank of your reel or below the first guide of your rod. Has a little clip to hold things down. Very convenient.

BEVIN-WILCOX

top of the line

LEW CHILDRE. An interesting idea in the rapidly changing baitcasting field is this tapered line, available in brown, green and clear and in 10-, 15- and 20-pound test varieties on the 170-yard spool. The idea behind this Fuji-made, Lew Childre-imported product is simple: the front end is clear and 70 yards long; the middle section is green, also 20-pound test, and 85 yards long; the tail end is green and 15 yards long, giving you extra strength with a running fish. Available in three different models for the experimental baitcaster who wants to test the claim that this line is more wind resistant, offers less drag and causes you fewer backlash problems.

CORTLAND NYLORFI. That wonderful tippet material sold by Cortland — Nylorfi — also makes a wonderful spinning line. Made in France, it has a relatively small diameter, controlled elongation and its neutral grey is almost invisible. Takes a knot very well, too. Comes in 100-yard spools or in 2000-yard bulk. One of the best.

GLADDING. Gladding sells a very fine variety of mono lines for the spincaster, open-facer or baitcaster in any pound-test imaginable. Their Mercury is an ultra-soft monofilament; Clearon is transparent for crystalline waters, Super Monofilament is a limp spincasting line. Other types are sold for the angler who has progressed to the enviable point of knowing what he wants.

GLADDING BASSIN' MAN ALL-PRO MAGNUM BASS LINE. Gladding's Bassin' Man "All Pro" Magnum Bass Line has been designed for use with worming rods and other big-time bass tackle. A good product but an example of overkill. The line is invisible grey and Gladding boasts that

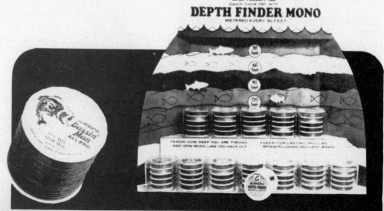

LEW CHILDRE

GUDEBROD GT

it was produced to maximize "lunker-generated sudden strains." Sold from 10- to 22-pound test.

GLADDING DEPTH-FINDER MONOFILAMENT. An idea that has kicked around fishing circles for quite a few years is colored line for trolling and casting that will tell you how deep your bait or lure is. Gladding has a Depth-Finder monofilament packaged in 100- or 200-yard spools available from 2- to 30-pound test which changes color every 10 yards. Can be useful to those going down under.

GLADDING INVINCIBLE. One of the better nylon baitcasting lines around is Gladding's Invincible, available in black, white and multi-color in most standard-pound tests. This floating line has a heat finish and is quite smooth enough for easy casting.

GLADDING MARK V. Another good deep-trolling line is Gladding's Mark V. It changes color every 10 yards and is dacron-braided over its core. Vinyl coated and sold from 18- to 60-pound test. Gladding also has a Special Mark V dacron metered lead core line that offers a smaller diameter and less elongation. To minimize the drag, this one has braided nylon over its lead core that's similar to many modern fly lines.

GUDEBROD GT. A fine, heavy-duty dacron ice fishing line available from No. 15 through No. 72 in 100-yard spools. Teflon coating makes it ideal for winter angling.

GUDEBROD MUSKIE SPECIAL. A good, heavy-duty dacron casting line sold in 50-yard spools in test-pounds of 25, 30, 35 and 40. Also available in six fifty-yard spools and in Greenspot and Bluespot colors.

THE LAST HATCH
A FISHING MYSTERY
HARMON HENKIN

(continued from page 277)

"I don't know yet," Paul said. "But it's one of this group for sure." The burden of the investigation had shifted from Sid to himself with remarkable speed.

"Let's have a conference, Paul," Sid whispered. Paul nodded in agreement.

"All right, folks," Sid announced with all the authority he could muster. "We're zeroing in on the culprit but we just need a little time to clean up the details. I want you all to stay around. Don't nobody try anything sneaky. I'll call you all back in here when we're ready."

"But sheriff," Belle cooed, "I was supposed to go to Olympia, Washington, tomorrow to visit my dear mother."

"And I was scheduled to fly to New Jersey," Wormer added.

Everyone except Hewitt, Dun and Tups joined the chorus of whines about missed planes and botched schedules.

"Well, I'm real glad to know that everyone wants to leave but none of you are going anywhere till we get to the bottom of this." He stared them down one by one. Paul headed for the patio and Sid followed as the group broke into a couple of knots, which whispered and eyed each other.

Sid sat down next to Paul on the patio.

"You know what I've been thinking, buddy?"

"Nope."

"I'd sure like to have one of Halford's rods."

"What a self-serving cynic you are," Paul said lightly. "You're supposed to be solving the crime of the century in this county and you're worried about fly rods."

"Yeah, but so far the only leads in this case have come from fishing."

"I don't know how far that will take us. How long can you keep this case out of the papers?"

"Not much longer. I figure I was supposed to call whoever the sheriff calls at times like this already. Probably the state cops in Helena and maybe even the FBI. But if I do that the place will be swarming with uniforms."

Julie wandered over and sat on the grass.

"Solved it yet, boys?"

"Why couldn't he have gotten killed in Key West?" Sid moaned.

(continued on page 287)

top of the line

MAXIMA. Maxima's Chameleon monofilament, available in tests from 1- to 40-pound tests, is one of the best. It's not cheap, but a much better buy in the maxi-spool with over 650 yards, than in the 250-yard spools. Also sold in Service Spools in lengths from 3200 to 2600 yards depending on the pound test.

QUICK DAMYL. Like the rest of Quick's stuff, the Damyl line has been around for a while. It comes in a variety of packaging, including twin packs of 100-yard spools in gold coloration from 2 pound test to 60. This soft monofilament is also available in camouflage green and clear in larger packages, including a 300-yard pack. Damyl is time-tested, a lot to say these days about any tackle!

QUICK DAMYL

GAMEFISH: FLOUNDER

NAMES
Fluke, flatfish. *(Paralichthys dentatus)*

DISTRIBUTION
The summer flounder ranges from Maine to Texas. It is plentiful off the coast of South Carolina.

DESCRIPTION
The summer flounder is a member of the flatfish family. Its body is flat and both of its eyes are situated on the left side of the body. The side of its body that is directed towards the surface is a pale brown or grey with dark spots. The side that faces the ocean floor is generally whitish. The summer flounder has a large mouth and strong canine teeth.

SIZE
The average summer flounder weighs 2 to 8 pounds although they do go as large as 25 pounds or more.

HABITAT
The summer flounder is most often found in shallow waters around bays and harbors. They often lie in the mud or sand but in the winter move into deeper waters.

FEEDING HABITS
The summer flounder feeds on crabs and shrimp as well as small fish. They are often taken in the surf and at anight.

TACKLE
Like the saltwater sunfish, the flounder is most often sought by casual anglers looking for something good to eat. But surfcasters with tackle as light as possible enjoy them as do pier anglers using cut baits.

MAXIMA CHAMELEON

A rod twelve feet long and
  a ring of wire.
a winder and barrel, will
  help thy desire
In killing a Pike; but the
  forked stick,
With a slit and a bladder —
  and that other fine trick,
Which our artists call snap,
  with a goose or a duck,
Will kill two for one, if you
  have any luck.

Thomas Barker
The Art of Angling

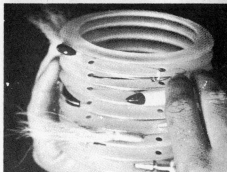

PBI LEADER-KEEPER

PBI's model 300 Leader-Keeper is a collapsible storage unit for your leaders that keeps them organized and out of the way in your tackle box. Whether wire or mono, the plastic rollers, which take eight leaders, will even hold small lures on the end. It can be tied to your belt or boat. A very convenient accessory.

The specialized art of baitfishing

By Harmon Henkin

Though many anglers think of baitfishing and its paraphernalia as the most basic and primitive form of fishing, it actually has become much more specialized recently.

The key to choosing baits, weights, swivels, snaps, leaders and other accessories is to have a specific task. These accessories have been designed with a narrow function in mind and that's what they should be used for.

There should also be a harmony between various baitfishing components. The nightcrawler should be impaled on a hook that will hold it firmly yet not be too large or small. The weight, swivel and monofilament leader should also be in balance. Too many baitfishermen think whatever they can find in a discount house is correct.

Steelheaders are probably the most sophisticated bait anglers around. Their tiny gold-plated hooks are made for a certain number of salmon eggs and the weights are available in graduations precise enough that the eggs can be bumped along the bottom, which is the way any bait should be fished in moving water.

The most successful carp and catfish seekers also develop their own formulas for bait size and weight. With sensitive bottom feeders it becomes crucial not to let the quarry sniffing around a doughball or cut bait sense a lot of extra weight.

And while threading a worm isn't as intricate as matching a trout stream hatch, it is a world with its own equipment and rules. Baitfishing is the most popu-

(continued on page 294)

Baitfishing is a world with its own rules and equipment.

A brief history of Norwegian fish hooks

These Stone Age bone fish hooks are at least 5000 years old. They were found in the Skipshelleren cave, Straume, Nordhordland in Norway, site of hunters' and fishermen's settlements which lasted into the Viking Age (A.D. 800-1030). Actual length: 1.8—4.3 cm.

Large, Stone Age bone fish hook from Skipshelleren, source of the largest and most varied collection of fish hooks found at any prehistoric settlement in Scandinavia. Inhabitants also used gaffs, lances, harpoons and needles of bone and antler. Actual length: 7.4 cm.

Two simple bone hook patterns from the Stone Age. Over 5000 years old, they came to light in the Vistehula cave near Stravanger, Norway, once situated on the Stone Age coast line. The early residents caught seal, gathered shellfish, fished for cod, coalfish. Actual length: 1.6—2.9 cm.

Bone fish hooks made by Lapps at Kjelmoy on the Varanger Fiord in northern Norway, some 1500 years ago. Lacking contact with the Iron Age people, living farther south in Norway, they made tools and hooks from bone and antler instead of iron and bronze. Actual length: 7.2—10.2 cm.

(continued on page 294)

THE LAST HATCH
A FISHING MYSTERY
HARMON HENKIN

(continued from page 284)

"They're used to that stuff down there. I sure don't want to go back to Philadelphia." He chewed on a fingernail and frowned. "Look, I gotta go make those calls. Think of something, Paul. We'll have to arrest Julie otherwise, just to make me look good."

"It'd take more than that to make you look good, Sid. At least in this case."

Sid wandered back into the house mumbling to himself about crime, brown trout and graduate school.

"How come you're not fishing, Paul?" Julie asked. "That's your usual response to crisis."

"Still bitter?"

"No. Just wiser."

"Things change."

"But the fishes don't and, I think I can assume, you don't either."

"I still care for you."

"Getting romantic in your old age, aren't you. No more love 'em and leave 'em?"

"Let's take a walk."

They strolled along the creek, now covered by late-afternoon shadows. Julie sat down on a log half submerged in the water and dangled her feet. Paul crouched on the bank.

"Ever think of settling down, Julie?"

"Almost never. I can't feature a future filled with cooking trout in your run-down cabin. It qualifies as a disaster area."

"God, Julie. People have ups and downs. They can change. You bring back lots of memories."

"Yeah but some people are as transparent as this water. I didn't know this was your spawning season. Do you want to swim upstream?"

"God, you're hard, Julie. I still love you. And I still love fishing."

"Sentimentality was never your strong suit, Paul."

He sat down next to her on the log and put his arm around her shoulder. After a moment's hesitation she leaned against him.

"You were always my weak spot."

"We've both matured and so have my feelings toward you."

He put his fingers under her chin and lowered his head toward her. Their lips met gently and they held each other tenderly. Then his left eye opened just a smidgen. An enormous brown trout had taken a grass-

(continued on page 291)

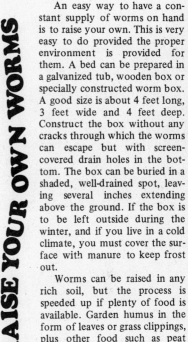

RAISE YOUR OWN WORMS

An easy way to have a constant supply of worms on hand is to raise your own. This is very easy to do provided the proper environment is provided for them. A bed can be prepared in a galvanized tub, wooden box or specially constructed worm box. A good size is about 4 feet long, 3 feet wide and 4 feet deep. Construct the box without any cracks through which the worms can escape but with screen-covered drain holes in the bottom. The box can be buried in a shaded, well-drained spot, leaving several inches extending above the ground. If the box is to be left outside during the winter, and if you live in a cold climate, you must cover the surface with manure to keep frost out.

Worms can be raised in any rich soil, but the process is speeded up if plenty of food is available. Garden humus in the form of leaves or grass clippings, plus other food such as peat moss, or manure mixed with soil and to which food is added periodically, makes an excellent bed. The worms can be fed almost anything: all kinds of table garbage, corn meal, chicken mash, grease drippings, bread crumbs, ground oats, cattle feed and other forms of animal or vegetable matter. The soil should be slightly moistened to keep the worms healthy.

After preparing the bed, I would then add several hundred worms, the exact number depending upon the size of the container. With proper care and enough feed you should breed enough worms to provide yourself with a good supply all the year round.

Worms that are to be kept for short periods of time may be kept in sphagnum moss, leaves or peat moss with a small amount of feed. Before being used, worms ought to be placed in your bait container with sphagnum moss (the kind obtained from a florist) to be scoured. This means the worms get rid of the earth inside of them while in the moss and become more transparent, and, at the same time, tougher and more lively.

From *America's Favorite Fishing* by F. Philip Rice. (C) 1964 by F. Philip Rice. Used by permission of Outdoor Life Books.

SHOSHONI POCKET PAK
SALMON EGGS

BUSS WORM BEDDING

The Buss people keep turning out products to make your worm's life more bearable. Just add water and it will hold some 50 crawlers per pound. Sold in packages of 1, 2, 5 and 25 pounds.

Facts About Nightcrawlers
By George Sroda

Everything you wanted to know about nightcrawlers but were afraid to ask. This fully illustrated, 100-page booklet presents all the information you need about the care, raising and fishing of the beasties in a very folksy, easy-to-read style. Fun and informative reading from America's self-proclaimed "Worm Czar."

---

top of the line

Bait

KEGARA FOAMBAITS. Foambaits sold by Kegara are bits of material impregnated with fish oil for baitfishing. They stay on the hook even after taking a fish, yet are very soft. Good for icefishing, too. Easy to transport.

LUHR JENSEN IMITATION SALMON EGGS. Luhr Jensen is marketing a Jensenegg soft plastic imitation salmon egg in either red or orange. Good for emergency use. They also sell a "gooey-blob," which, as the name implies, is a soft plastic slump of eggs.

SHOSHONI POCKET PAK SALMON EGGS. Boise's Earlybird Company sells pocket packages of salmon eggs for the angler with little room to spare. They come in red, cheese and natural.

SIBERIAN SALMON EGGS. The Siberian Salmon Egg Company packages not only individual salmon eggs but also clusters of them in varying styles. Available in many sizes and in red and yellow, too. Everything the preserved bait angler needs.

UNCLE JOSH. Ole Uncle Josh puts out a line of packaged baits to fit the needs of any still angler. It includes a panfish bait with a fruity taste, a carp bait a-la blue doughballs and a blood bait made of, well, maybe you better not know. There's also a variety of trout and catfish cheese baits. Baits available in 6- and 12-ounce packs and they do well for chummers, too.

LUHR JENSEN IMITATION
SALMON EGGS

UNCLE JOSH BAITS

top of the line

UNCLE JOSH PORK RINDS. Uncle Josh's Pork Rinds have been around catching all sorts of fish long before rubber worms and their kin burst on the scene. These rinds, made in such shapes as Pork Frog, Pork Chunk, Pollywogger, Eel, Twin and Triple Tail and Porkcrawler, add life to any spoon, jig or whatever. They are also available for saltwater use down to tiny fly flicks. A venerable old tradition that still works.

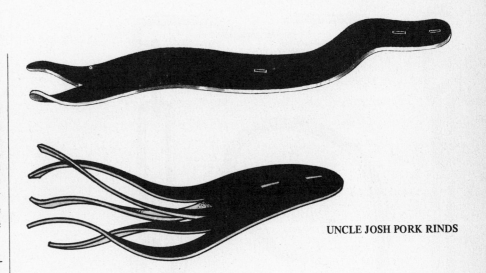

UNCLE JOSH PORK RINDS

UNCLE JOSH SALMON EGGS. Uncle Josh has a pretty complete line of salmon eggs and clusters, which they've been putting out for years. There's yellow, fluorescent and cheese-flavored. Also Soft-Textured, Husky, Span Sacs and what have you. Good for steelheading and trouting where legal.

Hooks

EAGLE CLAW BAITHOLDER. Eagle Claw baitholder hooks, available in gold or bronze finish, eye-offset straight or down, are the standard of the breed for bait anglers and have been for a long time. They range in size from 5/0 to No. 10 and come snelled or straight. Eagle Claw also sells a very complete line of other hooks, which have been their mainstay in the tackle business for a long time. In addition, they produce hooks for the home jig maker, bass bugger and plug constructor.

KEGARA BAIT HOLDER. This product has been around with varying degrees of success for a number of years. It's a plastic container that holds any sort of bait, including small minnows. The fish allegedly attack the container but wind up on the trebles. May attract only fishy window shoppers, however.

UNCLE JOSH SALMON EGGS

KEGARA BAIT HOLDER

HARDEE HOOK FILE

This hook file, designed for steelhead salmon and saltwater fishing, is something that every fisherman should have within easy access. The file is designed to put a needle point on large hooks.

Crayfish, By Lou Calala

Unlike worms, grubs, hellgrammites and Mepps spinners, crayfish are not only fishable but very edible as well. Lou Calala has produced a small booklet that covers the basics of crayfish raising and their use as a fine bass bait. Covers what you'll need to know in 24 pages. A good starting place.

LUHR JENSEN EGG LUG

Luhr Jensen's Egg Lug simplifies life for the salmon egg fisherman. It attaches to your belt. You screw on the jar of eggs and the spring-loaded top pops back on at a touch. The lid can be used as a tray to hold the three or four eggs you're putting on. Been around for 15 years.

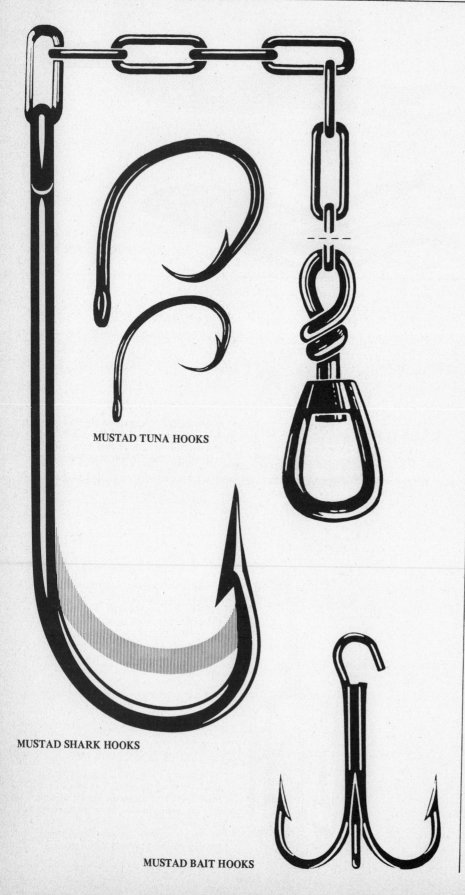

MUSTAD TUNA HOOKS

MUSTAD SHARK HOOKS

MUSTAD BAIT HOOKS

top of the line

MUSTAD BAIT HOOKS. Mustad has bait hooks in every style an angler could want, ranging from tuna circle hooks, giant tuna hooks, pike hooks, tarpon hooks, halibut hooks and other specialized items. They also market the gamut of more mundane bait hooks for nightcrawlers, salmon eggs and other simple fare. Take a look at them if you're searching for just the right thing to present that favorite bait of yours.

MUSTAD SHARK HOOKS. Impressed by *Jaws*? Well, the famous Mustad Hook Company of Norway has a surprise for you: shark hooks. They have ringed, tinned, kirbed hooks in sizes ranging from 6 inches to 1 foot with intermediate stops. Besides the variations of model 4480, they have the same style of hooks with swivels and 3/4 meter chains attached. Top quality, like all Mustad stuff.

PEQUEA HOOKS. Pequea has a lot of specialized bait fishing rigs not available in other places, including minnow rigs with a nylon leader, a bait needle and a swivel in sizes No. 6 through No. 12. They also market goodies like panfish rigs, salmon egg rigs, universal trout rigs, Pocono trout rigs and worm-gang rigs. They also sell rigs for the ocean fishermen as well. All this proves again that bait fishing is more than tossing out a worm.

PEQUEA SNELLED HOOKS. Pequea takes some of those fine Mustad hooks and snells them lots of ways for various sorts of fishing. They do the job with beak, Aberdeen, Carlisle, Cincinnati Bass, Grand Central, Salmon Egg, Perfect Trout

top of the line

and other styles. Good for the specialist bait angler.

PFLUEGER HANDY PACK. This little tin of assorted bait hooks by Pflueger has been around for a long time serving anglers. Good for the bottom of tackle boxes when you don't know what's next.

Miscellany

EEL SKIN JIG. The Bead Chain Company's Eel Skin Jig is a finely-made skeleton for the salty rubber goods user. With a jig head of polished nickel, a swiveled safety chain and an 8/0 O'Shaughnessy hook, it will take on the big ones once you put on the eel.

HARPER-HOOKER. Here's something for the fastidious bait angler from the Harper-Willis Bait Company. Use it with one of their or anyone else's cheese or dough baits. Works with any size single or treble hooks. No human odor.

HERRING MAGIC. Luhr Jensen has a clear plastic action-imparting head for use when trolling or casting natural fish baits. In five sizes from No. 0 to No. 4, the scoops help move things along.

Rigs & Sinkers

CABELA SINKER MOLDS. For the hard-core, do-it-yourselfer, Cabela is still selling a wide variety of sinker molds. It's work but some en-

THE LAST HATCH
A FISHING MYSTERY
HARMON HENKIN

(continued from page 287)

hopper from the surface and smacked the water with his tail.

Paul leaped up, almost knocking Julie into the creek. "My God, did you see that fish?" He dashed toward the house, where he had left his rod, yelling as he ran.

"I'll be right back, Julie Don't go anywhere. I love you. I love you! But that fish! Don't worry, I'll get him for you."

When he returned a few minutes later she was gone. The big brown was eyeing another hopper. Paul thought for a moment — less than a moment — about looking for her.

The trout was still snacking as Paul threaded the No. 5 line through his 7½-foot Winston rod. He missed two guides in his anxiety and had to do it all over again. He searched through his dry fly box, the one where he kept his small specialty flies. He selected a newer pattern, a Dave's Hopper with a clipped deer hair head — the one he had tied last winter. He attached it to a 3X tippet, very heavy for this water, but this was a big fish.

He fell to his knees and began to crawl toward the water, being very careful not to let his shadow cross the water. Cautiously he began feeding out the double-tapered line with smooth false-casts. Any small error would ruin his chances. The fish swooped the surface again as another hopper miscalculated a landing. How big was that fish? Six, maybe seven pounds? Huge.

Paul's fly drifted back and forth in the air in response to his casts and then casually floated to the surface, hitting before the line and leader — exactly as the more demanding books command. It landed a foot upstream from the fish. Freely, without a trace of its binding leader showing, it drifted downstream with the current. The brown noticed it and began to rise to the surface in anticipation. A couple of smaller fish, Paul could see, were interested too but were afraid to intrude on the brown's territory. The brown opened his mouth a few inches from the fly, baring a ridge of teeth. Very impressive, Paul thought. He felt himself begin to tremble as he prepared to set the hook on the biggest trout of his angling life.

Suddenly the water exploded. The rock had just missed the brown trout, which, by the time Paul jumped to his feet with a roar, was on its way to Seattle.

"What the Hell is going on!!??"

(continued on page 297)

top of the line

joy it. Also available is a variety of lead-head jig molds and all the accessories to make your own and maybe even some money.

DRAGON FLY OCEAN RIGS. As fine a selection of pre-strung ocean bait fishing rigs as possible. The Dragon Fly Company offers models with spinner blades and others with weights and tandem-rigged hooks. Geared for specific species and ways of fishing and snelled onto the correct size hooks. You can buy them for snapper, bass, channel bass, drum, flounder, tautog, stripers, mackerel, weakfish and so on. Choose your adversary.

IDEAL SNAPPER. Sure, split-shot is pretty much split-shot, but the difference in this Snapper Brand is in its packaging. Available in all the standard sizes and in a variety pack, this shot can be taken out one at a time from its plastic package. Helps eliminate wasting split-shot!

KEATING FLOATING SINKER. The Keating Floating Sinker Company is making, as the name implies, a floating sinker. In weights of 1/8, 1/6 and 1/4 of an ounce, sinkers will keep your bait slightly off the bottom. If you have such a need for this thing, you'll have a need for this thing.

MR. TWISTER RIGS. Mr. Twister, the curly-cue tail people, have a line of live bait rigs including floater rigs for live minnows, leech rigs, spinner rigs and floating jigheads. They're all well-made and have all the components like swivels, snaps, spinners and snelled hooks.

WATER GREMLIN WORM LEADS. In the ongoing process of

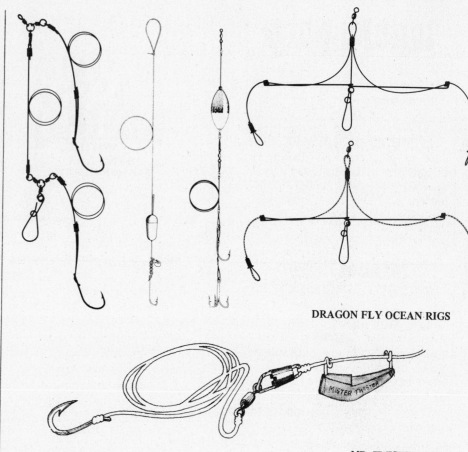

DRAGON FLY OCEAN RIGS

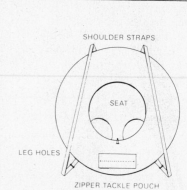

MR. TWISTER RIGS

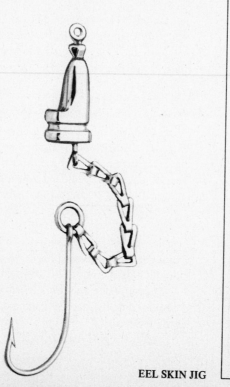

EEL SKIN JIG

TUCKER FLOATS

SHOULDER STRAPS

SEAT

LEG HOLES

ZIPPER TACKLE POUCH

The Tucker Company makes the original fishing floats, those innertube harness contraptions that anglers can use to float a lake while fishing. Not recommended for rivers, of course, for obvious reasons of safety. They are very convenient to carry in your car. And all you need to really zip up your act is the Tucker Duck Fins to paddle you along on your fishing float. The float comes in either medium or large sizes.

BEAD CHAIN

top of the line

the wormization of fishing, Water Gremlin offers a selection of worm lead sinkers in a pick-a-sinker plastic container. Convenient.

Snaps & Swivels

BEAD CHAIN TACKLE COMPANY. The Bead Chain Company of Bridgeport, Connecticut, makes a fine line of snaps, swivels and chains for the angler. Their variety includes single snaps, lock snaps, double snaps, chain leaders, three-way swivels and more. They also make a full range of casting and trolling chains. All well-made.

BERKLEY SWIVELS. If you're in the market for snaps or swivels, try the well-made Berkley variety. They sell swivels from 3/0 to 10 and snaps from 1 to 6. Good stuff.

SAMPO. The Sampo line of swivels, snaps and snap-swivels is available in a variety of sizes for every purpose. There are even models that come equipped with ball bearings. Sampo also produces a steelhead leader and one for toothy muskies made from stainless steel wire coated with nylon. A good line of products.

MAGIC WORM BEDDING COMPANY

Don't be cruel to your worms. They're the best fishing friend you'll ever have. The Magic Worm Bedding Company has developed a total environment for those segmented creatures that contains proteins, minerals and vitamins. In short everything you'll need for nice organic worms. The bedding is available in 1½-, 4½- and 25-pound bags. They also sell a portable magic worm farm for the bait angler on the go.

BEAD

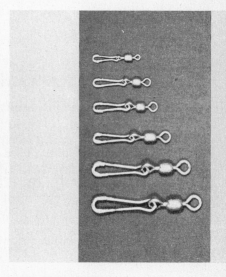

BERKLEY SWIVELS

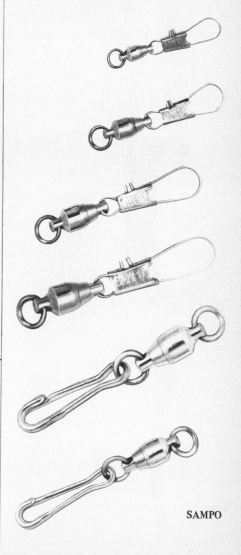

SAMPO

The specialized art of baitfishing

(continued from page 286)

lar way to go with many more adherents than the other forms of fishing combined. Like the other types of angling, whole books have been written on the subject and knowledge about its fine points can be as closely guarded as any fishing secrets.

It really pays off for the angler to know the various types of bait hooks available and which are best suited for each particular type of fishing. Ditto with sinker types and leader rigs, which are almost as varied as the species themselves.

Some of the better mail-order houses such as Herter's have a large variety of bait-fishing equipment. This type of establishment is sometimes far better to deal with than shops, which just want to sell you whatever they have in stock.

In essence, baitfishing is a rigorous process of learning like any other form of fishing; a combination of the theory of equipment with the practice that comes from learning where your favorite fish hangs out and where and what it likes to eat. That's the formula for success.

Like any variant of the sport, baitfishing is a rigorous process of learning.

More Norwegian fish hooks

(continued from page 286)

Dating from the late Stone Age (1800-1500 B.C.), this flint fish hook was discovered at Sele, Klepp, Rogaland in Norway. An extremely rare item throughout Scandinavia, it is painstakingly hewn with a wide top for attaching fishing lines. Actual length: 4.4 cm.

Bronze fish hooks from the Middle Age (A.D. 1030-1536), found on the shore of Lake Mjosa, site of the ancient market town of Hamar, Norway. It was an episcopal residence of churches, convents, monasteries and schools, where fishing was an important source of income. Actual length: 3.4—5.7 cm.

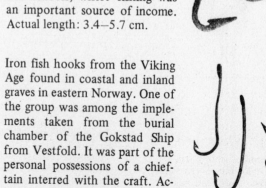

Similar to the bronze hooks used during the Bronze Age in Denmark (1500-500 B.C.), this rugged pattern was found in a wealthy man's grave from about 150 A.D. at Fagerheim, Stande in Vestfold. It is the oldest bronze fish hook found, so far, in Norway. Actual length: 8.4 cm.

Iron fish hooks from the Viking Age found in coastal and inland graves in eastern Norway. One of the group was among the implements taken from the burial chamber of the Gokstad Ship from Vestfold. It was part of the personal possessions of a chieftain interred with the craft. Actual length: 4.8—8.0 cm.

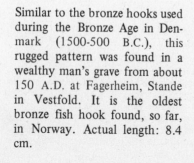

Courtesy of the Mustad Hook Company

Nineteenth-Century
bait pails and minnow
buckets.

WHALE BRAND

The Whale Enterprises people have a complete line of nylon minnow seines in a variety of mesh sizes and lengths, enough to round up the little critters you need. Well-made product for the bait gatherer. They also make seine poles and other netting accessories.

HOW I LEARNED TO DITCH-FISH

By Harmon Henkin

It had been a glorious summer of fishing. I had taken at least as many dunkings as I had fish, but that was all right too. I had learned a lot and felt more confident fishing in Montana.

Rock Creek looked especially fine in early fall. The colors of the trees were glorious, the creek relatively low and clear and the fish hungry. What a great combination.

I stopped my car at a spot overlooking the stream. A hatch of small caddis flies started up in the warm sunlight. Fish started rising. Most of them were in the foot-long category, but on the far shore a bigger trout was moving. It was exciting to watch him slurp down flies in a quick rhythm.

It was so nice out I just assembled my rod, grabbed a small plastic box of flies and ran down the bank without waders or vest, one of the few times in years I had done this.

The water was deep, even this late in the year, but I carefully waded across downstream from where the trout was rising. When I got near the other bank, I tied on a small brown caddis fly and stealthily maneuvered it within 30 feet of the fish. I made a couple of false casts and then let the fly drop above its head. A split second later there was a slurp and the fly was gone. I set the hook and was onto a good fish. It jumped — a rainbow about three pounds. It jumped again and then once more before heading straight downstream past me. The fish had most of the No. 5 line out so I followed him, stumbling along the creek bottom. There were too many snags to let the fish have its own way. He made a big mistake and ended up in the shallows right above the rapids that probably would have meant freedom. Keeping pressure on by holding the rod tip high, I managed to approach the fish and get it ashore. I sat down on the bank and looked at it. Beautiful! It would make a fine dinner.

I waded back across the stream with rod in one hand and the fish in the other, scrambling up the bank to the car. A vehicle with New Jersey plates was parked next to mine. A family inside it watched me.

A man got out and approached me.

"Gosh, that's a beautiful fish."

I nodded my head in response.

He looked down at the fast-moving creek. "We're out here on vacation from the East and I'm having a heck of a time catching any fish. Are you from around here?"

I nodded my head again.

"You know," he said, "I'm considered a pretty good fisherman back there, but around here I can hardly wade, can't figure what fly to use and the trout might as well be from Mars for all the interest they show in my stuff."

Then he looked back at his wife and kids and flicked his rod a couple of times. "You western anglers are a different breed."

I reached into my fly box and handed him a couple of caddis fly imitations, pointed out some likely looking spots and gave him a few tips on wading in fast water.

Before I climbed back into my car I turned to the vacationer and said in my best new western drawl.

"I reckon that the best way to fish out here is to keep on trying."

Then I quickly drove away before the old rancher who had seen me fish that barren irrigation ditch a year earlier came by and spilled the beans.

Reprinted from *Montana Outdoors* July/August 1974.

There's a tackle box for every need

By Harmon Henkin

Not only do things change quickly, so do the things we put the things into. Tackle boxes, which were once minor second cousins to tool boxes, have been taking on a life of their own and can be bought with as many accessories as a Dodge pickup truck. The technological and social developments ushered in by bass fishing are prime factors in this evolution. And all the new choices are good for anglers.

In the first place, when you're looking for a tackle box and puzzling about what size you should get, remember that you will fill it up. Even if your box is as tall as the Empire State Building and you're on welfare somehow it will get filled, then overcrowded. It's a law of nature. Henkin's postulate.

Be reasonable — how many lures will you buy and how many will you use? Some anglers get a multi-drawered tackle box and leave it in the garage or in the car, filling a pocket-sized box from it for each day's trip. That makes

sense, especially if you use only one rod and reel.

If you just must get one of those oversized boxes with the drawers and compartments that go on and on, you might as well go all the way. Get one of those big piggy-back types that you can sit on in your boat and that double as insulated cold-hot chests. That's the ticket if you're going all the way.

Most likely you're going to wind up with big and little tackle boxes, so there doesn't seem to be any urgency about the matter. Since almost all boxes are made out of plastic with plastic hinges (except some good old Umcos and related types made from aluminum) rust and corrosion aren't much of a problem.

Ditto with the fragility of the newer boxes. Herds of elephants could charge over them without any damage to your favorite Old Cracker Tandem Spinner Baits.

Actually, there are no generalizations that have to be made about the new tackle boxes. There's something for every need.

The new boxes could survive elephant stampedes and aren't bothered by rust or corrosion.

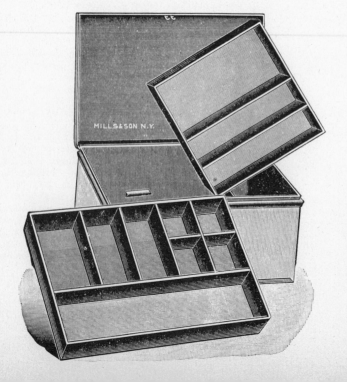

William Mills & Son marketed the Manhattan Company's "electric" tackle box in the early 1900s. Especially adapted for saltwater tackle, it was 12 3/8 inches long by 8½ inches wide and sold for $2.25. The author of this book is also confused about why it was called electric.

A SHORT GUIDE TO TACKLE BOXES

Most tackle boxes marketed today are either of steel, aluminum or plastic. A few wooden boxes are available here and there. Aluminum is lighter than plastic, but the latter takes hard knocks better and isn't as noisy. Steel is stronger than aluminum, but heavier and will rust. I use aluminum and plastic boxes.

When choosing a box give particular attention to the fittings, to the hinges and the latches. They should be well made and rustproof, for they are often the first points of a box to give trouble. I prefer a box with a lock, to discourage meddling and prevent theft of items in the box.

Except for size of the box itself, your most important consideration in the selection is the size and arrangement of the compartments in the trays of the box. Examine as wide a selection as you can, and try to visualize just what you'll be putting in those compartments. If you like to use big plug-casting lures, make sure the tackle box you choose has some compartments big enough for them. Many boxes do not.

If you confine your fishing to the use of small lures, usually identified as spinning size, get a box with many small compartments. Most of us use some of both and prefer a variety of compartment sizes. The depth of the area beneath the trays varies considerably; select the arrangement which suits you best.

The size of the box, too, is up to you. We've said that your first ones will probably be too small, but just how big you care to go depends on factors which only you can evaluate. Hip-roof boxes are manufactured which have a dozen trays in them.

Depending upon the boat you normally use, it may be better to have two or three smaller boxes than one big one. I find it convenient, for instance, to use a separate, small box for my plastic-worm fishing material. It contains worms, hooks, sinkers, leadheads, jigs and jars of pork eel. Keep your plastic worms in a clear plastic bag, one for each color, and you'll keep your tackle box a lot neater.

Clean your tackle box out periodically. Most important, leave it open overnight after you've been fishing. Air circulates through it and evaporates any moisture which would rust hooks, knives and other metal items. A drop or two of oil on metal working parts, such as hinges and latches, will keep them in good condition.

Taken from *Bait Fishing* by Grits Gresham. (C) 1966 by Grits Gresham. Used by permission of Outdoor Life Books and Harper & Row.

THE LAST HATCH
A FISHING MYSTERY
HARMON HENKIN

(continued from page 291)

He shook his fist north, south, east and west. *West*: Julie was standing 20 yards away partially hidden behind a Ponderosa pine. Her hands were draped on her hips. Her eyes were soft.

"But Paul, honey, we're so much more mature now."

"Julie . . . you rotten . . . " He put the rod down carefully and chased after her as she dashed laughing through the woods. As they hit the driveway he almost caught her, but tripped with a thud onto the gravel.

She skipped over to the fallen warrior and plopped down on his back.

"Wimp. Still prefer those fish to me?"

"Julie, let's get married."

"No, let's not. You might convince me to play house for a long weekend after fishing season, but that's my limit."

"Lordy. A weekend with your alabaster thighs."

"Sexist. Where'd you learn about alabaster thighs? All you used to know about were slimy fins."

"In Halford's latest and, alas, uncompleted novel."

"His writing had become horrible," Julie said. "Rumor has it even Hollywood wasn't interested anymore. That's the pits. But everyone thought he had so much money. Why was he going to shred this place?"

"I don't know. He needed a lot of cash for something. And he didn't have much of a career left."

"It would help 'the investigation,' " she sneered, "to know why."

"Wine, women or song. The usual reasons."

Julie shrieked as Sid jumped out from behind a bush at them.

"My job's on the line here and you two are playing doctor and nurse. Where you been?"

"Off making passionate love in the grassy glen," she replied, hands on heart.

"Him? Hah. He was probably poaching Halford's water one last time. I know the lad's values."

"So do I, alas. Have you found anything out?"

"Just that everyone in the world will be here tomorrow. Nobody seems to have much faith in the Vassar School of Advanced Forensics. Two state investigators, a pair of FBI men from Butte — their Siberia — and somebody from the National Librarian's Guild. Help!"

(continued on page 307)

top of the line

Tackle Boxes

ADVENTURER. The Adventurer line of tackle boxes offers a few models that are variations on the traditional theme. For instance, their model 2000 — made from plastic like all of them — consists of nine color-coded cartridges — smaller boxes that can be loaded with particular types of lures in different sizes and then filed back into the main box. Adventurer's 1745 model consists of 45 plastic sleeves which can be lifted out as a whole unit, and takes large size lures. Among other interesting models is their 1985 Select-O-Matic, which has covered trays and swing-out drawers.

BROOKSTONE TOOL CHEST. Want to outsnob those people with their plastic tackle boxes? Get a Brookstone walnut tool chest with its three plastic foldback trays and 21 compartments. Large storage area underneath the trays. A satin lacquer finish, dovetailed joints and nickel-plated steel fittings with rubber on the bottom. Elegant.

FLAMBEAU. Flambeau's line of clear unbreakable plastic lure boxes will do the job for any sort of angler not interested in lugging a tackle box around. An assortment of different sizes and compartment arrangements is available, including one that is a specialized plastic worm box for the popular range of worms. Like worms, these boxes are segmented.

LUHR JENSEN DOUBLE LURE CASE. An excellent way for ultra-light spin persons to carry their lure selection. The Double Lure Case holds small spinners and spoons on the top and small lures in the bottom

WHAT WE LOOKED FOR IN QUALITY

Bass anglers are the most avid consumers of tackle boxes, and we recognized this factor. A tackle box should be big enough to allow easy access to its nooks and crannies. We looked for boxes that had large capacities in the various size groupings, wouldn't rust or fall apart and were relatively lightweight. Since there are lots of these, we just took a sampling of interesting ones.

BROOKSTONE

FLAMBEAU

ADVENTURER POCKET WORM BOX

ADVENTURER "MINI" WORM BOX

ADVENTURER WORM TAMER

LUHR JENSEN

top of the line

six compartments. There's also a small compartment for weights, hooks and swivels. Made from plastic and around for quite a while, this is still the best luggage for the owner of the small, small lure collection. Also available in one-sided five-lure or two-lure cases.

OLD PAL BAIT BOX. This traditional heavy gauge steel box with belt clip is just the thing for the worm or cricket angler on the go. Very sleek and chic.

OLD PAL LIBRARY BOX. This rugged plastic split-roof box, which opens wide for easy access, has 32 compartments and 3 removable trays. But what makes this box so interesting is that the tray support is adjustable to permit other trays to be put in — up to 6 of them. The angler can build a library of trays, each stocked with a different size or type of lure. Very nice idea.

OLD PAL THREE-WAY BOX. A yellow polypropylene box for carrying one or two types of bait. Or it can be filled with water for use as a wading minnow can. Has a strap and can be carried over the shoulder or around the waist.

OLD PAL WADER LURE BOX. Old Pal's wader lure box will carry enough lures and gear for any angler to go after warm-water species. Has a removable rack for hanging lures, and can be carried over the shoulder or around the waist.

PLANO. The Plano Company is marketing a nice polypropylene tackle box which is worm-proof and has 42 compartments. The three lines of trays are deep enough for most popular lures. The trays are ribbed to

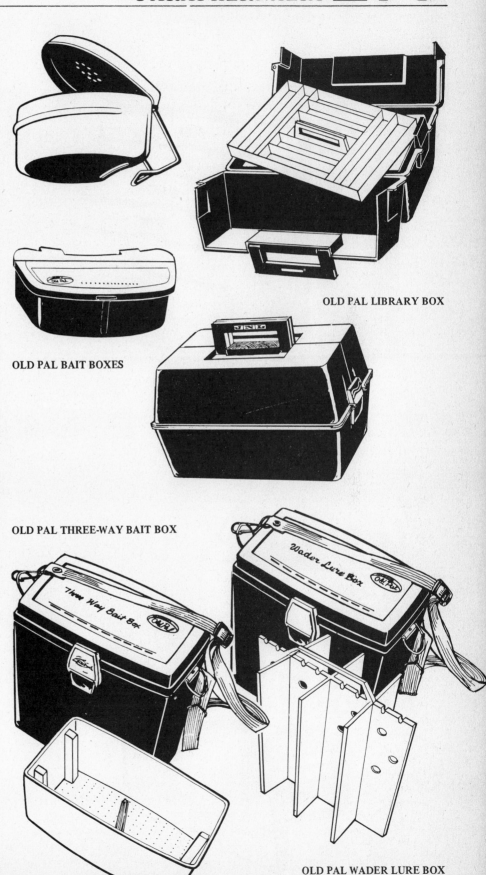

OLD PAL LIBRARY BOX

OLD PAL BAIT BOXES

OLD PAL THREE-WAY BAIT BOX

OLD PAL WADER LURE BOX

"It is not human to be quite happy with an empty creel."
THEODORE GORDON

PLANO 777

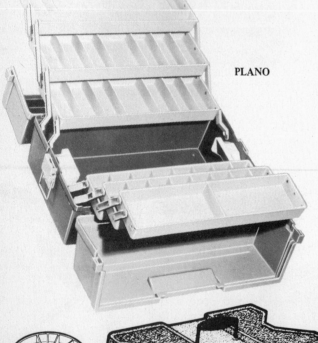

PLANO

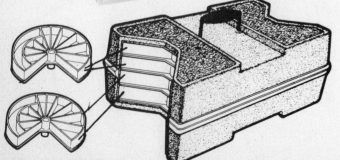

TACKLE TAMER

top of the line

keep moisture away. A nice box from a company that makes lots of nice boxes.

PLANO MODEL 777. Plano's model 777 is a really big tackle box with slide-out drawers. Though it can be customized, the standard arrangement consists of six drawers in increasingly large sizes down to the bottom, which can hold all your spinning and bait casting reels. Plastic construction and very well made. This will do the job if you haul around a lot of gear.

TACKLE TAMER. The Tackle Tamer is an interesting idea. There's nothing really to open. It has 5 revolving doors, just like a refrigerator, that you merely slide around. Made of tough plastic, it holds all sizes of lures.

UMCO HIP ROOF AND POSSUM BELLIES. Umco advertises its 3000 series tackle boxes as the largest made — they're probably right. The biggest model, the one that Godzilla would have probably used, has 10 trays and 84 compartments swinging out from the center. It weighs in at 11½ pounds, has special worm compartments, interchangeable tray layouts and is strong enough to sit on. But that ain't all. Umco has a Possum Belly for its hip roof models that gives even them a greater capacity. The bellies are insulated for food, beverages, etc., or non-insulated for extra gear that needs protection. Ingenious and functional equipment.

UMCO MINI BOXES. One of the nicest ideas around for the spin angler is Umco's mini-box — a combination tackle and live-bait box. On one side of the 9-inch by 4¼-inch by 1 5/8-inch box is a regular compart-

UMCO

UMCO POSSUM BELLY BOX

UMCO MINI-BOX

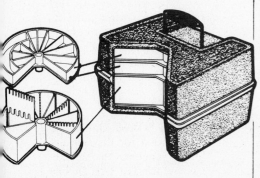

ANOTHER TACKLE TAMER

top of the line

mentalized tray and on the other side are two live-bait wells that work with worms or salmon eggs. Has a clip on top to attach to your belt. Umco also makes a foam-lined box for the fly angler and a combo for flies and tackle in the Aluminum mini-box series.

VELURE. Velure utility boxes by Adventurer are made from crush-proof polypropylene, have snap latch covers and are available in a great variety of shapes and sizes, some with adjustable inserts. Perfect for the rubber wormer or ultra-light bluff who angles with a back-pocket box.

Miscellany

AUTO-GAFF. An interesting idea is Auto-gaff's combination gaff-and-scale. Available in sizes from 32 to 60 inches, the scale, which works right out of the handle, is exposed in 5-pound gradients. Will give you a pretty good idea of how much your trophy weighs but still leaves enough leeway for exaggeration. Not accurate, but nice.

CHRIS' DELUXE FISH STRINGER. After the one that didn't get away got away what do you do? Use Chris' Deluxe fish stringer. It has 10 swiveled stainless steel hooks, a solid six-foot long brass chain and double safety locks. Well-made.

E-Z CORD STRINGER. A new twist on an old idea is the E-Z Cord Stringer, which eliminates the necessity of tying knots and the like. Just put your catch on and twist it to the left and the fish is locked on. Handy.

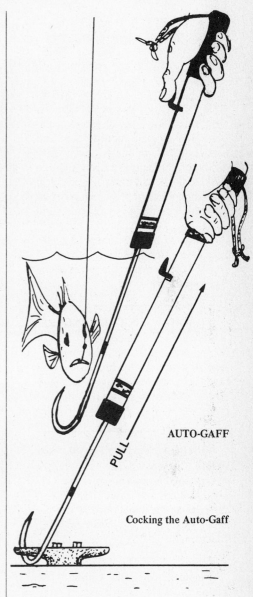

AUTO-GAFF

Cocking the Auto-Gaff

E-Z CORD STRINGER

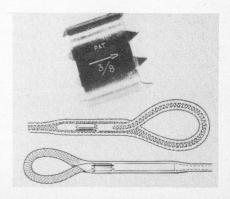

top of the line

FALLS CITY MINNOW BUCK-ETS. Falls City's model 601 minnow bucket is a slight modification of the old Orvis all-glass minnow trap and carrier. Live minnows swim into either of the funnel-shaped ends, to nibble at the goodies, i.e., bait, in the compartment. Once in, they're trapped. The design has been around since the 19th Century, and is still as effective as any. Falls City also sells a very large variety of other minnow buckets to suit the needs of the bait angler.

FRABILL FISH STRINGERS. The Frabill Company sells a very complete line of chain and polyethylene stringers. All the models are well made and can be bought cadmium plated to handle anybody's limit of fish.

FRABILL GAFF HOOK. The Frabill Company makes gaff hooks of polished stainless steel on embossed aluminum handles with plastic grips and a shock cord. These are well made items and simply functional.

FLAMBEAU ROD CASES. The Flambeau Company makes a very complete line of replacement and/or first time rod cases made from an unbreakable plastic. These cases are available in telescoping and set sizes in a variety of diameters. Not beautiful, but they'll sure do the job.

FRABILL WIRE FISH BASKETS. Wire fish baskets are the nicest thing this side of live fish boxes on fancy boats. Frabill's baskets, collapsible and available in sizes as large as 19 by 30 inches, have ¾-inch mesh blue anodized finishes and spring-loaded hinged trap lids at top and bottom.

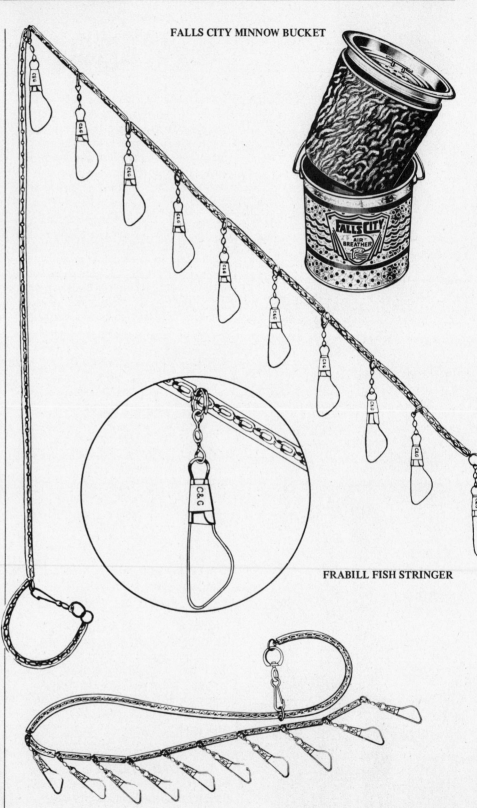

FALLS CITY MINNOW BUCKET

FRABILL FISH STRINGER

CHRIS' DELUXE FISH STRINGER

GAMEFISH: BLUEFISH

top of the line

NAMES
Tailor, skipjack, snapper blue, chopper, jumbo. *(Pomatomus saltatrix)*

DISTRIBUTION
The bluefish is found in waters throughout the world. It is found in the Atlantic from Argentina to Nova Scotia. It is abundant off New England, Florida and the Carolinas.

DESCRIPTION
The bluefish is iridescent blue on the back shading into grey and silver on the sides with a silver belly. The fins are dark and the large mouth contains strong, uneven teeth.

SIZE
This savage fish averages 2 to 5 pounds in weight. At times, schools of blues will average about 10 to 15 pounds.

HABITAT
The bluefish is a school fish that is rarely found close to shore. When it does venture into shallow waters, it is usually in pursuit of baitfish. They are extensive travelers and in the winter are most numerous in the waters off Florida.

POWERSCOPIC GAFFS. The Powerscopic rod people, who make those nice telescoping rods, are also making a fine line of fiberglass gaffs in lengths of 11, 32 and 48 inches. They have cork handles, stainless steel needle-point hooks and windings of the type found on rods. Good items.

RELIABLE GAFF COMPANY. Reliable gaffs are just that. They're guaranteed for life. All metal parts are guaranteed against defects in materials and workmanship. Just send it to the maker for a free repair or replacement. Available in all sorts of sizes with stainless steel hook and anodized aluminum shaft. Can be bought with all sorts of shaft sizes and some are collapsible. Reliable also makes custom models in sizes up to 8 feet.

GH48

GH32

GH11

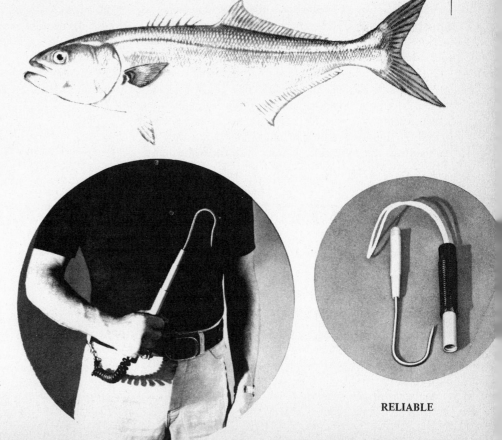

POWERSCOPIC

RELIABLE

WINTER IN THE BLOOD

I slid down the riverbank behind the house, After a half-hour search in the heat of the granary, I had found a red and white spoon in my father's toolbox. The treble hook was rusty and the paint on the spoon flecked with rust. I cast across the water just short of the opposite bank. There was almost no current. As I retrieved the lure, three mallards whirred across my line of vision and were gone upriver.

The sugar beet factory up by Chinook had died seven years before. Everybody had thought the factory caused the river to be milky but the water never cleared. The white men from the fish department came in their green trucks and stocked the river with pike. They were enthusiastic and dumped thousands of pike of all sizes into the river. But the river ignored the fish and the fish ignored the river; they refused even to die there. They simply vanished. The white men made tests; they stuck electric rods into the water; they scraped muck from the bottom; they even collected bugs from the fields next to the river; they dumped other kinds of fish in the river. Nothing worked. The fish disappeared. Then the men from the fish department disappeared, and the Indians put away their new fishing poles. But every now and then, a report would trickle down the valley that someone, an irrigator perhaps, had seen an ash-colored swirl suck in a muskrat, and out would come the fishing gear. Nobody ever caught one of these swirls, but it was always worth a try.

I cast the spoon again, this time retrieving faster.

The toolbox had held my father's tools and it was said in those days that he could fix anything made of iron. He overhauled machinery in the fall. It was said that when the leaves turned, First Raise's yard was full of iron; when they fell, the yard was full of leaves. He drank with the white men of Dodson. Not a quiet man, he told them stories and made them laugh. He charged them plenty for fixing their machines. Twenty dollars to kick a baler awake — one dollar for the kick and nineteen for knowing where to kick. He made them laugh until the thirty-below morning ten years ago we found him sleeping in the borrow pit across from Earthboy's place.

He had had dreams. Every fall, before the first cold wind, he dreamed of taking elk in Glacier Park. He planned. He figured the mileage and the time it would take him to reach the park, and the time it would take to kill an elk and drag it back across the boundary to his waiting pickup. He made a list of the food and supplies. He inquired around, trying to find out what the penalty would be if they caught him. He wasn't crafty like Lame Bull or the white men of Dodson, so he had to know the penalty, almost as though the penalty would be the inevitable result of his hunt.

He never got caught because he never made the trip. The dream, the planning and preparation were all part of a ritual — something to be done when the haying was over and the cattle brought down from the hills. In the evening, as he oiled his .30-30, he explained that it was better to shoot a cow elk because the bulls were tough and stringy. He had everything figured out, but he never made the trip.

My lure caught a windfall trunk and the brittle nylon line snapped. A magpie squawked from deep in the woods on the other side of the river.

From *Winter in the Blood* by James Welch.
(C) 1974 by James Welch. Used by permission of Bantam Books.

WHAT TO LOOK FOR IN GAFF HOOKS

Gaff hooks now on the market range from high carbon steel to stainless, with handles fashioned from tubular fiberglass and hardwood. All are effective as long as certain considerations are taken into effect.

A gaff hook must be sharp. Some of the stainless models are blunt and must be filed or honed to a fine, tapering edge. Carbon steel hooks seem to differ in design from the stainless steel product, being well tapered down to a needle point, a feature which is all-important.

Unfortunately, the well-shaped high carbon steel hook rusts. An angler must provide constant maintenance, with a regular touching-up prior to any fishing trip. On the credit side, they're strong, less likely to blunt than the stainless article, and are inexpensive. Some of the best sell for pennies, say 50c for a good three inch hook.

Everyday anglers use inexpensive gaffs, as do commercial fishermen, yet there is much to be said for the stainless steel hook. First off, of course, it does not rust or corrode. While slightly more expensive, it has a greater life expectancy. On the debit side, a stainless steel gaff must be ground down to a needle point — and then touched up more often than the time-honored high carbon steel article.

Any gaff is lost without an adequate handle. Initially, all gaff handles were fashioned of hardwood, and the only criterion was grain which would suffer great stress without splintering. Nowadays the fiberglass handle has become commonplace, and there are new requirements, yet modern hooks fill the bill.

From *Tackle Talk* by Henry Lyman and Frank Woolner. (C) 1971 by Henry Lyman and Frank Woolner. Used by permission of A.S. Barnes & Co., Inc.

BOOKS ARE PRIMARY FISHING TACKLE

Books don't look like other kinds of fishing tackle — they don't have gleaming metal scales, twirling nickel blades, smooth cork grips or hooks. But in a real sense books are primary fishing tackle. A night spent with a good one will often make the difference that a hundred lure changes and a hundred dollars' worth of graphite cannot. A copy of *Practical Fishing Knots* may be the final link between you and that bonefish trophy over the mantel.

Books are still one of the best investments the thinking angler can make. For the price of a few spinners you can buy a lot of fishing skill. In fact, thanks to Gutenberg, you can take fishing lessons from the best anglers of the last three centuries, anytime you want.

And there is a special pleasure that comes with experimenting with ideas from books — an extra dimension of thoughtfulness that gives angling a new depth and vitality and often a whole new challenge. If you got skunked on the reservoir yesterday, you're better off looking for the answer in *Practical Black Bass Fishing* than drowning your sorrows in $11 worth of hula poppers.

There are books for the angler's every need, from Garcia's penny-wise pocket library to A. J. McClane's $40 *New Fishing Encyclopedia*. *Outdoor Life* offers a boxed Tackle Box Library that will actually fit into a Plano 777 — something for the thorough angler who gets easily bored. More and more, fishing books are appearing as paperbacks, which puts them in the reach of every angler.

top of the line

Books

All About Surf Fishing
By Jack Fallon

Jack Fallon has presented a solid treatment of the latest techniques in this rapidly changing field, including the intricacies of choosing lures and rigging up baits. It covers the necessary ground quite well, and the beginner can get a firm grip on things with it.

Published by: Winchester. **Price** $8.95.

Bait Angling for Common Fishes
By Louis Rhead

This is one of a short stringer of paperback reprints of angling classics available from the Tuttle Company, which includes C. F. Orvis' *Fishing with the Fly* ($8.95) and Ogden Bigelow's *Mulberry Trout* — all pleasant little books. Full of the kind of 19th-Century writing that can only be had for a considerably higher price as cloth reprints and rare books. Rhead's drawings make his book especially pleasant when they're not biting. And it can yield a few nuggets that may help them start.

Published by: Charles E. Tuttle Co. **Price:** $3.95.

The Book of Lures
By Charles K. Fox

Charlie Fox's book on lures has for all practical purposes the field to itself. It's a wondrous journey through the world of wooden lures of another time as well as today's offerings. He knows vintage lures as well as anyone and explains their history clearly and concisely. There's also information on how to make your own wooden copies of the oldies and goodies. A great book just

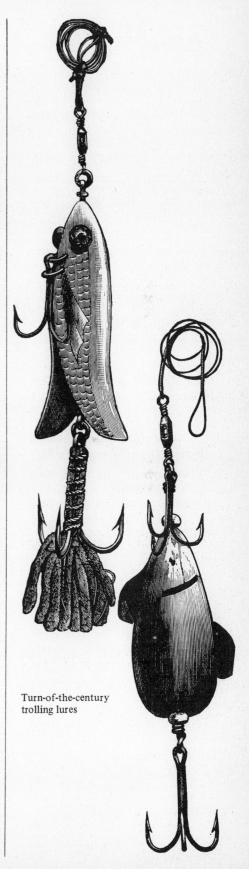

Turn-of-the-century trolling lures

top of the line

for looking at, especially for the modern basser who believes the history of the sport commenced with rubber worms.

Published by: Freshet Press. **Price:** $14.95.

The Complete Book of the Striped Bass
By Nicholas Karas

Nicholas Karas, an experienced outdoor writer, covers this fascinating fish which was transplanted across the continent to the Pacific in the late 19th Century and recently to some large inland lakes. It's a magnificent fish and Karas covers it completely and with the seriousness it deserves.

Published by: Winchester. **Price:** $10.

The Complete Book of Weakfishing
By Henry Lyman and Frank Woolner

If you've caught sea trout fever (weakfish, or sea trout, have made a dramatic comeback along the East Coast in the last few years) here's a cure for the ailment. Two of the best salty types in the business, Woolner and Lyman have put together a very readable book of the sea trout well worth its modest price to the offshore angler. Sea trout are about as much fun as you can have in a small saltwater craft, and the authors of *The Complete Book of Weakfishing* have tried to take the guesswork and broken leaders out of finding it. Complete with tackle and boat accessories.

Published by: A. S. Barnes. **Price:** $5.95.

Fishing the Pacific
By Don Holmes

Despite the beliefs of some New York publishers, there is a West Coast, and Don Holmes takes the angler on a trip up and down it. He

Charles K. Fox

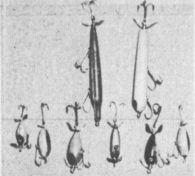

the book of LURES

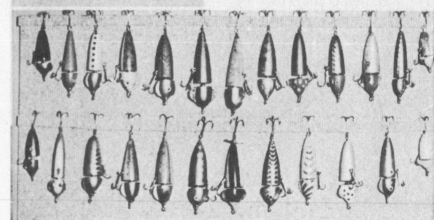

Of trolling for lake trout

The following is an excerpt taken from Frank Forester's classic Fish and Fishing of the United States and British Provinces of North America. *The book was illustrated with beautiful woodcuts — some of which appear in* The Complete Fisherman's Catalog *— and a plate of hand-painted flies.* Fish and Fishing *was first published by the W.A. Townsend Company of New York in 1859. "Of Trolling For Lake Trout" was written, according to the editors of the second edition of the book, by "a special correspondent."*

I propose, in this connexion, to treat of this fine and exciting sport, describing

1st, The rod;
2nd, The reel;
3rd, The line,
4th, The leader, and train of hooks;
5th, The bait and flies;
6th, The bait-kettle;
7th, The boat and oarsman, or guide;
8th, The manner of striking the fish, when the bait is taken. And lastly,
9th. How to play, and gaff the fish.

1st. THE ROD.—A mutual friend of ours, who writes occasionally for the *"Spirit,"* and who is a most skilful troller, wrote an article which appeared in the "Spirit" in the fall of 1848, signed "M., Maspeth, Long Island," in

(continued on page 312)

s &37

An Outdoor Life Book

How to Find Fish—and Make Them Strike

Joseph D. Bates

SECRET FRESH AND SALT WATER FISHING TRICKS OF THE WORLD'S FIFTY BEST PROFESSIONAL FISHERMEN

saltwater fisherman. Not as authoritative as Woolner's *Modern Saltwater Sport Fishing* — or as stylish — but a good investment for the beginning saltwater angler in the East.

Published by: Doubleday. **Price**: $8.95.

How to Find Fish — and Make Them Strike
By Joseph D. Bates, Jr.

Joseph Bates' book is a very good one for the beginner trying to understand the nuances of that difficult art — reading the water. Diagrammed in detail showing the likeliest spots for fish to be hanging out, the information is easily transferrable to actual stream conditions. He also goes into the wherewithals of getting them to strike, covering all of the basic methods. Very handy.

Published by: Harper & Row. **Price**: $8.95.

Modern Salt Water Fishing
By Vic Dunaway

Vic Dunaway has been one of the standard sources for the written word on saltwater fishing for a long time, and the magazine writer puts it together in this book. It is one of the better all-around guides through this burgeoning field and is a good starting point for the angler.

Published by: Winchester. **Price**: $10.

Secret Fresh and Salt Water Tricks of the Fifty Best Professional Fishermen
By George Leonard Herter

Another massive tome from the gala mail-order people who have been dishing it out for eons. Some 600-plus pages with relevant and wonderfully irrelevant information, this book is a delight, especially for the advanced angler who will marvel at

"Mr. Briggs tries for many hours a likely place for a perch."
(from the pages of *Punch* in a 19th Century issue)

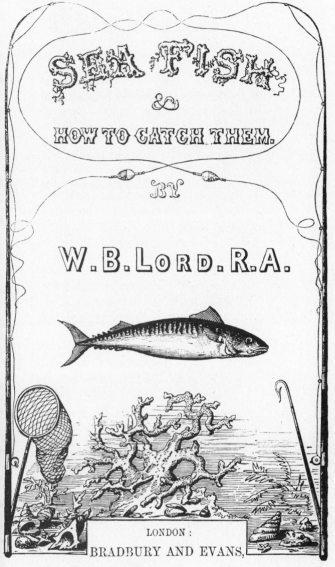

Books from the past: (left) a British volume on saltwater fishing published in 1863. (below) The Orvis Company sold Mary Orvis Marbury's treatment of popular flies at the turn of the century for $5. It contained 32 colored plates of flies.

GAMEFISH: HUMPBACK SALMON

NAMES
Pink salmon, humpy, humpback. *(Oncorhynchus gorbuscha)*

DISTRIBUTION
The humpback is found from northern California to Canada and into Alaska. It is most prevalent in the northern part of its range.

DESCRIPTION
The humpback salmon is silver in color with a dark blue back. Dark, oval spots are scattered over the tail and upper sides. During spawning, their coloring will change from silver to brown or reddish. The male develops a bony hump on its back during spawning.

SIZE
The humpback is a small fish that averages about 3 pounds. A weight of 10 pounds is considered the maximum size for this fish.

HABITAT
The humpback salmon is an anadromous fish that migrates into fresh water during spawning season. It usually prefers to spawn close to the sea and prefers tidal waters where gravel beds can be found.

FEEDING HABITS
The humpback feeds primarily on small baitfish, crustaceans and plankton.

top of the line

some of its information. Herter's guarantees it will double or triple your fishing catch or your money back. Let's see Schwiebert or Swisher equal that!

Published by: Herter's (Waseca, MN). **Price:** $3.79.

Successful Bluefishing
By Henry Lyman

The publisher of *The Salt Water Sportsman* magazine goes after the most popular small ocean gamefish of all with a wide range of tackle, including surf-fishing gear. Anyone who fishes offshore, or even in tidal bays, sooner or later will run into a school of blues, and Lyman can show you how to make the most of it. He includes a sniffing technique for smelling out subsurface schools. A really complete book worth having if you do a fair amount of saltwater fishing offshore.

Published by: International Marine Publishing. **Price:** $10.

Successful Ocean Game Fishing
By Frank T. Moss

A heady mix of the big game fisherman's tales and techniques, including contributions by other big game matadors on swordfish, bonito, and everything salty down to bluefish and stripers (bottom fish need not apply). If you're going to go out beyond sight of land looking for a fight with a tuna, get this book first to even the odds a little. For saltwater thrill-seekers only.

Published by: A. S. Barnes. **Price:** $12.50.

Successful Striped Bass Fishing
By Frank T. Moss

Striped bass are the saltwater angler's fetish fish. They come big and fight like their freshwater coun-

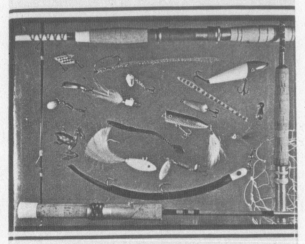

C. Boyd Pfeiffer
TACKLE CRAFT

The art of making, maintaining, and repairing your own rods, plugs, spinners, bucktails, nets, si...

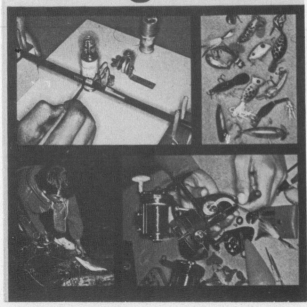

Dick Lewers
Understanding Fishing Tackle

terparts, and every year coastal fishermen wait for them, surf rods in hand, to appear on their way to spawning grounds in inland waters and bays. The Moss book has an edge of authority in its tackle and techniques treatment, and includes some valuable information on the natural history and migration patterns of the bass, one of the most interesting fish life stories to be found anywhere. Striped-bass anglers will understand the language here, and those just coming into the first stages of fanaticism could do no better for improving their angling success.

Published by: International Marine Publishing. **Price**: $12.50.

Tackle Craft
By Boyd Pfeiffer

Boyd Pfeiffer's book is by far the best thing ever done on the care and management of every sort of tackle. An invaluable volume that earns its keep by saving lots of money. Well-illustrated and complete. It's for sure a should-have work by the ex-*Washington Post* columnist.

Published by: Crown. **Price**: $9.95.

Understanding Fishing Tackle
By Dick Lewers

This book, little-known to Americans, is wonderful. It treats fishing tackle systematically and in detail, covering everything from the intricacies of monofilament to the ins and outs of sinkers, floats, rods and reels. It's done in a simple style that informs the angler as well as any book on the subject. Illustrated with many good charts and diagrams. Everything from rod building to casting. Deserves a wide readership.

Published by: A. H. & A. W. Reed, PTY, Ltd. **Price**: $16.50.

"The angler is always an optimist. He lives upon hopes and dreams of the future."

THEODORE GORDON

BOOKS & PERIODICALS 311

Fishing Annuals

Angler's Bible

Until 1976, this was just a section in the *Shooter's Bible*. Now on its own, the *Angler's Bible* is more bookish than magazinish — 1½ inches thick and almost 500 pages long. About half of that is devoted to "Techniques and Tools" features on a goodly cross-section of angling topics ranging from basics like "How to Choose a Casting Rod" to garnishes like "How Primitive Man Fished" and a delightful selection of old-time "Angling Classics." If you already know what you're looking for in tackle the "Specifications" section for tackle and accessories can serve as a good defense against over-anxious clerks. But like the "Reference and Directory" section, which lists books in print, fishing organizations and governmental agencies, the lack of recommendations and a point of view makes all this stuff of only passing interest. The *Bible* hits the stands in January-February and by the time you get through the last reel specification the snow will have melted and it'll be time to get a license.

Published by: Stoeger Publishing Company. **Address:** 55 Ruta Court, South Hackensack, NJ 07606. **Price:** $7.95.

Argosy Fishing Annual

The *Argosy* Fishing annual has been around as long as any of the perennials, and will probably outlast its namesake. It's better than the run-of-the-line annuals if you look closely, reading more like a single issue of one of the big magazines, which is a good enough reason to buy it in January, when the Big Three are off hunting in the snow.

Published by: Popular Publica-

Fishing annuals: don't expect nirvana

Fishing annuals are really a magazine species all their own. They spawn in early spring and appear on local newsstands just as the sun is beginning to warm the streams — and fishermen's blood.

Screamer headlines promise angling nirvana ("Bass Riot At Alcatraz!" was the leader in the 1976 Bob Zwirz annual) and every year one or two species of fish are "discovered" in far-off Wisconsin. Then there's the new tackle news, which is often hard to distinguish from the ads in these heavily advertised mags. It's a heady mix for a dollar and some change, and the angling annuals usually beat the subscription magazines' pre-season issues to the punch every year. They're hard to resist — and they do make good bus reading — but don't expect angling salvation.

These once-a-year flashes are always a grab bag of basics and far-flung fishing topics. And, after all, a buck fifty will get you a new Rappala and some change. Individual issues may carry a single article by a good angling authority on your fishing preferences that will make all the difference. And there are some leaders in this field that seem, over the years, to consistently bring in solid stuff that will carry you over until the season opens.

top of the line

tions. **Address:** 420 Lexington Ave., New York, NY 10017. **Price:** $1.50.

Bob Zwirz's
Fishing Annual, Fishing Report,
Fisherman Annual, Maco's
Fishing Guidebook,
Maco's Fishing Annual.

Bob Zwirz's *Fishing Annual* stands a hair above the other magazine-format annuals. The twins, *Fishing Report* and *Fisherman Annual*, are almost indistinguishable from each other, except that the *Report* focuses on fishing for given species and the *Annual* covers the same territory from the perspective of technique. The Maco annuals could be described with the same division, but at this level of competence, why bother: take a quick look at the tables of contents in these things before you part with your money. You can't plan your tackle shopping from them simply because their reports are too commercially oriented.

Fishing Annual. **Published by:** Charger Publications. **Address:** 34249 Camino Capistrano, Capistrano Beach, CA 92624. **Price:** $1.50.

Cord Sportsfacts Fisherman Annual, Cord Sportsfacts Fishing Report. **Published by:** Cord Communications Corporation. **Address:** 25 West 43rd Street, New York, NY 10036. **Price:** $1 each.

Maco's Fishing Annual, Maco's Fishing Guidebook. **Published by:** Maco Publications. **Address:** 699 Madison Avenue, New York, NY 10021. **Prices:** $1 (*Annual*), $1.25 (*Guidebook*).

Garcia Fishing Annual

The *Annual* is really half magazine, half Garcia catalog — double trouble for the tackle-hungry snowbound angler. That super-commercial combination also brings with it a wider — and better — selection of fishing

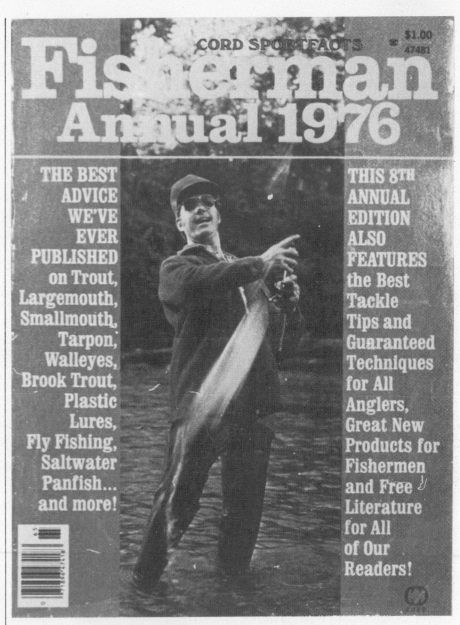

CORD SPORTSFACTS $1.00   47481

Fisherman Annual 1976

THE BEST ADVICE WE'VE EVER PUBLISHED on Trout, Largemouth, Smallmouth, Tarpon, Walleyes, Brook Trout, Plastic Lures, Fly Fishing, Saltwater Panfish... and more!

THIS 8TH ANNUAL EDITION ALSO FEATURES the Best Tackle Tips and Guaranteed Techniques for All Anglers, Great New Products for Fishermen and Free Literature for All of Our Readers!

Of trolling for lake trout

(continued from page 306)

which he gave a capital description on most of the above heads. I wish you had the paper, as it is all that is to be said on the subject.

The trolling-rod spoken of by you on page 327, would answer, to wit: the barbed rod. * * * had two of the most perfect trolling rods I have ever seen; they were made by Ben Welch, of Cherry-street, and are all bamboo cane. I had one made by George Karr, of Grand-street, which I like very much; and I will describe it the best way I can, although it is no easy matter to describe on paper a rod of any kind:—Length from eleven to thirteen feet; butt of ash, thoroughly seasoned, about one and a quarter inches in diameter, or about

as thick as an ordinary Bass-rod. The butt should be hollow, to contain spare tips. The second, third and fourth joints should be bamboo, so that when the rod is put together, it will be about twelve feet.

The rod should have two spare tips; one should be stronger and shorter than the other, to vary the fishing according to the state of the weather, and circumstances.

The fourth or last joint, tip, should be about three feet, thinner, and more pliant than the spare tops which fit in the bored butt. The first spare top should be two feet long, stiffer and stronger than the original top. The second spare top should be about

(continued on next page)

top of the line

topics, both salt- and freshwater, still for only a handful of pocket change. Almost an *Angler's Bible* in content, the Garcia annual has a real edge on the others its own price. Tackle, of course, can be ordered directly through the magazine.

Published by: The Garcia Corporation. **Address**: 329 Alfred Avenue, Teaneck, NJ 07666. **Price**: $1.50.

Sports Afield Fishing Annual
Editorially speaking, the most solid of them all. But like all the annuals, the features are spread thin over a wide range of fishing styles and species. The quality of writing and black and white photography is comparable to the parent magazine. The 1976 *SA Annual* excerpted the heart of *Fly Casting with Lefty Kreh* at half the price of the book. Many fresh- and saltwater adventures, book reviews, boating and tackle features and all the wisdom a dollar and a quarter can buy.

Published by: Sports Afield. **Address**: P.O. Box 604, New York, NY 10019. **Price**: $1.25.

Of trolling for lake trout

(continued from preceding page)

fourteen inches long, strong and stiff; and in heavy weather, this strong, stiff top will be the one to use.

Rod-making has been brought to such perfection, it would be a waste of time to give further instructions; but still I only know two men in this city who can make a true trolling-rod, viz:—Ben Welch, of Cherry-street, and George Karr, of Grand-street, near Broadway.

Rings should never be used on rods of this character. The "rail-road" through which the line travels, constitutes one of the peculiarities of this rod. Rings interfere with, and impede the line, and should not be used. The guides used by Welch are the only true ones —

they are neat, light, with a thin flat shank, about one-fourth of an inch in length, which is firmly secured on the different joints. There should be very few guides on the rod — five, I consider sufficient, exclusive of the metal case at the top of each tip. This metal case should have a rounded surface, perfectly smooth, and sufficiently large to allow the line to run without the slightest obstruction or friction.

Let me give one hint before I take leave of the rod. I recommend that all trolling-rods should have guides on both sides — that is, a guide on the opposite side of the other: *not on the butt,* but on all joints from the butt to the end; and why? In this kind of fishing there is powerful pressure on the rod; and the

very best will, from hard work, become bent, and remain bent, and thus lose its elasticity. To obviate this, turn around the joints, slip the line through the spare guides, and in a few hours the rod is "all straight."

2nd. THE REEL.—To give an explanation of this to you, would be absurd. I will simply say, that No. 3 is about the proper size for a trolling-rod, without stop, click, or multiplier. The line cannot run off too free. According to my opinion, John Conroy can make the best reel in the world.

3rd. THE LINE.—One hundred yards is abundant. Twisted silk is the best line for

(continued on next page)

Magazines: fishing through the mail

Fishing tackle catalogs have been called the opiate of the angler. If that's true, then the traditional outdoors magazines and new fishing periodicals must be our bourbon. What's more, they're socially acceptable — you can get them through the mail or at your dentist's office. A subscription to one of the mostly-monthly outdoors periodicals often comes as a pleasant reminder that you should get out again before the season closes and a consolation when you don't.

Angling never exhausts itself, and there is real pleasure and anticipation in even the most overworked "Monster Muskie" story, complete with you-shoulda-been-there photos in splashy color. Like other magazines, the outdoors press is often forced to promise more than it can deliver.

Almost all of us want to fish more than we can, and there are plenty of vicarious angling thrills to be had in *Outdoor Life*, *The Pennsylvania Angler*, *Fly Fisherman*, etc. — every month, rain or shine, right after supper. And until we develop a national angler's TV network, the magazines will remain the best way to keep on top of the latest developments in tackle and learn new fishing secrets — or more often, old ones — from those enviable guys who fish and get paid for it.

Magazines are by nature a very changeable commodity; all three superstars — *Sports Afield*, *Outdoor Life*, and *Field & Stream* — have changed their format and, more subtly, their content over the last few years. That is, at least partly because of another development in the magazine publishing industry which has finally affected the outdoors information media: the appearance of specialized angling magazines like *Bassmaster*, *Fly Fisherman* and *Saltwater Sportsman*. Still, all-outdoors magazines are generally worth their lower newsstand price.

For the purposes of our evaluation, we're considering any periodical which *consistently* offers material of interest and value to fishermen. We're excluding your local newspaper, of course, and the high-ad content outdoorsman's newspapers which have started to appear in some states, except where they've proven their worth over a number of years.

Of trolling for lake trout

(continued from preceding page)

trolling. I know they kink, when new; but very little use will put an end to it — *id est*, knock the kink out of it.

Plaited lines are very good and cheap, and do not kink; but they absorb the water, and do not run free from the rod.

A mixture of hair in lines, is my abomination. It is the most dangerous and uncertain stuff a man can use. You can never depend on it; the hairs will give way with but little strain; and when you hook the heaviest fish, the greater danger is to be apprehended. I hate them.

4th. THE LEADER AND TRAIN OF HOOKS.—This word "leader" goes against my grain. The old familiar English-Irish sound of "casting-line," has a charm for my ear, equalled only by the still, silent noise of

"Ballynahinch or Costello's flowing waters."

Most trollers use twisted gut for leader, with a small swivel attached to one end. The other end is fastened to the reel-line, either by loop or knot, but a knot is by far preferable. The leader should be two yards long — some good and old hands use three yards. I never use twisted gut. I prefer a leader of good round Salmon-gut.

The train of hooks is attached to the eye of the swivel, at the end of the leader. The train is made of five hooks, and made on the very best and most perfect gut, single. The strand upon which the hooks are tied, is fastened by a knot to another equally strong and perfect strand, which is fastened

(continued on next page)

top of the line

The big three

Field & Stream

Long considered the class magazine among the big three, *Field & Stream* has settled comfortably into its own image as a keeper of America's finer sporting traditions. If *Outdoor Life* is a bass trip to a reservoir for bass and *Sports Afield* an RV trip to Flaming Gorge for overgrown brown trout, *Field & Stream* is a charter flight to a Canadian grayling lodge complete with roaring fireplace, Ed Zern, Ernie Schwiebert and a bed once slept in by Theodore Gordon. True to form, *F & S* is the only big monthly with a European editor.

The angler who appreciates vicarious fishing pleasures will find them in *F & S*, supplied by Ed Zern, Ted Trueblood, Ken Schulz, a bevy of field editors and a big cast of contributors. Regular fishing departments include the basic: Boating, Camping, Vehicles, Conservation — but they're presented with a bit more polish and style than the other two biggies. The monthly fishing column — a kind of op-ed feature that's more often sentiment than not — is now in the hands of former Northeast field editor Jim Bashline. Ken Schulz balances this foray with various angling practicalities. Smaller regular features fall in between: a cheese-cakey "Fly of the Month" column, a kind of *Popular Mechanics* approach to angling called "Tap's Tips" and the best review system in the outdoors press for books and flicks called "Books and Comments." And no matter how serious George Reiger gets in the conservation column, you will, my friend, "Exit, Laughing" with Ed Zern.

All outdoors magazines seem to revolve around the notion that there's some *secret* to finding really memorable fishing and hunting ex-

periences; *Field & Stream* looks for it in more faraway places than any of the others.

Executive Editor A. J. McClane keeps a tight balance between angling facts and fancies, but the magazine's real heart is in the good story well told. Yet they sometimes get caught with a *National Enquirer*-size gap between the hard-sell cover headline and the article inside — be it ever so pleasant to read. *F & S*, to the good of all, still publishes occasional fiction and book excerpts, along with a humor piece now and then. It's the best substitute ever invented for good weather in April.

Published by: CBS Publications. **Address:** 383 Madison Ave., New York, NY 10017. **Price:** One year (12 issues), $7.95.

Outdoor Life

The difference between the three big general editorial outdoors magazines, like the difference between top-quality spinning reels, lies in the eye of the beholder. You pays your money and you takes your chances. That's what magazine publishing in America is all about.

Still, there are subtle differences. If you subscribe to *Outdoor Life*, *Field & Stream* or *Sports Afield*, you get a full year's worth of not only angling, but boating, hunting and many other outdoors pursuits. In this sense, *Outdoor Life* is weighted to non-angling interests, so if you carry your sporting life beyond fishing into wingshooting, skeet, dogs, big game — and if you like a little true-life adventure to spice things up — *OL* may be your best year-round companion.

With the September '76 issue, *Outdoor Life* took on a new, cleaner look. And the editorial content has gradually shifted, too. Its hallmark is still hard-core, no-nonsense information, but it has a wider range of editorial departments. All the standard

Of trolling for lake trout

(continued from preceding page)

by a loop to the swivel at the end of the leader. Thus you have the rod, reel, line, leader, and train of hooks. Perhaps a sketch of the train of hooks will be better than an explanation. Here it is:

This train, you will perceive, is made of five hooks. The lip-hook could be a size or two smaller than the tail-hooks — say No. 5 for the tail, No. 6 for the middle, and No. 7 for the lip. These hooks are joined shank to

(continued on next page)

Outdoor Life

JULY 1976   75¢

New ways to find, catch **BASS** in hot weather

HOW TO...freeze fish... rig grasshopper bait

Life with the **PORCUPINE,** nature's comic oaf

DUCK news! Comeback of the 'can'

Tips to trick big **BLUEGILLS,** twilight **TROUT**

Guide to best whitewater float trips

SHARK! What's behind the new fishing craze

WHERE TO HUNT & FISH IN YOUR REGION

Of trolling for lake trout

(continued from preceding page)

shank, with the gut between them, and then firmly tied with waxed silk. But I procured from Ireland a set of hooks welded or united together, and they are far superior to single hooks joined by tying together, for they frequently double up, and become very troublesome. George Karr, before named, can rig this kind of train better than any man in this city, as far as my experience goes.

5th. THE BAIT AND FLIES.—The proper bait is the Shiner, which can be plentifully procured in all the lakes of Hamilton county. They are taken with the smallest kind of hook, No. 12, with worm bait; and when secured, are put into the bait-kettle, and preserved until used. The mode of putting the Shiner on the train is simple: put the lip or single hook through the lip, the middle hook in the belly, the end hook in the tail.

Unlike Trout-fishing proper, I loop on my flies when trolling. About thirty-six inches from the Shiner I loop on the leader — a large fly; and thirty inches from that fly I loop a smaller-sized one, and then I am rigged to "throw out."

6th. THE BAIT-KETTLE.—This is a most indispensable article for the troller — he can't get along without it. It should be made of strong tin, painted green outside and white inside. The bottom should be wider than the top, but sloping gradually. Conroy has now in his store some very good and complete; but

(continued on next page)

ones are there: Fishing, Boating, Camping, a surprisingly good cooking column and perhaps the best conservation features to be found in the major monthlies. The most distinctive feature of the magazine is a "yellow pages" of regional information in each issue — divided into six areas of the country, each with a separate editor and staffers. Although it's a good theory, the odds against getting detailed information about your locale are still pretty high. *OL*'s new field use reports, "New Equipment and Ideas," really are field *use* reports, not sops to the advertisers. (Times-Mirror magazines, and *OL* in particular, with its 2 million-plus circulation, are beholden to no one.)

Fishing editor Jerry Gibbs relies heavily on his staffers, and they stay pretty close to home — bait fishing and spinning for bass (of course), and the popular salt- and freshwater game fish. *Outdoor Life* rarely casts a fly, but then again, it brought fly fishermen "The Secret of the Neversink Skater," by Vince Marinaro — an angling scoop if there ever was one.

The "Outdoor Life Field Guide" is a tear-me-out section, usually a little step-by-step photo essay on a minor outdoor skill worth acquiring — boning a panfish, for example. A nice, practical section worth accumulating (and tearing out of the old issues).

Outdoor Life features are seldom puffy. One article about a new hook-sharpening method came complete with electron-microscope photographs that could have passed in a metallurgical journal. The magazine is not above a personal profile or interview, but you'll always find more fishing fact than fancy in one issue. And that's its big appeal to the working angler.

Published by: *Outdoor Life.* **Address:** P.O. Box 2851, Boulder, CO 80302. **Price:** One year (12 issues), $7.94.

topoftheline

Sports Afield

Sports Afield has gone through an extensive overhaul in the last several years, perhaps to keep pace with its sister Hearst publication, *Cosmopolitan.* ("I like my fishing and hunting, and I'd go anywhere my RV will take me and Bosco. I guess you could say I'm that *Sports Afield* guy.") In any case, it's all to the good of its readers, and its angling readers in particular.

A look at *SA*'s easy-to-catch contents page tells the story: a full fishing features department, additional editors' reports on boating, saltwater and *angling* (not fishing) and, on occasion, a special-section treatment of hunting and fishing topics plus the mandatory stuff about recreation vehicles, shooting and the like. *Sports Afield* has been trying harder to get an edge on the competition and lots of people seem to agree that it's there.

For the angler, *SA* has perhaps the widest range of editorial opinion. Angling editor Homer Circle draws on the likes of Lee Wulff, Ernest Schwiebert and Dave Harbour to round out a far-flung list of contributors. The magazine's drive for editorial appeal stops just short of sensationalism ("Bass Wired for Sound!") and any given issue will often balance a hard-hitting bass article by Dr. Jekyll against a more lyrical trouting essay by Mr. Hyde.

Regular departments also hold lots of interest for anglers, at least during the season. "Report Afield," a long newsfeature-style gathering of short subjects, often drops useful evaluations of new tackle and important changes in fishing regulations, discoveries from the fisheries biologists, conservation, etc. On the practical side, there's an irregular tackle-making feature and a handy sportsman's "household hints" column called "Why Didn't I Think of That?" which is open to submissions from the readers. "Ask The Editors"

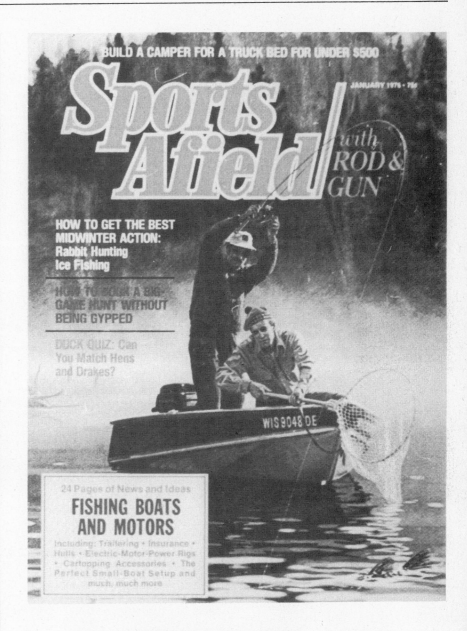

BUILD A CAMPER FOR A TRUCK BED FOR UNDER $500

Sports Afield with ROD & GUN

JANUARY 1978 · 75¢

HOW TO GET THE BEST MIDWINTER ACTION: Rabbit Hunting Ice Fishing

HOW TO BOOK A BIG-GAME HUNT WITHOUT BEING GYPPED

DUCK QUIZ: Can You Match Hens and Drakes?

WIS 9048 DE

24 Pages of News and Ideas
FISHING BOATS AND MOTORS
Including: Trailering · Insurance · Hulls · Electric-Motor-Power Rigs · Cartopping Accessories · The Perfect Small-Boat Setup and much, much more

Of trolling for lake trout

(continued from preceding page)

there is one great improvement, *to have the handle lie or fall inside the lid.* I recommend a small gauze ladle, with a short handle, to take the bait from the kettle when required – it will save much trouble, and injury, if not death, to the "dear little creatures."

The kettle should be replenished with water every hour; and one unerring sign that the Shiner needs fresh water, is when he pokes his nose to the surface. When the fishing is over, sink the kettle in the shoal water, and secure it, so that it cannot be tossed about by "wind or weather."

7th. **THE BOAT AND OARSMAN, OR GUIDE.**—Here you must trust to luck – "first

come, first served." But any person going to the house of John C. Holmes, at Lake Pleasant, will find good accommodation, and "honest John" will secure a good guide and a good boat; and from experience I can safely recommend Cowles, Batchellor, and Morrell, of Lake Pleasant, as faithful, honest, persevering, safe and skilful guides and oarsmen.

Trolling is solely done from the boat. The troller sits with his face to the stern; the oarsman in the middle, or rather near the bow, and rows slowly and gently along the lake; about one and a half or two miles an hour is the proper speed.

(continued on next page)

Magazines with home-state flavor

In the last few years lots of enterprising outdoors types have decided to become editors and publishers, and no matter how ragged the margins, the hallmark of their tabloids and magazines is local information — and local advertising. On the other hand, many state fish and game agencies publish slick, colorful all-outdoors and sometimes angling-only magazines at very reasonable subscription prices.

What you're buying is the home-state flavor, stocking schedules (or tides) and other up-to-the-minute information including perhaps some interesting features that will inspire a weekend fishing expedition or an angling vacation. The best fishing may be at your own back door.

top of the line

(continued from page 317)

is a handy Ann Landers service for confused anglers. Gene Hill's "Tail Feathers" is not designed to tickle your funnybone, but to provide part of *Sports Afield*'s attempt to balance hard angling information with sporting aesthetics and traditions.

The newest feature, the *Sports Afield* "Almanac" section, is a light mixture of tips, do-it-yourself items, wildlife curiosities, and news that often includes angling items. Not something that will make you buy the magazine, but it's perfect bathroom reading, and it's available from *Sports Afield* as an annual.

No matter what you put on the end of your leader, you'll find some of it dangling on the cover of *Sports Afield* sometime during the year. Fly fishermen are not neglected and *Sports Afield* has been acting as though the bass was a fossil fish that has recently been discovered alive in American waters. Tom Paugh keeps things salty, and every now and then, an editor takes a fishing junket to the Arctic that's worth tagging along for if you're not doing anything that night. *Sports Afield* may be the angler's best friend among the general outdoors publications.

Published by: The Hearst Corporation. **Address:** P.O. Box 604, New York, NY 10019. **Price:** one year (12 issues), $7.

Local Magazines

Fishing & Hunting News

Fishing and Hunting News, published weekly out of Seattle, is sort of *National Enquirer* of the outdoor press. There are eight separate editions of the tabloid directed at sportspersons in Eastern Washington, Western Washington, Northern California, Southern California, Oregon, Mon-

Of trolling for lake trout

(continued from preceding page)

8th. THE MANNER OF STRIKING THE FISH WHEN THE BAIT IS TAKEN.—Should there be much wind, thirty-five yards of line is sufficient to run out — if calm, say forty-five or fifty. When a fish is felt, the tip of the rod should be eased off, or given to the fish, in order that he have time to take hold; then give a good surge of the rod, and you will rarely miss striking him. Should you be fishing with two rods, which is almost always the case, pass the other rod to the oarsman. Never give the fish an inch, unless by actual compulsion; invariably keep him in hand — feel him at a distance, but still be kind and gentle, not rude or rough. Do not show the gaff until you know that the fish is "used up;" if a small fish, run the net *under* him; and if the fish is spent or exhausted, he will fall into it; but if he shows life, draw him *over* the net. If a large fish, use the gaff, which pass under him, with the point downwards; then turn it up inside, and strike as near the *shoulder* as possible. I say *shoulder* instead of *tail*.

I believe that I have now done with this branch; but let me say, that no good troller uses lead or sinker of any kind. I have seen it used, but used to the destruction of sport and tackle. Sinkers carry the hooks to the bottom, and there you stick either to root or rock.

When trolling, you take, on the average, more fine Brook Trout than Lake Trout. I think that two to one is correct.

MONTANA
FISHING and
HUNTING
®**NEWS**

Volume 32; Issue 21
May 22, 1976

35¢

The Fish Are There

Bear Cr. Gives Up Pike

Kalispell Bruins Stir

Yellowstone Park Mapped

The Crusader: Worth Wait

Trap Shoot: Family Fun

EASY OVEN FISH

2 1-3 pound trout
salt
pepper
paprika
juice from 1/2 lemon or lime

After removing the heads from the trout, split the fish along the spine to the tail, but not through the skin. Lay the fish, skin side down, on a shallow foil-covered baking dish and sprinkle with the spices; pour the juice over the top. Place fish in 425 degree oven. When all the juices around the fish and in the pan are gone, the fish are done.

If a crustier top is desired, put under the broiler until brown. Remove the fish by sliding a fork between the skin and meat, leaving the skin on the foil.

This is an easy and delicious way to prepare fish that will please diners and dishwashers alike. — H. M. Burrell, Libby, Montana.

top of the line

tana, Colorado, Idaho, Utah and Wyoming but they have basically the same content with local comments gathered from phone calls. Sometimes gets hysterical over gun laws and Indian rights but has a smattering of decent regional information.

Published by: *Fishing & Hunting News*. **Address**: P.O. Box C-19000, Seattle, WA 98109. **Price**: one year (52 issues), $12.

Fishing in Maryland and the Mid-Atlantic

Not quite big enough to be called a book (it's actually a glorified atlas) and too regional to be an annual, this once-a-year guide to the Chesapeake and surrounding freshwater systems is nonetheless indispensable for anglers who get out to the Bay more than once a year. Fishermen investigating the ever-shifting bay waters can count on this game guide for good up-to-the-last-season information about the activities of the migratory fish that make the bay an angler's smorgasbord. It's composed of advertisements with a few feature articles thrown in for window dressing. The real value of this "magazine" lies in the foldout maps of the bay and local rivers and lakes, which are studded with fish silhouettes marking last year's hot spots, navigation guides, tides, dock facilities, etc. Well worth the investment for anglers in Maryland, Virginia, Pennsylvania and New Jersey.

Published by: Fishing in Maryland and the Mid-Atlantic. **Address**: Box 1892, Baltimore, MD 21203. **Price**: $3.95.

Florida Sportsman

The Sportsman's editorial territory really extends to the adjacent Gulf and Central American waters, including the Keys and the Bahamas. The high quality of its angling features makes it somewhat of an exception among state-oriented magazines. A nice saltwater fisherman's wish book. If you're going to Florida for a vacation that just might include some fishing, pick up a copy.

Published by: Wickstrom Publishers, Inc. **Address:** 2701 South Bayshore Drive, Miami, FA 33133. **Price:** One year (six issues), $5.95; one issue, $1.

Great Lakes Sportsman

This Great Lakes regional publication is oriented more towards the outdoors and family fun than just fishing, but it does carry fish recipes and good information about stockings, tournaments and, during the season, features on Great Lakes species and general interest fishing. A bit top-heavy in the ad department, though. You may find it useful for planning local vacations. "Great Lakes" here means Wisconsin, Michigan, Minnesota, Indiana, Illinois and Ohio.

Published by: Great Lakes Publications, Inc. **Address:** 31360 Northwestern Highway, Farmington Hills, MI 48024. **Price:** One year (six issues), $5.

The Long Island Fisherman

The Long Island Fisherman, The New Jersey Fisherman and *The Connecticut Fisherman* are tabloid newspapers issued from the same editorial offices. They serve readers in states where there's a heavy emphasis on saltwater opportunities. These lightweights are good for local fishing information, tide reports, charter boat sailings, etc. Their local news on lakes and streams is reliable. Not slick, but the angling "Believe It or Not!" page, illustrated and written by Ted Gardineer, is worth the trip to the mailbox every week.

FRIED CATFISH

6 skinned, pan-dressed catfish, about 1 pound each
2 t salt
1/4 t pepper
2 eggs
2 T milk
2 c cornmeal

Sprinkle both sides of fish with salt and pepper. Beat eggs lightly and blend with milk. Dip fish in egg mixture and roll in cornmeal.

Fish may then be fried at a moderate heat in a fry pan that contains 1/8 inch cooking oil — or they may be deep fried. Brown well on both sides. Serves 6. — *Michigan Natural Resources.*

top of the line

Published by: *The Long Island Fisherman.* **Address:** P.O. Box 143, Deer Park, NY 11729. **Price:** One year (weekly), $9.

New England Sportsman

A sister publication of the *Great Lakes Sportsman*, NES often carries identical fishing features, supplemented with the appropriate local information and local contributors. Again, a pretty fair all-around outdoors magazine for families. "New England" is everybody north of the Mason-Dixon Line.

Published by: New England Publications, Inc. **Address:** 31360 Northwestern Highway, Farmington Hills, MI 48024. **Price:** One year (six issues), $5.

Southern Outdoors

Ever since B.A.S.S. took over this "fishin' and huntin' in Dixie" magazine, it's gotten slicker and better without losing any of its Southern flavor. There's an emphasis on bass, of course, but that's really because it's the South's most popular game fish; panfish and the saltwater scrappers of the Gulf and Florida coast are not neglected. Lots of good travel information and tackle tips in what might really be called the Southern edition of *Outdoor Life*. The "South" here is everybody from Oklahoma east to Maryland.

Published by: Southern Outdoors. **Address:** 101 Bell Road, Montgomery, AL 36109. **Price:** One year (6 issues), $2.

Western Outdoors

West Coast anglers have long moaned and groaned about the lack of coverage given to them by what they consider the Eastern outdoor press. *Western Outdoors* is an attempt to cover that void. It can vary greatly from issue to issue. Satisfied mostly with varying sorts of "Me and Joe" articles, it will sometimes have excellent how-to articles. It is a good place to look when planning a trip as many of its pieces have detailed info on what to expect when you get to some western locale or another.

Published by: Western Outdoors Publications. **Address:** Box 2027, Newport Beach, CA 92663. **Price:** $6.60 (one year), 11 issues.

Magazines

Bassmaster

Bassmaster is the official magazine of the Bass Anglers Sportsman Society (B.A.S.S.), the high-powered all-bass club you'll find heavily advertised in lots of outdoors magazines. A one-year membership fee of $12 includes a year's subscription to *Bassmaster* — the only way you can subscribe. The magazine is the most substantial benefit of the membership package; your subscription includes the *Bassmaster Fishing Annual*, which you won't find on the newsstands either.

Bassmaster takes an all-star approach, and all of the big bass tournament personalities appear — Bill Dance, Mark Sosin, Roland Martin, et al. There are plenty of articles devoted to new bass technology and tackle and mapped-out travel tips to bass hot spots. B.A.S.S. president Ray Scott lends a nice fishin' club tone to the experts' screamer articles on every imaginable way to take bass ("Raise 'Em with a Ruckus"). If you're a born-again bass fisherman, *Bassmaster* is the evangelical truth and hope for more strikes. But remember, you have to join B.A.S.S. to get a subscription. *Sports Afield* and other major outdoors magazines have all taken up the bass banner,

GAMEFISH: MONTANA GREYLING

NAMES
Michigan greyling, American greyling. *(thymallus signifer tricolor)*

DISTRIBUTION
The Montana greyling is found throughout Canada and Alaska from the Northwest Territories to British Columbia. In the United States, it is found in the higher elevations of Montana and parts of Wyoming, where it has been transplanted.

DESCRIPTION
The Montana greyling is a member of the family that includes the Michigan greyling (now extinct) and the Arctic greyling, which is found primarily in Alaska and Canada. It is a beautiful fish of dark blue or grey on the back with silver or silvery-purple sides. Dark, irregular spots mark the forebody. Its most distinctive feature is its large dorsal fin, which is grey to blue-green in color and is marked by rows of purple or reddish spots. Coloration depends on where the fish is located.

SIZE
The Montana greyling is a small fish that rarely exceeds 2 pounds. The average is about 1 pound.

HABITAT
The Montana greyling is only found in clear cold waters such as mountain streams and high timberline lakes. It cannot survive in polluted waters and tends to seek out deep pools.

FEEDING HABITS
These fish survive mainly on insects and insect larvae although they have been known to eat worms. They are an active fish that often travels in schools.

TACKLE
The not-too-abundant Montana greyling is usually found in small streams and is a downright sucker for small wet and dry flies or tiny spinners flung from an ultra-light outfit. Small fly rods are all that's needed.

top of the line

too, and you're bound to read about the sport somewhere else.

Address: P.O. Box 3044, Montgomery AL 36109.

Fishing World

"The largest-circulation magazine for sport fishermen" is probably also the best of the new angling-only magazines. The editorial staff is always a chorus of good advice from good fishermen: Lefty Kreh on inshore fishing, Charles Waterman on trout, et al., Tom McNally, Frank Moss and others. A nice-looking magazine, *Fishing World* casts a line between fishing practicalities and well-told tales. It hardly ever sensationalizes, perhaps because it's not involved in circulation wars with the Big Three. Just good, friendly, readable fishing information here. *Fishing World* is available as part of the Fishing Club of America membership package ($7) which includes travel and services and discounts on books and movies, and of course an FCA patch.

Published by: *Fishing World.* **Address:** 51 Atlantic Ave., Floral Park, NY 11001. **Price:** one year (6 issues), $4.

Fishing Tackle Trade News

The *Fishing Tackle Trade News* won't tell you how to catch fish but it certainly will keep you apprised of developments in the industry. You'll learn who is going to market with what new products, what changes there are in company personnel and how the industry is doing financially. Lots of interesting products are advertised and some of them you won't see around otherwise. No great shakes as far as articles go but sometimes good writers like Mark Sosin get some general-interest stuff in.

Published by: Fishing Tackle Trade News. **Address:** P.O. Box 70, Wilmette, IL 60091. **Price:** one year (10 issues), $4.

ultimate commodity

*Russell Chatham by Francis Golden
Spring, 1976*

Gray's Sporting Journal

At a time when good sporting writing seems particularly hard to find in the outdoors magazines, *Gray's Sporting Journal* appears like a phoenix. Visually and editorially, *Gray's* makes all the others seem slightly pornographic; it's a beautiful magazine.

The editorial lineup is simply today's best, and yet it manages to avoid trading on the cult of personality that has invaded the other larger magazines: Frank Woolner, Poul Jorgensen, Charles Waterman, Charles Dickey, Russ Chatham, Nick Lyons and many others familiar and unfamiliar — not the least of which is the editor and publisher of this noble undertaking, one Edward Gray. His "Gray's Journal" opening feature is consistently thoughtful, without any of the preachiness that spoils too many published attempts at communicating what it is we're after out there.

The articles themselves range from purely whimsical but gorgeous photo-essays on trout streams and bass coverts, to deep-background stories on tackle, travelogues, short stories and pure yarns. *Gray's* is not without its practicalities; there's lots of armchair travel available, and each

issue features gourmet-level game recipes and a profile of fly-tyers, guides and gamekeepers you may never get to meet otherwise. None of angling's varied pleasures is neglected. The subscription price makes *Gray's* seem, like split bamboo, a

luxury you can well do without — until you own one. Individual issues are available a la carte ($2.75) in better tackle stores everywhere. Really only three of the seven annual issues are directly concerned with angling: "Trout and Salmon," "Bass and Pike," "Trophy Fishing" and indirectly, "Expeditions and Outings." (The other three issues are solid hunting.)

Graphically, *Gray's* is a feast of full-color photography, handsome watercolors (usually an original on each distinctive, heavy-bound cover), and quaint drawings that will make you want to tear them out to paste in your scrapbook. But don't; you'll have this magazine on your bedstand a lot longer than any other, and you'll be pleasantly surprised that you didn't really miss a penny of that subscription price. Each angling and hunting issue is released about a month before the appropriate season. *Gray's Sporting Journal* is altogether a movable feast of fine writing about the outdoors.

Published by: *Gray's Sporting Journal.* **Address:** P.O. Box 70, Farmingdale, NY 11735. **Price:** One year (7 issues), $18.

THE LAST HATCH
A FISHING MYSTERY
HARMON HENKIN

(continued from page 307)

"Who did it, Dun?"

"What?" He was stunned by the question. "Who did what, sir?"

"Who killed your boss? We ain't interested in Cock Robin today."

"I can assure you, sir, I haven't the faintest idea. A man of Mr. Halford's stature and accomplishments was much beloved by everybody." He lifted his eyes towards heaven reverentially.

Paul took over. "Dun, we all know your feelings toward your employer."

"Oh, he was much more than an employer. He was a shepherd in my life."

"But someone around here disliked him enough to kill. That's a powerful amount of dislike."

"Of course there are always jealousies and grudges held against someone of Mr. Halford's eminence."

"Now we're getting somewhere," Sid mumbled.

"Had there been a higher level of these 'jealousies and grudges' lately?" Paul asked.

"Well . . ."

"Come on now."

"Well, I guess the truth will out. This is a private conversation between three gentlemen, is it not?" He paused to make sure everyone was a gentleman, then continued.

"Some people felt Mr. Halford was undergoing some major changes recently. He even revealed to me once that he was sick of the same old rut. For the first time in his career, he was having trouble with his writing. His publisher, Berner & Sons, was even wondering whether it should publish the novel he finished last spring, *Of Moose and Men*. But every great career has its ups and downs. Am I not correct?"

He paused again to make sure they agreed. They nodded. Paul could tell that Sid was bored with literary talk. He'd had his fill in college.

"Now, many people believed Mr. Halford had an unlimited supply of money. But he didn't. What with high taxes, alimony payments to three wives and the full, joyous style of life he was living, he was having a severe cash-flow problem. Just last week he told me he wanted to sell this place so he could start fresh somewhere else."

(continued on page 334)

top of the line

Fishing Facts

This splashy, all-angling magazine is actually a combination tackle catalog (you can order a variety of freshwater tackle and accessories directly from the publisher) and freshwater fishing publication. It's a likely combination, and the whole thing has a dead serious fishin' tone. Most of the feature writing is handled by staffers after muskie, bass, panfish, trout, walleye and other common freshwater catches. The close-to-home adventures are complemented by lots of color snapshots of readers' catches. Despite the me-and-Joe-went-fishin' tone, this is an expensive magazine. The tackle service makes an interesting 18-month unconditional guarantee on lures and other accessories and the publisher offers some nice-sized plastic worm kits and rigs and complete "nightcrawler kits" consisting of bait hooks and weights in various styles. Patriarch Buck Perry has some dogmatic, inbred ideas about freshwater fishing, but all in all, this is good, clean family fishing fun.

Published by: Northwoods Publishing Company. **Address:** P.O. Box 609, Menomonee Falls, WI 53051. **Price:** One year (12 issues), $12.

Fly Fisherman

Fly Fisherman came along at the right time. When Don Zahner introduced it nine years ago the market was ready. The current revival in fly fishing was just underway and fly anglers were discouraged by the Big Three's treatment of their sport. At times it has some good, helpful articles but lots of it is relatively mundane stuff. It is very much a part of the angling establishment and tends toward being quite bland. Its virtual obliviousness to conservation matters is not only irresponsible but tends to make the Big Three seem radical in comparison. But *Fly Fisherman* is de-

"The main tendencies of modern American fly-tying largely stem from Theodore Gordon, the old master of American fly fishing, familiar to most fishermen through his Quill Gordon Fly."
JOHN McDONALD

BOOKS & PERIODICALS 325

top of the line

voted solely to fly fishing, has lots of nice ads and a fine back page column by Nick Lyons that can make it all seem worthwhile at times. Its strongest features are on fly patterns and tackle maintenance. Its weakness is uptown "Me and Joe" things told with pomp and circumstance.

Published by: Fisherman Magazine, Inc. **Address:** Manchester Village, VT 05254. **Price:** one year (7 issues), $10.

Fur-Fish-Game

The venerable old *Harding's Magazine*, as *Fur-Fish-Game* was originally called, is traditionally the publication that many teenagers graduated to from *Boy's Life*. There's usually more fur than fish, though John Weiss' "Fish & Tackle" column is always solid. The magazine has a "Midwest — Heart of America" kind of tone, though on occasion fishing and hunting articles range further. Some true-life adventures spice up the regular Travel, Camping, Vacationing and Hunting departments. It's the only national magazine with a focus on trapping, which makes it a good year-round companion for the yeoman sportsman.

Published by: Harding's Magazine. **Address:** P.O. Box 1320, Columbus, Ohio 43209. **Price:** One year (12 issues), $4.50.

The Lunker Gazette

This Fenwick house newsletter won't go away, and keeps getting better and better. It's an almost even mixture of good, sometimes very localized information and news about Fenwick tackle. It includes an order form for their mail-order service. Good tackle tips, for which the Gazette pays $10, appear among the Fenwick T-shirts, caps, patches and feature articles by name outdoor

Notes on a fishing trip with Riley

By Peter Adler

Vashon Island, Washington

turtle lazy, fishing
on a tanker dock

the ocean, flat, calm
veined with seaweed

sign on pier
    NO SMOKING OR FISHING

". . . pound for pound, by god, a large-mouth bass is the finest fish there is . . ."

on a knot of timbers
baiting: crabs, grubs,
helgemites, chunks of
fish, a snot of tired
worms

beer

starfish, ling cod, sole, and
batfish

talking story: " . . . and then when John-the-Christian took this new guy out to teach him how to spin cast, he snagged old John through the cheek with a red and white daredevil. John stuck a chew of Copenhagen in beside the hook and hoofed it down to have the hook cut off his face. Walked three miles and never said a word . . ."

slime scales, and fish shit

the Quinault Indians
catch good red salmon
and trade it off for hamburger

fishing
pissing off the dock
ocean perch

" . . . the only ones with spine and fiber left these days are us and the fish . . ."

cold Sound water,
washing off the
worm and fish

sunburned fishline

Taken from *Tantalus*, Spring 1974.
(C) 1974 by Tantalus Press. Used
by permission of Tantalus Press,
Honolulu, Hawaii.

top of the line

writers. If you're brand-name conscious, or you just can't read enough about fishing, try it. Fenwick will send free copies to members of your fishing club if you send them your roster. You know what that means.
Published by: Fenwick-Sevenstrand. **Address:** P.O. Box 729, Westminster, CA 92683. **Price:** One year (6 issues), $1.

Salmon, Trout, Steelheader

Salmon, Trout, Steelheader has come a long way from its skimpy beginnings not too long ago. More and more anglers looking for information about West Coast angling experiences turn to this magazine. Sometimes its understanding of such touchy issues as the Indian Fishing Rights controversy is limited but otherwise it is an excellent place to learn about the intricacies of the Pacific Northwest.
Published by: Salmon Trout Steelheader. **Address:** Box 02112, Portland, Ore. 97202. **Price:** one year (6 issues), $4.50.

Saltwater Sportsman

"The voice of the coastal fisherman," the masthead proclaims. This is a magazine for the serious, full-time saltwater angler. Vacationers need not apply. If your skin is a year-round burnt orange, and your idea of angling is intimately tied up with salt air, classy big-game equipment, the glorious solitude of fishing in open water and live baits that would pass for a day's limit ashore, then you probably already subscribe. If not, here's what you're missing: regular boating departments — two of them, usually, since there's a lot more to be said about marine boats and accessories than any of the general outdoor mags have space to devote; detailed fishing conditions from the Maritime Provinces and around the coast of America to

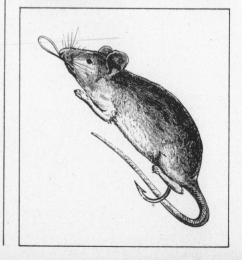

top of the line

Oregon; reliable tackle talk, and features from harbors and havens all over the Americas. The Caribbean is part of the *Sportsman's* turf. Even though saltwater sportfishing is almost by its very nature sensational, all the splashing and thrashing is recreated by writers, whose names you'll recognize from other angling publications, in a remarkably low-keyed tone. Editor Frank Woolner and publisher Henry Lyman share a regular "Tackle Talk" feature covering everything from their favorite plugs to heavyweight tarpon tackle. The "Marine Clinic," an ask-the-editors feature, guarantees an answer to your knottiest saltwater question. Charles Waterman's "Sideswipes" is an interesting mixture of yarn and here-and-now tackle advice. There's even a cookery column. The whole magazine has the flavor of a conversation over beers at the end of the day.

Altogether, *Saltwater Sportsman* is black-and-white proof that saltwater fishermen are a separate tribe in the angling world — and it's the best way to even the odds on a bluefin tuna.

Published by: Saltwater Sportsman. **Address:** P.O. Box 6050, Marion, OH 43302. **Price:** One year (12 issues), $7.50.

Trout

The official organ of Trout Unlimited, *Trout* fortunately is available outside of the membership (TU members receive *Trout* as part of their $12.50 annual dues). Even with a staple of trout and salmon features, including some fiction and humor, *Trout* comes as close to being a fisheries biology journal as it dares. But the true salmaniac will not be put off by the frequent appearance of scientific studies like "The Reseting and Feeding Behavior of the Brown Trout" and stream management sur-

MONTANA TROUT BAKED IN WINE

3-4 good-sized trout (8-10 inches long)
6 T butter
3/4 c onion, chopped
1/2 c parsley, chopped
1 c dry white wine

Clean trout, leaving head and tail on. Sauté the onion and parsley in the butter. Spread 1/3 of the mixture on the bottom of a baking dish. Fill the cavity of the fish with 1/3 of the mixture and place the rest on top.

Pour the dry white wine over the top and cover. Bake at 350 degrees until done (25-30 minutes). Uncover and sprinkle with bread crumbs. — Virginia Burns; Polson, Montana.

How not to scare fish

Fish are frightened with any the least sight or motion, therefore by all means keep out of sight, either by sheltring your self behind some bush or tree, or by standing so far off the Rivers side, that you can see nothing but your flie or flote; to effect this, a long Rod at ground, and a long Line with the artificial flie may be of use to you. And here I meet with two different opinions & practices, some always cast their flie & bait up the water, and so they say nothing occurreth to the Fishes sight but the Line: others fish down the River, and so suppose (the Rod and Line being long) the quantity of water takes away, or at least lesseneth the Fishes sight; but the other affirm, that Rod and Line, and perhaps your self, are seen also.

The Experienced Angler
(1662) **By Col. Robert Venables**

top of the line

veys that are complete with graphs and charts — all mixed in with travelogues, book reviews, and news of the TU chapters. These studies are usually made available as free reprints from TU headquarters, and close attention may yield a fishing application or two. "Washington Billboard" is often grim reading, but it's the best legislative report going. A nice mix for the serious trout fisherman, and a bargain at the subscription price.

Published by: Trout Unlimited. **Address:** 4260 East Evans Street, Denver CO 80222. **Price:** One year (4 issues), $2.

Trout and Salmon

This mostly English publication has been around for a long time informing readers in the British Isles what is going on in their sport which they take very seriously. Sometimes it's a bit obscure for the American angler but at other times its articles on fishing in lakes for trout is very valuable and its articles on salmon angling are worthwhile, too. Its general approach to the sport can be enchanting, especially for a Yank a little jaded with our periodicals.

Published by: Trout and Salmon, **Address:** Park House, 117 Park Road, Peterborough, England PE1 2TS. **Price:** About 50 cents per issue.

SERVICES & ACCESSORIES

IN SEARCH OF WILD FISH

The backpacking angler's first principles are austerity and simplicity

By Richard Eggert

Backpack fishing — getting away from the beaten path and the madding crowd — is an adventure in angling's first principles.

In the first place, only in remote regions of North America can wild fish still be found. The homebred fish in roadside streams and lakes survive only because they have developed successful ways of dealing with civilization. They are not wild. In the swamps and bogs of the upper Midwest and the deep South and the mountains of New England ar.d the West the fish grow big, brawny and cocky by obeying their simplest instincts and following the most primitive of laws.

To find them, the fisherman must sacrifice a measure of sophistication. To do that, you have to throw out the junk.

The roadside, lowland angler is burdened by an incredible array of supportive tackle which has little or nothing to do with the act and art of catching fish. For every ounce of essential gear — rod, reel, line and lures — there is a pound of fluff. So another first principle the wild fish should obey is simplicity. The venerated ancients of the sport; Dame Juliana Burners and the poet J. D. (*Secrets of Angling*) gave us a few simple tools. They told us we could store everything we needed in the butts of our rods and hike to our fishing with tackle concealed in what appears to be a walking stick so we "will not be thought idle."

I know backpack anglers who take this suggestion almost literally by cramming everything they think they will need into a two-piece rod case.

Another principle in backpack angling is austerity. Discover what your minimum tackle requirements are and strictly limit yourself to that amount. One way is to find a container — such as a rod case — and restrict your tackle needs to what will fit. Another approach is to decide on a maximum weight limit — say 1½ pounds — and fit your requirements around it.

Tackle requirements start with a rod. For fly fishing you should aim for one at least 7½ feet long that will carry a No. 5 or No. 6 line. Spin fishermen can probably get away with an ultra-light outfit that will carry a 6 pound test line.

Most rod makers offer three- or more-piece back pack models. Some are

A 6-strip bamboo rod marketed in 1897 by Abbey & Imbrie for $4. An 8-footer, it weighed 9 ounces, had nickel-plated mountings and was wound in red and black silk.

good, many are sheer garbage. The principle of multi-piece rods is, of course, to create more compact carrying packages. A four-piece eight footer breaks down into a package of about 28 inches (including case). The problem in multiple-section rods is the cumulative effect of extra ferrules on the action of the rod. If you do decide to go into a multiple piece rod, you are probably better off with light-weight, flexible glass-to-glass type ferrules.

Another option is to put your regular two-piece rod into a heavy duty, shock absorbing rod case-walking stick. The top and bottom of the case should be insulated with thick disks of sponge rubber and the rod should fit snugly into a heavy cloth bag to protect it from impact with the side of the case. You should wrap a leather or tape handle at the top of the case and fix it with a sling-lanyard for carrying on your back while scrambling among rocks or beating through brush.

The reel should be the lightest you can afford which will carry enough line and backing. Ultra-light spinning reels with breakdown handles are nice because they form smaller packages.

Reels can be jammed into a small, nylon bag along

(continued on next page)

Buy hiking and camping gear from a specialist

(continued from preceding page)

with one box of flies or lures. Wild fish generally are not as demanding as their more human-wise cousins and a copious menu is not necessary. Bright, basic flies — dry, wet and streamers — and spinners and spoons are usually sufficient. Fly fishermen would be wise to carry extra tippits and an extra leader, which also fit into the bag.

But that is all you really need. You may not be comfortable without your net, sink-tip line reel, vest and three volume entomology identification set; and nothing I can say will prevent you from carrying them on your first trip into the wilds. But nothing anybody could say would convince you to carry them on your second trip.

The main reason for developing simple needs in tackle is the amount of camping and hiking gear also required for backpack fishing. Here is a checklist of the things you need and some other things you probably already have which you will want in the wilds. A suggestion: when you shop for specialized camping and hiking gear, go to a specialist. Mountain climbing shops have developed lines of equipment which have been proven rugged, comfortable and light by thousands of high mountain climbers and hikers. Many fishing tackle shops carry hiking equipment, but much of it is overstuffed and overpriced.

BOOTS

There are more boots on the market today than you would want to shake a leg at. They range from campus waffle stompers to Alpine technical boots. For spring, winter and fall hiking, look for a pair of Vibram-soled, padded ankle boots weighing about 4½ pounds in a No. 10. These are usually known as light climbing-hiking boots and most good manufacturers have a model that will fit.

In fitting, you probably should go a good half-size larger than street shoes to compensate for thick socks and swelling. I have found that Italian and Austrian boots are better built and engineered than most others but there are a few firms in the U.S. making fine hiking footwear. Signs of quality are good — tight outside and inside stitching (some cheap boots have glued-in liners or no liners at all in the toe section of the boot). A reputable mountaineer shop should put you into a good pair of boots. You will be spending $50 to $65.

(Above and far right) Abercrombie & Fitch collapsible cups from the early 1900s.

SOCKS

No big deal? Try wearing rayon hose sometime. Buy heavy duty Norwegian type rag socks and carry at least one pair for every day you intend to be out.

TENNIS SHOES

The only considerations here are weight (you will be carrying them in your pack) and some support in the sole. Leather won't put up

A turn-of-the-century silverplated, engraved pocket flask.

with much wading so try canvas or nylon duck.

PACKS

There are a lot of different styles, sizes and functions available. For light weekend packing you will want one that has enough support to hold 30 pounds and from 3000 to 4000 cubic centimeters comfortably. The obvious ticket is the standby frame back, which you can use for longer-heavier trips too. Mountaineer stores can fit you nicely for $40 to $60.

A recent alternative to the frame is the soft, self-frame or monochoke style. These packs don't have a

frame at all but take on a rigid, body-forming configuration as you load them. They can carry 30 pounds on your back like a shirt and don't throw your center of gravity backwards as frame backs do sometimes. Many of these are available now but only a few have proven worthwhile. Don't buy one that doesn't come in a number of sizes — the fit is critical. You will also have to pay more — from $60 to $75 — and you will only find these at mountaineer supply shops.

SLEEPING BAGS

Everybody makes sleeping bags these days and there are a number of very good ones. And there is junk. Price does not necessarily separate them. You are looking for a three-season bag with a comfort range down to say 15° or 20° F. The best weight-warmth engineered bags are the mummy or semi-rectangular styles. If you go in for a bag with more foot room, you are carrying around a lot of extra weight.

The shell should be made of rip-stop nylon because it's tough and strong, yet light. The filling is a matter of function and finances. Goose down is the traditional favorite and still preferred by most mountaineers. It is resilient, lofts (inches of insulation) better than any other insulation, weighs less and drapes over your body better. It also costs considerably more. A quality goose down bag in the three-season category will squeeze you $100 to $125 — enough to lose sleep

as down. But a lot of very serious mountaineers are using them and they may be the best suited for the budget-minded backpack angler.

Compromises: duck down is a half-step lower than goose down. It is almost as good and almost as expensive. Another option being played with by a number of manufacturers is a bag with a down top and a synthetic fiber bottom. The down lofts and drapes where it should and the synthetic insulates and resists compression where it should. Prices are generally in between the two fillers.

sleeping bags to stoves

withstand Himalayan storms and days of incarceration. You don't really need one of these either.

What you do need is a rain-proof, insect-resistant, three-season shelter that's as light as it is rugged. There are a number of really excellent tents made by various mountaineering firms selling from $80 to $125 and weighing from 5½ to 6 pounds. Don't spend more on a tent and don't get one that weighs much more.

All tents in this category normally have A-frame fronts with A or I rears. They have one entrance in the front. They are made of either rip-stop or taffeta nylon with an extra coated fly (don't buy a tent without a fly because they tend to sweat, swelter and steam). There are some dome and aerodynamically designed tents available but they are either too expensive, too heavy or both.

STOVES

Campfires are nice and correspond to the mood. But they are also messy,

Abercrombie & Fitch "Matchless" prepared foods from the early 1900s were heated by adding water to quicklime sealed in an outer container.

slow and sometimes unreliable. A nice rule of thumb is: never build a fire where one has not been built before. Another good rule is to have a stove in case it rains or you want to heat something in a hurry. Lightweight stoves come in several different styles, shapes and functions. For summer use a heat-vaporizing white

(continued on next page)

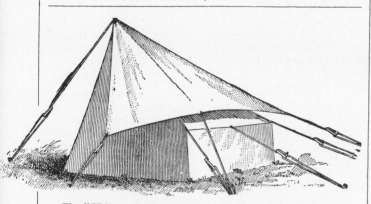

The Wilkinson Co. began selling the "Protean Tent" in the 1890s. Made in various sizes, it sold for from $4.18 to $10.10.

over no matter how cozy.

Two new synthetic fibers called Polarguard and Fiberfill II are taking shots at down's primacy. Both are cheaper ($60 to $75 for bags in our range), quicker drying and less prone to absorb water than down. They are not as weight-warmth efficient as down, are not as compressible and are not yet as uniformly insulating

TENTS

Backpacking tents range in price from $50 to $200 with neither extreme really suitable for backpack angling. Cheap tents are cheap — they probably won't function well to begin with or will fall apart quickly. Expensive tents are generally specially designed high-altitude winter jobs made to

The "Kamp Kook's Kit" was a 21-piece extravaganza the H. H. Kiffe Co. sold for $5.50 in the early 1900s. It weighed 15 pounds.

(continued from preceding page)

gas stove — it's lighter, cheaper and sufficient.

FOOD

The object of the trip into the wilds is to catch and eat fish, but it often doesn't work out that way. If you are eating fish never — but never — keep more than you intend to eat at the next meal. It is incredibly easy to wipe out a high mountain lake where it takes a native cutthroat four years to mature. And keeping fish

Folding Abercrombie & Fitch wash basins. At bottom is a rubber bath tub.

around camp can lead to awesome bear problems.

Some commercial freeze-dried foods are very tasty but finding good ones is a hit-and-miss proposition. They are also incredibly expensive, which leaves market testing well out of the reach of most people. However, there are a number of grocery shelf dried foods which are reasonable and can be rendered into good wholesome meals.

Dried fruits such as raisins, apricots and apples are excellent snacks. So are granola, cereals and nuts. With powdered milk, you can make a lavish breakfast or lunch.

Powdered soups — such as Chinese noodles — with powdered eggs and garnishes make good dinners. Remember to bring powdered coffee, tea bags and cocoa, too.

Another consideration in foods is packaging — you are going to have to dispose of what you don't use. It is not a particularly good idea to burn plastics but it is better than leaving them around. Messy aluminum trays or tins won't burn so they will have to be hauled out.

COOKWARE

For one person, the old Boy Scout mess kit is hard to beat. There are also several nesting aluminum cook kits large enough to prepare meals for several persons.

A good plan is for all travelers to carry their own Boy Scout kit and spoon

food to first aid kits

(forks are a bit of an affectation in the sticks) and to divide the community pot and fry pan among the packs.

KNIVES

One of the most important items in your camp kit is a good stout knife. I used to carry a large Air Force Survival sheath knife into the hills but recently have found that the folding lock-blades will do as much with only a fraction of the bulk and weight. And with folding lock-blades you can show your pocketbook a vast variety of makers and styles — all seem to be fairly good.

CLOTHING

Clothing should be suited to the area you are hiking. In the mountains, for instance, warmies should always be carried — even in July. I bring both a light, closely woven wool sweater and a superlight down sweater. I also have a waterproof nylon poncho in my pack along with an extra change of blue jeans and sweat shirt. A couple of handkerchiefs are handy for sweat-headbands, flag signals and blowing your nose.

FIRST AID KITS

It is very easy to justify bringing an army field station along with two qualified surgeons — but one must be practical. I carry a small pouch similar to items sold by several mountaineer shops known as "hiker"

kits. This will get me through the normal routine of wilderness cuts and contusions and I rely on a good sense of discretion to keep me out of larger troubles. I also bring along an elastic pin bandage for sprains and flareups of old knee injuries.

DON'T FORGETS

Among the things you probably already have that should go into your pack are: compass, waterproofed matches, toilet paper, belt, cup, sewing and repair kit, notebook and pen, dime novel, light flashlight and insect repellent (especially in the swamps and marshes).

One more thing. It is always a good idea to know how to get to where you are going and back again (not necessarily the same way). The U.S. Geological Service and most local mountaineering shops will sell you topo maps of the area you intend to hike and fish. Take the maps around to people who have been there before to find the easiest way up and down and what problems you may encounter.

DEALING GRACEFULLY WITH THE UNKNOWN IS WHAT IT'S ALL ABOUT

By Harmon Henkin

Backpack angling is usually pictured as a peaceful jaunt to a highcountry trout lake. But it can also be a lot more, including an overnighter on a deserted beach, a three-day excursion along a southern bass river or disappearing for a week to a wilderness pike lake.

Though the mountain trouter considers himself the backpacker par excellence, actually any angler who seeks the out-of-the-way under his own power is a backpacker and should choose equipment with the same high standards.

Both support camping gear and tackle itself should be picked with lightness and durability as big considerations. The farther and more arduous the backpack excursion, the more crucial these qualities become. It is in hauling a piece of tackle uphill that ounces become tons and a little reel screw that didn't seem to have any purpose becomes the key to the angler's universe.

In choosing a rod, especially a fly rod, portability becomes a factor. The fad for two-piece rods in the past few decades doesn't help the angler who wants to take along something longer than eight feet. If you get a three- or four-piece rod that has the same good feel and action as a two-piece, do it. Just don't sacrifice too much quality for handiness. That's a bad tradeoff and these days, with the variety of pack rods available, it shouldn't have to be made.

There are lots of multi-pieced glass ferruled fiberglass rods that are made in models for the fly fisher, spin fisher or anglers who go both ways. Beware of inexpensive three- or four-piece rods that have metal ferrules. They usually have awful actions.

Unless a metal ferruled rod carries a big price tag like the $300-range Orvis and Leonard bamboo pack types, it's probably less of a rod than one with a glass ferrule. The price of good metal ferrules — when they are available at all — usually starts at $10 and therefore aren't found on inexpensive rods. Cheap metal ferrules transmit casting energy like a rubber fish transmits love and affection.

Unless you restrict yourself to one type of pack angling under one set of water conditions, get a rod that's a compromise. You can never be sure of what you'll find away from civilization.

In a fly rod for Western mountain use get something about eight feet that takes around a No. 6 line. Although not best at either extreme, that kind of eight-footer can handle in a pinch anything from a No. 20 midge to a No. 2 streamer. It should ideally come in three or four pieces.

For a light spinning rod choose something about six feet long. The piece count isn't crucial but it should be able to handle monofilament from two to eight pounds and lures from 1/16 to 1/4 ounce, which are usually what's needed for mountain lakes and streams.

In reels, regardless of the type, durability has always seemed to be the prime requisite. Weight is secondary. But if you do suffer from a lightness mania, there's the featherlight Cortland graphite fly reels and such ultra-light open-faced reels as the Orvis and Alcedo Micron. Smaller still are the close-faced models such as those Shakespeare makes. Extra spools with lighter or heavier monofilament and sinking or sink tip line for fly casting will also help give you the versatility you need in the wilderness.

A larger than usual selection of flies and lures is also recommended, especially for unknown conditions. There is no place to buy them, thankfully. But then the unknown is what backcountry angling is all about.

THE LAST HATCH
A FISHING MYSTERY
HARMON HENKIN

(continued from page 324)

"He was going to give it all up?" Paul asked.

"That's correct, sir."

"But there must be more to it than that."

Both Paul and Sid leaned forward on their chairs.

"Mr. Halford told me he was in love. Real love. He said it was the first time he had ever felt that way. He said it was a strange and wonderful feeling. He was almost . . . boyish when he told me but he wouldn't say who he was in love with."

"Was he acting weird or anything? You know." Sid asked.

"Perhaps a bit giddy. His new attitude was upsetting some people, I must say. For instance, Mr. Wormer was afraid in his joy Mr. Halford would forget the land development. Mr. Wormer was putting pressure on him to sign the papers. And starting to get a little nasty about it."

"Anyone else unhappy?"

"Well, Miss Softhackle could see that her alimony payments might be cut off in the near future if Mr. Halford really did run away and start fresh. Mr. Tups was probably anxious for the same reason. Miss Softhackle supports him, you know. I really don't know about the Hewitts. Mr. Halford had met him on a fishing trip off the coast of Washington, which is where Belle Parmachene is from."

"What about Schielbacht?"

"He was very unhappy because Mr. Halford didn't seem interested in collaborating on a book, *Hatches I Have Matched.* Mr. Schielbacht hadn't been doing well since he got skunked on that segment last spring of *American Sportsman* and was counting, I suppose, on the new work to regenerate his reputation."

"How'd you stand with your boss after he fell in love? And remember, don't try to kid us. We have our ways of finding things out."

Sid nodded gravely in agreement.

"Well, I . . . uh. I took it for granted that Mr. Halford would have provided amply for me after all these years of devoted service even if he had changed his will."

"There was going to be lots of money in his estate?" Paul asked.

"Yes. As soon as this and a few other pieces of prime recreational real estate were disposed."

"Next time you use a phrase like 'prime recreational real estate,' you're in trouble," Sid barked.

(continued on page 349)

FLY BOXES FOR BACKPACKERS

The purpose of the fly box is to contain the flies that the angler wishes to carry and in so doing protect them from being damaged. Some fly boxes . . . are designed not only to contain flies but essentially to keep them separate from each other. While this distinct separation can be advantageous at times, for the backpacker who will no doubt purposely limit the number of flies that he wishes to carry, such facility is not a necessity. Of primary importance to the backpacker are the ever-present considerations of weight, durability, and capacity. . . .[P]lastic fly boxes best fit the needs of the backpacker. Of course personal preference dictates different fly boxes for different individuals, so for various reasons the aluminum boxes might be more desirable to some people. If you find this to indeed be the case, be careful to choose the type of fly box that can contain the type of fly you intend to carry.

Excerpted from *Fly Fishing for Backpackers* by R.A. Cordes. Published by Fenwick-Sevenstrand Inc. The complete book may be obtained by sending $2.50 to Fenwick, Box 279, Westminster, CA 92683.

Put together your own fishing first aid kit

By Marshall Bloom, M.D.

A first aid kit is an item frequently overlooked by anglers as they gather their tackle for a fishing expedition. Yet a well-considered kit is small, requires relatively few special purchases and is potentially the most important bit of gear in your pack or tackle box. The following list of first-aid materials is largely self-explanatory. The list is primarily for the freshwater angler, but really little effort is necessary to make the kit useful for saltwater fishing as well.

Anyone planning a trip longer than a day away from civilization (and such trips are requiring more and more ingenuity) should have a working knowledge of first aid essentials. The Boy Scout *First Aid Merit Badge Manual* is concise, inexpensive, up-to-date and easy to read. If you're headed into the real back country, read up on the area and beef up this kit appropriately for hazards you might encounter. Don't take chances — no first aid item is too heavy or too bulky. My philosophy is that a snakebite kit acts as a charm, and as long as I carry one, I'll never see a poisonous snake. Consider taking an emergency food cache along, too, separate from your regular menu. It should include instant energy, high-calorie food like hard candy as a guard against hypothermia.

No matter how long or short your fishing trip, sunglasses and a hat are good preventive first aid. Besides preventing sunburn and minimizing glare, a hat is good protection from the airborne missiles we call lures and flies. It's easier to remove a hook from a hat than from the back of the head.

A final, very unconventional item of first aid is a barbless hook. Having hooked myself and others in various locations, I have concluded that none of the methods of hook removal are sufficiently easy or painless to be of practical value, even the new quick-yank methods. A barbless hook circumvents all the difficulties of hook removal from even the most inaccessible places and has saved me from ruining several sweaters in the frenzy of good fly hatches besides. The present-day barbless hooks are actually sharper than their barbed counterparts, seem to hold just as well and when the fish is in hand or net the hook is easily backed out with minimal damage to the fish.

And speaking of fish, it is rapidly becoming clear that fish are in much greater need of first aid than are fishermen. Trout streams are being silted, bull-dozed, dammed and ruined at an alarming rate. Studies suggest that in a few years the lower Madison River in Montana will be too warm for trout. Not only are cold water fisheries in trouble — industrial pollution is ruining both warm water and saltwater fisheries in all parts of the country; development threatens the eutrophication of many lakes and ponds. It seems ludicrous to debate the merits of flesh-colored Band-Aids or Polaroid sunglasses while such devastation is going on. The complete first-aid kit for fishermen in the contemporary world must include a membership card for at least one of the organizations devoted to giving first aid to fish. (A directory of these organizations is located in the chapter "United We Stand").

The essentials

SQUARE GAUZE BANDAGES 4"x4", VARIOUS SIZE BAND AIDS	for minor cuts and contusions
MOLESKIN	good protection against blisters if you're hiking
ANTISEPTIC	the easiest kind to carry are the disposable premedicated swabs available in drug stores; the cardinal rule for lacerations is to keep them clean
ADHESIVE TAPE	for fixing bandages, splints, reels and guides
RUBBER BANDS, ELASTIC BANDAGES	for sprained joints and old injuries
SMALL PIECE OF SOAP	good for washing down if you get into poison ivy — also good for lubricating ferrules
SALT TABLETS	even if you sweat profusely, you lose more water than salt, so these tablets can be *very dangerous* unless you take them with lots of water
ASPIRIN	nothing can ruin a fishing trip like a headache, and aspirin *is* effective
SPECIAL PRESCRIPTION MEDICATION	antihistamines, insulin, etc. Special kits of injection medication for those who suffer from severe systemic reactions to insect bites are now available; ask your doctor
SMELLING SALTS	primarily if you're going where the fish are big and you are faint-hearted.

Abercrombie & Fitch sold its "Midget" hypodermic syringe in the early 1900s for $2.50. It weighed only 2 5/8 ounces; 3¼ inches long.

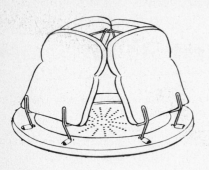

CAMP STOVE TOASTER

WHAT WE LOOKED FOR IN QUALITY

In recommending camping equipment for the angler we tried to choose components which would complete outfits for almost every budget. Backpacking is now a very voguish pastime for many Americans and there is a swarm of equipment from the sublime to the ridiculous.

Using the general standards of quality construction, convenience and availability we have put together a representative sampling of current products. We have listed, for example, synthetic and natural insulation in sleeping bags (each has certain advantages), large and small tents and other gear necessary for the portable fisherman.

Anyone who plans to invest the hundreds of dollars involved in getting a top notch backpacking outfit would be advised to glom onto as many catalogs as possible from the listing at the rear of the book.

top of the line

Cookware

CAMP STOVE TOASTER. Distributed by Cabela's, Inc., this gadget holds four pieces of toast over your campstove. For the fastidious. Just the thing for your butler to pack in.

EDDIE BAUER PORCELAIN ON STEEL CAMP WARE SET. For the more sedentary camper, Eddie Bauer has an 18-piece Porcelain on Steel Camp Ware Set with the famous old blue-and-white pattern. It has four plates, bowls and cups, a ladle, a frying pan, a 7-quart kettle, an 8-cup coffee pot and that's plenty. Chow's on, as they say.

OPTIMUS A-R CAMP STOVE. One of the best of the small backpacking stoves. Available in larger sizes from this careful manufacturer. The A-R will do the job for two people with ease. Other Optimus stoves are available to burn kerosene, which is more readily available in other parts of the world.

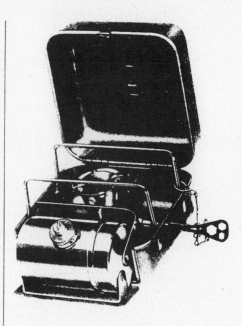

OPTIMUS A-R CAMP STOVE

BROOKSTONE CAMP GRILL

Camping where there's no firewood and you don't have charcoal along? Well, put this book or boring old newspapers in the grill. It will do in a steak in 7 minutes. Will cook fish (if you're lucky) and anything else. Wonder if the *New York Times* is better for gourmets than the *Washington Post*? Reasonably priced and handy for the car camper.

HOBSON ACCESSORIES

The Hobson outfit is offering a line of camping accessories of interest to the angler or anyone else not cooped up inside. Packaged conveniently, there is a sun-wind-frost protector, germicidal tablets for emergency drinking water, an all-purpose, completely biodegradable cleanser, a pan coat for clean camp cooking and a flying insect killer. All work well.

BROOKSTONE WOODMAN'S PAL

Brookstone's Woodman's Pal has lots of uses for the backpacking angler. It can cut firewood, lop off branches, dig holes, clear away brush and other related tasks. Comes with a sharpening stone in its zippered sheath.

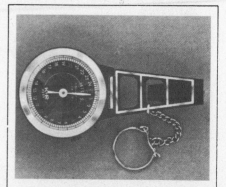

EDDIE BAUER PEDOMETER

If that secret lake you've heard about is seven and a half miles up the first trail to the left, you might consider getting a decent pedometer. The Eddie Bauer people sell one that records up to 25 miles. Clips on to your belt and is adjustable for your stride. Read like a watch.

top of the line

OPTIMUS CAMP OVEN. For the decadent, Optimus is now producing a backpacking oven that weighs only 15½ ounces. It works in conjunction with the mini-backpacking stoves that are so popular. This easy-to-pack three-piece item is a welcome accessory for those to whom pan-fried back country food is getting stale.

SIGG ALUMINUM NESTING POTS. These Swiss-made aluminum pots and plates are still the best around. Each pot fits inside the next size for compact storing and carrying. A good buy even at the price.

SIERRA CLUB PACK CUP. One of the traditional accessories of the seasoned backpacker. With a clamp handle that can be hooked onto the belt, the cup can be used for cooking if necessary. Impress your friends.

SVEA PACK STOVE. The Svea, which burns for 45 minutes on 1/3 pint of gasoline and heats 1½ pints of water in just five minutes, is one of the best packing stoves around. Made of brass, and weighing 1 pound 4 ounces, the Svea never needs priming or pumping. It's about the same size as a soup can. A good buy.

Packs

CAMP TRAILS SKYLINE COMBINATION. A very standard pack found in stores around the country. Has large padded hipbelt and welded tubular aluminum frame. The skyline bag has five outside pockets, a map pocket and all the other goodies required in a frame pack. For the angler going out for a few days at a time.

OPTIMUS MINI-OVEN/FRYING PAN

PACK STOVE

top of the line

CARIBOU FANNY PACK. Fanny pack is a nice item for anglers who are bothered by having to carry all their gear in vests or shoulder bags. Has two large compartments — one for fishing gear, the other for a sweater and lunch. Outside pocket with zipper for small things like dry fly dope.

JANSPORT FRAME SACK. A very large day pack or overnighter. This serves the needs of most anglers very well. Available in a medium size for people up to 5' 8" and large for those over, it has an assortment of zippered side-compartments, shoulder pads and a padded waistbelt. The bottom is leather covered for some protection against sharp rocks.

KELTY. The Kelty line has something for just about every backpacker and angler. They're one of the standard outfits for this kind of gear. Their frames and bags are sold separately, but models like the D4, the Basic pack and the expedition backpacks will surely do the job for any camper. They come with a padded waist belt and other paraphernalia which have changed backpacking so much in the last decade.

SIERRA DESIGNS BELT PACK. A very convenient way for the ultralight angler to carry enough gear for a day's fishing. It measures 6-by-9 inches.

SIERRA DESIGNS SUMMIT. A fine multi-compartmented frameless pack, which works as a heavy-duty day pack or a light overnighter. Will take your sleeping bag on the bottom and most everything else inside. The backpacking angler with one of these usually doesn't need a frame pack.

CARIBOU FANNY PACK

KELTY TOURPACK

SIERRA SUMMIT PACK

Suunto Compass

Suunto's Scandanavian-built compasses are probably the best around for the hiking angler. More features than the average lost soul will ever need. Extremely well-built, their top-of-the-line model, KB-14/360R, which comes in a leather-type case, is made of a lightweight non-corrosive alloy. It's accurate to 1/6th of a degree, has a sighting aperture with a crosshair and a lanyard with a neck loop. A precision piece of equipment sold by Precise.

ALTIMETER BAROMETER

Getting high? Find out exactly how high with this Eddie Bauer Altimeter. It's expensive and very well made. Measures up to 16,000 feet, plenty for any backpacking angler. But more importantly, it is also a barometer for the many who believe that barometric pressure is crucial in fishy response. Real class.

"The carp is a bad fish to catch, for he is so strongly reinforced in the mouth that no weak tackle can hold him." DAME JULIANA BERNERS

Fishing The Highcountry
By Trey Combs

Trey Combs' 89-page booklet is different from most of the introductory backpacking works in that it deals with spinning tackle and techniques rather than fly stuff. Though fly fishing in the backcountry is the most glamorous way to go, the spinning gear described by Combs is used by more anglers. Solid information and a good place to start.

ultimate commodity

Russ Peak Pack Rods

Russ Peak, the glass craftsman from Pasadena, California, made it and it fits all the qualifications for the ultimate pack rod. Despite its $200 tab — still less than the Orvis and Leonard pack type cane rods — it seems the perfect fly rod for backpacking. Pack rods are often used and even accidentally abused during long odysseys. Glass seems to withstand rough treatment better than wood. This rod, which duplicates as well as technically possible the action on my Paul Young Para 15 bamboo rod, is eight feet long, somewhere under 4 ounces and casts a No. 6 line under almost any conditions. It's the most versatile glass imaginable. And, with its slow semi-parabolic action, it's probably as close to a universal rod as has ever been built. It has all the painstaking craftsmanship that has come to characterize Peak rods over the years.

Broken down into two-foot sections, Russ' rod has been attached in a leather case to my pack for years of coast-to-coast trips. I've never wished for that "other rod." — H. H.

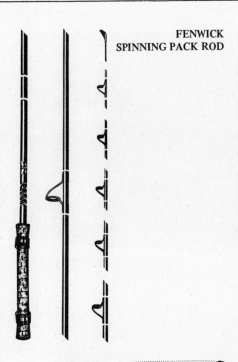

FENWICK SPINNING PACK ROD

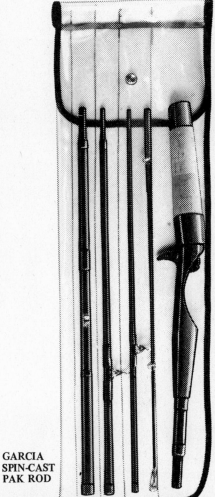

GARCIA SPIN-CAST PAK ROD

top of the line

Pack Rods

ABERCROMBIE & FITCH. The tiniest backpacking rod of them all. Coming in its own passport-sized case, its 11 (count 'em) 11 six-inch sections assemble to make a 4 foot, 9 inch fly or spinning rod that weighs only 2 ounces. Keep it in your back pocket for those real emergencies.

FENWICK SPIN & FLY RODS. Fenwick has been putting out very decent pack rods in a variety of fly, spinning and combination-of-the-two for a long time. With the introduction of their glass ferrules they could provide a reasonably priced rod that had a nice action, something the competition, laboring with cheap metal ferrules, couldn't match. For the fly rodder they have a 7½ and 8 footer for No. 6 lines that break down into four pieces; also an 8½ footer for No. 6 line and an 8½ footer for No. 8 line that break down into five sections. In addition, they make a pack spinner from 5 feet 9 inches to 7 feet in four sections. And don't forget their combination rods in 7 feet and 7½ feet lengths. Goody-goody.

GARCIA SUPER-LIGHT PAK RODS. A pair of okay backpack rods are the Garcia Super-Light Pak Rods in spinning and fly models. The 6-foot light spinner is a four-piecer and has five stainless steel guides and a chromed tip-top. Designed with a cork handle with reel bands for lines from No. 4 to No. 8. The fly rod is a 7½-foot dry fly action, which is okay but not great. It breaks down into a convenient 3.6-ounce five-piece package with stainless snake guides, chromed stripper and, yes, takes a No. 6 or No. 7 line.

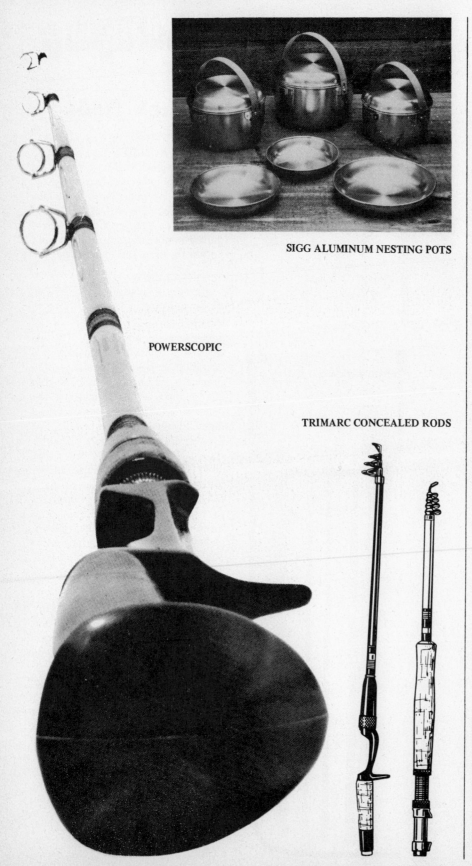

SIGG ALUMINUM NESTING POTS

POWERSCOPIC

TRIMARC CONCEALED RODS

top of the line

POWERSCOPIC. Some of the best of the telescoping rods on the market are the Powerscopics, which scope down to small sizes ranging from 15 to 20 inches. Plenty portable for any sort of angling. Powerscopic makes their rods in models for spincasting, spinning and fly fishing. Besides a pack rod, some of their other model lines, which slide down to 13 inches, are perfect as back-up rods for travelers or in tackle boxes. Some of the better models have aluminum oxide guides, special cork handles and other features that mark decent rods. Now Powerscopic rods are available for tournament-type bass fishing, as well. Well worthwhile.

SCOTT POWR-PLY RODS. Scott Powr-Ply Rods makes a very interesting item for the backpacker. It's a 5-piece, 8-foot fly rod that weighs in at 3¼ ounces and takes an all-around No. 6 line. They also make a 5-piece, 7-foot model for No. 4 or 5 line and a 4-piece, 7½-footer for a No. 5 line. They aren't the prettiest rods in the world, but they are among the smoothest-actioned glass. Glass ferrules, natch. Good buys.

TIMBERLINE RODS. Timberline Rods in New Hampshire offers six well-thought-out models of 4-section pack rods including fly, spin and combinations thereof. The rods range from 5 to 7 feet and weigh from 1.8 to 3.4 ounces. They are also available in kits for the home finisher.

TRIMARC. Trimarc makes a complete line of telescoping rods popular with some traveling and packing anglers. Their Concealed Rods are made of tubular fiberglass with solid glass tip sections and stainless steel double-bridged guides. Available in styles for the baitcaster, spincaster, spinner and fly angler and combinations thereof. Folded, they measure from

CAMP TRAILS SKYLINE PACK

EMS BERKSHIRE SLEEPER

top of the line

15 to 22 inches. An okay rod, especially for the non-specialized fisherman.

Sleepware

EASTERN MOUNTAIN SPORTS ESTES. The Estes and the Teton are two Eastern Mountain Sports semi-rectangular down bags that are fine investments for those who find mummy bags too confining. Though not as warm in extreme conditions as a mummy bag, they work well for the fair-weather campers most anglers are. These bags also come with down hoods for additional snugness. EMS also offers the relatively inexpensive Sandpiper as a nice light down summer bag.

EASTERN MOUNTAIN SPORTS MINI-LIGHT. This Eastern Mountain bag is probably the lightest of the light-weights — 2 pounds, 12 ounces, and 2 more ounces for the large size. Designed with most of the down on top, rather than the bottom where the body compresses the feathers. The company rates this bag at 58°F.

EMS POLAR GUARD. Eastern Mountain Sports' line of Polar Guard polyester sleeping bags are a fine, reasonably priced substitute for down. Models like the Blue Ridge Franconia and the Berkshire work better than down, in fact, in places with high humidity and moisture. For use when considerations other than weight are critical. Most backpack anglers would be better off with a synthetic rather than the real thing.

GERRY CAMPER. Available in either regular or large size, the camper is a good pre-season down bag

POWERSCOPIC

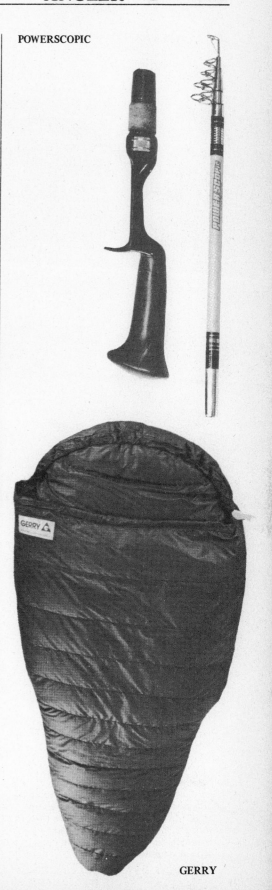

GERRY

SIERRA SUPER NIGHT

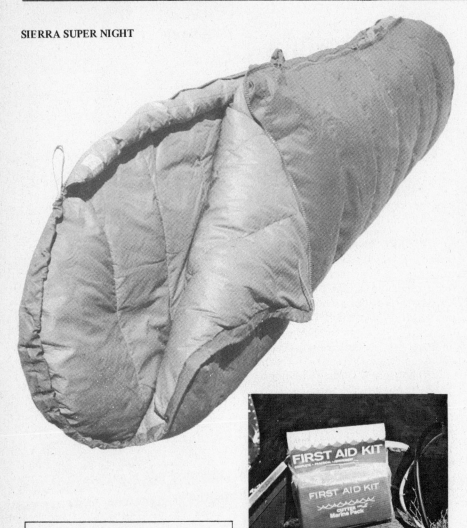

top of the line

with a 25° comfort range. Has slant box baffles and other features that go into a quality down bag.

NORTH FACE SUPER LIGHT. Another top-quality lightweight bag at 3 pounds, 5 ounces, and 4 ounces more for the large. Very slender girth dimensions on this one, but an excellent buy. Rated at 15° F. For those who don't mind that closed-in feeling.

SIERRA DESIGNS DOUBLE MUMMY. A very large bag suitable for one gargantuan or two people. Saves energy for the couple by using body heat. A fine, luxurious sleeping bag of top quality for those long evenings when the fish aren't biting. It has a 10° F. rating and will accommodate people up to 6' 3". Will zip into other double mummy bags for couples into that sort of thing.

SIERRA DESIGNS SUPER NIGHT. The Sierra Designs Super Night is a very fine, very light (3 lbs., 2 oz.) mummy bag at a fairly reasonable price. Designed for use from mid-spring to mid-fall, it will zip together with other mummy bags if you fish with a friend. Caution: for persons up to six foot tall only.

Survival Kits

CUTTER FIRST AID KIT. The Cutter Pocket Pack, which, as its name implies, fits in your back pocket, is an important accessory. Only 2 7/8 inches wide, 4½ inches high and ½ inch thick, it contains Band-Aids, wound wipes, Anacin tablets, alcohol prep pads, a knuckle bandage and a gauze pad. It weighs only 1½ ounces. They also make more exten-

CUTTER MARINE PACK FIRST AID KIT

TRAK KIT

The kit contains a concentrated cold water soap for such things as washing a person's face or body and washing dishes or clothes. Sold through Eastern Mountain Sports. Also contains two reusable towels and a mouthwash. Kit lasts one person about a month. Fish, after all, like clean people.

CUTTER TRAIL PACK FIRST AID KIT

top of the line

sive first aid kits for backpacks, traveling, camp use and for marine injuries. Worth it.

EDDIE BAUER SURVIVAL KIT. For the angler going back, back and further back in places like Alaska, the Eddie Bauer Survival Kit may be very worthwhile. It can save you for up to 25 hours (gulp) with the goods in this 7½- by 5- by 2-inch, 23-ounce container. Stuff includes emergency fire starting equipment, 8 feet of plastic tube for shelter, soup, tea, honey, signal mirror, whistle, candle, wire, tape, pocketknife, compass, nylon cord, foil, first aid gear, fish hooks, line and weights plus a survival manual. Doesn't hurt to have this around.

Tents

COLEMAN BACKPACK TENT. The swell lantern people are also producing a very light (5 pounds) backpacking tent for two. Though Coleman boasts that it's very roomy, it's best that the pair be friends. Zippered sidedoor, mosquito netting and it all rolls up into a very packable sack.

COLUMBIA SPORTSWEAR. Makes a couple of very interesting tents for the back country angler. One, the High Cascade Bug Eater, weighs only 1½ pounds, has a nylon floor and super heavy duty nylon mesh walls to keep beasties away. A fine idea if you're not in rain country. They also make an emergency tent at 1¼ pounds that's fine for basic overnight use.

SIERRA DESIGNS. The top of the line Glacier will keep you snug almost regardless of where you are. This A-framed tent, which weighs 7 pounds, 11 oz., offers room for two

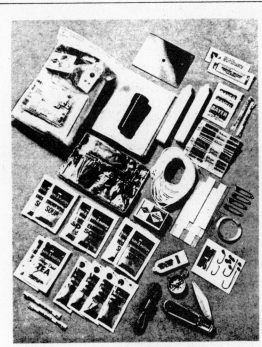

EDDIE BAUER SURVIVAL KIT

COLEMAN
BACKPACK TENT

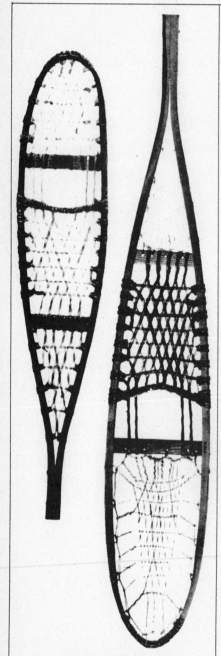

TUBBS SNOW SHOES

The Tubbs Company of Wallingford, Vermont, where they know about such things, sells a very complete line of snow shoes for the walk-in ice angler. Available in all the popular styles, such as Alaska trapper, flat bear paw, Michigan and Adirondack, these are very well-made traditional snow shoes hewn from New England white ash. All snow shoes available with either rawhide or neoprene. These people also make a nice line of snow-shoe-type furniture with aluminized fabrics.

top of the line

plus lots of gear. One end of the tent has a large zipper door and the other has a fully-enclosed alcove with a tunnel door and cook hole. Both doors are backed by insect netting. A very glamorous item for the backpacking angler.

Sierra Designs also makes other fine tents, including some for families, both natural and extended.

SIERRA DESIGNS TARP TENT. An effective, inexpensive tarp tent that can be used in a variety of ways for improvised shelter. Good for the overnight angler who may or may not need a tent. Can be tied up in trees, rocks, bushes, etc. Convenient to have around for emergencies.

THERMOS POP TENTS. These pop tents have been around for a long time. They set up in seconds. Though a bit heavy, either the camp model or the giant pop tent — which holds skads of people — are ideal for the station-wagon-camping angler.

EUREKA DRAWTITE. Available in sizes from one to six persons. These reasonably priced tents are fine for everyone except the ultra-serious backpacker, something most anglers have more sense than to become. Made from flame retardent material, these tents can be set up in five minutes on rock, sand, snow or ice. A good buy.

Backpacking for Fly Fishermen
By Ron Cordes

Ron Cordes, under the Fenwick imprimatur, has written a good basic guide for the backpacker. His 95-page booklet contains very little fluff. Covers the tackle, techniques, trout species and packing equipment needed for high-country fishing in lakes and streams. There's a lot more that could be said on the subject but this is the place to begin.

SIERRA DESIGNS TARP TENT

THERMOS CAMPERS POP TENT

EUREKA DRAWTITE

INTERALPCERROTORRE ICE AXE

An all-metal axe sold through Eastern Mountain Sports. One of the finest ice axes for technical climbing. However, if you need one of these, I can assure you, you're playing the wrong sport. A wonderful thing to own, anyway.

GAMEFISH: MUSKELLUNGE

NAMES
Muskie, pike, Great Lakes muskellunge, blue pike, Jack, spotted muskellunge, tiger muskellunge, Ohio muskellunge, lunge, great pike. *(Esox masquinongy)*

DISTRIBUTION
The muskellunge is only found in the eastern part of America. Its usual range covers an area from southern Canada into the Great Lakes region and down into Ohio and Tennessee. It is quite prevalent in Wisconsin, Minnesota and Michigan.

DESCRIPTION
The muskellunge is a large, predatory member of the pike family that ranges in color from grey to green to brown with silver or brownish sides. Its entire body is covered with dark, irregular spots. Only the upper half of the gill cover and the cheek are scaled. The muskellunge sports a set of large teeth.

SIZE
The size of the muskellunge ranges anywhere from 15 to 35 pounds. Large catches of 50 to 70 pounds have been reported.

HABITAT
The muskellunge prefers cool temperatures and is found in large slow moving rivers and in large clear lakes. It usually inhabits shallow waters and tends to hide near submerged logs and weed beds where it lies in wait for prey.

FEEDING HABITS
The muskellunge is a voracious feeder that readily attacks almost any moving prey. It feeds primarily on other fish, including smaller muskellunge, but will also consume frogs, ducklings, mice and snakes. It is, however, considered an unpredictable fish, passing up the most luring of baits. In the hot summer months, the muskellunge will usually disappear into deeper, cooler waters.

BEST FEEDING TEMPERATURES
Between 60 and 75 degrees.

TACKLE
This fearful sounding dentist's dream is most often fished for with heavy trolling gear, huge plugs and prayers. It's also a favorite for heavy-duty baitcasting or spinning gear with plugs or large spoons. Sometimes, but rarely, it will also take a large streamer from a hefty fly rod.

ultimate commodity

Warmlite

You know you're not dealing with a regular camping gear manufacturer when you thumb through Stephenson's Warmlite color catalog and see mounds of flesh beaming back at you.

Well, before you go slobbering off for a copy, consider that all that tent and sleeping bag cheesecake is dressing up the best line of products in the country. No question about it. Unless you need specialized equipment or have a low budget, get one of their sleeping bags or tents.

Besides sparkling general quality, their bags feature zippers on either side, down on three sides and a foam bottom both for comfort and protection (compressed down doesn't insulate anyway). A simple but very effective idea. Stephenson is a perfectionist on a par with the most finicky custom rod makers. He's concerned with such things as the quality of down used to stuff his bags and is forever coming up with variations such as bags with the bottom open for air circulation in warmer climes. They're really not much more expensive than the better down bags made by bigger manufacturers. And, of course, they zip together.

His tents are much lighter than other quality tents and are available in a variety of models. For instance, his five-person tent weighs only 5 pounds, 13 ounces. There are many options he offers, too.

Stephenson also sells some selected accessories like their own packs, some pack boats and the like.

Great camping equipment and lovely naked bodies.

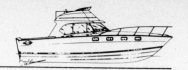

Go with simple, classic boats

By Harmon Henkin

Not so many years ago boats were very simple, functional things. They did their job and that was that. But today boats are imbued with as much mystique as cars and are just about as expensive and durable.

This is true whether you're buying a simple sort of craft like a canoe or raft or something more complex like a bass boat or an off-shore cruiser. In the same way that a reasonable consumer asks himself if that Cadillac is really what he needs for work around the ranch, the boater should ask himself whether that 175-horsepower Evinrude is really necessary for taking crappies from the Old Mill Pond.

That may be an extreme example but there are lots of people buying boats that are much too over-powered. If you're going to run dangerous Montana rivers you might need an ultra-sturdy Avon raft for $1000, but for plopping around in a little lake one of those inexpensive Japanese or Taiwanese rafts might do the job just as well.

Over-consuming may be the American way but it's becoming more and more expensive. The worst abuses are in the area of tourney-type bass boats. These highly specialized, gadget-filled things may be a joy to behold but they sure aren't for everyone. They have been the object of real hard sells pushing them as all-around craft. Well, they aren't, unless you make a living as a bass fisherman.

Actually, it's a rule of thumb in modern industrial societies that the more it can break down, it will. The soothing powers of angling can be evaporated by cranky electronic equipment that needs lots of attention. When fishing becomes a mechanical act its charm disappears and many of the people who have been pressured into one of those deluxe boats rue the day. Life with one ain't as simple as it looks in the films or in the ads.

There is no such thing as an all-around boat. The best ones, the ones that retain at least a semblance of a resale, are the classically designed single-purpose models. Leave the fancy stuff for other parts of your life.

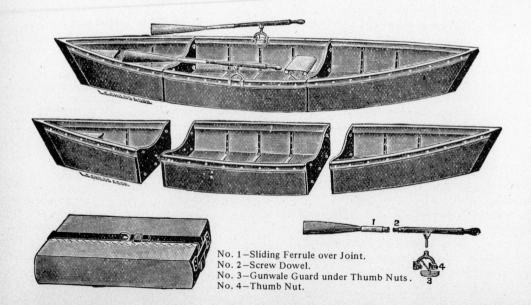

No. 1—Sliding Ferrule over Joint.
No. 2—Screw Dowel.
No. 3—Gunwale Guard under Thumb Nuts.
No. 4—Thumb Nut.

The Wilkinson Co. of Chicago advertised it in the 1890s as the "Clark-Divine Patent Nesting Carry Boat." It carried two or three people and 300 pounds of gear. Wilkinson claimed it would with proper care last a man "as long as he can see to drop a duck, or cast a fly or bait." The Clark-Divine, which weighed 75 pounds and folded into the package at lower left, sold for $40.

Surviving a Montana maelstrom

By Harmon Henkin

Dick Eggert and I should have known enough not to get into a boat together. In the Marine Corps I had been in most every type of vessel known to man and Dick had done a lot of canoeing in the Midwest. But together we were a mixture of nitro and glycerine.

While attending college in Michigan, Dick and I dropped a $100 portable radio overboard while bait fishing on a peaceful lake one Sunday afternoon. Early one morning on another lake we got caught in a mini-tornado that almost cost the world two of its more inept anglers.

But the Bitterroot was running high this year, and we had heard the sporting goods store gossip all winter that it had some lunker trout. We drove along it a number of times during the first weeks of fishing season and on one outing even took a couple of nice fish on spinning tackle and bait.

So when Dick suggested we try out his new deluxe four-man raft, I threw good sense to the wind and agreed. We drove upstream about 50 miles from Missoula, inflated the yellow craft and it was anchors aweigh.

I became nervous looking at the river. Though natives said it was merely high, I decided that the Bitterroot must have looked that way during Noah's angling days. The water was murky, with branches and small trees floating by. If a house had drifted past, it wouldn't have shocked me.

But the river didn't look like it had rough rapids even though it was overflowing its banks when we took off. As we floated down, I made several fruitless casts with my spinning outfit and Dick amused himself by giving me advice and bragging about how easy it was to run a river in a raft.

We kept pretty close to the middle of the water, moving along at a good clip and trying to work out a good handling technique. After two miles we were confident — no, actually overconfident.

Then we went around a large bend and the river doubled in size and slowed down. Dick got bored, claiming the sport was too dull

for the likes of him. But a weird feeling started gnawing at me.

"Dick, do you hear a funny noise?"

"No."

He was facing downstream.

"Dick, are you sure you don't hear a roar?"

I didn't need an answer. All it took was the look on his face. Whirling around I could see a solid sheet of white in the distance. It couldn't be mere rapids. It was a dam. Neither of us knew the river and nobody ever said there was a dam on it. But on the other hand, no one had ever said there wasn't a dam, either.

From my past experience with the Corps of Engineers, I knew they might have slapped up a 500-foot dam during the winter without telling anyone. The types of dams I knew intimately were monsters like the behemoth Con-

owingo on the Susquehanna in Maryland which frightened me even when I fished below it.

Then began the most frantic paddling effort in the history of rowing. But the tiny paddles that came with the raft wouldn't have

been enough to get us across a bathtub.

The tempo of the river picked up. We couldn't make it to either shore. All we could see was a white maelstrom drawing us quickly toward it. The term "utter panic" is too mild to describe our feelings at the time.

As I composed my epitaph, the only concrete thing I could remember about rafting was that the craft should always face straight downriver. The advice might as well have urged us to get the raft airborne.

At the lip of the dam, Dick, like W. C. Fields, decided that he would rather be in Philadelphia and started to climb out. Over the roar, I bellowed for him to get back. As he fell backward he bumped the raft hard and I was tossed out. Then I slid down the dam face and disappeared into the whiteness.

After bouncing around on the bottom for what seemed a few thousand years, I decided the only way to survive was to push off the bottom and get back into the main current, wherever that was. Somehow I did it and felt myself rushing downriver.

I bobbed up 50 yards downstream and after breathing the freshest air I had ever tasted, the first thing that caught my eye was Dick, who I was sure had already been canonized in the Anglers' Hall of Fame. He was sitting in the raft 20 feet away, keeping pace with my downriver flow. I splashed over to him and breath-

Boats for one kind of fishing

By Zack Taylor

The evolution of the modern bass boat over the last 20 years stands out as one of the most startling developments in all boating history. Amazingly, as we head into the last part of the 1970s, the thirst for these $4000 to $7000 machines specialized for one kind of fishing — indeed, one kind of fish — remains undiminished.

It all started in the early 1950s when a Shreveport, Louisiana, bass fisherman designed a 13-foot, easily trailerable, narrow vessel he called the Skeeter. Instead of conventional boat seats he installed high pedestal seats so he could sit up high enough to study his retrieve. Plastic worms were just coming into

vogue and often a strike was signaled by the tiniest movement of the line. So the boat could be controlled from the front pedestal, he steered with a stick at his side. To further aid his fishing he turned to another machine then appearing on the market — foot-controlled electric outboard motors. These operated from a battery and by pedals and floor switches could control both the direction and the speed of the boat. Even with a wind blowing, the angler could maneuver the boat along choice fishing spots with both hands free to cast and retrieve. Anglers use the larger gas motors to speed to hot spots, then lower the silent electric to stalk into position without

(continued on next page)

(continued on next page)

Boats for one kind of fishing

(continued from preceding page)

alarming fish. Yet another development was to change fishing forever. This was the near-universal acceptance of depth sounders to locate "structure." These are underwater irregularities — dead trees, house foundations, original stream beds, rock walls — that show up clearly on screens that read rapid electronic pulses to the bottom and back. So-called "Fish Finders" soon became so sensitive, schools and even individual fish could be spotted on them.

The new breed of boat would probably have remained the relatively modest vessel it started out to be except for another phenomenon of the 1970s. In 1969 the newly formed Bass Anglers Sportsman Society began sponsoring bass fishing tournaments with huge cash prizes. The "pro" fishermen who competed in these contests — usually held on big reservoirs — demanded larger 16- and 18-foot bass boats with the highest horsepower. Stick steering, dangerous at high speeds, was replaced by sit-down consoles. Electric motors advanced from 12 to 24 volts to better control the larger craft. And since more tournament points were amassed for bass kept alive, elaborately created live wells were built into the boats. All manner of rod and gear storage compartments held the bewildering assortment of tackle routinely carried by the pros. The boats bristle with gadgetry: electric motors raise and lower anchors at the touch of a switch, depth sounders at console

and forward pedestal allow continual bottom monitoring, "boat reins," i.e., dock lines, are stored on self-winding concealed drums, multi-position hydraulic-cushioned seats insure a soft ride. Indoor-outdoor carpeting softens boat noise and adds a colorful interior. Colorful signs and promotional advertising soon became standard with sides sporting such gaily painted nicknames as "Hawg Hunter," "Red Baron," or "Super Sport," and the names of such top money winners as Ricky Green, Roland Martin and Bill Dance.

While the boats sold first in the South and Southwest, they have long since invaded northern markets as more and more local clubs sponsor bass tournaments of their own. As long as bass remain to be caught (and they are a relatively easily managed warm-water fish), bass boats

from unpretentiously rigged johnboats to superboats with 200-hp outboards and black-mirror finishes would appear to be integral additions to America's fishing scene.

Montana maelstrom

(continued from preceding page)

lessly threw a hand on the rubber boat.

His first question was enough to make me sink to the bottom.

"Did you lose your rod?"

My answer is not fit for a family publication.

When we made it to shore and looked back at the dam, we discovered it was the biggest 10-foot dam in the universe. I have returned to that structure many times in the ensuing years and still can't believe how ferocious it seemed that day.

After I had fallen out, the front end of the raft had bobbed up and Dick rode straight through the holocaust, getting little more than a bit wet in the process.

Oh, yes, I lost my tackle box as well as my rod, and my camera had to be sent back to the factory for un-water clogging. I think it still gurgles when I use it.

Dick never suggests we go out in a boat anymore. It makes his insurance premiums cheaper.

This article appeared originally in *Montana Outdoors,* July/August 1974.

CHRIS-CRAFT STROBILITE

Chris-Craft's electronic flashing Strobilite is a good thing to have when you need emergency help, especially out on the water. It's an ultra-bright flashing stroboscopic-type unit whose flash can be seen miles away. It weighs only 11 ounces and floats, too. Using C batteries it will flash for almost seven hours. Comes with wrist strap.

THE LAST HATCH
A FISHING MYSTERY
HARMON HENKIN

(continued from page 334)

Dun looked frantic for a moment and could not have known that the threat came from Sid's primitive abhorrence of advertising agency language.

Paul tried to get back to the subject at hand. "Tell me some more about the will."

"I had been one of the major beneficiaries in the old one, along with his ex-wives. I guess that will is still in effect. He hadn't mentioned that the new will was finished. But if it is, there may have been some big changes."

"Including you?"

"I, uh. Oh no, sir."

"Okay, Dun. You can go." Paul said. "Send in Wormer."

"Suddenly lots of motives," Sid said as Dun shut the door.

"Halford was even slimier than I thought."

Their conversation was interrupted as a nervous Wormer walked into the room at a fast clip. He sat down on the couch and lit a cigarette.

"Okay, whatta you boys want? I have an honest reputation. Nothing to hide."

"One main thing. And don't try to lie to us. Did Halford ever sign the development papers?"

"We had a verbal agreement. Courts will accept that, you know."

"But he never did sign the papers?"

"Nah. First he was real hot to trot. But he'd been stalling lately. Like he was waiting for something to happen."

"Like what?" Sid asked.

"What did I care? I'm a rich man. Didn't really need him, anyway." Wormer lit another cigarette from the butt of his first.

Paul took a shot in the dark, as detective novelists started saying 40 years ago.

"That's not true, Wormer. Sid's investigators checked over your financial reports and you're in real trouble. You need this development to stay afloat."

Bingo! Wormer dropped his cigarette and flushed.

"You don't have any right to search my private financial records. Just having a little liquidation problem. That's all."

"How much did you stand to make on this little deal?" Sid asked.

"Let's see . . . a hundred lots at $10,000 a crack. That's about a mil-

(continued on page 354)

GAMEFISH: BLUEGILL

NAMES
Bream, bluegill sunfish, brim, copperhead, pumpkinseed, blue sunfish, sun perch, blue perch, red-breasted bream. *(Lepomis machrochirus)*

DISTRIBUTION
The bluegill is found throughout the continental United States and into southern Canada.

DESCRIPTION
The coloration of the bluegill varies according to its environment. It can range from brown to green to purple. The sides are marked with vertical bars and the gill cover is entirely black. The forepart of the body and the belly may be a bright orange or red.

SIZE
The average weight of a bluegill is about ½ pound and the average length is 5 inches.

HABITAT
The bluegill can be found in both rivers and lakes. It prefers quiet waters with weed beds and submerged debris. It likes to hang around the shoreline hidden in protective growth.

FEEDING HABITS
The bluegill's diet consists of aquatic insects, small crustaceans, minnows and worms. It is not a fussy eater and usually travels in schools. In the evening it can be found feeding on the surface.

BEST FEEDING TEMPERATURE
Between 65° and 75°.

TACKLE
Everybody's favorite fish is a sucker for almost anything from flies to tiny plugs to all kinds of bait. Good as a beginner's quarry sought with a pole, bobber, sinker and worm or an elaborate light bamboo fly rod with small popping bugs or flies. This scrapper is also fun with ultra-light spinning gear and tiny spinners or small jigs.

CHRIS-CRAFT DATA PACK

Chris-Craft's Boating Data Pack provides a mass of information for the angler when this information is needed quickly. The two assortments of cards are on index-tabbed waterproof cards. One has things like rules of the road, buoy and light phases, fog and distress signals, first aid and artificial respiration and useful knot and line handling. The other pack deals with visual weather forecasting, engine trouble-shooting, anchoring techniques, Morse code and phonetic alphabet and emergency procedures. Can be a life saver.

BRUSH ANCHOR

A Brush Anchor is a convenient gadget to take along on your next rafting expedition. It will hold up to 500 pounds when you clip it onto a tree branch or sturdy bush. It's simple and works.

Boating scenes from the 19th Century

top of the line

ABERCROMBIE & FITCH BACKPACKING RAFT. This little two-man raft is a very handy item for the backpacker. It's so convenient because its 450-pound capacity can be reduced to only 7 square inches and weighs less than 3½ pounds. It can be blown up in under 4 minutes using its 4-ounce inflator carrying case. If that isn't enough to perk up your dreams of high country lakes, then think about the two-piece aluminum oars that weigh less than 8 ounces apiece. Comes with a neoprene carrying case.

AMERICAN TRI-JON. The Jon boat style of craft is one of the more stable. The Tri-Jon from American comes in 12-foot and 14-foot plastic and fiberglass models and is perfect for the casual angler or one who just needs a part-time boat. They have aluminum gunnels, molded keels, varnished cross-seats and a large drain plug.

BART HATHAWAY. Bart Hathaway's 10½-foot pack canoe weighs a minuscule 18 pounds. Nothing elegant, natch, but it can be handled with a double- or single-edged paddle, has foam floatation under the decks and a foam seat. And yeah, please don't forget those 18 little pounds.

BASS BUDDY FLOAT. A variation of the inner-tube float harness especially popular in mountain lakes and southern ponds. Made of high-density polyethylene, it has a built-in seat, backrest, trays, keel and rod holder. A battery-operated trolling motor can be had as an accessory. Not the ticket for everyone but a float can be a fish-catching necessity if it's the only craft.

ABERCROMBIE & FITCH BACKPACKING RAFT

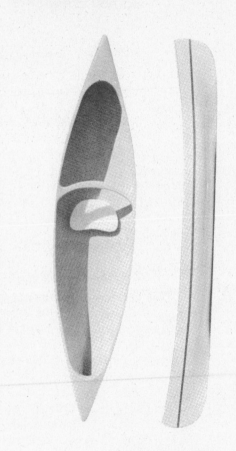

BART HATHAWAY

WEEDMASTER WEEDGUARD

Protect your motor when you skim into the lettuce with a Weedmaster Weedguard for electric motors. It looks like a giant badminton birdie. Installs quickly around your troller and keeps you from getting snagged up.

"It is useful advice to pay more attention to the size of the artificials and the manner of fishing them than to the dressing."
W. J. HOWES, *Fly Fishing for Coarse Fish.*

BOATS 351

top of the line

BASS CLASSIC. A one-purpose, highly developed boat made by well-known Ranger Boats. With a high-powered 175 Johnson engine, the 17-foot behemoth has everything the technologically oriented bass angler would want. It comes equipped with a Silvertail Trailer, a Silvertrol Trolling motor, a Lowrance Fish Lo-K-Tor, a Lowrance surface temperature gauge, an electric anchor and lots more. Whew. Now if you can just nab a few largemouths.

CRESTLINER VOYAGERS. Solid, all-around freshwater boats. Crestliner's Voyager 18 and 16 (which describes their length) have mechanical steering, steering consoles, running lights and vinyl-covered decks. The 16 has a swivel seat for convenient casting, a side seat with a 6-foot-rod storage space and an upholstered, padded seat. The 18 has a 7-foot-rod storage box, forward casting platform, a forward storage locker and a stern pan. Good boats.

FUNBOAT. A convenient and simple boat for the angler not tangling rough waters is the Electric Feather. Twelve feet long and weighing 67 pounds, it's powered by a Shakespeare electric trolling motor and will hold one or two people. Can turn in its own length for absolute maneuverability.

GREGOR BOAT COMPANY. A good line of welded aluminum fishing boats. They have five models but the U-151, which is 15 feet, 1 inch long, is designed for roomy loads and relative safety for two anglers. It has big, deep sides, a wide hull and it can be had with extra framing and reinforced transom. All the models have options like a side-steering binnacle, a self-bailing motor well and a bow deck.

CRESTLINER VOYAGERS

FUNBOAT

GREGOR BOAT COMPANY

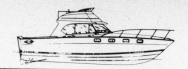

GRUMMAN

MIRRO-CRAFT FISHERMAN

top of the line

GRUMMAN. One of the more adaptable-to-fishing canoes from the famous Grumman Company is the 15-foot, 3-inch Sportcanoe, which can handle up to a 5-horsepower motor and weighs 112 pounds. Has three seats as standard, spray rails, closed-cell floatation, aluminum oar-locks and a mast clip, if you want to buy one of Grumman's sails as a delightful accessory.

LANDAU ALUMINUM BASS BOATS. It's not as elegant as some, but the Landau Aluminum Bass Boat certainly has all the basics. It's 16 feet long, has four seats and will take up to a 50-horsepower engine. It has a live well, console steering, a padded captain's chair, running lights, trolling motor mount, raised rear seat on an elevated deck, bow storage compartment and on and on. Well made.

McKENZIE RIVER BOATS. Alumaweld's Deluxe Guide McKenzie Drift Boat is an excellent craft for running rough rivers. It comes in 16- and 18-foot models with high sides to keep the water out, a removable front deck and with, as an option, three dry-storage compartments. Simple, well-constructed boats that can safely hold over 1000 pounds of humanity in search of fishes.

MIRRO-CRAFT FISHERMAN. A good, small boat for anglers who might find themselves in roughish water. It has a wide 63-inch beam with a deep 30-inch bow depth and is 14 feet long. It weighs a hefty 202 pounds and can handle up to 950 pounds and a 35-horsepower outboard. All the standard features.

top of the line

MISSISQUOI BY MAD RIVER. The Missisquoi is a 13-foot canoe with an 860-pound capacity that weighs only 75 pounds. It has been designed for use with an outboard. Drains easily and maneuvers well. Stable — an important quality for the caster.

MOOR AND MOUNTAIN WOOD AND CANVAS CANOES. Wood and canvas, like lots of fine things that were once standard, are now mostly historical oddities. But it's possible to still find handcrafters in the north country who will construct one in lengths from 16 to 20 feet. They aren't real lightweights but like a bamboo fly rod, a hand-carved wooden plug or a customized gun, they're the real thing. If you like the best, you'll have to get one.

OLD TOWN CANOES. Old Town has been synonymous with canoe in this country for almost a century and they continue to make the widest variety of top-quality craft. They use a multi-laminated cross-linked vinyl fiberglass called Oltonar. Other models, of course, are made of the much beloved canvas and wood. They have canoes for every angling possibility, many other sleek boats and even some models that take sails. Top-notch stuff.

QUETICO BY ALUMAWELD. The 18-foot, 5-inch Quetico Cruising Canoe, which can carry a lot of gear in its aluminum hull, is a good, stable craft for the angler. And it weighs only 71 pounds for easy portage. A carrying yoke is basic equipment and portage pads are an accessory.

McKENZIE RIVER BOATS

MOOR AND MOUNTAIN
WOOD AND CANVAS CANOES

OLD TOWN CANOES

(continued from page 349)

lion bucks before expenses. After we took care of them, I guess, we'd make about $400,000 between us over the next eighty years. The customer had to put down $500 and pay $100 a month. A real deal. We were going to advertise the lots everywhere."

"Why was Halford hedging?"

"I don't know. He said he needed money right away. That I could have the whole deal myself for $200,000 cash. But I didn't have that kind of money on hand. I told him it would take time to raise it, but he said he didn't have much time."

"So now what?"

"I haven't talked to his heirs yet, but I figure the verbal agreement will stand."

"We'll see about that," Paul said icily.

"Get outa here, Wormer," Sid said. "And send in the next one."

Alexandrea Softhackle made a gracious entrance, smiling, and sat down primly. "What can I do for you fellows?"

"Lots," Sid said. "But I'm on duty now." He got a snarl for his effort.

"Did you know that Halford was planning to sell the place and leave?" Paul asked.

"Dear Frederick was forever making plans but he always wanted his Alex around." She blinked demurely.

"Then you don't think he was going to cut you out of his new will."

"What new will?"

"Had he mentioned your allowance?"

"That money was a . . . loan. He said I could keep it as long as I needed it."

"Do you have your own source of income?"

"I'm currently planning to come out of retirement. I have an audition next week for a major part in the new Roger Foreman romance, *Porgy and Bass.* A great role."

They shrugged. Sid coughed. "That's enough for now."

"Thanks fellahs."

She walked out slowly, smiled at the door before disappearing and returned a few seconds later with Tups on her arm.

"Here's my baby. You be nice to him, hear?"

(continued on page 358)

top of the line

SEA EAGLE. Sea Eagle makes some excellent inflatable canoes that can handle very rough water. The Explorer 340, designed for one person, weighs 34 pounds and can handle 600 pounds. The 380 weighs 36 pounds, can handle two people and has a capacity of 750 pounds. Both come complete with bellows pump, repair kit and carrying bag.

TRAILCRAFT CANOE KIT. The Trailcraft people have an interesting idea in their wood and canvas canoe kits, which can be put together without special tools. The 16-foot Explorer weighs 80 pounds completed and will take 850 pounds of gear and people. The kit includes pre-cut wood, keel-curved end pieces, ribs, deck pieces, hardware, glue, canvas and step-by-step instructions. A fine way to spend a winter and get something swell in the bargain. They make lots of other canoe kits as well.

CHRIS-CRAFT FIRST AID KIT

Chris-Craft markets a very complete first aid kit put up in a tackle box and designed for the seagoing angler. It has more than 220 individualized items for emergency injury treatment plus specialized things for diarrhea, heat fatigue, eye strain, poisoning and dizziness. Especially important for the fisherman who stays out on the water for long periods.

Choosing a charter or party boat

By Frank Woolner

Seagoing party and charter boats fall into two general categories, but there are differences between the Atlantic and Pacific coasts, and there are wheels within wheels in a given area. For basic purposes, define a charter craft as one which hosts a very limited number of people on each trip — say four to six at most — and usually takes dead aim at big game or specialty fishes. They are expensive.

Party boats normally carry a far greater number of paying passengers, so the cost per angler diminishes. Often these vessels seek bottom-feeding species, yet this is generalization. There are, in either case, half-day, full-day, or long-range trips which may encompass several days or even a couple of weeks. It is the angler's prerogative to choose that which best suits his desire.

There are thousands of party boats operating on a daily schedule out of well-advertised slips. Often there is no need for reservation, since it is "first come, first served," so plan to arrive well before departure time to ensure passage.

However, on practically all of the long-range trips or those where specialty fishing is stressed, reservations are in or-

der and should be made well ahead of time. If you're confused, a telephone call to the skipper or his landing will provide necessary information.

Practically all true charter boat skippers demand that a reservation be made and that the booking angler deposit part of the agreed-upon fee beforehand. Sometimes you can reserve a day ahead, but rarely when the captain is in demand. This usually happens at metropolitan marinas where a number of boats vie for daily customers. It can be tricky.

In chartering, know what you want and ask questions. Most boats provide tackle, but it will be medium to heavy: therefore, if you want to use light stuff, then it will be your own. Take the skipper's advice about the best possible gear for a task at hand. Also, determine whether he keeps the fish caught, or whether you get all or a percentage of those personally brought to gaff. Ask about any policy that bothers you. Skippers are honest men and they prefer to level with a customer.

Patronize charter (and party) boats that have built good reputations. The sea is no place to gamble, so it is unwise to book aboard any questionable

cheapie craft. You'll almost always get precisely what you pay for.

If there is ample time for study, stroll down to the docks and eyeball returning vessels. See which disgorge happy anglers carrying game fish. Favor those craft which not only succeed, but are clean, functional, and well-equipped with aids to navigation. If your local newspaper outdoor columnist dwells on marine angling, ask him to recommend a boat. Seek information from the best available sources — and *listen!*

Ask about peak seasons of the fish you want to catch, and book then. Inquire about proper tackle, baits and lures. See whether there's a galley aboard, or whether you'll have to tote lunch. Determine proper clothing for the trip, and find out whether you should lug an icebox aboard to take your catch. Inquisitive folk are respected—jugheads and know-alls are not.

If it's a charter, you'll be expected to tip the mate. Ask the going rate. After that, if you're happy at day's end, anything extra is up to you. Usually, on a party boat, you will be expected to tip crewmen who dress out your catch. Inquire about the policy.

Go with success. Go with the skippers who have proven themselves. Go with the boats that are clean and modern and operate on schedule.

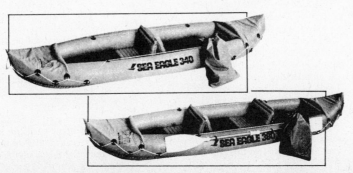

SEA EAGLE

THE TERRY
BEST BASS BOAT

After twenty years of searching I have found what I consider the best bass-fishing boat available. With it I can efficiently fish the ma--jority of bass waters which can be fished with any other boat — with the pirogue or the cruiser. This boat is made of fiberglass, and has an inverted "W" bow design which scoops in air to help smooth out the bumps. It has a double bottom with floatation foamed in between. It is 14'9" along the centerline, 54" wide and weighs 280 pounds. It will handle a maximum of 40 horsepower on the stern, but I use a 20-hp outboard and get an honest 20-25 miles per hour, depending upon how clean the hull is. A faster rig is helpful at times, but this speed covers a lot of water and the decreased gasoline consumption is a decided advantage.

My boat has two seats plus a small deck up front. A third middle seat is optional, But I prefer to have the center area open. If it's necessary to accommodate a third fisherman, I place a low, folding chair in the middle, or just let him sit on an ice box.

I operate the boat from the forward seat, which requires remote controls for starting (electric starting outboard), gearshift, throttle and steering. The first three are positioned on the starboard side of the boat and, since they are common, need no further comment.

Remote steering, on the other hand, usually involves a steering wheel, which is an abomination on a bass-fishing boat. Instead of a wheel, I use stick steering which is positioned on the port side of the boat for left-hand operation.

Stick steering is not common in most parts of the country, but has become very popular in my home area. Jim Dockery is the man who developed the Jim Stick several years ago, and in 1965 improved it with a geared version which is smoother, easier to operate, and which removes the effect of big outboard torque. For details about the Jim Stick write Dockery at Reeves Marine Center, 3210 Lakeshore Drive, Shreveport, Louisiana.

Why operate the boat from the bow? Visibility is tremendously improved. You can avoid obstructions which would not be possible to see from the stern seat. You never have a blind spot caused by a front-seat passenger, because there's never anyone in front of you. Also, when you stop the outboard and begin to fish, you're in the best fishing position there in the bow.

On the bow of my boat I have a Motor-Guide, one of the greatest boons to the bass fisherman ever invented. It is an electric motor which is controlled entirely with one foot pedal. Pressure of that one foot starts or stops the motor, and guides the boat in any direction — even backwards. This allows the fisherman to do more fishing in a specified time, to keep his lure in the water. With it he can position the boat properly to fish each area and keep it there as long as he chooses. He can fish more efficiently for longer periods of time because he is not tired from fighting a paddle, a particularly frustrating and fatiguing chore if the wind is blowing. The Motor-Guide is manufactured by the Herschede Hall Clock Company, Starkville, Mississippi.

Power for the electric starter on the outboard, and for the electric motor, is provided on my boat by a single 12-volt battery. I have it in a metal box with a battery charger, fastened to the floor between the stern seat and the transom. Each night when I end the fishing day I plug the charger in to the nearest outlet. I carry a 100-foot extension cord for this purpose. If you're out of reach of electricity, of course, better take an extra battery or use the one sparingly.

There's room behind that stern seat for a gasoline tank for the outboard, which frees the working area of the boat from tank or fuel line.

The floor of the boat is *level*, and this is important. If it is slanted toward the middle all gear gravitates together with each bump. I like to stand up in the boat and fish from time to time. It gets the kinks out of your legs, and you can fish better because you can see better and have more freedom of action. If the floor of the boat isn't level, standing on it is tiring and your platform is much less stable. There is nothing wrong with standing in a boat in which it is safe to stand.

My boat is a Terry Bass Boat, built by Bass Boats Incorporated, P.O. Box 635, Hurst, Texas. Another similar boat is the Kingfisher. Also similar, and excellent fishing boats although not quite as comfortable, or as dry in a chop, are the Skeeter and Hustler.

From *Bass Fishing* by Grits Gresham. (C) 1966 by Grits Gresham. Used by permission of Outdoor Life Books, Harper & Row.

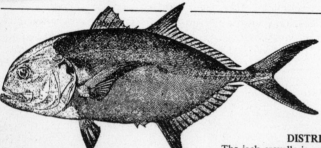

GAMEFISH: JACK CREVALLE

NAMES
Jack, common jack, crevalle, cavalla, horse crevalle, tourist tarpon. *(Caranx hippos)*

DISTRIBUTION
The jack crevalle is a fish of the Atlantic and Gulf of Mexico. It is also found in the Pacific although not in great abundance. It is found in number off the coasts of Florida and Texas.

DESCRIPTION
The jack crevalle is a husky fish of yellow-green color on the back with silver and yellow sides. At the back of the gill cover, there is a dark spot. The pectoral fins are long and curved.

SIZE
The average size of the jack is about 2 to 5 pounds, although fish of up to 70 pounds have been reported.

HABITAT
The jack is a school fish that is found near reefs, inlets, pilings and other shallow environments. Larger specimens tend to inhabit deeper waters and often travel alone.

FEEDING HABITS
The jack crevalle feeds on smaller fish, shrimp and crabs. It will strike in both the day and the evening.

TACKLE
Use medium to light casting or spinning equipment and artificials as well as cut baits. A good fighter, it can be taken by still anglers and all kinds of casters.

Knives around water
Look for quality materials and utilitarian design

By Harmon Henkin

There are two kinds of knives of interest to most anglers — all-around camp knives and filleting knives — and many others of a more specialized function. But they all should be made from a good hard metal that's able to withstand repeated sharpenings.

Modern knives are usually forged from metal alloys that are hardened to various degrees on the so-called Rockwell Scale. Now it would be possible to harden a particular steel alloy to an incredible level but then of course it would be impossible to sharpen it when it dulled. What knife makers seek is that happy medium. For anglers, the real differences in blades, especially stainless steel blades, is minimal. Most of them are made from 440-C steel, which is a good enough compromise since few anglers hack their way through any substantial resistance. If the knife you're after is made from a steel like this you don't have much to worry about. Even many of the better Japanese imports are made from pretty good metal these days.

As well as carrying a serviceable blade, the knife's handle should be made of something that won't get hurt by repeated contact with water. That brings us to another point. Should the angler use a folding knife or a sheath model?

No definitive answer, of course, but there are lots of factors that favor a small sheath knife, especially the fact that it has no hidden recesses where rust can grow. You have to clean a pocket knife with oil after each use.

But if you lean towards a folder get something that really folds. There has been a tendency by manufacturers recently to put out huge folding knives to be worn on the belt — that seems to me to be neither fish nor fowl. A folding knife should fit comfortably in the pocket and a belt knife should be rigid. Some

of the newer 3- to 4-inch sheath knives are much more convenient than their big folding counterparts. Except for hacking, a small blade is much more usable than a mammoth one.

Going back to the handle for a moment, the best all-around material for the angler is Micarta, an almost indestructible plastic that resembles ivory in white and teak in black. It's being used by some very expensive custom knifemakers like Bob Loveless and will undoubtedly find general use soon. Buck puts a very nice hard plastic

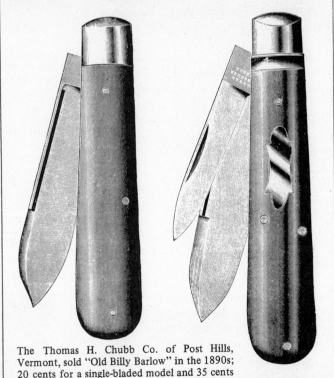

The Thomas H. Chubb Co. of Post Hills, Vermont, sold "Old Billy Barlow" in the 1890s; 20 cents for a single-bladed model and 35 cents for a double.

handle on both their folders and sheath models and companies like Case and Western aren't far behind. Look for any sign of space between the metal and the handle material. That's where rust and stain can build up.

A filleting knife should have a thin blade that you can move back and forth easily with your fingers. Its dexterity in maneuvering around fish flesh is important. Almost any knife can clean a fish but it takes a specialized one to fillet it.

The filleting blade can be as long as you need. There's no need to use a 7-inch blade on bluegills. The handle should be made from either wood or a synthetic, but the plastic will last longer. Good filleting knives that won't cripple your budget are made by Nor-Mark and Western, among many others.

There are many specialized knives available these days, including the wonderful blade combinations possible in the so-called Swiss Army knives and their Japanese Army imitations, expensive boater's knives with blades to help you tie knots and splice rope, fly fisherman's knives with pointed awls, scissors and tweezers and knives for the bass fisherman with pliers and long main blades.

But quality materials and utilitarian design are the standards to which all your cutlery should comply.

THE LAST HATCH
A FISHING MYSTERY
HARMON HENKIN

(continued from page 354)

Tups stood awkwardly in front of the desk, tapping his toe to some imaginary music. "You guys know anyplace to surf around here?"

"In Montana?" they both asked.

"Never hurts to ask."

"Did you like Halford?" Paul asked.

"He was a cool dude, if you can dig it. He had his gig and I got mine."

"But his gig supported your trip."

"Yeah."

"Did you know he was going to change his will?"

"No, man. I didn't know any Will. Never met the dude. But I could dig where the cat was coming from, if you know what I mean."

"That's enough, Tups. Split."

"It's your trip, baby."

Schielbacht was next. He was cranky. "Can we hurry up, gentlemen? I'm expecting a call from Pennsylvania. The local fly fishing club at Boiling Springs is paying me $1500 to fish terrestrials in the Yellow Breeches."

"I guess they'll have to wait. Maybe they could get someone to demonstrate fishing with blasting caps to replace you," Sid said.

"So you weren't happy that Halford didn't want to work on the book with you?" Paul asked.

"As a leading trout and salmon authority it would have been a pleasure working with Mr. Halford, but I didn't need him to be successful. There's quite a bit of money in the business these days."

"What do you know about his plans?"

"Not much, I assure you. He talked to me one day about going into partnership in a bass tournament venture. Said it would be like a ballet dancer playing pro football. We would employ the graceful techniques of fly fishing in the bass circuit and possibly revolutionize the whole sport. He wanted to write an epic poem about the largemouth bass, buy one of those fancy Terry boats and a Lowrance Fishfinder."

"That interest you?"

"Oh, no. Not at all. I like the idea of fishing for money but my fans would never accept me as a spinning and baitcasting angler. The two groups, as I'm sure you're aware, don't mix at all. Also, I'd look terrible in a bass fishing jump suit. As you can see, I'm more the tweed type. But he always wanted to do strange things. He once wanted to enter the

(continued on page 368)

GAMEFISH: CARP

NAMES
Common Carp, Mirror Carp, Leather Carp, Scaled Carp, European Carp, German Carp, Sewer Bass. *(Cyprinus carpio)*

DISTRIBUTION
An extremely prolific fish, the carp was first introduced to the United States in 1872 by way of Europe from Asia. It is now found in every part of the country. A cousin of the common goldfish.

DESCRIPTION
A large, strong fish, the carp is colored olive, bronze or golden brown on the back shading into yellow or gold on the sides with a yellowish white belly. It is a large scaled fish that possesses a toothless mouth with a projecting upper jaw and two barbels on the side of the mouth. Its long dorsal fin is located in the middle of its body.

SIZE
Although the average size of a carp is 3 to 8 pounds, fish weighing up to 20 pounds are not considered unusual. They have been known to reach a maximum of 60 pounds.

HABITAT
The carp is a very versatile fish that can be found in almost any type of environment. It prefers muddy lakes and rivers with warm, quiet waters.

FEEDING HABITS
The carp is primarily a bottom feeder and a vegetarian although they do feed on insect larvae, crustaceans and small fish. They like to root up bottom vegetation in search of tender roots. In doing so they constantly roil the water, disturbing other vegetable and aquatic life. Carp are attracted to such bait as doughballs, bits of corn and cooked potato.

TACKLE
In Europe carp angling is a science, in America barely a pastime. Light and medium spinning gear or baitcasting gear is usually required for this tackle-busting brute who shows finesse when sniffing around doughballs. Great moments in angling occur on those ultra-rare occasions when carp are feeding on certain blossoms on the surface and will take flies like the White Miller, which passably imitate the blossoms. Hold on to your hat and carry a stout fly rod!

BUCK FOLDING
HUNTING KNIFE

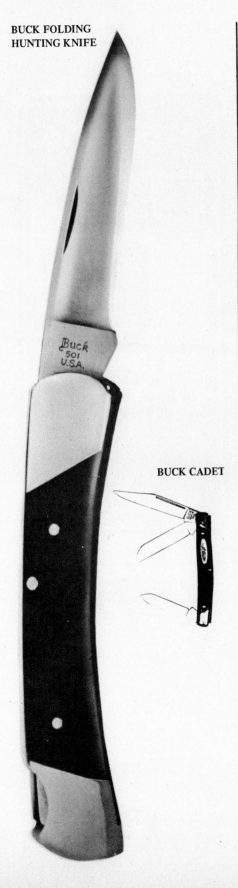

BUCK CADET

top of the line

Knives

ANGLER'S MAIL. The Angler's Mail Company is featuring a nice-sized knife with a 2½-inch blade made of 440-stainless steel 1/8 inch thick. Designed for the trout and salmon angler, this small belt knife, created by Rick Darby, can be had with either micarta, Brazilian rosewood or cocoa bolo handle, though the chemically constructed micarta is the best for use around water. This well-made cutlery is available with scrimshaw or engraving at an extra price. Should last a lifetime.

BEAN'S TROUT KNIFE. Bean sells an inexpensive and functional 4-inch blade trout-cleaning knife made from highly polished steel. It has a rosewood handle held in place with nickel rivets. Comes in a leather sheath.

BUCK. The renowned Buck line of pocket knives are very well made and excellent tools for general outdoor use. Small models like their Lancer, Trapper or Muskrat work well for fishy work. And their Yachtsman model, with a three inch blade, is designed for boat use.

BUCK FISHERMAN'S KNIFE. Those nice knife-making folks at Buck are producing a fisherman's model that has a smooth curving 10-inch blade designed for easy filleting jobs. Has a black leather sheath to protect the high carbon-steel blade and a technologically developed handle that resists everything.

CASE FLY FISHERMAN'S KNIFE. Case, which makes a very high quality knife, has been turning out this fly fishing knife at an ever increasing price over the years.

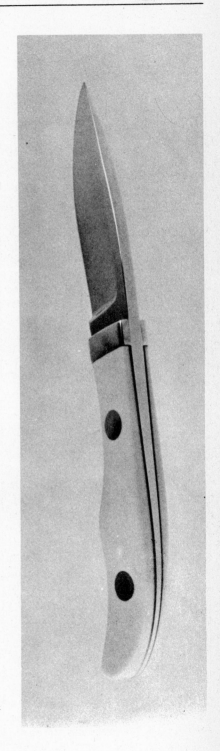

ANGLER'S MAIL

top of the line

It has a stainless-steel handle with a cutting blade and scissors on one side plus a pick file and disgorger on the other side. There is a measuring scale in inches on one side. All this only weighs 2 ounces. Highly recommended.

GLADDING. This is a fine line of filleting and cleaning knives made from all stainless steel. They have going in their favor single-piece construction, which makes them easy to clean. These knives can be purchased in sheath models with blades from 4 7/8 inches to over 9 inches or in a folder with a 4-inch blade. No fishy remains can clog up wooden recesses and there are no bolts to loosen or rust. A good buy, even though stainless steel is difficult to sharpen.

G-96 COMPANY. The G-96 offerings, which began as Japanese import imitations of Buck and other folding knives, have now branched off into original things. Among the well-made knives in this line is a folding fisherman with a small hook-sharpening stone embedded in the wood of the handle. Has a regular blade, a scaler and a hook remover. G-96 also makes a nice line of filleting knives, some small boat gaffs and a whole variety of other filleting and scaling models. Well worth the money.

PUMA. Puma's fisherman's knife is unique. The big folder has a 3¾-inch stainless-steel blade for cleaning, a notched back for scaling and a heavy nob at the end for conking the fish upside the head. But the really interesting thing about the knife is that it's a scale or balance, too. Fish up to 12 pounds can be weighed by balancing on the end. Very interesting but too heavy to carry around comfortably. Perfect for boats and tackle boxes. Comes with a leather strap.

GLADDING'S KING FILLET AND FISHERMAN KNIVES

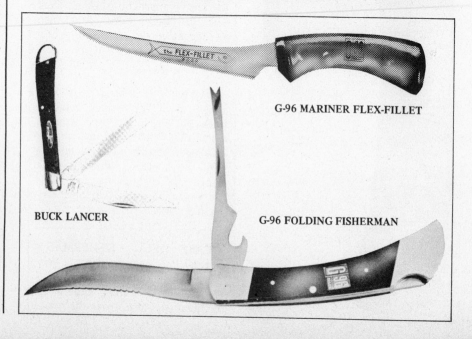

G-96 MARINER FLEX-FILLET

BUCK LANCER

G-96 FOLDING FISHERMAN

ultimate commodity

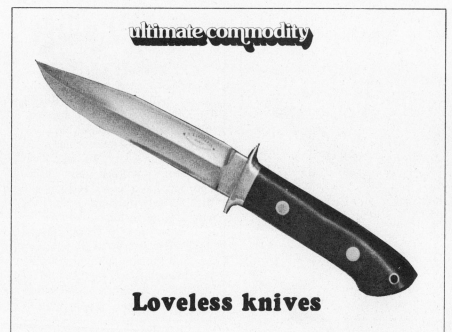

Loveless knives

There are some ultimate commodities that are ultimate because of their ingenious machinery or ornate workmanship.

Not so with Bob Loveless knives. The Californian's sheath knives are the ultimate in large part because they are the ultimate in simplicity. Nothing fancy.

The normal Loveless knife, which starts off these days around $300 and a two-year wait, has a smallish 3- to 4½-inch blade. His most influential knives have a cleanly designed drop point blade found on so many other custom knives these days. But the Loveless drop point was the first.

His choice of blade steel is almost a maximum compromise between hardness and sharpening capabilities. His favored handle material is micarta, a space-age plastic that's almost unbreakable and in white very difficult to tell at first look from ivory.

But like many very fine fly rods, reels and guns, most Loveless knives are owned by collectors who wouldn't know how to use a knife in the field if their lives depended on it. They buy Loveless because of their value, which increases from year to year.

Loveless will make you anything special you want and is capable of making the greatest filleting knives of all time. They are things of beauty for a lifetime.

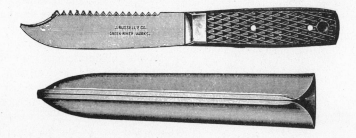

A. J. Russell & Co. fish knife sold between 1910 and 1920 for 35 cents. For another 15 cents you could get a leather sheath.

top of the line

PUUKKO KNIFE. The Finnish-made Puukko is an all-around knife designed in a traditional stream-lined shape. Available with a 4- or 3 3/8-inch blade of stainless steel. The Puukko has a black nylon handle with brass fittings and a leather sheath. Sturdily constructed. A good angler's knife for the money.

BUD LILLY BELT SHEATH

Here's a nice little sheath for your Swiss Army knife sold by Bud Lilly. Well-made with a snap closure. See page 363.

BUD LILLY KNIFE LANYARD

If you don't always hang onto your fancy pocket knife, get a 15-inch chain lanyard that will attach to any knife with a shackle. The other side clips onto your sheath or belt loop.

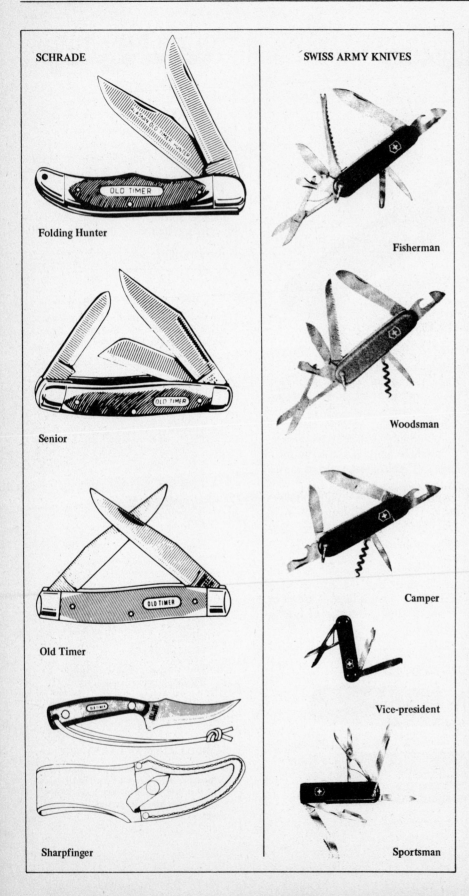

SCHRADE

Folding Hunter

Senior

Old Timer

Sharpfinger

SWISS ARMY KNIVES

Fisherman

Woodsman

Camper

Vice-president

Sportsman

top of the line

A. G. RUSSELL. One of the most elegant but expensive places to buy a fishing knife is the A. G. Russell Company in Arkansas. No discount-store bargains here. Russell has many of the best custom knives being made in the world today. He sells them new, and on occasion, second-hand. You can buy classics such as the Marble Safety Fisherman's Knife for only $150, or a thin-bladed Loveless (the man generally considered the best knife maker in the world today) for $300 or more. It's fun getting on the mailing list, anyway. And he occasionally does have very fine knives for less than $50.

SCHRADE CUTLERY COMPANY. Schrade's Old Timer pocket knives remain some of the best of the inexpensive items on the market today. Available in lots of blade configurations from two to five inches, they're nice and long-lasting.

SHARK FILLETING KNIFE. This Canadian-made knife has one very fine feature. It floats. Available in 5-, 6- or 7½-inch lengths, it has an orange tip for quick locating, a Solingen steel blade, an unbreakable handle and a sheath that locks in the knife. A good product.

WENGER SWISS ARMY KNIVES. Certainly the most versatile knives ever devised, though the Swiss have yet to test them in combat. For the outdoorsperson who doesn't worry about major tasks like skinning animals. Like a component system, they can be bought in a grand variety, with blades ranging from magnifying glasses and screwdrivers (standard and Phillips, no less), universal can openers, fish scalers and hook removers, tweezers, scissors, reamers, files and on and on and on. There's even an Izaak Walton model designed specifically for fishing, but almost any of the knives from the tiniest to

"If you can't stand the heat get out of the water below a nuclear power plant."
ANON.

CUTLERY **363**

SWISS ARMY KNIFE

Champion

FOLDING SCISSORS

WALTON'S THUMB

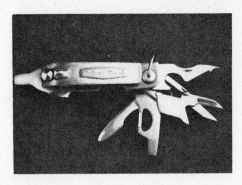

Listed below are some of the sportsman folding knife features:
1. Long pincher nose
2. Clipper.
3. Cold forged knife blade.
4. Split ring opener.
5. Screwdriver.
6. Self sharpening scissors.
7. Stiletto or hook eye cleaner and knot picker.
8. Lanyard ring.
9. Knot tag crimper.
10. Split shot opener.

top of the line

the largest will sure do the job. Sold by Precise.

WESTERN CUTLERY. The Western Cutlery Company has begun turning out a really excellent line of fish-filleting knives that have lots of uses around the kitchen. Their super fillet model has a 9 inch blade and is 14 inches in length. Laminated hardwood handles and stainless-steel blades. Also available in a cheese model with a 4-, 6- or 9-inch blade.

WILKINSON. Wilkinson's in England is selling a very practical fly-fisherman's knife with a 2 1/8-inch knife blade, heavy duty scissors, tweezers, file and hook disgorger. Also has a bottle cap lifter and a hole for the thumb.

Miscellany

FOLDING SCISSORS. One of the gadgets that's swept the fly fishing world recently. Much more elegant than mere clippers and more functional to some anglers, they can be hooked to the vest and unfolded safely whenever needed. Only weighing a couple ounces and only a little bit over 3 inches long, they are very useful for the price.

HARDY SCISSOR PLIERS. This is one of those gadgets that the old-time English company makes for fly fishermen, but which any kind of angler can use. These scissor pliers, which have a good serrated blade and plier jaws, make a handy tool for cutting nylon or breaking off barbs.

WALTON'S THUMB. Walton's Thumb, produced by Colorado's Hank Roberts, is enough to send the confirmed gadgeteer over the edge.

WESTERN CUTLERY SUPER FILLET

WESTERN CUTLERY FISH FILLET

BUD LILLY BELT SHEATH

top of the line

Expensive and well-made, the Thumb is to the old angler's clipper what the atomic bomb is to the firecracker. Made from stainless steel and surprisingly light, it has blades that include a tiny pincer pliers, side-positioned clipper, small knife blade, split ring opener, split shot remover, scissors, reel-sized screwdriver, hook eye cleaner, knot tag crimper and bottle opener. The parts are replaceable and it is guaranteed. Really swell. Get one for Christmas.

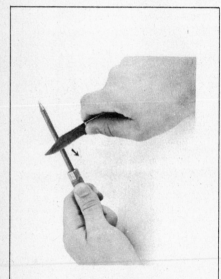

E.Z.E. LAP

The E.Z.E. Lap knife sharpener, made of diamond-impregnated steel, is just the thing for sharpening those knives used for filleting fish. Very expensive, but it surely does the job probably better than anything else.

LEONARD PIN RING AND LANYARD

These two leather gadgets are handy ways to carry the assortment of knives, scissors, nets and pliers that anglers seem to accumulate like flies. The pin ring has a 1½-inch split ring and the lanyard is 8 inches overall, with a buckle on one end and a split ring on the other.

ultimate commodity

Henry Frank's Pocket Knives

Henry Frank. Whitefish, Montana. That's the ultimate word about pocket knives. There's lots of good ones these days but Frank's are at the top.

Of course they are ultra-expensive — $300 and up. And there's a wait lasting years. But even the simplest lock-blade models with minimal engraving put Frank's work in a league by itself. Many of the other custom pocket knife makers display Teutonic overstatement that Frank only hints at even with his most gaudy special orders.

A picture doesn't do a Frank knife much justice. You have to pick one up and fondle it to appreciate its fine balance and the minute scrollwork worthy of the best English shotguns.

There are lots of styles offered, most with one locking blade and varying degrees of engraving. They're made of good steel and everything else you could dream of in a folder. Few, and I stress few, ever get used for anything more than opening envelopes!

Remembrances of fishing past: Howie

By Harmon Henkin

It may be the cruelest thing I've ever done, but he sure deserved it.

We were at a small pond that fed off a river flowing into the Chesapeake Bay. He — let's call him Howie — was pestering me with incessant questions. He was just beginning to fish and had to have every little thing explained in detail, over and over and over and over again and then once or twice more.

It was getting on to dusk and I wanted to plink off some small panfish that were rising everywhere on the two-acre pond. Since the fish had access to the river and then the bay there was an incredible variety of species there depending on the season. But Howie hadn't given me much time. Most of it

had been spent showing him how to put a worm on his hook and cast it. But that wasn't enough. He wanted a precise description of the whole eco-system.

So I put on a glob of worms, cast his rig out as far as possible and ran around to the far side of the pond for a tad of peace. His questions skittered across the water like flat rocks but I ignored most of them. Finally he had a bite.

"Hey. Something's starting to tug."

"Let him swallow it, Howie."

"Hey. It's starting to swallow it."

"Let him run with the line."

"Hey. He's starting to run with the line."

"Pick the rod up and jerk, Howie."

Howie more than compensated for his lack of tact with strength.

He jerked the rod like it was the sword Excalibur imbedded in granite. I expected to see bluegills leaping for the sun. But lo and behold it was an eel. A long fat eel that had come up from the Bay.

Howie screamed as it flew.

"Arghh. What is it?"

I don't really know where my reflexive answer came from. Probably some deep, mean recess of my being.

"Rattler! Howie, you hooked a rattler!"

Howie shot another look at the menace hurling through space at him,

dropped the rod and ran off howling through the woods.

I found him at dark huddling in the car. I handed him his rod.

"Did ya kill the snake?" he asked.

"No. Howie. He got away."

Howie was silent on the way back to town. What a relief. If you didn't want him to go fishing with you, all you had to say was that you were going back to the pond.

That was the least you could say for that place.

Stainless and high-carbon steel

Having acquired a blade shape and length that best lends itself to the carving of bait or the rough-dressing of table fish, an angler must select one or two basic metals. These are, roughly, time-honored high-carbon steel and stainless steel. Reputable American makers offer many alloys, and the custom blade may be well worth its healthy price. Object, of course, is the development of a blade which is tough, holds a fine edge and resists — if it does not entirely defeat — the ravages of rust and corrosion.

Stainless steel would seem to be the answer in our field, yet it has never displaced the high-carbon steel article, nor is it likely to do so until such time as the stainless blade proves able to take and hold an edge as well and as long as its competition. Because stainless steel knives require more working over with a stone to keep them reasonably sharp, many believe that a blade forged of this material cannot be honed to a fine edge. This is not true: it simply takes more effort to maintain the harder, more resilient metal at peak cutting efficiency. Some think the game hardly worth the candle.

Therefore professionals still use basic high-carbon steel blades, and wage a constant battle with rust. They feel that the excellence of this material, together with its staying power, is a worthy combination. Stainless cutlery boasts some advantages, but it has yet to be accepted by commercial fisheries workers or by butchers in the hinterlands.

Regardless of obvious faults, jackknives fabricated of stainless steel may be practical tools for a great many marine anglers, precisely because they resist corrosion and rust. Blades may not be as sharp as a man might desire, but neither will they be welded into one immovable lump by rust after a week or so of neglect. In salt water, we prefer the stainless steel clasp knife.

From *Tackle Talk* by Henry Lyman and Frank Woolner. (C) 1971 by Henry Lyman and Frank Woolner. Used by permission of A.S. Barnes & Co., Inc.

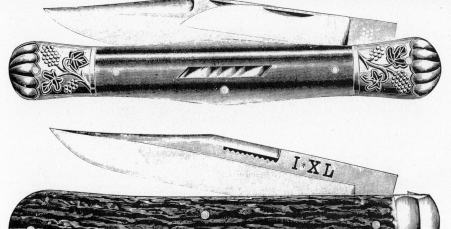

The Thomas H. Chubb Co. of Post Hills, Vermont, sold these folding knives in the 1890s.

Something for every boat

If you look back a mere decade, you'll note that electronics were designed almost entirely for larger craft. Radiotelephone, Loran, radar and depthfinding equipment were used only on boats 30 feet in length or longer. Today most of that same equipment has been miniaturized to such an extent that it is suitable for boats under 20 feet as well. You can buy radiotelephones and depthfinders that are not much larger than a cigar box and portable radars about the size of an attache case.

Electronics for boats have changed considerably during the past ten years, and it would appear that these changes have just begun. As the boatman's needs for navigation, communications and understanding of the waters that surround his craft become more complex and sophisticated, it is reasonable to assume that the electronic equipment designed to meet these needs will follow suit.

Boatmen of the mid-Seventies need more electronics, especially the angler. He not only needs to know exactly where he is (i.e. to locate and fish a particular wreck, reef or other bottom structure), but also what's in the water around and under the craft. He might also want to know water temperature, not only at the surface but at depth as well, since some species of fish are very temperature-sensitive.

And, he might find it necessary to communicate with anglers in other boats to compare his results and findings with theirs. Thus, when it comes to selecting the electronics he will actually need to pursue his favorite sport, he will have to consider his own requirements very carefully in order to make intelligent selections.

If, for example, his procedures involve long, offshore runs to fish particular known concentration areas such as the canyons, he'll need electronic aids to navigation. Loran, Omega and radio direction finding receivers are items he must consider. He may need only one of these, or possibly all three, depending upon his area. As the size of the instruments continues to decrease and the reliability increases, they'll find a spot on smaller and smaller boats. Even now it's not uncommon to see Loran receivers on boats under 20 feet.

There are a wide variety of depthfinders now on the market, and new ones appearing every day. They range from simple flashers and digital meters to sophisticated recorders and more recently from units that could look only straight down beneath the hull to rotating scanners that look horizontally as well as down. Even as this is being written at least one company, Vexilar, is developing an ultra-compact "straight line" depthfinder that records on a CRT (cathode ray tube) much like a miniature TV set.

The better depthfinders are capable of great sensitivity and can depict fine details at considerable depths. They can show fish near the bottom in several hundred feet of

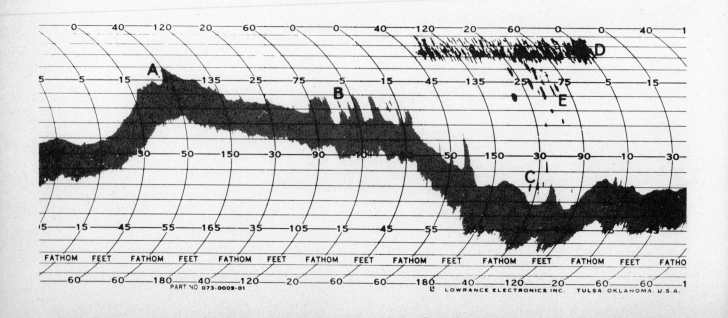

Amazing shrinking electronic gear

By Bob Stearns

What's next? Miniaturized computers coupled with all kinds of angling and boating electronics.

...ater, but they're expensive (usually costing ...700-$2000 or more). In many cases a less ...phisticated unit will fit the angler's needs, ...d it would be unwise to buy "more" than ...needed. They're made to work on a large ...nge of boats and are common on craft ...om as small as 14 feet to the largest afloat.

Electronic temperature sensors are rapid-... becoming popular. They're usually de-...gned around the thermistor, a temperature-...nsitive resistor that can be calibrated to ...reat accuracy and fast response. Mounted ...n the boat's hull underwater, they help the ...ngler detect subtle surface temperature ...hanges that indicate the special currents ...any gamefish find attractive. When used in ...onjunction with downriggers, they provide ... vertical profile of the water temperature, ...us helping locate that layer most desirable ...o the species of fish sought.

Radiotelephones are now commonplace ...n all sizes of fishing craft. They range from ...mple, hand-held walkie-talkies in canoes and rowboats to ultra-sophisticated, long-range, single-sideband gear that can reach out over thousands of miles. Some, like the walkie-talkies, are very short-range only. Others, such as VHF, are line-of-sight and cannot get past the curvature of the earth. Selection of the right type of equipment here is tricky: long-range equipment, such as SSB, is useless for short-range work and often medium distance too. Some types can be used with shoreside stations (i.e. VHF) to tie into telephone landlines, while others (Citizens Band) cannot.

What does the future hold? More versatile, compact and reliable versions of the items described above. Also miniaturized computers that can be coupled with one or more types of boating electronics to further utilize the information they can provide. It's a sure bet that anything we see only on larger boats now will be scaled down in the near future to be used on anything from a bass boat to a mini-offshore fishing machine.

At left is a sample of the graphic printout made by scanning a stretch of off-shore water using a Lowrance Fish Lo-K-Tor. It shows bottom contours, structure and fish in schools and alone. The bottom depth varies from 12 to 42 feet. The high spot at A rises to a depth of 12 feet. At B, thin markings show vegetation: a kelp bed. The pinnacle at C rises slightly to a depth of 36 feet. Structural irregularities like kelp beds and pinnacles attract gamefish — the markings immediately above C prove that they're there. But the concentration of fish is at a shallow depth: a school of baitfish (D) gathered between 6 and 12 feet and the gamefish below them (E) at 15 feet.

Illustration and text taken from *New Guide to the Fun of Electronic Fishing.* (C) 1975 by Lowrance Electronics, Inc. Used by permission of Lowrance Electronics, Inc., Tulsa, Oklahoma.

"I hate these cunning tricks of making gifts, when presents are baited hooks. All know how the greedy wrasse swallows the fly and is fooled."
MARTIAL, CIRCA 150 A.D.

GAMEFISH: TIGER SHARK

NAMES
Leopard shark. *(Galeocerdo arcticus)*

DISTRIBUTION
The tiger shark is found throughout tropical waters. It is also found as far north as Woods Hole, Massachusetts. Most often it is found in the Caribbean.

DESCRIPTION
The color of the tiger shark is grey to brown on the back with a white belly. The sides are often marked by dark, vertical bars. It has a short, sharp snout and the upper lobe of the tail is long and slender.

SIZE
Although there have been specimens reported of over 30 feet, the average is about 12 feet. A fish of that length will weigh about 1000 pounds.

HABITAT
The tiger shark is usually found near the surface at night. They can be found in both deep and shallow water. At times, they come quite close to shore.

FEEDING HABITS
The tiger shark has been known to eat anything from turtles to its own kind. It will feed on squid, crab, sea lions and they have been known to attack humans.

THE LAST HATCH
A FISHING MYSTERY
HARMON HENKIN

(continued from page 358)

Grand Prix Des Snowmobiles in Montreal. Halford really liked me, though. He wanted me to be his literary executor. He told me so last year."

"In his old will or new?"

"The old one, I guess."

"That would have meant money for editing his stuff, new editions and movies, right?"

"I want my lawyer . . . who isn't a bass fly tier, by the way. He took the Schielbacht Famous Tiers Course and —"

"Get the Hell out of here," Sid barked. "And send in Hewitt."

Schielbacht disappeared and was replaced by a scowling, aristocratic Hewitt.

"How may I aid the idiot savants of forensics?"

"First of all, by telling us how well you knew Halford," Sid said.

"Not very well, actually. I met him steelheading last winter. My wife knew him much better. She had read all his books and especially liked *The Plastic Eskimo: Progress Comes to Alaska.* We had dinner together one night in Seattle. He invited us out to fish but I find trout boring. They're so small and cowardly. Anyway, I may have seen him a dozen times. That's all. It was enough."

"You didn't care for him?" Paul asked.

"No, why should I have? Did you?"

"No comment. We're asking the questions. Send your wife in."

Belle Parmachene entered. She was frightened.

"Did you have a close relationship with Halford?" Paul asked.

"Why, whatever do you mean?"

"Whatever you want it to mean."

"I'm a student of the written word. Frederick was the unquestioned master of our time."

"That's debatable," Sid said softly.

"This is not the proper time to discuss art, sheriff. I met him at a literary conference last year and we talked from time to time about life and the novel."

"Did you ever discuss the birds and the bees?" Sid asked. Paul smiled.

"I resent that question. I'm a happily married woman."

(continued on page 371)

top of the line

AQUASCAN. The Aquascan, put out by the Flip-Tail Lure people, is a very sophisticated piece of fish-finding gear. It's like an underwater radar unit that produces a 360° look at the subsurface for about 300 feet. It'll even tell you where the fish are with blips that appear on the TV-like screen. The sound waves are picked up on the transducer which translates them for the TV tube and screen. A complicated, specialized and expensive piece of gear.

FISH HAWK MODEL 530. The Fish Hawk Model 530 Digital Depth/Light Density-Temperature Meter is something of a triple threat. It'll tell you the depth of the water, the temperature at that depth and also the light density, which is an important factor in deciding lure color. It's sophisticated, but mastery of its nuances can be a great leap forward in consistent angling success. Not a beginner's piece, but then few electronic gadgets really are.

GARCIA ELECTRO-SONIC FLASHER/RECORD. One of Garcia's better entrants in the electronic fishing equipment derby. It has a 3-speed graph choice that allows the angler the option of depth ranges of 0 to 60 feet, 60 to 120 feet, 120 to 180 feet and 180 to 240 feet. It has a flip-up window on the chart to allow for notations. It will work independently or in conjunction with the graph recorder.

GARCIA OXYGEN-TEMPERA-TURE PROBE. A handy, though delicate, piece of electronic equipment. Garcia makes a reasonably priced model that helps you locate fish by finding out the amount of dissolved oxygen in a given piece of water, a very important consideration for fish, especially in late sum-

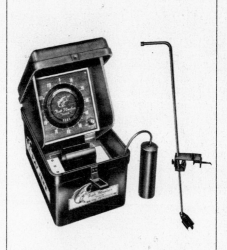

RAY JEFFERSON FISH FLASHER

GARCIA ELECTRO-SONIC 9500 FLASHER/CHART RECORDER

FISH HAWK MODEL 530

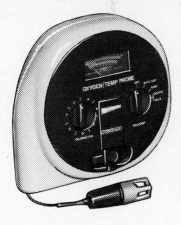

GARCIA 8500 OXYGEN-TEMPERATURE PROBE

top of the line

mer. It also probes the water for temperature, another very important factor in finding fish. The unit is self-contained with batteries, probe, probe cable and built-in reel for the whole apparatus.

HUMMINBIRD. The most interesting thing about the Humminbird line of depth sounders is that they're completely waterproof just the way they come. Don't need any fancy housing units to keep the wet off. Humminbird has a complete set of finders for any sort of use.

RAY JEFFERSON. Ray Jefferson is a very solid producer of electronic sport fishing gear. He's been in business for almost 30 years now making boating-related equipment. One of the most popular of his outfit's finders is the Model 170 Fish Flasher, a moderate-priced transistorized unit that is less than 5 inches square. It reads down to 70 feet, which is enough for most bass fishing, though limited for some other species.

RAY JEFFERSON BEEPER. The Ray Jefferson Model 6010 operates up to depths of 240 feet and has a delightful feature: a beeper that sounds off with an audible signal when something fishy (or an underwater obstruction) places itself between the sounder and the bottom. You can concentrate on steering the boat or on trolling without constant stares at the unit. A good one.

LOWRANCE FISHFINDERS. Lowrance was one of the first manufacturers to really get into producing equipment for the electronically inclined angler. Its line has grown and grown and it still has a good hunk of a market that has become ever more competitive. Starting with the low-

HUMMINBIRD SIXTY

LOWRANCE FLASHER-GRAPH

THE LAST HATCH
A FISHING MYSTERY
HARMON HENKIN

(continued from page 368)

"That's not exactly the impression I get from your husband," Paul said.

"We pursue our own interests."

"So your relationship with Halford was carried out on a perpendicular rather than horizontal level?" Sid was enjoying himself for the first time all day.

"What?"

"That's all for now," Paul said.

She left them alone.

"Well, Paul. What do you think? I'm lost."

"Not a lot. They could all be covering up a skeleton in the closet or they could all be guilty. It's like those times on the river when the fish are active but they aren't taking anything in particular. We have to get more specific. Let's get Dun back in here. He's our best source of information."

Dun walked in a few steps behind Julie. "Ms. Berners wanted to come, too," Dun said.

"Why, Julie?" Paul asked.

"I want to play cops and robbers, too. I'm bored sitting around with those sots."

"Okay. Dun, how long have the guests been here?"

"Five days, sir. Most came at the beginning of last week."

"Did Halford spend more time with one in particular?"

"No, not really. He wasn't like that. He spoke to the whole group at night by the fire. During the day, as far as I could see, he would chat with each of them separately."

"Did he do anything special this week. Anything out of the ordinary?"

"He seemed a little more secretive. He made a number of phone calls himself. I usually did most of his telephoning. He also disappeared for short periods of time. But he did fish each afternoon and always filled his journal in the evening."

Paul was thumbing through Halford's leather-bound journal, ignoring Dun. He noticed that Halford made his entries in prose rather than the angling shorthand most fishermen use to compile their ups and downs. Normally journals include only the date, time, weather conditions, fish

(continued on page 375)

end models — the LFP 150 and LFG 150 — up to the more specialized high end of the scale, Lowrance makes enough equipment to satisfy even the hard core. Good stuff.

LOWRANCE FISH-N-TEMP. Lowrance's Fish-n-Temp is a completely portable underwater temperature gauge that can read even extreme variations very quickly. It's a very small unit that fits in any tackle box and will give you depth and degree readings up to 100 feet. Works in fresh or salt water.

LOWRANCE LRG 600 FLASHER-GRAPH. The Lowrance LRG 600 Flasher-Graph is a finely-made unit that will work in up to 360 feet of water. This fairly expensive unit is equipped with both a flashing dial depth finder and a graph recorder with a 2-speed paper drive mechanism. It can even be used for a quick glance around a strange lake when the boat is moving at maximum speed.

LOWRANCE LTD 200. If you want to know the surface temperature (something that may or may not be useful to the angler) then get a Lowrance Surface Fish-n-Temp and mount it permanently on your boat. Reads from 35° to 90° even as you zip along at high speed. Includes a large scale for quick readings.

SEA-DEEP STRUCTURE RE-CORDER. Sea-Deep's Model 1200 is one of the more interesting structure recorders. All-solid state, it has a 4-inch paper with two linear recording scales of 0 to 100 feet and 0 to 200 feet. Has a night light and is easy to remove from its brackets. A good piece of equipment.

"It is a reasonable surmise that before the fourth century the fly must have been known to anglers in the salmon rivers of the West (England)."
ALFRED JOSHUA BUTLER, *Sport in Classic Times.*

top of the line

VEXILAR DEPTHERM. The most basic piece of electronic equipment any angler can obtain is a depth thermometer and one of the most handy on the market is the Deptherm II by Vexilar, one of the better manufacturers of such things. It uses a 'C' battery and operates like this: you dial the fish zone you want and lower the probe until the needle hits that mark. The wire is calibrated in feet and will give you the exact depth to 30 feet. Measures temperatures from 35° to 95°. Good stuff.

VEXILAR SONA-GRAF. Vexilar makes one of the most respected of all the lines of electronic fishing aids currently flooding the market. Experts agree that Vexilar's equipment is dependable and functional. The Sona-Graf range of models, especially the 155, 155D and HE-33, cover the broad needs of the modern deep water angler. Check them out if you want to plug yourself in.

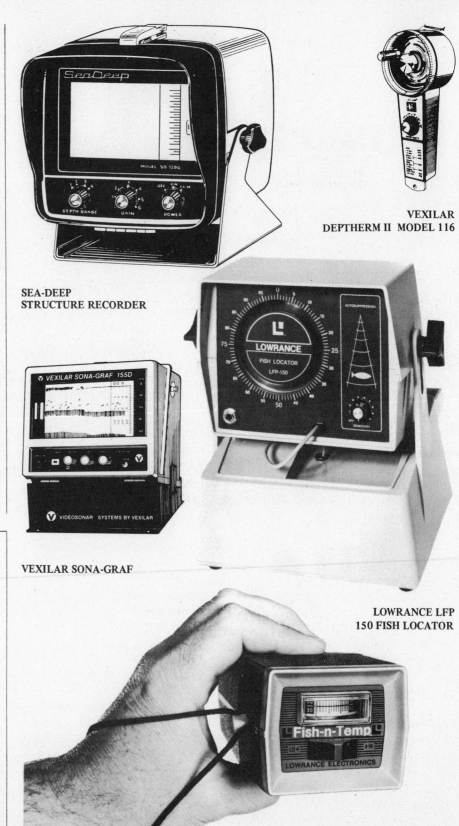

VEXILAR DEPTHERM II MODEL 116

SEA-DEEP STRUCTURE RECORDER

VEXILAR SONA-GRAF

LOWRANCE LFP 150 FISH LOCATOR

HUMMINBIRD ELECTRONIC CLOCK

Can't bear to be separated from your transducer? Spend endless hours at work dreaming of great depths? Well, get a Humminbird electronic clock for your house or office. It looks just like their well-known depth sounder. You have to look at it a few times to realize that it's really a clock. A neat gadget for the hard-core electronic basser.

LOWRANCE LTP 100 FISH-N-TEMP

Well-dressed anglers are suited for the occasion

By Harmon Henkin

There are some very tradition-minded anglers who fully believe that one does not have to dress like a slob to catch fish. They feel that fish, most especially trout and salmon, are aristocratic enough to spurn the offerings of anyone who doesn't have the decency to attire themselves properly.

Well, that may or may not be true, since you see successful anglers in many outfits. But unless you're fishing off a dock belonging to a nudist colony, clothing is a crucial accessory for any angler. It's difficult, however, to make generalizations about high fashion for fishers.

Sure, it should be comfortable and functional but what that means varies widely from place to place; sometimes tweeds and sometimes jump suits are *de rigueur*. Your dress simply should be suited for the occasion. Yet there are a few things that could be considered.

Your pants, shirt, jacket or whatever should be large enough to allow for movement. Unless you're meditating on the bank waiting for an inquisitive fish

"A sure protection against mosquitoes and flies," William Mills & Son said of their angler's bug net. It sold in the 1890s for 75 cents.

to sniff out your nightcrawler, you'll be doing lots of casting and therefore moving arms and legs. It's not the most strenuous exercise in the world but it does qualify as exercise. Tight-fitting clothes might be elegant but aren't good for fishing. The fish ain't impressed.

If you're fishing in a way that involves getting wet, clothes should be relatively quick drying. Cotton dries off

in the air much quicker than denim, for instance, and many wet waders in the West prefer shedding their Levis for cotton trousers.

Pockets are another consideration no matter how many compartments are in your tackle box or vest. There's always stuff you will want to shove in them. Also, you should always be able to add or shed an extra layer of clothes during the course of a day. Weather has the peculiar habit of changing and it's a shame to have an outing ruined because you over- or under-heat.

Hats are another thing to keep in mind. Hooks have the unnerving habit of hitting upside one's noggin. Besides acting as a helmet of sorts, hats also act as sunshades.

That all sounds simple and it is. It's a lot more difficult to pick a spincasting reel than a pair of pants. Everyone has had more experience with clothes — remember, it's one leg at a time.

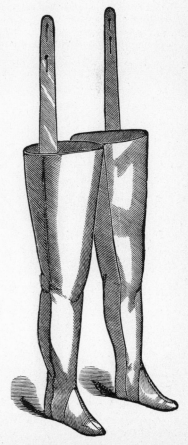

(left) The "Izaak Walton" fishing suit, marketed in the 1880s by Dame, Stoddard & Kendall of Boston, came with coat, vest and pants for $9.25. (above) This rubber trouting cape weighed 9½ ounces and was sold in the early 1900s for $3. (right) Wading stockings from the 1890s, sold by Abbey & Imbrie for $7.50.

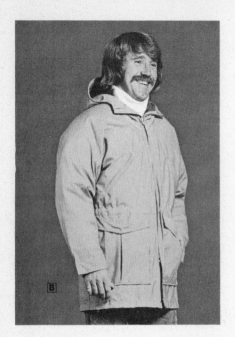

GERRY PARKA

**SPORTSMAN'S
FELT COMPANY SOLES**

Most felt soles for waders and wading shoes come in one piece, but the Sportsman's Felt Company has two-pieces, one for the heel and one for the sole for ease in getting it on. Well made.

MARATHON RAINSUIT

---

top of the line

Coats & Jackets

ANGLER'S MAIL. The Durham jacket made by England's J. Barbour and Sons, Ltd., is sold in this country by the Angler's Mail Company. Weighing only 27 ounces, it folds up nicely and has rainproof pockets, adjustable cuffs, double shoulders and a hood. It's made of Egyptian cotton, which is superior in many ways to 60-40 materials. A nice coat.

CLIMBER'S CAGOULE. Cagoule is a fancy word for an alpinist's poncho. They shed wind, rain and snow and fit over other clothing, adding warmth because body heat is trapped. The double-layered, waterproof coated nylon is probably the best thing around for shedding heavy doses of moisture. But they're a bit much for strenuous activity, and more suited for sitting around a camp. Sold through Sierra Designs.

GERRY PARKA. The Gerry all-weather parka is without a doubt the most convenient and functional raincoat I've ever owned, says Harmon Henkin, author of this book. It weighs only a few ounces, folds up into a fishing vest, pack or anywhere else. This one really is a raincoat, unlike some that say they are. Everything you need for wet weather protection.

MARATHON RAINSUIT. A two-piece rainsuit can be handy for the hard-core angler or camper who will not be denied. Marathon has designed their suit to accommodate casting. It weighs only 19 ounces, including top and bottom. It folds down to obscurity and will keep you dry regardless.

THE DUNHAM JACKET

CLIMBER'S CAGOULE

GUDEBROD SEWING KIT

Gudebrod is marketing a handy sportsman's emergency sewing kit. Has 16 colors of thread to match the opening hatch on your clothing. Also has two needles, two safety pins, two buttons, two pins, a pin cushion and a needle threader. Don't be sloppy, Mother Nature doesn't like surprises.

top of the line

SIERRA DESIGNS 60-40. Sierra Designs, which made the original 60-40 parka, continues to produce these fine coats. With seven pleated pockets, these mountaineering coats are made of 60 per cent cotton and 40 per cent nylon. They're highly water-repellent and offer good, lightweight protection against the chill. They are currently available with either a light wool lining, which will help keep you warm even if the coat gets soaked, or with a Polarguard lining. Good, though somewhat expensive, protection against the elements.

Footware

L. L. BEAN MAINE HIKING SHOE. If you're looking for an inexpensive, lightweight beat-around shoe for light hiking or use around the water, try the L. L. Bean Hiking Shoe. Made of canvas, this sneaker-like shoe has been around for decades. Has a vulcanized sole for good traction. Very comfortable.

CLARK'S RHINO. A comfortable shoe to wear on your fishing expedition is the English Rhino Shoe by Clark. It's made of a tough canvas with a bonded rubber sole and is very sure-footed for steep hiking. The canvas uppers dry quickly and there is a removable hemp inner sole. Men have the option of an ankle-high boot or Oxford style and women have the Oxford. Lots of sizes in tan.

DUNHAM HIKING BOOTS. Dunham's Duraflex line of boots is a good one for the hiking angler who wants a well-made pair of European shoes. They are totally waterproof but have the flexibility and breathability offered by leather. Available in a variety of styles, including Wellingtons. Good things.

THE LAST HATCH
A FISHING MYSTERY
HARMON HENKIN

(continued from page 371)

activity, patterns used and fish caught. Halford had all this stuff but also included, in his turgid style

TUESDAY, JULY 20. 4:30 PM. Fished the Big Pool with the 8-foot, No. 4 line Leonard. It was a glorious day. Trout actively nymphing on an assortment of immature caddis and stonefly. Using an Otter Nymph, I took rainbows of 16, 18 and 20 inches. The larger fellow leaped as if possessed by the wind, struggling to the marrow of its life force. I landed the speckled beauty and released it to fight another day. A noble creature.

THURSDAY, JULY 22. 3:30 PM. Fished the upper end of the spring creek with the 7½-foot Paul Young Perfectionist, carrying a No. 4 weight-forward line. A cloudy, very overcast day reminding me of my youth in London. I used a Quill Gordon to fish the Isonychia hatch. The perfectly correct imitation. Took two-score trout ranging from 10 to 20 inches. All in all, one of those limestone creek days that keep alive the glorious traditions and values of Izaak Walton.

Paul slammed down the cover with a bang that made everyone jump. "He glorified the values of fishing and was going to cut up the creek. What a contradiction! Besides being a rotten writer he was a hypocritical ass!"

"Please, please, don't speak ill of him," Dun said softly.

Paul shook his head and stood up. "Let's go fishing, Sid."

"I didn't bring a rod."

"Use mine, I'll use one of Halford's. I'm sure Mr. Dun won't object and I know Halford won't."

Dun looked for an instant like he wanted to object. But he didn't dare.

The group in the bar had scattered. Tups and Alexandrea were hypnotized by a *Wild Kingdom* special on life insurance for plant-eating animals. Paul didn't hesitate. He walked to the rod rack in the alcove and took out Halford's 8-foot Payne. It was made in the 1950s by Jim

(continued on page 384)

(left) SIERRA
60-40 COAT
(below) DUNHAM
DURAFLEX
HIKING BOOTS
(bottom left)
BEAN MAINE
HIKING BOOT
(bottom right)
BEAN RUBBER
MOCCASIN

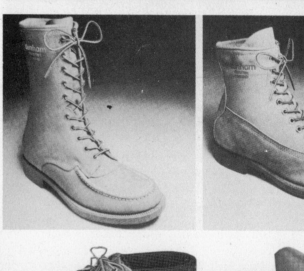

top of the line

DUNHAM SNAKE BOOTS. Going into rattler country? That's where the good fishing sometimes is, especially in the West. Well, one of Europe's best-known booters, the Dunham people, have a boot 16 inches high made from smooth leather with a vamp strap and Vibram soles. Let the buggers try to bite through these.

L. L. BEAN. Bean's rubber moccasins are a very convenient shoe for the angler who doesn't want to get in too deep. Works especially well in canoes and other boats. Leather tops and rubber lower halves. They are available with chain tread or featherweight bottoms. Very comfortable.

Gloves

MILLARMITT. These wool half-finger mittens are made in Great Britain for the serious alpinist. However, they make a very excellent glove for the angler plying his wares in very cold weather. The fawn-colored mittens, available in small, medium and large, allow for finger mobility, but keep the palm and other parts warm.

VISA-THERM CLOTHING. Been sitting jigging for pike through the ice too long? Are fingers that used to feel like they were attached to your body no longer responsive? Maybe you could use heated mittens from Visa-Therm. Made of nylon with leather strips across the front for gripping, they're coated with Polar-guard inside. They have a circuit activated by D-cell batteries to warm fingertips in extreme conditions. They also make them with slits to remove fingers for handling things. They also make a fine line of insulat-

"Then if you want to be crafty in angling, you must first learn to make your tackle."
DAME JULIANA BERNERS

top of the line

ed socks, electrically warmed innersoles and a Heatalator vest. Heavy duty stuff for the extreme cold.

Hats

EDDIE BAUER HARRIS TWEED SLOUCH HAT. For the angler who's going to spend a country weekend fishing for trout there's nothin' like a Tweed Slouch Hat from Eddie Bauer. It can be shaped to taste and is sold in sizes from 6¾ to 7¾ in a blend of autumn weave. Nice and elegant.

HERTER'S HATS. Dr. Watson, I presume? No, it's just you in your Herter's Sherlock Holmes fishing cap with a long visor and a back shade. Especially good for saltwater angling. Also available is a Hemingway model with a 4½-inch long translucent visor and an adjustable strap on the back.

BUD LILLY'S. Dubbed Greg's Leather Hat, this is a very fancy cap. Ages very well, but don't take too many dunks wearing it.

NORM THOMPSON CLOTHING. For the angler looking for more than a touch of elegance, Norm Thompson sells an Irish Fishing Hat moldable to your personality. All the head sizes for men and women plus either a grey or brown tweed mix. You shape it with an iron.

ORVIS YEAR-ROUNDER. This Orvis fishing helmet, despite an inflated price tag that grows by leaps and bounds, is a very practical and long-lasting item. It has air-vent pockets on either side that make onlookers cock their heads at first sight. It's a cool hat that gives protection from the sun, flies and stray hooks.

GREG'S LEATHER HAT

FENWICK BELT BUCKLES
A Fenwick solid-pewter belt buckle will probably deflect speeding torpedo lures if necessary but at any rate, the Western-style buckle with the familiar Fenwick emblem just looks okay. A solid brass clip on the back clutches your favorite leather belt.

VISA-THERM HEATED MITTENS

MILLARMITT

ORVIS YEAR-ROUNDER

EDDIE BAUER HARRIS TWEED HAT

NORM THOMPSON IRISH FISHING HAT

WALLS ACTION FISHING SUIT

HERTER'S HATS

CUTTER INSECT REPELLENT

EDDIE BAUER HAND-KNIT SOX

top of the line

Miscellany

EDDIE BAUER HAND-KNIT INDIAN SOX. A real deluxe item. Undyed and unbleached wool is used for added warmth. They work well even when wet. Outstanding under waders.

JUMP SUITS. Like to fish in a jump suit? Well, the Walls Action Fishing Suit, sold in green, gold and brown in all sizes for men, is a nice one. Made from a dacron-poplin blend, it has big pockets and even an emblem of a fish over the pocket just in case you forgot why you and your buddies and those six packs ever got on the boat in the first place. Available from a Bass Pro Shop.

Repellents

BUG NET. Insect repellent, shminsect repellent. There ain't nothing like a bug net. The only sure thing to keep nature's harpies away. Should be worn over a wide-brimmed hat. Available from Eastern Mountain Sports.

CUTTER. Cutter insect repellent is the best of the generally available bug lotions. It keeps the beasties away, though like all of them, it isn't perfect. Most anglers keep one of the small containers in their vest or tackle box. For extreme conditions rub a little in Vaseline. It stays on you longer.

MUSKOL. The ultimate weapon in the war against bugs is a Canadian import. Considered the best there is and with a walloping big price tag,

HOBSON STING RELIEF SPRAY

A handy potion to have along on all your spring and summer fish-catching outings is Hobson's sting relief spray. It will alleviate the pain and itching from bees, wasps, spiders, mosquitoes and even jellyfish if they sneak up behind you. Reduces swelling and neutralizes the venom. Works well and at times can be a trip saver.

RONNING ELECTRIC BOOT DRYER

If you're in the habit of taking lots of spills when wading, the Ronning Electric Boot Dryer is just the thing. It plugs into a 110-volt AC or DC outlet and dries your boots overnight. Will not harm rubber or leather. Quickest way for safe drying. Sold by Dan Bailey's.

BASS TIES

It used to be that only fly casters could have their emblem on an elegant tie. No more. The B.A.S.S. folks are merchandising a tie made from 100 per cent polyester in maroon, yellow, green, navy or brown with a jumping bass illustration. Don't get mistaken for a carp angler. Get a tie.

MUSKOL

top of the line

it's sold with the warning *"Keep away from paint and plastics."* But if you need such a potion, Muskol is a mixture based with Toulamide, a powerful repellent used by the Army in World War II. It will keep mosquitos and flies away for six to nine hours and is not diluted by sweat or rain. Muskol Mark II, which is cheaper and less potent, is advertised as giving "reasonable protection."

SHOOBUG. The armored personnel carrier approach in the war against bugs is the Shoobug Jacket made by Cole Outdoor Products. It's a wide-mesh fabric jacket that's worn over other clothing. Space Shield II Repellent is applied to the jacket and the mesh retains the repellent for weeks or months depending on the conditions under which it is used. It can be recharged with more repellent and is available in sizes from small to extra large. As a last resort in swamps or mountain lakes, it can be a trip saver effective for all categories of insect pests.

Shirts

CHAMOIS SHIRT. These shirts, pioneered by L. L. Bean, are now the rage and sold by many outfits to those who want a heavy but soft machine-washable cotton shirt. It has lots of uses for the angler, especially in the spring and fall. They last years, and are well worth their price.

EDDIE BAUER DOWNLIGHT SHIRTS. If you're fishing in the cold, you need special gear like the Eddie Bauer Downlight Shirt, available in red, Scotch mist green and taupe. It weighs less than 16 ounces and gives wonderful protection under a jacket or shirt. Made with quilted down covered by nylon taffeta. Fine item.

BEAN CHAMOIS SHIRTS

SHOOBUG

ROYAL FLEXNET CASTING SHIRT

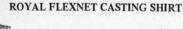

COLUMBIA
FURNACE CREEK VEST

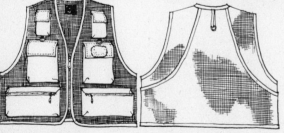

MAGIC PATCH

Here's a handy accessory for all waders regardless of race, creed or type of rubber. It's the Magic Patch and it will work even without taking your waders off. Dry the hole area, rough the surface with a twig or something, heat the blade of a knife and smear it on. Works very well.

top of the line

ROYAL FLEXNET CASTING SHIRT. Hallelujah! A rain jacket designed for someone other than a mummy. The Flexnet Casting Shirt from Royal is available in the company's 360 Batwing design, which means in essence that you have room to do the kind of arm flapping that goes on during casting, especially fly casting. Well made and in a field tan that won't offend sensitive fish. A handy knee-length product. Also available with the same drawcord hood, waterproof zipper and snap-closing front pocket, but without the batwing excess for the more sedentary trolling types.

WOOLRICH SAFARI SHIRT. The Woolrich Safari is a fine fishing shirt, even for those not actually on safari. It's designed in the "bush" style and made from a polyester/cotton blend. Has button closing pockets. Sold in poplin or chambray for men. Just poplin for women. Long or short sleeves.

Vests

BIB VEST. Advertised as "very feminine," this blue denim bib vest, available for sizes under 5 feet, 6 inches and over, has lots of pockets and works well. Fine for walking around Beverly Hills, too. Available from Bud Lilly.

COLUMBIA SPORTSWEAR. The Columbia Sportswear people are putting out a very complete line of fly fishing vests to suit every need. They make a Furnace Creek vest from nylon mesh that's the ultimate for hot-weather angling. All of their models have lots of pockets. Worth looking at.

top of the line

Wading Gear

CONVERSE WADERS. The Converse line of waders, despite their Asian point of origin, remains one of the best. Converse cleated or felt-sole nylon waders are offered in a large assortment of sizes including those for women. Converse also makes a nylon stocking-foot wader and other quality wading gear. They also make some lesser-priced lines that will do the job but not for as long or as comfortably.

FLY FISHERMAN'S BOOKCASE WADERS FOR CHILDREN. Kids deserve comfort, too. Get them a pair of these children's hip boots with harness and steel shank. Sizes from 3 through 6, olive drab and with a semi-hard toe. Start 'em right and they won't steal yours in a few years.

GRA-LITE. A new entry in the quality wader market are these Gra-Lites, available in boot or stocking foot with felt soles as an option. They will also custom-fit them for an additional $20. Developed for industrial use around those charming chemicals that are so hazardous to workers' health, they are guaranteed not to crack for five years or to deteriorate in any other way. Interesting.

LAKESTREAM FELT-SOLE WADING SANDALS. Available in either men's or women's sizes, these slip-on sandals with their felt soles will give added security to those wading tricky or treacherous waters. They fit on underneath any boots or waders, as well. They also work with sneakers for the bare wader.

(above) BLUE DENIM BIB VEST FOR LADIES
(above right) LAKESTREAM WADING SANDALS
(right) CONVERSE WADERS

Cheap waders have no place

They're everywhere — but not in this book.

I mean those inexpensive waders found in all the discount houses and many tackle shops trying to tie down a share of the, well, budget market. Usually made in Korea, Singapore and places like that, they probably make up the bulk of the wader business today.

The reason that these chest highs, hippers and soft rubber stocking feet are not in the book is simple. As Ronald Reagan said of redwood trees once, if you seen one, you seen 'em all. From a practical standpoint we were not able to detect much difference in the various and changing brands.

Now it's easy to make a case for buying these low-priced things. With very little care they will last a season and many anglers prefer buying a cheap pair of waders they don't have to worry about for $10 or so to shelling out $50 or more for a top-of-the-line product. And there is merit in this approach especially if you do your wading in areas where factors such as the soling material are not crucial and where insulation is important.

For the casual angler, as well, these imports might be fine and we have no argument with that attitude. But as regards the standards of this book, they just didn't fit in.
—H.H.

If you seen one, you seen 'em all.

MARATHON WADERS

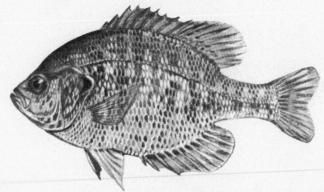

GAMEFISH: REDEAR SUNFISH

NAMES
Shellcracker, redear, stumpknocker. *(Lepomis microlophus)*

DISTRIBUTION
The redear ranges throughout Ohio and Indiana into the South and Florida and west to Texas and New Mexico.

DESCRIPTION
The redear closely resembles the bluegill in its coloring. It is generally olive green on the back with lighter sides. The sides are marked with olive spots and the ear flap is bordered with red. It has a small mouth and pointed pectoral fins.

SIZE
The redear is the largest of the sunfish and usually averages about 1 to 1½ pounds.

HABITAT
The redear is found in large, quiet rivers and lakes with abundant growth. It favors weed-beds and submerged debris near shorelines.

FEEDING HABITS
The favorite food of the redear is snails although it also feeds on worms and small crustaceans. It usually feeds on the bottom.

TACKLE
This big southernish sunfish is great on still-fishing rigs baited with worms. It'll also hit spinners on the end of light spinning outfits and flies, too.

top of the line

MARATHON CUSTOM-MADE WADERS. For an extra $10, Marathon will build a special pair of waders for the hard-to-fit. You need someone to take your exact and complete measurements. These waders are non-returnable, of course, but they do make for extra comfort. Worth it. They'll last longer if they fit right.

MARATHON HIP BOOTS. Marathon makes a complete set of hip boots for those who prefer them to waders. They are sold in stocking-foot, shoe-foot and Marathon's unique over-the-shoe models for quick use. Any size for men and most women available.

MARATHON WADERS. The Marathon Company of Wausau, Wisconsin, has been making good quality waders and hip boots for a long time. They also make other practical outer wear. The waders are made from industrial nylon fabric coated with natural rubber to provide puncture and abrasion resistance. Even if poked or cut, they will not tear. Available with action or felt sole. In men's and women's body type. Also available are stocking foot waders and a model that can be worn over regular shoes.

RETCO WADING SHOES. Retco's reasonably priced hiking shoe, with its laminated nylon body, fabric-lined, speed-lace eyelets, steel shank and molded rubber sole, also works very well as a wading shoe. Much cheaper than most regulation wading shoes, it's available in standard sizes.

SEAL-DRI WADERS. These are pretty good stocking-foot waders, made of latex rubber with suspenders and a large inside pocket. They

Front and back views of L.L. Bean's Fishing Coat, sold at the start of the Depression in 1931. At bottom is a pair of Bean's "Automatic Fishing Pant" — automatic means it had zippers at the cuffs.

top of the line

stretch for maneuverability and are extra light. Okay, but you have to remember that there's no such thing as the perfect wader.

ANGLER'S WORLD BOOT CHAINS

A convenience for the angler taking off through rough waters. Made from galvanized steel in a harness of stretchy rubber. They pull over your shoes or boots for added traction on slippery things like moss. They weigh under 6 ounces and can be a real lifesaver.

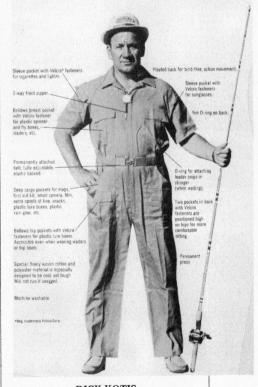

Sleeve pocket with Velcro* fasteners for cigarettes and lighter.

2-way front zipper.

Bellows breast pocket with Velcro fastener for plastic spinner and fly boxes, leaders, etc.

Permanently attached belt, fully adjustable, elastic backed.

Deep cargo pockets for maps, first aid kit, small camera, film, extra spools of line, snack, plastic lure boxes, plastic rain gear, etc.

Bellows hip pockets with Velcro fasteners for plastic lure boxes. Accessible even when wearing waders or hip boots.

Special, finely woven cotton and polyester material is especially designed to be cool, yet tough. Will not run if snagged.

Machine washable.

*Reg. trademark Velcro Corp.

Pleated back for bind-free, action movement.

Sleeve pocket with Velcro fasteners for sunglasses.

Net D-ring on back.

D-ring for attaching leader snips or stringer (when wading).

Two pockets in back with Velcro fasteners are positioned high on hips for more comfortable fitting.

Permanent press

DICK KOTIS ALL POCKET FISHING SUIT

Pockets galore, enough for any kind of fishing. Lots of this stuff has hit the market recently because of the fishing tournament boom, but the Kotis suit remains one of the best. A blend of cotton and polyester in a deep green color.

RETCO WADING SHOES

WADER CLIPS

Wader clips are a very handy way of taking good care of your waders or hip boots after use. You simply hang them downward, which provides for good circulation of air. Helps keep them in working shape.

DUNHAM SNAKE BOOTS

D-BOONE MINK OIL

Water takes a terrific toll on your leather products if you don't protect them. Old-fashioned mink oil can handle those problems, including salt stain. It waterproofs and conditions anything that once mooed.

CONVERSE FELT SOLE REPLACEMENT KIT

For those who want to replace their worn-out felt or put on felt for the first time, Converse offers such a thing. The kit includes soling material, a tube of cement and a scraper to rough up the bottom of your boots. Makes things seem a lot firmer.

THE LAST HATCH
A FISHING MYSTERY
HARMON HENKIN

(continued from page 375)

Payne, generally considered the best rod maker ever. In good used condition, like this one, they were worth more than $500. Like almost all fly anglers, Paul had always wanted to own one. He got his vest and they walked out the door, leaving a dejected Julie to curl up on the sofa in the den with a copy of *National Geographic*.

As they strolled down the path, Sid flicked Paul's Winston rod.

"You still like this bamboo stuff, don't you?"

"Nothing like it."

"I'll take my Fenwick glass any time. You don't have to worry about them falling apart and costing a fortune to repair. God, you can't find a decent bamboo rod for less than $300 anymore. You can buy a half dozen good glass rods for that."

"That's true, but bamboo is more sensitive."

"Just like me."

They put their outfits together where an old log crossed the stream underwater — a likely hiding place for trout.

"What are you going to fish with?" Sid asked.

Paul tied on a No. 20 light Cahill that passably imitated the light-colored mayflies that were emerging from the surface of the creek. His 1-pound test nylon tippet gave little room for error in playing or landing a fish. But anything heavier on the crystalline water would have been like a hawser holding a newt.

Sid tied on a Quill Gordon, that all-American pattern named after its creator. They roamed the bank casting at rising fish, trying to put their flies inches from the snouts of feeding trout, as they do on England's chalkstreams. But because of the abundance of natural flies, the phonies were received like wax fruit in the Garden of Eden.

There was an amazing variety of hatches. The simultaneous emergence of many kinds of insects is a hallmark of the spring creek, which are unlike rivers, where only one hatch at a time occurs and sometimes none at all. The problem facing anglers is to figure what pattern among a myriad of possibilities would interest a fish, a fickle matter of taste that can change in minutes.

Paul had a couple of strikes from fish so small and audacious that he shook them off his hook. He was more interested in the graceful arc of the Payne rod than in troutettes.

(continued on page 390)

TAKE THE PLUNGE: OPTICS ADD THAT EXTRA FLAVOR

By Harmon Henkin

Binoculars, cameras, magnifying glasses and other lensy things aren't what many anglers consider basic accessories but they can turn out to be the spice that gives a fishing trip that extra flavor.

How many times have you wished you could bring back some sort of record of that special vacation? Or needed something to get that blue heron into focus? Or wanted to magnify a tiny mayfly to determine its exact coloration?

Weight or bulk is no longer an excuse for not packing some optics. Modern photographic equipment and roof prisms have made it a game of ounces. Tiny, exquisite magnifying glasses can be had from suppliers like Orvis or Hardy as well as from entomological supply houses.

In cameras, 35mm is the best film size because of the variety available. But the inexpensive Kodak Instamatics work well too, especially those 110 models with glass rather than plastic lenses. Unless you have a Nikonos or a camera with full housings, don't dunk your camera. It's very expensive to get them dried out. Keep your camera in a plastic lock-top bag if you are susceptible to dunkings or spillings. They are better protection, especially around salt water, than a mere camera case, which offers only knock protection.

The advice about plastic bags holds true with binoculars too. Tiny roof-prism

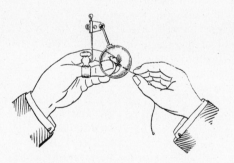

Hardy Brothers sold this magnifier designed to help those "with defective sight" thread a leader through the eye of a hook. It sold between 1910 and 1919 for $6.

models like the Nikons work very well and don't interfere with your activities. Roof prisms can be had for less than $60 if you're in the right place at the right time.

Though the old-fashioned "opera glasses" are about the same size, they don't have the roof-prisms for light gathering ability, an important optical development.

Magnifying lenses of intermediate power are the most useful for the angler examining the stomach contents of a trout. The type of casing isn't as important as the glass itself, and most times just the lens itself is enough, even the variety store variety.

So take the plunge. For the price of that extra fishing outfit you were going to splurge on you can have accessories that'll make your present equipment and trips more fun.

"Catching an occasional fish is to the enjoy-joyment of trout fishing what encountering an occasional oyster is to the enjoyment of oyster stew: gratifying, yes, but far from everything."
ROBERT TRAVER

A FEW OF MY FAVORITE CAMERAS

By Harley Hettick

Photography and the great outdoors, photography and fishing are, at best, compromises. When the hatch is on and the trout are moving, I find it difficult to get very serious about photography. More often than not a fly rod materializes in my hand instead of my Nikon. After working 40 hours a week as soft photographer for a small Montana daily newspaper, I am tempted to leave the cameras at home. But if I do, I inevitably see the photo of a lifetime.

If, after long and very deliberate consideration, I come to the conclusion that my main object in the great outdoors is photography, I pack all the equipment I feel will be necessary to do the job. But if I decide my main object is fishing, I pack only my trusty Nikonos or possibly my small pocket Rollei T. Any additional weight or bulk becomes an unnecessary

burden that takes a lot of the fun out of my fishing.

The Nikonos is the perfect camera for boat fishing, deep wading and the congenital klutz. I once lost some very fine Nikons in a rafting accident, but my Nikonos came through unscathed.

Both the Nikonos and the Rollei T use 35mm film and cast a pretty fine negative. With the Nikonos you will have to carry a small hand meter. The Rollei T has a fine meter built right into the camera which can handle most situations. If you are uncertain of your exposure, bracket the hell out of it. If the photo is worth taking at all, it's worth some film.

If you feel you want consistently super photos you will probably go to the heavy stuff. This to me means my Nikon, and I have five or six bodies and nine lenses. The latest Nikon F2 model is a little heavier than most

ROLLEI T

35mm cameras, but it is certainly well made.

If you are just starting outdoor photography you may want to consider the Olympus OM system. These cameras are quite a bit lighter and smaller than Nikons or Leicas and feature some pretty fair optics. Their price will make a believer out of you if their weight and size don't.

The Leicaflex camera system is that company's answer to Nikon. Although they are super expensive and a little bulky, they are beautifully engineered and deliver one hell of a fine negative. Leica also offers a wide selection of lenses and many other accessories.

For general outdoor work I recommend the Leica CL, a fine lightweight camera which offers 28mm, 40mm, 50mm

and 90mm lenses, plus a very accurate CDS through-the-lens meter. All the viewer has to do is look through the view finder and all the exposure options are right in front of his or her eyes.

But remember, no meter is perfect. Keep track of your shots, writing down exposure time and aperture size for each photograph, so you can analyze your results. Test your meter continually. Make sure you know what it does under various conditions. Become as familiar with your photo eye as you are with your shotgun or fly rod. When you get the fumbling and bumbling out of your photo shooting, the fun and joy of the great outdoors will be something you can take home with you in the form of fine photos.

NIKONOS

EMOSKOP

FOSTER GRANT GLASSES

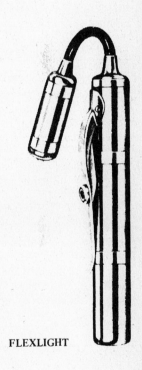

FLEXLIGHT

top of the line

BROOKSTONE EMOSKOP. Brookstone offers a very handy gadget for the angler on outings. The Emoskop functions as a 3-power telescope or a magnifier ranging from 3X to 30X. It's only 2¼ inches long and 4 ounces light. Just re-arrange the three elements to get the desired power to zoom in on anything from a bird to that tiny mayfly you want to imitate.

EDDIE BAUER POLARIZED SPORTS GLASSES. Eddie Bauer offers three ground-glass shades of polarizing sunglasses, essential if you spend much time looking at the water. There's a light grey for average conditions, tan for overcast days and dark grey for intense glare. Plastic frames molded over a spring wire core make this a well-made product.

CABELA'S TIE FOCAL. Having trouble focusing the old tired eyes? Get Cabela's tie focal, which clips onto your shirt or vest. It has a small battery-operated light and a magnifying glass to help you get that last lure or fly tied on before dark, when the big ones start cruising.

FLEXLIGHT. A well made flashlight that fits into your pocket has an extended head that can be bent in any direction. The off and on mechanism isn't the world's greatest, but it will put a beam of light where you want it while freeing your hands. An important accessory for anyone going out after dark.

FOSTER GRANT POLARIZED GLASSES. Those well-known sunglass people make a pair of polarized models to help anglers in their everlasting search for fish. Model 6252 fits over prescription sunglasses or can be worn by themselves. Available

WHAT WE LOOKED FOR IN QUALITY

Optics are available today for almost any acitivity, but the angler needs specialized products. They have to be light, water-resistant and well-made to be hauled around on a boat or along a streamside.

FLIP-AWAY LOUPE

A nice accessory for the serious hatch-matcher is this 3X loupe, which clips to your eyeglasses or shades and will flip out of the way when not needed. Perfect for drawing a color and form bead on those tiny midges or threading a 7X leader through a No. 22 fly as dark approaches. Gold-plated nickel-silver. A small joy available from Angler's World.

"But as time passes perhaps the gravest threat to inland fishing of all kinds is from the water polluters and contaminators, who come in all shapes and sizes to fit all occasions."
ROBERT TRAVER

top of the line

in brown or grey lenses. Model 6254 is available in the same colors but offers more complete glare protection with a topside cover and a cheek-snuggling design.

MAGNA SIGHTER. Makes you look like a spaceman. The Magna Sighter is a real help to the fly tyer who needs extra help. Four models of these optical glass goggles with 1¾-, 2¼-, 2¾- and 3½-power magnifications are available. Now you can get on those midges.

VENIARD MAGNIFIER. England's Veniard fly tying supply outfit has a 3-inch glass lens that attaches onto your vise for magnifying those small things you want to tie. The focal length is adjustable through a 5-inch range and the whole thing can be turned to any angle.

ZEISS CENTER FOCUS. These German-made 8 x 20 mini-binoculars are one of the very best around. They are well worth the money for the very serious backpacker, but a bit steep for the rest of us mortals.

VENIARD MAGNIFIER

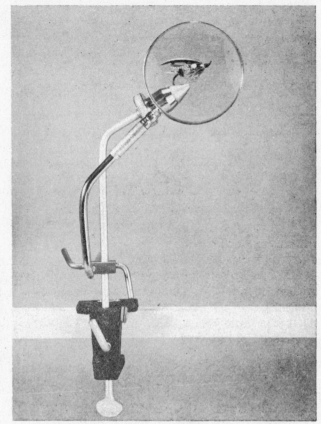

MAGNA SIGHTER

ZEISS CENTER FOCUS

LUXO MAGNIFYING LAMP

A really deluxe accessory for the hard-core fly tyer. It's a circular lamp surrounding a 5-inch ground-glass magnifier. It turns in any direction. The fluorescent light it shines on your vise won't heat things up. Just clamp it onto your bench and get busy. Available from Fly Fisherman's Bookcase.

BROILED STEELHEAD

Fish steaks, about 3/4-inch thick
2 T onion, finely chopped
2 T butter
salt and pepper, to taste
1/4 to 1/2 t marjoram
parsley

After chopping the onion, cream it with about 2 T butter. Add the salt, pepper and marjoram. Spread part of this mixture on the steaks; broil at 375 degrees on a greased broiler pan. When browned, turn the steaks, spread other side with the mixture and broil until done. (It will take about 5 minutes per side, depending on thickness of the steak.) Garnish with parsley and serve.

This quick, easy recipe works well with salmon, too. — *Idaho Wildlife Reivew.*

Leica CL & Nikon Nikonos

Depending on how intimate you are with water you might want to get either a Leica CL or a Nikon Nikonos. Each has its advantages and they're both ultimate joys.

Both models are extremely portable and use 35-mm film, which is extremely versatile. This cassette-loaded film can be bought at various sensitivities and speeds in black and white or color. And it's available anywhere in the world — the real advantage.

Unlike the glamorous Hasselblads and Nikons, the Nikonos and Leica CL are very easy to haul around and both are ruggedly constructed to withstand shaking boats or back country hikes.

Lenses for the two are limited, though the CL will take many of the regular Leica lenses, which are generally considered to be the finest ever made. The CL normally comes with a very lightweight 40-mm lens; a matching 90-mm semi-telephoto is also available.

The big advantage of the Nikonos is that it's totally waterproof. You can even take it underwater with nothing but the case it comes with. If you're fishing and the lens gets dirty, just dunk it.

Dials and levers for the Nikonos are oversized for ease of handling in cold weather or underwater. It doesn't have a rangefinder or a built-in light meter like the CL but that's a minor irritation once you get used to a particular film.

Trinovid Binoculars

Though hard-pressed by the larger and more rugged Zeiss-Ikons, Leica's German-made Trinovids are the best binoculars around.

Available in all the popular powers, Trinovids have a tremendous light-gathering capability and they are also very, very compact. You can put them in your vest for bird watching while fishing mountain streams or in your tackle box for checking out the action on the Florida Keys.

Binoculars can be a very useful angling accessory; breathest there an angler with soul so dead that he's never wished to have a pair handy? At any rate, Trinovids are the best all-around lenses, although you might want to consider a bulkier Zeiss-Ikon, which looks as if it was ripped off a German tank, if you're going to hang your binoculars in one place most of the time.

NICHOLL BROTHERS FLASHLIGHTS

Nicholl Brothers' line of flashlights are a long lasting, sturdy group in a variety of sizes that work well for fishing at night or for general use around the camp.

BURKE'S EYEGLASS SNUGGLER

Just the thing for the bespectacled angler. They hold your glasses even if you take a spill or dip. Can be a trip-saver.

390

"The Walleye is everyman's fish."
PARKER BAUER

OPTICS

THE LAST HATCH

A FISHING MYSTERY
HARMON HENKIN

GAMEFISH: WALLEYE

NAMES
Walleye pike, pike perch, pike, jack salmon, walleye perch, yellow pickerel, blue pickerel, dore. *(Stizostedion vitreum)*

DISTRIBUTION
The walleye is found throughout Canada, from the Great Slave Lake to Labrador, and down to the Great Lakes region and south to Tennessee and Alabama. It has also been widely stocked throughout the states except for the Deep South and the Far West.

DESCRIPTION
The walleye is a member of the pike family and is a robust fish with an ample set of canine teeth. It is olive green or brown-yellow on the back with lighter sides. The sides are marked with dark, patternless mottlings. Its large, glassy, opaque eye gives the fish its name. At the lower end of its dorsal fin membrane there is a black blotch.

SIZE
The average size of the walleye is about 2 to 5 pounds. A fish of 5 pounds and up is considered a large catch.

HABITAT
The walleye prefers clear, cold waters in northern climates. They are found in both large lakes and rivers with gravel or sandy bottoms and tend to seek out deep holes and areas close to rocky ledges. The walleye spends most of its time in very deep water.

FEEDING HABITS
The walleye is a voracious feeder that eats all types of small fish. It will also feed on crustaceans and insects. At night, they can be found feeding in the shallows. They are a school fish that can often be caught in the worst of weather conditions.

BEST FEEDING TEMPERATURE
Between 55 and 70°.

TACKLE
When the walleye is deep, light or medium trolling rigs equipped with baitcasting rods and reels work well but when it's near the surface light tackle does the job. It likes small plugs or spoons, jigs and live minnows.

(continued from page 384)

"It's a good thing I tie my own flies," Sid called from downstream. "I'd hate to spend 85 cents apiece on these guppies. Where are the real fish?"

"Probably laughing at us."

"It'd be great if there was a huge hatch on like the other day when Halford was fishing here. Those big yellow mayflies are beautiful."

As if on command, one of the last Isonychia of the season fluttered its gossamer wings and disappeared over the top of a tree.

"Imagine all those luscious beauties swarming this place Thursday. And I had to spend the day chasing down speeders from Iowa. A cop's life ain't easy."

"What?"

"I caught some speeders going 35. No big deal. I didn't beat them or anything. And I got wet standing in the rain."

"Run through that first bit again, Sid."

"I gave some people from Iowa a ticket?"

"And?"

"And, uh, I got wet and didn't fish?"

Paul doubled his fist and brought it down on an imaginary table. "God! I should have known! There was no *Isonychia* hatch Thursday."

Sid stopped in mid-cast and the line fell on him in a heap. "What do you mean?"

"I was in Helena Thursday. Indoors all day. But it was cloudy and rainy here?"

"Yeah. Very overcast. So what?"

"Simple. That species of mayfly doesn't hatch on rainy days. Only when the sun is out. Rain would knock them into the water. It's a species adaptation mechanism. No hatch on Thursday."

"Halford lied a lot about what he caught. We all do that. But why would he lie about what hatch he was fishing?"

Paul began putting up his outfit as the sun dropped behind the highest hills.

"He probably wasn't fishing."

"But why didn't he want anyone to know he wasn't fishing?"

"That's another key to this business."

Sid reluctantly drew back the line in his guides and tugged at the ferrules lightly.

(continued on page 392)

"No art, worthy of the name, was ever learned without perseverance and unceasing practice."
WILLIAM BAYARD STURGIS, *Fly Tying*

SOURCEBOOKS 391

Catalogs: you can't get skunked

By Harmon Henkin

Some anglers do their best fishing in catalogs. As long as you have money you can't get skunked.

Catalogs have always been an integral part of American angling. Only the names of the products and the language of the boasts have changed. A hundred years ago manufacturers were claiming that "the Devon is the most deadly of all spinning baits," and today companies make the same sort of claim for rubber worms. History repeats itself, first as tragedy then as farce!

Fishing remains basically a fair-weather sport that allows plenty of space for dreaming. As cannon fodder for our fantasies, catalogs function best. For we are no longer a rural people who depend on Sears Roebuck for our tackle.

Catalogs are able to offer gear that's often more interesting than the stuff in our local tackle shops simply because they're more centralized. A good mail-order place spends almost its entire advertising budget on its catalog, which must be a minor masterpiece if the business is to succeed. Though catalogs are geared for various economic levels — taste, they call it — they also need to be varied and offer at least a smidgin of something for everyone.

It isn't enough for a catalog to merely dress up a product with flowery language. It should contain enough descriptive information to let the angler make at least minimal comparisons between, say, Zebco's and Daiwa's open-faced spinning reels.

It is, however, the unique products that give the best of the catalogs their flavor. Bassmaster, Orvis and Herter, most especially, offer lots of things not obtainable anywhere else. Sure, the claims will be extravagant but the claims for all commodities in an advertising-dominated culture are extravagant.

That doesn't detract from the pleasure of browsing, waiting for those lists of mid-year bargains from the companies and dreaming of the big one that one day won't get away.

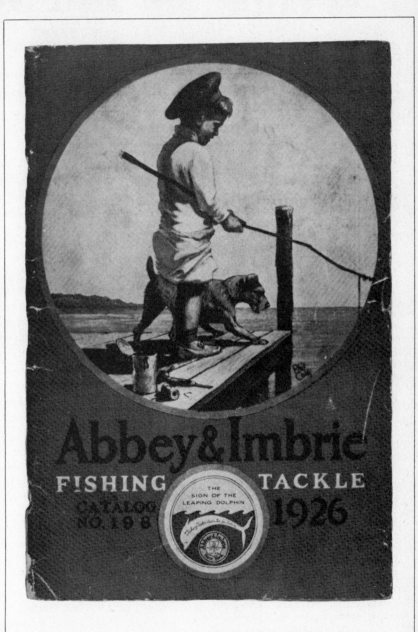

Abbey & Imbrie's 1926 tackle offerings featured the "Glowbody Minnow," a clear plastic trolling lure filled with a luminous chemical. It was developed to help celebrate the New York company's 100th birthday.

You gotta have faith

By Harmon Henkin

It was the kind of hangover that only a brain transplant could help.

But being the merciless fellows that we were, Pete and I loaded Alvin into the rear of the decrepit old English Ford and headed out from Baltimore towards the small bass and panfish lake — our Sunday ritual.

Even our coffee layover on the far side of Chesapeake Bay Bridge did nothing to create a humanoid condition in the semi-catatonic Alvin, whom any reasonable doctor would have certified dead. Despite a periodic moan from the back seat, Pete and I engaged in a lively discussion of our angling game plans. We systematically went through a roundup of new spin tackle gleaned from incessant visits to local sporting goods stores and studious examinations of catalogs that would have made the efforts of medieval monks seem superficial.

However, there was another reason for our high spirits that early morning. If the uncrowned king wasn't really dead, at least he was in no condition to defend his crown against usurpers. The night's heavy carousing had taken its troll and Alvin was very vulnerable to a palace revolt. An unspoken rivalry had grown up in the years we had fished together, a competition he always won. Alvin was, without doubt, the most consistently successful fisherman we had ever met. I wouldn't have taken odds on his getting skunked in a toilet bowl. He methodically and magically took bass, bluegills, chain pickerel and crappie from the string of lakes and ponds stretching from Easton to Pocomoke, Maryland — despite such incidentals as weather, water conditions and even fish population.

There was still a distinct chill in the air from a summer storm rolling in off the Chesapeake Bay as we reached the

(continued on page 397)

THE LAST HATCH
A FISHING MYSTERY
HARMON HENKIN

(continued from page 390)

"Here. You take this stuff apart. I don't want to hurt it."

Paul took down his rod with automatic precision, then held the two sections in his hands.

"Halford did his journal year after year. It told him what would be hatching when. A quick glance at the entries for July 20 last year and the years before that would show him, I think, that it was usually a good day for the Isonychia hatch. It doesn't rain much here this time of year."

They began walking back to the house.

"What does that have to do with anything?"

"Simple. If Halford was going to falsify his journal so that someone wouldn't know where he really was he would use his journal to cover his tracks. It was Halford's diary, only it was almost a public document since he left it open on the desk all the time."

"But he must have known that if the weather was bad, there wouldn't be a hatch."

"Yeah, that's a harder one to figure out."

The main room was empty except for Julie, who was curled up on the couch asleep with a copy of Halford's atrocious *Over the Trees, Into the River* draped across her face.

"That's the only socially redeeming value of a Halford novel," Sid muttered.

Paul was motioning for the sheriff at the desk and pointing with the other hand at the journal. "There are two ways we can look at this, Sid. We can figure out first who was likely to check over the journal."

Sid picked up on the thread. "Dun, probably out of the habit of calculating his boss' output. Hewitt, because he did some fishing and would naturally be attracted to the journal. And Schielbacht, checking out the competition. Nobody else."

"Or we can look at it another way," Paul said. "Who would have the sense to pick out an obvious lie in the journal? Probably not Dun. He would have learned a basic bit of fishing lore from working for Halford but since he didn't fish he wouldn't know the fine points."

"That leaves us Schielbacht and Hewitt."

"They both had good motives."

"But what's Hewitt's. He seems awfully aloof from all this."

"His wife."

(continued on page 405)

The inward gifts of the angler

Vi[ator]. Why then, I pray you, what gifts must he have that shall be of your company?

Pi[scator]. 1. He must have faith, believing that there is fish where he cometh to angle. 2. He must have hope that they will bite. 3. Love to the owner of the game. 4. Also patience, if they will not bite, or any mishap come by losing of the fish, hook, or otherwise. 5. Humility to stoop, if need be to kneel or lie down on his belly, as you did today. 6. Fortitude, with manly courage, to deal with the biggest that cometh. 7. Knowledge adjoined to wisdom, to devise all manner of ways how to make them bite and to find the fault. 8. Liberality in feeding of them. 9. A content mind with a sufficient mess, yea, and though you go home without. 10. Also he must use prayer, knowing that it is God that doth bring both fowl to the net and fish to the bait. 11. Fasting he may not be offended withal, but acquaint himself with it, if it be from morning until night, to abide and seek for the bite. 12. Also he must do alms deeds; that is to say, if he meet a sickly poor body or doth know any such in the parish that would be glad of a few fishes to make a little broth withal (as often times is desired of sick persons), then he may not stick to send them some or altogether. And if he have none, yet with all diligence that may be [he] try with his angle to get some for the diseased person. 13. The last point of all the inward gifts that doth belong to an angler, is memory, that is, that he forget nothing at home when he setteth out, nor anything behind him at his return.

The Arte of Angling (1577).
Anonymous.

Ordering tackle by mail: some rules

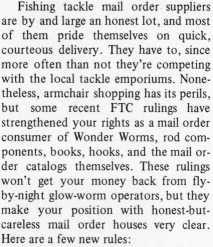

Fishing tackle mail order suppliers are by and large an honest lot, and most of them pride themselves on quick, courteous delivery. They have to, since more often than not they're competing with the local tackle emporiums. Nonetheless, armchair shopping has its perils, but some recent FTC rulings have strengthened your rights as a mail order consumer of Wonder Worms, rod components, books, hooks, and the mail order catalogs themselves. These rulings won't get your money back from fly-by-night glow-worm operators, but they make your position with honest-but-careless mail order houses very clear. Here are a few new rules:

Mail order firms must *ship* (not deliver) merchandise within 30 days of receiving your order; if, however, the firm has advertised "delivery within a week," or some other promise, it must ship within that pledged time.

If the seller cannot ship within 30 days of the stated shipping date, it must notify you and give you the option of cancelling and receiving a full refund within 7 days of your reply. This option must be made free, in the form of a postage-paid envelope or postcard. Silence is interpreted as consent to the delay.

If the delay is more than an additional 30 days after the original time period, the firm *must* return your money, unless you consent to the extra delay.

There are several significant exceptions to this ruling: C.O.D. orders, services (such as repairs) and serial publications (magazines), if the initial copy has been sent and received. Specific complaints are handled by your postal authorities.

GAMEFISH: FRESHWATER DRUM

NAMES
Sheepshead, grey bass, white perch, jewelhead, gaspergou, grunter. *(Aplodinotus grunniens)*

DISTRIBUTION
The freshwater drum ranges from Canada south to the Gulf states. It is found in Mexico, the Great Lakes region and Louisiana and Texas.

DESCRIPTION
The freshwater drum is grey or silver on the back with silver sides and a white belly. The body is covered with large scales and the back has a humped appearance. A lateral line runs from the gill covers to the tail. The freshwater drum is also one of the few fish capable of making noise. It does this by contracting abdominal muscles against the air bladder.

SIZE
This fish has been known to reach weights of up to 50 pounds, but the average is around 1 to 3 pounds.

HABITAT
Large lakes and rivers are the preferred environments of the freshwater drum. It favors muddy or silty bottoms and modest depths. In the spring and summer, they gather in large numbers below dams.

FEEDING HABITS
The freshwater drum feeds primarily on mollusks, which it shells with its lower throat teeth. It also feeds on small baitfish, crayfish and crustaceans. These fish feed primarily at night and travel in schools.

top of the line

BROOKSTONE. Brookstone in Peterborough, New Hampshire, doesn't offer items of direct interest to the angler but lots of things of indirect value. Its specialty is hard-to-find tools and it has all kinds of glues, gadgets, specialized equipment and other goodies that the do-it-your-selfer and tackle-fixer can use.

FLY FISHERMAN'S BOOK-CASE. The Fly Fisherman's Book-case has come a long way quickly. Along with probably the best selection of books on the sport (usually discounted), Sam Melner and Eric Leiser also market rods, reels, lines, an excellent selection of flies and the other accessories that make an angler's life better. They also have some outstanding fly tying gear, some not available elsewhere. A must catalog for the serious fly fisher.

HERTER'S. The Herter's catalog is the sourcebook of all sourcebooks. Though some disgruntled fly caster types might not like the grade of all its equipment, the catalog contains just about everything in the world described in a prose that is truly amazing. Herter's mostly makes its own stuff, which it sells reasonably, including some very strange books. They have clothing, hunting stuff, bows, all manner of fishing gear and on and on and on. You must not be without this one for reading as well as ordering.

LEONARD. This catalog, like little Topsey, has grown by leaps and bounds since Leonard was taken over by a New Jersey-based corporation. Resembling the style and approach of the Orvis has done wonders for its interior decoration. In the old days — before the late 60s — the tradition-bound William Mills emporium of

HERTER'S

Old World Craftsmanship   SINCE 1893   New World Production
MANUFACTURERS, IMPORTERS, EXPORTERS
THE AUTHENTIC WORLD SOURCE FOR FISHERMEN, HUNTERS, GUIDES, GUNSMITHS, TACKLEMAKERS, FOREST RANGERS, COMMERCIAL FISHERMEN, TRAPPERS, EXPLORERS, EXPEDITIONS, BACKPACKERS.

$1.00 $1.00

1976—CATALOG NO. 86

MAKERS OF CUSTOM FISHING TACKLE — MAKERS OF CUSTOM ARCHERY — MAKERS OF CUSTOM AMMUNITION RELOADING AND LOADING MACHINES — MAKERS OF DOWN SLEEPING BAGS — MAKERS OF DOWN GARMENTS — MAKERS OF BACKPACKERS PACKS — MAKERS OF SNOWMOBILES — MAKERS OF HUNTING DECOYS — MAKERS OF SHEFFIELD STEEL FISH HOOKS — MAKERS OF FIBERGLAS AND ALUMINUM BOATS — MAKERS OF CUSTOM GUNSTOCKS — MAKERS OF THE FINEST QUALITY BINOCULARS AND TELESCOPE SIGHTS — MAKERS OF CLAY TARGETS — MAKERS OF THE FINEST SURVIVAL AND CAMPING EQUIPMENT — MAKERS OF GAME CALLS — MAKERS OF RIFLES — MAKERS OF VENTILATED SHOTGUN RIBS — MAKERS OF TRAIL MOTORCYCLES — MAKERS OF SONAR EQUIPMENT — MAKERS OF JEWELRY

HERTER'S INC.,

MITCHELL, SOUTH DAKOTA • WASECA, MINNESOTA • OLYMPIA, WASHINGTON
BEAVER DAM, WISCONSIN • GLENWOOD, MINNESOTA

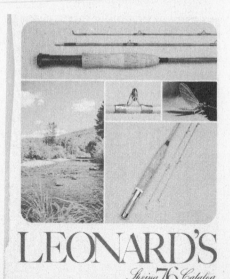

"The angler's true skill or knowledge is not measured by the
size of his quarry."
CHARLES WATERMAN

SOURCEBOOKS 395

top of the line

Park Avenue used to handle
Leonard's retail sales. The Mills catalog was a model of propriety, often
making Orvis seem like Herter's. But
today, when merchandising is the
name of the mail-order game,
Leonard is putting out a glossy
sourcebook that is also a must with
its now-limited line of cane rods,
glass and graphite. Lots of other
knick-knacks including a grand selection of flies. Leonard's Central Valley store also puts out lists of previously owned rods, reels and miscellaneous goodies that make for good
reading.

ORVIS. Orvis usually publishes
the dominant catalog of the fishing
season. Everyone should get it. The
advertising copy isn't abrasive and
the color pictures of the flies are simply great. It's a big catalog that
comes out a couple of times a year
with seasonal supplements. Along with
Orvis cane, glass and graphite rods it
features the CFO reels, every manner
of angling accessory (some not found
elsewhere), lots of clothing for
sporty and outdoorsy use and even
hunting gear. It was the first of the
uptown catalogs that started the fly
fishing renaissance during the 60s.

PAYNE. For their first catalog
since the revival the reborn Payne
Rod Company has chosen a cover
from one of the old Payne catalogs.
The 20-page booklet contains essays
from George LaBranche, John Alden
Knight and Edward Hewitt that also
appeared in the vintage catalogs
when Jim Payne was building a reputation as the best cane rod maker of
them all. Nostalgic format and illustrations of the new Paynes make this
a very nice little catalog and one
worth sending for even if you're not
going to mortgage the house for a

Kaufmann's
Streamborn Fly Shop
1976 Edition

rod. Has lines, reels and some other goodies as well as the standard Payne rods.

PEZON ET MICHEL. Like pretty pictures of cane rods? Then get ahold of the Pezon et Michel catalog. The French-made top-quality rods are now distributed by the Stoeger Arms folks. The catalog is a beautifully done, full-color, 25-page booklet that puts most American catalogs to shame. Besides illustrations of mostly parabolic rods, it also has angling scenes that are knockouts. Get one if you can.

RANDALL KAUFMANN'S. Randall Kaufmann's Streamborn Fly Shop has rapidly become one of the best sources on the West Coast for fly fishing gear and his catalog is very complete. Has everything from super grizzly necks, steelhead flies, Kaufmann's own nymph patterns, rods, reels and other gear for taking on the big western waters. Not as snobby as some outfits and a first place the westerner or someone heading out for a vacation should look.

RANGELEY REGION SPORTS SHOP. Another long-time outfit that produces a downhome catalog from its Maine headquarters in what was once the brook trout capital of America. There are lots of fly tying things, fly tying boxes and good quality glass and graphite rods. It has everything the fly angler needs, unless his tastes have become jaded.

THOMAS & THOMAS ROD- MAKERS. This relative newcomer to the cane rodmaking market offers a very large selection of models. It recently merged with New Jersey's Len Codella, who handles second-hand cane rods and a very, very large as-

top of the line

sortment of fly fishing accessories. Codella had quietly become the producer of perhaps the most interesting catalog for hard-core fly casters with lots of quality items as well as more pedestrian ones for beginners or those few people who consider food more important than rods and reels. Everything you'll need and lots more you don't need but will buy anyway.

DERMOT WILSON. Old England might not be what it once was but Britisher Dermot Wilson has a very complete tackle catalog. The real buys are in the area of clothes with that distinctive English Touch, flies, Pezon et Michel rods from France and those long rods favored by the British. Best to write first to find out exchange rates, customs and postage, but Wilson's Orvis Shop certainly is a reputable outfit and one that a good many Americans would enjoy dealing with.

Fly Fisherman's Bookcase and Tackle Service

SPRING 1976

WELCOME To THE FLY FISHERMAN'S BOOKCASE
Doug Swisher

A CHOICE OF TACKLE 1976

Dermot Wilson

NETHER WALLOP MILL

You gotta have faith

(continued from page 392)

picturesque pond near Easton. We turned to see Alvin lost in a drugged sleep. It took a massive amount of yelling and shaking to even arouse him slightly. But we didn't want to win by default.

We pulled him out of the car and dressed him in his old vest stuffed with tackle consisting of 1/8 ounce Abu-Reflex spinners, some small Mepps, a Hula Popper in case the bass were shopping on top, scads of pinheads, small homemade leadhead jigs with flared marabou and a Hawaiian Wiggler — which had never been used in man's memory. He staggered the 100 yards to the nearest bank with the enthusiasm of someone walking the last mile. As usual, his spinning outfit was assembled and ready for an action that seemed unlikely.

Pete immediately put his game plan into action and began plumbing the shallow depths with a rubber worm. I used a Panther Martin. Alvin's eyes were closed, his head pointed down.

But there was something about the gentle plops and splashes of our lures hitting the ruffled surface of the water that sparked a primordial reflex in Alvin. He began casting a 1/32 ounce yellow pinhead. He took a crappie. Then another one. Then another one. Pete eyed this with increasing fury from the bank. He began to change lures. Every few casts Alvin would connect with something, bring it ashore like an automatic fishing machine, unhook it blindly and throw it back.

Pete and I went through a repertoire of lures that included spinners, spoons,

(continued on next page)

You gotta have faith

(continued from preceding page)

subsurface plugs and even the then newly introduced Rappalas — the atom bomb of warm water species lures. Nothing.

Finally Pete could stand it no longer. He put on a yellow pinhead and tossed it out almost maniacally. The storm was getting closer. We didn't have much time. I put down my rod and sighed. But Pete was no quitter. But then he wasn't catching fish either.

Alvin continued taking fish in the 12-15-inch range. Pete kept on getting skunked. He drifted slyly closer and closer to Alvin's vantage point, which must have looked on the repository of all the lake's fishes. Pete began mimicking the distance Alvin cast. Nothing. He began duplicating the retrieve exactly. Nothing. Alvin still took fish. He could have been on Mars, as alert as he was to his surroundings.

Then Pete was within a few feet. I thought he was going to break his Garcia rod over Alvin's head. But he didn't. Alvin didn't notice the intrusion on his turf. He was oblivious.

Alvin would cast — plop. Pete would cast — plop. Their identical pinheads landed literally inches apart. Alvin would give the handle one turn. So would Pete. It was maddening. Alvin took fish. Pete didn't have a hit.

Then the rains came. Alvin didn't notice. When your world is all pain what's one more insult?

Pete to his credit waited till he was soaking before retreating to the car, where I was comfortably waiting. We both stared out at Alvin standing there in the downpour still flicking out the pinhead. Not out of common decency but from a fear that we would be arrested for negligent homicide, we went out and grabbed him and hauled him back to the Ford.

I began driving back to Baltimore. Alvin's eyes were closed. He hadn't said a word all morning. Pete just stared at him until he couldn't take it any longer. He crawled into the back seat and began shaking Alvin.

"All right, you bastard. Tell me. What did you have out there that I didn't."

Alvin clumsily cocked one eye open — quite a job — and blinked at Pete. "Faith."

That's all. Alvin had faith in his tackle. Pete didn't. That was the difference and the wisdom of it struck us immediately. And if you don't think that faith in your method of fishing is important — you got a long way to go in the sport.

And that's the truth.

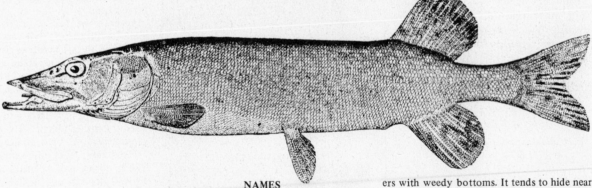

GAMEFISH: NORTHERN PIKE

NAMES
Northern, great northern, snake, jack, jackfish, pike. *(Esox lucius)*

DISTRIBUTION
The range of the northern pike extends from Alaska and Canada southward into the Mississippi Valley and the Great Lakes. It has been extensively stocked throughout the western states, most notably in Montana, New Mexico and Colorado.

DESCRIPTION
The coloring of the northern pike ranges from light green to dark olive on the back, shading into light green on the sides with a white belly. It is entirely covered with light, oval spots and the fins are marked with darker spots. It can be distinguished from the muskellunge by its scaled cheek.

SIZE
The average size of the northern pike is about 3 to 4 pounds, yet catches of up to 15 pounds are not considered unusual.

HABITAT
The northern pike prefers cold lakes and rivers with weedy bottoms. It tends to hide near submerged logs and thick aquatic growth where it can hide in wait for passing prey. It favors muddy waters and at times hides in deep holes.

FEEDING HABITS
The northern pike is considered a ferocious fish due to its aggressive feeding habits. It will eat almost anything that moves, from small fish to larger prey such as ducklings, mice and frogs. In the spring, the northern pike can be found in fairly shallow water.

BEST FEEDING TEMPERATURE
Between 60 and 75 degrees.

TACKLE
This toothsome fish comes in pretty decent sizes and requires some equalizing tackle. Medium and sometimes heavy baitcasting tackle with large spoons or live minnows at the end work well. In smaller northern lakes light spinning tackle with darting plugs can be the ticket and at times streamers from 9-foot fly rods do it.

HOW TO CHOOSE
A CONSERVATION GROUP
EXAMINE ITS NATIONAL PERFORMANCE

By Harmon Henkin

For many anglers, joining a conservation group is as routine as giving to charity. They hear a little about the group's lofty goals and fine ideals from a friend who's a member and decide to join or at least donate a little money. After the cash changes hands, they might go to the yearly banquet, featuring a fishing superstar making the circuit, or even attend a meeting or two. But that's about it.

Like any piece of angling equipment, some conservation groups work much better than others. And in order to judge the effectiveness of the organization you have to look at it nationwide.

For instance, some Montana anglers have mixed feelings about Trout Unlimited — considered one of the most effective groups by other anglers around the country. The hesitation is based on a contradiction: TU's stated goal is the perpetuation and betterment of trout fishing, yet some of its high-ranking members own large chunks of Montana real estate, which they heavily post. Now these non-joiners will admit that TU has done some minor wonders in stream rehabilitation all over the country but they resent the "No Trespassing" signs they see on their home rivers, oftentimes erected by wealthy non-residents who want to keep their fishing private.

The same sort of objection about wealth and privilege have been raised

(continued on page 410)

A DEBATE
BASS TOURNAMENTS: CASES FOR AND AGAINST

AGAINST:
They're a sad commentary on the way we live

FOR:
The future of fishing is brighter because of them

By Harmon Henkin

Fishing contests and extravaganzas have been a part of the angling scene for a long time but today's bass tournaments are as different from their predecessors as the rubber worm is from the real thing.

Older tournaments, whether the various Florida saltwater outings or those like the annual Livingston, Montana, trout competition on the Yellowstone River, are one-shot affairs, not really connected with day-in, day-out sport fishing. Sure, companies have always bragged when their tackle broke this or that world record. But there never was a direct connection between tackle manufacturers and the contests. Also, the competitiveness was isolated from the mainstream of angling.

The current bass tourneys are very much a product of the South, where they originated, and of the times in which we live — a blending of the

By Bob Cobb

In the once tranquil domain of freshwater fishing, nothing has ever stirred up bigger or more controversial waves than competitive bass fishing, the organized cast-for-cash sport.

In ten short years, organized tournament-style fishing has done more than anything else to create an entirely new breed of fisherman, a wondrously equipped, unprecedentedly aggressive and scientifically calibrated angler — the bass fishing pro.

Understandably, these guys make many onlookers jittery and other veteran bass anglers fume — especially when up to 250 of them compete against each other and gang up on the fish. The old-time bass-fishing enthusiast charges, "They're prostituting our noble sport!" The creek bank conservationists scream, "They're raping the lakes and ruining the streams."

These outcries have stirred rumblings

(continued on next page)

(continued on next page)

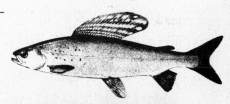

Advanced hucksterism and sports mania

(continued from preceding page)

virtues of good ol' boy professionalism in sports and advanced hucksterism. Professional competitive sports invaded the U.S. in the 1960s. It's a matter of speculation whether the losing war in Southeast Asia evoked sports professionalism as a replacement for the patriotism and volunteer spirit that characterized America's earlier military undertakings. Nonetheless as our Army grew more professional and tried to apply "scientific principles" so did our athletes, their managers and the industry.

Angling was pretty much untouched by this social phenomenon. Egos would get slightly bruised when the fisher was outsmarted by a bunch of creatures not much higher on the evolutionary scale than a cockroach, or outcaught by the dimwitted neighbor down the street, but it was a personal matter. Anglers were delighted that on weekends most people were glued to the TV set watching basket-foot-base-ball. More room on the lake.

Being a savvy fisher or hunter has always merited some esteem in this country, which has lived so long with wilderness and a frontier, but that respect was reserved for the rugged individual.

In the South, however, fishing and hunting were more directly related to social identity than in other areas of the country. The development of sonar devices, depth-finders, underwater temperature gauges and an increase in the effectiveness in bass fishing techniques, combined with Dixie sports mania to make the South an area where manufacturers and promoters began to sense money in fishing.

Tournaments offering prize money became a growing business. All the paraphernalia of professionalism grew, too.

(continued on next page)

The birth of the bass tournament

(continued from preceding page)

in some states that restrictive measures should be taken to limit organized tournament fishing. Others have suggested that a special user tax should be levied against tournament bassers.

Yet there is evidence that organization has been helpful to the sport, and its future is even brighter as the result of it. To see why, let's review the whole phenomenon — the evolution of this serene, contemplative sport, the emergence of a new life-style, that of the professional bass fisherman, and the direction competitive bass fishing is headed.

In the massive crowd of more than 50 million American fishermen, one individual has had as much responsibility as any in charting the changing course of bass fishing: Ray Wilson Scott, now a 42-year-old former insurance salesman from Montgomery, Alabama.

Since 1968, Scott's promotional and organizational abilities have united more than 265,000 bass anglers into the Bass Anglers Sportsman Society — B.A.S.S. Bass hunters are being enrolled at the rate of over 25,000 a year. They are organized into over 1200 chapters with members in all 50 U.S. states and in Canada, Mexico and far-flung locales such as Spain and Rhodesia.

Scott's basic publicity tool is the B.A.S.S. Tournament Trail. Clutching his bass angler's bible (Henshall's *Book of the Black Bass*) in one hand and a bullhorn in the other, he swept across the southern Bass Belt spreading the gospel.

A chain of events in the late 1950s laid the foundation for the sudden surge in bass fishing interest. The U.S. Army Engineers and state and city governments plunged into dam building. The lakes and reservoirs were constructed to harness the flood waters, to provide

(continued on next page)

GAMEFISH: ARCTIC GREYLING

NAMES
Alaska greyling, greyling, American greyling, sailfin greyling, poisson blue. *(Thymallus signifer)*

DISTRIBUTION
The Arctic greyling is found throughout Canada and Alaska. It is plentiful in the Yukon and the Northwest Territories.

DESCRIPTION
The Arctic greyling is quite similar to the Montana greyling although its dorsal fin is larger and its color brighter. The back is usually greyish blue in color, often with brown overtones, and the sides are silver-blue. The forepart of the body is marked with several small dark spots. The long dorsal fin is grey or blue with rows of blue or purplish red spots. Like the Montana greyling, the color of the fish varies according to location.

SIZE
The average size of the Arctic greyling is around 1 pound. A fish of 2 pounds is considered a good catch.

HABITAT
The Arctic greyling can only be found in clear, unpolluted mountain lakes and streams. It is abundant in high mountain lakes.

FEEDING HABITS
Like the Montana greyling, the Arctic greyling's diet consists primarily of insects and insect larvae. They often travel in schools near the surface.

TACKLE
Another fish made for fly fishing, the Arctic greyling will hit small and colorful flies just like the brookie, but sometimes is sought with ultra-light spinning gear and small spinners or, alas, bait. Non-discriminating and not much of a fighter but loads of fun.

A vile competition against nature

(continued from preceding page)

Certain types of equipment — baits, boats, rods and reels — became *de rigueur*. Tournament anglers began endorsing products. The jump suits became a fishing uniform. The language became technical. (Understanding the new bass fishing jargon became important for the feeling that one was an insider, privy to the secrets of the sport. If you didn't understand what a "blitz" was you couldn't be a real football fan; ditto for bass fishing and terms like "crank baits.")

Looking over the "brand new" carefully, it's obvious to many fishers who know the history of bass angling that they aren't discoveries but a mere re-introduction of ideas from the sport's past. The names of the top anglers have become bywords and endorsement by one of the top prizewinners is as important to a product as Jimmy Connor being seen at Wimbledon with his Wilson Racquet.

People have become enthused about the tournaments because the tactics and techniques developed by the pros seem to promise the individual angler more success — and that's an important word in this society. The real promise of angling has rarely been involved with nailing lots of big fish, but with fishing itself. That was the joy of the sport from its beginnings in the 15th Century.

The real danger in the commercialism of bass fishing and the contest mentality is not merely in its competitiveness. That would be a small thing to be concerned about if it were just another example of people competing against each other. It's more the fact that they are competing against nature at a time when that has become a vile and foolish thing to do.

(continued on next page)

The environment: What one person can do

There isn't much the individual can do in the environmental struggle. It takes lots of people joining the battle before any progress is made but there is something the individual angler can do and perhaps help his catch, too.

Get in the habit of maintaining a journal when you fish familiar nearby waters and carry along some litmus paper and a thermometer. Just keep a dated record of water temperature and PH of the stream or lake and compare it over the years.

In this way a sudden change in the acidity or alkalinity of the water or a temperature many degrees higher than the previous years on the same date will become immediately apparent. These rapid changes always indicate that something strange is going on and the strangeness can often be traced by fisheries people to unwanted "additives" in the form of pollutants.

The information will be useful to your angling if you also keep track of the temperature and PH balance of the water when you're most successful.

If you do notice water degradation, call your state fish and game department, write a letter to the editor or start hollering. It's a start anyway.   —H. H.

A modern fishing revolution

(continued from preceding page)

electric power and to help navigation, but their deep waters, rocky or wooded inlets were made to order for the large-mouth bass. Long classed in the minor leagues by the lordly trout and salmon societies, the Micropterus clan was soon to dominate angling interest. The South's discovery of her greatest native gamefish was soon to trigger a modern fishing revolution.

The first big splash heard around the angling world was made by Nick Creme, an Ohio bass fishing enthusiast who developed the first "rubber worms." Others are credited with improving these plastic fakes, but it now matters little who actually first came up with the idea. Suffice to say that before rubber worms, bass were considered finicky feeders an angler had to pursue at early light or dusk, or on those magic spring days or again in the fall when water temperatures and weather conditions moved the largemouths into the banks and shallows.

But suddenly the plastic worm made the largemouth more vulnerable. The weedless rigged, weighted plastic fakes gave the bass angler an effective deep-water, bottom-bumping weapon.

And, in Joplin, Missouri, Carl Lowrance was about to open his "little green box." His Fish Locator was to become the bassman's birddog — his underwater eyes that search out the largemouth's hideouts with much the same kind of sonar savvy used to track submarines.

The last, but hardly the least, development in the South's rising interest in bass fishing has been the design of a proper craft. The "bass boat" was designed to speed the angler quickly to his chosen "honey hole" and once there to shuttle him about with an electric bow-mounted trolling motor that left his hands free for casting and took the hard

(continued on page 404)

top of the line

Organizations

AMERICAN LEAGUE OF ANGLERS. The American League of Anglers has become an important group in a short time in the area of "direct political action." This means the organization, with Curt Gowdy as Chairman of the Board, directly tries to influence legislation involving the interests of anglers by lobbying legislators in Washington and at a local level. The names on its masthead range from I. W. Abel, president of the United Steelworkers, to Bing Crosby. It often acts as an activist front for other environmental groups which don't want to endanger their tax-exempt status by overt political action.

Current membership: still organizing. **National staff**: 4. **Address**: 810 18th St., N.W., Washington, D.C., 20006.

FEDERATION OF FLY FISHERMEN. The Federation of Fly Fishermen was formed when the Theodore Gordon Flyfishers of Manhattan, a Trout Unlimited Chapter, broke off and began contacting other independent fly fishing groups around the country. At times it and TU shamefully overlap, since their goals and many of their methods are the same. There have been some efforts in the past to merge FFF and TU but they haven't come to anything yet. It takes membership applications but the formation of a local group which has a full say in the national council is the most efficient way to proceed with FFF. Its magazine *The Flyfisher*, edited by Steve Raymond, has some excellent articles.

Current membership: 20,000. **Distribution**: 30 states. **National staff**: 4. **Address**: 519 Main St., El Segundo, CA 90245.

Tournaments are another commercial spectacle

(continued from preceding page)

Anyone who has even the vaguest ecological awareness knows that time is running out for the environment. Anglers are painfully aware of the degradation. It is not technology that is going to allow our species to survive but a change of consciousness about the inter-relationship of man and his natural world. That's the bottom line.

Now it's not going to cause grave damage for a bunch of men (women now, too) to get paid to haul a mess of fish from a lake and have pictures taken. The danger comes from the attitude it spawns. Despite the claims of tournament organizers that the lake's eco-system is not harmed by fishing tournaments, that the Bass Anglers Sportsman Society (B.A.S.S.) sponsors research into bass habitat and that pro anglers release many of their fish, there is real damage being done.

Kids are growing up thinking that fishing is a competitive sport; even worse, they are growing up with the attitude that an overpowered, gas-eating boat, fancy electronic gear and certain types of tackle are necessary to be happy outdoors. That's nonsense.

Manufacturers are delighted with a consumerism that foists off expensive products on people who can really ill-afford them, encouraged by tournament anglers who are delighted to be able to earn a living fishing. It's a cozy arrangement.

Fishing information has traditionally been part of a folklore passed on from generation to generation. Now it's owned by professionals who make thousands of dollars from their ability to organize highly technical equipment in such a

(continued on page 406)

Bass tournaments are now headlined

(continued from preceding page)

labor out of angling. Today's high-performance vessels are truly "fishing machines" with all the comfort, safety, luxury, convenience and fish-finding ability a bassman's budget can afford.

In the late 1960s there were not more than a small handful of boat builders, most notably Stemco Manufacturing Company of Longview, Texas, which made popular the "Skeeter" type hull, the prototype bass boat. But today the manufacturing of bass rigs is big business. It isn't unusual for a dedicated basser to sink $8000 in his fishing boat.

Then, while Ray Scott was prospecting for insurance clients in Jackson, Mississippi, he happened to read an article in a waiting room about a new bass fishing hot spot on the famed White River. The idea of an invitational bass tournament, similar to golf's play-for-pay events, hit him so hard he "sat straight up in bed and hollered."

The next morning, he drove 450 miles to Springdale, Arkansas, and Beaver Lake. "The lake was far enough away from home, if my idea failed I could slip back without anyone knowing about it," recalled Scott.

Local Chamber of Commerce officials listened politely, but said, "no thanks" to Scott's announced plans for the first All-American Invitational Bass Tournament. B.A.S.S. might have died on the spot, but a Springdale physician quietly advanced Scott $2000 to "put Beaver Lake on the fishing map."

With more than $1200 of the sum, Scott rented a WATS telephone line. Dialing tackle shops, marinas, boat docks and newspapers around the country, he compiled a list of top bass-catching experts who were well-known in their areas.

Remarkably, Scott lured 106 anglers from 13 states to plunk down $100

(continued on page 406)

From a cover story in *Not Man Apart,* the official publication of Friends of the Earth.

THE IZAAK WALTON LEAGUE OF AMERICA
INCORPORATED

top of the line

FRIENDS OF THE EARTH. This group began as a dissident offshoot of the Sierra Club a few years back in the heyday of environmental militancy and has withstood the test of time. It's a very sincere group headed by David Brower with chapters around the earth. It takes a classical ecological stance in all matters pertaining to the outdoors and has a very fine bi-weekly publication, *Not Man Apart.* A good one for those serious about preserving the environment.

Current membership: 20,000. **Distribution:** National and international. **National staff:** varies. **Address:** 529 Commercial, San Francisco, CA 94111.

THE INTERNATIONAL GAME FISH ASSOCIATION. Functions as a repository for marine records, a place to study such problems as the relationship between game and commercial fisheries, and as a gatherer of data on fish habits and habitat. A fighter for the sport fisher's rights. It puts out a pretty complete newsletter as well.

Current membership: 770. **Distribution:** National and international. **Address:** 3000 E. Las Olas Blvd., Fort Lauderdale, FA 33316.

IZAAK WALTON LEAGUE. With a name like that how can you go wrong? Well you can't if you're looking for a national conservation group that's constructed more like a traditional sportsmen's club than one of the modern ecology groups. The League involves itself with bread-and-butter pollution issues but doesn't usually get too offensive to the powers that be. Very good with wildlife and local problems.

Current membership: 50,000. **Distribution:** 36 states. **National staff:** 15. **Address:** Suite 806, 1800 North Kent St., Arlington, VA 22209.

"If you only carry a few fly patterns you will become very bored when skunked."
HARMON HENKIN

UNITED WE STAND 405

top of the line

NATIONAL WILDLIFE FEDER-ATION. A mammoth national organization that has plenty of weight to throw around. Located ideologically somewhere between a sportsman's and an environmental group, it gets concerned about gun legislation — which it's against — and endangered species — which it's for. Its magazine is an educational delight.

Current membership: 3,500,000. **Distribution:** National and international. **National staff:** 25 staff members, 324 employees. **Address:** 1412 16th St., N.W., Washington, D.C. 20036.

RESTORATION OF THE AT-LANTIC SALMON IN AMERICA, INC. This group is just what its name suggests. Richard Buck, a TU activist, heads the smallish organization that has some impressive names in its membership. It helps spread information about the noble fish now endangered from a variety of sources.

Current membership: 400. **Distribution:** U.S., England, France, China. **National staff:** 3. **Address:** Box 164, Hancock, N.H. 03449.

SIERRA CLUB. The Sierra Club became the most powerful conservation group in the country during the late 1960s when the ecology movement was really getting going. Now that things have quieted down it's not as much in the limelight. Started in San Francisco by John Muir and others in the late 19th Century, this group has always attracted some articulate and perceptive spokespeople in the big fights it has taken on. Sometimes at odds with hard-core "sportsmen" types, since it is not directly oriented towards hunting and fishing, it remains one of the

THE LAST HATCH
A FISHING MYSTERY
HARMON HENKIN

(continued from page 392)

"I thought she and Halford had a platonic relationship, as they said at Vassar."

"When someone says that, there's only one question: whose place are they using?"

"Yeah. Dun did say that Halford was in love."

"But Hewitt seemed blind to it."

"As Claudius said, 'Sometimes blindness is the only way to save the eyes' pain.'"

"Well, we know Schielbacht's motive. You go talk to him and I'll try Hewitt. Meet you back here."

Paul walked quietly through the room to avoid waking Julie and down the hall to Hewitt's room. He knocked quietly.

"Come in."

Hewitt was lounging in a chair by the lamp reading *Moby Dick*. A briar pipe rested in an ashtray. He held up the book. "This is my idea of a fishing story."

"Melville 35, Halford 0. Final score."

"No contest. These Hemingway clones have gotten awfully boring."

Paul sat in a wicker chair by the window. "What did you think of the development on the creek?"

"Another little trout stream down the drain like hundreds of others. A symptom of the times in which we live — or exist. But I can't be bothered or excited about the machinations of greedy people who want to destroy everything."

Paul puzzled over the meaning of that line.

"So you don't think the environment is worth fighting for?"

"The only things worth fighting for are those you can either win or draw a good fight from. If you spend your life battling the Halfords and Wormers there isn't time left to live. That's why I enjoy Ahab. That was a titanic struggle."

"The attitude of the rich."

"Which is precisely what I am. Should I pretend I'm a poor working man simply for your amusement?"

Paul changed the subject. There were no victories to be had here. "Do you fish for trout much?"

"Rarely anymore. I do so occasionally when I find myself trapped in a place like this. I just purchased one of those new graphite rods. It's the finest I've ever seen. It weighs just an ounce-and-a-half. Makes trout

(continued on page 409)

Tournament pay-offs are climbing

(continued from page 404)

each to help underwrite the cost of the event and furnish the $5000 in prizes. Anglers paired two to a boat competed against the clock, and using artificial lures attempted to catch the most pounds of black bass (largemouth, smallmouth or spotted Kentucky bass) within the legal daily limit. There were three fishing rounds.

When it was all over, Stan Sloan, a Nashville, Tennessee, cop, was the winner with 37 pounds, 8 ounces. As have many others, Sloan has since abandoned his former occupation, and is now a "bass pro" and a fishing tackle manufacturer.

B.A.S.S. tournaments have done for bass fishing what auto racing has done for the family driver. Safer, more comfortable, and more efficient bass boats have resulted from the tournament pros' demands for better rigs. Bass fishing skills and success techniques have accumulated among more anglers over the past seven years than at any period. B.A.S.S. pros like Bill Dance, Roland Martin, Tom Mann, who have become among the "names" in the sport, share their secrets.

Unlike other professional sports, bass fishing tournaments are a business oddity. "We don't conduct B.A.S.S. tournaments to make a profit," says Scott. "The majority of the entry fees are returned to the fishermen, or as in the past a portion donated to bass fishing research."

With a prize fund approaching $400,000 in awards in 1976, B.A.S.S. tournaments have certainly moved into big-time sports. Even more amazing than its success is the fact that bass tournament fishing hasn't been spawned by today's sports television dollar. It isn't considered a spectator sport, but some 1400 fans swamped some borrowed high school football bleachers in

(continued on next page)

Tournaments are doing real damage

(continued from page 403)

way as to catch more fish than their rivals.

It's become a sad commentary on the way we live our lives. We have to buy more, waste more and become technicians to enjoy even the basic pleasures of fishing. The sins of the fathers are always visited on the sons. The legacy of the commercial exploitation of angling with its competitiveness and aggression towards the natural world will become a sad legacy, long after spectators get bored with watching grown men and women battle a few pounds of bass and have moved on to another spectacle geared to selling products.

That's what our kids will have to live with.

best hopes the environmental movement has.

Current membership: 164,000. **Distribution:** National and international. **National staff:** 100. **Address:** 530 Bush St., San Francisco, CA 94108.

TROUT UNLIMITED. Trout Unlimited is the best-known of the postwar fish conservation groups. From relatively humble origins in Michigan it has become the most powerful and successful of all the groups engaged in the battle for trout habitat.

With chapters around the country, TU has garnered many of the biggest names in angling to aid in its local and national projects. It was very instrumental in thwarting the fiendish plans for Reichle Dam on Montana's Big Hole River and also with the Hat Creek project of stream renovation in California.

Though at times it has had a stridency that has turned some people off, it has been a very effective voice at times and deserves widespread support. It's best joined at a regional or local level where the good fights originate.

The TU Magazine is capable of some excellent stuff.

Current membership: 22,000. **Distribution:** National and international. **National staff:** 7. **Address:** 4260 E. Evans Ave., Denver, CO 80222.

THE WILDERNESS SOCIETY. The Society has been a very important voice in fighting for the establishment of untouched areas where fish, game and man can rejuvenate. It has a pretty good-sized national membership, which is sure to get stirred up on the right side of any battle over wilderness areas and it has a very high level of expertise as well.

Current Membership: 70,000. **Distribution:** National and international. **National staff:** 50. **Address:** 1901 Pennsylvania Avenue, N.W., Washington, D.C. 20006.

FENWICK FLY FISHING SCHOOLS

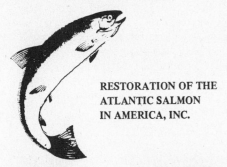

RESTORATION OF THE ATLANTIC SALMON IN AMERICA, INC.

GLADDING MUSEUM

topoftheline

Schools

FENWICK. Fenwick was one of the pioneers in the fly fishing school business with their pond and small building outside West Yellowstone, Montana. Now they're more sophisticated and operate schools throughout the country all season long. They have special schools for the advanced angler and the beginner. Instruction is geared for the locale, of course, and there are such regional specialties as courses on Pennsylvania spring creeks and Montana's big rivers. The Cal-Tech of fly-fishing schools.

LEONARD. For the past few seasons Leonard has been running what amounts to the Harvard of fly fishing schools at its Central Valley Store in New York. It lasts 20 weeks and is held one night a week. There are assignments, homework and textbooks, just like college. Students learn such requisites as fly tying and casting to more arcane aspects of the sport like stream etiquette, conservation and tackle. Not very expensive but lots of work for the serious angler. They also run weekend courses in June and July on the Beaverkill.

BUD LILLY. Bud Lilly's Trout Shop in West Yellowstone, Montana, sponsors an excellent fly fishing school. As well as offering the basic classes, Bud has pioneered a "ladies only" school taught by his daughter and also more informal schools consisting of days astream with so-called professional fly fishermen. A very knowledgeable outfit with plenty to offer anglers interested in any level of Western fishing.

Organization has been helpful to fishing

(continued from preceding page)

May 1976 at the $50,000 South Carolina Invitational at Santee-Cooper Lakes to watch the fish weigh-in.

There's no free ball night, ten-cent beer, or free baseball bats to promote a gate-paying crowd. The tournament pros pay their own way. A Texas basser on the road with his family estimated it cost $1000 for the week's stay at the 1976 Tennessee Invitational at Cordell Hull. The Texan finished 27th in the 201-man field gathered from 26 states. He collected a check for $205.

Competitive bass fishing hasn't reached the level of golf's huge, TV-packed purses, but the publicity afforded winners and heroes on the established B.A.S.S. Tournament Trail, does have its rewards. The pay-offs are climbing — up to $50,000 split among the top 35 anglers for a full 250-man limit contest. This compares to $5000 in Scott's first contest in 1967. The annual B.A.S.S. circuit features six qualifying tournaments, usually with a top prize of $14,000 — including $9000 cash and a deluxe Ranger bass boat rig worth $5000 — leading to the hook and line world finals of bass fishing — the BASS Masters Classic.

The BASS Classic is the "Super Bowl" for bass pros. It's the $50,000 pot of gold at the end of the season's rainbow. To earn a chance at casting for the $25,000 first prize, a Bassmaster must survive the "test of the best," and rank among the season's top 24 anglers over the span of six tournaments.

The Classic contenders are treated to an all-expense paid fishing junket for a week to a "mystery lake." The suspense is thick enough to be cut with a fillet knife — when Ray Scott finally reveals to the top pros their destination aboard an unannounced charter flight, usually in late October or November. The plot has unfolded in such romantic settings

(continued on next page)

Fishing habits and techniques have changed

(continued from preceding page)

as Lake Mead near Las Vegas, a posh but remote backwoods state lodge on Clark Hill, South Carolina, and a surprise landing at Currituck Sound on North Carolina's Outer Banks.

While Stan Sloan's first win in the All-American in 1967 led him into the tackle business, Tom Mann of Eufaula, Alabama, a fishing tackle manufacturer, has parlayed his tournament success into excellent promotion for his "tournament proven" lures. Other tackle, outdoor products, boat builders, and marine dealers have discovered the value of tournament publicity and promotion. As a result, more and more experts are finding full-time jobs as public relations or sales promotion managers for bass fishing related companies. Other lure "field testers" and top tournament regulars have gained the status of factory-supported fishermen with paid entry fees, boats, equipment and expenses.

B.A.S.S.-conducted tournaments are now treated with headlines and carried on the newspaper's sports pages along with football, baseball and golf results. A dozen or so of the more consistent "bass pros" have sprung from the unsung ranks to become full-fledged celebrities, whose magic words of . . . "I caught my fish on . . . " or . . . "I use . . . " means increased tackle sales and endorsement checks.

Bill Dance, a former Memphis, Tennessee furniture salesman, was the first super star. Only 34 years old now, Dance is already a bass fishing legend. A seven-time tournament winner, Dance was the 1974 B.A.S.S. Angler-of-the-Year. His career B.A.S.S. winnings amount to over $40,000. Today, while still actively fishing tournaments, Dance is the star of a syndicated television show, "Bill Dance Outdoors," author of books on bass fishing, and serves as public relations and sales promoter for boat and lure companies.

Roland Martin, a former school teacher and Santee-Cooper, South Carolina, fishing guide, is another golden boy. Martin, 36, started later, but has climbed to the top of the pro bass fishing ladder. Winner of over $50,000 in B.A.S.S. rewards, including eight tournament wins, four B.A.S.S. Angler-of-the-Year awards, which in 1975 earned a $1000 bonus from the DuPont Stren folks, Martin also now has his own television show, "Fishing With Roland Martin," and is actively engaged in fishing tackle sales promotion and fishing schools and clinics.

The tournament bass fisherman has been characterized as an emotionless "fishing machine." A burly brute armed with a pool cue for a rod, a winch for a reel, and a tow line with which defenseless bass are derricked out of the water, and quickly stringered or rejected without feelings of joy — then back to the cold cash business of catching bass.

In the early days, heavy tackle *was* the rule. But fishing habits and techniques have changed drastically as the B.A.S.S. pros honed their success methods. Changes in scoring methods and attitudes have also been altered. These folks may still refer to a largemouth as a "hawg," but today's tournament boats are equipped with special aerated live-wells geared to the bass' comforts.

This special treatment may be due to the fact that a "bonus" ounce is awarded for each live bass weighed-in, but in reality there is a new awareness among Bassmasters of the value of this fish. Previously, fishermen lugged home stringers of bass to show off to the neighbors. Today, the B.A.S.S. tournament's "Don't Kill Your Catch" release program has spread outside the arena.

(continued on next page)

top of the line

ORVIS. Orvis has had one of the longest-running fly-fishing schools in the country. They're basically three-day sessions in Vermont complete with instructors, stocked pond and fishing on the Battenkill. The course covers entomology, casting, fly selection and all the basics. Graduates say it's a very enjoyable experience.

Museums

GLADDING MUSEUM. The Gladding Company has provided a service to anglers with its International Sport Fishing Museum in South Otselic, New York. The non-profit museum, which boasts the largest collection of fishing memorabilia in the world, has rare old antique fishing rods, reels, old catalogs and famous paintings dating back to the 1970s. There's more recent gear, as well, plus lots of other goodies that make up a fine collection. Free admission. It's open from mid-May to early November.

MUSEUM OF FLY FISHING. The Museum of Fly Fishing, curated by Austin Hogan, is a testament to the popularity of the sport. It's up in Manchester, Vermont (where Orvis is headquartered) and puts out a quarterly magazine, *The American Fly Fisher*, just like any other legitimate museum. It has such goodies on display as gear belonging to Presidents Eisenhower and Hoover, reels from as far back as 1826 and some of the exquisite vintage tackle available from the 19th and early 20th Centuries. Membership starts at $10 for which you get the magazine. Very fancy fly fishermen belong. Why not you?

Bass tournaments are a business oddity

(continued from preceding page)

B.A.S.S. boss Ray Scott points with pride that since the catch and release program was started in 1972 in national B.A.S.S. contests, over 32,000 bass have been released alive. This represents almost 80 per cent of the total fish weighed-in. He says, "Delayed mortality studies by fisheries scientists have indicated the release program works, providing specific techniques are used for handling the fish."

Scott says B.A.S.S. tournament publicity has created "thousands of new enthusiasts for freshwater fishing," who are contributing support, interest, and resources into state and national fisheries programs. Tournaments have obviously been a tremendous influence on the growth of fishing, boating and the marine industries. The Bass Research Foundation (BRF) was established in 1974. The BRF's purposes are to promote results-oriented research on the black bass, to give the bass angler a better understanding of scientific bass management, and to give the bass manager a better understanding of the needs and desires of the bass angler. In the past, profits from the B.A.S.S. tournament circuit have been donated to the Bass Research Foundation, which now has its national headquarters in Starkville, Mississippi.

B.A.S.S. tournaments are also being used as a scientific tool for collecting information. "Using conventional techniques, it takes the scientist days to obtain results that can be accumulated in a few hours during a B.A.S.S. tournament," points out Scott.

All right, you may be thinking, all this sounds okay, but what about the bass? Does all this fishing pressure, publicity and floating fishing machines threaten the future of bass fishing?

The balance sheet thus far says, "no" — for the several reasons pointed out.

(continued on next page)

THE LAST HATCH
A FISHING MYSTERY
HARMON HENKIN

(continued from page 405)

fishing seem more sporting than it really is. I prefer large fish, not these puny freshwater beasts. It doesn't matter to me whether a 12-inch brown takes my fly or not as long as I have the chance to land a 25-pound steelhead or a 300-pound tuna."

"But don't you find trout fishing the most intellectually stimulating of all sports?" Paul couldn't resist the debate.

"That is for birdbrains like Schielbacht and that pretentious lot."

"The mysteries of trout don't excite your thinking at all?"

"Just a little. But as Goethe said, 'Man's trouble begins when he starts to think.' "

"You're sounding like the sheriff."

"A potentially interesting chap. He'd like big game fishing, I venture."

"But do you know a lot about trout fishing?"

"Of course. I grew up on our family's estate in Northern California. There was an excellent stream cutting across the property and I had three miles of private water at my disposal. As a youngster I researched the literature quite thoroughly and was tutored by the best. I discovered quite a bit about the fish before going on to bigger things."

Paul got up to leave, then stopped. "If you don't mind me asking, where's Mrs. Hewitt?"

"I don't mind you asking. She's in her room. A relationship like ours requires a minimum of contact."

He dropped his eyes back to his book and began reading as if Paul had already left.

Sid was waiting for him in the den and pawing through the journal again.

"Discover anything, Sid?"

"Just that Schielbacht's a bigger bore than I would have suspected. Can talk about nothing except his adoring fans."

"Nothing else?"

"A little. He knows a tad about saltwater fishing but didn't want to admit that he knew anything about gaffs, of course. And we were right: he was in the habit of scanning Halford's journal, probably looking for ideas he could steal."

"Hewitt's a strange duck. He talks in riddles. But he sure knows saltwater fishing and he sure knows trout fishing. He's still an A-1 suspect."

"I can't figure out what Halford would be hiding from Schielbacht.

(continued on page 416)

WHAT YOU SHOULD ASK A CONSERVATION GROUP

(continued from page 399)

about members of the Federation of Fly Fishing Clubs, a rather loose union of local and regional organizations which was started as a breakaway from Trout Unlimited. For more than a decade the two groups have fought for the same things but because of personality differences and slight disagreements about approach each goes its way alone, though quite a few people belong to both groups.

The Theodore Gordon Flyfishers of New York City, once a chapter of TU, split because the Gothamites didn't like TU's former Michigan headquarters dictating national policy.

Objections of another sort can be thrown at The Bass Anglers Sportsman's Society, which some feel has the same relationship to the average fisherman that the National Football League has to a touch-football team. Though B.A.S.S. claims to be ecologically oriented, and donates money for bass habitat research, etc., it is also heavily involved with the promotion of fishing tackle and sports professionalism.

But this is not to pick on these three groups. Their limitations are all too typical. The Sierra Club and Friends of the Earth, for example, are far more preservationist oriented than most sportsmen can tolerate. The National Wildlife Federation tries to take a middle-ground approach to the problem of using outdoor resources but at times comes out heavily on one side or another, much to the chagrin of its members. There have even been cases in recent years where one sportsman's organization in the Pacific Northwest was actually a front group for the logging industry. And others have been intimate with real estate developers.

There are some basic questions that anyone thinking about becoming a member of a conservation group should ask. If the organization doesn't answer them to your satisfaction, look elsewhere.

(1) How much money does the group take in and where does the money go?

It is important to see what portion of the group's revenues are chewed up internally by its administrative machinery.

(2) What is the political slant of the group?

If it's a basically Republican group and you're a Democrat it might be wise for you to look elsewhere. Most groups will claim to be apolitical or un-political but that's not the way they really work. Are their friends in Congress liberals or conservatives? Are their friends and associates individuals who claim on one hand to be conservationists yet oppose strip-mining legislation on the other?

(3) What kind of people are on the group's board of directors?

If they're all corporation presidents or realtors who like subdivisions that's a strong indication that environmentally they won't be fighting much. If you're just a working stiff your interests might be very different from those of a $250,000-a-year oil company executive.

(4) What is the general environmental approach of the group?

Is the group interested in a piecemeal approach to ecological problems? Does it realize that all things are interrelated? Do they see the whole picture? Some organizations fighting for the steelhead in Washington and Oregon are actually thinly veiled anti-Indian groups who want to keep Native Americans away from their traditional waters.

(5) What has the group really done?

Aside from clichés, has your prospective group really done anything for the environment? Has it been able to mobilize its membership and public support for its goals or is it satisfied merely to talk? They have to put up or shut up.

Even after taking these questions into consideration there will be lots of things that rub you wrong about the group unless you are blindly uncritical. Join the most responsive one and work from within for change.

B.A.S.S. tournaments aren't for everyone

(continued from preceding page)

Also, despite his over $6000 worth of fancy bass boat and related accessories, despite the hot tips and new secret weapons, the *average* so-called bass fishing professional, according to the B.A.S.S. record book, in a full day of frantic fishing — usually catches no more than two keeper-size (12-inch) tournament bass.

B.A.S.S. tournament style fishing is not everyone's bag — just as tournament golf isn't every duffer's game. But by the same token, competitive fishing tournament anglers are far from the despoilers of bass fishing; they are among the vanguard in seeking improvements — for it is they, who will suffer, too, if the effort is not made.

CA/90 CLEANER

Anglers are never satisfied, which is why the CA/90 people designed their "Fish-Free." First we want to get around fish, then we don't want to smell like them. Fish-Free, when sprayed on the hands or whatever after washing, will remove that tell-tale odor. Also supposed to de-fish coolers, refrigerators and live wells by substituting a cool, clean citrus scent.

What's a nice product like you doing in a book like this?

Down comforters, clocks, fish replicas, money belts! What are those things doing in a book supposedly about fishing tackle?

It's simple. "Fishing tackle" is a broad category that includes all kinds of interests and enthusiasms. The arena of modern tackle has more than three rings and there are all sorts of things that are related to something an angler does or might want to do at some time.

That's what this chapter is about: things of direct interest like big game fighting seats and angler's priests and things of indirect interest like warm, cozy down comforters. So just relax and enjoy it. What have you got to lose?

—W.T.V.

COLLAPSIBLE FISH BASKET

Aside from a built-in live box on your boat, the best way to keep your catch alive until you decide whether to keep it or not is to get one of these French-made fish baskets, which can be hung in the water from your craft or pier. The Maillnox baskets are available in a 15¾-inch diameter that will float even if filled with fish, a 13¾-inch standard model and a gigantic 35-inch-high bonzo with a 23½-inch diameter. None are expensive and are lots better than stringers for keeping things alive.

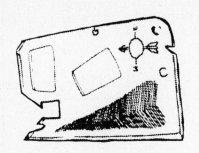

WALLE-HAWK

The Walle-Hawk is one of those strange gadgets that sort of defy classification. But it must be useful. This 1/16-inch thick stainless steel tool will fit into your wallet for emergencies. Can be used as a screwdriver, can opener, wood or metal file, compass, signal mirror, something to make fish hooks from wire, nails or pins and it will even skin animals or fish in a pinch. A great conversation piece anyway.

THE DAVY-PACK

The Davy-pack, made in England, consists of a belt with pouches on either side. When you fall in over your head you merely squeeze the pack and you activate the CO_2 mechanism and the bag fully inflates in seconds. The inflated tube may then be passed over your head and under your arms and used to aid other people, if you've taken a communal dunk. Helpful in rougher terrain, like big steelhead rivers.

NU-INVENTIONS HOOK REMOVER

Here we go again. Another one-second hook remover. This one by the Nu-Inventions Company down in Pearland, Texas, is spring-operated and works by holding the hook in its mechanism. Then you squeeze the handle and the fish is free. Give it a try.

POMPANETTE FILLETING TRAY

If you're into filleting in a severe way get a Pompanette all-anodized aluminum tray, which is designed for use on your big boat. Works as a bait preparation table, too. Easy to keep clean and non-odoriferous.

LEONARD ANGLER'S LOG

These logs provide the place where you can keep an exact directory of your fly fishing success and failure through the years. Comparing each season's lies, as it were. Simply check the appropriate box or circle a number to complete entries on air and water temperatures, weather, wind, water level, etc. Refill pages also available.

ANGLERS' WORLD WADING STAFF

The Anglers' World Scotch Hazelwood wading staff is, at $85, another one of those wonderfully decadent accessories. These Scot-made wonders have a staghorn grip and detachable lanyard. They're 57 inches long and weigh 13 ounces. Lots a luck.

FOLSTAF WADING STAFF

Going, going — oops — not gone if you have a Folstaf wading staff with you. It folds up to 10½ inches and extends to 44. An elastic cord pulls and holds the sections together and it has a cork handle and carrying case with a belt hook. A tough tungsten carbide tip helps you dig into rough river bottoms. Good for use in a pinch.

Folstaf Wading Staff

CASCADE LAKES AQUATIC INSECT NET

The specialized, matching-the-hatch addict will appreciate this fine-mesh, cherry-wood handled insect net sold by Cascade Lakes Development. It's 13 inches long by 2 inches wide and can be attached to your landing net for deeper water captures of nymphs. Well made.

NO BONE KEY

Giving up on those delicious panfish because it's a pain in the anal fin to clean them? Try a No Bone Key from Farm Pond Harvest. Not a filleting knife, it removes ribs after the fish has been fried. With the price of meat being what it is you can't afford to pass this one by. Will really work for you.

GEM FISHERMEN'S PAL ANGLER'S PLIERS

Gem's Angler's Pliers is a handy gadget. It's a pliers, scissors, lead weight crimper, screwdriver and hook sharpening file. It doesn't weigh much and earns its keep quickly.

NORM THOMPSON

Shikari Kit Bags (duffel bags) are elegant variations on a very traditional way for outdoorsy people to carry their gear. In three sizes — 21, 30 and 34 inches — they have soft leather handles, are water repellent and rip proof and have a compartment on the side for grabbing small things in a hurry. Lovely.

Pond Management, By Lou Calala

A simply written 42-page booklet that will give you a basic outline of what you'll need to get started in a home-grown, warm water fishery. It covers the essentials.

FISH BELL

Still fish with your eyes closed? Let the fish awaken you with its first run. Get a fish pole bell from Cabela's to clip onto your rod. Tinkle, tinkle.

LUHR JENSEN REELOCK

Those rings holding your reel together getting loose with age? Luhr Jensen's surgical rubber stretch band will hold the reel together tightly. A good product to keep your reel from coming apart at the seams when fighting a mean fish.

MARATHON WADING BELT

A simple elastic wader belt by Marathon is good insurance for those dipping into dangerous waters. Easy to secure and release. It keeps your waders stationary, too.

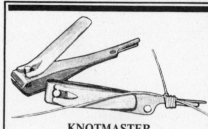

KNOTMASTER

For those who need help in tying knots, the Knotmaster is an aid for tying all sorts of things, including nail knots for that line-to-leader connection.

DATASPORT TABLES

For those who feel Old John Alden Knight's Solunar tables are out of date, the Datasport, Inc., people have a really advanced version. Derived from a digital computer, the charts take a variety of factors into consideration to come up with a daily feeding forecast chart consisting of 365 curves with nine pages of theory and instruction. Also included are sunset and sunrise tables, moon phase charts, logging and mapping grids and other like info. Quite an interesting product.

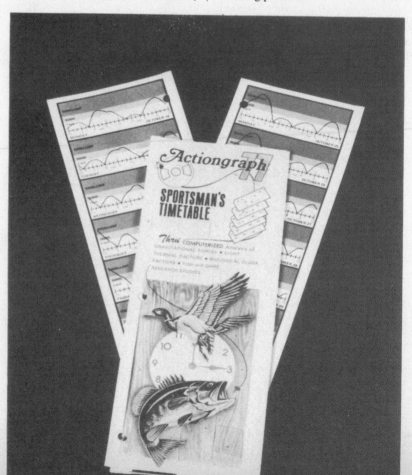

ultimate commodity

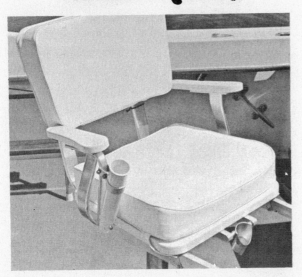

SALT WATER FIGHTING CHAIR FROM POMPANETTE

Everything you need or could ever need in a fighting chair for heavy-duty ocean work is in Pompanette's F Series. All parts are either stainless steel or chrome-plated brass. The swiveling mechanism is ball bearing-operated and it will lock in any position. Has an adjustable headrest, back, arms, footrest and gimbal. Height of the chair is optional. It has a turning radius of 40 inches and is a little over 28 inches wide. You'll need to sit in it when you hear the price!

GAMEFISH: WHITE PERCH

NAMES

Silver perch, sea perch, silver bass. *(Roccus americanus)*

DISTRIBUTION

The white perch is found along the Atlantic coast from North Carolina to Nova Scotia. It is also found throughout New England and in New York State.

DESCRIPTION

The white perch is not a perch but is a member of the sea-bass family. It is an anadromous fish that is found both in salt water and in brackish waters. It is green on the back with bright silver sides. Pale stripes are often visible on the sides.

SIZE

The white perch is a small fish that averages about one pound. Specimens of up to 5 pounds have been reported, however.

HABITAT

An unusually adaptable fish, the white perch is at home in salt, brackish and fresh water. In saltwater, it is generally found in tidal pools, backwaters and small bays. Inland, the white perch does very well in deep lakes with sand or gravel bottoms. Those fish that live in salt or brackish waters will migrate into fresh water during spawning.

FEEDING HABITS

The diet of the saltwater white perch consists of shrimp, crabs and small baitfish. In fresh water, they feed on worms, insects, insect larvae and small crustaceans. They are a school fish that likes to feed at night, often moving into the shallows at evening in search of food.

BEST FEEDING TEMPERATURE

Between 55° and 70°.

NORM THOMPSON

One of the most convenient bags for hauling gear around, especially in a station wagon or camper, is Norm Thompson's trek bag. It's made of lightweight nylon, can hold a rod across its 21-inch top and has large compartments along both ends and the side.

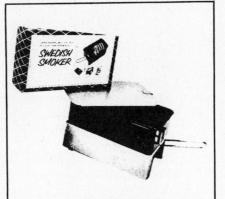

SWEDISH SMOKER

Like those smoked fish that cost so much at the neighborhood delicatessen? Get a Swedish Smoker and make your own from your next full stringer. It's lightweight and small — just 3 pounds. Waterproof and comes with a pound of wood chips that smokes 100 pounds of yummy fish.

416 THE ANGLER'S GRAB BAG

"No one catches bass every time. Some say they do. They lie a little."
HOMER CIRCLE

POMPANETTE GAME FISH REPLICAS

Want to see your quarry all year round? Get a gamefish replica from Pompanette. Large sizes like sailfish and blue marlin available and smaller species, too. All realistically hand-painted.

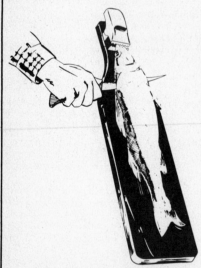

IPCO FILLETING BOARDS

Ipco puts out a line of filleting boards that work very well in preparing fish for the table. They have a clamp at one end to hold the head and a v-ribbed cleaning surface. Very convenient for the sometimes not-so-pleasant job of filleting fish.

THE LAST HATCH
A FISHING MYSTERY
HARMON HENKIN

(continued from page 409)

A time warp that put him on another planet where there are nothing but 6-pound browns?"

"You've watched one *Star Trek* too many, Sheriff Gordon. Anyway, in Hewitt's case it's Belle. If Halford was sneaking off in the bushes with her, he would naturally want Hewitt thrown off the trail."

"But why kill him now?"

"Maybe he just found out about it."

"But if Halford was being so careful how would Hewitt find out?"

"I don't know. Husbands and wives have a way of knowing those things."

"What should I do. Arrest him?"

"No, we need some hard, cold facts, as they say. Maybe something will break overnight."

"Then everyone will have to stay."

"There's no choice."

Paul walked out onto the patio and gazed at the moon. A few minutes later Julie wandered out and sat across the table from him. She was still sleepy. "Hi. What are you doing?"

"Pondering."

"What?"

"Truth, beauty and man's fate in a changing world."

"Didn't know you still thought about me."

"Very funny."

"Sid just told me that we all have to stay here until tomorrow. Unless you plan to fish all night you better be nice to me."

"That almost sounds like an invitation."

"It could be."

There was nothing to do but smile and grab a sleeping bag from her VW. They walked holding hands to the creek and began building a nest of sorts in the grass.

[Interested readers may find more information on this subject in Hawkin's memorable study, *Biological Cycles of Warm-Blooded North American Species*.]

The morning was as clear and chilly as summer mornings usually are at the 5000-foot level. Paul and Julie walked back to the house and gratefully accepted some of Dun's Jamaican Blue Mountain coffee. The others staggered onto the patio in various shades of grumpy until they had all congregated at 10. No one said anything. Dun read to them

(continued on page 429)

SECRET COMPARTMENT MONEY BELT

Just struck it rich at a bass tournament? Get a Secret Compartment Money Belt made of 1½-inch tanned cowhide from Eddie Bauer and the muggers won't know how well you can handle those crank baits. All sorts of sizes in dark brown or black. Other uses for the angler, too.

STRIKE PRODUCTS

Do fish stink to you? Do you stink to fish? Well, the Strike Products Company has a solution designed mainly for bass fishermen. Their bass x-citers supposedly stimulate fish to make them strike. Formula 2 eliminates human odors, which some anglers believe is an important factor. The Original Formula and Fish X-Citer is for freshwater fish like crappies and bass.

LOWRANCE FISH-N-FLOAT

Sometimes in their rush to go electronic, anglers forget the basics such as how to find that spot where they were hitting yesterday. Well, the Lowrance Company has a solution — their Fish-N-Float. It contains six markers, weights, nylon line and instructions on its use. The only problem is if someone else spots the marker and gets there first in the morning!

UPSON SCALER

The Upson Tool Company is marketing a magic scaler with "free floating" plastic fingers which act as a rapid scrubber in removing the scales from panfish. Since it's plastic, it doesn't damage the flesh and works quite well.

LEONARD'S SALMON TROUT PRIEST

These swell little hickory-stemmed brass head priests with their leather thongs are certainly an elegant way to put a fish out of the misery of being hooked by a clod like you. Actually a very convenient way to kill fish you intend to put on the table.

E-Z MOUNT FISH MOUNTING KIT

OK. Caught that trophy-sized lunker? Now what? Simple — mount it. The E-Z Mount fish mounting kit has everything the home taxidermist needs to set things up including preservative, foam, universal fish eye, plastic fin backing, oil paints and knife, needle and thread. They claim even a beginner can do the job in only three hours. If so, it will save lots of money in professional mounting costs. You have nothing to lose . . . . except your trophy.

INSECT JEWELRY

If your fly fishing mania has progressed to the point that you've begun to rescue mayflies from spiderwebs, perhaps you'll be glad to learn of these gold and silver aquatic insect totems from Tom Satterthwaite (a working jeweler by profession), who is offering mayfly and stonefly lapel pins. At $28-plus for the gold versions and $14.50 for the silver ones, they're definitely luxuries, but then you won't find them at Tiffany's. For the fly fisherman of distinction.

HAMMACHER-SCHLEMMER SERVING PLATTER

Serve your catches on this elegant marble inlaid serving platter from Hammacher-Schlemmer. Available in either silver or gold finish, it will dazzle your dinner guests. Hammacher's catalog is a fine place to shop for kitchen aids. It's worth getting on their mailing list.

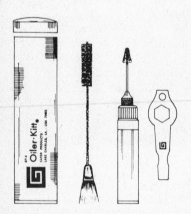

GP-4 OILER-KITT

The GP-4 Oiler Kitt is an everything you'll need to keep your reel functioning. It has an oiler, wrench and brush set-up that fits into a waterproof plastic oval tube. Can be very convenient. Available from Bass Pro Shops.

FAO SCHWARZ FISHING GAME

If you really hate to take an off-season break, try FAO Schwarz's *Gone Fishing*. The best toy shop in the world offers two "anglers" a game in which they try to catch 30 fish of various point values from a rotating table-top pond. A good game and great for the tournament angler who wants to keep in shape.

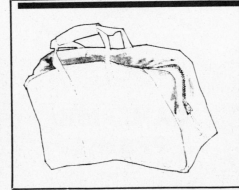

GERRY AIR BAG

This is an oversized bag for the angler on the move that can hold everything including a smallish full pack. The Gerry bag is 25 by 16 by 9 inches in the regular size and 32 by 16½ by 11½ inches in the large size. Good protection — the nylon material is padded with urethane foam.

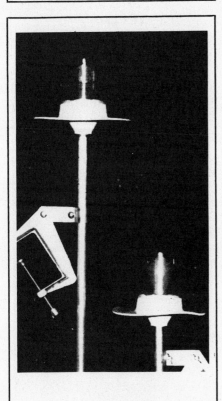

MILBOLAC

We don't exactly know what the Milbolac multilight can be used for, but there are undoubtedly thousands of things. It's a light bulb enclosed in glass mounted on a pole with a 40-inch bendable stem. The 50-watt light, which can be maintained for six to eight hours on a fully-charged 12-volt battery, will work completely submerged under water. It can also be used around camp and in lots of other places. Comes with a clamp and adjustable bracket. Nothing quite like it.

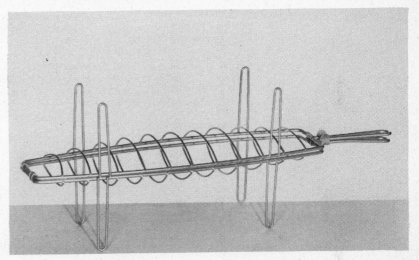

FISH GRILLS

Ye old frying pan always seems to make a trout look comfortable over an open fire, but here's an improved cooking utensil from the gourmet's bag of gadgetry. A fish grill allows for cooking both sides without turning (and usually breaking) even the big ones, and you can bake a fish over low heat on an open campfire, a charcoal grill or even in the oven; a simple buttery baste or your own sauce adds a lot. There are a variety of fish grills — mostly imported ones — available at gourmet gear stores (this American-made Hoan model FG20 is $17), and legless models that travel well on the outside of a pack. (The old-fashioned weenie-roaster will do almost as well in a pinch, but these stand-up, fish-shaped grills make for a nice, even cooking job.)

If you're aspiring to the upper realms of fish cookery, you might eventually want to invest in a fish poacher (and we do mean invest — poachers cost anywhere from $60 and up) — a very flashy piece of kitchen tackle that good cooks swear by. Just be sure it's lined with tin; any other metal (except gold or silver, which is available) will taint the delicate wine sauces you'll be concocting from your wine cellar, of course.

FAO SCHWARZ GIFTMAKER SET

The toy people at FAO Schwarz have a nifty "Preserve Forever" Giftmaker Set the angler can use to preserve small things like a favorite fly, lure, mayfly or the like in a clear plastic. Make bookends or paperweights from your Royal Coachmen. Lots of uses on those cold winter evenings.

DICK KOTIS SINGS. Though not on a par with the Beachboy's Greatest Hits, Dick Kotis, lead singer for the Fred Arbogast Singers, has done more than a credible job on his new album *Fishing Farm Ponds and Strip Pits* (the flip side is *Fishing Large Impoundments and Reservoirs*). Included in the latest Arbogast catalog, this album has plenty of basic programmed info for the beginner and even some insights for the more advanced. Three or four minutes well spent.

THE HORNBLOWER

This is an ultimate commodity for the meditative angler so engrossed in deep thought that he's unaware when a fish is tugging away. The Hornblower toots like mad when a fish swallows your bait. Just stick one of its steel spikes in the ground, install a "C" battery and chant "Om—om" until a fish takes. Honk, Honk, Honk.

FLY-O-KIT

A neat device dreamed up by master caster Lee Wulff and marketed by Garcia. Fly-O-Kit is a clever outfit to help you learn and practice casting even indoors. It's essentially a bulky line attached to the end of a rod, which allows you to see exactly what's happening while you cast. Ingenious, with practical results.

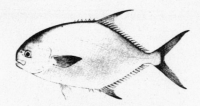

GAMEFISH: PERMIT

NAMES
Great pompano, round pompano, Key West permit, palometo. *(trachinotus goodei)*

DISTRIBUTION
The permit is found along the Atlantic coast from Brazil to New England. It is most abundant throughout the West Indies, the Gulf of Mexico and off the coast of Florida.

DESCRIPTION
The permit is a chunky fish colored blue on the back with silver-blue sides. Larger fish may be silver with blue overtones. The fins are dark and the dorsal lobe is not prolonged.

SIZE
The average size of the permit is about 8 to 15 pounds. Specimens weighing up to 40 pounds have been reported.

HABITAT
Permit prefer the shallow waters around reefs and inlets. At times, they are taken in the surf or at the mouth of tidal rivers.

FEEDING HABITS
Permit feed on fish, crustaceans and mollusks. They are bottom feeders.

TACKLE
A great fish when it strikes a fly — a rare happening that defies logic. But it also is taken in the shallows on varying kinds of artificials. An outstanding fish on any kind of light tackle. Most often taken on bait.

MIYA EPOCH ELECTRIC REELS

There is really just one reason for buying an electric fishing reel: if you're disabled. Otherwise they seem to steal the joy of battling a big fish. The Miya Epochs are available in models for trolling and deep sea fishing. Their big No. 1000 carries 900 yards of 90-pound nylon. They also make a model for surf casting or boat fishing. Miya's electric reels can mean the difference between fishing and not fishing for the handicapped and are excellent in this regard. All the accessories, including batteries, are available from the company.

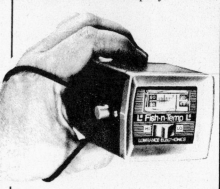

LOWRANCE LTD 200

If you want to know the surface temperature (something that may or may not be useful to the angler), then get a Lowrance Surface Fish-n-Temp and mount it permanently on your boat. Reads from 35° to 90°.

GAMEFISH: WHITE STURGEON

NAMES

Sturgeon. *(Acipenser transmontanus)*

DISTRIBUTION

The white sturgeon is found on the Pacific coast from California to Alaska. It has also been reported in Flathead Lake, Montana.

DESCRIPTION

The white sturgeon is the largest of the inland fish found in the United States. It has an elongated body of grey or brown coloring. Its body is covered with bony plates and its skeleton is cartilage rather than bone.

SIZE

It is difficult to determine the average size of the white sturgeon. Specimens of up to 1800 pounds have been reported in recent years. They are an extremely large fish that can range anywhere from 50 to 1500 pounds.

HABITAT

The white sturgeon is an anadromous fish but many of them are landlocked and thus spend their whole life in fresh water. They are sometimes found in brackish waters and prefer deep holes in rivers. In recent years dams have inhibited the propagation of this migratory fish by altering their natural environment.

FEEDING HABITS

The white sturgeon is not particular about its diet and with its sucking mouth will consume almost anything available. Favorite foods include mollusks, crustaceans, lampreys and insects. They are bottom feeders that feed voraciously during the spring and summer.

DICK SPLAINE FISHING REPORT

An old tradition in American pursuits is the one-shot, how-to newsletter purporting to give secrets on how to beat the horses, lose weight, pick up women or catch fish. Continuing in that tradition is the Dick Splaine Fishing Report. It gives you the inside skinny on how to make and use his Squeteager Lure, which is actually a fly. A very folksy approach, revealing his history, theory on fishing and detailed tying instructions. Interesting reading.

THE LITTLE GEM

If you're planning an angling trip to Lilliput, or you've got 150 dollars left over from your inheritance and there's just no reels left to buy, here's a small addition — very small. The Little Gem is just a shade tinier than a dime (not including the reel foot) but it works like a Walker: 23 working parts of nickel silver give off the satisfying muted click of a full-sized reel. Angling craftsman Tom Satterthwaite is making the Little Gem in a limited edition of 150, including a miniature suede reel bag, at the full-size price of $150, and rumor has it that there will be a 21-inch 6-strip bamboo rod available in the future. Also good for dace fishing, but use lots of backing if you're going after shiners.

The "Little Gem" pictured with a normal-sized fly reel.

ANGLING BOOKS SHOULD IMPROVE
OUR CHANCES OF TAKING FISH

By Nick Lyons

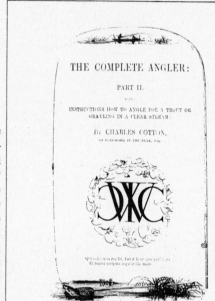

THE COMPLETE ANGLER:

PART II.

INSTRUCTIONS HOW TO ANGLE FOR A TROUT OR
GRAYLING IN A CLEAR STREAM

By CHARLES COTTON,
OF BERESFORD IN THE PEAK, ESQ.

A cover page from Izaak Walton's *The Complete Angler.* Pictured is the beginning of Charles Cotton's contribution to one of the hundreds of editions of Walton's classic, which, since its original publication in 1653, has become the best-selling fishing book of all time.

If I really knew a recipe for concocting angling best-sellers, I'd patent it, make a fortune, and retire to a valley I know in Colorado where the rainbows are long and lithe and wild and come readily to a Rio Grande King. The sad fact is, combined profits from my own three fishing books would barely pay for one ill-used bamboo rod with a bad warp. Sparse Grey Hackle, one of the few really durable angling writers of our time, once estimated that he'd earned less than 10 cents an hour for all his writing efforts. Raising worms pays much better.

Still, as an ex-editor of the fishing books of others, I had the pleasure of seeing several books sell enough copies to qualify as best-sellers and have studied the success of others. Art Flick's wise, down-to-earth *New Streamside Guide to Naturals and Their Imitations* has sold more than 50,000 copies and continues to sell steadily seven years after publication. Art spent three years, every day of the season, collecting entomological data, and then condensed it into a little book that is pure gold. Its success is easy to understand: there's not a word of bunk in the text, it's highly practical, and — since it recommends only about ten fly patterns,

which are all Flick uses to this day — it vastly simplifies the great mystery about which fly to use. Flick is so knowledgeable he says a lot in a very few words.

Books that reveal innovations do extremely well — if the innovations are more than gimmicks. Swisher and Richards' *Selective Trout,* which popularized the no-hackle fly, must have proved its worth to anglers, for it sold more than 50,000 copies. Len Wright's fine *Fishing the Dry Fly as a Living Insect,* which initiated the current caddis-fly boom, rightly deserved the broad attention and good sales it enjoyed: it was surely fresh and innovative. Practical angling books should genuinely improve our chances of taking fish.

Though most of the successful books in recent years have been narrowly focused

— perhaps because the state of the art has truly advanced — several others contain so much practical information that their breadth becomes an asset. A. J. McClane's *Standard Fishing Encyclopedia,* which probably has sold twice as many copies as its nearest competitor, appeals to all fishermen because of the thoroughness, solidity, and reliability of its information. Somewhat more specialized is Ray Bergman's *Trout,* which has continued to sell well for more than 40 years because of the wealth of practical information it contains on all aspects of trout fishing and its genial, down-to-earth style. Ernest Schwiebert's *Nymphs* is vastly knowledgeable, and nymph fishing continues to attract more and more fly fishermen. Boyd Pfeiffer's *Tackle Craft,* which explains how to make and repair all kinds of tackle, has

appealed to all breeds of angler because it is genuinely helpful and comprehensive. You must know your subject extremely well. Good illustrations help.

Though the more substantial literary fare of Roderick L. Haig-Brown, William Humphrey and (most recently) Norman Maclean will have a good chance to survive the moment, they do not survive nearly so well as practical books. There are no recipes for literature: each work will bear the unique impress of its author's character in all its complexity and richness. Ultimately, I suspect, there are no recipes for the practical book, either. You must have the breadth of McClane, the earthy practicality of Flick, the innovative spirit of Swisher and Richards if you want the angling community to beat a path to your door. The book must derive from hard experience, careful study; your "discoveries" must have demonstrable value; it helps if you can write clearly.

But if you do write such a best-seller, you may be too busy answering letters or delivering lectures to fish any more.

Me? I'll keep writing shaggy fish stories — and try to make my fortune elsewhere.

For a review see page 429

top of the line

Books

The Angler's Coast
By Russell Chatham

In an age of fly fishing specialization, when whole tomes are written on that or this little bug, Russ Chatham is a pleasant surprise. Not only is his collection of essays on fishing with flies for anadromous and ocean fish a delight in itself but his illustrations give the book an added depth. Chatham is not only a knowledgeable angler but he's a fine artist and a good story-teller — what else could you want?

Published by: Doubleday. **Price:** $7.95.

Backpack Fishing
By Charles Farmer

Part of the excitement of going fishing is in the going, and backpack fishing is a way of making the going an angling adventure in itself. It is a pleasant confusion of angling ends and means. Charlie Farmer's paperback book is a fly-spin combo approach to backcountry angling that covers everything from the beginning of the trail to a campfire-cooked meal by the lake. The beginning camper will find all the basic warnings and advice about planning a hike and buying backpack gear. There are also lots of manufacturers' photos of tents, bags, cooking utensils. Farmer's emphasis on timing high-country trips is good. There's a lot of western flavor, though the travel and information references cover the East, too. Not a basic fishing book, but a good hiking book for the beginner.

Published by: Jolex. **Price:** $6.95.

THE JOYS OF SPORTING BOOKS

By Sparse Grey Hackle

Herein are some astonishing opportunities for anglers to acquire, for a small initial investment, a lifetime of free sport.

No rods or lures to buy, no tackle to pay for. Everything is free after that first small cost. No posted or restricted waters, or guards to bother you, no closed seasons, and no limits. Occasionally it may rain or snow but incredibly enough you will not get either wet or cold.

And where is this earthly paradise to be found? Why, in the pages of sporting books. A good fishing book, one you really like, will last you a lifetime and still exist to divert and fascinate the sportsman who comes after you. Such a book, a couple of years after you read it and enjoyed it the first time, will fairly cry out to you from its shelf to be read again. And you will be surprised to find that you enjoy the second reading as much as the first.

A long while ago, writing of my boyhood trips of fancy through the pages of a drawerful of sporting goods catalogs, I said: "Those were the best trips I ever took. I caught more fish and shot more game and saw more wonderful woods than on any trips I ever really took. And it never rained."

I still believe it, and I invite you to increase your enjoyment of the best sporting grounds in the world through the medium of books, some of which are listed and described here.

Backpack Hiking: The First Steps
By Richard Eggert

A pocket-sized book which covers most of what you need to know about backpacking in the U.S. The book assumes reasonable intelligence but no previous experience as it takes prospective hikers through the first steps of getting into the wilderness. This includes an evaluation of the equipment needed and suggestions on how to save money, locating suitable places to hike and where to get accurate information on them, how to pick foods that won't break your back or attack your stomach, plants, animals and bugs to watch for and how to avoid them — how to find directions accurately without being a mathematician, and a detailed review of the process and ethics of wilderness fishing. A good one for beginners.

Published by: Stackpole. **Price:** $2.95.

Basic Fishing:
From the Worm to the Fly
By Harlan Major

Basic Fishing is another example of the economics of publishing at work for the angler; Major's book is a vintage (1947) work of the kind that no one but the most obsessive collector would want at $8.95. But as a $1.95 paperback revival it's a delightful slice of recent angling history with something to say, even 20 years later. You will look far to find any better information on "Raising Maggots Outdoors" (and indoors, of course); the use of macaroni as bait; making horsehair lines; bottle fishing, jugging, kegging, and many other fishing techniques that vanished with the arrival of monofilament and fiberglass. (Major is one of the old-time angling democrats to whom catching fish was the penultimate goal, and the subtitle is not meant to imply any evolution of means.) But *Basic Fishing* is more than an angling curiosity; for the price of a new

Mepps you can learn how to make a landing net from a branched limb, hackle pliers from a clothespin and several other sensible tackle items; the simple chapter on the hydraulics of lures is a gem. You may wonder what you'll ever do with the ideas Major presents, but you'll never be sorry you spent a couple of bucks to read about them.

Published by: Funk & Wagnalls. **Price:** $1.95.

Consumer Guide – Complete Buying Guide To Fishing Equipment

Consumer Guides have a well-earned reputation for honesty and objectivity unlike some publications that have a vested interest in keeping advertisers happy. There's lots of solid information in their treatment of fishing tackle but some peculiar surprises such as their listing of the tiny, highly specialized Orvis 6½-foot Flea Rod as their first choice. Some other selections seem to indicate that their choices and those of anglers may be based on different standards. A good book anyway when thinking about major purchases, especially electronic gear and boats.

Published by: Signet. **Price:** $1.95.

Fiberglass Rod Making
By Dale Clemens

This book has become the basic text for the home builder regardless of the level of proficiency. In a profusely illustrated text, Clemens goes into intricate detail describing various techniques of rod wrapping of all types of rods. Putting together a fiberglass or graphite rod makes sense when done along with Clemens, who practices what he preaches with a custom rod shop in Pennsylvania.

Published by: Winchester. **Price:** $10.

GAMEFISH: ATLANTIC SALMON

NAMES
Kennebec salmon. *(Salmo salar)*

DISTRIBUTION
The Atlantic salmon was originally found in the coastal rivers of the Atlantic from Delaware to southern Canada, Nova Scotia and New Brunswick. Due to the encroachment of civilization and its attendant pollution, the Atlantic salmon is becoming a scarce species. It is now most often found in the rivers of Maine and southern Canada. It is also native to the eastern coast of the Atlantic.

DESCRIPTION
The Atlantic salmon is a dark blue fish with silver sides that are covered with X-shaped markings. While spawning, an adult salmon will turn darker in color with a reddish underside. A young salmon, known as a parr, takes on a brownish hue with distinctive vertical markings called parr marks. When parrs begin to migrate to the sea, they turn a light blue-green with silver sides. A fish about two years old that migrates prematurely into fresh water is called a grilse. They are generally lighter in color than an adult salmon.

SIZE
The Atlantic salmon is a large fish that ranges in size from 10 to 50 pounds. The average, however, is around 12 to 15 pounds.

HABITAT
The Atlantic salmon is an anadromous fish that spends most of its life in saltwater but migrates into freshwater to spawn. Salmon runs begin in early spring and continue until fall when the fish reach their spawning grounds. They prefer clear, moving water, although they like to find deep quiet pools where they can find protection. When spawning, they will seek out shallow water with gravel bottoms where they can bury their spawn.

"Caddis flies are among the most important trout stream insects and constitute a large part of the trout's diet."
DAN BAILEY

BOOKS **425**

Fiberglass Rod Making

DALE P. CLEMENS

top of the line

A Fine Kettle of Fish Stories
By Ed Zern

Field & Stream columnist Ed Zern is certainly the master outdoor humorist of our time. No real competition. In the Mark Twain tradition and with a superb writing style, Zern's latest book of some of his more memorable Exit Laughing columns is a gem. Some places make you laugh and others make you very sad. That's the mark of a fine writer, and Zern is.

Published by: Winchester. **Price**: $5.95.

Fisherman's Bounty
Edited by Nick Lyons

No angling collection is really complete without at least one anthology, and *Fisherman's Bounty* is the best and biggest collection on the market. Lyons is a fine angling storyteller in his own right (*Fishing Widows, The Seasonable Angler*) and his grouping of the best angling writers of yesterday and today is like a 72-course dinner — you always seem to have room for another taste of fishing joys, big fish and near disasters, and a few sorrows and belly laughs. Stories you will have a hard time finding in original (and expensive) old editions are here for the asking; Foote's "The Wedding Gift," "When All the World Was Young" and an Ed Zern story, "A Day's Fishing, 1946," that is un-Zernly serious. De Maupassant, Kipling, and other storytellers shine their light on the mysteries of angling. For this varied and satisfying book of the very best angling writing, "Bounty" is the right word.

Published by: Crown. **Price**: $6.95.

SMALLMOUTH BUFFALO FISH STEAKS

1 pound smallmouth steaks, fresh or frozen
1 1¾-ounce can condensed tomato soup
2 T parsley, snipped
¼ t dried basil leaves, crushed
6 thin lemon slices

Thaw frozen steaks. Sprinkle fish with salt and pepper. Place the steaks in well-greased shallow baking pan. Combine soup, parsley and basil. Pour over fish and top with lemon slices. Bake at 350 degrees until fish flakes easily when tested with a fork, 20-25 minutes. Serves 3-4. — Leona Schrupp, Billings, Montana.

The Fishing in Print
By Arnold Gingrich

This last book by the late Arnold Gingrich combines the author's chatty style with an anthology of some of the most important sources in fly-fishing's history. It puts in one place much of the material that was difficult for the non-bibliophile to gather, and a reading of it provides a good background for understanding where the sport of fly fishing for trout has come from. Good listing of books in the bibliography as well. A great starting point for the would-be serious scholars of angling.
   Published by: Winchester. **Price:** $12.95.

Fishing in America
By Charles Waterman

The Sherman Anti-Trust Act will soon have to be applied to Charlie Waterman, who's beginning to create a monopoly on really pretty pictorial angling books. This latest one is a vivid look at the past and present of sport fishing in America with some gorgeous color pictures and facsimiles from 19th-Century sources. It's a real "oooh" and "aaaah" book especially if you've been to the places he photographs. Informative text, as well.
   Published by: Holt, Rinehart & Winston. **Price:** $19.95.

Fishing Widows
By Nick Lyons

Nick Lyons' *Fishing Widows* represents one of the high points of the literary element of angling literature. Lyons understands the nuances of angling from a social perspective often ignored by most other angler writers who are only concerned with catching whoppers. He carries on the prose traditions of the sport in a

From Indians to today's sportsman: The epic story of fishing and tackle.

by Charles F. Waterman

PARADE-DRESSED WHITEFISH
2 pounds whitefish fillets or other fish fillets, fresh or frozen
1 t salt
dash pepper
2 T melted fat or oil
Thaw frozen fillets. Sprinkle them with salt and pepper. Place half of fillets, skin side down, in a well-greased 12x8x2 baking dish.

1 c onion, chopped
1/4 c melted fat or oil
2 c toasted or dry bread cubes
1 c cheddar cheese, grated
2 T parsley, chopped
2 t powdered mustard
1/2 t salt
dash pepper
Cook onion in fat until tender. Add remaining ingredients and mix thoroughly. Place the above stuffing on fish and cover with remaining fillets. Brush fish with fat and sprinkle with paprika. Bake in a 350-degree oven 30-35 minutes or until fish flakes easily when tested with a fork. Serves 6. — *Water, Woods & Wildlife.*

top of the line

superb way and one that should be sampled by more anglers.

Published by: Crown. **Price:** $5.95.

Fishless Days, Angling Nights
By Sparse Grey Hackle

A winsome collection of fishing stories (including an adult children's bedtime story) that makes the grandfatherly image of Mr. Hackle (a *nom de pêche*) on the jacket come alive as a warm and talented storyteller. Sparse Grey Hackle's reminiscences bridge the gap from the halcyon days of Gordon to our quasi-technological age with grace and show that there are consolations to "fishless days" and mighty satisfying ones at that. "The Quest for Theodore Gordon" (his final resting place, that is) is a first-rate piece of angling journalism, and "Murder" will indeed make you wonder why it is you fish.

Published by: Crown. **Price:** $7.50.

The Garcia Outdoor Library

In *Complete Fisherman's Catalog* terminology these little pocket-size fishing books might be called "Minimum Commodities." If you still don't believe there's any connection between better fishing and book learnin', invest $1.50 in one of the *Garcia Outdoor Library* fishing titles of your choice. With the exception perhaps of Howard Brant's *Trout*, an identification and techniques book, they're a solid school of good fishing techniques — concise and well-illustrated too. You'll find the bare basics of each fishing topic covered with enough photographs or line work to help even the beginner visualize what he's really trying to do with that Garcia rod (there's a certain amount of Garcia advertising free with every book). Mark Sosin, Lefty Kreh, Homer Circle, Vlad Evanoff —

GAMEFISH: OCEANIC BONITO

NAMES
Skipjack, Arctic bonito, bonito, Victor fish, striped tuna. *(Katsuwonus pelamis)*

DISTRIBUTION
The oceanic bonito is a fish of warm waters that prefers the southern ranges of the Atlantic and Pacific oceans. It is found off the coast of California and Florida.

DESCRIPTION
The oceanic bonito is a beautiful fish colored blue on the back, with silver sides and shaded yellow and red. Across the sides and belly four horizontal stripes run from the pectoral fin to the tail. The oceanic bonito has no scales except in an area surrounding the pectoral fin.

SIZE
The oceanic bonito is a small fish that usually does not weigh over 20 pounds. The average weight is between 10 and 18 pounds.

HABITAT
The oceanic bonito travels in schools and prefers open waters. They will, however, come close to shore if they are following food. They feed on the surface. In the fall and winter, they are found in southern waters.

FEEDING HABITS
The oceanic bonito feeds on all varieties of fish including mackerel, flying fish and sardines.

BEST FEEDING TEMPERATURE
About 64°.

TACKLE
This fish is a good candidate for the still-fisher casting from piers with cut baits but can also be caught by trolling or casting with medium-weight baitcasting or spinning gear.

GARCIA OUTDOOR LIBRARY

top of the line

they've all authored more expensive books, but you can get the gist of it in these Garcia editions at one-fifth the price. Lefty Kreh's *Fly Fishing* may be the exception, but even intermediate flycasters will probably learn a trick or two here. His *Tips and Tricks for Spinning* must be worth twice the price. They're good preparation for a change-of-pace fishing trip that may spark a whole new angling enthusiasm. You'll find them at Garcia tackle stores, or you can order direct from the company.

Great Fishing Tackle Catalogs of the Golden Age
By Samuel Melner and Hermann Kessler

This is a charming book and it will teach you plenty about the history of a sport in which there is little under the sun that's really new. Covers excerpts from the major manufacturers' catalogs starting in the late 19th Century and finishing with post-1922 stuff. The startling new ideas have come and gone. The solid ideas remain.
Published by: Crown. **Price:** $6.95.

How to Fish Good
By Dave Bascom

If you think that fishing is ultimately silly, you'll love this work by ex-advertising man Dave Bascom. "A fishing comic book," is how some anglers describe this otherwise indescribable book. Lots of yuks. Lots more yuks. No solid information. Thank goodness.
Published by: Winchester. **Price:** $2.95.

In Trout Country
Edited by Peter Corodimas

A recent but out-of-print collection

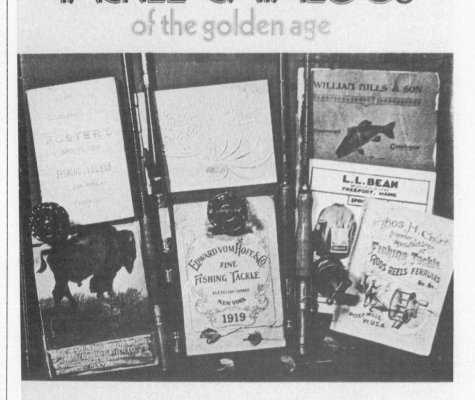

GREAT FISHING TACKLE CATALOGS
of the golden age

Edited by Samuel Melner and Hermann Kessler
Commentary by Sparse Grey Hackle

top of the line

worth finding if only for the wide range of modern angling stories it presents; from Brautigan's "The Hunchback Trout" to Ed Zern's "Something Was Fishy About Stonehenge" and a gathering of the golden-age writers in between: Robert Traver, Jesse Hill Ford, Donald O'Brien and 25 others. Something for everybody.

Published by: Little Brown. **Price:** $8.95.

Jonah's Dream
By Sven Berlin

This book by Englishman Sven Berlin is unusual. It's a metaphysical journey through the higher realms of the sport. A little difficult for those used to the "me and Joe school" of outdoorsy writing, it's a worthwhile trip for those meditative enough to relax and go along for the descriptive ride.

Published by: William Kaufman (Los Altos, California). **Price:** $5.95.

Moby Dick
By Herman Melville

A longish novel that illustrates very well the dangers of going out after lunkers with inadequate tackle. Considering that it's only a fish story, some of the book dwells too heavily on the relationships between people. Nonetheless, it's an important source for anyone considering managing a fishing boat, even though it will never replace A. G. Watson's *Commercial Deep Sea Angling.*

Power Boats in Rough Seas
By Dag Pike

This book should be looked at by every angler who sometimes goes a little too far and winds up in open seas. Covers boat and engine capabilities, emergencies, storms, weather interpretation, wave dynamics and

THE LAST HATCH
A FISHING MYSTERY
HARMON HENKIN

(continued from page 416)

from the *Missoulian*, the local daily, a small, boxed announcement of Halford's death. It was printed next to a big interview with a Kiwanis Club president who had just returned from South Africa with a report that thousands of Black African Communists were going to invade Montana. The president was worried about declining property values.

Paul became restless as Wormer and Schielbacht discussed the ups and downs of pork bellies on the Chicago futures market. He went back into the house and began browsing through books. Except for a couple classic works on angling, there wasn't much there to interest him. As he was examining the rod rack for the umpteenth time, the phone rang. He hesitated before picking it up.

"Hello?"

"This is Fran Hailey's Fly Shop. Mr. Halford called us last Thursday and ordered a dozen Skykomish Specials. Said he needed them right away in big sizes. I called yesterday morning to tell him they were finished. Some guy answered the phone and said he'd tell him. But nobody picked 'em up and today I read he's dead. What's going on?"

"Who answered the phone?"

"I dunno. Said he was just visiting. Seemed to know a lot about those kind of steelhead flies, though."

"Would you recognize the voice?"

"Sure. We talked for five minutes or so. Why? What's this all about?"

"That's great. Just hold the flies. I'll get back to you. This is Paul Skues."

He found Sid standing by the stable, looking dejected.

"Damn it, Paul. The investigators are going to be swarming the place in a little while. What am I going to tell them?"

"Simple. That you know who did it and have proof."

"Who? What? When?"

"Gather everyone back in the living room and I'll show you."

Julie had been watching them from a branch ten feet off the ground.

"I solved it, Julie."

"I won't come down until you tell me I'm the fairest in the land."

"I have proof."

(continued on page 435)

BARBECUED LING

4 ling
4 slices bacon
1 small onion, chopped
1/2 clove garlic
1 bay leaf
1/4 t sweet basil
1 t salt
dash cayenne pepper
1 t brown sugar
3 ounces tomato paste + 3/4 c water OR 1 No. 2 can tomatoes

Prepare ling as you would for broiling.

Fry bacon. Add onion and garlic. Sauté, until lightly browned. Add remaining ingredients to bacon mixture and simmer, covered, for 10 minutes.

Place fish in greased shallow baking dish and pour sauce over fish. Bake one hour in 375-degree oven. Serve over steamed rice. Serves 4. — Connie Miller, Grand Junction, Colorado.

top of the line

operating procedures in storms. Excellent.

Published by: International Marine Publishers. **Price:** $10.95.

Practical Fishing Knots
By Lefty Kreh and Mark Sosin

Kreh and Sosin are two of the best technical-minded anglers in the country and this knotty work is the standard for the field. Regardless of what particular kinds of angling you practice they have a way to get it together. Not only are the knots themselves fully illustrated but they also list breaking strengths and everything else you've wanted to know about them. Excellent book.

Published by: Crown. **Price:** $5.95.

The Spawning Run
By William Humphrey

This is more like literature than a fishing book but that shouldn't scare anglers away. It's a deliciously funny story about an American on a British salmon river — one of the cleverest angling books written in a long time. a modern classic.

Published by: Knopf. **Price:** $4.50.

Sport in Classic Time
By Alfred Joshua Butler

William Kaufman's California publishing house has done anglers a real service by reprinting Alfred Butler's *Sport in Classic Time*. It was originally printed in England in 1930. The new edition, which includes an introduction by the late Roderick Haig-Brown, contains excellent material on the roots of angling in antiquity — Greek and Roman times — plus information on hunting and fowling too. A sourcebook for fishermen in the true sense of the term.

Published by: William Kaufman (Los Altos, California). **Price:** $9.95.

top of the line

Teaching Your Children to Fish
By Jack Fallon

A good one for the parent who isn't an angler himself but whose kids have somehow got the bug. Covering all the basic modes of angling from the parent's point of view, it'll fool the kids into thinking you're an expert even if you've never wet a line.

Published by: Macmillan. **Price:** $6.95.

Through the Fish's Eye
By Mark Sosin and John Clark

An important and informative book that does just what the title suggests. It gives the world view of a fish: how they see, what they see, effects of color on them and on and on and on. It's a very complete book covering the diet preferences and biological reactions of the species that anglers covet most. Fine work.

Published by: Harper & Row. **Price:** $8.95.

Trout Fishing in America
By Richard Brautigan

Trout Fishing in America was described in a tackle shop in West Yellowstone, Montana, as, "That hippie fishing book." Well, yes, it's the same kind of fishing literature as *Moby Dick* or Hemingway's *Big Two-Hearted River*. But this poetic odyssey is a vision of our times and as such is not really a story at all but a metaphor. And a difficult one to describe. Yet it somehow manages to get to the soul of fishing more than the outdoor writers do every month in the magazines.

Published by: Dell. **Price:** $1.25.

*Where the Pools
Are Bright and Deep*
By Dana S. Lamb

This book is a fine series of what used to be called vignettes of the life

GAMEFISH: DOLLY VARDEN

NAMES

Dolly, bull trout, western char, red-speckled trout, salmon trout. *(Salvelinus malma)*

DISTRIBUTION

The Dolly Varden is found from northern California into Canada and Alaska. It is also native to Montana and parts of Idaho.

DESCRIPTION

Like the brook trout, the Dolly Varden is a member of the char family. Its elongated body is brownish-green on the back with yellow and red spots on the sides. The fins are bordered with a white or yellow stripe and the tail is forked. In salt water, these fish take on a silver cast.

SIZE

The size of the Dolly Varden varies according to where it lives. In small streams, the average is about ½ to 1 pound but in large lakes, they can attain weights of up to 6 pounds.

HABITAT

Although the Dolly Varden is considered a freshwater fish, in the northern part of its range it sometimes can be found in saltwater. It prefers cold lakes and large streams where it seeks out deep pools and eddies. In lakes, it tends to hide close to submerged debris and near ledges and reefs.

FEEDING HABITS

The Dolly Varden has acquired a notorious reputation among anglers due to its fondness for the spawn of other fish. It does, however, eat flies, insects and baitfish as well as trout and salmon young. It is primarily a bottom feeder that is not particular about its diet.

TACKLE

The Dolly, which ain't the greatest fighter in the world in its smaller sizes, can be a brute in the bigger lengths requiring heavy fly tackle with big streamers or medium spinning or baitcasting outfits with spoons, plugs and live minnows. Sometimes trolled.

top of the line

of an angler in all of its aspects. Lamb is a delicate writer not given to overstatement and the series of miniatures he paints with words come through loudly and clearly to anyone who cares about days on the stream. An excellent little book.

Published by: Winchester. **Price:** $8.95.

Children's Books

Fishing
By Tom McNally

If your angler offspring insists on having his or her own book, the McNally All Star Sports series book (ages 8 and up, notes the publisher) will probably fit the bill. It's an all-purpose introduction to fishing with all the safety and tackle care admonitions that you are probably already making yourself. A book like this can't take the place of good instruction and a few bites now and then, but it will get young Walton started on the road to angling literacy.

Published by: Follett Publishing Co. **Price:** $3.95.

For a review see page 429

Jonah's Dream

A MEDITATION ON FISHI

Sven Berl

For a review see page 426

Our chef suggests....

Since most angling books take you only as far as landing (or releasing) your fish, it pays to have a specialty fish cookbook on hand for those times when you haul out the season's frozen catch and have a fiesta. After all, fish is one of the few entrees both low in calories and high in protein. Properly prepared it can be a real delicacy. And it seems fool-hardy to spend $89.99 on a spinning rod, read 12 bass books, travel to northern Mexico's Lake Chichihuahua, and then drown your catch in a sea of vegetable oil. Carry the angling cere-mony through to the end with careful if not necessarily gourmet-level fish cookery and you may find your friends and family encouraging your fishing trips.

There are quite literally thousands of cookbooks in print and almost all gener-al ones have good basic fish recipes. Craig Claiborne's *New York Times Cookbook* is the best all-purpose guide. Ethnic cookbooks (the French are no-toriously good fish cooks) usually offer interesting and not always exotic rec-ipes, and upper-crust gourmet cook-books like Simone Beck and Julia Child's *Mastering the Art of French Cooking* (Volume I is better for fish) represent fish cooking as a discipline in itself. Even if your tastes are simpler, you should know the basics of good fish cooking, including a few recipe alterna-tives to frying. (If you must fry, fry quickly).

Proper fish cookery may be summed up in a sentence from The Fishery Council of New York: "Fish is cooked to develop flavor, not to make it ten-der." Use a sauce, try poaching fish or steam it — but don't overcook. It's done when the meat flakes away from the bones at the touch of a fork.

Here is a good selection of fish cook-books from our New York chef in a va-riety of angling tastes and prices. Gour-met cookbooks are included, even though they often call for fish more often available at the market than any-where else. — J.H.

top of the line

In a Running Brook
By Winifred and Cecil Lubell

Fish and How They Reproduce
By Dorothy Hinshaw Patent

Here are two recent "young adult" books that ironically are also the best introductory books for adults too. These are not cute little fishy stories, and they will help you try to instill basic conservation principles in young anglers. You'll learn a few things yourself, too. At children's book prices they're both bargains.

In a Running Brook by the Lubells has a pleasant and yet biolog-ically accurate story line perfect for younger freshwater anglers or chil-dren who visit streams a lot. Don't be bashful about reading it yourself; it's probably second only to Brian Curtis' *The Life of the Fish* (Dover) for recommended adult reading about fish from a non-angling view-point.
Published by: Rand McNally & Co. **Price:** $4.95.

Fish and How They Reproduce is a nicely illustrated, simple all-pur-pose reference to fish, including all the popular game species as well as ocean creatures and oddities. A good book for the serious young icthyolo-gist and the angler who wants to learn all the fish biology he needs and no more. This one should settle all the questions your young fishers will raise about where fish come from, but it may lead to others about the higher species. Be prepared.
Published by: Holiday House. **Price:** $6.95.

Fish Cookery

Art of Fish Cookery
By Milo Miloradovich

Not as stylish as Beard, but still a good gourmet approach; it does as-sume some familiarity with fancy cookin'. Our chef recommends the

Rolled Carp Fillet. (Available in a $1 paperback edition from Bantam).

The Blue Sea Cookbook
By Sarah D. Alberson
Edited by Eleanor Porter
A good seafood guide with less emphasis on shellfish than other salty cookbooks. Seafood cookbooks are not in short supply but if you're really after fresh seafood experiences, try this one.
Published by: Hastings. **Price:** $8.95.

Fish Cookery of North America
By Frances MacIlquham
MacIlquham does Dunaway's "from hook to table" treatment a lot more stylishly and sometimes approaches the Beard school in its gourmet reaches but still includes handling and preparation. A good book for making the transition from cook to *chef de peche.*
Published by: Winchester. **Price:** $10.

From Hook to Table: An Angler's Guide to Good Eating
By Vic Dunaway
A cookbook by an angler for anglers. Dunaway's compilation does not reach the gastronomic heights that Beard's does, but he does prove the point that even the humble catfish can be made into a memorable meal. A good choice from an angler's point of view, since there are recipes and preparation tips for the more common catches across the country.
Published by: Macmillan. **Price:** $6.95.

The Home Book of Smoke-Cooking Meat, Fish, and Game
As a preliminary step, or as an alternative to freezing fish you don't want to eat right away, try smoke-

CRANBERRY CATCH

2 pounds thick fish fillets
1 c celery, sliced
1/3 c onion, chopped
6 T margarine or cooking oil
4 c soft bread cubes
1/2 c pecans, chopped
1 1/4 t salt
1 t orange rind, grated
1/4 c orange juice

Cut fillets into 6 portions. Cook celery and onions in a 10-inch frying pan in 4 T margarine or cooking oil until tender but not brown. Stir in bread cubes, pecans, 1/4 t salt, orange rind and orange juice. Turn stuffing into well-greased baking dish 12x8x2 inches. Arrange fish in a single layer on stuffing. Drizzle remaining 2 T melted margarine or cooking oil over fish. Sprinkle with 1 t salt. Bake in 350-degree oven 25-30 minutes, or until fish flakes easily when tested with fork. Serve with Cranberry-Orange Sauce.

CRANBERRY-ORANGE SAUCE

1/3 c sugar
2 t cornstarch
1/2 c orange juice
1/2 c water
1 c cranberries, raw
2 t orange rind, grated

Combine sugar and cornstarch in a 2-quart saucepan and mix. Add orange juice and water; cook, stirring constantly, until mixture comes to a boil. Add cranberries and cook 5 minutes or until skins on cranberries pop. Stir occasionally. Fold in orange rind. Serve with fish. Makes 1 1/4 c sauce. Serves 6. — *U.S. Conservation News.*

TROUT WITH ALMONDS

4 trout, each about 8 inches long
flour, salt and pepper
1/4 c butter or margarine
1/4 c almonds, slivered
3 T butter or margarine

Dredge trout in flour, salt and pepper. Fry them in 1/4 c butter or margarine until done. Remove to a platter. To the frying pan add 3 T butter or margarine and 1/4 c slivered almonds. Cook the almonds until the butter is browned. Pour butter-almond mixture over the fish and serve immediately. — Mrs. Liter Spence, Helena, Montana.

top of the line

cooking. There's almost no fish that can't be made palatable by smoking it, and homemade smokers are pretty easy to rig. A good guide to smoke-cooking, including plans for building simple fish-sized smokers.

Published by: Stackpole. **Price:** $7.95.

International Fish Dishes
By Nina Froud and Tamara Lo

A round-the-world selection of ethnic fish dishes; not always exotic, but adds an international spice to the job of cooking. It includes some of the under-appreciated Chinese and Japanese fish dishes that everyone shies away from in restaurants.

Published by: Hippocrene Books. **Price:** $8.95.

New Fish Cookery
By James Beard

A new edition of one of the best of the gourmet-level cookbooks. This revised version includes some supposedly fool-proof" cooking methods discovered by the Canadian Fisheries Council for just-right fish every time. (A paperback version of the original edition is available from Paperback Library for 95 cents.)

THE LAST HATCH
A FISHING MYSTERY
HARMON HENKIN

(continued from page 429)

"That I'm the fairest?"

"Be serious."

"That's what I've been telling you for years."

She leaped off the tree and almost knocked him down. "Let's go, Prince Charming, and vanquish this mystery."

Half an hour later everyone had finally assembled. The meeting had the feel of an Academy Awards, or at least the naming of the Sweetheart of Sigma Chi. Paul was nervous and Julie tried to calm him down.

"Let's get to it, folks," Paul said, standing. They heard cars roll into the driveway.

"Hurry up, Paul," Sid whispered. "They're coming."

"Just keep them outside until I finish this. It won't take more than a few minutes."

He turned back to the group. "Now everyone here had a clear and decent motive for killing Halford, the all-American scoundrel. And you all had the opportunity and machinery to kill him. The gaff was always available and it only took a few minutes after lunch."

Everyone agreed reluctantly.

"But it took either a spectacularly lucky blow to kill him instantly, which I think we can rule out, or someone who knew how to use a gaff."

The glances went to Schielbacht and then to Hewitt.

"We've discovered that Halford lied in his journal to cover up where he was really going last Thursday. And it would take someone very familiar with trout fishing to catch the lie."

Eyes still flowed between Hewitt and Schielbacht.

"But the key came this morning. Hailey's Fly Shop called and said that Halford had placed a special rush order for a dozen Skykomish Specials."

Everyone was puzzled.

"What's that got to do with anything?" Wormer demanded.

"The Skykomish is a pattern used solely for steelhead, mainly on the Olympic Peninsula of Washington. Despite Schielbacht's claims of universal competence there's only one person who would really understand what that fly was going to be used for. And that person would know that Halford was about to leave here to start a new life. He would also know where he was going."

(continued on page 438)

Oh, you who've been a-fishing will endorse
me when I say
That it always *is* the biggest fish you catch
that gets away!
EUGENE FIELD, *Our Biggest Fish.*

Coffee table books: reading trophies

Angling books come in almost as many sizes and weight classes as fish, from Art Flick's compact little *New Streamside Guide* to the salmon-sized *Salmon of the World*. These big productions are angling's answer to what is called in the book trade a "coffee table book": oversized and lavishly illustrated and bound, they usually cost as much as a coffee table. Some like the Freshet Press limited edition reprints of 19th Century classics in handsome leather bindings are collector's pieces well worth having to maintain a tenuous bond to the era when 5-pound brook trout could be found on Long Island streams. Others are strictly for conspicuous angling consumption — but no less a joy to own for the real bibliophile. Don't worry if you can't afford these trophy books; like the trip you always wanted to take to Newfoundland they're usually just as much fun in your imagination as they are on a bookshelf.

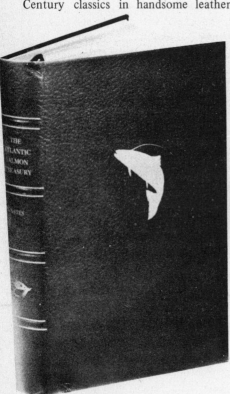

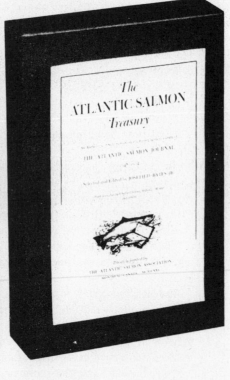

PADDLEFISH WITH ONION RICE

3/4 c onion soup
3/4 c instant rice
12 ounces paddlefish, cut in 1-inch cubes
1 c mushroom soup
1 c water
1/2 c mixed red and green sweet peppers and celery

Bring the onion soup to boil. Add the instant rice and stir. Cover for 5 minutes. Keep hot. Parboil the paddlefish for 2 minutes. Drain. (Save the broth for pet food.) Add the mushroom soup diluted with the water. Bring to boil and simmer for 2 minutes. Pour fish mixture over onion rice. Garnish with the mixed vegetables. Serves 2-3. — Nancy Olson, Billings, Montana.

top of the line

Lunkers

The Atlantic Salmon Treasury
Edited by Joseph D. Bates, Jr.

The Atlantic Salmon Association, on the occasion of the 25th anniversary of its *Journal*, published a 1000-copy limited edition of *Journal* writings: "gems of angling literature, with valuable, factual information on the lore of the salmon, the lure of the rivers, and on the tackle and tactics for hooking our 'King of Fishes' and bringing the trophy to net or beach." All that in a gold-stamped, morocco-bound and boxed book illustrated with line drawings and color work by the likes of Mill Weiler and Charles DeFeo and photographs. The team of salmon worshippers includes some stellar names — Dana Lamb, Lee Wulff, Austin Hogan and others from the salmon-fishing constellation. It's a happy coincidence that those articles also happen to be well-written, in a wide range from anecdotal stories to precise histories of salmon flies. Some international material makes this the salmon fisherman's dreamiest opium, at only slightly less than the price of a trip to the Miramichi.

Published by: The Atlantic Salmon Association. **Price:** $125.

---

*The Compleatest Angling Booke
That Ever Was Writ*
By Joseph Crawhall

A boxed edition with luxurious binding and stampings, the hallmark of this aristocratic angling press. The Crawhall book is one of an early and modern series of classics from Freshet that includes John Atherton's *The Fly and the Fish* ($12.95), *Greased Line Salmon Fishing* by Jock Scott ($10.75), Bus Grove's lyrical *The Lure and the*

top of the line

Lore of Trout Fishing ($9.95), and Charlie Fox's *The Wonderful World of Trout* ($35). For William Schaldach fans there is *Coverts and Cats* and *Currents and Eddies* combined for $25, and their special *Wind on Your Cheek* contains a Schaldach engraving "Evening on the River" created especially for the Freshet edition. In a publishing era when rising production costs force most publishers to take short cuts among the frills that book lovers love, these handsome editions are exceptionally well-produced. Certainly not everyone's idea of fishing accessories, nonetheless, like snelled salmon flies and solid brass baitcasting reels, it's nice to know this kind of quality's still around.

Published by: Freshet Press. **Price:** $27.50.

Game Fishes of the United States
By S. A. Kilbourne
With text by G. Goode Brown

Winchester's limited edition of the classic 19th-Century study of American game fishes features framable color plates, Kilbourne's renderings of fresh- and saltwater fish, including most of the salmonids and some saltwater fellows, too. When you see the fine (and somewhat formal) printed text, which carries some nice line illustrations of its own, you'll hesitate to separate them. For the angler of distinction.

Published by: Winchester Press. **Price:** $75.

The Lore of Sport Fishing
Edited by Frank Moss

A lavish book of tackle and gamefish, with some solid fishing basics added, in the style of *The Lore of Trains* and other forebears. Colorful and hefty (420 pages), it may tempt you away from more sensible titles

GEFILTE GOLDEYE

1/2 pound goldeye fillets, fresh or frozen
6 c water
2 medium carrots, sliced
2 medium onions, chopped
1 T salt
1/8 t pepper
2 eggs
2 T ice water
2 T matzo meal or cracker meal
1/2 t salt
dash pepper

Thaw frozen fish. In large saucepan, combine the water, half the carrots, half the onions, salt and pepper. Bring to boiling and simmer, covered, 30 minutes. Finely grind the fish and remaining vegetables. Place in large mixing bowl; add eggs, ice water, meal, salt and pepper. Beat at high speed until fluffy. Shape into balls or fingers, using 3 T for each. Place in broth. Cover; simmer 20 minutes. Drain; serve hot or cold.

THE LAST HATCH
A FISHING MYSTERY
HARMON HENKIN

(continued from page 435)

Hewitt leaped up. Everyone gasped.

"Me. I'm the only person in this gaggle of dullards who would know what and where that pattern was going to be used."

"And your wife said she was planning a trip to Washington this morning. When you picked up the phone yesterday morning and found out about Halford's order for flies you put it all together and knew your wife was going to run off with him. You had to act."

Belle was crying softly. Hewitt slumped back into his chair.

"Very good, young man. It was getting intolerable. Belle was forever running off with some wretch or another. If it wasn't a novelist it was a poet or a musician. Besides being unfaithful, she had awful taste. But I drew the line with Halford. Enough was never enough for her. What a revolting couple they would have made."

"Honey," Belle said, reaching out for him, "I wasn't going to leave with him. We had a little, well, romance but I told him three days ago it was over. He was becoming such a crushing bore. As a farewell sop he begged me to loan him my family's cabin on the Peninsula, the one at Quinault."

"You weren't running off with him?" Paul gasped.

"Never."

"What a stinking waste," Hewitt snarled.

"Well, who was he going away with?" Paul asked.

"Me."

They all turned. Tups was smiling.

"That's right, man. He was older but we could have worked it out. We were going to start a commune based on Spartan principles and doughball fishing in the mountains. I could dig that trip, if you know what I mean."

Everyone was dumbfounded. Tups shrugged. Dun had gone off into a corner to sob again.

Schielbacht had broken into a big smile.

"Now I'm the greatest angling expert in the world."

The door burst open and a mob of cops and librarians swarmed in, pushing Sid out of the way.

"Arrest that man," Paul ordered, pointing at Hewitt.

As they led him away he turned. "With my money and influence and

(continued on page 440)

that cover the same information for a third the price. *The Lore of Sport Fishing* is probably one of the more useful of the big-ticket books except, of course, for *McClane's New Standard Fishing Encyclopedia*. Includes some basic tackle material.

Published by: Crown. **Price:** $29.95.

Salmon of the World
By Ernest Schwiebert

Herr Schwiebert's monument to the salmon he has known and loved. You'll love them, too, when you see the 30 paintings he's created for this book. Fine talk about salmon fishing and the rivers of Europe and North America for those who can afford to indulge their salmania to this level.

Published by: Winchester Press. **Price:** $100.

McClane's New Standard Fishing Encyclopedia
Edited by A. J. McClane

One of the larger encyclopedic books really worth its price tag in practicalities, *McClane's* is the angler's answer to the *Britannica*, *Guinness Book of World Records* and the *Oxford English Dictionary* all in one. Over 6000 alphabetized entries from "aawa" to "zooplankton" that makes for diverting reading, even if you never get to fish for the Okefenokee pigmy sunfish or speckled hind. There are lots of practical bits of information on fly tying and other tackle crafts — over 1400 pages of it — but the lack of an index is vexing. Dive right in — you're bound to find something useful within four pages, and you probably won't look up for twenty. A hefty book for a hefty price, but read it closely and you can probably win back the $40 in bets the first year.

Published by: Holt, Rinehart and Winston. **Price:** $40.

The science behind the sport: find out what it's like down there

As you get deeper into angling, sooner or later you will come to see the fish as a member of a stream (lake, ocean, etc.) community of critters. After all, beyond the level of chuck-it-and-chance-it, sportfishing might be widely described as the attempt to enter the fishes' world by some artifice — bait, fly, spinner or live-hooked lunker — and bring them back to ours. It helps to know what it's like down there. Call it an "ecosystem," "food chain" or just good fifth-grade biology, understanding of fish and their natural history adds a dimension to fishing that you can't buy in the tackle store. And just as often it makes the difference that a shiny new Wonder Wobbler won't. Familiarity with the habits and habitat of your favorite quarry is more than just background music; it's really the whole symphony. Listening and learning to understand what you hear will make a big difference in your appreciation of the time you spend fishing, and in your success.

Fortunately or unfortunately, there exists a huge body of scientific literature on fish, stream biology, oceanography, aquatic entomology and fisheries management. Not every angler would want to read these books, even if they were readily available; many are the results of ex-haustive studies and are necessarily large, expensive and sometimes hard to find (scientific books tend to go out of print quickly). But there are several books that bring essential information from the laboratory to the fisherman's den with ease, grace and a modest cash outlay. These are the kinds of books you'll find yourself referring to again and again, and re-reading over the winter, even though in most cases they weren't written with anglers in mind.

On the other hand, the economic value of some fish species as game fish or as food has brought down upon them the full wrath of science (B.A.S.S. has founded the Bass Research Institute), and which in turn has led to some thorough studies of individual habitats and species. Once again, it's tough going, but the dedicated angler may find the spark of a new fishing technique or lure here (don't read these in the bathtub). And, perhaps most importantly, these books will give you an appreciation for the complexity of the aquatic world that you cast over, but seldom really know. It's harder to dump soapsuds into the water — and easier to prove the wrong in it to others — when you know what it does to the folks who live there.

top of the line

Science & Fish

American Food and Game Fishes
By David S. Jordan and Barton Everman

A quasi-scientific treatment of the edible fish species found in North American waters, including up-to-date range information, where possible, and a full life history and profile that yields an angling application or two. A bargain reference book for the angler.
Published by: Dover. **Price:** $5.

Ecology and Field Biology
By Robert L. Smith

A good step back to the relationship of running water to the larger ecological network; a bit textbookish, but understandable and authoritative. A good reference to use on the stand when testifying against real estate developers who think it's just a creek.
Published by: Harper & Row. **Price:** $14.95.

The Ecology of Running Waters
By H. N. B. Hynes

Wide and deep as the Mississippi, Hynes' book is recognized as the standard encyclopedia and reference work on the biology of running water. Chapters on plant life, aquatic insects, stream dynamics and fish and their feeding habits are studied with references to scientific works. Yet the whole remains clear and intelligible to the layman. Taken a little at a time, it will give a baccalaureate grounding in stream biology that justifies its price.
Published by: University of Toronto Press. **Price:** $25.

> "The line with its rod is a long instrument whose lesser end holds a small reptile, while the other is held by a great fool."
> GUYET

THE LAST HATCH
A FISHING MYSTERY
HARMON HENKIN

(continued from page 438)

your flimsy evidence, what do you think the odds are of getting me convicted? Justice might not be for sale in this country but it's certainly for rent."

"Good struggle, Hewitt. Hope you enjoy the rest of the fight."

As Alexandrea backed Tups into a corner, screeching and shaking her fist, Julie grabbed her coat and walked for the door. Paul followed her.

"Hey, how about dinner at my place tonight?"

"Trout?"

"Of course."

She nodded and grinned. Paul clapped his hands once.

"Sid, let's go fishing!"

FINIS.

POACHED CARP WITH HORSERADISH SAUCE

1 3-pound pan-dressed carp, fresh or frozen
1 medium onion, sliced
2 parsley sprigs
1 bay leaf
3 whole peppercorns
salt

HORSERADISH SAUCE

1 c dairy sour cream
3 T prepared horseradish, drained
1/4 t salt
dash paprika

Thaw frozen fish. Pour water into poacher or large skillet to depth of 1/2 inch. Add onion, parsley, bay leaf, peppercorns and salt (use 1/2 t salt per cup of water). Bring to boiling. Place carp on greased rack and set into poacher. Cover and cook until fish flakes easily when tested with a fork, about 20-25 minutes. Drain; serve hot or cold with Horseradish Sauce.

top of the line

Fishes of the World
By J. S. Nelson

A handsome Encyclopedia Britannica of fish, including detailed evolutionary relationships of modern forms. For the serious angler.

Published by: John Wiley & Sons. **Price:** $24.

Fresh-Water Invertebrates of the United States
By Robert W. Pennak

You could probably find a cheaper field guide to the freshwater fishes of the United States, but the illustrations and profiles of trout, bass, perch, et al., carry the authority of icthyology, and Pennak is considered the last word in that circle. Should settle any barroom arguments with ease.

Published by: The Ronald Press Co. **Price:** $15.

The Life Story of the Fish
By Brian Curtis

A gem of scientific writing for the layman that takes you down to the bottom of the evolutionary stream for a vivid look at fish as a life form — no mean task for a scientist-writer. Curtis' work will help put all the others in focus, and you'll learn a little icthyology in spite of yourself. Highly recommended for curious anglers.

Published by: Dover. **Price:** $3.50.

The New Field Book of Freshwater Life
By Elsie B. Klots

The Klots book is the publisher's successor to the admirable *Field Book of Ponds and Streams* by Ann Haven Morgan (out of print but not out of mind). It includes color plates and handy keys which were missing in

top of the line

that title. A good field guide, and perfect streamside reading.

Published by: G. P. Putnam's Sons. **Price:** $5.95.

The Stream Conservation Handbook
Edited by J. Michael Migel

The Stream Conservation Handbook is a round-table of conservationists who set forth in essays on basic stream biology, legal resources, group actions, stream improvements and other stream-health topics. It's not really a "handbook," although the chapters by Don Ecker on "Stream Surveillance" and Maury Otis on "Stream Improvement" are functional, and Dave Whitlock's Vibert Box essay is real angling news. There's more information on all these topics available from other sources, and of course no amount of reading is going to clean up our abused waters. But this book does help bring all the scattered elements of the issues into focus. In fact, *The Stream Conservation Handbook* raises more questions and unsettles more issues than it answers, but perhaps that's the first step. Read it once a year, at least.

Published by: Crown. **Price:** $7.95.

Trout Streams
By Paul R. Needham

The classic study of trout stream management and ecology, including comprehensive material on the entomology of cold waters.

Published by: Winchester. Out of print but worth finding.

Used Books

ANGLER'S & SHOOTER'S BOOKSHELF. Colonel Henry Siegel's Angler's and Shooter's Book-

shelf has been pushing vintage and semi-contemporary volumes for quite a while. It sets the pace for much of the market. Although the Colonel ain't known for his bargains, he is known for his completeness. The Bookshelf catalog, which comes out in two sections — "A to K" and the rest — is itself a minor education in the literature of the sport. Some thousands of books are offered — enough to convince even the diehard that the idea of writing a book about your outdoorsy experiences is not a unique experience. A must.

THE CHARLES DALY COLLECTION. A good source of used fishing books. The Charles Daly collection also has a wide selection of prints and oil paintings. It's a place for the specialist to look for that one book that means everything. Prices are in keeping with the market averages and they will search free-of-charge for the book you want. They sometimes trade and buy, as well.

RISING TROUT SPORTING BOOKS. This Guelph, Canada, shop offers a free list of used trouting books. They claim to have lots of valuable and rare titles.

SPORTING BOOK SERVICE. They're back in action with their annual list you can get for $1. May have some very offbeat titles.

GAMEFISH: LANDLOCKED SALMON

NAMES
Sebago salmon, lake Atlantic salmon, landlock, ouananiche. *(Salmosalar sebago)*

DISTRIBUTION
The landlock was originally found in the cold lakes of New England and southern Canada. Due to transplantation, it is now found in the lakes of New York state and in South America.

DESCRIPTION
The landlocked salmon is almost identical in appearance to the Atlantic salmon. It is dark, steel blue on the back, with silver-blue sides and a silvery white belly. The upper sides are marked with dark, shaped markings.

SIZE
A smaller fish than its cousin, the Atlantic salmon, the landlock averages about 4 pounds. A 10-pound fish is not considered unusual.

HABITAT
The landlocked salmon is a subspecies of the Atlantic salmon that was trapped inland thousands of years ago. It does not migrate from the ocean but spends its entire life in freshwater. It prefers clear, cold lakes and can usually be found in shallow waters. Favorite haunts include rocky shorelines and submerged reefs. In the late summer, these fish head for deeper, cooler water.

FEEDING HABITS
Like the Atlantic salmon, the landlock feeds primarily on fish, smelt in particular. They also eat small insects and worms. The spring is the best time to fish for landlocks because they can be found in shallow waters at that time.

BEST FEEDING TEMPERATURE
Between 45° and 50°.

Addresses of Manufacturers

Abercrombie & Fitch
P.O. Box 4266, Grand Central Station
New York, NY 10017

Tony Accetta & Son
932 Avenue E
Riviera Beach, FL 33404

Acme Tackle Company
69 Bucklin Street
Providence, RI 02907

Adventurer Tackle Boxes
VLCHEK Plastics Company
Middlefield, OH 44062

Al's Goldfish Lure Co.
Indian Orchard, MA 01051

Alumaweld Boats Inc.
4665 Crater Lake Highway
Medford, OR 97501

American Fiber-Lite
P.O. Box 67
Marion, IL 62959

American Fishing Tackle Manufacturers
    Association
20 N. Wacker Dr.
Chicago, IL 60606

Ande Inc.
1500 53rd St.
W. Palm Beach, FL 33407

Angler's & Shooter's Bookshelf
Goshen, CT 06756

Angler's Mail
6497 Pearl Road
Cleveland, OH 44130

Angler's World
16 East 53rd Street
New York, NY 10022

Angling Specialties
Box 97
Ancaster, Ontario L96 3L3
Canada

Applied Oceanographic Tech. Corp. (Lu
    Division)
199 Warfield Way
Southampton, NY 11968

Fred Arbogast Company
313 West North Street
Akron, OH 44303

Avon Inflatables Ltd.
Dafen, Llanelli Dyfed
South Wales, Great Britain

B and B Tackle Company
P.O. Box 220
Lufkin, TX 75901

Dan Bailey Flies & Tackle
209 West Park Street
Box 1019
Livingston, MT 59047

Dennis Bailey
Principal
Coventry & Birmingham School
288 Allesley Old Road
Coventry, CV586H, England

Bass Buster Inc.
301 Main
Amsterdam, MO 64723

Bass Pro Shops
2023 South Glenstone
Box 4411
Springfield, MO 65804

Eddie Bauer
1737 Airport Way South
Seattle, WA 98134

Bay De Noc Lure Company
14 Central Avenue
Gladstone, MI 49837

Bead Chain Tackle Company
110 Mountain Grove Street
Bridgeport, CT 06605

L. L. Bean, Inc.
Freeport, ME 04032

Berkley & Company, Inc.
Highway 9 & 71
1617 Hill Avenue
Spirit Lake, IA 51360

Betts Tackle, Ltd.
P.O. Box 57
Highway 42 West
Fuquay-Varina, NC 27526

Bevin-Wilcox Line Company
Division — Brownell and Co. Inc.
Main Street
Moodus, CT 06469

Big-Jon Inc.
14393 Peninsula Drive
Traverse City, MI 49684

Bobber Products Inc.
2500 — A
East Fender Avenue
P.O. Box 3175
Fullerton, CA 92631

Bodmer's Fly Shop
2400 Naegele Road
Colorado Springs, CO 80904

Bomber Bait Co.
Box 1506
Gainesville, TX 76240

Boone Bait Company
Forsyth Road
P.O. Box 571
Winter Park, FL 32789

Brookstone Company
123 Vose Farm Road
Peterborough, NH 03458

Browning Arms Company
Route 1
Morgan, UT 84050

Buck Knives
Box 1267
El Cajon, CA 92022

Burke Fishing Lures
1969 South Airport Road
Traverse City, MI 49684

Buss Manufacturing Co.
Box 87
Lanark, IL 61046

Buz's Fly and Tackle Shop
805 West Tulare Avenue
Visalia, CA 93277

Cabela's, Inc.
812 13th Avenue
Sidney, NE 69162

Calala's Water Haven, Inc.
Dept. FS-6
R.D. 2, Route 60
New London, OH 44851

Camp Trails
4111 West Clarendon
Phoenix, AZ 85019

Cascade Lakes Development Operation
6 Berkley Square
Scotia, NY 12302

Cascade Tackle Company
2425 Diamond Lake Blvd.
Roseburg, OR 97470

W. R. Case & Sons Cutlery Co.
20 Russell Blvd.
Bradford, PA 16701

Lew Childre and Sons Inc.
P.O. Box 535
Foley, AL 36535

Chris-Craft
Algonac, MI 48001

The Classic Gun & Reel
P.O. Box 1035
Livingston, MT 59047

F. M. Claudio Rod Company
1482 38th Avenue
San Francisco, CA 94122

Dale Clemons Custom Tackle
Rt. 3, Box 415-F
Allentown, PA 18104

Len Codella's Anglers Den Inc.
5 S. Wood Ave.
Box 701
Linden, NJ 07036

Charlie Cole
6052 Montgomery Bend
San Jose, CA 95135

Cole Outdoor Products of America, Inc.
801 P Street
Lincoln, NE 68501

The Coleman Company Inc.
250 North St. Francis Street
Wichita, KS 67201

Columbia Sportswear Co.
6600 N. Baltimore St.
Portland, OR 97203

Common Sense
A. J. Gallager
319 Delsea Drive
Westville, NJ 08093

Converse Rubber Co.
55 Fordham Road
Wilmington, MA 01887

Cordell Tackle Inc.
P.O. Box 2020
Hot Springs, AR 71901

Coren's Rod and Reel Service
6619 North Clark
Chicago, IL 60626

Cortland Line Company
Cortland, NY 13045

Creek Chub Bait Co.
113 Keyser St., East
Garrett, IN 46738

Crestliner
609 13th Avenue, N.E.
Little Falls, MN 56345

J. Lee Cuddy Associates Inc.
450 N. E. 79th Street
Miami, FL 33138

Ed Cummings Inc.
P.O. Box 6186
Flint, MI 48508

Vince Cummings Custom Rods
73 Main Street
Dobbs Ferry, NY 10522

Cutter Laboratories Inc.
Fourth and Parker Streets
Berkeley, CA 94710

The Charles Daly Collection
36 Golf Lane
Ridgefield, CT 06877

D-Boone Enterprises Inc.
P.O. Box 8
High Spire, PA 17034

Daiwa Corporation
14011 South Normandie Avenue
Gardena, CA 90249

Les Davis Fishing Tackle Company
1565 Center Street
Tacoma, WA 98409

Dewitt Plastics
P.O. Box 400
Auburn, NY 13021

Dickey Tackle Company
Little Portage Lake Road
Land O' Lakes, WI 54540

Dragon Fly Company
823 Broad Street
Sumter, SC 29150

The Dunham Company
P.O. Box 813
Brattleboro, VT 05301

E-Z Action Products Company
1053 Riverside Drive
Battle Creek, MI 49916

E. Z. Mount, Inc.
735 North Snelling Avenue
St. Paul, MN 55104

Eastern Mountain Sports
Box 662
Boston, MA 02215

John B. Emery
7770 Sunset Drive
Miami, FL 33143

Eureka Tent Inc.
P.O. Box 966
Binghamton, NY 10932

Glen L. Evans
Caldwell, ID 83605

Farm Pond Harvest
372 South East Ave.
Kankakee, IL 60901

Featherweight Products
3454-58 Ocean View Blvd.
Glendale, CA 91208

Fenwick/Sevenstrand
P.O. Box 729
14799 Chestnut Street
Westminster, CA 92683

Fireside Angler, Inc.
P.O. Box 823
Melville, NY 11746

Fish-Hawk Waller Corporation
Box 340
4220 Waller Drive (Ridgefield)
Crystal Lake, IL 60014

Fishing Tackle Trade News
P.O. Box 70
Wilmette, IL 60091

Flambeau Products Corporation
801 Lynn Avenue
Baraboo, WI 53913

Fly Fisherman's Bookcase
Route 9A
Croton-on-Hudson, NY 10520

Foster Grant Co.
289 North Main Street
Leominster, MA 01453

Frabill Manufacturing Company
2018 South First Street
Milwaukee, WI 53207

Henry Frank
1 Mountain Meadow Road
Whitefish, MT 59937

The Gaines Co.
Gaines, PA 16921

Gapen Tackle Company
Highway 10
Big Lake, MN 55309

The Garcia Corporation
110 Charlotte Place
Englewood Cliffs, NJ 07632

G-96 Brand
Division of Jet-Aer Corporation
100 Sixth Avenue
Paterson, NJ 07524

Gerry Company
5450 North Valley Highway
Denver, CO 80216

Gladding — South Bend
South Otselic, NY 13155

Gladiator
Via Bonacini N. 4
41011 Campogalliano
Italy

Gregor Boat Co.
3564 N. Hazel
Fresno, CA 93705

Grumman Boats
Marathon, NY 13803

Gudebrod Brothers Silk Company, Inc.
12 South 12th Street
Philadelphia, PA 19107

Hackle & Tackle Co.
533 N. Salina St.
Syracuse, NY 13208

Hammacher Schlemmer
147 East 57th St.
New York, NY 10022

Harper Willis Bait Co.
Rt. 5, Box 53
Abilene, TX 79605

Harrington & Richardson, Inc.
Industrial Rowe
Gardner, MA 01440

Harrison-Hoge Ind. Inc. and Leisure
   Imports Inc.
104 Arlington Avenue
St. James, NY 11780

Hathaway Kayaks
640 Boston Post Road
Weston, MA 02193

Heddon (James Heddon's Sons Co.)
Dowagiac, MI 49047

Helin Tackle Company
4075 Beaufait
Detroit, MI 48207

Heritage Rod and Reel
P.O. Box 1035
Livingston, MT 59047

Herter's
Route 1
Waseca, MN 56093

Hildebrandt Corporation
Box 50
Logansport, IN 46947

E. Hille
P.O. Box 269
Williamsport, PA 17701

Hobson Company
3283 Lakeshore Avenue
Oakland, CA 94610

Hoffman's Hackle Farm
P.O. Box 130
Warrenton, OR 97146

Hummingbird
Allied Sports Company
One Hummingbird Lane
Eufaula, AL 36027

IPCO Inc.
331 Lake Hazeltine Dr.
Chaska, MN 55318

Ray Jefferson
Main and Cotton Streets
Philadelphia, PA 19127

Luhr Jensen and Sons Inc.
P.O. Box 297
Hood River, OR 97031

Jet-Aer Corporation
100 Sixth Avenue
Paterson, NJ 07524

Jiffy Jigger
Max H. Merrill
R.F.D. Rutland, VT 05701

Johnson Reels Company
Johnson Park
Mankato, MN 56001

Poul Jorgensen
604 Providence Road
Towson, MD 21204

Jorgensen Brothers
P.O. Box 69
Pleasanton, CA 94566

Kaufmann's Streamborn Flies
P.O. Box 23032
Portland, OR 97223

Kegara Manufacturing Company
P.O. Box 46322
Cincinnati, OH 45246

Kelty
1801 Victory Blvd.
Glendale, CA 91201

Kencor Sports Inc.
2184 W. 190th St.
Torrance, CA 90504

Keystone Fishing Corp.
1344 W. 37th St.
Chicago, IL 60609

Knight Manufacturing Company Inc.
Box 3162
Tyler, TX 75701

Knotmaster Industries, Inc.
P.O. Box 23201
San Diego, CA 92123

Kodiak Corporation
Box 467
Ironwood, MI 49938

Lake Products Co.
P.O. Box 116
Utica, MI 48087

Lakeland Industries
Isle, MN 56342

Lamiglass, Inc.
237 Davidson
Woodland, WA 98674

Landau Boat Company
P.O. Box 750
1015 Jefferson
Lebanon, MO 65536

H. L. Leonard Rod Company
25 Cottage Street
Midland Park, NJ 07432

H. L. Leonard Store
P.O. Box 491
Central Valley, NY 10917

Bud Lilly's Trout Shop
Box 387
West Yellowstone, MT 59758

Lowrance Electronics
12000 East Skelly Drive
Tulsa, OK 74128

Lure-craft
P.O. Box 1418
Bloomington, IN 47401

LusterLure
Box 594
Oak Ridge, MI 48073

M-F Manufacturing Company Inc.
1003 East Loop 820 South
Fort Worth, TX 76118

Mac-Jac Manufacturing Company
P.O. Box 821
Muskegon, MI 49443

Mad River Canoe
P.O. Box 363
Waitsfield, VT 05673

Magic Match Patch Company
625 Lk. Angelus Road
Pontiac, MI 48055

Magic Worm Bedding Company, Inc.
Amherst Junction, WI 54407

Magnuflex Rod Company
1771 West Flagler
Miami, FL 33135

Mann's Bait Company
P.O. Box 604
Eufaula, AL 36027

Marathon Rubber Products Co.
P.O. Box 1264
510 Sherman Street
Wausau, WI 54401

Marathon Tackle Company
Route 2, Highway XX
Mosinee, WI 54455

Martin Reel Co.
30 E. Main St.
Mohawk, NY 13407

Mepps
c/o Sheldons Inc.
P.O. Box 508
Antigo, WI 54409

Mildrum Manufacturing Company
230 Berlin Street
East Berlin, CT 06023

William Mills & Son, Inc.
21 Park Place
New York 8, NY

Mirrocraft
804 Pecor Street
Oconto, WI 54153

Mister Twister Inc.
P.O. Drawer 996
Minden, LA 71055

Muskol Enterprises Ltd.
P.O. Box 644
Truro, N.S., Canada B2M 5E5

O. Mustad & Son Inc.
P.O. Box 838
185 Clark Street
Auburn, NY 13021

Nebco National Expert Inc.
2928 Stevens Ave.
Minneapolis, MN 55408

Nelson Sales Co.
626 Broadway
Kansas City, MO 64142

The Netcraft Company
Box 5510
Toledo, OH 43613

Nicholl Brothers Inc.
1204 West 27th Street
Kansas City, MO 64108

Norman Manufacturing Co.
Highway 96 East
P.O. Box H
Greenwood, AR 72936

Normark Corporation
1710 E. 78th Street
Minneapolis, MN 55423

The North Face
1234 5th Street
Berkeley, CA 94710

Old Town Canoe Company
Old Town, ME 04468

Olympic Fishing Tackle Co., LTD.
1294 Shimofujisawa, Iruma, Saitama
Japan

Omega
266 Border Street
East Boston, MA 02128

Optimus-Princess, Inc.
12423 E. Florence Ave., Box 3448
Santa Fe Springs, CA 90670

The Orvis Company, Inc.
10 River Road
Manchester, VT 05254

Paducah Tackle Co.
P.O. Box 23
Paducah, KY 42001

E. F. Payne Rod Co. Inc.
Highland Mills, NY 10930

PBI, Inc.
4840 N. E. 10 Terrace
Fort Lauderdale, FL 33334

Russ Peak
21 North Allen Avenue
Pasadena, CA 91106

Penn Fishing Tackle Mfg. Co.
3028 W. Hunting Park Ave.
Philadelphia, PA 19132

Pequea Fishing Tackle Company
19 Miller Street
Strasburg, PA 17579

Perrine
Aladdin Laboratories, Inc.
620 S. 8th St.
Minneapolis, MN 55404

Pezon et Michel
21 Route De Tours
37400 Amboise, France

Pflueger Corporation
Sporting Goods Division
P.O. Box 310
Hallandale, FL 33009

Phillips Fly & Tackle Co.
P.O. Box 188
Alexandria, PA 16611

Phillipson Rods/3M Company
Leisure Time Products Division
3M Center
St. Paul, MN 55101

Plano Molding Company
Plano, IL 60545

Plastilite Corporation
P.O. Box 12235
Omaha, NE 68112

Pompanette, Inc.
190 Bryan Road
Dania, FL 33004

Powell Rod Co.
1148 West 8th Ave.
Chico, CA 95926

Powerscopic Corporation
P.O. Box 278
Westwood, NJ 07675

Precise Imports Corporation
3 Chestnut Street
Suffern, NY 10901

Prescott Spinner Co.
1000 Fairview Ave.
Hamilton, OH 45015

G. Pucci & Sons, Inc.
480 Princeton St.
San Francisco, CA 94340

Quick Corporation of America
620 Terminal Way
Costa Mesa, CA 92627

Rangeley Region Sports Shop
Box 850
Rangeley, ME 04970

Record
RecTack of America
P.O. Box 36
Downey, CA 90241

Reed Tackle
Box 390
Caldwell, NJ 07006

Reel-Assist Corporation
Drawer 3053
240 S. Wolcott
Casper, WY 82601

Reliable Gaff Company
4160 Merrick Road
Massapequa, NY 11758

The Richardsons' Fly Box
Osceola Mills, PA 16666

Mike Riedel
3203 Overland 6149
Los Angeles, CA 90034

Riviera Manufacturing
3859 Roger Chaffee Blvd., S. E.
Grand Rapids, MI 49508

Hank Roberts
Box 308
1033 Walnut Street
Boulder, CO 80302

Royal Sports Clothing
17 N. E. Fourth St.
Washington, IN 47501

A. G. Russell
1705 Hiway 71 North
Springdale, AR 72764

Ryobi
1555 Carmen Drive
Elk Grove Village, IL 60007

Sampo Inc.
North St.
Barneveld, NY 13304

Tom Satterthwaite
401 Garden Road
Springfield, PA 19064

Schrade Cutlery Corp.
Ellenville, NY 12428

FAO Schwarz
P. O. Box 218
Parsippany, NJ 07054

Scientific Anglers
Box 2001
Midland, MI 48640

Scotty Manufacturing Company Inc.
14139 21st Avenue North
Plymouth, MN 55441

Seal Dri Division
Wichita Canvas Supply, Inc.
P. O. Box 16006
Wichita, KS 67216

Seamaster Fishing Reels
4615 Le Jeune Road
Coral Gables, FL 33146

Seaway
7200 North Oak Park Avenue
Miles, IL 60648

T. R. Seidel Company
P.O. Box 268
Arvada, CO 80001

Seneca Tackle Co. Inc.
P.O. Box 2841-D
Elmwood Station
Providence, RI 02909

Sevenstrand Tackle Mfg. Co.
748 Lincoln
Westminster, CA 92683

Shakespeare Fishing Tackle Division
P.O. Box 246
Columbia, SC 29202

Sierra Designs
4th & Addison St.
Berkeley, CA 94710

Skyline Industries
P.O. Box 821
Fort Worth, TX 76101

Sportsman's Felt Co.
368 Prospect Ave.
Hartford, CT 06105

Stearns Manufacturing Company
St. Cloud, MN 56301

Stillfish Corporation
P.O. Box 6466
4005 Vermaas
Toledo, OH 43612

Strader Tackle, Inc.
P.O. Box 4029
Tallahassee, FL 32303

Strike Master Inc.
411 N. Washington Ave.
Minneapolis, MN 55401

Strike Products Inc.
702 N. Carl
P.O. Box 427
Siloam Springs, AR 72761

Sunrise India
233/5 Jogadish Bose Rd.
Calcutta-20, India

Sunset Line & Twine Company
Petaluma, CA 94952

Super Sport Inc.
P.O. Box 696
Bishop, CA 93514

Tacklecraft
Chippewa Falls, WI 54729

Tack-L-Tyers Sport Mart
939 D, Chicago Avenue
Evanston, IL 60202

Thomas & Thomas
4 Fiske Ave.
Greenfield, MA 01301

Norm Thompson
1805 N.W. Thurman Street
Portland, OR 97209

3M Company
3M Center, Bldg. 224-BW
St. Paul, MN 55101

Thunder River Flies
Box 821
Basalt, CO 81621

Timberline Rods
Box 774
North Main Street
North Conway, NH 03860

Trailcraft
Box 60614
Concordia, KS 66901

Trimarc Corporation
Premium Division
High Point Plaza
Hillside, IL 60162

Al Troth
P.O. Box 1307
Dillon, MT 59725

True Temper
1623 Euclid Avenue
Cleveland, OH 44115

Tubbs Snowshoes
Vermont Tubbs Sales
P.O. Box 98
Warrenville, CT 06278

Tubby Tackle Inc.
P.O. Box 426
Norman, OK 73069

Tucker Duck & Rubber Company
2701 Kelley Hiway
Fort Smith, AR 72901

UMCO
P.O. Box 608
Watertown, MN 55388

Uncle Josh Bait Company
Fort Atkinson, WI 53538

Upson Tools Inc.
P.O. Box 4750
Rochester, NY 14612

Uslan Rods
18679 W. Dixie Highway
North Miami Beach, FL 33160

Varmac Manufacturing Company
4201 Redwood Ave.
Los Angeles, CA 90066

E. Veniard
Paramount Warehouses
138 Northwood Road
Thornton Heath
England

Vexilar Inc.
9345 Penn Ave., S.
Minneapolis, MN 55431

Visa-Therm Products Company, Inc.
247 Madison Avenue
Bridgeport, CT 06604

Walker International
1901 W. Lafayette Blvd.
Detroit, MI 48216

Walle-Hawk Corp.
30 Archibald St.
Burlington, VT 05401

Warmlite
Stephenson's
23206 Hatleras St.
Woodland Hills, CA 91364

Weber Tackle Company
1039 Ellis Street
Stevens Point, WI 54481

Weedless Bait Company
Rogers, MN 55374

Weir & Son
101 W. Main St.
Los Gatos, CA 95030

Western Cutlery
5311 Western Ave.
Boulder, CO 80302

Wheatley Fly Boxes
Richard Wheatley & Son Ltd.
M. Sharf & Company Inc.
200 McGrath Highway
Somerville, MA 02143

Whopper Stomper Inc.
P.O. Box 1111
Sherman, TX 75090

R. L. Winston Rod Co.
475 Third St.
San Francisco, CA 94107

Woolrich Inc.
Woolrich, PA 17779

The Worth Company
P.O. Box 88
Stevens Point, WI 54481

Wright & McGill Co.
P.O. Box 16011
Stockyard Station
4245 East 46th Ave.
Denver, CO 80216

Yakima Bait Co.
Box 310
Granger, WA 98932

Paul H. Young
14039 Peninsula Drive
Traverse City, MI 49684

Zebco
P.O. Box 270
Tulsa, OK 74101

Index